CW00971995

HARLAXTON MEDIEVAL STUDIES

VOLUME SIX

MONASTERIES AND SOCIETY
IN MEDIEVAL BRITAIN

HARLAXTON MEDIEVAL STUDIES

NEW SERIES

1. ORMROD, W. M. (ed.), *England in the Thirteenth Century*, Proceedings of the 1989 Harlaxton Symposium (1991).
2. HICKS, Carola (ed.), *England in the Eleventh Century*, Proceedings of the 1990 Harlaxton Symposium (1992).
3. ROGERS, Nicholas (ed.), *England in the Fourteenth Century*, Proceedings of the 1991 Harlaxton Symposium (1993).
4. ROGERS, Nicholas (ed.), *England in the Fifteenth Century*, Proceedings of the 1992 Harlaxton Symposium (1994).
5. THOMPSON, Benjamin (ed.), *The Reign of Henry VII*, Proceedings of the 1993 Harlaxton Symposium (1995).
6. THOMPSON, Benjamin (ed.), *Monasteries and Society in Medieval Britain*, Proceedings of the 1994 Harlaxton Symposium (1999).
7. STRICKLAND, Matthew (ed.), *Armies, Chivalry and Warfare in Medieval Britain and France*, Proceedings of the 1995 Harlaxton Symposium (1998).

OLD SERIES

1. ORMROD, W. M. (ed.), *England in the Thirteenth Century*, Proceedings of the 1984 Harlaxton Symposium (Harlaxton, 1985).
   (1b. Sheets of the above paperback reissued with a new title-page in hardback by Boydell & Brewer, Woodbridge, 1986).
2. ORMROD, W. M. (ed.), *England in the Fourteenth Century*, Proceedings of the 1985 Harlaxton Symposium (Woodbridge, 1986).
3. WILLIAMS, Daniel (ed.), *England in the Fifteenth Century*, Proceedings of the 1986 Harlaxton Symposium (Woodbridge, 1987).
4. WILLIAMS, Daniel (ed.), *Early Tudor England*, Proceedings of the 1987 Harlaxton Symposium (Woodbridge, 1989).
5. WILLIAMS, Daniel (ed.), *England in the Twelfth Century*, Proceedings of the 1988 Harlaxton Symposium (Woodbridge, 1990).

HARLAXTON MEDIEVAL STUDIES, VI

MONASTERIES AND SOCIETY IN MEDIEVAL BRITAIN

Proceedings of the 1994
Harlaxton Symposium

Edited by
Benjamin Thompson

PAUL WATKINS

STAMFORD

1999

Published in 1999 by
Paul Watkins
18, Adelaide Street,
Stamford,
Lincolnshire, PE9 2EN

ISBN
1 871615 88 7

Typeset from the discs and essays of the authors
by Paul Watkins (Publishing)

Printed on long-life paper

Printed and bound by Woolnoughs of Irthlingborough

CONTENTS

LIST OF CONTRIBUTORS

Roger Bowers   Jesus College, University of Cambridge
Janet Burton   University of Wales, Lampeter
Lynda Dennison   St Mary's School, Wantage
Barrie Dobson   Christ's College, University of Cambridge
Marsha Dutton   University of Ohio
Sarah Foot   University of Sheffield
Joan Greatrex   Robinson College, Cambridge
Isabel Henderson   Newnham College, Cambridge
Jack Higham   Peterborough Cathedral
Donald Mackreth   Peterborough Cathedral
Nigel Morgan   University of Oslo
David Postles   University of Leicester
David Rollason   University of Durham
Lynda Rollason   University of Durham
Nicholas Rogers   Sidney Sussex College, Cambridge
Benjamin Thompson   Somerville College, University of Oxford

ABBREVIATIONS

BL   London, British Library
Bodleian   Oxford, Bodeian Library
CUL   Cambridge, University Library
EH   *Bede's Ecclesiastical History of the English People*, ed. and trans. B. Colgrave and R. A. B. Mynors (Oxford, 1969)
VCH   *Victoria History of the County of...*
TRHS   *Transactions of the Royal Historical Society*

PREFACE

This volume records the first of the Harlaxton Symposia to be organized around a theme rather than a chronological period. In choosing monasticism for this change of direction, the Committee enabled a programme to be constructed which covered a millennium of history on a subject which, because it was central to medieval society for much of the time, touches on many aspects of medieval life. It therefore fits well into the Harlaxton inter-disciplinary tradition. I am grateful to the Committee for entrusting to me the task of drawing up the programme, and for their continuing support (and patience) since; I am especially grateful to the Chairman, Barrie Dobson, for his tactful oversight of the process of production and tolerant understanding in less-than-ideal circumstances.

The Symposium visited Peterborough under the knowledgeable guidance of Donald Mackreth and Jack Higham, for which we are grateful; they also warmed us up with two papers which neatly provide this collection with an account of the interaction between a single monastery and its environment over one thousand years.

Barbara Harvey and Sarah Foot kindly read and commented constructively on two papers (although they are not responsible for their contents).

The staff at Harlaxton and the Principal, Dr Robert Stepsis, were as accommodating and hospitable as ever; Dr Stepsis' presence on the Committee provides valuable support to the Symposium, and his generosity has allowed it to cover its costs and now make a contribution towards the printing of these proceedings. Sean O'Harrow, the first Conference Secretary external to Harlaxton, ran the Symposium with efficiency and good humour, and relieved the Editor and Committee of a great deal of the burden of routine administration.

Institutions which have given permission for the reproduction of plates are gratefully acknowledged; and they are individually identified in the list of illustrations. Shaun Tyas has maintained his customary cheerfulness while having his patience somewhat tested. The Committee and I are most grateful to him for all the personal effort he puts into the publication of these volumes, to an ever-higher standard.

Benjamin Thompson
Somerville College, Oxford

LIST OF ILLUSTRATIONS

Plates

13 (Dennison) Holkham Hall, Norfolk, MS 26, fol. 7 (photo: Conway Library, Courtauld Institute, University of London, and by kind permission of the earl of Leicester)

14 (Dennison) New York, Pierpont Morgan Library, MS Glazier 53, fol. 6 (photo: Conway Library, Courtauld Institute, University of London, and The Pierpont Morgan Library, New York)

15 (Dennison) Holkham Hall, Norfolk, MS 26, fol. 56 (photo: Conway Library, Courtauld Institute, University of London, and by kind permission of the earl of Leicester)

16 (Dennison) Bodleian, MS Bodley 316, fol. 8 (photo: copyright The Bodleian Library, Oxford)

17 (Dennison) Holkham Hall, Norfolk, MS 26, fol. 48v (photo: Conway Library, Courtauld Institute, University of London, and by kind permission of the earl of Leicester)

18 (Dennison) Durham Cathedral Library, MS A.1.3, fol 1 (photo: by kind permission of The Dean and Chapter of Durham)

19 (Dennison) CUL, MS Ii.2.24, fol. 13 (photo: by permission of the Syndics of Cambridge University Library)

20 (Dennison) BL, Royal MS 14.C.ix, fol. 9 (photo: copyright the British Library Board)

21 (Dennison) Holkham Hall, Norfolk, MS 26, fol. 27v (photo: Conway Library, Courtauld Institute, University of London, and by kind permission of the earl of Leicester)

22 (Dennison) New York, Pierpont Morgan Library, MS Glazier 53, fol. 36v, detail (photo: Conway Library, Courtauld Institute, University of London, and the Pierpont Morgan Library)

23 (Dennison) Holkham Hall, Norfolk, MS 26, fol. 22 (photo: Conway Library, Courtauld Institute, University of London, and by kind permission of the earl of Leicester)

24 (Dennison) Bodleian, MS Rawlinson G.185, fol. 32v (photo: copyright The Bodleian Library, Oxford)

25 (Dennison) Bodleian, MS Don. b.5, fol. 7 (photo: copyright The Bodleian Library, Oxford)

26 (Dennison) Bodleian, MS Rawlinson G.185, fol. 20 (photo: copyright The Bodleian Library, Oxford)

27 (Dennison) Bodleian, MS Don. b.5, fol. 172v, detail (photo: copyright The Bodleian Library)

Figures

Introduction:
Monasteries and Medieval Society

BENJAMIN THOMPSON

> When historians write of the church as if it could be separated from secular history, they are simply repeating the mistake made by medieval ecclesiastical reformers, who were never more clearly the captives of their environment than when they spoke of their freedom from it.[1]
>
> R. W. Southern

Deeply engrained in the medieval mind was a series of dualisms, between spiritual and temporal, the heavenly and earthly cities, soul and body, good and evil, the church and the world, and many more. The last, our major concern here, was ultimately derived from the gospels: for instance, St John reports Christ enjoining the apostles, having been called 'out of the world', to be 'not of the world'.[2] Monasteries were part of the church – indeed at times they led it – so that our title appears to present a simple dichotomy between two entities which were distinct: the monasteries were to be not 'of' the world. Indeed monastic thinkers generally thought of monasteries as that part of the church which rejected the world most completely.[3] What 'the world' meant, however, varied considerably between different types of monasticism,

---

[1]   R. W. Southern, *Western Society and the Church in the Middle Ages* (Harmondsworth, 1970), pp. 15-16. In the attempt which follows to provide a broad context for the essays in this volume, I refer to them by their author's name only.

[2]   John, xv. 19, xvii. 6, 15-16.

[3]   St Benedict's Rule barely mentions the world outside, and when he does it is as a place of evil, to be avoided. See his directions for brethren sent on a journey (c. 67): on their return, they are to prostrate themselves in church and confess to any faults they may have committed, such as anything evil they have seen or heard, and must not tell anyone about anything they have seen or heard 'for that does much harm'. Going out of the enclosure of the monastery without permission is to be punished: the underlying assumption is that the world beyond the monastery is likely to contaminate anyone coming into contact with it. There are numerous editions of the Rule: for a parallel text with notes, *RB 1980: the Rule of St Benedict in Latin and English with Notes*, ed. T. Fry (Collegeville, Minnesota, 1981).

1

and between different times and places. Before we assume that the relationship between monasteries and society – an unproblematic term if we take it to mean simply everything which involves human activity[4] – was the same as that between monasteries and the world, a preliminary survey of monasticism is necessary.

The essential quality of 'the religious' was that they took a vow to live in a particular manner, in the service of God; the 'regulars', another term wider than 'monk', equally pinpoints the notion of living under a 'rule' of life different from the ordinary. There were different forms of such ways of life.[5] At one end of the spectrum is the hermit who fled from the world into the desert to live as a solitary, represented by St Paul and St Anthony. The essential aim was to make direct contact with God by renouncing the clutter of the world and the life of the flesh, and facing the demons of temptation directly. Hermits might live in groups, with less or more contact between them, especially when preparing for the eremitical life.[6] Thus the cenobitic monastery – in the centre of the spectrum – functioned partly as a training-ground for hermits, even though, since it was also accepted that most would not reach the stage of solitary eremitism, it was also a way of life in its own right. This is the monastery described by Benedict in his 'little rule for beginners', characterized by charity and patience to those learning to live under vows, rather than over-rigorous demands – difficult enough though even his envisaged way of life would be for most of us. Life was lived away from the world but in common, the whole community worshipping collectively eight times a day; there was to be no private property, and each monk was under complete obedience to the abbot.[7]

The function of the clergy to minister to the Christian laity, especially by serving churches, was in principle quite different from that of monks; they could not physically remove themselves from society. But they still might live in common and under vows, a tradition which became established from the fourth century for what came to be labelled 'canons'. This ideal was reinforced by the Carolingian reforms, brought to fruition in 816–17, which also attempted to establish the Benedictine Rule as standard for monks and to draw a clear distinction between the two orders. In the central period, the

---

[4]   For recent, if tongue-in-cheek, doubt about whether there was any such thing as society for post-conquest England, see George Garnett in *The Oxford Illustrated History of Medieval England*, ed. Nigel Saul (Oxford, 1997), p. 80.

[5]   A survey is provided by C. H. Lawrence, *Medieval Monasticism: Forms of Religious Life in Western Europe in the Middle Ages*, 2nd edn (Harlow, 1989).

[6]   Lawrence, *Medieval Monasticism*, ch. 1 & pp. 152ff; Henrietta Leyser, *Hermits and the New Monasticism: a Study of Religious Communities in Western Europe, 1000–1150* (London, 1984).

[7]   *Rule of Benedict, passim*; hermits are also mentioned in the Rule as having been trained as monks; c. 1.

canons acquired the label 'Augustinian' because a rule expanded from some advice of St Augustine (who was particularly insistent on clergy living the common life) became standard by the mid-twelfth century.[8] The friars, partly an Augustinian offshoot, developed this form of religious life fully by basing themselves in the densest centres of population, the cities, and renouncing landed property as their means of funding in favour of mendicancy, begging for alms.[9] Throughout the middle ages there were communities of clergy, living variously regulated lives, who are on the cusp of the regular and the 'secular' life, at the opposite end of the monastic spectrum from the hermits.[10]

Women could participate in principle in all these forms of life, except that they could not perform the ministry of active clergy. Anchoresses were prominent in some societies, but otherwise women tended to occupy the middle of the monastic spectrum, as nuns (even when under a Franciscan or Augustinian rule).[11] They are seen here in Marsha Dutton's discussion of Chaucer's two nuns, whom she shows to represent the ideal and the practice of female monastic life: the almost invisible second nun conformed to the pure archetype, whereas the ignorant, noisy and over-decorated prioress was a tawdry reality.[12]

There was, therefore, a range of possible ideals and models of the religious life, which was diversified further in the central middle ages with the proliferation of different orders.[13] The crusading orders of knights even strikingly combined the regular life with an active vocation of knighthood.[14] All of them in some sense rejected 'the world', but precisely what was being rejected varied considerably, from society itself and its physical location, to some standard aspects of human existence, most commonly material consumption and sex. We have to beware, therefore, of not measuring

---

[8]   J. C. Dickinson, *The Origins of the Austin Canons and their Introduction into England* (London, 1950), pp. 7–72.

[9]   C. H. Lawrence, *The Friars: the Impact of the Early Mendicant Movement on Western Society* (Harlow, 1994). The friars are not the focus of attention in this collection, which is confined to a narrower definition of monasticism, as is most of this introduction, except where friars are specifically mentioned.

[10]   Dickinson, *Augustinian Canons*, pp. 241–4; see below on secular colleges, pp. 28, 30–1.

[11]   Sally Thompson, *Women Religious: the Founding of English Nunneries after the Norman Conquest* (Oxford, 1991); Eileen Power, *English Medieval Nunneries, c.1275–1525* (Cambridge, 1922); A. K. Warren, *Anchorites and their Patrons in Medieval England* (Berkeley & London, 1985).

[12]   Below, Dutton, pp. 296–311.

[13]   The Premonstratensians are a good example, combining the canonical ideal with Cistercian ascetic customs; H. M. Colvin, *The White Canons in England* (Oxford, 1951).

[14]   A. J. Forey, *The Military Orders from the Twelfth to the Early Fourteenth Centuries* (Basingstoke, 1992).

monasticism by a single ideal standard, since few societies accepted one as such. The Rule of Benedict has, however, tended take centre stage in discussion of monasticism, partly because of its dominance – although not exclusive – in the west from the ninth century onwards, and partly because it occupies the centre of the spectrum sketched above.[15] But because it was flexible, we would find it difficult to agree what true 'Benedictinism' should be, and it was appropriated in different ways at different times to produce rather different forms of life. In one of the great episodes of monastic history, the conflict in the early twelfth century between the new Cistercians and the Cluniacs (representing the established 'black' or 'Benedictine' monks), both sides claimed the Rule as their warrant.[16] Although, therefore, the Rule is fundamental to any discussion of monasticism, it is essential to identify for any particular situation the ideals of monastic founders, innovators and reformers, and the practice of the religious life which the application of these engendered.

If we narrow our focus, therefore, and try to discern what was necessary to the foundation and functioning of a religious community, we may be able to acquire a more tangible sense of what monasticism entailed.[17] One pre-requisite for setting up a monastery was religious inspiration, a set of ideas in which some form of monastic life was deemed to be important; more specifically this would be a model to guide structure and practice in the form of a pre-existing monastery or order, or a rule. These would necessarily have to exist in, or have been imported into, the culture of the society founding the monastery, even if the aim was to react against that society or flee from it:

---

[15]   It is one possible criticism of David Knowles' fundamental *The Monastic Order in England*, 2nd edn (Cambridge, 1963), and *The Religious Orders in England*, 3 vols (Cambridge, 1948–59), that his own Benedictine assumptions tend to infect the text. But this is not without warrant for much of the middle ages, when the Rule was regarded as so central; even many communities of canons were effectively communities of monks, whose only pastoral role was to keep up the liturgy; see Dickinson, *Augustinian Canons*, pp. 197–241.

[16]   David Knowles, *Cistercians and Cluniacs: the Controversy between St Bernard and Peter the Venerable* (Oxford, 1955), reprinted in his *The Historian and Character and Other Essays* (Cambridge, 1963), 50–75.

[17]   There is no space here to give an outline of the monastic history of Britain, although the following touches on many aspects, and a broad chronology is attempted on pp. 27–32. It is given in brief in David Knowles and R. N. Hadcock, *Medieval Religious Houses: England and Wales*, 2nd edn (Harlow, 1971), pp. 8–47, and in full in Knowles, *Monastic Order in England*, and *Religious Orders*. Part of the story is more recently told by Janet Burton, *Monastic and Religious Orders in Britain, 1000–1300* (Cambridge, 1994). A brief chronology of the monasteries of Norfolk is in Benjamin Thompson, 'Monasteries and their Patrons at Foundation and Dissolution', *TRHS*, 6th ser. 4 (1994), 103–25.

world-rejection, of whatever sort, must begin in the world. The relationship between monasteries and society is unlikely to be simple.

Second, convents need people to occupy them, whether as hermits, monks, nuns, canons, or friars. These too had to come from society, although the first occupants might have travelled from elsewhere. Because of the vow of chastity taken by almost all those whom we would accept as religious, regular communities were not self-perpetuating, but required constant replenishment from outside. They had to answer some need in society in order to persuade people to join them. This might be a spiritual motivation similar to that of the founding religious of the community – an individual's desire to devote a life to God whether through contemplation, communal worship, or ministry, as above.[18] Many recruits in the twelfth century were inspired by the renewal of devotion in the new orders. Alternatively, recruitment might answer the needs of others, most obviously families, who put members into monasteries, often – especially in the early middle ages – at a young age through the oblation of children.[19]

Monks (to use the term loosely as an inadequate synonym for religious) were generally supposed to put off their worldly selves inside the monastery, to exchange their secular identity for a spiritual persona. This involved losing their existence before the law, and was often symbolized by a change of name.[20] Needless to say, in practice monks often maintained their ties with the society they had come from, and brought the world into the monastery with them by maintaining much of its culture and mores. Sarah Foot shows how early Anglo-Saxon monasteries replicated secular patterns of association in the familia, the aristocratic household.[21] Since many religious were put there by their families who were benefactors through the gifts which accompanied the oblates, it is not surprising that contact was sustained: life-long prayers for their kin would be the return, and Lynda Rollason shows that such links were also perpetuated in the later middle ages at Durham.[22] Roger Bowers reveals how monks in the larger later medieval English monasteries educated boys

---

[18]   Milis insists that the spiritual vocation is the defining characteristic of monasteries, and therefore what their contribution to society should be judged by: Ludo J. R. Milis, *Angelic Monks and Earthly Men* (Woodbridge, 1992), pp. vii–x. See the incisive but tolerant review by Barbara Harvey, *English Historical Review* 110 (1995), pp. 970–1, and further below, pp. 28–31.

[19]   David Williams, *The Cistercians in the Early Middle Ages* (Leominster, 1998), pp. 61–5; Lawrence, *Medieval Monasticism*, pp. 36–8, 71–2, 124–7, 174–88; Jean Leclercq, *Monks and Love in Twelfth-Century France: Psycho-Historical Essays* (Oxford, 1979), pp. 9–12 & ff. Oblation is envisaged in the Rule, c.59.

[20]   Knowles, *Religious Orders*, I, p. 271; F. Pollock & F. W. Maitland, *The History of English Law before the Time of Edward I*, 2nd edn, 2 vols (Cambridge, 1898, repr. 1968), I, pp. 433–8; see below, p. 290.

[21]   Below, pp. 38–44.

[22]   Below, pp. 290–3.

from their own families in convents' almonry schools.[23] Later medieval monks seem to have retained more of their individual identity (in contradistinction to the ideal of losing it in the community), especially the superiors and obedientiaries running their own offices; obedientiaries and senior monks followed abbots and priors in acquiring their own accommodation, and, so Nicholas Rogers finds, were buried elsewhere than in the monastic cemetery.[24] Even St Bernard did not think secular imagery inappropriate to theology and devotion; his sermons, preached to adult recruits who had lived in the world rather than life-long inmates, were full of images of knights and warfare, of love and marriage.[25] If the aim was to spiritualize these secular modes of conduct, it nevertheless emphasizes the extent to which monasteries existed in the culture of their own society, and drew on it.

Many of the ways in which the religious maintained contact with the world would have been put down by theologians to human weakness, the simple but inevitable falling away from ideal standards of conduct which is, in the Christian framework, inherent to the human condition. The glamour and status-consciousness of Chaucer's prioress contrasts with her humble and unnoticed chaplain, and her tale is about merciless vengeance rather than Marian mercy.[26] Food and drink were natural temptations: Chaucer aside, Barbara Harvey has shown how late-medieval monks at Westminster consumed large amounts of protein and alcoholic drink.[27] A common complaint of late-medieval visitations, seen below in Jack Higham's evidence from Peterborough, was that monks were out on the town boozing the night away, and womanizing was often part of the entertainment; one abbot was alleged to have kept three mistresses in the town. Moreover, the individualization of the quarters of monastic obedientiaries opened up the possibility of filling them with semi-permanent company, particularly of the bed-warming kind.[28]

While sex, like hunting (another vice revealed in texts both early and late),[29] was a temptation which monastic ideology firmly rejected, with the necessities of life it was a question of degree. Monks needed buildings, but

[23] Below, pp. 194-9.
[24] Knowles, *Monastic Order*, pp. 404-6; *Religious Orders*, I, p. 273, n. 4; Barbara Harvey, *Living and Dying in Medieval England: the Monastic Experience* (Oxford, 1993), p. 77; below, Rogers, pp. 262-76. For the gradual improvement of a superior's house through the centuries, see F. J. E. Raby and P. K. Baillie Reynolds, *Castle Acre Priory, Norfolk*, 2nd edn (London, 1952), pp. 8-13, 16-20.
[25] Leclercq, *Monks and Love, passim*, esp. ch. V.
[26] Below, Dutton, pp. 296-311.
[27] Harvey, *Living and Dying*, pp. 46-71.
[28] Below, pp. 171-4; *Visitations of the Diocese of Norwich, A.D. 1492-1532*, ed. A. Jessopp, Camden Society, new ser. 43 (1888), pp. 96-100.
[29] See below, pp. 43-4, 174.

were often housed in some of the greatest edifices of their times, which glorified God but also exhibited the greatness of a monastery and its order: the legendary Cluny III, built in the later eleventh century by St Hugh, was the largest church in Christendom for five centuries, and was concomitantly denounced along with Cluniac building in general for grandeur and ostentation.[30] Cistercian asceticism equally rejected art and decoration as unnecessary, yet monasteries were fundamental to religious art – and vice versa – in the early and central middle ages, and not irrelevant to it later.[31] Just as monasteries needed manuscripts, so they needed music, and even processions, for the ceaseless round of liturgy; but not only might it get too long and elaborate (another Cistercian complaint against the Cluniacs), it was also not always possible to resist the temptation of less devotional music and entertainment, denounced, for instance, by the Council of *Clofesho* in 747.[32]

Wealth of some sort was equally necessary to survival, but again, it was too easy to start to pursue it for its own sake, rather than solely for the needs of the community; the prohibition on monks holding individual property could also break down, even to the extent of receiving wages.[33] Power was a concomitant temptation, since it went with wealth in the form of lordship; Peterborough (which the conference visited) was dominated by its abbey for nearly six centuries, and the abbot was one of those who sat with the lords in parliament from the thirteenth century.[34] The heads of the greater monasteries took their place amongst the nobility in lifestyle and power. Administering a monastery's estates and itself became an increasingly complex and time-consuming task: the proliferation of different offices and administrative operations from the twelfth century would seem to denote an increasing involvement with simply keeping the institution going, and a consequent loss of time to spiritual activity, as well as accompanying careerism.[35] Perhaps,

---

[30] Noreen Hunt, *Cluny under St Hugh, 1049–1109* (1967), pp. 83, 109–10; Knowles, *Cistercians and Cluniacs*, p. 19/63.

[31] See below, pp. 19–20.

[32] Below, pp. 35, 43–4; John Harper, *The Forms and Orders of Western Liturgy, from the Tenth to the Eighteenth Century* (Oxford, 1991).

[33] Knowles, *Religious Orders*, I, pp. 287–89, II, pp. 240–4; Harvey, *Living and Dying*, pp. 136–7, 153.

[34] Below, Mackreth and Higham, pp. 137–76; Knowles, *Religious Orders*, II, p. 304.

[35] One half to two-thirds of monks had an office in the greatest monasteries by the early sixteenth century: R. B. Dobson, 'The English Monastic Cathedrals in the Fifteenth Century', *TRHS* 6th ser. 1 (1991), 151–72, p. 170. The centralization of the thirteenth century, superseding the acquisition of autonomy by obedientiaries in the late twelfth, and partly implemented in order to facilitate the direct management of estates, added to rather than detracted from the complexity of administration, as the complex internal accounting, and the account rolls which survive from that century onwards, show; Burton, *Monastic and Religious Orders*, pp. 251–2; Knowles, *Religious Orders*, I, pp. 55–63, II, pp. 309–10ff.

indeed, the form of 'worldliness' most to be feared was creeping apathy and loss of fervour, which threatened to deprive the religious of their sense of living a distinct life and following a separate calling. Yet such decline was a recurring part of the cyclical history of monasticism: maintaining the barriers between the 'world' and the monastery was not only difficult, but in Christian theology impossible, because its inhabitants were human and therefore fallen.

A third pre-requisite for the establishment of a monastery was a material base sufficient to support the community. Initially a site was needed, on which appropriate buildings would have to be constructed in due course, possibly by the monks themselves. Then a means of livelihood had to be found. The friars' mendicancy has been touched upon, and at the other end of the spectrum hermits (who might not even need buildings if they could occupy caves) could live on very little. Most religious, however, would need food, drink and clothing, and some basic liturgical tools, or cash with which to buy them in the short term; and, in the not-too-long-term, capital which would produce a permanent income. The gift of landed property and other rights is the invariable focus of charters of foundation, although they might be drawn up some time after a convent came into existence.[36] Capital in land was a necessary concomitant of the desire for monasteries to last for ever, and to be independent of worldly demands; hence the ideal of 'free alms' tenure developed in the eleventh and twelfth centuries to signal the disburdening of secular service so that the land could be entirely used to support the monastery and its religious purposes, in perpetuity.[37]

The circumstances of the foundation of convents varied enormously, but most subsequently aimed to increase their property, whether because they wanted to expand their activities or because they had not yet reached a secure level of endowment. They encouraged and often needed a never-ending flow of gifts in all forms, but especially in land and money, with which they engaged in the purchase of further land. As David Postles shows in the case of Garendon Abbey in the twelfth century, most of its property was derived not from the founder's meagre initial gifts, but from subsequent purchase, which presupposes success in attracting donations in cash.[38]

---

[36] A large collection of charters is in *Monasticon Anglicanum*, ed. William Dugdale, 2nd edn, ed. J. Caley, H. Ellis, B. Bandinel, 6 vols. in 8 (London, 1817–30). V. H. Galbraith, 'Monastic Foundation Charters of the Eleventh and Twelfth Centuries', *Cambridge Historical Journal* 4 (1934), 205–22; Paul R. Hyams, 'The Charter as a Source for the Early Common Law', *Journal of Legal History* 12 (1991), 173–89, p. 174.

[37] Benjamin Thompson, 'Free Alms Tenure in the Twelfth Century', *Anglo-Norman Studies* 16 (1994), 221–43.

[38] Below, pp. 105–115; on the church and the land market in later medieval England, see Sandra Raban, *Mortmain Legislation and the English Church, 1279–1500*

For land to become income it had to worked and administered. The original Benedictine ideal, revived by the Cistercians in the twelfth century, was for the monks to work the land themselves, which was not only of moral benefit to them, but also removed one area of contact with society.[39] This was socially unacceptable to the aristocratic aura of early medieval monasteries, but in any case it was difficult to effect if the lands were at all widespread, since monks could not also then perform the monastic office; even the Cistercians resorted to using lay-brothers. Most other religious exploited their lands in the same way as other lords, through peasants and serfs and hired labour; indeed without the records of monasteries our knowledge of the medieval economy would be very much thinner.[40] Moreover, English monasteries did not have compact blocks of land around them which could be isolated from the rest of society; the richer houses had widespread lands, and, with the initial exception of some of the northern Cistercians, the rest fitted into the patchwork patterns of English land tenure in which manors and smaller holdings within them were intermingled.[41] Monks had secular neighbours, and had to travel across others' land to get to many of their own, unless they hired secular agents to do it for them.[42] Either way, the land which was intended to guarantee the monastery's independence also necessitated its involvement with society.

Changes in economic circumstances through the centuries reinforce this point: some of their effects are seen in the Peterborough evidence, notably in the twelfth- and thirteenth-century expansion, and the crisis and adjustment which followed in the fourteenth, particularly following the Black Death.[43] Monasteries were not immune to these any more than nuclear-free zones are to radiation. And the worst did sometimes happen: some of the smaller monasteries folded through economic weakness in the fifteenth century, being inadequately endowed to meet the downturn for lords, and subsequently unable to attract adequate further benefactions to shore up their position.[44]

(Cambridge, 1982), esp. chs 5–6.

[39] Lawrence, *Medieval Monasticism*, pp. 34–5, 177–81.

[40] See below, pp. 47–8, for the early period. For one of many modern accounts of monastic estates with implications for the economy as a whole, see Barbara Harvey, *Westminster Abbey and its Estates in the Middle Ages* (Oxford, 1977).

[41] Robin Fleming, 'Domesday Book and the Tenurial Revolution', *Anglo-Norman Studies* 9 (1987), 87–102; *King and Lords in Conquest England* (Cambridge, 1991). See Postles' map of Garendon, below, figure 4, p. 111.

[42] Both methods are evident in the accounts of Creake Abbey, Norfolk, for 1331–2: 'A Cellarer's Account Roll of Creake Abbey, 5 & 6 Edward III', ed. G. A. Carthew, *Norfolk Archaeology* 6 (1864), 314–59, pp. 320–2, 330–4.

[43] Below, Mackreth and Higham, pp. 137–76, esp. pp. 159–67. See also Harvey, *Westminster Abbey*, esp. chs 5–9.

[44] Thompson, 'Monasteries and Patrons', pp. 115–16.

'The changes and chances of this fleeting world' did not leave monasteries untouched.

The religious also had to protect their lands, especially in turbulent political and social circumstances. Since the Tenth-Century Reformation was in part political, it is not surprising that it was followed by a political reaction in which Peterborough temporarily lost some of its lands; equally the Norman Conquest required adjustment to a new regime, including housing then finding land for sixty knights which were imposed as the abbey's military quota.[45] In the former episode, a protector was at hand in Aelfwine, earl of East Anglia, and early medieval monasteries commonly looked to an advocate or lay abbot to fulfil precisely this function of earthly lord and protector.[46] Often the founder and his descendants would be the natural lord, especially since, after the Conquest and the development of the tenurial structure of lordship ('the feudal system'), he was also a convent's tenurial lord as the donor of its initial properties.[47] But for many reasons – notably the failure of the lineage, or because the patron was the king who could hardly take a personal interest in all the monasteries within his direct lordship – monasteries often had to look elsewhere, as Garendon did in turning for support from the earl of Leicester, who soon lost interest in his foundation, to the local gentry.[48] In the later centuries, many English monasteries employed lay stewards to run their estates, who in practice could play a bigger role as informal patrons and protectors of monks' interests; William Paston, the judge and founder of the letter-writing family's fortunes, was such for Bromholm Priory in Norfolk in the early fifteenth century.[49] Thus the normal pattern of medieval lordship – 'bastard feudal' rather than 'feudal' – in which lordship and clientage were exchanged in more flexible and varying

---

[45] Below, pp. 137–40, 147–52.

[46] Lawrence, *Medieval Monasticism*, pp. 75–6, 82–3, 132; *The New Cambridge Medieval History*, II: *c.700–c.900*, ed. Rosamond McKitterick (Cambridge, 1995), pp. 135–6, 634–6; J. M. Wallace-Hadrill, *The Frankish Church* (Oxford, 1983), pp. 270–1, 289–91.

[47] See below for the mutual exchange between monastery and patron, pp. 12–16.

[48] Below, pp. 105–15; also Bowers and Lynda Rollason on Durham's contacts with the local dominant nobility, below, pp. 197, 286–90, and n. 131 here. Susan Wood, *English Monasteries and their Patrons in the Thirteenth Century* (Oxford, 1955), pp. 16–21; for the failure of patronal lineages, see Thompson, 'Monasteries and Patrons', pp. 119–25.

[49] Knowles, *Religious Orders*, II, pp. 284–5; R. B. Dobson, *Durham Priory, 1400–1450* (Cambridge, 1973), pp. 123ff.; *The Cellarer's Account for Bromholm Priory, Norfolk, 1415–16*, ed. L. J. Redstone, Norfolk Record Society 35 (Norwich, 1944), no. 50; for further relations between Paston and the priory, *The Paston Letters*, ed. James Gairdner, 6 vols (1904; repr. Gloucester, 1983), II, pp. 19–24, 32–4, 56, 63–4, etc. A lay steward of Durham was recorded in the *Liber Vitae*, below, p. 287.

patterns than the simple relationship of tenurial lord and tenant, reasserted itself.

At the top of the hierarchy of earthly powers which had a potential influence on monasteries was the king, especially in England where he gained significant political control by supporting the Tenth-Century Reformation and thus influence over monasteries outside Wessex in place of local families.[50] Such control was reinforced by the Conquest, with its assertion of royal lordship over all existing houses,[51] although the competing claims of the papacy to jurisdiction over all ecclesiastical institutions and personnel came to fruition at the same time. It may have seemed for a moment in the early twelfth century that canon law and the new hierarchy of ecclesiastical jurisdictions up to the pope would provide the best protection for monastic property, especially with Henry I's concession of investiture to Anselm and Pascal II and the failure of royal lordship under Stephen. Becket and Alexander III felt able to reject clause nine of Henry II's constitutions of Clarendon, in which a preliminary hearing as to whether land under dispute was 'lay fee' or 'free alms' would be held in the royal court. But despite Becket's victory, ecclesiastical landholders voted with their feet: the common law, guaranteed ultimately by royal power, offered the best security, and when the plea rolls bring the operation of the royal courts into view from the end of the twelfth century, we see churches and monasteries using the royal writs and actions habitually in their property disputes and dealings. Tenure in 'free alms' did not preclude a preference for protection from a secular authority best placed to provide it.[52]

In concluding this survey of the essential ingredients for religious houses, therefore, we come to the unsurprising conclusion that the support of the society in which a house was founded was essential to its initial foundation and to its continued prosperity, or just survival, thereafter. In some particular circumstances, monastic movements managed to distance themselves from society further than was the norm, as the Cistercians did most spectacularly, but by no means exclusively: Cluny, which came to represent worldliness at its worst for its critics, had been founded on the same ideal of world-rejection.

---

[50] Eric John, 'The King and Monks in the Tenth-Century Reformation', in his *Orbis Brittanniae* (London, 1966), 154–80; the importance of kings to the early Christianization of England is attested throughout Bede, e.g. *EH*, I. 25–6, III. 25.

[51] Much debated, but now accepted: J. H. Round, 'The Introduction of Knight Service into England', in his *Feudal England: Historical Studies on the XIth and XIIth Centuries* (London, 1895), 225–314; J. C. Holt, 'The Introduction of Knight Service in England', *Anglo-Norman Studies* 6 (1984), 89–106; Brian Golding, *Conquest and Colonization: the Normans in Britain, 1066–1100* (London, 1994), pp. 135–8. For Peterborough, see above, n. 45.

[52] I have sketched this story towards the end of 'Free Alms Tenure', pp. 236–41, and intend to tell it in more detail soon.

Even so, not only did those ideals spring from the societies which were rejected, but the initial endowment and continuing recruitment had to be supplied from society. Few such movements maintained their distance for long: the Cistercians both got rich, and eventually did many of the same things as other monasteries such as praying for their benefactors' souls.[53] Perhaps only the Carthusians, on a small scale, were successful in maintaining a tangible isolation from society over centuries.[54] Monasteries could not be created and sustained without the support of society.

What did society expect in return for this investment of people and resources?[55] It must be assumed that it thought the investment worthwhile, and that, at its most obvious, it thought it worth supporting the ideals of the religious, as laid out by a rule or order, for their own sake. This naturally depended on the ability of spiritual leaders to persuade society of the importance of those activities, whether they were contemplation, communal worship, or ministry in the world. But there was a more direct return for benefactors than this, in the first place because using their resources to support a worthwhile spiritual activity redounded to their spiritual credit. The fact of making a grant to a convent was recognized as beneficial to the donor, as the common identification of God as the recipient of the gift suggests.[56] The monks' activities in addition provided continuing benefits to their founders: often the point of a foundation must have been to have a church on the doorstep to minister to the aristocratic household, whether a minster on an early medieval estate, a Cluniac house functioning as the virtual household-chapel for a Norman castle, or an Augustinian house near a manor-house.[57] Even without the connection of locality, the house would

[53] Lawrence, *Medieval Monasticism*, pp. 197–202; Wood, *Monasteries and Patrons*, p. 134.
[54] Lawrence, *Medieval Monasticism*, pp. 159–63; E. M. Thompson, *The Carthusian Order in England* (London, 1930). Even then, Carthusian foundations in later medieval England operated within the usual frameworks of lordship and prestige: see the group founded in Richard II's reign (*ibid.*, pp. 199–238), plus Henry V's Syon, and Henry VII's patronage of it; Neil Beckett, 'Henry VII and Sheen Charterhouse', in *The Reign of Henry VII: Proceedings of the 1993 Harlaxton Symposium*, ed. Benjamin Thompson (Stamford, 1995), 117–32.
[55] For recent thoughts, Christopher Holdsworth, *The Piper and the Tune: Medieval Patrons and Monks*, Stenton Lecture 1990 (Reading, 1991).
[56] On grants to monasteries in twelfth-century England and what was expected in return, see Thompson, 'Free Alms Tenure', pp. 224–31; 'From "Alms" to "Spiritual Services": the Function and Status of Monastic Property in Medieval England', *Monastic Studies* 2, ed. Judith Loades (Bangor, 1991), 227–61.
[57] Below, pp. 42–6; Brian Golding, 'The Coming of the Cluniacs', *Anglo-Norman Studies* 3 (1980), 164–77, esp. p. 168; David Crouch, 'Geoffrey de Clinton and Roger, Earl of Warwick: New Men and Magnates in the Reign of Henry I',

provide continual prayers for the family's good estate and, especially, their souls. Monastic founders were invariably members of the confraternity, whose core-members were the religious of the particular house and order; other benefactors too might have it granted to them, commonly in the form that they would participate 'in all the benefits and prayers which will be performed in this church for ever'.[58] From the early period monasteries kept a *Liber Vitae*, such as that of Durham Cathedral Priory, analysed here by Lynda Rollason, in which the names of benefactors and friends were entered to ensure their continued remembrance in and benefit from the monastery's round of prayer.[59]

Even in the twelfth century, a more precise spiritual return might be specified by donors, such as a light, an anniversary mass (obit), or a specific prayer or mass added to the monastic timetable.[60] This became increasingly common in the thirteenth and fourteenth centuries with the diffusion of the doctrine of purgatory, which opened up the possibility of securing salvation after death partly through suffrages performed on earth.[61] Hence the emergence of the chantry, the daily mass said in perpetuity principally for the soul of an individual benefactor.[62] Spiritual services became increasingly directed to the individual, as the proliferation of names in the later medieval part of the Durham *Liber Vitae* shows.[63] Equally, Nicholas Rogers shows that abbots and other monks singled themselves out from the monastic throng and by the thirteenth century had begun to be buried in their monastery-

---

Bulletin of the Institute of Historical Research 55 (1982), 113–24, pp. 116–17; Benjamin Thompson, '*Habendum et Tenendum*: Lay and Ecclesiastical Attitudes to the Property of the Church', in *Religious Belief and Ecclesiastical Careers in Late Medieval England*, ed. Christopher Harper-Bill (Woodbridge, 1991), 197–238, pp. 235–6; Wood, *Monasteries and Patrons*, p. 116. See also below on foundation and locality, p. 15.

58 '... in singulis beneficiis et oracionibus que de cetero fient in ecclesia sua imperpetuum'; *Stoke by Clare Cartulary, BL Cotton Appx. xxi*, ed. Christopher Harper-Bill & Richard Mortimer, 3 vols, Suffolk Records Society: Suffolk Charters 4–6 (Woodbridge, 1982–4), nos. 11, 14, 15 (I, pp. 9, 11). For further references, Thompson, 'From "Alms" to "Spiritual Services"', pp. 234–5. See Postles' table of the counter-gifts to Garendon, the spiritual of which were burial or fraternity; below, p. 116.

59 Below, Lynda Rollason, pp. 277–95.

60 Thompson, 'Free Alms Tenure', p. 227 & n. 35; *Stoke by Clare Cartulary*, III, p. 12, nos. 572–646 *passim*, and index *s.v.* anniversary, lamps, and lights.

61 Clive Burgess, '"A Fond Thing Vainly Invented": an Essay on Purgatory and Pious Motive in Later Medieval England', in *Parish, Church, and People: Local Studies in Lay Religion, 1350–1750*, ed. S. J. Wright (London, 1988), 56–84, pp. 59–62; R. W. Southern, 'Between Heaven and Hell', *Times Literary Supplement*, 18 June 1982, 651–2 (review of J. Le Goff, *La Naissance du Purgatoire*).

62 Kathleen Wood-Legh, *Perpetual Chantries in Britain* (Cambridge, 1965).

63 Below, Lynda Rollason, esp. pp. 279, 282–6, pl. 43.

churches, round the high altar and elsewhere, like lay benefactors, rather than relying on their general participation in the monastery's spiritual benefits.[64]

Burial was indeed one of the benefits which founders and patrons expected, and which other benefactors also sought (as in the Garendon evidence presented by David Postles).[65] Many monasteries in fact performed the function of mausoleum to their founding family, as did Lewes Priory, the first Cluniac house to be founded in England (1077), for the Earls Warenne between the late eleventh and mid-fourteenth centuries.[66] Some spectacular collections of tombs still survive, such as the Plantagenets at Fontevrault, and the Dukes of Norfolk at Framlingham, some moved from Thetford Priory after the Dissolution.[67] The physical presence of the remains of the founder and subsequent patrons and family-members reinforced the monks' continual intercession for them by prayer and the mass down the centuries. In this exchange between the dead and the living, the dead had not only given what made the monastery what it was in the form of its initial, and often main, endowments, but continued to proclaim the status of a house (increasingly bound up with its antiquity) in connection with its aristocratic founders.

The subsequent patrons equally benefited from this visible assertion of lordship: the secular benefits which monasteries could offer to their benefactors were important to the package.[68] Since churches were, alongside castles and manor-houses, the most impressive buildings to be found in the landscape, the aristocracy did not miss the chance of using them to advertize their local eminence, partly bound up with their antiquity. As well as their tombs, patrons stamped their houses with their arms to assert their identity, as on the gatehouse of Castleacre Priory in Norfolk, another Warenne house in another area of Warenne lordship.[69] The lengths to which Henry VII went to proclaim his new royal lordship in his new chapel at Westminster Abbey (described in the previous Harlaxton volume), only took to extremes a common practice of the nobility.[70]

---

[64]   Below, Rogers, pp. 262–76, esp. pp. 263–4, 268 ff.

[65]   Below, p. 116; Brian Golding, 'Burials and Benefactions: an Aspect of Monastic Patronage in Thirteenth-Century England', in *England in the Thirteenth Century: Proceedings of the 1984 Harlaxton Symposium*, ed. W. M. Ormrod (Nottingham & Woodbridge, 1985), 64–74.

[66]   *VCH, Sussex*, II, pp. 64–71; GEC, *The Complete Peerage*, ed. V. Gibbs et al., 12 vols in 13 (London, 1910–59), XII/i, pp. 493–512.

[67]   *The Plantagenet Chronicles*, ed. E. M. Hallam (London, 1986), pp. 253–7; Lawrence Stone and Howard Colvin, *The Howard Tombs at Framlingham, Suffolk* (London, 1966).

[68]   Benett D. Hill is particularly insistent on these for Cistercian foundations: *English Cistercian Monasteries and their Patrons in the Twelfth Century* (London, 1968), esp. pp. 53–77; this is confirmed by Postles, below, pp. 100–5.

[69]   Raby and Baillie Reynolds, *Castle Acre*, p. 7.

[70]   Richard Marks, 'The Glazing of Henry VII's Chapel, Westminster Abbey', in *The*

Since monasteries both reflected and exercised entrenched lordship, in areas where local influence was disputed competition was partly played out through monastic foundation and control, as Sarah Foot suggests for the early Thames Valley, the border between Wessex and Mercia.[71] Equally, in the early twelfth century some of the many Cistercian foundations emanated from the intense competition for local lordship, especially in the midlands between the earls of Chester and Leicester: Garendon is just one such house, having been founded by the earl of Leicester in the earl of Chester's sphere of influence and using land taken from a Chester tenant.[72] In this case the political motives would seem to be essential to understanding the foundation, and at least equal to any spiritual intentions on the part of the founder. Similarly, Sarah Foot reminds us of Bede's complaint in 734 that magnates were founding minsters – and even turning their households into them – as a tax-dodge, to benefit from the immunity from secular burdens conferred on ecclesiastical property by kings.[73] Even where the primary purpose of a gift was to fund religious activities, however, residual secular services might be reserved, especially to the donor's overlord: this was a way of passing on an inconvenient obligation.[74]

There were many other secular benefits available, perhaps more as spin-offs to later generations than primary motives for foundation. We have touched upon the practice of putting sons and daughters (often as children) into convents: common in the early middle ages, it was by no means abandoned as a result of the high-medieval challenge to child-oblation, especially for daughters for whom the option of a career as a secular cleric was not open; in 1273 Carrow Abbey in Norwich had to get a papal bull allowing it to refuse further aristocratic daughters because it had become so burdened with them.[75] Not only did this provide a living for children, although not necessarily cheaply since gifts were expected to accompany them into the convent,[76] but it also might extend a family's dominance, since its religious members were part of institutions which themselves controlled lands and exercised lordship, and it created a more direct connection through which spiritual benefits specifically for the family would be maintained.

Reign of Henry VII, ed. Thompson, 157–74 and pls 24–42.

[71] Below, p. 46.

[72] Below, p. 102; further examples are summarized in Burton, *Monastic and Religious Orders*, pp. 72–3.

[73] Below, p. 46.

[74] David Postles, 'Tenure in Frankalmoin and Knight Service in Twelfth-Century England: Interpretation of the Charters', *Journal of the Society of Archivists* 13 (1992), 18–28.

[75] *Monasticon*, IV, p. 71.

[76] Envisaged in the Rule, c. 59; see the various Beauchamp daughters at Shouldham Priory, Norfolk, throughout the fourteenth century; William Dugdale, *The Baronage of England*, 2 vols (London, 1675), I, pp. 226–38.

Monasteries were expected to house and entertain their patrons when they visited, sometimes with large households, a privilege whose abuse Edward I sought to limit by legislation.[77] Because of their virtually-guaranteed permanence, perpetual institutions could provide services which aristocratic families – temporally and geographically less stable – could not do for themselves so easily, such as banking.[78] Monasteries could provide other administrative and clerical services to patrons to help them run their households and estates, perhaps especially when they were situated amongst the patron's lands, where they remained when the patron was away.[79] In the earlier period, where literate clerks were rare, founding a community might be the best way of securing a supply of them.[80] There was always the temptation to exploit the monastery's property more or less directly, for instance by retiring superannuated servants into corrodies, or getting the convent to present a particular clerk to a benefice.[81] One of the striking features of medieval monasteries, therefore, is the great range of benefits which they offered to their patrons.

Furthermore, it was not only patrons, benefactors and recruits who benefited from religious houses. Because they were in principle perpetual and stable institutions and able to transmit knowledge and traditions continuously down the generations in the same place, they could perform useful functions not easily found elsewhere. Most obvious, again, is prayer and supplication, a virtual monastic monopoly in the early middle ages: prayers for king and people, for the safety of kingdoms and the salvation of their people, were staples of monastic prayer, stipulated for instance at the Council of *Clofesho* in 747, and in the *Regularis Concordia* of 970.[82] It was precisely the continual round of prayer for society which made Cluny and its congregation so prestigious and valued from the tenth century onwards.[83] Monasteries also habitually provided a tangible ministry to the poor and destitute through alms-giving, enjoined by the Rule. The tendency to institutionalize alms-giving resulted in the creation of hospitals, as at Peterborough, and the general obligation to receive travellers led to the building of guest-halls.[84]

---

[77] Wood, *Monasteries and Patrons*, pp. 101–6; *Statutes of the Realm*, 11 vols in 12 (London, 1810–28), I, p. 26.

[78] Wood, *Monasteries and Patrons*, p. 118.

[79] Wood, *Monasteries and Patrons*, pp. 119–21.

[80] Below, p. 49.

[81] Wood, *Monasteries and Patrons*, pp. 107–15.

[82] Below, p. 52; *Tenth-Century Studies: Essays in Commemoration of the Millennium of the Council of Winchester and* Regularis Concordia, ed. David Parsons (London, 1975), pp. 44, 95–6.

[83] John van Engen, '"The Crisis of Cenobitism" Reconsidered: Benedictine Monasticism in the years 1050–1150', *Speculum* 71 (1986), 269–304, pp. 292–7; Hunt, *Cluny under St Hugh*, pp. 99–114.

[84] Rule, c. 53; Harvey, *Living and Dying*, pp. 7–33, esp. 17–20; below, pp. 54, 157–8,

Benedict rejected pastoral work in the community as a task unsuitable for monks, who were to turn their backs on the world, and in the eleventh and twelfth centuries, the distinction between monks and other clergy was re-emphasized.[85] Some orders, however, existed to provide a direct pastoral ministry to their localities; the friars' continuing popularity through the late middle ages was based on their successful provision of a ministry of preaching, confession, burial and spiritual suffrages beyond that of the secular clergy.[86] The extent to which monks in the earlier period in practice also did so is complex. In the period of conversion, minsters were established as the source of evangelization and of missionizing clergy; the problem is to decide whether we should define these as monks or secular clergy, and the answer may be that in England before the tenth century definitions of vocation were not so clear. Indeed, Sarah Foot argues strongly that the lack of distinction between an enclosed monastery and a church with a community of priests serving a locality means we must adopt the term 'minster' to cover the ambiguity.[87]

The debate on the 'minster hypothesis' highlights the problem.[88] John Blair has suggested that minsters in pre-Viking England were just such communities with a double function, and bishops intended to create a systematic network of them through the country to provide pastoral care. David Rollason here and elsewhere (with Eric Cambridge) refutes this view, arguing that the model has become self-justifying since any piece of evidence for part of the system is taken as proof of the whole; moreover, he argues that in practice the minsters were unevenly distributed. Rollason wishes to distinguish between pastoral communities and enclosed contemplatives, on the Benedictine model, before the Tenth-Century Reformation – and therefore between monks and clergy. Sarah Foot here and elsewhere takes a middle position: she agrees that the evidence for a systematic network of minsters is inadequate, but equally argues that there is no evidence for a clear distinction between monks and clergy in the early period, even if some communities did more pastoral work than others.[89] Certainly, Bede's argument that new episcopal sees should be based on 'monasteries' suggests

167–8; the guest-house at Norton Priory has been dated to the early thirteenth century, J. Patrick Greene, *Norton Priory* (Cambridge, 1989), pp. 122–3. For the channelling of alms into education in the almonry schools, including for the monks' kin, see Bowers, *passim*, esp. pp. 184, 194–9.

85 Giles Constable, *Monastic Tithes* (Cambridge, 1964), pp. 136–65.
86 Lawrence, *Friars*, pp. 102–26.
87 Below, Foot, pp. 35ff.
88 See below, David Rollason, pp. 59–74, and his notes for full references; note the 'Debate' in *Early Medieval Europe* 4 (1995), to which Rollason's paper is supplementary, and Foot's a contribution. Further rounds are promised in forthcoming editions of that journal. See especially *Pastoral Care before the Parish*, ed. John Blair and Richard Sharpe (Leicester, 1992).
89 Below, Foot, esp. pp. 38–9, 44–6, 52–7.

that these were the churches offering the highest level of activity, the ecclesiastical centres of society.[90] Foot successfully shows how central the minsters were to Anglo-Saxon society, a conclusion which Rollason does not dispute.[91] In a period with so few educated clerics, bishops simply could not afford to ignore the resources of the monasteries in mission and pastoral work; the veneer of Christianization was still very thin for much of the population, and minsters were perhaps primarily part of aristocratic society, to which they ministered and for which they prayed – activities between which it is hard to envisage a clear distinction. They constituted the church of that society. Similarly, Isabel Henderson's evidence of Pictish sculpture suggests a lack of precise distinction between monasteries, church and society, a spectrum which makes the very interpretation of the evidence, with little back-up from literary sources, highly problematic.[92]

The reform of the tenth century, seen here through the Peterborough experience by Donald Mackreth, sought to introduce – or revive, as the reformers assumed – a much more Benedictine-based monasticism into England.[93] There is evidence for reform focusing on regional centres; Peterborough was to be the reformed monastery for Northamptonshire. One of the peculiar legacies of the reform was that many English cathedrals— central ministry churches *par excellence* – were staffed by communities of monks not secular canons, a feature which the Normans accepted and reinforced.[94] Nevertheless, an essential transformation of the tenth, eleventh and twelfth centuries was the creation of a network of parish churches providing complete coverage of pastoral ministry to the localities of England.[95] In principle this had the potential to free monks from responsibilities to the world and retreat to contemplation, which some of the movements of the time such as the Cistercians certainly envisaged. But another of the church's aims was to remove churches and tithes from the control of lay lords (who nevertheless were founding many of the new parish churches); they were encouraged to give them to monasteries, who thus ended up with control over many parish churches and over much tithe income.[96] In

---

[90] Below, pp. 63–4.

[91] Below, Foot, *passim*, Rollason, pp. 64–5, 66–7.

[92] Below, Henderson, pp. 75–96.

[93] Below, pp. 137–40; see *Tenth-Century Studies*, ed. Parsons; John, 'King and Monks'; and F. M. Stenton, *Anglo-Saxon England*, 3rd edn (Oxford, 1971), pp. 446–57.

[94] Knowles, *Monastic Order*, pp. 129–34.

[95] *Minsters and Parish Churches: the Local Church in Transition, 950–1200*, ed. John Blair (Oxford, 1988).

[96] Constable, *Monastic Tithes*, pp. 83–136. The ecclesiastical taxation of 1291 in England shows the result, many churches and portions and pensions of tithes being owned by monasteries; *Taxatio Ecclesiastica Angliae et Walliae auctoritate papae Nicholai IV, circa 1291* (London, 1802).

the course of the twelfth and thirteenth centuries bishops did, however, sideline monks – and canons too – from direct pastoral responsibility, a development made easier by the increasing availability of secular clergy.[97] But many conventual naves still retained parochial responsibility, even if a secular chaplain was employed to do the work; Janet Burton's contribution on Kirkham Priory and its parish turns on a late-fifteenth-century dispute about parochial jurisdiction.[98] Her evidence provides a rare and detailed glimpse of the extensive use parishioners made of the priory nave, although in the fifteenth century the canons stopped serving the parochial nave themselves and built a separate chapel in an attempt to remove the local laity and their distracting activities.[99] Even without parochial responsibility, many monasteries must have remained the focus of their communities, and it was difficult to deny access to devoted laity wishing to observe the monastic liturgy, albeit from the nave through a screen.[100] The theoretical separation between the monastic and ministerial vocations failed, ultimately, to remove monasteries from some role in ministry to the people among whom they lived.

Society used its monasteries for functions other than spiritual: literacy and culture were for some time virtual monopolies of monks, who preserved much of the heritage of antiquity through the early middle ages.[101] Manuscript production, essential for monastic liturgy, and learning, for theological study and preaching, had to be maintained within monasteries, providing monks with skills which might be drawn upon by others, for instance in drawing up charters or providing a forum for judicial processes and agreements.[102] When such abilities became more widespread, especially in the twelfth century, monasteries were far less necessary to their provision. They still, however, played an essential part in manuscript production: Nigel Morgan shows how monastic liturgical books were made in monasteries for laity, and Lynda Dennison, in investigating one particular psalter from Ramsey Abbey, probes

---

[97] Marjorie Chibnall, 'Monks and Pastoral Work: a Problem in Anglo-Norman History', *Journal of Ecclesiastical History* 18 (1967), 165–72; Knowles, *Monastic Order*, pp. 596–600; Burton, *Monastic and Religious Orders*, pp. 44–9; Dickinson, *Augustinian Canons*, pp. 197–241; R. A. R. Hartridge, *A History of Vicarages in the Middle Ages* (Cambridge,1930).

[98] Below, Burton, esp. pp. 330–3.

[99] See also the parish church at Peterborough, discussed by Higham, pp. 170–1. The parishoners were buried in a cemetery next to the abbey.

[100] See Rogers on St Albans, below, pp. 275–6. Van Engen, 'Crisis of Cenobitism', pp. 298–9, comments on the centrality of Benedictine churches to communities.

[101] Care must be taken with such a generalization: see for instance Rosamond McKitterick, *The Carolingians and the Written Word* (Cambridge, 1989).

[102] See below, pp. 49–51. The pages of James Campbell, Eric John and Patrick Wormald, *The Anglo-Saxons* (London, 1982; repr. 1991), are decorated with many examples of manuscripts.

the complex world of later medieval production in which monasteries and laity were inextricably intertwined.[103] A symptom of this is the impossibility of being certain whether a particular illuminator or scribe was a monk or a laymen, although illuminators were probably more often laymen, who worked on texts written by monastic scribes; it is certain that laymen and monks worked together, and that monasteries were centres of exchange of texts and of exemplars of images. Here again, it was the permanence of monasteries which ensured their continuing utility even after laymen had acquired the same skills; lay workshops might be wiped out by plague or business failure, whereas monasteries kept their books and perpetuated their skills down the generations.[104]

Monasteries equally lost their dominance of education in the twelfth century, with the creation of cathedral schools and universities and the proliferation of a network of more or less formal places of education at all levels.[105] Monastic education thereafter was in the first place directed at those being trained for the cloister. The changing centre of gravity is revealed by the fact that later medieval monks went to – and Benedictines after 1336 were obliged to go to – the secular universities to get their education, and established halls and colleges there to accommodate their monks. Joan Greatrex traces the relationship between Ely Cathedral Priory and Cambridge University.[106] However, monasteries, like other great churches, could still provide local education: Roger Bowers shows that monasteries educated not only the sons of the great to whom they felt obliged, but also considerable numbers of local boys located in the monastic almonry, many of whom were paid for as part of the house's almsgiving. Since local fee-paying boys were also admitted, monasteries were providing a valuable service to local society. If such was the origin of Westminster School, for instance, known to have such an almonry school from the early fourteenth century, it suggests an additional origin of the English public school to the secular foundations of Winchester and Eton.[107]

The early medieval cultural and educational prestige of monasteries ensured that they supplied the church with many of its leading and greatest clergy – from St Augustine and Archbishop Theodore to Lanfranc and

[103] Below, pp. 135–6, Dennison, pp. 223–61.
[104] In England, music and liturgy was not so directly influenced by monasteries, since the predominant use of the Salisbury liturgy was derived from a secular church; Harper, *Western Liturgy*, pp. 202–3.
[105] Nicholas Orme, *English Schools in the Middle Ages* (London, 1973), especially pp. 167ff., 224–51.
[106] Below, pp. 312–28.
[107] Below, Bowers, pp. 177–222, *passim*, esp. pp. 199–204, 206–8, 213–16; see also Burton, p. 338.

Anselm.[108] Thereafter more high ecclesiastics were seculars, Becket in the mid-twelfth century perhaps neatly representing (if a little late) the shift, but a steady if small stream of bishops continued to emanate from the religious houses.[109] Barrie Dobson closes this volume with a survey of the last century of the monk-bishop, few either particularly distinguished or in very prominent sees.[110] Rather, chosen for the administrative competence demonstrated in running their large abbeys, and equipped with a university education, they efficiently set about the ordinary episcopal task in their dioceses. Moreover, the monastic contribution to the work of the secular church was increased by the tenure, by monk-bishops of impoverished – usually Welsh – sees, of their (richer) abbeys *in commendam*, whose resources were thus diverted to the support of ministry in some of the more difficult areas of the kingdom: all four Welsh cathedrals were restored by monk-bishops in this century.

There were other ways in which kings exploited monasteries. King Edgar allied with monastic reformers in the Tenth-Century Reformation to reinforce royal power, especially beyond the boundaries of Wessex, by gaining control of a network of reformed monasteries and their resources, and to focus the prayers of the whole kingdom on himself as the symbol of its salvation and unity.[111] The usefulness of such monasteries to the governance of the realm is seen in the wide jurisdictional rights which they were granted, such as Peterborough's 'soke' of eight hundred hides which gave it the rule of north-east Northamptonshire, just as much of Suffolk was carved up between Bury St Edmund's and the abbot of Ely.[112] William the Conqueror therefore had to secure control over the monasteries, and a process of Normanization was inevitable, although not inexorably comprehensive: Peterborough's abbot was confirmed, but then died to be replaced by the notorious Abbot Thorold of Glastonbury. William ensured that he both asserted his superiority over the Old English monasteries and used their vast resources to bolster the new conquest regime, by demanding quotas of knights; Peterborough's, at sixty, was at the top end of the scale.[113] Later kings tended to see, and tax, monasteries as part of the English church in general, as with John's

---

[108] The high point in England was reached after the tenth-century reform, up to the Conquest; Knowles, *Monastic Order*, pp. 65–7 and appendix IV.

[109] Knowles, *Monastic Order*, appendix XII; *Religious Orders*, I, appendix I; II, appendix III.

[110] Below, pp. 348–67.

[111] See above, nn. 50, 82; below, pp. 137–40.

[112] Below, pp. 147–51. H. M. Cam, *Liberties and Communities in Medieval England* (Cambridge, 1944), pp. 100–1, 182–204; Edward Miller, *The Abbey and Bishopric of Ely* (Cambridge,1951), pp. 25–35, 199–246.

[113] Burton, *Monastic and Religious Orders*, pp. 21–9; Knowles, *Monastic Order*, pp. 100–27; below, pp. 151–2; for the debate see above, n. 51.

confiscation of property in the interdict, although Edward I's removal of monies stored for papal taxation was perceived as an attack on the monasteries where they were housed.[114] During the Hundred Years' War, property and priories belonging to French mother-houses were taken into royal hands and used to support the war, a deprivation made permanent in the fifteenth century through the confiscation and redistribution of the alien priories (a story I told at Harlaxton in 1992).[115]

The landowners benefited considerably from this dissolution, as they did from the later one. A land-hungry aristocracy was always on the look out for opportunities to gain control over, or even to appropriate, the resources of a significant but potentially vulnerable sector of the landlords, especially where their spiritual activities offered them little. Early medieval nobles diverted monastic land to themselves and their kin through lay abbacies and, in eighth-century England, the fiction of bookland.[116] The subinfeudation of knights onto the estates of the Old English abbeys after the Conquest constituted a major redistribution of land; nor was simple annexation beyond the thinkable in turbulent times such as the Anglo-Norman period.[117] Later, gentry aimed to influence or control monastic property by filling the office of steward, as William Paston did at Bromholm, and by leasing estates, when this became normal in the fifteenth century.[118]

Other ways in which the aristocracy used monastic resources have been illustrated above in the discussion of patrons, since non-patrons, in the guise of benefactors, advocates, or otherwise, could avail themselves of such benefits by persuasion or coercion. The rest of society might receive from religious houses ministry and alms or might take opportunities of employment,

---

[114] Sidney Painter, *The Reign of King John* (Baltimore, 1949), pp. 174–6, 183-4; J. H. Denton, *Robert Winchelsey and the Crown, 1294–1313* (Cambridge, 1980), pp. 63–9.

[115] Benjamin Thompson, 'The Laity, the Alien Priories and the Redistribution of Ecclesiastical Property', *England in the Fifteenth Century: Proceedings of the 1992 Harlaxton Symposium*, Harlaxton Medieval Studies V, ed. Nicholas Rogers (Stamford, 1994), 19–41.

[116] Above, n. 73; Bede, Letter to Ecgberht, § 11, in *Venerabilis Baedae Opera Historica*, 2 vols (Oxford, 1896), I, pp. 414–17.

[117] Above, n. 45; see the restorations of Nigel d'Aubigny in the early twelfth century: *Charters of the Honour of Mowbray 1107–1191*, ed. D. E. Greenway (London, 1972), nos 2–8; and, famously, J. H. Round, *Geoffrey de Mandeville* (London, 1892), pp. 209–22. See also the more subtle ways of using monastic resources at n. 81 above.

[118] Above, n. 49; Christine Carpenter, *Locality and Polity: a Study of Warwickshire Landed Society, 1401–1499* (Cambridge, 1992), p. 33, and e.g. pp. 129, 186, 250 n.23, 325: following the fortunes of religious houses through the index of this massive work gives one a good sense of their involvement in the rough and tumble of local politics.

especially as monasteries increasingly employed laypeople and admitted servants.[119] The larger monasteries naturally became the focus of local economies: particularly those houses in existence in the tenth century when the European economy began to take off, like Cluny and Peterborough, found that people gathered round for livelihood and protection, and generated markets and towns.[120] Monastic intentions to flee from world and keep it at bay were subverted by the world coming to the monasteries.

The papers in this volume show the world intruding itself into the cloister in many ways, as it did in most religious houses at most times: the cacophony of parishioners at Kirkham, even when seeking the monastery's ministry in marriage or baptism, caused the monks to try to remove them from the priory nave; parties of the monks' kin came into Durham to be received into the confraternity; lay servants, traders and administrators came and went, keeping the wheels of the monastic economy and administration turning; almonry boys were housed within the walls or came from nearby for their lessons and to sing in the Lady Chapel; illuminators on the monastic circuit stayed for a time to work up a few pages of a lavish manuscript; guests from great lords and their households downwards abounded alongside the poor; 'poets, harpists, musicians and clowns' had to be warned off in 747; and when it came to burying the great and the good, or the monastery's servants, no doubt their kin turned up in large numbers, as did the poor to receive their clothing and doles.[121] Such are only some of the most direct and graphic images of the continuous contact of monasteries with their world, and the ways in which they were shaped by it.

We may now be able to answer our original question, what is a monastery? For it is sufficiently clear that, both in supplying monasticism with the preconditions of existence in ideas, people, and resources, and in demanding a return on that investment, monasteries were what society made them. Our title is a tautology, a false dichotomy. Monasteries could only be established if society entertained the ideology which legitimated their existence. They needed a continuous flow of recruits from society, who unceasingly brought the world into the cloister. They needed constant external support in many forms. Society demanded a perpetual return on its investment in equally varied ways. Times changed and brought different pressures. The symbiosis between religious houses and their world was a continuous and dynamic negotiation. Monasteries were thus always shaped by forces beyond their control; the notion that flight from the world was

[119] For a recent discussion of servants, Harvey, *Living and Dying*, ch. V.
[120] Below, pp. 140-7; 152-7, 159-62; M. D. Lobel, *The Borough of Bury St Edmund's: a Study in the Government and Development of a Monastic Town* (Oxford, 1935), pp. 5-6, 9-11.
[121] *Clofesho* is quoted below by Foot, pp. 35, 43. For a lavish funeral, see John Paston's at Bromholm in 1466, *Paston Letters*, IV, pp. 227-31.

possible was a fantasy, albeit one that was sometimes briefly realized by institutions and individuals. Even when trying to be separate from it, monasteries were inherently and centrally part of medieval society.

Religious houses, however, were not only passive, ineluctably moulded by external influences. In the many ways in which they contributed to the world, they also shaped it in return. Religious innovation usually came from a monastic milieu before the later middle ages, most spectacularly in the papal reform of the eleventh century with its insistence on distinguishing the clergy as a separate order of society on the monastic model of world-rejection.[122] Anglo-Saxon kingdoms were converted by monks; tenth-century reformers revitalized its religion, and the eleventh- and twelfth-century reform of the English church was carried out under the leadership of monks such as Lanfranc and Anselm. The friars had an enormous impact in the later medieval evangelization of the population which Christianized society more thoroughly from top to bottom.[123] Even Henry VII, in appointing ten monastic bishops in the course of his reign, seems to have made a half-hearted attempt at religious reform under monastic leadership.[124] Not that changing the world was always the preferred task of those who had chosen to reject it: such spiritual leaders often oscillated between their enclosed contemplative lives and the world which called them to reform it. This pattern can be discerned from Fursa and Cuthbert, through Peter Damian, Anselm and Bernard, to later medieval hermits and anchorites such as Julian of Norwich, and even the more observant fifteenth-century monastic bishops and the Carthusians, Bridgettines and Franciscan Observants around Henry VII.[125] Yet the tension is revealing: those who most successfully fled from the world and communed with God were also those most needed to pass on some of their insight and experience to lesser mortals. The paradox may be that, when the spirituality of world-rejection was at its most vibrant, it was most influential in the world.

At a less intense level much later medieval liturgy and lay piety had monastic roots. Nigel Morgan traces some of the specific ways in which

---

[122] H. E. J. Cowdrey, *The Cluniacs and the Gregorian Reform* (Oxford, 1970), esp. pp. 141–56.

[123] Above, n. 86. I use the term, of course, neutrally, not to suggest that people were any better or worse, but simply that Christian ideas, beliefs and practices now thoroughly infused their lives in a way that they had not earlier; see Rosalind and Christopher Brooke, *Popular Religion in the Middle Ages* (London, 1984), and the comprehensive account of Eamon Duffy, *The Stripping of the Altars: Traditional Religion in England, 1400–1580* (New Haven & London, 1992), part I.

[124] Below, pp. 350–1.

[125] Below, pp. 35–6, 356–7, 361; Lawrence, *Medieval Monasticism*, pp. 154–6, 183–4; R. W. Southern, *St Anselm: Portrait in a Landscape* (Cambridge, 1990), pp. 168–71, 183, 189–94, ch. 10, etc.; Beckett, 'Henry VII and Sheen', pp. 124–5.

monastic piety and devotion spread from the monastery to the rest of society: Marian liturgy and images were developed in religious houses in the twelfth century, which were transmitted to the secular church and the laity to create the Marian devotion central to later medieval piety.[126] The orders which retained their spiritual vitality, including the Bridgettines, maintained this influence: at the tip of an iceberg, on the eve of the Reformation a monk of the Bridgettine monastery of Syon produced an immediately popular manual of lay spirituality, informed by monastic practice, *A Work for Householders*.[127] It is indeed a criticism sometimes levelled at the later medieval church that its piety was too monastic, too much based on sin and penitence and not offering enough of a distinctly lay pattern of devotion.[128] This looks less convincing now that rich studies of later religious practice have shown how in their thorough internalization of Christianity the laity also appropriated and reshaped it to their needs.[129] But the fact that such a criticism could be made reflects the enormous monastic (including mendicant) contribution to the late medieval success, even once most monks had perhaps played their part and retired to the background in a world where innovation was more likely to come from seculars.

The role of monks called from the cloister was not confined to religion. The church was a powerful and influential part of society, and in leading it they also played an important political role. The high profile of a St Hugh on the later eleventh-century stage was replicated at lower levels. The monks in the Tenth-Century Reformation must be mentioned again, as well the post-Conquest archbishops – Lanfranc leading the Normanization and reform of the English church, Anselm loyally leading resistance to rebellions against Rufus and Henry I.[130] Politics at whatever level was an unavoidable concomitant of conspicuous office and control of land; bishops, abbots and priors were part of political society, both nationally (reflected in, but not confined to, the participation of the greatest in parliament as lords) and locally, where they controlled the land on which power was based, and were necessarily part of the local aristocracy.[131] Since local stability was more

---

[126] Below, pp. 117–36.

[127] Duffy, *Stripping of the Altars*, pp. 86–7.

[128] Steven Ozment, *The Age of Reform, 1250–1550* (New Haven and London, 1980), pp. 220–2.

[129] E.g. Duffy, *Stripping of the Altars*.

[130] Golding, *Conquest and Colonization*, pp. 146–76; Margaret Gibson, *Lanfranc of Bec* (Oxford, 1978), pp. 113–61; Frank Barlow, *William Rufus* (London, 1983), pp. 349–51; Southern, *Anselm*, p. 293.

[131] Discussion of the role of ecclesiastical lords in local politics and power ('bastard feudalism') is found in Dobson, *Durham Priory*, pp. 183–202; and see Christine Carpenter, *Locality and Polity*, cited in n. 118, and the many local studies of the later middle ages; a few comments are found below in Bowers, pp. 179, 194–5, 197, Lynda Rollason, pp. 281, 286–90, and Dobson, pp. 362–3. See also my

crucial to them than lay lords, who in the last resort could defend themselves, it may be that they attempted to use that influence to reduce tensions and prevent disputes getting out of hand: this was how Prior Wessington of Durham played his hand in the gradual breakdown of order in the north-east in the first half of the fifteenth century.[132]

The ways in which monasteries shaped the world might be very tangible, therefore. Monastic landlords could maintain consistent management of their estates without the changes of ownership, personnel and location, suffered by lay lineages and even episcopal administrations. Their lordship therefore tended to be conservative, and whether it bore down on peasants harder or not, it was probably different from lay lordship.[133] In a different way, even the Cistercians who most dramatically and physically attempted to reject society by placing themselves in marginal areas (the north) and accepting marginal and unexploited land, ended up moulding its economy: they colonized that land, expanding the boundaries of cultivation, and, by running millions of sheep on it, stimulated and grew rich upon the booming wool trade.[134]

The greater monasteries naturally controlled their environments more than any others, both through their extensive jurisdiction over manors and hundreds, and their wide economic interests, with the markets and towns which developed round them. Donald Mackreth shows how Martin de Bec, abbot of Peterborough in the mid-twelfth century, completely relocated the town from the old burh, which was taken into the monastic precinct, in order to rebuild the abbey and presumably to expand the increasingly wealthy town.[135] Like other such great houses, relations with those at the door could be difficult because of these monasteries' insistence on retaining manorial control and refusal to grant the autonomy of a borough charter. Even though Jack Higham in taking up the story shows that the townsmen were given some freedom and certainly prospered, they still had frustrations to express in the revolt of 1381 when, with manorial tenants from round about, they marched on the abbey. They were less lucky than rebels elsewhere, however, such as those at St Albans, and Bury, where they killed the prior and paraded his head on a spike; Henry Despenser, bishop of Norwich, happened to be passing Peterborough and put down the attack with brutal severity.[136] That

---

forthcoming book, although there is a subject here still awaiting a systematic investigation.

[132] Dobson, *Durham Priory*, pp. 188–202.

[133] Edward Miller and John Hatcher, *Medieval England: Rural Society and Economic Change, 1086–1348* (London, 1978), pp. 182–3, 190–1, 199–203, 204–5. *The Agrarian History of England and Wales*, III: *1348–1500*, ed. Edward Miller (Cambridge, 1991), pp. 571, 574, 578–9.

[134] Burton, *Monastic and Religious Orders*, pp. 253–60.

[135] Below, pp. 152–6.

[136] Below, pp, 159–67; *The Peasants' Revolt of 1381*, ed. R.B. Dobson (London, 1970),

monasteries could provoke such a reaction from those around them – and could continue to until the sixteenth century, if not on the same scale – testifies to their great secular power, to their enormous influence on the world. Medieval society was partly what monasticism made it.

It was not opposition from peasants and townspeople which eventually destroyed the monasteries. The support of more powerful people had to be forfeited before there was any serious threat to their existence. Yet it is clear that maintaining such support was absolutely necessary to survival, let alone prosperity. At any particular time the world might ask itself whether it was getting what it needed and valued from its houses in return for its investment.[137] Religious therefore had to be adaptable to society's needs, and the ways in which that could be done have been illustrated; they included persuading society that what it needed was what monasteries provided. Such adaptation might, however, ease an institution or order away from its original aims and ideal. It might constitute what reformers would denounce as 'corruption', or 'secularization' (as in the 'secular domination' of monasteries criticized in the tenth century). Yet even the constant renewal and redefinition of monasticism by reforming movements was part of its adaptation, in so far as it fitted demands in society, or moulded those demands. Monasticism was highly successful in the middle ages, and that success was built upon satisfying a great range of needs and desires. The religious ideals of reformers could strike a chord with numbers of recruits, at the same time as attracting the wider support of benefactors who in turn received worthwhile commodities. The Cluniac priory of the central middle ages, for example, represented a well-wrought balance between society's perceived need for intercession, the recruit's need for a structured spiritual lifestyle, and the patron's desire for ministry in his castle, prayers for his soul, and visible demonstration of his lordship.[138]

The need to maintain this balance through changing times (changes partly brought about by monks) dictates that the medieval history of monasticism was dynamic, a constantly shifting panorama rather than a story of stability and peace.[139] Early medieval monasticism was at the centre of the Christianizing project, yet monasteries were liable to be subjected to the

---

pp. 243–8, 269–84, 297–300; Lobel, *Bury St Edmund's*, pp. 118–70, esp. pp. 150–5. For some tensions in other boroughs before 1381, Burton, *Monastic and Religious Orders*, p. 244.

[137] The laity put this into words in parliament: Thompson, '*Habendum et Tenendum*', pp. 214–17.

[138] A theme underlying the argument of Van Engen, 'Crisis of Cenobitism'; see Golding, 'Coming of the Cluniacs'.

[139] The following inevitably simplifies vast swathes of medieval history, but is an attempt to trace some of the essential developments.

domination of the lay nobles who funded and peopled them, often draining their spiritual vitality: hence Bede's complaints, and Charlemagne's then Cluny's (and Dunstan's) reforms based on the Benedictine Rule. Such reforms often relied on – and strengthened the hand of – the king against the nobles, so that when royal power failed or was disrupted, it could no longer preserve monasteries from renewed 'secularization'. New waves of reformers then attempted to revitalize the whole church through the papacy on monastic principles of world-rejection, at first in alliance with the emperor, then, with Gregory VII, spectacularly in opposition to his secular power. Reform was now focused on the secular church, in order to equip it to provide spiritual ministry and leadership throughout society. Paradoxically, therefore, this process also involved the monks losing their leadership of Christianity: popes became lawyers, and canons, and later friars, now represented the combination of asceticism and ministry which early medieval monks had embodied. This allowed monks to retreat more fully from society than had been possible earlier on: the monastic movements which rose in parallel with papal reform, most obviously the Cistercians, emphasized the original Benedictine ideal of isolation from the world, stiffened with a more eremitical emphasis, seen at its fullest in the Carthusians.

While this was an opportunity for monks to concentrate on their own spiritual exercises, it thereby deprived them of their pre-eminence in learning, culture and education, as well as ministry. Theological creativity largely passed to the cathedral schools and then the universities, who trained the higher clergy, and educated those who trained the lower. This threatened to reduce drastically what monasteries gave to society, but for the moment they retained their function of intercession, on the all-pervasive Cluniac model to which even the Cistercians and Carthusians eventually succumbed, since it was compatible with a degree of isolation.[140] They continued to attract benefactors needing suffrages, and to retain their support. Yet this threatened to re-secularize the monasteries, both because of the range of secular benefits which patrons sought, and more insidiously in the hardening of the exchange-mentality through which spiritual services were bought, and monasteries were threatened with disendowment for failure to perform them.[141] Moreover, this function was increasingly taken over by the secular clergy in the fourteenth and fifteenth centuries, with the emergence of the chantry and the secular college. It seemed possible, when attacks were launched on the monks by Wyclif and others, that monasteries would be left without a useful role in society, only vast properties. The lay powers certainly did not hesitate to dissolve those institutions which they perceived as offering nothing to them, such as the alien priories, and to redeploy their resources in

---

[140] See n. 53, and for the character of Charterhouses as federations of chantries, Thompson, *Carthusian Order*, pp. 172–5, 200–5, 210–13, 219–21, 230, 234.

[141] Thompson, 'From "Alms" to "Spiritual Services"', and n. 137.

more useful ways, primarily secular and academic colleges.[142]

This may provide the context in which to place the renewed integration of monasteries into society in the later middle ages. The monasteries seem to have made an effort, particularly in the fifteenth century, to open themselves out to society, and in particular to their own localities. Much of this survey, and the papers below, illustrate this.[143] The membrane between the cloister and the world, which had always allowed osmosis, became so thin as to be transparent. The religious houses transmitted their devotion to the laity through the liturgy and the production of books, while equally religious absorbed secular learning by being sent away to the universities. The almonry schools of at least thirty houses provided a fundamental local service. The pages of the Durham *Liber Vitae* were increasingly crowded in the later middle ages with many local names – of family groups of monks, of benefactors and friends from the aristocracy to townspeople, and also the tenants of the priory and their connections. Perhaps, paradoxically, in integrating more closely into the locality, monasticism narrowed the original breadth of its spiritual vision. Indeed it seems likely that more laypeople were buried in the cloister as time went on.[144] Barrie Dobson suggests that black monks were playing an increasingly active role in the ordinary life of the English church in the fifteenth century, as preachers, penitentiaries, spiritual mentors and suffragan bishops.[145] Monastic writers were aware of this: in redefining the role of monastic life in the church, Thomas Walsingham emphasized the centrality of monks to the life of the community, not their separation from it.[146]

One might wonder, indeed, how distinct later medieval English monasteries were: how different did they look from secular churches of the time? In style they were very similar, and although their cloisters presented a different aspect, the updating of their buildings narrowed the difference.[147] Royal edifices such as Henry VII's chapel and St George's, Windsor, were built by a group of architects who worked on other buildings, both secular

---

[142] Thompson, '*Habendum et Tendendum*', pp. 224–36; 'Laity and the Alien Priories'.

[143] An exception is Janet Burton's evidence, which suggests that Kirkham Priory distanced itself from the parish in the fifteenth century by building a parochial chapel and appointing parochial chaplains. Yet these were Augustinians, and the reason may have been simply to avoid infection by plague, below, pp. 335–7.

[144] Below: Morgan, Dennison, Greatrex, Bowers, Lynda Rollason, Rogers.

[145] Below, pp. 357–8.

[146] James Clark, 'Intellectual Life at the Abbey of St Albans and the Nature of Monastic Learning in England, *c.*1350–*c.*1440: the Work of Thomas Walsingham in Context', unpublished D. Phil. dissertation, University of Oxford (1997), pp. 282–90. I am indebted to Dr Clark for this reference, and for discussing the point with me.

[147] See Castle Acre, above, n. 24.

and monastic, and who occupied the same milieu.[148] Lady Chapel choirs were imported into monasteries in imitation of the secular church at the end of the fourteenth century, and monasteries employed secular choir-trainers who also worked in secular churches, just as illuminators moved easily between monastic and secular workshops.[149] The almonry schools were less a distinct development in the provision of local education than an addition to the available provision. Lay schoolmasters taught in the almonry schools just as they did in secular schools, and sometimes both at once; local boys, some of them external fee-payers, experienced little difference between the two types of education, especially since some almonry boys were sent to the local grammar school.[150] University education was common to the most successful clergy in both spheres. The increasing individualization of spiritual services for and the burials of monks paralleled developments in the lay and secular spheres. Quite apart from the scandals revealed in the visitations, the increasingly porous precinct of the monastery was the location for a way of life which was becoming less distinct: monks had private property, slept and ate less communally, ate an ordinary (in fact rather aristocratic, protein-filled) diet, held private property, even kept women, and spent much of their time administering their own complex and internally-differentiated institutions as obedientiaries.[151] The monastic bishops were selected to take charge of a diocese primarily because of their success in running another great ecclesiastical institution, a monastery which was usually richer than their see; the fact that they often ran both concurrently makes the point neatly.[152]

Shrines and images were located in both monastic and secular churches; indeed the major pilgrimage centres of late-medieval England were monasteries, such as Walsingham, which accommodated a large and constant flow of pilgrims.[153] Half of the English cathedrals had been monastic since the eleventh century, requiring monks to play a public and ministerial role to some extent; one wonders how different from the secular cathedrals they were or had remained, especially in view of the smooth transformation of many priories (and indeed of other abbeys such as Peterborough) into secular cathedral chapters at the Dissolution, with many of the same personnel, in the

---

[148]   Christopher Wilson, 'The Designer of Henry VII's Chapel, WestminsterAbbey', in *The Reign of Henry VII*, ed. Thompson, 133–56.

[149]   Below, pp. 208ff., 241ff., 258–61; Magnus Williamson, 'The Eton Choir book: Collegiate Music-Making in the Reign of Henry VII', in *The Reign of Henry VII*, ed. Thompson, 213–28, p. 225: John Tucke was educated at Winchester, and worked at Higham Ferrers College and Gloucester Abbey.

[150]   Below, Bowers, *passim*, esp. pp. 181–2, 191–2, 194, 200–4, 207–8, 217.

[151]   Harvey, *Living and Dying*, illustrates many of these themes *passim*.

[152]   Below, pp. 355–8.

[153]   J. C. Dickinson, *The Shrine of Our Lady of Walsingham* (Cambridge, 1956). See generally R. C. Finucane, *Miracles and Pilgrims: Popular Beliefs in Medieval England* (1977).

same buildings.[154] Later medieval secular colleges were established often to fulfil the same role as high-medieval Benedictine priories, to provide intercession and ministry to a noble family.[155] Some black-monk houses were indeed transformed into secular colleges in the fifteenth century (such as Stoke-by-Clare), and at the Dissolution some nobles hoped to be able to do the same, as the duke of Norfolk envisaged for Thetford Priory.[156] One priory of canons founded in fourteenth-century Norfolk at Ingham was in fact part of a group of secular colleges founded in a short space of time by inter-connected families, and was sometimes called 'college' rather than 'priory'.[157] Some failing, smaller houses were dissolved and transformed into chantries.[158] The interchangeability of secular and monastic forms may not only be an index of what was deemed efficient and useful; it may have been that their differences had become too small to justify retaining distinctions.

This may make the central point: monasteries were clearly doing, and making an effort to do, plenty of useful things for society in the later middle ages, for which they were valued. But fewer and fewer of these functions were exclusive to them, because, like illumination and intercession, the secular church and world had learnt how to do them and had even taken over leadership in them – and, further, because the monks responded by trying to imitate what the secular world was doing, like education and ministry, thus further diluting their particularity. It was not that the monasteries were making no contribution to society, just that that contribution did not have to be made by monks. The very few enclosed religious who maintained the observance of the specifically monastic vocation (Carthusians, Bridgettines, Franciscan Observants) indeed retained the respect of society and its support.[159] They were the exceptions that prove the rule: it is understandable that most monasteries could be perceived to have lost their *raison d'être*. Why not convert them into collegiate churches, which could do the things which were valued such as intercession, education and almsgiving, and strip off the unnecessary paraphernalia of monasticism and the vast edifice of administration it had evolved?

That is not, of course, an account of what actually happened in the 1530s and '40s. For that, both the particular motives of kings, ministers and landowners or potential landowners, and the new religious ideals of more extreme reformers have to be taken into account; since the Dissolution was

---

[154] Knowles, *Religious Orders*, III, pp. 359, 389–92.

[155] Both were also established by bishops, as their chantries.

[156] Thompson, 'Monasteries and their Patrons', pp. 113–14, 118–19.

[157] Thompson, '*Habendum et Tenendum*', pp. 233–6 for a sketch; Norfolk Record Office, Norwich Episcopal Registers, V, fol. 2v. My forthcoming book will deal with secular colleges in detail.

[158] Thompson, 'Monasteries and their Patrons', pp. 114–16.

[159] Knowles, *Religious Orders*, III, pp. 206–40.

not a universal phenomenon in Europe, some of its causes must have been particular to time and place, and they explain why the Reformation that did happen was not necessarily the one that might have been predicted or regarded as desirable. But such an analysis may help to explain the general condition of the monasteries which made the Dissolution possible (preceding much of the Reformation in England), and thus why it was relatively easy to accomplish.[160]

Monasteries were necessarily part of society, while through the conceptualization of separation from it they were also conceived as having a relationship with it, a relationship which these essays shows to have been symbiotic, complex and changing. In the early centuries, while the monks provided Christian leadership, their position was secure; but monastic ideologues would hardly have approved of them as monks – their role was more that of clergy, active in the world. Their success was not specifically monastic success, but the success of institutions which happened to participate more or less in monastic forms. When religious and cultural leadership passed elsewhere, therefore, monks could focus more specifically on the monastic vocation. But to do that, they needed to retain social support, which required them to respond to social demands, or to persuade society of its need for what the monks were offering. Since these tended to focus on what laypeople wanted, and therefore to 'secularize' monastic activities in various different ways, this, as well as simple weakness, made it harder for monks to maintain their distinct religious function, especially once intercession had been replicated in secular churches and was no longer a monastic monopoly. Whether we blame the religious or society for this is beside the point. More important is to notice that this joint failure was a religious one: monks failed to maintain performance of their distinct contemplative vocation, and society no longer believed that its widespread practice was something essential to it. We should not be surprised that social institutions evolve, fail and are replaced: the river of time runs on, and eventually it leaves even its most durable and flexible bodies washed up on its banks, having failed just once too often to keep up with – or to mould – the times. But they had handed on to other institutions and other parts of society almost all of the important functions which they had performed; the survival of these may seem more important than the destruction of the structures which had embodied them.

The history of monasticism over a millennium and more was a dynamic process of constant change, in which new institutions were continually being founded, and older ones evolving and being transformed; the Dissolution was in many respects a natural extension of that process. We should end,

[160] J. J. Scarisbrick, *The Reformation and the English People* (Oxford, 1984), and Christopher Haigh, *English Reformations* (Oxford, 1993) show that the Reformation was more difficult and longer term than was thought, but do not change the picture on the Dissolution significantly.

therefore, by focusing not so much on the ultimate failure as on the long-lived success of the monasteries, who sustained themselves for centuries, even a millennium: they exercised an enormous influence on medieval society, and left a rich legacy to the modern world.

The Role of the Minster in Earlier Anglo-Saxon Society[1]

SARAH FOOT

At the reforming council held at *Clofesho* in 747 the English bishops were charged to ensure that the *monasteria* in their dioceses, 'as their names imply, be virtuous dwellings of stillness and of those who quietly labour for the Lord; they should not be refuges for those indulging in boisterous arts, that is poets, harpists, musicians, or clowns, but habitations of prayer, reading and the praise of God, of sober and continent living and psalmody'.[2] This tension between the quiet contemplation of the cloister and the lively noise of the hall lies at the heart of the Anglo-Saxon monastic experience, reflecting not just the social origins and enduring tastes of so many monks and nuns, but also their continued contact with the secular world. This was not, of course, a difficulty peculiar to English circumstances; early Irish monasteries were similarly integrated into their secular environment.[3] Fursa had first left Ireland because he could not endure the noise of the crowds who thronged to him, but coming to England he found his minster in East Anglia no more peaceful and left charge of it and the care of its souls to his brother in order to become a hermit.[4] Even hermits could not escape external pressures. St

---

1   Many of the arguments advanced in this paper are explored at greater length in my forthcoming book on Anglo-Saxon minsters for the Cambridge University Press series, Studies in Anglo-Saxon England. I am grateful to Michael Bentley, John Blair, Katy Cubitt and particularly to Julia Smith for discussing various points of detail with me and commenting on an earlier draft.

2   Council of *Clofesho*, 747, c. 20 in *Councils and Ecclesiastical Documents Relating to Great Britain and Ireland*, ed. A. W. Haddan and W. Stubbs, 3 vols (Oxford, 1869–78), III, 362–76, p. 369.

3   K. Hughes, *Church and Society in Ireland AD 400–1200*, ed. D. Dumville (Aldershot, 1987), nos VIII and IX, and for 'monastic towns' in Ireland see also R. Sharpe, 'Some Problems Concerning the Organisation of the Church in Early Medieval Ireland', *Peritia* 3 (1984), 230–70, pp. 260–2.

4   *EH*, III. 19 (pp. 274–7). Compare the yearning of ninth-century Irish religious for 'hidden secluded little huts' where in austere surroundings there might be 'attention to reading, renunciation of fighting and visiting, a calm, easy conscience': G. Murphy, *Early Irish Lyrics, Eighth to Twelfth Century* (Oxford, 1956), no. 9, pp. 18–20, and cf. no. 8, p. 10; cited by Hughes, *Church and Society*,

Cuthbert was taken unwillingly from his hermitage on Farne in order to return to the world as a bishop,[5] while others found that the world came to them. A Northumbrian nobleman, Wilgils, gave up his worldly career to live in solitary austerity by the Humber estuary, serving God through fasting, prayer and vigils in a little oratory there, but his fame having attracted crowds wanting to hear his teaching, he soon found himself heading a small congregation of servants of God, endowed with some small estates beside the headland to build a church.[6]

The inability of Wilgils to achieve social isolation was a typical experience: rumour of sanctity might often lead to the congregation of followers around solitaries. Would-be Merovingian ascetics had met with the same experience.[7] Gregory of Tours told a markedly similar story of the Auvergnat saint, Martius, who cut for himself a cave out of the mountain rock a little way outside the city of Clermont, and lived in lonely austerity, but his holiness became known and 'attracted by the fame of such a great man, some men began to gather near him, wishing to instruct themselves by his teaching. ... He brought men together, made them monks, and rendered them perfect in the work of God'.[8] It is indeed the case that these episodes belong to the stock of hagiographical commonplace, such an incident being related in the *Life of St Anthony*, as Rollason and Cambridge have recently reminded us.[9] The tension created by the apparent inevitability of incursion from the secular world into the monastic life was not unique to the Anglo-Saxon experience, and coloured much medieval writing on the proper pursuit of the monastic ideal.[10] The English response, however, was to create a church

---

VIII, p. 112.

[5] Anon, *Vita S. Cuthberti*, III. 1, in *Two Lives of St Cuthbert*, ed. and transl. B. Colgrave (Cambridge, 1940, repr. 1985), 60–139, pp. 94–7.

[6] Alcuin, *Vita S. Willibrordi*, ch. 1; ed. W. Levison, Monumenta Germaniae Historica [MGH], *Scriptores Rerum Merovingicarum [SSRM]*, ed. B. Krusch, 7 vols (Hanover, 1884–1920), VII, 81–141, p. 116.

[7] I. Wood, 'A Prelude to Columbanus: the Monastic Achievement in the Burgundian Territories', in *Columbanus and Merovingian Monasticism*, ed. H. B. Clarke and M. Brennan, British Archaeological Reports, International Series 113 (1981), 3–32, pp. 5–6.

[8] Gregory of Tours, *Liber vitae patrum*, XIV.2, in MGH, *SSRM*, I.2, 661–744, p. 719; cited by G. Fournier, *Le peuplement rural en basse Auvergne durant le haut moyen âge* (Paris, 1962), pp. 412–15.

[9] E. Cambridge and D. Rollason, 'Debate: the Pastoral Organisation of the Anglo-Saxon Church: a Review of the "Minster Hypothesis"', *Early Medieval Europe* 4 (1995), 87–104, p. 93, n. 27, citing Life of St Anthony, c. 13: J.-P. Migne, *Patrologiae Cursus Completus: Series Latina*, 221 vols (Paris, 1844–64), LXXIII, col. 134.

[10] For general discussion of the monastic ideal and the influence of the secular world

in which communities of religious lay closer to the integrated than the separated end of the spectrum of possible responses to this dilemma, which solution this paper seeks to explore.

It is not only impossible, but arguably inappropriate, to separate the Anglo-Saxon church from the world in which it was situated, of which its clerical members were born, with whose secular families the members of religious communities retained important links beyond their entry to the cloister. For their survival religious communities were dependent on being sufficiently of the world to obtain the physical nourishment necessary to sustain their prayerful, otherworldly, life. This is not to deny that secular and spiritual spheres were perceptibly different: in social, legal and ecclesiastical terms there was indeed a sharp distinction between what it was to be a king's thegn and a soldier of Christ, a bride of man and a bride of Christ. One of the major concerns of church legislators in this period, reflected also in the secular codes, was to ensure that such distinctions were rigorously maintained.[11] The dichotomy between the church and the world is, however, at its sharpest and most visible at the extremes which separated the two societies: it is best defined by the contrast between earthly wealth and individual poverty within the minster, between abundance and self-denial, luxury and ascetic rigour, earthly warfare and spiritual conflict.[12] At the points where lay and religious lives converged, where the church came into direct contact with the world, the areas of separation are less susceptible to precise definition.

Investigation of the nature of the exchange between these two worlds, and their mutual involvement in each other's lives, may serve to illuminate the theme central to the conference on monasteries and society from which these papers derive. After some general remarks about the internal organ-isation of religious communities, the roles performed by these congregations within Anglo-Saxon lay society in the pre-Viking period will be examined under three heads: the insights offered by the evidence for the motives inspiring the creation of minsters; the apparent centrality of churches in the physical and social landscape; and information relating to the services, sacramental and charitable, performed by religious on behalf of their lay

---

on its expression see L. J. R. Milis, *Angelic Monks and Earthly Men: Monasticism and its Meaning to Medieval Society* (Woodbridge, 1992). Nor were these tensions peculiar to the Christian west; see, for example, R. Morris, 'Spiritual Fathers and Temporal Patrons: Logic and Contradiction in Byzantine Monasticism in the Tenth Century', *Revue Bénédictine* 103 (1993), 273–88, pp. 273–6.

[11] For example, council of *Clofesho*, 747, cc. 19, 28 (*Councils*, III, pp. 368–9, 374).

[12] On the conflict between spiritual perfection and material prosperity in the monastic ideal see J. van Engen, 'The "Crisis of Cenobitism" Reconsidered: Benedictine Monasticism in the Years 1050–1150', *Speculum* 61 (1986), 269–304, pp. 285–92.

neighbours. Examples employed are drawn primarily from the period before the monastic revolution of King Edgar's reign, which led to a substantial rethinking of the nature of the communal religious life, and clear articulation for the first time of the roles appropriate to those living according to a rule.

Religious Families

At the outset it is necessary to clarify the terms in which I shall be defining the communities with which I am concerned, particularly since I depart somewhat from the conclusions reached by David Rollason elsewhere in this volume.[13] It is clear from the contemporary literature relating to early Anglo-Saxon ecclesiastical organisation that all religious lived within organised communities; church councils in the seventh and eighth centuries reiterated injunctions against wandering clergy, asserting the importance of the ties between religious and their houses of origin and imposing penalties on those who sheltered clergy away from their homes.[14] The sources do not, however, distinguish between the kinds of community in which such religious may have dwelt; they are generally called by the blanket term *monasterium*, or its Old English equivalent, *mynster*.[15] Houses are not differentiated in any other way, not according to the number, gender, or clerical rank of their occupants, nor with reference to their internal organisation, method of regulation and manner of spiritual observance, nor by reason of the function or role performed by the institutions and their members within lay society. It is on this basis that I have suggested that we, too, should adopt one blanket

---

[13]   These conference proceedings are not the most appropriate place at which to enter into the complexities of the so-called 'minster debate'; see rather the paper by Cambridge and Rollason, 'Pastoral Organisation' and the reply by J. Blair, 'Debate: Ecclesiastical Organisation and Pastoral Care in Anglo-Saxon England', *Early Medieval Europe* 4 (1995), 193–212.

[14]   Council of Hertford 672/3, cc. 4–5 (*EH*, IV. 5, pp. 350–1); council of *Clofesho* 747, c. 29 (*Councils*, III, pp. 374–5); legatine synod 786, c. 6 (ed. E. Dümmler, MGH Epistolae IV, *Epistolae Karolini Aevi*, II (Berlin, 1895), 19–29, p. 22, no. 3); council of Chelsea 816, c. 5 (*Councils*, III, 579–85, p. 581). Compare also laws of Wihtred, c. 7; *Die Gesetze der Angelsachsen*, ed. F. Liebermann, 3 vols (Halle, 1903–16), I, pp. 12–13. See further S. Foot, 'Parochial Ministry in Early Anglo-Saxon England: the Role of Monastic Communities', *The Ministry: Clerical and Lay*, Studies in Church History 26 (1989), 43–54, pp. 48–50.

[15]   *Monasterium* is not the only word used to describe communities of religious but it is the most usual term; *coenobium* and *locus* are also found in early texts, as, less frequently, are *cella* and *monasteriolum*. The words *ecclesia* and *oratorium* are more often used of church buildings than of the institutions serving them or dwelling around them. For detailed consideration of this issue see Foot, 'Anglo-Saxon Minsters: a Review of Terminology', in *Pastoral Care Before the Parish*, ed. J. Blair and R. Sharpe (Leicester, 1992), 212–25, and Blair, 'Debate', pp. 194–6.

term to describe all communal religious establishments, with the exception of cathedral churches, in earlier Anglo-Saxon England. The word monastery to the modern ear carries connotations of Benedictine regularity that are inappropriate to pre-Viking England, and use of a vocabulary more appropriate to later periods tends to reinforce a teleological approach to the Anglo-Saxon church, which measures it against the achievements of the high middle ages and denies the distinctiveness of its own contribution. Minster is a more neutral term. I have not defined minster as meaning 'a church with a community of clergy responsible for the pastoral organisation of a defined area', although others have defined the word thus.[16] Minster is used here to mean nothing more than a religious congregation, a community of those nominally engaged in non-secular pursuits, living together in dwellings including at least an altar, but more likely one or more churches.[17] Since the contemporary sources make no differentiation between types of community, it is inappropriate for us to impose an artificial taxonomy of active and contemplative institutions onto the early Anglo-Saxon evidence.

What did distinguish religious houses from congregations of lay people, at least in theory, was the fact that as brothers and sisters in Christ their members shared their earthly and spiritual lives as one territorially coherent family, ostensibly devoted to some aspect of the service of God. These religious families were, however, so well integrated into early Germanic kinship structures that they appear markedly similar to contemporary secular social groupings, most notably to aristocratic households.[18] There was not even a new vocabulary for an ecclesiastical family (as opposed to the institution its members collectively represented): like its secular counterpart a monastic congregation was a *familia*, a household, the word encompassing all persons, including retainers or servants, not just the immediate kin group, or in monastic terms, the professed religious.[19] The same word denoted the

---

[16] M. Franklin, 'The Identification of Minsters in the Midlands', *Anglo-Norman Studies* 7 (1984), 69–87, p. 69.

[17] J. Blair, 'Anglo-Saxon Minsters: a Topographical Review', in *Pastoral Care Before the Parish*, 226–66, pp. 246–58.

[18] P. Wormald, 'Bede, "Beowulf" and the Conversion of the Anglo-Saxon Aristocracy', in *Bede and Anglo-Saxon England*, ed. R. T. Farrell, British Archaeological Reports, British Series 46 (Oxford, 1978), 32–95, pp. 52–4; P. Stafford, *The East Midlands in the Early Middle Ages* (Leicester, 1985), pp. 97–102. Irish and Frankish monasteries show the same close resemblance to noble households and to the ideals of the noble life-style: Hughes, *Church and Society*, nos VIII and IX; F. Prinz, *Frühes Mönchtum im Frankenreich* (Vienna, 1965), pp. 489–501.

[19] *Dictionary of Medieval Latin from British Sources* (Oxford, 1975–), fasc. IV, s.v. *familia*. For discussion of the change in the meaning of *familia* between the classical and early medieval periods see D. Herlihy, *Medieval Households*

nominal unit of land on which the community dwelt, the hide.[20] The vernacular terms were similarly ambiguous: Old English *hired* denoted both secular and religious communities,[21] and the Old English words for hide, *hid* and *hiwisc*, carried the same dual meaning of land and family.[22] A religious family reflected the same elements of separation from and integration with the world as any other kin group: in some spheres it was separate, self-supporting and introspective, but at others integrated, dependent and outward-looking. Like an earthly family, a minster incorporated all stages of human experience, accommodating people at all life stages from young children to elderly widows.[23] Where religious families differed from their temporal counterparts was that their kinship lay not within a blood group, but with Christ, and often their founder or patron saint.

This spiritual affinity, the sense in which a religious family was both a model of and a replacement for earthly relations, is illustrated in the homily Bede wrote for the feast of Benedict Biscop:

> The children which [Benedict] had disdained to have in a fleshly way he deserved to receive a hundredfold as spiritual children. ... Now we are his children, since as a pious provider he brought us into this monastic house. We are his children since he has made us to be gathered spiritually into one family of holy profession, although in terms of the flesh we were brought forth of different parents. [24]

Bishop Wilfrid's congregations also saw themselves as bound by familial ties. When Wilfrid was struck down with his final illness, his biographer Stephen

---

(Cambridge, Mass. and London, 1985), pp. 2–3 and 57.

[20] Defined by Bede as *terra unius familiae* in the context of the establishment of Hild's first minster on one hide of land on the north side of the Wear: *EH*, IV. 23 (pp. 406–7).

[21] For a tenth-century example see the text entered into the gospel-book of St Augustine's Canterbury, BL, Royal MS 1.B.vii, fol. 15v, recording King Æthelstan's manumission of Eadhelm 'immediately after he first became king', with the witness of various individuals and 'the community' (presumably of St Augustine's): 'ðæs wæs on gewitnesse Ælfheah mæssepreost 7 se hired ...'. Printed by W. de G. Birch, *Cartularium Saxonicum*, 3 vols (London, 1885–98), no. 639; translated *English Historical Documents*, I: *ca 500–1042*, ed. D. Whitelock, 2nd edn (London, 1979), no. 140. See also below, n. 71.

[22] T. M. Charles-Edwards, 'Kinship, Status and the Origins of the Hide', *Past and Present* 56 (1972), 3–33.

[23] Bede's account of the minster at Barking refers both to a child of three (*EH*, IV. 8, pp. 358–9) and to an older brother *quidam de fratribus senior* (IV. 7, pp. 358–9), as well as to two severely disabled, and presumably aged, nuns, who lived in the community for some years (IV. 9, pp. 360–3).

[24] Bede, *Homilia*, I. 13; ed. D. Hurst, Corpus Christianorum Series Latina 122, 88–94, p. 92.

reported that his whole *familia* prayed that he would be granted an extension of life, 'at any rate so that he could speak to them, and dispose of his minsters and divide his possessions, and not leave us as it were orphans, without any abbots'.[25] The force of this spiritual bond was also appreciated by others: Aldhelm wrote, possibly in 677 at the beginning of the troubles between Wilfrid and his clergy, to Wilfrid's abbots collectively, lamenting the recent 'raging and tempestuous disturbance' shaking the foundations of the church, and begging the 'sons of the same tribe' not to be sluggish in inactivity since they were required to go into exile with their bishop.

> What harsh or cruel burden in existence, I ask, would separate you and hold you apart from that bishop, who like a wet-nurse gently caressed you, his beloved foster children, warming you in the folds of his arms and nourishing you in the bosom of charity, and who brought you forward in his paternal love by rearing, teaching and castigating you from your very first exposure to the rudiments of education and from your early childhood and tender years up to the flower of your maturity. ... What then will be said of you if you cast into solitary exile the bishop who nourished and raised you?[26]

A community's common cause and hence its shared identity might be the more apparent when its members were linked by memory of their first founders; the minster at Lindisfarne, for example, was already described as the 'church of St Cuthbert' by Alcuin writing in the 790s.[27] As Catherine Cubitt has recently argued, the dead members of a community, whose memory was preserved in liturgical commemoration, both forged a congregation's identity and continued to inform and act upon the present.[28]

A religious family thus transcended kin loyalties and replaced the ties of blood with those of spiritual affinity; the act of joining a minster represented, in theory at least, a formal severance from obligation to earthly relations. Postulants left their own kin but still remained one of a group, in this case a new, spiritual family; in the sense of leaving one's father and mother this act resembled marriage, but the monk would henceforward cleave to Christ, a nun become a bride of Christ. The consequences of this in terms of the

---

[25] Stephen, *Vita S. Wilfridi*, c. 62; *The Life of Bishop Wilfrid by Eddius Stephanus*, ed. and trans. B. Colgrave (Cambridge, 1927, repr. 1985), pp. 134–5.

[26] Aldhelm, *Epistola XII*; *Aldhelmi Opera Omnia*, ed. R. Ehwald, MGH Auctores Antiquissimi XV (Berlin, 1919), p. 501; trans. M. Lapidge and M. Herren, *Aldhelm: The Prose Works* (Woodbridge, 1979), p. 169.

[27] Alcuin, *Epistolae* 16, 19; ed. E. Dümmler, MGH Epistolae IV, Karolini Ævi II (Berlin, 1895), pp. 42, 54. For vernacular references to the *hired* of St Cuthbert, see below, n. 72.

[28] C. Cubitt, 'Universal and Local Saints in Anglo-Saxon England', in *Local Saints and Local Churches*, ed. R. Sharpe and A. Thacker (Oxford, forthcoming); I am grateful to Dr Cubitt for letting me see a draft copy of her paper before publication.

payment of compensation for injury were made clear in the eighth-century *Dialogues of Ecgberht*:

> what ever layman kills a bishop, priest, deacon or monk, let him do penance according to the established measures, and pay the price of his blood to the church to which he belonged [at a given price on a diminishing scale according to ecclesiastical rank], unless the dignity of his birth or the nobility of his stock require a greater price; for it is unjust that those who serve the holy profession at a better grade should lose what those who live outside in the lay habit are known to claim by right of parentage. [29]

Clergy (and those not in clerical orders – the text goes on to make the same provision for 'abbots without orders') were thus not to lose their former social standing by suffering any loss of *wergild* through being in orders,[30] yet payment of the compensation appropriate to their rank was to go to their ecclesiastical not their earthly family. The most explicit statements that rule-law destroyed kin-law are found only, however, in late Anglo-Saxon law-codes: Æthelred's code of 1014 stated, 'no cloistered monk anywhere need by rights demand compensation in a feud nor pay compensation in a feud; he leaves the obligations of kinship when he submits to the monastic rule'.[31]

The ties of blood did, however, continue to have a good deal of relevance within the cloister, not least, it must be presumed, because of the predominance of royalty and nobility among the founders and inhabitants of early minsters and because of the creation of minsters in large part to cater for the needs of such noble families, especially in the world to come. Benedict Biscop was anxious towards the end of his life to ensure that rank and family influence counted for less than righteousness of life and soundness of doctrine in the election of an abbot, trying to ensure that his kin might not be able to assume control of his minsters of Wearmouth and Jarrow after his death.[32] Bishop Wilfrid, on the other hand, cheerfully appointed his kinsman to the abbacy of Ripon after him.[33] This, in fact, was patently the much more common occurrence.[34]

---

[29] *Dialogues of Ecgberht*, XII (*Councils*, III, p. 408).

[30] H. Mayr-Harting, *The Coming of Christianity to Anglo-Saxon England*, 3rd edn (London, 1991), pp. 251–2.

[31] VIII Æthelred, 25 (*Gesetze*, p. 266); I Cnut, 5.2d (*ibid.*, p. 286). H. Loyn, 'Kinship in Anglo-Saxon England', in his *Society and Peoples: Studies in the History of England and Wales, c.600–1200* (London, 1992), 45–64, p. 59.

[32] Anon, *Vita Ceolfridi*, c. 16; *Venerabilis Baedae Opera Historica*, ed. C. Plummer, 2 vols (Oxford, 1896), I, 388–404, pp. 393–4. Compare Bede, *Historia Abbatum*, c. 11; *ibid.*, I, 364–87, p. 375.

[33] Stephen, *Vita Wilfridi*, c. 63 (*Life of Bishop Wilfrid*, pp. 136–9).

[34] Among many examples see Bede, *EH*, III. 23, IV. 19, 26 (pp. 288–9, 392–5, 428–31); Æthelwulf, *De Abbatibus*, cc. 13–15; ed. A. Campbell (Oxford, 1967), pp. 33–41.

That its social organisation was derived from secular kinship models explains much about early Anglo-Saxon monastic organisation and also demonstrates why it can be so difficult to define precisely where in so many spheres, beyond those of prayerful contemplation, this life differed from that of the secular world. In terms of the most ascetic lifestyles adopted by saints such as Cuthbert the hagiographical literature makes the contrast with secular activity obvious, and is indeed designed to concentrate on the extremes and point up as many of the distinctive features as possible. As James Campbell has demonstrated, the majority of religious failed to live up to these sorts of ideals, a fact which was well-known to the hagiographers, who deliberately presented a distorted picture in order to accentuate the asceticism of their subjects. The presence of so many of noble and especially royal birth within minsters inevitably affected the conduct of their internal life, as much as their continuing relations with exterior royal society.[35] The prescriptive literature, such as it is, attempted to clarify the distinctiveness of the monastic life, urging monks and nuns to dress appropriately to their profession (not in garish secular apparel),[36] to strive after austerity and reject luxury, to be moderate in eating and more so in drinking, to live in chastity and devote themselves to education and, above all, prayer.[37] On the other hand it is quite clear that many failed to adhere to this model. The 747 council of *Clofesho* tried to direct that solemn festivals should be properly observed in minsters and not consigned to games, horse-racing and feasting;[38] other texts refer to harpists, to the ownership of horses, to hawking, fox-hunting and hare-coursing.[39] There is no account in an English source equivalent to

---

[35]   J. Campbell, 'Elements in the Background to the Life of St Cuthbert and his Early Cult', in *St Cuthbert, his Cult and his Community to AD 1200*, ed. G. Bonner, D. Rollason and C. Stancliffe (Woodbridge, 1989), 3–19, pp. 15, 11. Aristocratic ideals and social hierarchy were not given up in Merovingian monasteries either; see F. Irsigler, 'On the Aristocratic Character of Early Frankish Society', in *The Medieval Nobility*, ed. T. Reuter (Amsterdam, New York and Oxford, 1978), 105–36, pp. 113–14, 121–2.

[36]   See for example Aldhelm, *De Virginitate*, c. 58 (*Aldhelmi Opera Omnia*, pp. 317–18); Boniface, *Epistola 78* (*Die Briefe des Bonifatius und Lullus*, ed. M. Tangl, MGH Epistolae Selectae 1 (Berlin, 1916), p. 170); council of *Clofesho*, 747, c. 19 (*Councils*, III, pp. 368–9); Alcuin, *Epistolae 20, 40* (ed. Dümmler, pp. 58, 86); and the legatine councils of 786, c. 4 (*ibid.*, p. 22).

[37]   Council of *Clofesho*, 747, c. 20 (*Councils*, III, p. 369); Campbell, 'Elements in the Background', p. 14, n. 74.

[38]   Council of *Clofesho*, 747, c. 16 (*Councils*, III, p. 368).

[39]   Boniface, *Epistolae 78, 116* (pp. 163, 251–2); *EH*, V. 6 (pp. 466–7); Alcuin, *Epistolae 19, 114* (pp. 55, 168); Campbell, 'Elements in the Background', p. 12; Wormald, 'Bede, "Beowulf"', pp. 54–5. On the ownership of horses by Frankish religious see Irsigler, 'On the Aristocratic Character', pp. 121–2.

Gregory of Tours' reference to the charge that the abbess of Poitiers played backgammon, and her extraordinary defence: 'As to the backgammon [*tabulae*] she used to play during the lifetime of the Lady Radegund, she saw nothing wrong in it, and it was not expressly forbidden in the Rule, or in the canons'.[40] But it seems more than likely that Anglo-Saxon religious enjoyed similar amusements; the early eleventh-century text known as the 'Canons of Edgar' states that 'it is right that a priest be not a hunter or a hawker or a gambler, but amuse himself with his books as befits his order'.[41]

The minster may thus have offered an ideal of withdrawal from earthly concerns, but its expression was couched in the shape of a community modelled in the image of the secular family and providing for its needs forever.[42] This is surely one reason why it is so difficult confidently to distinguish monastic sites from high status secular enclosures on the ground, as witnessed for example by the debate about the purpose of recently excavated sites at Brandon in Suffolk, and Flixborough in Lincolnshire.[43] There are, however, a number of features of the monastic life as practised in earlier Anglo-Saxon England which are peculiar to those societies, exploration of which can help to determine the role performed by such communities within the contemporary world.

The Founding of Minsters

The motives inspiring individuals to found or endow monastic houses offer a valuable insight into the purpose their founders envisaged minsters might fulfil and can thereby illuminate the roles their members were intended to perform. Many of the first minsters established within each Anglo-Saxon kingdom were designed to act as mission stations, bringing the faith to the royal court in the first instance, and thereafter to the wider population.[44] These missionaries lived and worked as communities, mixing their evangelising activities with some corporate worship and devotion; their contact with the laity continued after the latter's nominal conversion, for the

---

[40]   Gregory of Tours, *Decem Libri Historiarum*, X. 16; ed. B. Krush and W. Levison, MGH, *SSRM*, I.1, p. 428. I owe this reference to Julia Smith.

[41]   'Canons of Edgar', §65; *Councils and Synods with other Documents Relating to the English Church, I: 871–1204*, ed. D. Whitelock, C. N. L. Brooke and M. Brett, 2 vols (Oxford, 1981), I, pp. 334–5.

[42]   Stafford, *The East Midlands*, p. 101.

[43]   See L. Webster and J. Backhouse, *The Making of England: Anglo-Saxon Art and Culture, AD 600–900* (London, 1991), pp. 81–8 (Brandon), 95–101 (Flixborough).

[44]   J. Campbell, *Essays in Anglo-Saxon History* (London, 1986), pp. 73–8; C. Stancliffe, 'Kings and Conversion: Some Comparisons between the Roman Mission to England and Patrick's to Ireland', *Frühmittelalterliche Studien* 14 (1980), 59–94, pp. 70–7.

maintenance of regular pastoral care still devolved upon the religious in such houses. The importance of providing continuity in the provision of spiritual services was expressed by Archbishop Theodore; the penitential attributed to him stipulated that if the site of a minster were moved, 'a priest should be released for the ministry of the church in the former place'.[45] Beyond the first phase of conversion, minsters might still be founded specifically to meet the wider pastoral needs of the lay population as for example is stated in the foundation charter for the minster at Bath dated 676, and was apparently also relevant in the creation of Breedon-on-the-Hill in Leicestershire in the later seventh century.[46]

Other minsters appear to have been created as a physical expression of their founders' devotional piety. The South Saxon king, Nothhelm, for example, for the relief of his soul made a grant of thirty-eight hides in Sussex to his sister, Nothgyth, to found a minster and build a church to be devoted to the divine praises and honouring of the saints, saying 'I know that whatever I devote from my own possessions to the members of Christ will benefit me in the future'.[47] Statements to the effect that grants were made for the benefit of the founder's soul, or the remission of sins, should be taken as a reflection of genuine religious fervour, for all that they may be recorded in formulaic terms by charter scribes. Literary sources attribute the same motives to founders, echoing the language of the charters.[48] Donations were made to create some houses in order that they might serve as burial places in the future, as for example in the case of the foundation of Lastingham by King Œthelwald, who wanted to establish a minster so that during his lifetime he might go there to pray and hear the Word, and that after his death he might

---

[45] Theodore, *Penitential*, II. vi. 7, in *Die Canones Theodori Cantuariensis und ihre Überlieferungsformen*, ed. P. W. Finsterwalder (Weimar, 1929), p. 320.

[46] Bath was created as part of a scheme for increasing male and female minsters 'for the increase of the catholic and orthodox faith': P. H. Sawyer, *Anglo-Saxon Charters: an Annotated List and Bibliography* (London, 1968) [S], no. 51; P. Sims-Williams, 'St Wilfrid and Two Charters dated AD 676 and 680', *Journal of Ecclesiastical History* 39 (1988), 163–83, pp. 167–74. Breedon-on-the-Hill was allegedly founded to provide pastorally for an ill-served area, because of an increase in the number of Christians throughout Britain: S 1803 (datable to 675x692); F. M. Stenton, 'Medeshamstede and its Colonies', in *Preparatory to Anglo-Saxon England*, ed. D. M. Stenton (Oxford, 1970), 179–92, pp. 182–4. For a rather different interpretation of S 1803–6 see R. Morris, *Churches in the Landscape* (London, 1989), p. 132.

[47] S 45.

[48] See, for example, Bede, *Vita S. Cuthberti*, c. 7 (*Two Lives of St Cuthbert*, pp. 174–5); or Stephen, *Vita S Wilfridi*, c. 14 (*Life of Bishop Wilfrid*, pp. 30–1); R. Abels, *Lordship and Military Obligation in Anglo-Saxon England* (Berkeley, Los Angeles and London, 1988), pp. 47–9, 224, n. 26.

be buried there, 'for he firmly believed that the daily prayers of those who served God there would greatly help him'.[49] Houses were sometimes founded to maintain or promote the cults of individuals or families, as were Minster in Thanet and Gilling, for example.[50]

New foundations could, however, be inspired by rather more worldly motives. The potential of political rivalry may have lain behind the creation of many new minsters, especially those on the borders of disputed territory; the density of minsters in the Thames valley and along the border between Wessex and Mercia is striking in this context.[51] Complex reasons will equally have determined whether or not an established minster recruited additional members. Just as a successful warleader attracted more followers to his warband, so a thriving church might act as a magnet not only for the pious, but for those who saw an opportunity to profit – spiritually or materially – from its prosperity.[52] Bede alleged in his 734 letter to Ecgberht, bishop of York, that some Northumbrian nobles were so tempted by the exemption of ecclesiastical land from secular taxation that they fraudulently created minsters on their own estates, or converted their own households into minsters without in fact intending to abandoning their secular way of life and devote themselves to God.[53] It is, however, important to remember that the patronage of the nobility was essential for the establishment of sufficient religious institutions in the early Christian period; many of these family minsters were to become significant sources of pastoral services for their lay neighbours, even if their first founders did not envisage them functioning as such.[54]

In exploring the roles newly created minsters may have been meant to perform it is more important to appreciate the complexity of interconnected motives governing their first members' actions within the cloister and outside

[49] *EH*, III. 23 (pp. 286–7). Compare also SS Peter and Paul (later St Augustine's) Canterbury, created to serve as the mausoleum for the kings of Kent and bishops of Canterbury: *EH*, I. 33 (pp. 114–15).

[50] D. Rollason, *The Mildrith Legend: a Study in Early Medieval Hagiography in England* (Leicester, 1982), pp. 49–51, 56; Bede, *EH*, III. 14, 24 (pp. 256–7, 292–3).

[51] This issue is discussed further in my forthcoming book, *Anglo-Saxon Minsters*.

[52] This parallel was suggested to me by one of my Sheffield students, Richard Collins.

[53] Bede, letter to Ecgberht, §§ 11–13 (*Baedae Opera*, I, pp. 414–17).

[54] J. Blair, 'Minster Churches in the Landscape', in *Anglo-Saxon Settlements*, ed. D. Hooke (Oxford, 1988), 35–58, pp. 39–40. For continental examples of the pastoral role of family foundations see U. Stutz, 'The Proprietary Church as an Element of Mediaeval Germanic Ecclesiastical Law', in *Mediaeval Germany 911–1250: Essays by German Historians*, trans. G. Barraclough, 2 vols (Oxford, 1938), II, 35–70. The treatment of some Irish churches as hereditary property by their founding families has been discussed by Sharpe, 'Some Problems', pp. 257–8.

in the wider world, than it is to attempt to disentangle this web into threads of worldly or pious ambition. Even the most exclusive and inward-looking devotional aspirations may also have been hard to sustain in practice, as the example of Wilgils cited earlier suggests. The centrality of many minsters within the secular landscape and the correspondence of minster sites with administrative centres or other lay settlements indicates that, as in Gaul, Ireland and northern Britain, many religious communities were prominently, not remotely, situated within the world.[55]

Minsters as Central Places

Within its local agrarian economy no minster could fail to be a significant participant, for the pursuit of the religious life was dependent on the permanent acquisition of a landed endowment sufficient to free the members of the community from the necessity of engaging in subsistence agriculture, enabling them rather to devote themselves to prayer.[56] Wealth was an essential prerequisite for monastic founders, further accentuating the similarities between theirs and noble households. A minster community might indeed be seen as a unit of lordship in terms of the obligations of its head to feed, clothe and care for its members just as a lord had responsibility for the well-being of his retinue, as James Campbell has shown.[57] The possession of lands – granted 'with fields and men' in the formulaic language of the charter, the written evidence of the inalienability of their estates and privileges[58] – inevitably turned minsters into temporal lords, with responsibilities to their tenants and slaves and obligations to collect produce and revenues and organise the contribution to the fyrd, even if their land was freed from other secular burdens.[59] A community's success was in large part dependent on its ability to

[55] C. Thomas, *The Early Christian Archaeology of North Britain* (Oxford, 1971), pp. 27–32; Blair, 'Anglo-Saxon Minsters', p. 227.
[56] This was not necessarily true of houses without adequate endowments, but there is some evidence that houses without independent economic viability proved unsustainable as spiritual centres. One example is Bede's explanation for Cwichhelm's abandoning of the see of Rochester: *prae inopia rerum* (*EH*, IV. 12, pp. 368–9). See further my forthcoming book, *Anglo-Saxon Minsters*, ch. 4.
[57] Campbell, 'Elements in the Background', p. 13, citing council of *Clofesho*, 747, c. 28 (*Councils*, III, p. 374). Both Boniface and Wilfrid demonstrated concern for the material well-being of their retinues after their deaths: Stephen, *Vita S. Wilfridi*, c. 63 (*Life of Bishop Wilfrid*, pp. 136–9); Boniface, *Epistola* 93 (*Die Briefe*, pp. 212–14).
[58] P. Wormald, *Bede and the Conversion of England: the Charter Evidence*, Jarrow Lecture 1984 (Jarrow, 1985), pp. 21–3; E. John, *Land Tenure in Early England: a Discussion of Some Problems* (Leicester, 1964), pp. 10–11, 24–5; Abels, *Lordship*, pp. 45–7.
[59] N. Brooks, 'The Development of Military Obligations in Eighth- and Ninth-Century England', in *England Before the Conquest*, ed. P. Clemoes and K.

exploit its material resources effectively, to farm its lands with maximum efficiency, but also to profit from any industrial or manufacturing activity carried out on its estates. Charters refer to the involvement of churches in the salt industry, in iron- and lead-working, for example, and archaeological evidence from excavated monastic sites further witnesses to the range of craft activities pursued at such places.[60]

Minsters were thus economically active within their locality, and to some extent on a wider scale. Merchants were attracted to churches' estates as potential markets for luxury products – those commodities such as silk, precious stones, spices, pigments, oil and often wine which minsters could not themselves produce – and as places which might themselves have an agricultural surplus to sell. The close correspondence between churches and markets in Domesday Book, together with the efforts of kings from Æthelstan onwards to prohibit the holding of markets on Sundays, suggest that markets and fairs were often held at a minster's gates.[61] Minsters may themselves have taken a more active part in long-distance trade; minsters are frequently found lying at or near harbours, and one minster at least had its own ships.[62] Minsters thus provided a central focus for their locality, both by stimulating nearby settlement and commercial activity, and as a consequence of the association between the sites of minsters and centres of royal government, particularly the royal *tun*.[63]

Hughes (Cambridge, 1971), 69–84, pp. 82–4; Abels, *Lordship*, pp. 43–57.

[60] Salt-works are mentioned, for instance, in S 102 and 23; lead in S 190; iron-working may have been carried out at Crayke, which is possibly to be identified with the minster of Æthelwulf's poem *De Abbatibus*: see M. Lapidge, 'Aediluulf and the School of York', in *Lateinische Kultur im VIII. Jahrhundert: Traube-gedenkschrift*, ed. A. Lehner and W. Berschin (St Ottilien, 1990), 161–78, and for iron-smelting sites, pp. 176–7. For discussion of some of the archaeological evidence see R. Cramp, 'Northumbria and Ireland', in *Sources of Anglo-Saxon Culture*, ed. P. E. Szarmach and V. D. Oggins (Kalamazoo, Michigan, 1986), 185–99, pp. 192–4.

[61] Blair, 'Minster Churches in the Landscape', pp. 47–50; P. H. Sawyer, 'Early Fairs and Markets in England and Scandinavia', in *The Market in History*, ed. B. L. Anderson and A. J. H. Latham (London, 1986), 59–77, pp. 64–5. See also the later medieval accounts of Saints Aldhelm and Ecgwine preaching to traders and craftsmen at, respectively, Malmesbury and Alcester discussed by G. Rosser, 'The Cure of Souls in English Towns Before 1100', in *Pastoral Care Before the Parish*, ed. Blair and Sharpe, 267–84, pp. 268–9. For Irish parallels see Sharpe, 'Some Problems', pp. 260–2, 267.

[62] S. Kelly, 'Eighth-Century Trading Privileges from Anglo-Saxon England', *Early Medieval Europe* 1 (1992), 3–28.

[63] Campbell, *Essays*, pp. 140–2.

There were various ways in which minsters fulfilled quasi-official functions within the operation of royal government, notably in the making of written records, but also in other routine affairs. Abbots – and for that matter, abbesses, if the example of Hild of Whitby is not to be seen as exceptional[64] – were consulted by kings and are prominent among the witnesses of royal councils.[65] Councils, meetings of the king, his nobles and leading churchmen, enacting royal as well as ecclesiastical business, were sometimes held at minsters where such written record as might prove desirable could be readily produced.[66] As those most likely to possess literate skills, the members of minster communities were sought out by lay people for the production of written documents, whether records of decisions reached in councils, of the conveyance of land or of the terms of the settlement of disputes, or private documents such as wills. The survival of charters exempting minsters from the obligation to provide hospitality for royal servants and mounted men, or feeding and lodging messengers including those from other kingdoms, or in one unique instance 'praecones from across the sea', sheds further light on the governmental responsibilities of minsters.[67] Although church land was nominally exempt from secular dues including food-rents and the obligation to provide labour to king or ealdorman,[68] it may be that the three common burdens (military service, building fortresses and constructing bridges) were always exacted from all lands including those booked by means of charter to the church. Minsters presumably arranged for their tenants to perform these duties, rather than the monks themselves. Boniface may have had further labours than these in mind when he wrote to

---

[64] Hild's counsel was said to have been sought by kings and princes when in difficulties: *EH*, IV. 23 (pp. 408–9).

[65] For the importance of certain Middle Anglian minsters in eighth- and ninth-century Mercia see S. Keynes, *The Councils of 'Clofesho'*, Eleventh Brixworth Lecture, Vaughan paper 38 (Leicester, 1984), pp. 30–48.

[66] C. Cubitt, *Anglo-Saxon Church Councils c.650–c.850* (London, 1995), pp. 27–39, and Appendix 2, 'The Sites of Synods'.

[67] S 197, a grant from Berhtwulf, king of the Mercians, and Humberht, *princeps* of the 'Tonseti', to Abbot Eanmund and his *familia* at Breedon-on-the-Hill, allowing the community to pay to exempt themselves from obligations of royal hospitality; see Keynes, *The Councils of 'Clofesho'*, p. 39; Bullough, 'What has Ingeld to do with Lindisfarne?', *Anglo-Saxon England* 22 (1993), 93–125, pp. 121–2. Compare also S 207, by which Burgred, king of the Mercians, accepted 300 silver shillings from Bishop Ealhhun of Worcester, in order that the minster of Blockley in Gloucestershire should be freed from the feeding and maintenance of hawks and falcons, huntsmen of the king or ealdorman, the Welsh border patrol (*walhfæreld*) and of all mounted men of the English race and foreigners.

[68] Exemption from secular dues has been discussed by Brooks, 'Development', p. 71; Abels, *Lordship*, p. 49.

Archbishop Cuthbert in 747 complaining about the forced labour of monks upon royal buildings and other works.[69]

The official role of minsters is visible, furthermore, in the judicial process. Churches could provide the setting for solemn judicial acts, the swearing of oaths at altars (sworn by the relics they contained), or the performing of manumissions, also at altars.[70] A written record of the act of freeing a slave was often made in a set of gospels or some other book belonging to the church where the manumission was made; for example several such transactions are recorded in the Bodmin Gospels, many referring to the performance of the manumission 'on the relics of St Petroc' and 'in the witness of the community', on þæs hirydes gewitnesse.[71] The first vernacular reference to the community of St Cuthbert is found in the record of the manumissions made by Ælfred lareow, priest of the church of Durham in the second quarter of the eleventh century, and entered on the last leaf of the gospel book which King Æthelstan had given the community in 934: 'these seven men Ælfrid hath freed, by the grace of God and of St Cuthbert, for himself and for his wife Kolawis, all the congregation (heored) of St Cuthbert being witness'.[72] Ordeals, too, could be conducted in certain churches, especially after the mid-tenth century, when the priest was assigned a central role in the prior preparation of the proband (in prayer and fasting within the church) as well as in the organisation and adjudication of the trial itself.[73]

---

[69] Boniface, Epistola 78 (Die Briefe, p. 171). Compare his letter of the same year to King Æthelbald of Mercia (Epistola 73) which refers to the violence and extortion with which the king's praefecti et comites have been treating monks and priests (ibid., p. 152). The privileges granted to churches at the synod of Gumley of 749 (S 92), may have been meant to meet some of Boniface's criticisms; it was on this occasion that the three common burdens were first explicitly reserved, although this was not necessarily an innovation: Brooks, 'The Development', pp. 73–8. Abels (Lordship, p. 49) has, however, argued that the common burdens were newly imposed on booked land by the eighth-century Mercian kings.

[70] The laws of seventh-century Kentish kings, Hlothhere and Eadric, and those of Wihtred make provision for the swearing of oaths at altars: Hlothhere and Eadric, laws, c. 16.2 (Gesetze, I, p. 11); Wihtred, laws, cc. 18–21 (ibid., pp. 13–14); Wihtred, c. 8 (ibid., p. 13) provides for performing manumissions.

[71] BL, Add. MS 9381, fols 1–7, 133v, 141; these are printed by B. Thorpe, Diplomatarium Anglicum Aevi Saxonici (London, 1865), pp. 623–31 and a selection in translation is found in English Historical Documents, nos 141–8.

[72] BL, Cotton MS Otho B.ix; N. R. Ker, Catalogue of Manuscripts Containing Anglo-Saxon (Oxford, 1957), no. 176, art. d; printed and translated H. H. E. Craster, 'Some Anglo-Saxon Records of the See of Durham', Archaeologia Aeliana, 4th ser. 1 (1925), 189–98, p. 190.

[73] II Æthelstan c. 23 (Gesetze, I, p. 162) ordered the accused to come to the mass-priest for three days' preparation before the ordeal itself. The tenth-century

Attempts seem to have been made later in the tenth century to centralise the performance of the ordeal: Æthelred ordered that all vouching to warranty and ordeals should be performed in royal boroughs,[74] and the privilege to hold ordeals may have been jealously guarded as is suggested by the surviving twelfth-century confirmation of the right of St Peter's, Northampton in this respect.[75] Churches could afford sanctuary to those who sought shelter within them; St Cuthbert would rather his body be buried on Farne 'on account of the influx of fugitives and guilty men of every sort who will perhaps flee to my body'.[76] Early Anglo-Saxon law-codes such as that of King Ine recognised the protection which churches could offer to criminals.[77] King Alfred decreed: 'if anyone for any guilt flees to any one of the monastic houses to which the king's food rent belongs, or to some other privileged community which is worthy of honour, he is to have a respite of three days to protect himself unless he wishes to be reconciled'.[78]

The wealth of minsters and their personal connections with the nobility and royalty, their importance in the agricultural and often the industrial economy, their role as places for exchange and their administrative and judicial functions all served to make minsters central places within their immediate locality and give them a political role at least within their own kingdom, if not further afield. One of the factors which seems to have alienated Bishop Wilfrid from the Northumbrian royal family was that his monastic empire transcended contemporary political boundaries, comprising

---

tract *Ordal* (*c.*936x958, or *c.*1000: *Gesetze*, I, pp. 383–7) gives details of the ceremony and may be compared with extant liturgical *ordines* for ordeal ceremonies; see P. R. Hyams, 'Trial by Ordeal: the Key to Proof in the Early Common Law', in *On the Laws and Customs of England: Essays in Honor of Samuel E. Thorne*, ed. M. S. Arnold *et al.* (Chapel Hill, North Carolina, 1981), 90–126, pp. 106–11; and the summary of the secular provisions given by Liebermann, *Gesetze*, II, pp. 601–4, s.v. *ordal*. For the development of the ordeal see R. Bartlett, *Trial by Fire and Water: the Medieval Judicial Ordeal* (Oxford, 1986), pp. 4–12.

[74] III Æthelred 6.1 (*Gesetze*, I, p. 230).

[75] F. Stenton, '*Acta Episcoporum*', in *Preparatory to Anglo-Saxon England*, 166–78, p. 177; discussed fully by M. Franklin, 'Minsters and Parish Churches: Northamptonshire Studies' (unpublished Ph.D. thesis, University of Cambridge, 1982), pp. 80–2.

[76] Bede, *Vita S. Cuthberti*, c. 37 (*Two Lives of Cuthbert*, pp. 278–9).

[77] Ine, laws, cc. 5, 5.1 (*Gesetze*, I, p. 90).

[78] Alfred, laws, c. 2 (*Gesetze*, I, p. 48). The same code also recognised that providing sanctuary could prove inconvenient for a minster and recommended: 'if the community have more need of their church [the fugitive] is to be kept in another building and it is to have no more doors than the church; the head of that church is to take care to give him food during that period': *ibid.*, 5.1–2 (p. 52), compare c. 42.2 (p. 76).

as it did houses in both Mercia and Northumbria. It was in order to break up this politically dangerous supra-regional alliance that Ecgfrith strove so hard to deprive Wilfrid of land and power.[79] While the extent of an individual minster's influence beyond its own gates was inevitably dependent on the scale of its endowment and the range of its lay connections, total isolation from lay concerns seems at best implausible, and was rarely sought. Conviviality, drinking and feasting were clearly as much a part of the ecclesiastical as of contemporary noble life, and as well as providing opportunities for the self-indulgence condemned in various texts, they were also occasions to be shared with friends still in the world, at which distinctly worldly entertainments might be expected.[80] But of the factors so far identified as involving minsters in secular society, most were also to be found in royal vills, even possibly the availability of literate skills.[81] It is in their liturgical and intercessory activities that the members of minster communities stand out most from their lay counterparts and where their lives were most distinctly different.

The Spiritual Role of the Minster

Prayer – for the king, his people, for the whole church, for a minster's benefactors, for the souls of those buried within its bounds – was the central spiritual role performed by the members of religious communities.[82] In recommending the correct observance of the seven canonical hours, the 747 council of *Clofesho* urged that at the proper hours of prayer ecclesiastics and monastics should remember to pray not just for themselves, but for kings and for the safety of Christian people; reference was also made at the council to the intercessions made by priests to God for the atonement of the sins of the people.[83] It is not necessary to presume that this petitionary prayer was

---

[79]   E. John, 'The Social and Political Problems of the Early English Church', in *Land, Church and People: Essays Presented to H. P. R. Finberg*, ed. J. Thirsk, *Agricultural History Review* 18 (1970), supplement, 39–63, p. 51.

[80]   Campbell, 'Elements in the Background', p. 12; D. Bullough, *Friends, Neighbours and Fellow-Drinkers: Aspects of Community and Conflict in the Early Medieval West*, H. M. Chadwick Memorial Lecture 1 (Cambridge, 1991), pp. 8–11; Bullough, 'What has Ingeld to do with Lindisfarne?', pp. 105–8. The *prandium* had similar importance in Frankish aristocratic and hence monastic life: Irsigler, 'On the Aristocratic Character', pp. 120–1.

[81]   S. Kelly, 'Anglo-Saxon Lay Society and the Written Word', in *The Uses of Literacy in Early Medieval Europe*, ed. R. McKitterick (Cambridge, 1990), 36–62.

[82]   Van Engen, 'The "Crisis of Cenobitism"', pp. 292–4.

[83]   Council of *Clofesho*, 737, cc. 10, 15 (*Councils*, III, pp. 366–7). For a later example of the centrality of intercession in the lives of those serving the true God in the monastic order see S 745 (A.D. 966), the foundation charter for the New Minster, Winchester, cited by van Engen, 'The "Crisis of Cenobitism"', p. 292, n. 108.

performed only by such religious as had direct contact with lay people; if there were certain monks or nuns who led a more enclosed life, they would surely have shared in, or even taken a major role in, such intercession. The maintenance of the cults of the dead buried at minsters through the celebration of masses and singing of psalms, as well as prayer for their souls and those of their other benefactors, was an equally important responsibility.[84] As has already been seen, some communities were created specifically to promote particular cults, and laymen might make bequests to their local minsters as well as to their eventual place of burial for the future benefit of their souls.[85] In confirming the bequest made by Oswulf and Beornthryth to Christ Church, Canterbury, Archbishop Wulfred specified the religious offices the community were to perform on the anniversaries of their deaths, the singing of masses, the reading of passions and the singing of fifties of psalms.[86]

Mention has already been made of the centrality of minster enclosures within the local landscape and the extent to which such places acted as magnets for the laity, not just relatives of inmates, but those who had been invited to meetings or feasts, travellers and pilgrims, or people attracted by the availability of goods to buy or sell. An ecclesiastical community might further provide a stimulus for the expression of lay devotion, the intercession and contemplation of its members acting as a focus for individual piety. In the regular round of the liturgical year, on Sundays and at major festivals, churches were enjoined to invite the laity to be present at the sacrament of the mass and for the preaching of sermons,[87] and various texts recommended lay communion, although some restricted receipt of the sacrament to those not sexually active.[88] The 747 Clofesho council directed lay penitents first to pray for themselves, but then to bring as many servants of God as they could to

[84] See M. McLaughlin, *Consorting with Saints: Prayer for the Dead in Early Medieval France* (Ithaca and London, 1994), especially ch. 2. Monastic promotion of the cults of the dead is investigated by Catherine Cubitt in her forthcoming paper, 'Universal and Local Saints'.

[85] See, for example, S 1187, 1482, 1515. J. Blair, 'Introduction: from Minster to Parish Church', in *Minsters and Parish Churches: the Local Church in Transition 950–1200*, ed. Blair (Oxford, 1988), 1–19, pp. 3–6; and J. Blair, 'Local Churches in Domesday Book and Before', in *Domesday Studies*, ed. J. C. Holt (Woodbridge, 1987), 265–78, pp. 269–71.

[86] S 1188.

[87] Council of *Clofesho*, 747, c. 14 (*Councils*, III, p. 367).

[88] *Ibid.*, c. 23 (p. 370); Theodore, *Penitential*, I. xii. 3; I. xiv. 1; II. xii. 1–4 (*Canones Theodori*, pp. 305, 306, 326); Bede, letter to Ecgberht, §15 (*Baedae Opera*, p. 419); and see A. Thacker, 'Monks, Preaching and Pastoral Care in Early Anglo-Saxon England', in *Pastoral Care*, ed. Blair and Sharpe, 137–70, pp. 155–6.

make their common prayers to God for them.[89] Minsters recommended themselves furthermore to the indigent, drawn by the promise of physical solace or material largesse. The spiritual obligation to give alms to the poor fell nominally on all Christians, who were urged to give alms for the good of their own souls,[90] but it was particularly enjoined upon the members of religious houses, thereby bringing them into contact with social groups other than the nobility.[91] Many lay people indeed preferred to delegate the responsibility for the actual administration of charity to minsters, making gifts to churches for their members to distribute appropriately. For the poor, minsters thus represented promising sources of the basic necessities of existence (food, clothing and shelter), and the potential also for the alleviation of physical as well as spiritual ills. The presence of doctors, *medici*, within minsters is attested in a number of early sources, and should their remedies prove ineffective (as so often in the narratives of the saints' lives they did), there was always the hope that the shrines or relics of the saints within the church might prove more efficacious.[92]

Not all the services provided by minsters were inward-looking or provided within the bounds of the minster itself. Arising in part from the initial role many performed as mission stations, communities often had active pastoral responsibilities which they had perforce to maintain beyond the acceptance of the word of God by their lay neighbours. Quite how (or for that matter, whether) these obligations were centrally regulated is a matter of considerable current debate, but texts do refer to the assigning of particular groups of lay people to the charge of individual clergy or communities, and the importance of providing continuity in the provision of spiritual services.[93] The central importance of the provision of baptism to the laity beyond the conversion period is clear from the stress laid on its proper performance not only in the prescriptive literature of penitentials and church councils, but also

---

[89]   Council of *Clofesho*, 747, c. 27 (*Councils*, III, p. 373).

[90]   Christ's injunction to give to the poor is in Matthew xix. 21. Bede (*Homelia*, I. 9, p. 64) urged on all Christians the need for charity and care for the poor.

[91]   A number of texts from the early period stressed the importance of monastic alms-giving. Writing to Bishop Speratus in 797, Alcuin recommended that the bishop have in his retinue 'an experienced steward, to see to the care of the poor with proper concern. It is better that the poor should eat at your table than entertainers and persons of extravagant behaviour': Alcuin, *Epistola* 124 (p. 183). The recipient of this letter has now been identified by Donald Bullough as Bishop Unuuona of Leicester: 'What has Ingeld to do with Lindisfarne?' Compare also Alcuin, *Epistolae*, 36, 79, 102, 300 (pp. 78, 121, 149, 459).

[92]   For examples of *medici* within minsters, see Anon, *Vita S. Cuthberti*, IV. 17 (*Two Lives of Cuthbert*, pp. 136–7); Bede, *Vita S. Cuthberti*, c. 32 (*ibid.*, pp. 258–9); Stephen, *Vita S. Wilfridi*, c. 23 (pp. 46–7).

[93]   Theodore, Penitential, II. vi. 7 (*Canones Theodori*, p. 320), quoted above, p. 45.

in secular law-codes from throughout the Anglo-Saxon period, and it is clear that clerics travelled away from their minsters to carry the sacrament to the people.[94] The sources also mention lay demands for the services of the clergy on behalf of the sick and the dying, both in the hope of healing, as in the case of the woman ill with a pain in her head whom Cuthbert cured by anointing with holy chrism,[95] and in requests for the viaticum and for the hearing of final confession. The reeve Hildemer summoned Cuthbert to go to his wife's bedside in order that, although she was mad in life (she was afflicted by demons), she might through Cuthbert's ministry or that of another priest have peace in the grave.[96] The sacrament of the mass may also have been taken by travelling priests to local villages. Theodore's penitential, for example, made provision for the celebration of mass in a field. The early saints' lives, however, make no mention of their subjects' celebrating other than within their own churches, referring predominantly to the administration of baptism and above all to the preaching and teaching the saints provided for the laity.

The spiritual instruction of the laity, it is clear, lay at the centre of all pastoral ministry. Its proper provision was of great importance to Anglo-Saxon ecclesiastical legislators, and the failure of the church to provide proper teaching is frequently blamed for wider ills. Bede attributed the weaknesses he saw within the church of his own day to the lack of sufficient teachers of adequate learning, and ascribed responsibility for this task to all minster communities, not just those living round a bishop;[97] Alcuin similarly blamed a lack of teachers for the woes of the late eighth-century English church.[98] Many of the examples given in the sources of priests and other religious travelling out to preach do relate to the initial work of conversion, but peripatetic clergy are still to be found beyond the missionary period. The council of Hertford of 672/3 directed that clerics travelling outside their own dioceses should have the permission of the local bishop before exercising any priestly function, while stipulating for the behaviour of clergy within their

---

[94] See further S. Foot, "By Water in the Spirit": the Administration of Baptism in Early Anglo-Saxon England', in *Pastoral Care*, ed. Blair and Sharpe, 171–92.

[95] Anon, *Vita S. Cuthberti*, IV. 4 (*Two Lives of Cuthbert*, pp. 116–7).

[96] *Ibid.*, II. 8 (pp. 90–3). In Bede's account of the same story Hildemer is said to have asked for a priest to bring communion to his wife, and also that Cuthbert would permit her to be buried *in locis sanctis*: Bede, *Vita Cuthberti*, c. 15 (*ibid.*, pp. 204–7).

[97] Bede, letter to Ecgberht, §§ 7, 15 (*Baedae Opera*, pp. 410–11, 419); see my 'Parochial Ministry', pp. 47–8.

[98] Alcuin, *Epistola* 129 (pp. 191–2); compare *Epistola* 31 (p. 73): 'It is good to give alms to feed the poor with physical food, but satisfying the hungry soul with spiritual teaching is better'.

dioceses only that they should not wander about at will.[99] These chapters and the other frequent references in the narrative sources to clergy travelling away from their minsters to visit the laity suggest that travel within the diocese may have been a normal and expected part of the role of many religious and not merely those with Irish backgrounds.[100]

Conclusion

The first English text to attempt to lay down detailed specifications for the proper behaviour of the inhabitants of religious houses and the relationship of these institutions to the outside world was the *Regularis Concordia* of the early 970s.[101] For the earlier period the sources do provide some indications of contemporary perceptions of appropriate religious observance, but nothing approximating to a monastic customary. Such statements as there are cannot be interpreted in the light of the more rigid definition of the monastic ideal first articulated in the tenth century. Rather the early texts must be viewed afresh on their own terms, and their own inherent distortions recognised: the early saints' lives are as likely to magnify the spiritual virtues of their subjects at the expense of their more worldly habits, as the equally formulaic advisory literature is to exaggerate the inappropriate behaviour it seeks to correct.[102] Only then is it possible to reach any conclusions about the response of the early Anglo-Saxon church to the society in which it was enmeshed.

The question of the provision of pastoral care has been addressed last since it is only one element of this argument, albeit that part of the debate which has attracted the most discussion among historians recently. There can be no doubt that this aspect of the church's role was seen to be of great importance by contemporaries. Great stress was laid in church councils on its proper performance and the control of those ministers responsible for its provision, and there is a good deal of evidence that specific pastoral services, particularly but not exclusively baptism, were sought out by the laity. Nothing that can be determined about the nature of the religious life in earlier Anglo-Saxon England suggests that the provision of these services was incompatible with the highest ideals of monastic observance as they were then understood. This is not to argue that pastoral care was necessarily organised in an institutional system in which the positioning of houses, their relationships one to another and the precise services their members were to perform were all prescribed and controlled. There may well have been houses which took a minimal interest in regular pastoral ministry, and it is more than likely that

[99] Council of Hertford, cc. 6 and 5 (*EH*, IV. 5, pp. 350–3).
[100] See further Thacker, 'Monks, Preaching and Pastoral Care'.
[101] *Regularis Concordia*, ed. T. Symons (London, 1953).
[102] Compare the discussion of the distortions in the *vitae* of St Cuthbert by Campbell, 'Elements in the Background', pp. 18–19.

there were some within active communities who were not involved in external ministry. The sources from this period do not, however, provide evidence that separation and concentration solely on internally focused contemplative devotion was an ideal in the English church before the Benedictine revolution to the extent to which it had been for St Benedict, who asserted that the monastic profession and external priestly ministry were incompatible.[103] It has been argued that there were two distinct forms of monastic organisation in this period – communities of priests and other members of the clergy with a prime role in external mission and pastoral care, and other congregations of contemplatives – but these are not visible in the sources. The career of Boniface on the continent exemplifies the notion that community life and proselytising ministry were entirely compatible. One might rather question the prevalence of genuine 'monks' in this period, so inarticulate is the expression of the enclosed devotional ideal.

I return again in conclusion to the family model, which seems the most useful in helping to clarify these issues. It is arguable that for many minsters their role within lay society was little more than a familial, fraternal, caritative one: a community itself lacking a priest among its members was in no position to provide sacramental services for its lay clients, although it might satisfy a number of more general social needs for those within its lordship and their neighbours. But the family is itself a functional institution, not just a social classification, and further comparison with secular family structures and study of the interactions between separate family groups might contribute much to our understanding of the internal workings and external roles of minster communities. Minsters sat somewhat uncomfortably both within and without aristocratic kin groups. Inevitably they were tied into particular noble and royal networks, where they acted in many respects as secular lords, but being part also of the wider family of the church they could divorce themselves from kin (and king) by appeal to a higher authority: that of bishop, archbishop or even pope.[104] It is scarcely surprising that some of our most illuminating evidence for the church's attempts to define its place within the secular world derives from the deliberations of bishops and senior ecclesiastics in council. In this period we are looking at a developing church, not at fixed, solid structures but at religious trying to carve out functions for themselves, to define and create an identity, struggling with that very issue with which we have been most concerned: the fact that visible fusion with noble ideals did not assist those who desired separation. This relationship

---

[103] *Rule of St Benedict*, c. 60; ed. T. Fry (Collegeville, Minnesota, 1981), pp. 272–4. See U. Berlière, 'L'exercice du ministère paroissial par les moines dans le haut moyen-âge', *Revue Bénédictine* 39 (1927), 227–50; and my 'Parochial Ministry' and Thacker, 'Monks, Preaching and Pastoral Care'.

[104] Richard Collins drew this point to my attention.

between aristocracy and monasticism is crucial to our understanding of the nature of the early Anglo-Saxon church, and its role and place in society; if the models affecting the first aspiring religious were largely those of familial and noble communality, not separate solitary asceticism, these inevitably shaped communities on the lines to which their members were accustomed, producing in James Campbell's phrase something resembling much more 'a special kind of nobleman's club' than Benedict's Monte Cassino.[105] The challenge for those church leaders whose task it was to define an ideal appropriate to English circumstances was to recognise these factors as integral to the Anglo-Saxon monastic experience and to capitalise on ways in which the features they most admired could be integrated into a higher spiritual ideal; hence the tendency of the literature to dwell on extreme models of perfection. As Patrick Wormald has argued, 'Christianity in Anglo-Saxon England was successfully assimilated by a warrior nobility which had no intention of abandoning its culture, or seriously changing its way of life, but which was willing to throw its traditions, customs, tastes and loyalties into the articulation of the new faith'.[106] The church created by the Anglo-Saxon aristocracy carried over many of these noble, heroic ideals into an institution with defined spiritual and social roles, but one which was in essence very much of that world on which it was modelled.

---

[105] Campbell, 'Elements in the Background', p. 12.
[106] Wormald, 'Bede, "Beowulf" and the Conversion', p. 57.

Monasteries and Society in Early Medieval Northumbria

DAVID ROLLASON

This paper is a contribution to a debate which takes us to the very heart of this volume's theme: monasteries and society.[1] It concerns the role of monasteries in the earliest period of Christianity in England in maintaining a system of pastoral care, or, put another way, in spreading Christianity throughout all orders of society in all areas of the country. A well-known and widely diffused interpretation of this matter, which can for reasons which will appear be conveniently termed the 'minster hypothesis', maintains that in pre-Viking England, say in the seventh, eighth, and ninth centuries, all or most churches were served by communities of clergy, who formed in effect a team ministry for the purpose of exercising pastoral functions. Monasteries, including such as Bede's Monkwearmouth and Jarrow and St Cedd's Lastingham, could have such pastoral functions, which they exercised throughout large territories attached to them, embracing areas equivalent to several modern parishes. In pre-Viking England, then, the church reached all corners of the land and all levels of society by means of monasteries, which were pastoral as well as ascetic in character. They were, as the sources make clear, often associated with kings, so it is further argued that they formed a royally sponsored network covering England with monasteries often linked with royal vills. Since the proponents of this hypothesis about the organisation of the church in early England effectively deny the existence of monasteries of an exclusively ascetic and devotional character, they favour using 'minster' instead of modern English 'monastery' as a translation for both Latin *monasterium* and Old English *mynster*. To this they assign the very general meaning of a church served by a community of some sort. Hence my shorthand label: the 'minster hypothesis'. According to the hypothesis, the territories attached to minsters became fragmented particularly in the period

---

[1] See also David Rollason, 'The Ecclesiastical Context', in *The Origins of the Midland Village*, ed. Harold Fox, Papers prepared for a discussion session at the Economic History Society's annual conference, Leicester, April 1992 (Leicester, 1992), 73–90; Eric Cambridge and David Rollason, 'Debate: the Pastoral Organisation of the Anglo-Saxon Church: a Review of the "Minster Hypothesis"', and John Blair 'Debate: Ecclesiastical Organisation and Pastoral Care in Anglo-Saxon England', *Early Medieval Europe* 4 (1995), 87–104, 193–212.

between *c.*900 and *c.*1100 as private estate churches were founded within them, as bishops created new episcopal churches, and as large agrarian estates themselves fragmented. Thus the system of parishes and parish-churches familiar to us emerged, although, it is argued, the minsters retained residual traces of their earlier position and of their original territories.

Like many influential hypotheses about Anglo-Saxon history, the 'minster hypothesis' appeared in all its essentials in the pages of F. M. Stenton, in his 1936 article 'St Frideswide and her Times',[2] and then in his *Anglo-Saxon England*, in which he wrote:

> The word *mynster* is the Old English form of the Latin *monasterium*, and there is no doubt that many ancient parish churches actually represent early monasteries which have disappeared without trace. The missionary impulse was strong in early English monasticism, and the foundation of a monastery was a natural means of spreading Christianity among a backward people.

Monasterium, noted Stenton, need not mean a community of monks in the Benedictine sense. 'So far as can be seen', he continued, 'the earliest English parishes were large districts served by clergy from a bishop's *familia*, grouped round a central church'.[3]

Stenton's admission that 'no records of these communities have survived' might have been enough to cast doubt on his picture, but in fact the decades since he wrote have seen considerable development of it. Although there has been little attention paid to Stenton's suggestion that the churches responsible for pastoral work were episcopal, in other respects his views have been the starting point for most scholars who have worked on the subject:[4] Margaret Deanesly in her paper on double monasteries in Kent,[5] Dean Addleshaw in his 1963 Jarrow Lecture on the pastoral organisation of north-east England in Bede's day,[6] and most energetically in more recent years a series of scholars

---

[2]   *Preparatory to Anglo-Saxon England, being the Collected Papers of Frank Merry Stenton*, ed. D. M. Stenton (Oxford, 1970), pp. 231–2.

[3]   F. M. Stenton, *Anglo-Saxon England*, 3rd edn (Oxford, 1971), pp. 148–9.

[4]   Notable exceptions are P. Sims-William, *Religion and Literature in Western England, 600–800* (Cambridge, 1990), ch. 2; E. Cambridge, 'The Early Church in County Durham: a Reassessment', *Journal of the British Archaeological Association* 137 (1984), 65–85; Richard Morris, *Churches in the Landscape* (London, 1989), ch. 3; and C. Cubitt, 'Pastoral Care and the Conciliar Canons: the Provisions of the 747 Council of *Clofesho*', in *Pastoral Care before the Parish*, ed. J. Blair and R. Sharpe (Leicester, 1992), 193–211.

[5]   M. Deanesly, 'Early English and Gallic Minsters', *TRHS*, 4th ser. 23 (1941), 25–53.

[6]   G. W. O. Addleshaw, *The Pastoral Organisation of the Modern Dioceses of Durham and Newcastle in the Time of Bede*, Jarrow Lecture 1963 (Jarrow, 1964); for a more nuanced treatment by the same author, see his *The Beginnings of the Parochial System*, St Anthony's Hall Publications 3, 3rd edn (York, 1970), and *The Development of the Parochial System from Charlemagne (768–814) to Urban II*

whose work is best represented by the majority of the contributions to the two collections of papers edited by John Blair: *Minsters and Parish Churches: The Local Church in Transition 950–1200*, and *Pastoral Care before the Parish*, the latter edited with Richard Sharpe.[7] In the work of these scholars in these collections and elsewhere, we find Stenton's picture forming the essential framework for discussion and research. 'There is now a generally accepted view', wrote John Blair in the publication of his doctoral thesis on Surrey,

> of the process by which England acquired its rural churches. Kings, and bishops under their patronage, founded churches of a public character in important administrative centres. By the mid-eighth century, all or most of the English kingdoms had established a network of minster *parochiae*, typically covering between perhaps five and fifteen modern parishes and served by groups of itinerating priests from the central church.[8]

Not the least startling aspect of this claim is the assumption that the church in all or most of the English kingdoms developed in the same way in the pre-Viking period, and indeed studies by Blair and others have sought to include the rest of the British Isles and even the Continent in the same pattern of development.[9]

Turning now to Northumbria, how far is it demonstrable that monasteries exercised pastoral functions like other types of church? Certain passages in Bede's *Ecclesiastical History of the English People* seem at first sight to suggest that they did. Describing the pastoral activities of the Irish who evangelised Northumbria, Bede writes:

> Whenever a cleric (*clericus*) or a monk (*monachus*) went anywhere he was gladly received by all as God's servant. If they chanced to meet him by the roadside, they ran towards him and, bowing their heads, were eager either to be signed with the cross by his hand or to receive a blessing from his lips. Great attention was also paid to his exhortations, and on Sundays the people flocked eagerly to the church or monastery (*ad ecclesiam siue monasterium*), not to get food for the body but hear the word of God. If by chance a priest (*siquis sacerdotum*) came to a village, the villagers crowded together, eager to hear from him the word of life; for the priests and the clerics visited the villages for no other reason than to preach, to baptise, and to visit the sick, in

---

    (1088–1099), St Anthony's Hall Publications 6, 2nd edn (York, 1970).

[7]   The former is Oxford, 1988. In the latter, Cubitt, 'Pastoral Care and the Conciliar Canons', is notable for its criticism of the 'minster hypothesis' and its emphasis on the episcopal dimension of pastoral care.

[8]   John Blair, *Early Medieval Surrey: Landholding, Church and Settlement before 1300* (Stroud, 1991), p. 91.

[9]   See, for example, Huw Pryce, 'Pastoral Care in Early Medieval Wales', Alan Macquarrie, 'Early Christian Religious Houses in Scotland: Foundation and Function', and above all John Blair, 'Anglo-Saxon Minsters: a Topographical Review', all in *Pastoral Care*, ed. Blair and Sharpe, pp. 41–62, 110–33, 226–66.

brief to care for their souls.[10]

Setting aside the fact that monks are here distinguished from priests and clerics on whom the emphasis seems to be placed, the idealised character of the passage is obvious. This is Bede describing what he thinks ought to have happened – and ought to have been happening in his day. Are we really authorised to believe that villagers of his day were so enthusiastic to become Christians? The church inquisitors of a later age, who were so energetic in the imposition of Christianity, would have found this hard to envisage. Idealisation is equally apparent in Bede's treatment of St Cuthbert's preaching tours from Melrose and Lindisfarne. The saint, we are told, preached to villages amongst high mountains, which must surely be related to Bede's famous letter to Bishop Egbert of York in which he laments the slothfulness and worldliness of the bishops of his own day, and particularly their reluctance to penetrate into mountainous areas: 'many villages and hamlets of our people are situated in inaccessible mountains and dense woodlands, where there is never seen for many years a bishop to exhibit any ministry or celestial grace'.[11] Bede's descriptions of Cuthbert's preaching activities while a monk of Melrose are didactic not realistic. They are not a safe foundation for the 'minster hypothesis'.

Once we set them aside, it is clear that the *Ecclesiastical History* and contemporary texts provide little support for the 'minster hypothesis'. The functions of a number of monasteries are quite explicitly defined but in the case of none of them are we told that pastoral work – beyond spiritual services for the founder and his kin – was among them. King Œthelwald, Bede tells us, asked Bishop Cedd to 'accept a grant of land, on which to build a monastery [Lastingham] where he himself might frequently come to pray and hear the Word and where he might be buried; for he firmly believed that the daily prayers of those who served God there would greatly help him'.[12] When Oswine became a monk of Lastingham, we learn, he did so not 'for the sake of ease as some did, but to work hard', although in his case this meant manual labour rather than reading.[13] Pastoral care in any shape or form is not mentioned. For Chad, who held the monastery after Cedd, Lastingham was a place of retirement,[14] as was the monastery of Whitby for Trumwine after his flight from his bishopric at Abercorn, and the monastery of Coldingham for

[10]   *EH*, III. 26 (pp. 310–11).
[11]   *Two Lives of St Cuthbert*, ed. and trans. B. Colgrave (Cambridge, 1940; repr. 1985), ch. 9 (pp. 184–7); see also chs 12–16 (pp. 195–211). Boisil is also said to have preached from Melrose (pp. 186–7). For Bede's letter to Egbert, see *Venerabilis Baedae Opera Historica*, ed. C. Plummer, 2 vols (Oxford, 1896), I, p. 410.
[12]   *EH*, III. 23 (pp. 286–7).
[13]   *EH*, IV. 3 (pp. 338–9).
[14]   *EH*, V. 19 (pp. 522–3).

Æthelthryth after her separation from King Ecgfrith.[15] The role of the monks (*monachi*) in the twelve monasteries founded by King Oswiu as a thank-offering for his victory over King Penda of Mercia was 'to wage heavenly warfare and to pray with unceasing devotion that the race might win eternal peace'.[16] The monastery of Gilling was founded as a direct result of Oswiu's role in the killing of his colleague King Oswine: 'in it prayer was continually to be said for the eternal welfare of both kings, for the one who planned the murder and for his victim'.[17] If it is not explicitly stated that Whitby was founded as a burial-church for Northumbrian royalty, there is no doubt that it assumed that function.[18] The unidentified monastery described in Æthelwulf's poem *De Abbatibus* appears to have been founded as a refuge for Northumbrian aristocrats persecuted by their king.[19]

It could be argued, of course, that the failure of these texts to mention the pastoral role of monasteries derived from the fact that that role was too well-known and commonplace to deserve mention, but that is hardly the most economical interpretation, especially in view of the fact that in his letter to Bishop Egbert Bede set out a strategy for improving pastoral care in the Northumbrian church which relied on bishops and their clergy rather than on monasteries. He wrote:

> Because the distances between the places belonging to the rule of your diocese are too great for you alone to be able to traverse them all and preach the word of God in the several hamlets and homesteads even in the full course of a whole year, it is very necessary that you appoint several assistants for yourself in the sacred work, by ordaining priests and instituting teachers, who may devote themselves to preaching the word of God in the various villages and to celebrate the heavenly mysteries, and especially to performing the rites of holy baptism, wherever opportunity arises.[20]

We should notice that there is no mention here of preaching monks, no mention of monasteries, only a recommendation that the bishop should appoint clerks and priests. In the same letter Bede makes a further recommendation, namely that more bishoprics should be created and that sites for the new sees should be sought in the monasteries. Opposition from the abbot and monks of such should be bought off with permission to elect the bishop from amongst their number.[21] Although Sarah Foot has argued that this suggests

[15] *EH.* IV. 26 (24) (pp. 428–9); bk IV. 19 (pp. 392–3).
[16] *EH*, III. 24 (pp. 292–3).
[17] *Ibid.*
[18] *Ibid.*
[19] Æthelwulf, *De Abbatibus*, ed. A. Campbell (Oxford, 1967), chs 2–3.
[20] *Opera Historica*, ed. Plummer, I, p. 408; trans. *English Historical Documents*, I, *c.500–1042*, ed. D. Whitelock, 2nd edn (London, 1979), p. 801.
[21] *Opera Historica*, ed. Plummer, I, pp. 412–14.

that the monasteries were indeed engaged in pastoral work, it is hard to see how Bede's words can be interpreted in that way.[22] For him the framework of pastoral care was to be episcopal and not monastic.

The letter to Egbert shows, of course, that Bede envisaged that bishops' sees could be based in monasteries, as was indeed the case with Lindisfarne, Abercorn, Ripon and Hexham.[23] But it was not universally so, for Bede never described the church of York as a monastery even though it was evidently served by a religious community with (at least in the later eighth century) considerable claims to be a learned body.[24] In the case of Lindisfarne, Bede clearly anticipated that his readers would be surprised by the association of a bishop's see and a monastery on the island.[25] Nor need we suppose that the location of a bishop's see in a monastery necessarily meant that the monks were themselves involved in pastoral work. When in the late eleventh century, William of St Calais, bishop of Durham, constituted his cathedral chapter as a Benedictine monastery, even going so far as to appoint the prior as archdeacon, this did not mean that Durham monks immediately assumed pastoral roles. The cathedral priory was a monastic church devoted to study and the liturgy like any other.[26]

There is no doubt, of course, that pre-Viking monasteries had numerous contacts with the laity just like monasteries in other periods.[27] We have already noted the functions they fulfilled vis-à-vis their founders. It seems likely that they felt some pastoral responsibility, for, in the south, Wilfrid is said to have taken care to baptise the serfs on the landed endowment of his monastery at Selsey,[28] and it may have been to the peasants of the estates of

---

22 Sarah Foot, 'Parochial Ministry in Early Anglo-Saxon England: the Role of Monastic Communities', in *The Ministry: Clerical and Lay*, Studies in Church History 26 (1989), 43–54, p. 48.

23 E.g. *EH*, IV. 26 (pp. 428–9, Abercorn); IV. 27 (pp. 434–5, Lindisfarne); III. 28 and V. 1 (pp. 316–17, 454–5, Ripon); IV. 27 (pp. 430–1), and *The Life of Bishop Wilfrid by Eddius Stephanus*, ed. and trans. B. Colgrave (Cambridge, 1927; repr. 1985), ch. 44 (pp. 90–1, Hexham).

24 E.g. *EH*, II. 20 (pp. 206–7); Alcuin, *The Bishops, Kings, and Saints of York*, ed. and trans. P. Godman (Oxford, 1982), pp. lxi–lxxv. It is possible, but not certain, that *monasterium* in line 1417 of Alcuin's poem refers to the cathedral church of York.

25 *Two Lives of Cuthbert*, pp. 206–9. The size of the island seems to have been only an incidental reason for this surprise.

26 *Symeonis monachi opera omnia*, ed. T. Arnold, 2 vols, Rolls Series (London, 1882–5), I, pp. 120–1, 129; see also Symeon of Durham, *Libellus de exordio atque procursu istius, hoc est, Dunelmensis ecclesie*, ed. and trans. David Rollason (Oxford, forthcoming) and, for general background, *Anglo-Norman Durham 1093–1193*, ed. David Rollason, Margaret Harvey and Michael Prestwich (Woodbridge, 1994).

27 See, for example, Sarah Foot, 'The Role of the Minster', previous essay.

28 *EH*, IV. 13 (pp. 374–7).

Monkwearmouth/Jarrow that Bede expected to preach on feast-days.[29] Guests of various kinds were received in monasteries.[30] Abbots and abbesses were naturally involved with the ruling class of their day, especially as they were themselves often drawn from that class. The advice offered by Abbess Hild of Whitby to those who visited her,[31] and the demands on Abbot Benedict Bishop of Monkwearmouth/Jarrow to advise the king were a typical aspect of monastic life in the time of Bede. Monasteries could assume governmental roles, as in Mercia the monastery of Winchcombe is said to have been the repository for the royal archives,[32] and their wealth may have tended to make them centres of economic exploitation, as the siting of some monasteries at harbours and on routeways may perhaps suggest.[33] Such contacts with lay society, however, do not constitute pastoral functions, and are indeed characteristic of medieval monasticism generally, however much monastic founders may have desired to separate their monasteries from the world. Indeed, it is arguable that in England monasteries became more rather than less integrated with society from the ninth and tenth centuries onwards, as they began to develop pilgrimages and saints' cults on a considerable scale,[34] to found boroughs outside their gates,[35] and to assume responsibility for parishes from which they received tithes and for which they provided vicars.[36] Yet it was in this period, according to the 'minster hypothesis', that their pastoral functions were declining. In short, evidence for the general integration of monasteries with lay society is irrelevant to the putative pastoral functions of those monasteries.

If we cannot with confidence attribute pastoral functions to pre-Viking English monasteries, we should not accept that all churches of the period should be lumped together under the heading of 'minsters', however loose the terminology of some of our sources may be. That Bede should have used *monasterium* in an imprecise sense is *prima facie* unlikely. Indeed, a number of passages in the *Ecclesiastical History* suggest that his use of words deliberately

---

[29] Alan Thacker, 'Monks, Preaching and Pastoral Care in Early Anglo-Saxon England', in *Pastoral Care*, ed. Blair and Sharpe, 137–70, p. 140.

[30] E.g. *Two Lives of Cuthbert*, pp. 174–8.

[31] *EH*, IV. 23 (pp. 408–9).

[32] W. Levison, *England and the Continent in the Eighth Century* (Oxford, 1946), p. 252.

[33] Rosalind Hill, 'Christianity and Geography in Early Northumbria', *Studies in Church History* 3 (1966), 133–9.

[34] David Rollason, *Saints and Relics in Anglo-Saxon England* (Oxford, 1989), pp. 177–95.

[35] See, for example, M. D. Lobel, *The Borough of Bury St Edmund's: a Study in the Government and Development of a Monastic Town* (Oxford, 1935).

[36] G. Constable, *Monastic Tithes from their Origins to the Twelfth Century* (Cambridge, 1964), ch. 1.

distinguished *monasteria* from other types of church. After the conversion of Northumbria, 'churches (*ecclesie*) were built in various places and the people flocked together with joy to hear the Word; lands and property of other kinds were given by royal bounty to establish monasteries (*monasteria*)'.[37] On the Continent the Northumbrian missionary Willibrord 'built a number of churches (*ecclesias*) throughout those districts and established several monasteries (*monasteria*)'.[38] At the royal vill of *Campodunum*, where the 'minster hypothesis' would predispose us to expect a minster, Bede tells us there was a church (*basilica*). There was, it appears, a monastery (*monasterium*) in the forest of Elmet, at which the altar from *Campodunum* was preserved after the royal vill had been burned and superseded.[39] When the *paterfamilias* Drihthelm had a vision of heaven and hell, he went first to pray in the oratory (*oratorium*) of his village, but subsequently became a monk in the monastery (*monasterium*) of Melrose.[40] These are, of course, very well-known passages, but they seem to require reiteration in the face of the argument that Bede and his contemporaries did not perceive monasteries as functionally distinctive churches. On the contrary, Bede was acutely aware of what monasticism was about. 'I have spent all my life in this monastery,' he wrote, 'applying myself entirely to the study of the scriptures; and, amid the observance of the discipline of the Rule and the daily task of singing in church, it has always been my delight to learn or to teach or to write'.[41] There is no reason to suppose that the teaching in question was pastoral care in the 'minster hypothesis' sense, for the passage quoted is followed directly by Bede's list of his many erudite publications. Moreover, in his *History of the Abbots of Monkwearmouth and Jarrow*, he gave an outline of Abbot Eostorwine's praiseworthy way of life. Pastoral work is not mentioned, but manual labour, as laid down in the Rule of St Benedict, figures prominently.[42] Paramount, however, was the importance of the monastic liturgy. When plague swept Jarrow leaving only Abbot Ceolfrith and one small boy, what preoccupied them was not preaching or attending to the laity, but maintaining the appropriate antiphons.[43]

None of this is to deny the importance of monasteries in the Christianisation of England. They were numerous and wealthy; they must have reflected and extended the impact of Christianity on their founders; and by their range of functions set out above they must have played an important

[37] *EH*, III. 3 (pp. 220–1).
[38] *EH*, V. 11 (pp. 486–7).
[39] *EH*, II. 14 (pp. 188–9).
[40] *EH*, V. 12 (pp. 488–9).
[41] *EH*, V. 24 (pp. 566–7).
[42] *Opera Historica*, ed. Plummer, I, pp. 371–2.
[43] *Ibid.*, p. 393.

role in familiarising the lay population with the Christian religion. The evidence suggests, however, that they were functionally distinct from other types of church, and it in no way justifies the assertion that they formed the backbone of a pre-Viking system of pastoral care.

This is not to say, of course, that monks like Bede were not concerned with spreading Christianity to the laity. On the contrary, even on his death-bed he was concerned with producing gospel translations into Old English, and his exegetical and homiletic writings show an emphasis, as Alan Thacker has explained, on preachers and teachers, and a thirst for controlling the private lives of the laity at large along Christian lines which implies a preoccupation with pastoral work.[44] A preoccupation is one thing, however; being able to turn it into a reality is another. Bede's wish to impose higher standards of Christianity on the laity is no proof that the church possessed the machinery necessary to carry it out. This brings us to the second aspect of the 'minster hypothesis' which requires critical attention: the existence in the pre-Viking period of a 'network of minster *parochiae*'. Can it be shown that early monasteries – or indeed early churches of any kind – formed such a network?

If we restrict ourselves to early evidence, the answer would seem to be in the negative. Bede tells us that the monastery of Lastingham was deliberately founded 'amid steep and remote hills which seemed better fitted for the haunts of robbers and the dens of wild beasts than for human habitation'.[45] Even today the traveller can attest to the remoteness of the site, lying in the fastness of the North Yorkshire moors, well to the north of any major route-way; and a similar position is occupied by Hackness.[46] As for the monastery of Coldingham, the probability that it was in fact located on the wild and inaccessible St Abb's Head to the north of modern Coldingham underlines the extent to which its foundation derived from a wish to be remote from the world, rather than any need to be part of 'a network of minster *parochiae*'.[47] Whitby too would seem to have been favoured for its inaccessibility: even today road access to the modern town is steep and difficult.

Aside from these individual cases, where the distribution of churches which have documentary, sculptural, or architectural evidence for their early

---

[44]   Alan Thacker, 'Monks, Preaching and Pastoral Care', pp. 152–9, and *idem*, 'Bede's Ideal of Reform', in *Ideal and Reality in Frankish and Anglo-Saxon Society: Studies presented to J. M. Wallace-Hadrill*, ed. P. Wormald, D. Bullough and R. Collins (Oxford, 1983), 130–53.

[45]   *EH*, III. 23 (pp. 286–7).

[46]   On which see *EH*, IV. 23 (21) (pp. 412–14).

[47]   L. Alcock *et al.*, 'Reconnaissance Excavations on Early Historic Fortifications and Other Royal Sites in Scotland, 1974–84: 1, Excavations near St Abb's Head, Berwicks', *Proceedings of the Society of Antiquaries of Scotland* 116 (1986), 255–79.

date has been plotted, the resulting picture looks not at all like a 'network'. For County Durham, Eric Cambridge has shown that the distribution is characterised rather by clusters of churches, some of which, as in the case of Escomb and Auckland, may in fact be monasteries linked in the way that we know Monkwearmouth and Jarrow were.[48] In Yorkshire, there are similar clusters of known early churches, notably in the Vale of Pickering, where the nearby churches of Stonegrave, Hovingham, Middleton, and Kirkdale all have early evidence of pre-Viking date, contrasting with the large areas of Yorkshire which have no evidence for pre-Viking churches at all.[49] In Lancashire too, Cambridge has noted a concentration of early sculpture and early churches in the Lune valley and northwards, contrasting with its absence from the area between the Lune and Mersey valleys, despite the fact that the latter can be shown on the basis of place-names to have been early settled.[50] Cambridge concludes that the evidence of texts, sculpture, and architecture is showing us not a 'network of minster *parochiae*' but groupings of monasteries whose location was presumably dictated by that of the lands which they received from founders and benefactors. If a network of pastoral care existed at all, its constituent churches must have been separate from the monasteries, which is entirely consistent with our discussion of early references to monasteries above.[51]

John Blair has objected to Cambridge's views, arguing that, in the case of County Durham, the uneven distribution of known early churches is misleading and that extensive *parochiae* could in fact be drawn around them,[52] but there is no evidence and Blair's observation could apply to virtually any selection of points. In fact, Blair's 'network of minster *parochiae*' can only be postulated on the basis of later – often much later – sources. It is argued that as, in accordance with the hypothesis, minster parishes fragmented in the post-Viking period, the original minster churches formerly at the heart of large *parochiae* retained certain characteristics allowing them to be identified even in records of the high middle ages and later. Such characteristics might include the right to receive payments such as church-scot from other churches (which are interpreted as originally having been subsidiary churches within the minster *parochia*), the possession of chapels, the presence of more than one priest, ideally a college of priests, an exceptionally large parish (interpreted as the remnants of an even larger *parochia*), location at or near the centre of an actual or putative unit of royal government, and even the presence at the

---

[48] Cambridge, 'Early Church in County Durham'.

[49] Morris, *Churches in the Landscape*, pp. 122, 134, 137.

[50] Cambridge, 'Early Church in County Durham', p. 71.

[51] *Ibid.*, pp. 79–82.

[52] John Blair, 'Minster Churches in the Landscape', in *Anglo-Saxon Settlements*, ed. Della Hooke (Oxford, 1988), 35–58, p. 37 and n. 2.

church in question of pre-Viking architectural or sculptural remains.[53] Since any one or any combination of these characteristics has been held sufficient to identify an ancient minster church in the sense of the 'minster hypothesis', it will be seen at once that the matter depends on an *a priori* acceptance of the hypothesis. Once we accept the view that all early churches were minsters, then any demonstration of pre-Viking antiquity, however slight, will suffice to identify one such. Once we accept the concept of the fragmentation of minster *parochiae* any indication of superior status will be seen as marking a church out as a pre-Viking minster.

The premises involved in this, particularly regarding attributes of superior status as derived from the pre-Viking period, seem very doubtful. Consider the priory of Nostell in Yorkshire. This church originated as a group of hermits who were around 1100 granted permission to live beside the fishpond at Nostell and to take over the adjoining woods dedicated to St Oswald, the seventh-century Northumbrian king and martyr. They received generous aristocratic benefactions in the early twelfth century, and soon became a house of canons. Among the gifts to them were the church of St Oswald at Winwick in Makerfield, and the church of Bamburgh, also closely associated with that saint. Moreover, Nostell came to control a whole complex of churches in Yorkshire, and Nicholl argued that Thurstan was deliberately building up such control as a means of organising his diocese with churches like Nostell as in effect subsidiary diocesan centres. The net result of all this was, as Nicholl noted, that Nostell looked like a minster in the sense of the 'minster hypothesis'. It had ancient associations, namely its connection with Oswald; it was collegiate in constitution; it controlled subsidiary churches; and in addition it had freedom from episcopal exactions and a royal gift of 12*d.* from the farm of the shire. In the light of the 'minster hypothesis', all or any of these attributes would have been sufficient to identify Nostell as a pre-Viking minster; and that would be highly misleading. In fact we know for certain that it was the product of piety, patronage, and the planning of the archbishop of York in the early twelfth century.[54] Its minster attributes are thus late creations, not early relics. In the case of Nostell and of other Augustinian priories, confusion is unlikely because of the availability of evidence. But may it not be that many alleged 'minster' churches were in fact created in a similar way but in a less well-documented context?

Even in the 'minster hypothesis's' own terms, the evidence for Northumbria is far from convincing. As regards Yorkshire, David Palliser has recently noted that churches suggested as pre-Viking minsters 'on varying

[53] For example, Jane Croom, 'The Fragmentation of the Minster *Parochiae* of South-East Shropshire', in *Minsters and Parish Churches*, ed. Blair, 67–81, p. 71.

[54] For the above account of Nostell, see Donald Nicholl, *Thurstan, Archbishop of York (1114–1140)* (York, 1964), pp. 130–5.

evidence' include Beverley, Ripon, Bridlington, Conisborough, Dewsbury, Doncaster, Hemingbrough, Howden, Hunmanby, Ledsham, Masham, Pocklington, and Stonegrave.[55] The varying character of the evidence is indeed striking. Beverley and Ripon are well known early monasteries, the former founded by John of Beverley, the latter by St Wilfrid. By the high middle ages they had certainly become important mother churches, in effect subsidiary cathedrals, and were thus crucially important in pastoral organisation.[56] But it is quite unknown whether this situation derived from their pre-Viking status, or whether it was of much more recent origin.[57] It is instructive that the other church of comparable status in the diocese of York was Southwell which is first documented only in the tenth century.[58] Of the other churches in Palliser's list, Stonegrave is attested as a monastery in the eighth century and it preserves sculpture of the tenth and perhaps the ninth centuries; but nothing else is known of it, apart from the fact that its parish embraced four townships; it does not even appear as a church in Domesday Book.[59] Dewsbury has early sculpture and appears as the recipient of dues from other churches in fourteenth-century documents and in the *Valor Ecclesiasticus* of the sixteenth century,[60] but when these dues were awarded to it is quite unknown. Masham has a pre-Viking stone cross shaft, and part of the church's fabric may be of similar date.[61] Conisborough's name implies that it was a

---

[55] *The Yorkshire Domesday*, ed. and trans. D. Palliser, Alecto County Edition of Domesday Book 31 (London, 1992), p. 22.

[56] C. N. L. Brooke, 'Rural Ecclesiastical Institutions: the Search for their Origins', in *Cristianizzazione ed Organizzazione Ecclesiastice delle Campagne nell'Alto Medioevo: Espansione e Resistenze*, Settimane di Studio 28, 2 vols (Spoleto, 1982), II, 685–711, p. 695.

[57] For an account of the sources for Beverley and Ripon, which argues unconvincingly for continuity of religious life on the sites, see Richard Morris and Eric Cambridge, 'Beverley Minster before the Thirteenth Century', in *Medieval Art and Architecture in the East Riding of Yorkshire*, ed. C. Wilson, British Archaeological Association Conference Transactions for 1983 (London, 1989), 1–31, pp. 9–12.

[58] D. Knowles and R. N. Hadcock, *Medieval Religious Houses: England and Wales*, 2nd edn (London, 1971), p. 439.

[59] *Councils and Ecclesiastical Documents relating to Great Britain and Ireland*, ed. A. W. Haddan and W. Stubbs, 3 vols (Oxford, 1869–78), III, p. 395; *York and Eastern Yorkshire*, ed. James Lang, Corpus of Anglo-Saxon Stone Sculpture 3 (Oxford, 1991), pp. 215–20; *VCH, North Riding of Yorkshire*, I (London, 1914), p. 561.

[60] *West Yorkshire: An Archaeological Survey to A.D. 1500*, ed. M. L. Faull and S. A. Moorhouse, 3 vols and maps (Wakefield, 1981), III, pp. 216–18 and map 15.

[61] W. G. Collingwood, *Northumbrian Crosses of the Pre-Norman Age* (London, 1927), p. 43; and H. M. and Joan Taylor, *Anglo-Saxon Architecture*, 3 vols (Cambridge, 1965–78), II, p. 734.

royal burgh and thus a suitable location for a minster, according to the 'minster hypothesis'. It was certainly a large estate in the eleventh century, but the evidence suggests that this was of recent creation and that its church enjoyed no superior status over other churches.[62] Ledsham preserves an early church.[63] Hunmanby has some fragments of sculpture dated from the eighth to the tenth centuries, and it formerly had an extensive parish of 8,452 acres.[64] Bridlington and Pocklington originally had large parishes.[65] Doncaster was the head of a lordship in the eleventh century and became a deanery, but there seems no justification for the statement that an 'early minster was established in Doncaster'.[66] The evidence in short is to say the least of it uneven. Restricting ourselves to that of early texts, sculpture and architecture we learn no more than that there were early churches on some of the sites in question, but whether these had any functional continuity with the later parish churches is not demonstrable. As for the evidence of dues and extensive parishes, there is no way of establishing the date at which these originated. They may have resulted from diocesan organisation at any period, and there is no reason to refer them to a pre-Viking 'network of minster *parochiae*'.

Using the evidence of Domesday Book, Blair has mapped a different selection of churches as possible 'minsters' in Yorkshire: Morley, Topcliffe, Upper Poppleton, Wakefield, and Withernsea.[67] Although there is no doubt that these were churches of some importance in 1086, the entries for them in Domesday Book are of very diverse character, and neither this nor their uneven distribution encourages us to regard them as forming even part of a 'network of minster *parochiae*'.[68] Meanwhile in Cheshire, Nicholas Higham in a recent study has sought to identify the ancient ecclesiastical (and secular) territorial organisation of the county, with no early evidence whatsoever, but starting from 'basic assumptions', one of which is all too familiar to us: 'that the pre-Viking Age was characterised by comparatively few mother churches

---

62   David Hey, *Yorkshire from AD 1000* (London, 1986), p. 13; see now M. S. Parker, 'The Province of Hatfield', *Northern History* 28 (1992), 42–69, pp. 53–6.

63   Taylor and Taylor, *Anglo-Saxon Architecture*, I, pp. 378–84.

64   *VCH, East Riding of Yorkshire*, II (Oxford, 1974), p. 228, and *York and East Yorkshire*, ed. Lang, pp. 148–9.

65   *Ibid.*, p. 30; Morris, *Churches in the Landscape*, p. 136.

66   Arthur Raistrick, *The Making of the English Landscape: the West Riding of Yorkshire* (London, 1970), p. 31.

67   John Blair, 'Secular Minster Churches in Domesday Book', in *Domesday Book: a Reassessment*, ed. Peter Sawyer (London, 1985), p. 111; see also *Yorkshire Domesday*, ed. Palliser, p. 22, n. 134.

68   *Domesday Book: Yorkshire*, ed. M. L. Faull and M. Stinson, 2 vols (Chichester, 1986), 9W118, 13N17, 2W2, 1Y15, 14E4. For Withernsea's early parish, which was extensive, and other references, see *VCH, East Riding of Yorkshire*, V (Oxford, 1984), pp. 40, 45.

or minsters, with responsibility for large *parochiae* (minster parishes), which were later much reduced in size and authority through the establishment in the tenth, eleventh, and twelfth centuries of large numbers of lesser churches'.[69]

Returning to the north-east, the case of Hexham is an instructive one.[70] Well attested as a monastery and a bishop's see from the late seventh to the early ninth century, virtually nothing is known of it from then until *c.*1000, although the discovery there of sculpture of ninth- and tenth-century date shows that a church continued to function on the site.[71] From an account of the priesthood of Hexham preserved in London, British Library, MS Yates Thompson 26, however, it emerges that around the year 1000 the bishops of Durham, into whose diocese Hexham at that time fell, appointed priests of Hexham, men of some distinction who also held offices such as sacristan and treasurer in the church of Durham, and could on occasion appoint deputies to Hexham in their own right.[72] During the eleventh century then, Hexham may have been to the diocese of Durham what Beverley, Ripon, and Southwell were to the diocese of York. But was this in any way derived from Hexham's earlier history as a monastery? It may after all have been a legacy of Hexham's role as a bishop's see; or, and this would seem the most economical interpretation of the Yates Thompson 26 text, it may have assumed this role only in *c.*1000 when the priests of Hexham were appointed, a process which the text appears to regard as a new departure. Merely demonstrating the continuity of ecclesiastical life at Hexham does not, in other words, prove that the church had pastoral functions throughout the period from the seventh to the eleventh centuries, as the proponents of the 'minster hypothesis' would presumably suggest.

Evidence for other churches in the diocese of Durham is provided by a charter purportedly granted by William of St Calais, bishop of Durham (1080–96). The charter itself is unquestionably a forgery, but as Professor H. S. Offler noted, its witness list seems to derive from a genuine record of an episcopal synod.[73] Aside from the bishop himself, the witnesses are: Eilaf, priest of Hexham, Ælfwold, priest of Tynemouth, Wulfkill, priest of

---

[69] N. J. Higham, *The Origins of Cheshire* (Manchester, 1993), ch. 5, esp. p. 127.

[70] The best account is still *The Priory of Hexham*, ed. James Raine, 2 vols, Surtees Society 44, 46 (Durham, 1864–5), I, pp. xiv–lxviii.

[71] R. J. Cramp, *County Durham and Northumberland*, 2 vols, Corpus of Anglo-Saxon Stone Sculpture 1 (London, 1984), I, pp. 174–93.

[72] *Hexham*, ed. Raine, I, appendix, pp. vii–viii. The manuscript was formerly in the possession of Sir William Lawson. See also W. Longstaffe, 'The Hereditary Sacerdotage of Hexham', *Archaeologia Aeliana*, new ser. 4 (1860), 11–28.

[73] *Durham Episcopal Charters 1071–1152*, ed. H. S. Offler, Surtees Society 179 (Gateshead, 1968), pp. 39–45.

Sedgefield, Eilaf of Bedlington, Mærwin, priest of Chester-le-Street, Uhtred, priest of Auckland, Aldred, priest of Aycliffe, Gillo, priest of Eaglescliffe, and Hemming, priest of Brancepeth. The churches mentioned were presumably important ones in the pastoral structure of Durham in the late eleventh century. Aside from Hexham, only Tynemouth has any claim to have been an early monastery, and that is not a strong claim on the basis either of documentary evidence or of archaeological remains.[74] Certainly there was a church on its site in the ninth and tenth centuries as attested by the surviving sculpture,[75] but its status is uncertain. Auckland stood at the head of a shire in the late twelfth-century survey known as the *Boldon Book*, but the age of that shire is uncertain.[76] The church possessed a stone cross of some sophistication, suggesting that it was a monastic church perhaps linked with Escomb, but there is no early evidence for this apart from stylistic similarities between the sculpture from the two sites.[77] Chester-le-Street was the episcopal see for over a century before its establishment at Durham in 995.[78] Bedlington, like Auckland, was the head of a shire.[79] Sedgefield, Brancepeth, and Eaglescliffe all had extensive parishes. Brancepeth was dedicated to St Brandon, apparently an Irish saint; and Eaglescliffe preserves a carved baluster shaft of possibly eighth-century date.[80] In short, the list poses the same methodological problems as does the evidence for Yorkshire. Are we to perceive an early 'network of minster *parochiae*' lying behind the organisation of the eleventh-century diocese? Or may we rather suggest that some early churches, regardless of their original functions, had been absorbed into a pattern of diocesan organisation which as a whole may have been much more recent than the 'minster hypothesis' would presumably maintain?

We should, I suggest, accept the evidence at face value. Some of the important churches of Northumbria in the high middle ages and later had

---

[74] R. J. Cramp, 'Monastic Sites', in *The Archaeology of Anglo-Saxon England*, ed. David M. Wilson (Cambridge, 1976), 201–52, pp. 217–20.

[75] Cramp, *County Durham and Northumberland*, I, pp. 226–9.

[76] The case for the antiquity of this shire with citation of the available evidence is set out by Brian K. Roberts, *The Green Villages of County Durham: a Study in Historical Geography* (Durham, 1977), pp. 14–18.

[77] Cramp, *County Durham and Northumberland*, I, pp. 37–40, 77–9; Cambridge, 'Early Church in County Durham', pp. 75–6.

[78] G. Bonner, 'St Cuthbert at Chester le Street', in *St Cuthbert, his Cult and his Community to AD 1200*, ed. G. Bonner, D. Rollason and C. Stancliffe (Woodbridge, 1989), 387–95.

[79] *Domesday Book: Supplementary Volume; Boldon Book: Northumberland and Durham*, ed. D. Austin (Chichester, 1982), pp. 28–9.

[80] W. Fordyce, *History and Antiquities of the County Palatine of Durham*, 2 vols (Newcastle upon Tyne, n.d.), II, pp. 426–7, 524; *VCH, Durham*, III (London, 1928), p. 222; and Cramp, *Northumberland and Durham*, I, pp. 75–6.

been pre-Viking churches; others had not. There is certainly no compelling case for beginning from the assumption that there must have been a 'network of minster *parochiae*', or that early monasteries had an important pastoral role. It seems indeed much more likely that the seventh and eighth centuries were preoccupied with developing a framework of dioceses and archdioceses, with the work of Theodore and, in the eighth century, those who established the archbishopric of York and the short-lived archbishopric of Lichfield.[81] How far a pattern of subdiocesan organisation existed at all at that time is open to question, and it may well be that its development was the work of the ninth and tenth centuries and later.[82] In short, in their anxiety to demonstrate the existence of a coherent system of pastoral care in the pre-Viking period, the proponents of the 'minster hypothesis' are at risk of simplifying the process by which the English church took shape. That process may well have been protracted and complex, influenced no doubt by Continental developments, involving perhaps periods when pastoral care was barely available to the laity below the level of those who could found churches for themselves. Exploring that process requires an open-minded approach and will be hindered rather than helped by the adoption of the all-embracing models of the character of 'minsters' and of the 'network' of their *parochiae* which this paper has examined.

---

[81] H. Mayr-Harting, *The Coming of Christianity to Anglo-Saxon England*, 3rd edn (London, 1991), pp. 130–9; D. P. Kirby, *Bede's Historia Ecclesiastica Gentis Anglorum: its Contemporary Setting*, Jarrow Lecture 1992 (Jarrow, 1993), pp. 11–13; and Nicholas Brooks, *The Early History of the Church of Canterbury* (Leicester, 1984), pp. 118–27.

[82] As suggested in Cambridge and Rollason, 'Pastoral Organisation', pp. 97–103.

Monasteries and Sculpture in the Insular pre-Viking Age: the Pictish Evidence

ISABEL HENDERSON

Pictish territory lies north of a line drawn between the estuaries of the rivers Forth and Clyde (Fig. 1). The Picts spoke a P-Celtic language, and so were distinct from their neighbours in the west, the Q-Celtic speaking Irish who had colonised the south-western Pictish regions from northern Ireland. Within this Irish settlement, known as Dál Riata (modern Argyll) lay the great monastic centre of Iona. Around 850, these Irish speakers, later to be known as the Scots, moved into the eastern and northern Pictish lands and the Picts disappear from the political record before the end of the century.[1]

Much of the Pictish terrain is mountainous. Pictish sculpture, often the only evidence for settlement, occurs in river valleys generally, and in the south, in the flat lands of Strathmore and Fife.[2] In the north particularly fine sculpture is found in the area known as 'the Firthlands', those lands on the shores of the Moray, Cromarty and Dornoch firths (Fig. 2). All these districts have outcrops of sandstone, which carves well and breaks down into good agricultural soil.

The Picts are best known for their unique symbols. These are incised in groups, usually of two or three, on undressed erratic boulders – 'the symbol stones'. Symbols are also carved in relief, almost invariably with other ornament and iconography, on dressed slabs with full-length decorated crosses. We can only guess at what the symbols mean by noting their associations. For the incised monuments this amounts to a still not strong association with burials, and for the relief slabs, the cross, and the figural and decorative repertoire.[3]

---

[1] For a lively general survey see A. P. Smyth, *Warlords and Holy Men* (London, 1984).

[2] *An Historical Atlas of Scotland c.400–c.1600*, ed. P. McNeill and R. Nicholson (St Andrews, 1975).

[3] For excellent colour illustrations of Pictish symbol stones and relief sculpture see A. Ritchie, *Picts* (Edinburgh, 1989). For Pictish settlement archaeology see *Pictish Studies: Settlement, Burial and Art in Dark Age Northern Britain*, ed. J. G. P. Friell and W. G. Watson, British Archaeological Reports, British Series 125 (Oxford,

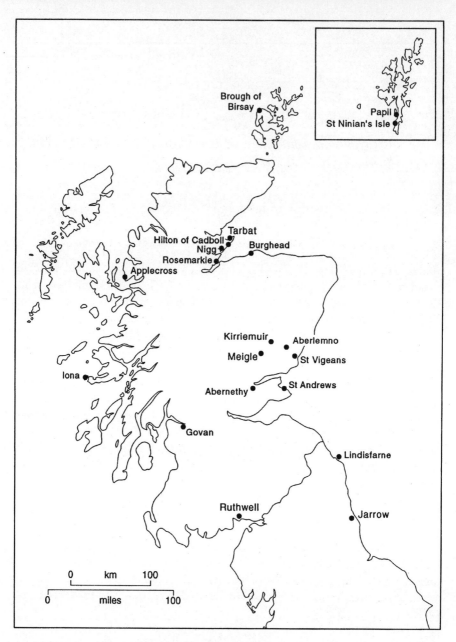

Figure 1: Places mentioned in the text.

Writing in 1980 in his book *Viking Age Sculpture*, Richard Bailey contrasted the contexts of the sculpture of the Viking Age with that of the preceding Anglian period. He pointed out that Anglian sculpture, unlike

1984).

76

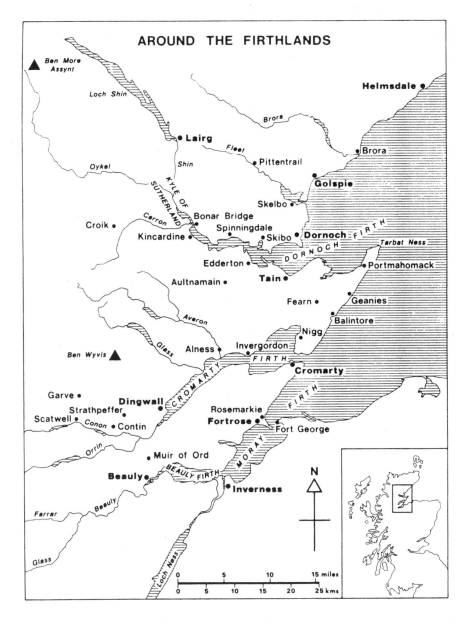

Figure 2: Around the Firthlands.

Viking sculpture, was concentrated at a few centres, and that those centres we know from written sources to have been monastic. With the decline of monasticism the quality of the sculpture declined, and by the time of the Viking Age patronage and manufacture had passed into lay hands. 'And even

77

when the documents fail us for other sites', he argues, 'it is reasonable to infer a similar monastic background' for the earlier sculpture, for those with inscriptions presuppose literacy, the by-product of monastic training, and others 'carry figural scenes with a monastic interest'.[4]

Bailey's views accord with those of Rosemary Cramp, who has argued that Anglo-Saxon sculpture had its beginnings in the decoration of monastic churches built in stone, and with those of Éamonn Ó Carragáin, who in a series of intricate papers has shown how sculpture in Ireland and England in the early medieval period reveals in its subject matter a shared pre-occupation with specifically monastic spirituality.[5]

Well over 200 examples of sculpture, which employ, with panache, a decorative repertoire familiar in the monastic arts of the rest of the British Isles, are found well-scattered in the Pictish regions of North Britain.[6] Yet the Picts are scarcely renowned for the richness of their monastic culture, and Julian Brown's suggestion that a Pictish provenance for the Book of Kells should at least be entertained was never taken seriously, for the simple reason that only one text can be attributed ultimately to a Pictish scriptorium.[7] So, one text and 200 or so pieces of potentially 'monastic' sculpture: this is the problem.

The case for Christianity, far less monasticism, flourishing among the Picts was dealt a blow by Kathleen Hughes in her Jarrow Lecture for 1970. Dr Hughes, relying on one writer's chronology for Pictish sculpture, maintained that since, it seemed, the Picts were still evolving the symbols on their 'pagan' symbol stones at the end of the seventh century, the Columban mission to the Picts, based on Iona, could have made negligible progress. For Dr Hughes it was not until the beginning of the eighth century, when, as Bede records, a Pictish king, Nechtan, had been in touch with Jarrow for help with promoting the acceptance of the orthodox calculation of the date of Easter among his clergy that Christianity had any significant influence on society.[8]

---

[4]   R. N. Bailey, *Viking Age Sculpture in Northern England* (London, 1980), pp. 81–4.

[5]   R. Cramp, *Early Northumbrian Sculpture*, Jarrow Lecture 1965 ([Jarrow], n.d.); É. Ó Carragáin, 'The Ruthwell Cross and Irish Crosses: Some Points of Comparison and Contrast', in *Ireland and Insular Art A.D. 500–1200*, ed. M. Ryan (Dublin, 1987), 118–23 (with references to his other papers).

[6]   J. R. Allen and J. Anderson, *The Early Christian Monuments of Scotland*, 3 parts (Edinburgh, 1903, repr. Belgavies, Forfar, 1993).

[7]   T. J. Brown, 'Northumbria and the Book of Kells', *Anglo-Saxon England* 1 (1972), 219–46; I. Henderson, 'Pictish Art and the Book of Kells', in *Ireland in Early Mediaeval Europe*, ed. D. Whitelock, R. McKitterick and D. Dumville (Cambridge, 1982), 79–105.

[8]   K. Hughes, *Early Christianity in Pictland*, Jarrow Lecture 1970 ([Jarrow], n.d.); Bede, *EH*, V. 21, pp. 532–53.

This abnormally sluggish progress of Christianity, Dr Hughes argued, accounted for the lack of Pictish written records. This analysis was promptly and effectively countered by David Kirby in the *Innes Review* for 1973, and as a consequence Dr Hughes modified her views somewhat.[9] But the damage was done and the influence of her Jarrow lecture lingers on, particularly among archaeologists of an interdisciplinary inclination.[10]

Marjorie Anderson's much less tendentious assessment of the reception of Christianity by the Picts was that while we simply do not know the extent and the effectiveness of the Columban mission in Pictland there is no good reason to doubt the claim of Columba's biographer Adomnán, writing around 700, that there were in his day, functioning normally within Pictish territory, Columban monasteries.[11] Nor indeed can Bede's account of King Nechtan be read naturally as anything other than an approach from a devout Christian, and a king of an officially Christian people, served by *ministri altaris ac monachi*, some of whom, apparently, were being recalcitrant in changing from the Columban to the Roman method of calculating Easter.[12]

Contemporary documentation for Pictish churches, whether native or foreign, which would flesh out the generalised statements of Bede and Adomnán, scarcely exists. King Nechtan arranged for the old Easter Tables to be obliterated, and for copies of the new ones to be made throughout his kingdom, but we do not know where these scribal activities took place. He also commissioned a stone church from Northumbrian architects to be dedicated to St Peter, but we cannot with certainty locate this Pictish St Peter's.[13] At a time of political crisis, like so many of his contemporaries, Nechtan withdrew into religion. Where this enclosed community was that gave him sanctuary is unknown.

---

[9] D. P. Kirby, 'Bede and the Pictish Church', *Innes Review* 24 (1973), 6–25, p. 12, n. 31; K. Hughes, 'Where are the Writings of Early Scotland?', in *Celtic Britain in the Early Middle Ages*, Studies in Celtic History 2, ed. D. Dumville (Woodbridge, 1980), 1–21, pp. 8–9.

[10] See C. D. Morris, *Church and Monastery in the Far North: an Archaeological Evaluation*, Jarrow Lecture 1989 ([Jarrow] n.d.), p. 5; S. M. Foster, 'The State of Pictland in the Age of Sutton Hoo', in *The Age of Sutton Hoo*, ed. M. O. H. Carver (Woodbridge, 1992), 217–34, p. 233.

[11] M. O. Anderson, 'Columba and Other Irish Saints in Scotland', in *Historical Studies 5, Papers read before the Sixth Conference of Irish Historians*, ed. J. L. McCracken (London, 1965), 26–36.

[12] *EH*, V. 21 (p. 552).

[13] For a discussion of the location of the church within a review of Scottish place-names containing the P-Celtic element *egles*, 'Christian church', see G. W. S. Barrow, 'The Childhood of Scottish Christianity: a Note on some Place-Name Evidence', *Scottish Studies* 27 (1983), 1–15.

The Irish chronicles enter the deaths of Pictish kings regularly. But although these obits, and other Pictish material, were taken from a chronicle kept on Iona, for some reason the obits of only three possibly Pictish clerics are recorded, and only one of these is styled 'abbot'. The abbot was called Tuathalán, and his monastery was at Cenrigmonaid, a place-name that can confidently be identified with Kinrimund, the old name for St Andrews in Fife. Abbot Tuathalán died in 747, so presumably there was a monastery at St Andrews at least from the earlier part of the eighth century.[14] The Irish chronicles also contain a series of entries, beginning in the late seventh century, concerning a monastic foundation of the Irish saint Maelrubai at Applecross, in Wester Ross, opposite the Isle of Skye – a useful indication that Columban monks were not the only clerics influential in Pictland in the seventh century.[15]

Finally there is the single Pictish text, a king-list which records the names of the kings and their reign-lengths. Marjorie Anderson has shown that the list was in writing by 724 and maintained thereafter.[16] The compilation of the list, with its pseudo-historical material for the pre-Columban period constructed on sophisticated mathematical principles, was a considerable cultural enterprise, displaying at the very least a concern for establishing in writing the nature of the nation's past, as well as providing a means for controlling its future.[17] But even if the compilation of the list was worked on by Pictish scholars and scribes in a monastic scriptorium, can one adduce here a truly monastic culture, in a way that one could have done had the one surviving Pictish text been, say, a martyrology, a Pictish saint's life or a biblical commentary? The king-list project looks like work for a royal archive.

Wendy Davies has detected the use of potentially Pictish charter-material in a note in the more purely Pictish of the two surviving versions of the king-list. It concerns a royal land grant to a community at Abernethy in Perthshire. This note has always been thought to indicate the provenance of the list but the further suggestion that its language reflects charter usage adds to our knowledge of the mechanisms, very normal ones, whereby land passed from a king to a community.

---

[14] M. O. Anderson, 'The Celtic Church in Kinrimund', *The Innes Review* 25 (1974), 67–76.

[15] For a plan of the monastic enclosure based on a field survey see C. Thomas, *The Early Christian Archaeology of North Britain* (London, 1971), p. 43, fig. 15.

[16] M. O. Anderson, *Kings and Kingship in Early Scotland* (Edinburgh, 1973, repr. 1980), pp. 88–90.

[17] On the methods of construction of the lists see M. Miller, 'The Disputed Historical Horizon of the Pictish King-Lists', *The Scottish Historical Review* 58 (1979), 1–34.

Another trace of the possible use of charters relevant to Pictish matters is embedded in a copy of the lost Register of St Andrews. It consists of part of a witness list confirming a royal foundation at St Andrews and claims to have been drawn up by a scribe in the ninth century in the royal *villa* at Meigle in Perthshire. The royal emphasis in this small collection of material is not surprising but is nonetheless noteworthy.[18]

The organisation of the Pictish church is perceived more clearly at the point at which it comes into contact with the Irish church of Dál Riata in the mid-ninth century. The fragmentary evidence, mostly in the text known as the Old Scottish Chronicle, may need re-assessment in the light of changing views of the organisation of the Irish church, but it is evident that the relationship between church and state in the Irish context of Dál Riata was different from that established in the Pictish kingdom, and that the Pictish church was remembered as being in some sense 'in servitude' to the king. This relationship could have relevance for elucidating the context of the Pictish cross-slabs.[19]

Archaeology provides the best hope for increase of knowledge of the Picts. This has already been amply fulfilled through recent re-assessment of the nature of the pre-Viking later Iron Age in the north and west of Scotland, and for the early medieval period in particular, by the systematic campaign of excavation of documented fortified sites by Leslie and Elizabeth Alcock.[20] No systematic work of this kind has been undertaken for potentially Pictish ecclesiastical sites. The Alcocks specifically pose the question, 'Where are [the churches] and the major ecclesiastical centres implied by clusters of Early Christian crosses and cross-slabs?'[21]

It is only in the undisturbed far north, in Orkney and Shetland, that ecclesiastical sites have been investigated and even there the nature of the evidence is not always clear.[22] The prolonged investigations at the Brough of Birsay, a tidal island off the north-west of mainland Orkney, demonstrate a

---

[18] W. Davies, 'The Latin Charter-Tradition in Western Britain, Brittany and Ireland in the Early Mediaeval Period', in *Ireland in Early Mediaeval Europe*, ed. Whitelock *et al.*, 258–80, p. 272 n. 47, p. 273 n. 55.

[19] M. O. Anderson, 'Dalriada and the Creation of the Kingdom of the Scots', in *Ireland in Early Mediaeval Europe*, 106–32, pp. 127–31.

[20] For the prehistoric period, see *Beyond the Brochs: Changing Perspectives on the Later Iron Age in Atlantic Scotland*, ed. I. Armit (Edinburgh, 1990). On the Alcocks' research programme see L. Alcock and E. A. Alcock, 'Reconnaissance Excavations on Early Historic Fortifications and Other Royal Sites in Scotland 1974–84', *The Proceedings of the Society of Antiquaries of Scotland* 122 (1992), 215–87, pp. 216–18.

[21] *Ibid.*, p. 227.

[22] For an authoritative review see Morris, *Church and Monastery*.

change of emphasis in interpretation. It was assumed by the early excavators that Birsay was the type of site favoured by the Celtic church and that the extent of the manufacture of artefacts there could only be accounted for by the existence of a monastic workshop. A vivid picture was called up of monastic craftsmen fleeing from the Vikings, dropping some of their artefacts in their haste. The more recent investigators, while not ruling out the possibility that there was an early church and monastery at Birsay, emphasise the ambiguity of the evidence. A Pictish slab was found at Birsay in the medieval graveyard. For many years it was claimed that it had stood over a triple burial, an attractive idea for the slab was carved in shallow relief with three warriors, one differentiated as the leader. It was suggested that three of the four symbols carved on the upper half of the slab related to the individual warriors, and that the fourth had a more general, perhaps tribal, significance. It was later shown that the relationship between the slab and the burials was illusory. The slab is unique in having no depiction of the cross; elsewhere the introduction of iconography additional to the symbols invariably brings with it the symbol of the cross. The shattered state of the slab and the geological structure of the stone might allow for a cross on the other side of the slab to have been sheered off, but if so, it is surprising that no fragment of it has been found.

Archaeologists cheerfully describe the warriors as a contemporary portrayal of a local Orkney war-lord with his bodyguard. Art-historians are uneasily aware of just how unusual such a 'portrait' would be in this period. However, no other relief stone sculpture has been found at Birsay and the slab may indeed be a secular monument of a so far unique kind, functioning within a primarily secular settlement.[23]

The excavations at St Ninian's Isle in Shetland are best known for the discovery of a cache of high-grade decorated silver.[24] The treasure included a sword chape with a specifically Christian inscription.[25] There was evidence at Birsay for manufacture on the site of a Pictish type of penannular brooch and twelve brooches of this type were part of the Shetland treasure. A case has been made for all the items in the hoard having a liturgical function, but the preferred explanation for the cache is that it is a collection of secular *de luxe*

---

[23] C. L. Curle, *Pictish and Norse Finds from the Brough of Birsay 1934–74*, Society of Antiquaries of Scotland Monograph Series 1 (Edinburgh, 1982), pp. 97–102; J. R. Hunter, *Rescue Excavations on the Brough of Birsay 1974–82*, Society of Antiquaries of Scotland Monograph Series 4 (Edinburgh, 1986). For an illustration of the Birsay slab see Ritchie, *Picts*, p. 52.

[24] *St Ninian's Isle and its Treasure*, ed. A. Small, C. Thomas and D. M. Wilson, 2 vols (London, 1973).

[25] E. Okasha, 'The Non-Ogam Inscriptions of Pictland', *Cambridge Medieval Celtic Studies* 9 (1985), 43–69, pp. 57–9.

metalwork placed in a church for safe-keeping, or amassed by the church itself as dues.[26] The site has a considerable collection of stone monuments which functioned unambiguously in the context of a Christian community. It includes plain cross-marked slabs, and at least two monuments generally described as shrines. A similar collection survives at Papil on the island of West Burra to the north of St Ninian's Isle. The significance of cross-marked stones in the Pictish area has been largely ignored, in spite of the fact that they might well have relevance for the work of the Columban mission, but the shrines have been fully studied by Charles Thomas.[27]

The shrines are of corner-post or corner-slab construction. The end and side panels are tenoned to fit grooves cut in the corner stones. Sometimes the shrine was double, a dividing panel being supported by two centrally placed grooved stones. A double shrine, with its small chambers, might reflect arrangements for the enshrinement of two saintly personages after a period of interment. A parallel in general function could be the 'founder's tomb' associated with remote Irish monastic sites, but the corner-post shrine seems to be unique to Pictland and Iona.[28] The sheer number of the monuments in Shetland is surprising; two double shrines on St Ninian's Isle and three on Papil. The St Ninian's Isle treasure certainly has an appropriate monumental context even though it has no architectural context and no documentation.

Thomas points out that the method of construction of the shrines is most closely paralleled in contemporary continental chancel screens and the like. Post and panel constructions were used for dividing up spaces in buildings and gardens from classical times. An example of the construction can be seen in Roman north Britain at Chesterholm (Vindolanda).[29] Another analogue for form is found in prehistoric burials in the Pictish area itself, where stone panels are supported by corner piers of layered stones to create a single or sometimes double burial chamber. This analogy, though remote in time,

[26]   D. McRoberts, 'The Ecclesiastical Significance of the St Ninian's Isle Treasure', *The Proceedings of the Society of Antiquaries of Scotland* 94 (1960), 301–13; D. M. Wilson, 'The Treasure', in *St Ninian's Isle and Its Treasure*, I, 45–148, p. 104.

[27]   C. Thomas, 'Sculptured Stones and Crosses from St Ninian's Isle and Papil', in *St Ninian's Isle and its Treasure*, I, 8–44, pp. 14–28; *Early Christian Archaeology of North Britain*, pp. 150–63; 'The Double Shrine "A" from St Ninian's Isle, Shetland', in *From the Stone Age to the 'Forty-Five: Studies Presented to R.B.K. Stevenson*, ed. A. O'Connor and D. V. Clarke, 285–92.

[28]   Only shrine-posts have survived at Iona. See Royal Commission on the Ancient and Historical Monuments of Scotland, *Argyll, an Inventory of the Monuments*, 4: *Iona*, pp. 217–18. For Irish *comparanda* see M. Herity, 'The Forms of the Tomb-Shrine of the Founder Saint in Ireland', in *The Age of Migrating Ideas: Early Medieval Art in Northern Britain and Ireland*, ed. R. M. Spearman and J. Higgitt (Edinburgh, 1993), 188–95.

[29]   D. J. Breeze and B. Dobson, *Hadrian's Wall* (Harmondsworth, 1978), pl. 15.

raises the possibility that the form had a long association with local pre-Christian funerary monuments rather than being solely derived from hypothetical prototypes from a Northumbrian monastic context as Thomas proposes.[30] If this were the case then the monuments could have primarily served a secular, conservative, clientele rather than a monastic one. Such a view is, of course, entirely speculative, and the side panel of one of the Papil shrines carved with three riders approaching a free-standing cross certainly appears to belong to a cultural centre that attracted pilgrimage to venerable monuments.[31]

At a recent conference on Govan, near Glasgow, an early Christian British site, Wendy Davies, on the basis of parallels in Wales and Brittany, made the point that comparatively few clerics would have been needed to oversee the shrine and the large collection of associated burial slabs there.[32] Large collections of sculpture need not, it seems, necessarily imply the existence of major ecclesiastical centres having an associated complex of buildings on the sites. Close association with such a centre would, however, seem to be a prerequisite for proper control of access and ceremonial.

There is no doubt that coastal, island or headland, sites were important to the Picts and their predecessors. Of the sites belonging to the early medieval period that at Burghead is perhaps the most impressive. It is located on a promontory on the south side of the Moray Firth, to the east of Inverness.[33] Its coastal defences and triple ramparts on the landward side were of massive construction. Much of the stonework was dismantled in the nineteenth century for harbour repairs. It is best known for its large number, originally, it seems, thirty or so, stone plaques incised with characteristically Pictish-style bulls, each most probably a variant of a single pattern or template.[34] These bulls could have formed part of an animal frieze or have decorated a wall surface. The use of animal plaques in architectural settings has a long history and there seems no necessity to make the further speculation that the bulls had a cultic or tribal significance. A tenoned fragment of a shrine, a grooved

---

[30] P. J. Ashmore, 'Low Cairns, Long Cists and Symbol Stones', *The Proceedings of the Society of Antiquaries of Scotland* 110 (1978–80), 346–55, p. 353.

[31] For the Papil pilgrimage stone see P. Moar, 'Newly Discovered Sculptured Stones from Papil, Shetland', *The Proceedings of the Society of Antiquaries of Scotland* 78 (1944), 91–9.

[32] W. Davies, 'Ecclesiastical Centres and Secular Society in the Brittonic World in the Tenth and Eleventh Centuries', in *Govan and its Early Medieval Sculpture*, ed. A. Ritchie (Stroud, 1994), 92–101, pp. 99–101.

[33] Ritchie, *Picts*, pp. 12–15, with plan and illustrations.

[34] The bull designs were adjusted to fit the stones selected. In a lecture given to the International Society of Anglo-Saxonists in Durham in 1989 I attempted to demonstrate that the variations of pose were achieved by the tilting of a template.

corner post, and other sculptured fragments decorated with insular ornament were found among debris on the promontory, and in the 'old burial-ground' at Burghead sited within the ramparts of the fort. Excavations at the site have never included investigation of the burial ground.[35]

The subject-matter of the shrine fragment, two lions attacking a stag, establishes that it must have formed part of a monument appropriate to the scale of the fort and the force of the multiple bull symbolism.[36] The exotic theme suggests prestigious gift-exchange of portable exotic art objects, a textile or an ivory, and it has often been proposed that Burghead could have had the role of a trading station within northern waters. It must certainly have controlled the Firthlands. The presence of lion-hunt rather than the native deer-hunt iconography gives us a glimpse of the cultural horizons of the Picts in the area.

In addition to the bulls and the animal combat theme, the Burghead repertoire consisted of interlace, spirals, and key-pattern, some of which is of fine quality, and a fragment of a typically Pictish profile rider. The context of this long-lived sculptural activity could be that of a nearby monastery or alternatively be more directly related to the activities of the fort itself, where sculptors worked for the occupants. If the latter were the case, then the lion shrine would take its place in a private funerary chapel.

When documents fail Bailey suggested that the presence of inscriptions could justify attribution of sculpture to a monastic milieu. Only four indisputably Pictish monuments have Latin inscriptions. The best known are those at St Vigeans and Tarbat.[37] St Vigeans may commemorate an Irish saint, Féchín, who died in 644. The church with its large collection of sculpture (now housed locally in a small museum) lies just north of Arbroath, with its twelfth-century royal abbey. Tarbat is in the Firthlands at the extreme tip of the Easter Ross peninsula. Its old church is dedicated to a Saint Colman. These two inscriptions are, therefore, geographically widely separated. Both

[35] For excavation at Burghead see A. Small, 'Burghead', *Scottish Archaeological Forum* 1 (1969), 61–8. For further analysis see K. J. Edwards and I. Ralston, 'New Dating and Environmental Evidence from Burghead Fort, Moray', *The Proceedings of the Society of Antiquaries of Scotland* 109 (1977–78), 202–10. The fullest account of the burial ground or 'chapel-yard' is still J. Macdonald, 'Historical Notices of "The Broch" or Burghead, in Moray, with an Account of its Antiquities', *ibid.*, 4 (1860–62), 321–68.

[36] J. R. Allen, in *Early Christian Monuments of Scotland*, 3, p. 137, fig. 138. Charles Thomas was the first to draw attention to the fact that the fragment came from a shrine. Allen described the animals leaping on the stag as 'beasts'. They are clearly lions.

[37] Okasha, 'Non-Ogam Inscriptions of Pictland', pp. 59–62; J. Higgitt, 'The Pictish Latin Inscription at Tarbat in Ross-shire', *The Proceedings of the Society of Antiquaries of Scotland* 112 (1982), 300–21.

appear to be primary and are carved within panels prepared for them. The St Vigeans inscription is within the lowest panel on the side of a symbol-bearing cross-slab. It is incised, with fair competence, in insular script that can be compared with the letter forms on the front of the St Ninian's Isle inscribed scabbard-chape. The Tarbat inscription is carved with display capitals in relief (Pl. 1). The analogies for its letter forms are to be found, as John Higgitt has demonstrated, in the display scripts of insular manuscripts of the second half of the eighth century and its technical brilliance is fully present in the sculpture on the site itself and in the other three great Pictish monuments on the peninsula which lies at the centre of the Firthlands, at Nigg, Hilton of Cadboll and Shandwick.[38]

The text of the St Vigeans inscription consists of three Pictish names and has no Christian invocation. The Tarbat inscription is specifically Christian, beginning *IN NOMINE IESU CHRISTI, CRUX CHRISTI*. As we shall see, there are other reasons for making a case for the monastic status of St Vigeans. For Tarbat, the inference must be that the sculptor of this accomplished work, described by Higgitt as 'one of the finest pieces of carved lettering to survive from dark age Britain', had direct access to a monastic scriptorium. This assumption is now given substance by the discovery by the archaeologist Jill Harden of what appears to be a *vallum* in the vicinity of Tarbat Old Church, Portmahomack. This is potentially Pictland's first *vallum monasterii*, and no doubt the excavations currently being conducted there by Martin Carver will shed light on the context of the remarkable artistic output of the site, and of Easter Ross in general.

A fairly recent find in Wester Ross, on the west coast, at the site of St Maelrubai's foundation at Applecross mentioned above,[39] demonstrates a specific decorative link (distinctive spiral work) between St Vigeans in the east and this documented western monastery. This shared trait is found on the cross-slab with the inscription. Some of the Pictish entries in the Irish chronicles may have come from an Applecross record. The name given there for Applecross, Aporcrosan, is P-Celtic, as are other names in the district, so the community at Applecross retained the Pictish place-name, recorded Pictish events and maintained cultural links with eastern Pictland.[40]

---

[38] The slab from Hilton of Cadboll and the slab at Nigg are illustrated in colour on pp. 9 and 35 of Ritchie, *Picts*. For Shandwick see Allen, *Early Christian Monuments of Scotland*, 3, pp. 68–73.

[39] The Applecross slab is illustrated in J. Close-Brooks, *The Highlands*, Exploring Scotland's Heritage Series (Edinburgh, 1986), p. 123.

[40] For the Applecross record see I. Henderson, 'North Pictland' in *The Dark Ages in the Highlands*, ed. E. Meldrum (Inverness, 1971), 37–52. For the place-name evidence see I. A. Fraser, 'Pictish Place-Names: Some Toponymic Evidence', in *The Picts: a New Look at Some Old Problems*, ed. A. Small (Dundee, 1987), 68–72,

Bailey's second indicator of sculpture having a monastic milieu was the portrayal of subject-matter of monastic interest. Some of the subject-matter on Pictish sculpture depicts monastic life in a very direct way, for at a number of sites there are carvings displaying tonsured clerics, or cowled figures carrying flabella, croziers or books, and sometimes having book-satchels suspended round their necks.[41]

The most remarkable of these 'clerical' slabs is at St Vigeans on the inscribed slab with the Applecross connection. It shows not only processing tonsured clerics with book-satchels but (to the right, facing, of the cross-shaft) an illustration of the story of the visit of St Anthony, the first Christian monk, to St Paul, the first hermit, as recounted in Jerome's *Life of Paul* (Pl. 2).[42] This is the kind of carving with monastic interest that Bailey has in mind. The Paul and Anthony theme is common on Irish high crosses and is best known on the Ruthwell cross where it has always been central to interpretations of the Ruthwell iconographic programme as having a bearing on the monastic life.

At St Vigeans the saints are seated, and in spite of damage one can just see the tip of the beak of the raven miraculously delivering a whole loaf, instead of its usual delivery of half a loaf, so that Paul can provide for the nourishment of his visitor.

At Ruthwell and St Vigeans the saints hold the loaf, which is scored through the middle, between them. The dividing line makes the point that the saints are in the act of pulling the loaf apart, so that in eating their share neither was put in the position of being served by the other. The division is depicted in the same way in another of the Pictish versions of the theme, at Kirriemuir, in Angus, where the saints, as at Ruthwell, stand holding the loaf between them.[43]

The fullest and most symbolically charged expression of the Paul and Anthony theme in insular sculpture is found on the Pictish slab at Nigg, Easter Ross (Pl. 3). The scene serves as a headline to the splendidly decorated 'empty' cross of resurrection below. The sculpture is fitted into an architectural pediment, which, daringly, does not wholly confine it. Neatly carved pleached trees representing St Paul's shelter of date-palms as described in Jerome's *Life* rise from little ridged mounds of earth to arch over the saints

---

pp. 70–1.

[41] These 'clerical' slabs deserve further study as a group. For a brief survey see I. Henderson, 'Sculpture North of the Forth after the Take-Over by the Scots', in *Anglo-Saxon and Viking Age Sculpture*, ed. J. Lang, British Archaeological Reports, British Series 49 (Oxford, 1978), 47–74, pp. 56–7.

[42] St Jerome, *Vita Sancti Pauli*, in J.-P. Migne, *Patrologiae Cursus Completus: Series Latina*, 221 vols (Paris, 1844–64), XXIII, cols 17–28.

[43] Allen, *Early Christian Monuments of Scotland*, 3, fig. 239b.

and spread their branches over the top edge of the slab. The whole loaf is in the beak of the descending raven, but the saints do not hold it and it is not scored for division. The bread is, however, in some sense already divided, for a segment is missing from the lower left (facing) quarter. Éamonn Ó Carragáin has made the perspicacious suggestion that while the more usual arrangement of the saints pulling the bread apart recalls the Irish rite of *co-fractio*, whereby when two priests were present, they together broke the communion bread, the missing segment of the Nigg loaf illustrates the further rite of *commixtio* as described in the Irish commentary on the mass in the Stowe Missal. Here this particular section of the bread was mingled with the consecrated wine in the chalice and a prayer said over it.[44] Recent personal examination leaves no doubt that it is the sculptor and not damage that is responsible for the missing section, which is shown as well-defined in photographs taken from a cast made around 1895.[45] The Nigg sculpture is therefore a very accurate depiction of the Eucharist, and the praying figures with their sacramentaries, like the standing figures at Ruthwell, are both Paul and Anthony and administering priests, just as the animals on either side of the chalice are both the lions who helped Anthony to bury Paul, and the two animals between whom Christ would be recognised, according to Jerome's exegesis of Habakkuk iii.2.[46]

One need have no hesitation then in claiming the Nigg slab as a product of monastic culture capable of producing religious imagery of a quality that can stand alongside contemporary Irish and English work.[47] Its intricate spiral and serpent-boss decoration has links with the decoration of the crosses on Iona, but it has its own delicacy and inventiveness and may well pre-date and so be an influence upon the Iona sculptures.[48]

The reverse of the slab was carved with a figure of David rending the jaws of the lion, set in a frame of panelled ornament that recalls the framed miniatures of David in the Durham manuscript of Cassiodorus's

---

[44] É. Ó Carragáin, 'The Meeting of Saint Paul and Saint Anthony: Visual and Literary Uses of a Eucharistic Motif', in *Keimelia: Studies in Medieval Archaeology and History in Memory of Tom Delaney*, ed. P. Wallace and G. Mac Niocaill (Galway, 1988), 1–58, pp. 7–14.

[45] Allen, *Early Christian Monuments of Scotland*, 3, fig. 72.

[46] Carragáin, 'The Meeting of Saint Paul and Saint Anthony', p. 11.

[47] On the iconography of SS Paul and Anthony in Irish sculpture, see P. Harbison, *The High Crosses of Ireland: an Iconographical and Photographic Study*, 3 vols (Bonn, 1992), I, pp. 302–9.

[48] For a fair and wide-ranging assessment of the relationship between Pictish sculpture and the Iona crosses see D. Mac Lean, 'Snake-bosses and Redemption at Iona and in Pictland', in *The Age of Migrating Ideas*, 245–53.

Commentary on the Psalms.[49] Most of its relief surfaces have been hammered off by iconoclasts, but a single symbol carved in relief, an eagle, has survived and there are traces of what may be a second symbol. The juxtaposition of the salvation theme of David protecting his flock from the lion, with Paul and Anthony celebrating mass, forms an explicit programme of salvation in the Old Testament, and salvation in the New, through the Eucharist.[50]

The most frequently occurring Old Testament iconography in Pictish sculpture concerns David. David was important both as the ancestor of Christ and as a type of Christian kingship. It was Donald Bullough who first made the connection between the frequency of David imagery and the secular character of much of the figurative art of the Picts.[51] And it is to this secular character that I now turn.

The best known Pictish cross-slab is the one standing in the churchyard at Aberlemno in Angus.[52] On the front, the cross is decorated with the full insular ornamental repertoire of interlace, spirals and key-pattern. The zoomorphic ornament in the background is of a type familiar in such central objects as the Lindisfarne Gospels and the Tara brooch.

When one moves to the back, apart from the marginal animals that frame the slab, the artistic context becomes strikingly particular to the Picts. There, two large symbols are carved above a battle-scene set out in three registers. The fate of the leader of the helmet-wearing side is clearly indicated at the bottom right (facing) by the pecking of his prostrate body by a carrion crow. If we set aside the possibility that the scene illustrates an Old Testament battle then it must be accepted as a remarkable piece of secular art, and one perhaps unlikely to have been 'of monastic interest'. The patron must surely have been the victor, bottom left (facing). If not the victor, then a king, who, like the Carolingian king who commissioned the fresco programme at Ingelheim, wanted to commemorate 'the deeds of his fathers' both as an act of piety and to strengthen his own position.[53]

49 Durham, Cathedral Library MS B.II.30; J. J. G. Alexander, *Insular Manuscripts, 6th to the 9th Century*, A Survey of Manuscripts Illuminated in the British Isles 1 (London, 1978), no. 17, ill. 74 & 75.

50 The preference for this programme, with varying Old Testament salvation imagery, may account for the lack of New Testament iconography on Pictish sculpture. Its limited range of biblical iconography should not be compared adversely with the rich store of imagery found on Irish sculpture, much of which is of a later date. The imagery on the surviving sculpture on Iona is similarly limited in range.

51 D. Bullough, "'Imagines Regum' and Their Significance in the Early Medieval West', in *Studies in Memory of David Talbot Rice*, ed. G. Robertson and G. Henderson (Edinburgh, 1975), 223–76.

52 Ritchie, *Picts*, the front of the Aberlemno cross-slab on p. 23, the reverse on p. 24.

53 Ermoldus Nigellus, 'The Paintings at Ingelheim', l. 267 in *Poetry of the*

A mile or so from the churchyard on the road that passes through the township of Aberlemno, there stands a larger, even more ambitious public monument.[54] Although still a slab it depicts a handsome ringed cross decorated in a manner strongly reminiscent of metalwork. On either side of the narrow cross-shaft two grieving angels bring to the mind of the viewer the full significance of Christ's crucifixion and resurrection. On the reverse, the arrangement on the churchyard slab is paralleled, in that large symbols are placed above the figural scene. The symbols, however, are a different pair, and the scene not of a battle, but of a hunt.

Hunting-scenes are very frequently depicted on Pictish cross-slabs and it is these and the associated symbols which have given Pictish sculpture its reputation for a pre-occupation with secular themes, thought by some somehow to accord with a lack of literate monastic culture.

There is a view, perhaps due for revival, that the hunting-scenes are, in fact, primarily Christian symbol-pictures. In Christian art the hunt has regularly been interpreted as a symbol of Christ pursuing the soul of the sinner. Certainly that the hunting-scenes should have conveyed an active message for the viewers seems entirely appropriate. It is difficult to regard them merely as the equivalent of sporting prints reproduced for the entertainment of simple hunt-loving folk by artists who could draw horses. Moreover one can detect, lying behind all the variants of the hunting-scene, a basic composition consisting of three hunters, a stag and two pursuing dogs. This model, a compressed symbol-picture of the hunt, though effectively naturalistic in its diagonal progression, is unlikely to be the product of a purely native hunters' art.

That the hunting-scenes are generally depicted in close proximity to the indisputably secular symbols has also to be taken into account. Is the hunting-scene telling us something relevant to the meaning of the adjacent symbols, rather than being relevant to the cross of resurrection on the front of the slab? Elsewhere, I have proposed that there is evidence on the slabs that the basic hunting-scene model was consciously modified so as to allow the expression of a kind of hierarchy, running from a single foot-hunter to a full-scale ceremonial hunt which included falconry.[55]

Janet Nelson has drawn attention to the importance of the hunt to the Carolingians, as what she terms one of 'the rituals of the court'. Hunting, and the feasting that went with it, was clearly one of the ways that a leader

---

Carolingian Renaissance, ed. P. Godman (London, 1985), pp. 254–5.

[54] Ritchie, *Picts*, p. 27.

[55] I. Henderson, 'The Picts: Written Records and Pictorial Images', in *Proceedings from the Conferences of the Pictish Art Society 1992*, ed. J. R. F. Burt, E. O. Bowman and N. M. R. Robertson (Edinburgh, 1994), 44–66, pp. 51–3.

strengthened his relationship with his retinue on whose loyalty he depended.[56]

Certainly the hunt depicted on the Aberlemno roadside cross-slab is no ordinary hunt. It is a ceremonial hunt accompanied by fanfaring trumpeters. The patron of the churchyard slab did not ask for Christian imagery other than the cross. The roadside patron added the grieving angels. There is a David scene on the reverse of the roadside slab but its lowly position, at the bottom right (facing) corner, and its miniature scale give it the status of a footnote.

The grade of a 'hunt-with-trumpeters' is carved on the slab from Hilton of Cadboll in Easter Ross, but here the model has been modified to give prominence to a female figure riding side-saddle (Pl. 4). A male figure rides alongside her, his head awkwardly inset in a panel and his mount conveyed by a simple outlining of that of his female companion. The Picts had a matrilinear system of succession so perhaps the female figure is the sister of the male rider, the female through whom the succession passed rather than his consort. So, perhaps some of the Pictish cross-slabs were not primarily the products of a monastery, but were set up by leaders as a secular ritual or symbolic act, a way of confirming publicly their title to power in the region (the symbols could have relevance here), their relationship with their retinues, and, through the explicit Christian content, their clerics. Of course, there is no reason to suppose that what happened at the court of Charlemagne happened at the courts of eighth-century Pictish kings, but, to use Patrick Wormald's phrase referring to another matter, 'to consider Charlemagne's empire, is at least to enlarge one's sense of eighth-century possibilities'.[57]

The most impressive Pictish hunt of all is that carved on a side-panel of a corner-slab shrine, known as the Sarcophagus, at St Andrews in Fife (Pl. 5). This monument has often been hailed as one of the finest pieces of sculpture in dark-age Europe but somehow it never manages to be included in such international compendia as Helmut Roth's *Kunst der Völkerwanderungszeit*.[58]

---

[56] J. L. Nelson, 'The Lord's Anointed and the People's Choice: Carolingian Royal Ritual', in *Rituals of Royalty: Power and Ceremonial in Traditional Societies*, ed. D. Cannadine and S. Price (Cambridge, 1987), 137–80. For a glimpse of royal hunting at the Northumbrian court see Bede's description of the 'tall and handsome' Oswine in Book III. 14 of the *Ecclesiastical History* (p. 259): 'The Bishop sat down in his own place and the king, who had just come in from hunting, stood warming himself by the fire with his thegns'.

[57] P. Wormald, in J. Campbell, E. John and P. Wormald, *The Anglo-Saxons* (Oxford, 1982), p. 114.

[58] H. Roth, *Kunst der Völkerwanderungszeit*, Propyläen Kunstgeschichte, Suppl. bd. 4 (Frankfurt am Main, 1979). For a recent assessment see I. Henderson, 'The Insular and Continental Context of the St Andrews Sarcophagus', in *Scotland in Dark Age Europe*, ed. B. E. Crawford (St Andrews, 1994), 71–102.

David is portrayed as a senatorial figure rather than as a shepherd boy, although he wears a distinctive hunting knife with a decorated scabbard and is accompanied by his dog. The adjacent hunting-scene, taken with minor modifications so obviously from a de-luxe treasury piece comparable to a sixth-century silver Sassanian dish, manifestly represents the very top end of the hierarchy of hunts; just as David is a type of Christian kingship, so the lion-hunt betokens imperial status.[59]

Such subject-matter is not appropriate for a saint's shrine, but it might indeed suit a monument for a royal founder. Another possibility is that it was commissioned as a monument for a lay member of an elite, to be placed in a royal funerary chapel within a monastery. The many royal connections of early and later medieval St Andrews begin with the days of Abbot Tuathalán, for his identifying place-name translates 'headland of the king's ridge'. In a recent survey made in connection with the excavations at San Vincenzo al Volturno, John Mitchell, as part of his re-assessment of the role of its crypt, reviews arrangements made in Europe of the eighth and ninth centuries for aristocratic lay burials. He points out that in the eighth century popes began to erect funerary chapels for themselves, and that their example must have been an important factor in the limited revival of the custom in other parts of Europe in the ninth century.[60] The St Andrews Sarcophagus could possibly have housed just such a lay burial, to be placed within a richly appointed private chapel or within the church of the monastery. In an Anglo-Saxon context, Bede records the burial, in the church of St Peter in the royal foundation of Whitby, of the founder, Oswy, and of King Edwin and *multi alii nobiles*. The early ninth-century church at Winchcombe in Gloucestershire is another example of a royal burial place, in this case for Mercian kings.[61]

The largest collection of Pictish sculpture is at Meigle in Perthshire.[62] Thirty-five monuments, most of which are reasonably complete, have survived, and many more were used locally as building material, or destroyed in the nineteenth century in a fire at the church. The sculpture includes cross-slabs of varying scale but mostly having the distinctive 'house-style' of a rounded top. There are also four full-length recumbent grave-markers. In all,

---

[59] For the silver dish analogy see C. L. Mowbray (Mrs Curle), 'Eastern Influence on Carvings at St Andrews and Nigg, Scotland', *Antiquity* 10 (1936), 428–40.

[60] J. Mitchell, 'The Crypt Reappraised', in *San Vincenzo al Volturno: the 1980–86 Excavations*, ed. R. Hodges (London, 1993–5), 2 vols, I, 75–114, pp. 111–14.

[61] J. Lang, *The Anglian Sculpture of Deira: the Classical Tradition*, Jarrow Lecture 1990 ([Jarrow], n.d.), p. 2; S. R. Bassett, 'A Probable Mercian Royal Mausoleum at Winchcombe, Gloucestershire', *The Antiquaries Journal* 65 (1985), 82–100.

[62] Royal Commission on the Ancient and Historical Monuments of Scotland, *South-East Perth: an Archaeological Landscape* (Edinburgh, 1994), pp. 99–102.

this is 'a remarkable assemblage unparalleled in Britain and Ireland', to use Thomas's description of the corpus of Shetland shrines. With the notable exception of the fine Daniel image on the largest of the cross-slabs there is no Christian iconography in the collection other than the cross. In spite of the expressive image of Daniel pacifying the lions, the Meigle repertoire is markedly obsessed with violence, violence between beasts and between men and beasts.[63]

The four recumbents give a strong impression of belonging together in a mausoleum or crypt similar to Mercian Repton or indeed Merovingian Jouarre, comparisons which neatly express the options of a mausoleum for seculars or religious.[64]

Above the Daniel image on the large cross-slab there is a cavalry procession where the basic hunt composition has been modified by omitting the quarry, and increasing the number of horsemen by showing three riding abreast on the lower register. A winged Victory is carved at the head of the leader's horse, a more succinct, sophisticated way of marking his military achievements than at Aberlemno churchyard, with its narrative battle-scene.[65]

The Meigle animal repertoire shows knowledge of a model containing illustrations of fabulous monsters. These are not invented forms and must come from an illustrated text on animal lore.[66] Such a work could have been housed in a monastic library, but it is just the sort of book a king might have owned. These fantastic creatures are found predominantly on cross-slabs in Perthshire, and this regional predilection leads to a final speculation.

A feature of monastic culture in this period is that it is frequently far-flung: texts known on Iona are used in Lindisfarne; books are borrowed; information is exchanged between north and south; forms and techniques are

---

[63] Henderson, 'Pictish Art and the Book of Kells', pp. 92–4.

[64] M. Biddle and B. Kjølby-Biddle, 'The Repton Stone', *Anglo-Saxon England* 14 (1986), 233–92. The paper starts with a useful review of the literature on the crypt. See also A. Grabar, 'Recherches sur les sculptures de l'Hypogée des Dunes, à Poitiers, et de la crypte Saint-Paul de Jouarre', *Journal des Savants*, janvier–mars 1974, 3–43.

[65] Ritchie, *Picts*, p. 57. Robert Stevenson's often quoted view that the winged figure is the Persian god Ahura Mazda is supported by the presence of images on other slabs in the collection (such as one of a possible camel) suggesting knowledge of oriental models. The use of a classical equestrian image of the victorious emperor with an adjacent small Victory, found on coins and other portable objects, seems altogether more probable.

[66] A full study of this material has yet to appear. For relevant discussions and references see C. Hicks, *Animals in Early Medieval Art* (Edinburgh, 1993). See also I. Henderson, 'Pictish Monsters: Symbol, Text and Image', H. M. Chadwick Memorial Lectures 7 (Cambridge, 1997), where the complexities of the Pictish fabulous monsters are explored.

replicated in Jarrow in the east and Ruthwell in the west. We do seem to have visual evidence for something of the sort in the sculptural connections between Iona, Nigg and St Andrews, and less dramatically in the links between St Vigeans in the east and Applecross in the west.[67] Some of these places are known to be monastic centres and the others may therefore have similar status. Networking of this quality seems more understandable in a monastic context than in any other.

The cases of Aberlemno and Meigle are somewhat different. Meigle in many ways stands apart from the other clusters of sculpture both stylistically and in its subject-matter, although its influence regionally can be discerned. Its firmest links are with Aberlemno. The two sites share the same lack of interest in biblical themes, and one of the Meigle cross-slabs shares motifs with those on the front of the Aberlemno churchyard slab. Both collections have battle imagery. The roadside slab has a learned centaur motif, also found at Meigle, and motifs of violence on either side of the bottom of its cross-shaft, of a type characteristic of the Meigle repertoire.[68]

Of all the notable clusters of sculpture Aberlemno alone has examples of the earlier symbol stones, which certainly relate to secular needs. Meigle is inland, but at a natural cross-roads which still has importance for communications within Scotland. Its importance as a central place, its 'royal villa' and its massive recumbents make it a prime candidate for a Pictish secular centre. As at Burghead, the great secular centre in the north, there is also some evidence for architectural sculpture in the form of an animal frieze (Pl. 6).[69]

The Easter Ross peninsula is particularly perplexing. Is the entire peninsula, as Jill Harden has tentatively suggested in a lecture, a single monastic estate with a centre and associated hermitages or cells?[70] Certainly the formidable monastic culture of the Firthlands balances the massive military strength of Burghead, a Lindisfarne to a Bamburgh. Does the spacing of the great monuments on the peninsula reflect a mixture of the secular (Hilton of Cadboll, and Shandwick, not discussed here) and the monastic (Nigg and Tarbat)? All the symbol-bearing cross-slabs need not have functioned in exactly the same way. Is it significant that sites with corner-post shrine monuments seem not to have had symbol-bearing cross-slabs?

---

[67] The sculpture at Rosemarkie in Ross-shire, not discussed here, may belong to the Applecross/St Vigeans network. See I. Henderson, *The Art and Function of Rosemarkie's Pictish Monuments*, Groam House Lecture 1 (Rosemarkie, 1990, repr. 1991), p. 20.

[68] Ritchie, *Picts*, p. 26.

[69] Allen, *Early Christian Monuments of Scotland*, 3, p. 337 and fig. 350.

[70] In a lecture given in the History of Art Department, University of Cambridge, 1994.

The cross-bearing sculpture is our only substantial source for the spread and nature of Christianity in Pictland. Thanks to new perceptions of the mixed nature of the organisation of the contemporary Irish and English church we may perhaps need no longer look for a major ecclesiastical centre behind every piece of accomplished Pictish sculpture.[71]

Archaeologists quite rightly want to see the sculpture working for society and not just standing in the landscape as passive works of art, and I have suggested one such active use for the sculpture carved with hunting- and battle-scenes.

But of course, Christian art is not passive, however much it may seem so for many twentieth-century viewers. We cannot assume, with Kathleen Hughes, that the church in Pictland was not, as elsewhere, from the start a significant factor in society at a political level, as well as in the spiritual lives of its servants, and in the lives of the secular faithful, few though they may have been in the earlier decades of the seventh century.

That the kings of the Picts were powerful effective leaders is known from the documented written records; but the power and effectiveness of the Pictish church is not documented, or as yet detectable in site archaeology. Both aspects of Pictish society are present in Pictish sculpture, and this is exactly what one would expect, but the role of the church, just because of the lack of sources, continues to need emphasis.[72]

---

[71] In an unpublished lecture on 'Pictish Art and the Church' given to the Society of Antiquaries of Scotland in 1990 John Higgitt made the point that some Pictish monasteries might have been more independent of secular control than others and that this could be traced in the sculpture. The strikingly consistent elements of the symbol-bearing cross-slabs make it tempting to see them all functioning in the same way. This strait-jacket seriously limits their usefulness in the effort to break down stereotyped views of the Picts. Several writers, including Higgitt, have detected hints of 'Romanism' in the iconography displayed on the cross-slabs. I have suggested that the most telling visual legacy of the Columban church was the lasting preference for a Latin cross with rounded arm-pits; see I. Henderson, 'The Shape and Decoration of the Cross on Pictish Cross-Slabs Carved in Relief', in *The Age of Migrating Ideas*, 209–18.

[72] Sculpture in this period will clearly have functioned as both political and ecclesiastical indicators. In this matter the recent discovery of an inscription bearing the name of a contemporary Scottish king on the Irish-style free-standing Dupplin cross, sited near the Picto-Scottish 'palace' of Forteviot in Perthshire, provides a rare possibility of proof rather than speculation. For this material, with a postscript on the Dupplin inscription, see Alcocks, 'Reconnaissance Excavations on Early Historic Fortifications', pp. 218–42, 282–3. It is not certain, however, that the cross stands in its original position.

ADDENDUM

After the completion of this paper the following studies have been published: T. O. Clancy, 'The Drosten Stone: a New Reading', *The Proceedings of the Society of Antiquaries of Scotland* 123 (1993), 345–53; this argues that the inscription contains a time expression involving the name of a Pictish king who reigned from A.D. 839 to 842. J. Harden, 'A Potential Archaeological Context for the Early Christian Sculptured Stones from Tarbat, Easter Ross', in *From the Isles of the North: Early Medieval Art in Ireland and Britain*, ed. C. Bourke (Belfast, 1995), 221–7; this shows that the ditch at Tarbat was found to contain organic material with a date span of A.D. 140 to 590. The ditch and its associated bank, therefore, will originally have surrounded a secular centre. Whether the bank later functioned as a monastic vallum is at present conjectural. For recent advances in perceptions of the Pictish symbols, the use of Old Testament imagery on Pictish sculpture, the Pictish church, and much else, see *The Worm, the Germ and the Thorn: Pictish and Related Studies Presented to Isabel Henderson*, ed. D. Henry (Belgavies, Forfar, 1997). For Bailey's response to current thinking about the nature of the pre-Viking Anglo-Saxon church vis-à-vis his view that sculpture of this period was primarily a monastic art, see his *England's Earliest Sculptors* (Toronto, Ontario, 1996), p. 76.

Defensores Astabimus: *Garendon Abbey and its Early Benefactors*[1]

DAVID POSTLES

Earlier notions that Cistercian houses were founded in remote, even 'waste', areas to promote the contemplative monastic life away from secular influence, are being revised. Indeed, perceptions of the Cistercian monasteries have altered so radically over the last decade or so, that it may be worth starting again to look in greater depth at the fortunes of individual houses.[2] To some extent, that process has already begun, for we already have fairly recent studies of Kirkstall and Fountains, as well as a slightly older introduction to Rufford, with continuing interest in Forde and Byland.[3] Superficially,

---

[1] I am grateful to Drs Janet Burton and Benjamin Thompson for reading drafts of this paper and making very helpful comments which have added immeasurably to the paper, but responsibility for any shortcomings remains my own.

[2] The most challenging recent work, as far as concerns Cistercian houses (excluding nunneries), is C. H. Berman, *Medieval Agriculture, the Southern French Countryside and the Early Cistercians: a Study of Forty-Three Monasteries*, Transactions of the American Philosophical Society, 76 (1986) and Isabel Alfonso, 'Cistercians and Feudalism', *Past & Present* 133 (1991), 3–30, and for this country, J. Burton, 'The Foundation of British Cistercian Houses', in *Cistercian Art and Architecture in the British Isles*, ed. C. Norton and D. Parks (Cambridge, 1988), 24–39. For slightly older studies, B. D. Hill, *English Cistercian Houses and their Patrons in the Twelfth Century* (Urbana, Illinois, 1968); C. Platt, *The Monastic Grange in Medieval England: a Reassessment* (London, 1969); and R. A. Donkin, *The Cistercians: Studies in the Geography of Medieval England and Wales* (Toronto, 1984). For 'Cistercian' nunneries, Sally Thompson, *Women Religious: the Foundation of English Nunneries after the Norman Conquest* (Oxford, 1991), pp. 94–112; *eadem*, 'The Problem of Cistercian Nuns in the Twelfth and Early Thirteenth Century', *Medieval Women*, Studies in Church History, Subsidia 1, ed. D. Baker (Oxford, 1978), 227–52.

[3] G. D. Barnes, *Kirkstall Abbey 1147–1539: an Historical Study*, Thoresby Society, 58 (Leeds, 1984); *Rufford Charters*, ed. C. J. Holdsworth, 4 vols, Thoroton Society Record Series, 29, 30, 32, 34 (Nottingham, 1972–81), I, pp. xx–lxiii; and J. Wardrop, *Fountains Abbey and its Benefactors 1132–1200* (Kalamazoo, Michigan, 1987). Marsha Dutton informed me of the interest in Forde and I learned of Janet Burton's work on Byland at this conference. Dr Burton also informed me of her forthcoming chapter on the economy of Rievaulx which will appear in a volume

Garendon presents many paradoxes, which, on closer inspection, turn out to be more representative of the early development of houses of the order than might be first expected.[4] The first paradox concerns the circumstances of its foundation. Although it pertained to the great belt of Cistercian houses which extended across the midlands, it was founded by the earl of Leicester, who manifestly had little clear interest in the Cistercians, and it was relatively shunned by the earl of Chester who seemed to have a greater empathy with the order. Secondly, despite being one of the earliest monasteries of the order, colonised from the initial house, Waverley, its endowments remained rather slender. Nevertheless, on further inspection, its economic position was not unlike that of many other houses of white monks. Garendon is then a reasonable place to start when re-examining the profile of the Cistercians in England.

The ensuing discussion takes something of the following form: some general comments about how Garendon fits into the overall profile of Cistercian houses in England; the circumstances of the foundation of Garendon, with particular emphasis on the very earliest endowments and acquisitions; and finally patronage of the house in the later twelfth century, which transformed the nature of its estates. It would be tedious, in the light of recent research, to belabour the difference between Cistercian theory (the rule of the order) and reality, but that divergence runs implicitly throughout the early development of Garendon.

Established in 1133 and colonised from Waverley, the first house of the order, established in 1128, Garendon was the fifth foundation of white monks. (For present purposes, the Savignacs are omitted from discussion, although they acceded to the Cistercian order in 1147.) The major foundations of Cistercian houses coincided with Stephen's reign, but with a few antecedent foundations in the late years of Henry I. Indeed, in 1152 the general chapter prohibited the foundation of further Cistercian houses,

---

on that house to be edited by P. Fergusson and G. Coppack.

[4] In this research, I have used the original MS of the Garendon cartularies (BL, Lansdowne MS 415), = G. R. C. Davis, *Medieval Cartularies of Great Britain* (London, 1958), p. 49 (no. 431). Davis describes the volume as several different cartularies and this is confirmed in D. Postles, 'The Garendon Cartularies in BL Lansdowne MS 415', *British Library Journal*, 22.2 (1996), 161–71. Davis also noted that substantial parts have been printed by J. Nichols, *The History and Antiquities of the County of Leicester*, 4 vols (London, 1795–1815), III (ii), pp. 804–31; in fact, Nichols prints elsewhere, in topographical sections, those other charters in the cartularies not at pp. 804–31 (for example volume II, pp. 133–7). His edition, however, is an uncritical transcription. Throughout I have used my own transcript from the original Lansdowne MS, but I give references to transcriptions in Nichols, as well as to any other place where the charters have been printed.

although a few, particularly royal, foundations or re-foundations occurred in England through into the early thirteenth century. By 1154 perhaps three-quarters of the full extent of Cistercian houses in England had already been founded.[5] In those years, two principal belts of houses were founded: the better-known houses in the north, particularly Yorkshire, of which many were daughter houses from Fountains (founded 1132); and the concentration across the midland counties, particularly from Worcestershire, through Warwickshire and Leicestershire, Nottinghamshire and into Lincolnshire. The character of most of these houses was a rather slender endowment, a general impecunity which may be illustrated by their financial resources at their dissolution, to which Garendon conforms.[6]

Traditional perceptions of the expansion of the Cistercian order in England in the early twelfth century emphasise the influence of the anarchy, territorial lordship, and the establishment of houses on marginal sites and lands.[7] Examination of the foundation and early development of Garendon

---

[5] Different figures are given by Hill, *English Cistercian Monasteries*, p. 27, who suggests forty without the Savignacs and fifty-four including them, and C. J. Holdsworth, 'The Cistercians in Devon', *Studies in Medieval History Presented to R. Allen Brown*, ed. C. Harper-Bill, C. J. Holdsworth and J. L. Nelson (Woodbridge, 1989), 179–91, p. 189. For the full list: D. Knowles and R. N. Hadcock, *Medieval Religious Houses: England and Wales*, 2nd edn (London, 1971), pp. 112–28.

[6] I have tried a number of statistical tests to place Garendon within the general context of the financial resources of English Cistercian houses. For want of earlier data, the tests have been run on those from the *Valor Ecclesiasticus* of 1535, abstracted from Knowles and Hadcock. Taking the *valor* alone, the mean figure for Cistercian houses founded before 1154 was £240 4s. with a standard deviation of 175.8, but, to counter the influence of Fountains (which had a *valor* of £1,115), the trimmed mean is more realistic, being £217 6s. (this figure is reached, using Minitab, by topslicing off the top 5% of values). The median level was £204. Garendon's *valor* was £159. There was, however, a general decline in acquisitions by Cistercian houses from the early thirteenth century and, indeed, the general chapter of 1180 prohibited the acquisition of land by purchase – a brake, if not an absolute one, on further expansion. The decline in numbers of monks and (especially) lay brethren in the later middle ages is serious, but it may have been that the minimum prescribed figures for Cistercian houses – an abbot and twelve professed monks – was in effect a norm or optimum number. For the decline in numbers of *conversi*, J. T. Donnelly, 'Changes in the Grange Economy of English and Welsh Cistercian Abbeys, 1300–1540', *Traditio* 10 (1954), 399–458, pp. 420–3. 'The Cistercian order in England owed its establishment and its development to the support of the feudal nobility and the history of the White Monks in England is inseparable from that of the nobility': Hill, *English Cistercian Monasteries*, p. 15. See also general comments on the mixed motives behind the foundation of religious houses during Stephen's reign, including pretensions to disputed

allows both a more intense analysis of these questions and, for some of them, a more nuanced picture.

Allusion has already been made by Edmund King in a wider discussion to the political circumstances of the foundation of Garendon, but its exact context can be considered profitably in even greater detail.[8] That foundation, although antedating the accession of Stephen, was informed by the localised political circumstances which became familiar in his reign, the competition for territorial control, lordship and integrity, especially in Leicestershire, particularly in the north of the county, and more explicitly in its north-western area. Discounting, for the moment, north-eastern Leicestershire and the Mowbray fees, north-west Leicestershire marked the confluence of two baronies, Ferrers (earls of Derby) and Chester, but in the contest between them the latter was dominant.[9]

Territorial rivalry, although having seeds at an earlier time, was intensified from c.1120, because of a number of contingent and coincidental events. In 1120, Richard, earl of Chester, died in the White Ship, and was succeeded by his nephew, Ranulph le Meschin.[10] In that year too, Robert le Bossu attained his majority and acceded to the earldom of Leicester after the

---

territory, by M. Chibnall, 'The Empress Matilda and Church Reform', *TRHS*, 5th ser. 38 (1988), 107–30, p. 109.

[8] E. King, 'Mountsorrel and its Region in King Stephen's Reign', *Huntington Library Quarterly* 44 (1980–1), 1–10; as King rightly indicates, the foundation of Garendon was a precursor of the territorial challenges of 1135–54.

[9] For the honour of Tutbury (Ferrers) and the contest with Chester, P. Golob, 'The Ferrers Earls of Derby: a Study of the Honour of Tutbury (1066–1279)', unpublished Ph.D. thesis (Cambridge, 1984), esp. pp. 67–8, 70, 121–43. Although largely centred elsewhere, the honour extended into north-west Leicestershire; these lands (Staunton Harold, Whitwick, Diseworth and Kilwarby) seem to have been acquired after 1086 and surrounded the Chester lands in the extreme north-west of the county: Golob, p. 70. The position of the family collapsed in 1153: Golob, pp. 140–2. For the Chester estates in Staffordshire, a belt across north Leicestershire centred on the *capud* of Barrow on Soar (acquired in the late eleventh century and formerly held by Earl Harold), and in Lincolnshire, see C. P. Lewis, 'The Formation of the Honour of Chester, 1066–1100', *The Earldom of Chester and its Charters: a Tribute to Geoffrey Barraclough*, ed. A. T. Thacker, Journal of the Chester Archaeological Society, special issue, 71 (1991), 37–68, pp. 42, 44–5. For detailed description of the Leicestershire fees, W. Farrer, *Honors and Knights' Fees*, 3 vols (1923–25), II, pp. 55–85.

[10] J. C. Holt, 'Politics and Property in Early Medieval England', *Past and Present* 57 (1972), 3–52, repr. in *Landlords, Peasants and Politics in Medieval England*, ed. T. H. Aston (Cambridge, 1987), 65–114, p. 113. For a similar conflict between the earl of Leicester and the bishop of Lincoln in Leicester and Leicestershire, D. Crouch, 'Earls and Bishops in Twelfth-Century Leicestershire', *Nottingham Medieval Studies* 37 (1993), 9–20.

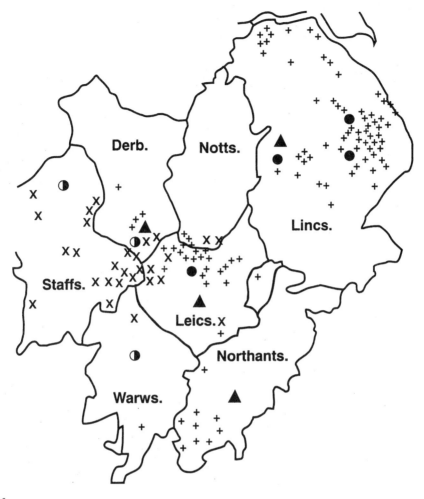

Key

- ● Principal demesne manors in 1086
- ◑ Principal manors acquired 1086 - 1100
- + Subinfeudated manors in 1086
- X Subinfeudated manors acquired 1086 - 1100
- ▲ Urban holdings

After C.P Lewis 'The formation of the honor of Chester, 1066 - 1100', p.44

Figure 3: The estates of the earldom of Chester in the Midlands.

death of Robert, count of Meulan, in June 1118. During Robert's minority, Henry I had established a council of wardship, which included Nigel d'Aubigny, a *curialis*, who had become a mesne tenant of Meulan in Warwickshire. That association paved the way for the *rapprochement* of the earl of Leicester with Henry I, which was sealed by Henry's arrangement of the marriage of Amice, heiress to the honour of Breteuil, to Robert; Amice had previously been promised to one of Henry's sons, Richard, who, like Henry's eldest son, William, was lost in the White Ship in 1120. During the 1120s, therefore, the earl of Leicester's influence at court was in the ascendant. That dominance was replicated in the localities, especially in Leicestershire, reinforced by the power of his honorial baronage, de Bosco and Asketil (the *antecessor* of the Harcourts).[11] The initial response of the earl of Chester may have been a flanking movement to the south through the arrangement of the Basset–Ridel marriage of 1123.[12]

The foundation of Garendon thus assumed a pivotal role in the latent struggle for territorial power. There seems little doubt that the house's foundation in 1133 in the heartland of the Chester estates in north-west Leicestershire was intended as a strategy to advance the earl of Leicester's influence in that area. Indeed, it seems quite probable that the house was founded by the earl of Leicester with the lands of a disseised tenant of the honour of Chester.[13] Thereafter, the earl of Chester appears to have concentrated his efforts on maintaining his territorial integrity and lordship in Lincolnshire in collusion with his brother, William de Roumare, earl of Lincoln.[14]

---

[11] D. Crouch, *The Beaumont Twins: the Roots and Branches of Power in the Twelfth Century* (Cambridge, 1986), pp. 3–4, 13–14, 28; *idem*, 'The Foundation of Leicester Abbey and Other Problems', *Midland History* 12 (1987), 1–13, pp. 4–5.

[12] For another interpretation of the marriage, R. C. DeAragon, 'In Pursuit of Aristocratic Women: a Key to Success in Norman England', *Albion* 14 (1982), 258–67, p. 263. For the details, *Regesta Regum Anglo-Normannorum 1066–1154*, II, ed. C. Johnson and H. A. Cronne (Oxford, 1956), p. 184 (no. 1389). For the later marriages probably arranged by the earl of Chester (in the 1140s) to secure his territorial advantage, T. Wales, 'The Knight in Twelfth-Century Lincolnshire', unpublished Ph.D. thesis (Cambridge, 1983), p. 6.

[13] Crouch, 'Foundation of Leicester Abbey', p. 5; King, 'Mountsorrel and its Region', pp. 5–6; for losses of lands from the earldom of Chester in this area, Farrer, *Honors and Knights' Fees*, II, p. 69 and King, 'Mountsorrel and its Region', pp. 3–6.

[14] P. Dalton, '*In neutro latere*: the Armed Neutrality of Ranulf II, Earl of Chester in King Stephen's Reign', *Anglo-Norman Studies* XIV, ed. M. Chibnall (Woodbridge, 1992), 39–60; *idem*, 'Aiming at the Impossible: Ranulf II, Earl of Chester, and Lincolnshire in the Reign of King Stephen', *Earldom of Chester and its Charters*, ed. Thacker, 109–34.

Therein lies a paradox. Whilst the earl of Chester may have been a genuine patron of the Cistercians – the 'greatest single benefactor of the Cistercians'[15] – the earl of Leicester's foundation of Garendon was rather calculating. Ranulf founded five Cistercian houses – Basingwerk (1131) before Garendon, Combermere and Calder (both 1135), Pipewell (1143), and Dieulacres (1153). In some way or another he was a benefactor of six other houses, including Revesby, founded in 1142 by his brother, William de Roumare.[16] Nevertheless, Ranulf's response to the foundation of Garendon reflected the political situation: he granted the abbey merely the right to have a ship on the river Dee, which the abbey found expedient to exchange with Ranulf III much later (1197x1207) for the right to have a cart in the earl's forest at Barrow.[17]

By comparison, the earl of Leicester's interest in the Cistercians may be most charitably described as fleeting. In equally charitable vein, Crouch described the earl's patronage of the religious as conventional, but eclectic, responding to the rapidly changing nature of opportunities for religious benefactions, as new orders were introduced into England.[18] Hill's reflections on the benefactions of the Leicester affinity to the Cistercians are rather disingenuous. Pointing to the foundation of Bordesley by the earl's brother, Waleran, count of Meulan, is rather ambiguous, since the house was founded on former royal demesne land alienated by Stephen to Waleran, which served to signify the power of the Leicester affinity in the west midlands.[19] Neither was the acquittance of knight service allowed to Garendon by the earl's cousin, the earl of Warwick, more than platitudinous familial loyalty. The gift of the manor of Baddesley was made by a tenant of Robert, earl of Warwick, but his son, William, recovered the manor.[20] The circumstances behind the

---

[15]   Hill, *English Cistercian Monasteries*, pp. 35–6.

[16]   *Ibid.*, pp. 35–6. Hill attributes Rufford (1146) to de Roumare, but C. J. Holdsworth demonstrates that the founder was Gilbert de Gant: *Rufford Charters*, I, p. xx. Hill's confusion may have arisen because both de Roumare and de Gant were granted the earldom during the troubles of the late 1140s. Pipewell may conceivably have been another southward flanking movement against the earl of Leicester and Revesby can be interpreted as de Roumare's confirmation of his territorial integrity in Lincolnshire.

[17]   BL, Lansdowne MS 415, fols 8, 26; Nichols, *Leicestershire*, III (ii), p. 809, IV (i), p. 411; King, 'Mountsorrel and its Region', p. 6; *The Charters of the Anglo-Norman Earldom of Chester c.1071–1207*, ed. G. Barraclough, Record Society of Lancashire and Cheshire, 126 (Gloucester, 1988), pp. 263–4 (nos 264–5). The date of the exchange follows Barraclough.

[18]   Crouch, *Beaumont Twins*, pp. 196–204.

[19]   Hill, *English Cistercian Monasteries*, pp. 33–4; M. Chibnall, *The Empress Matilda: Queen Consort, Queen Mother and Lady of the English* (Oxford, 1993), pp. 134–5.

[20]   BL, Lansdowne MS 415, fol 5; Nichols, III (ii), pp. 804–5; and see below, p. 108.

resumption of the property are not clear, but it may have been alienated without the consent of the superior lord. Whatever the case, an honorial tenant had been attracted by the house, but the earl compromised the benefaction.

The earl of Leicester's own patronage of religious houses was opportunistic. Like rites of passage, the earl's foundations occurred at significant points in his life, in many cases at minimal cost. The adoption as an oratory of an eremitical community in Whittlewood Forest (Northants) in 1124 reflected his majority.[21] A similarly minor endowment was involved in the adoption of another such community at Le Désert c.1120-5, marking his 'permanent arrival' as lord of Breteuil through marriage. The foundations in 1133-5 of first Garendon (Cistercian) and then Ulverscroft Priory (Austin canons), both in north-west Leicestershire, extended his territorial influence and challenged the earl of Chester, but with endowments of marginal lands. His most important foundation, Leicester Abbey (Austin canons) in c.1138-9, symbolised and confirmed the mediatisation of the borough of Leicester as well as challenging the bishop of Lincoln's influence in his liberty close by the site of the abbey, if not the episcopal presence to the south of the borough in Knighton.[22] The foundation of Bittlesden in 1147 was a renewal of the strategy of endowing religious houses with the lands of disseised tenants. The confiscated land in question was given by the earl to his steward, Arnold de Bosco, for the foundation of the house.[23] The earl's final act, the foundation of Nuneaton Priory in c.1147-53, was ambivalent. It could be interpreted either as initiated by his wife, Amice, who retired to the priory in her widowhood in 1168, or as the final reconciliation of the earl and Henry II, since the earl had supported Stephen, involving Leicester's recognition of the Angevin supremacy and symbolic integration into the Angevin political system.[24]

The other contestants for regional ascendancy in Leicestershire were equally prone to use monastic patronage for secular purposes. Allusion has been made to the foundation of Revesby confirming territorial integrity in Lincolnshire. Moreover, when, in 1141 at the Battle of Lincoln, Ranulf captured Roger de Mowbray, he immediately reasserted his influence in

---

[21] For the date, *Luffield Priory Charters*, ed. G. R. Elvey, 2 vols, Northamptonshire Record Society, 22, 26 (Oxford, 1968-75), I, pp. 15-16, nos 1-2; J. Hudson, *Land, Law and Lordship in Anglo-Norman England* (Oxford, 1994), p. 186.

[22] For details of these foundations, Crouch, *Beaumont Twins*, pp. 196-204, and 'Foundation of Leicester Abbey'.

[23] Hill, *English Cistercian Monasteries*, pp. 50-1.

[24] Compare Crouch, *Beaumont Twins*, pp. 190-207, with M. Chibnall, 'L'Ordre de Fontrevaud en Angleterre au xiiᵉ S.', *Cahiers de Civilisation Médiévale xᵉ-xiiᵉ Siècles* 29 (1986), 41-7, p. 43. Mlle A.-C. Dunet informed me of the last reference in 1992.

north-eastern Leicestershire by assuming the protection and patronage of Belvoir Priory.[25] Robert II de Ferrers attempted to assert influence in north-west Leicestershire through his refoundation of Breedon Priory (Austin canons), despite the significance of the familial house of Tutbury Priory.[26] Such acts, however, pale by comparison with the earl of Leicester's continuous political motivation.

The original endowment of Garendon was minimal and, in a sense, it conformed to the notion of 'wilderness' sometimes associated with the Cistercians, but the later acquisitions represent more closely the recent perception that the Cistercians were most successful where they intruded into existing settlements. Hill suggested that, after the original endowment, later benefactions to the Cistercians in the late twelfth century were parsimonious, reflecting the mediocre status of the donors.[27] Whilst that may have been true of some Cistercian houses in Yorkshire, the reverse applied in the case of Garendon. From a slender, even marginal, original endowment, the estate was transformed in the later twelfth century by the generous benefactions of honorial baronage and knightly families, from all local honours – Chester, Leicester and Mowbray. These gifts comprised consolidated blocks of land of considerable size, some explicitly demesne lands, others probably so. Moreover, the geography of the estate was radically altered, since these later benefactions formed a substantial nucleus of lands to the north-east, in the River–Wolds regions, the inter-related *pays* of the river valleys of the Wreake and Soar and the upland Wolds.[28]

The process of foundation conformed to that protracted series of events known to have characterised the establishment of many religious houses in the early twelfth century.[29] Although the foundation was initiated on 28 October 1133, no original foundation charter from Robert le Bossu survives, but there exists, as usual, the writ-charter of confirmation of Henry I.[30] The foundation thus consisted of an oral disposition. From the royal confirmation it is clear that the original endowment was slender for the support of an abbot and twelve monks. It comprised five carucates and three virgates at Garendon

[25] *Charters of the Honour of Mowbray 1107–1191*, ed. D. Greenway, British Academy Records of Social and Economic History, n.s. 1 (Oxford, 1972), pp. xxvii, 64, 66 (nos 51, 53–4).

[26] Golob, 'Ferrers Earls of Derby', Appendix, pp. 425–7 (no. 10) prints the charter.

[27] Hill, *English Cistercian Monasteries*, pp. 66–75.

[28] For the significance of the juncture of these two *pays*, H. S. A. Fox, 'The People of the Wolds in English Settlement History', in *The Rural Settlements of Medieval England*, ed. M. Aston, D. Austin and C. Dyer (Oxford, 1989), 77–101.

[29] V. H. Galbraith, 'Monastic Foundation Charters of the Eleventh and Twelfth Centuries', *Cambridge Historical Journal* 4 (1934), 205–22, 296–8.

[30] *Regesta Regum Anglo-Normannorum 1066–1154*, II, p. 268 (no. 1790).

with rights in the woods at Dishley and Shepshed. An additional four-and-a-half carucates in Dishley were provided by the earl before 21 November 1136, as also a house in the borough of Leicester, but again seemingly by oral disposition, as only the royal confirmation by Stephen informs us of this increment to the foundation.[31] Before 1154, two carucates were added in Ringlethorp (Thorpe Arnold), but without a charter, our knowledge deriving from memoranda at the end of the cartularies.[32] Subsequent increments were conveyed by charters of the founder, as, for example, when Robert added in 1150x1159 the land which Rabel de Seigneville had held in Dishley and woods in Shepshed extending to one-and-a-half leagues by one league in a charter specifically *ad incrementum*.[33] An earlier incremental charter of 1143x1151 allowed the monks a fishery on the Trent in the earl's manor of Lockington.[34] There remains in the cartularies a charter which purports to be either a foundation charter or a charter of general confirmation. In either case, the internal evidence is grossly inconsistent and it must be taken to be an intelligent reconstruction of what the monks assumed to have happened and one which borrows heavily from the confirmation charter of the earl's son, Robert III, which is the subsequent charter in the arrangement.[35] The foundation of the house thus happened orally without charters; initial additions to the endowment by the founder were also transferred without charters; and only later additions involved charters. The process of foundation was a protracted one. The founder's endowment was slender, concentrated almost exclusively at the site of the house with an outlying property in Dishley.

The response of the family and the honorial baronage of the earldom was dilatory and meagre.[36] The earl of Warwick's relative lack of interest has been demonstrated above; nor did Waleran, count of Meulan, the earl of Leicester's brother, exhibit any great interest. The principal benefactor from the honorial baronage was the earl's steward, Arnold de Bosco, who in 1143x1167 gave his manor (*manerium meum*) of Stanton-under-Bardon, in which he had recently been subinfeudated by Geoffrey de Clinton.[37] This gift probably followed

---

[31] *Regesta Regum Anglo-Normannorum 1066–1154*, III, ed. H. A. Cronne and R. H. C. Davis (Oxford, 1968), p. 128 (no. 338); BL, Lansdowne MS 415, fol. 22v. See also King, 'Mountsorrel', p. 5.

[32] BL, Lansdowne MS 415, fol. 34v.

[33] BL, Lansdowne MS 415, fols 14v–15; Nichols, *Leicestershire*, III (ii), p. 814.

[34] BL, Lansdowne MS 415, fol. 15.

[35] BL, Lansdowne MS 415, fol. 14; Nichols, *Leicestershire*, III (ii), p. 814; at fol. 14v is the *Carta Roberti Comitis Junioris de Geroldonia et Dixleia*.

[36] For the honorial baronage, Crouch, *Beaumont Twins*, pp. 115–32.

[37] For de Bosco, Crouch, *Beaumont Twins*, p. 149; BL, Lansdowne MS 415, fol. 16v; Nichols, *Leicestershire*, III (ii), p. 815.

closely Arnold's removal to England in 1141 to support the earl.[38] It may also have been Arnold who instigated the earl's incremental gift of two carucates in Ringlethorp to the abbey, since that place was in Thorpe Arnold, of which de Bosco was the eponymous tenant.[39] From a confirmation of Arnold's son, the homonymous Arnold III, it is also clear that de Bosco gave the abbey twelve acres and a pasture in Ringlethorp (Thorpe Arnold).[40]

The abbey's relationship with other honorial barons, such as the Tourvilles and Harcourts, was more ambivalent. The Tourvilles seem to have done no more than attest charters to the abbey. The important lands acquired from the Harcourts, which first significantly bolstered the slender endowment of the house, were received in special circumstances, the distress of the family. In 1148/9, William de Harcourt, with the consent of his brother and heir, Ivo, and mother, Agnes, alienated to Garendon the manor of Stanton-under-Bardon, which was specifically their *patrimonium*. One third of the manor was passed in free alms for 'unspecified' spiritual services, but the other two-thirds were an explicit sale for twenty marks and three horses to William, and symbolic counter-gifts of one horse to Ivo and one mark to Agnes.[41] The circumstances suggest that this sale, significantly of patrimonial lands according to the charters, was forced on the family by events during the anarchy.[42]

The relationship with another fee which belonged to the honour of Robert, count of Meulan, the father of the earl of Leicester, is just as complicated. In 1086, Ingenulf held six carucates in the whole vill and lordship of Ibstock.[43] His successor, Robert de Burton, alienated three carucates to Garendon, whilst Robert's son, Richard *filius Roberti*, gave a

---

[38]   Crouch, *Beaumont Twins*, p. 111.
[39]   BL, Lansdowne MS 415, fol. 34v.
[40]   BL, Lansdowne MS 415, fol. 11; Nichols, *Leicestershire*, III (ii), pp. 135–6.
[41]   BL, Lansdowne MS 415, fols 15v–16; Nichols, *Leicestershire*, III (ii), pp. 815, 823–4. The divided vill of Stanton had been in the lordship of Geoffrey la Guerche in 1086: Domesday Book, I, fol. 235c. Nevertheless, the charters of the Harcourts refer to *heres tocius patrimonii*. They also state its explicit nature: *emptio et uenditio*. The digest of charters in the cartularies have the following description: 'et inde habemus cartam Willelmi de vendicione et Iuonis fratris sui cuius fuit patrimonium'. On the meaning, but rarity, of this term at this time, J. C. Holt, 'Feudal Society and the Family in Early Medieval England: II, Notions of Patrimony', *TRHS*, 5th ser. 33 (1983), 193–220. The charter is dated 6 Ides of March [i.e 10 March] 1148 and 12 Stephen; difficulty is caused by there being no known standard for reckoning the beginning of the regnal year before the reign of Henry II.
[42]   It has to be said, however, that, in view of the Domesday tenure of Stanton, it is unclear how this manor could be regarded as patrimonial in its purest sense.
[43]   Domesday Book, I, fol. 237b.

further half a carucate in one Ibstock and another half a carucate in *alia* Ibstock.[44] Nevertheless, there are no charters for these benefactions, which are known purely from confirmations by Geoffrey de Clinton (possibly contemporaneously), William, earl of Warwick (later), William *filius Ricardi de Burtun* and Reginald *filius Ingenulfi*. The charters of de Clinton and the earl of Warwick pertained only to the knight service owing from the lands. The former's charter professed that the vill was held from him as one fee and he remitted the service of a third of a knight.[45] William, earl of Warwick, quitclaimed the service of half a knight owed by de Clinton and Robert de Burton.[46] By a further charter, however, William recovered Baddesley, which had been given to Garendon by a mesne tenant of his father, Robert, earl of Warwick, in return for which William gave the abbey ten marks and confirmed the quittance of knight service.[47]

---

[44]   It is possible that the vill was now divided into two lordships held by the same family from different superior lords.

[45]   BL, Lansdowne MS 415, fols 5, 15; Nichols, *Leicestershire*, III (ii), p. 805.

[46]   BL, Lansdowne MS 415, fols 5, 15v; Nichols, *Leicestershire*, III (ii), p. 805. The relationship of the earl of Warwick and de Clinton is described by D. Crouch, 'Geoffrey de Clinton and Roger, Earl of Warwick: New Men and Magnates in the Reign of Henry I', *Bulletin of the Institute of Historical Research* 55 (1982), 113–24.

[47]   BL, Lansdowne MS 415, fols 5, 15v. There are, however, numerous problems with these charters. That of de Clinton is especially odd. The *capitulum* in the cartulary attributes it to *G. Camerarius de Clintun* and that style is indeed used in the notification in the charter; that would suggest that the grantor is Geoffrey I de Clinton, the *novus homo* of Henry I (*fl.* 1108–35) (J. Green, *The Government of England under Henry I* (Cambridge, 1986), pp. 239–42). It is addressed to *R. episcopo de Cestria*; although the see was transferred from Chester to Coventry in 1102, the bishops retained the style 'of Chester': *Handbook of British Chronology*, ed. E. B. Fryde, D. E. Greenway, S. Porter and I. Roy (3rd edn, 1986), p. 253. This prelate must be Roger de Clinton, Geoffrey's brother, with the implication that the date is 1129x1148: *ibid* and Crouch, 'Geoffrey de Clinton and Roger, Earl of Warwick', p. 119. Since the principal witness is *R. comes de Ferr'*, it must antedate 1159 (I. J. Sanders, *English Baronies: a Study of their Origin and Descent 1086–1327* (Oxford, 1960), p. 148). That of William, earl of Warwick, must be between 1153 and 1184 (Sanders, *English Baronies*, p. 93). One version in the cartularies is attested by R. prior of Kenilworth, whilst the fuller version extends his name to Robert (BL, Lansdowne MS 415, fols 5 and 15v; Nichols, *Leicestershire*, III (ii), p. 805). It must therefore be after 1158 (D. Knowles, C. N. L. Brooke and V. C. M. London, *The Heads of Religious Houses: England and Wales 940–1216* (Cambridge, 1972), p. 167). The charter recovering Baddesley must be later than 1155, since it refers to the current abbot as T., that is Thurstan (*Heads of Religious Houses*, p. 135). The charter of de Clinton may thus be spurious, and that of William long after the first benefaction.

It is clear that the original acquisition of the three carucates had taken place before 1153–4, since they are confirmed in a bull of Anastasius IV.[48] The confirmations by the later members of the donor's family suggest an approximate date for the transaction. That of William *filius Ricardi de Burton* mentions the extent of assarting at 25 Henry II, so must not be much later than 1179. His charter and that of Reginald *filius Ingenulfi* allow a genealogy.

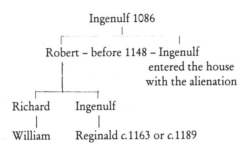

Since Reginald's charter is attested *R. electo sancto Andree* it must be either *c.*1163 or *c.*1189, when Richard and Roger were respectively elected to that see. Those considerations must push back the original transaction by Robert de Burton into the period of the anarchy.

The precise circumstances are revealed in the digest of charters at the end of the cartularies, for, although there is no charter and the transaction took place orally, the digest includes a memorandum of the events. The three carucates were sold by Robert for thirty marks (*pro xxx marcis argenti*) which the monks gave him to free him from his captivity (*quas monachi ei dederunt in liberacionem* [sic] *captiuitatis sue*). Furthermore, the additional carucate given by his son, Richard, the digest reveals, was in consideration of six marks paid by the monks towards Richard's relief (*ad redempcionem suam*).[49]

Two substantive points thus emerge about the early acquisitions by the abbey. Firstly, the honorial baronage of the earl of Leicester were more uninterested than disinterested in the foundation, which may reflect on the political circumstances of its foundation and lack of commitment of the founder. Secondly, in order to expand its original slender resources, the abbey had to enter the land market and take advantage of the political circumstances of the anarchy, when some mesne tenants found themselves in difficulty, particularly where there was a contest for local control.

The response of the honorial baronage was thus reticent. Nor were other baronial families effusive towards the earl of Leicester's house, probably again because of the fairly explicit political conditions surrounding its foundation.

48   BL, Lansdowne MS 415, fol 13v; Nichols, *Leicestershire*, III (ii), p. 813.
49   BL, Lansdowne MS 415, fol. 27.

As mentioned above, the principal target of the foundation, the earl of Chester, granted only a boat on the river Dee. Exceptionally, Gundreda (de Gournay), widow of Nigel d'Aubigny and mother of Roger de Mowbray, gave 32 acres in Thorpe Arnold (Ringlethorp), but that was the full extent of the patronage from the Mowbray quarter.[50] Benefactions from the Ferrers, earls of Derby, did not accrue until quite late, it seems. The bull of Alexander III (1159-81) referred to the *nova grangia* of the Peak, the earl having given land in Heathcote and Hardwick for a bercary.[51] The most significant early baronial benefactor was William (II?) Peverel who donated all his land in his lordship at Costock (Notts.) before 1153-4.[52] Peverel's gift was apparently in pure alms and not a concealed sale, for neither the charter nor the digest in the cartularies reflects any secular consideration.

The development of the estate of the house in the first half of the twelfth century was thus a qualified success. In the latter half of the century, however, a singular transformation occurred in the nature of the estate, as a result of benefactions from knightly families, through gifts consisting of consolidated blocks of land in a concentration of vills in north and north-east Leicestershire and adjacent southern Nottinghamshire. These substantial blocks acceded from all the principal honours in these areas. For example, lands from fees of the honour of Tickhill were received in Wysall, Costock and Rempstone, but equally from Burun fees in the last-named settlement. In Burton-on-the-Wolds, where the feudal structure was quite complicated, lands were held from fees in the honours of Despenser (Chester), Leicester and Mowbray. Lands from Mowbray fees were also held in Welby, as well as Albemarle fees in nearby Eastwell.

The size of these benefactions may be illustrated by some sample gifts. Thomas Despenser, a principal patron of the house, but an honorial tenant of the earl of Chester, gave ten bovates and five selions in Burton, Nigel de Luuetot 120 acres in Wysall, and the de Cortingestoca family six bovates in their eponymous vill.[53] Another seven carucates accrued in Burton from the

---

[50] BL, Lansdowne MS 415, fol. 21; Nichols, *Leicestershire*, III (ii), p. 215; *Charters of the Honour of Mowbray*, p. 116, nos 155-6.

[51] BL, Lansdowne MS 415, fols 12v, 13v; Nichols, *Leicestershire*, III (ii), pp. 812-14.

[52] BL, Lansdowne MS 415, fol. 6; Nichols, *Leicestershire*, III (ii), p. 812. The land was later described as ten bovates. William II's estates were confiscated by Henry of Anjou in 1153-4 and held by Ferrers for the crown thereafter (Sanders, *English Baronies*, p. 136); the lands at Costock are seemingly included in the bull of Anastasius, 1153x1154, which refers to four carucates in Costock. Peverel may have been an ally of the earl of Leicester, but was captured at the Battle of Lincoln in 1141: R. H. C. Davis, *King Stephen 1135-1154* (3rd edn, 1990), p. 50.

[53] For the Despensers, D. Crouch, 'The Administration of the Norman Earldom', *The Earldom of Chester and its Charters*, ed. Thacker, 69-96, pp. 78-9; Farrer,

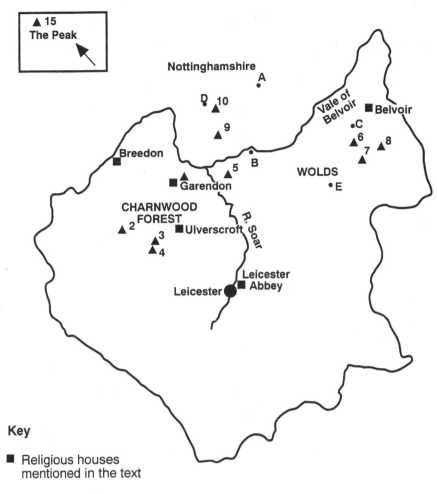

Key

■ Religious houses
mentioned in the text

▲ Granges of Garendon (+= by 1181)

1 Dishley (+)   6 Goadby Marwood (+)
2 Ibstock   7 Ringlethorp (+)
3 Swinfen (+)   8 Welby (+)
4 Stanton under Bardon (+)   9 Rempstone (+)
5 Burton on the Wolds (+)   10 Costock (+)

• Other lands (possibly attached to granges)

A Wysall   C Eastwell   E Sysonby
B Wymeswold   D East Leake

Figure 4: The estates of Garendon Abbey, *c.*1220.

gift of the de Berges family, as also four-and-a-half carucates there from the de Colevilles, six bovates from Frumentin, and another carucate from Putrel. Geoffrey Haget, an honorial baron of the Mowbrays, provided four carucates in Welby and Luke de Quatremars one carucate and fifteen acres in Goadby. John *constabularius* (of Chester) added ten bovates in Costock and Thomas I and II de Sextenebi gave respectively half a carucate and twenty-two selions in Sysonby. The de Aleby family gave successively half a carucate, thirteen acres, and eight acres in the eponymous Welby. These substantial blocks facilitated the establishment of granges in vills which were already populated and cultivated and certainly were not 'wilderness'.[54]

Unlike the earlier benefactions, some of these later gifts were inspired by social connections and kinship or genealogy. One of the earliest donors in this second phase was Hugh de Berges, whose superior lord for his land in Burton was Herbert de Queniburc', his brother. Hugh had two sons, Nigel and Asketil de Berges, the latter of whom augmented his father's benefactions to the abbey. Asketil's uncles were his superior lords and tenants of the honour of Mowbray, Ralph de Queniburc' and Ralph's brother, Thurstan de Queniburgo, successors of Herbert. Asketil, however, also held land in Burton from Thomas Despenser, himself another principal benefactor of Garendon. Asketil himself was superior lord of Gilbert *sacerdos* of

---

Honors and Knights' Fees, II, pp. 58–63.

[54] Figure 4 illustrates the disposition of these granges, many of which were mentioned as granges in the bull of Alexander III (1159–81) (BL, Lansdowne MS 415, fols 13v–14; Nichols, *Leicestershire*, III (ii) pp. 813–14). The use of the term *grangia* in such a formal context may have been common form for Cistercians rather than actuality. In fact, references in charters of donation also refer to the house's establishment of *grangie* before this time: 'infra fossatum grangie de Corting'; 'infra clausuram grangie sue de Burtun'; 'de altera parte grangie' [Burton]; 'totam clausuram eiusdem grangie' [Burton]; 'infra clausuram grangie monachorum ... prope grangiam ... in cultura proprinquiori grangie ... quicquid habent de feodo meo infra clausuram grangie' [all Sysonby]; 'infra fossata sue Grangie ... iuxta curiam eiusdem Grangie' [Costock] (BL, Lansdowne MS 415, fols 5v, 6, 8v, 9, 11v, 24, and 27; Nichols, *Leicestershire*, III (ii), pp. 136–7, 806–7, 811). A composition about the tithes of Prestwold refers to the *grangia* of Burton in 1177. For differing views on the sites of granges, R. A. Donkin, 'Settlement and Depopulation on Cistercian Estates during the Twelfth and Thirteenth Centuries', *Bulletin of the Institute of Historical Research* 33 (1960), 141–65; Platt, *The Monastic Grange*; Berman, *Medieval Agriculture and the Southern French Countryside*; R. H. Hilton, *A Medieval Society: the West Midlands at the End of the Thirteenth Century* (1966, repr. Cambridge, 1983), pp. 36–7; M. W. Barley, 'Cistercian Land Clearances in Nottinghamshire', *Nottingham Medieval Studies* 1 (1957), 75–89. The formation of these granges in the late twelfth century thus raises the prospect of the Cistercians being one influence in the general resumption of demesnes for direct demesne agriculture.

Walton-on-the-Wolds, who made a substantial gift of land there to the abbey.[55] This particular nexus of lordship and family was intense, but is simply illustrative of other ties between donors to the abbey in the late twelfth century. Garendon thus became in the late twelfth century the focal point for an emerging territorial knighthood whose inter-relationship was based increasingly on locality and neighbourhood rather than the honour.[56] This change in social relationships probably occurred independently of the patronage of Garendon which, rather, provided another focus for it.[57]

In its acquisition of the manors of Stanton and Ibstock in the early twelfth century, Garendon had expended a total of 57 marks as well as four horses. Counter-gifts were also elicited in the late twelfth century, but, with a few exceptions, on a much smaller scale. In many cases, the counter-gift consisted of burial or fraternity. Two major exceptions occurred. Asketil de Berges required sixteen marks as recompense for the performance of secular services, perhaps implicitly a concealed purchase. The other instance of a cash consideration reflected a more active intervention in the land market by the monks, but almost certainly antedated the prohibition of purchases by the Chapter General in 1180.[58] William de Evermu alienated to the abbey four carucates in Eastwell, two of which had been held by Leon de Arceles as a gage for the use (ad opus) of the abbey as collateral for twenty marks. The monks proffered a further twenty-five marks to acquire the four carucates in fee, probably c.1162–70.[59]

55 For example, BL, Lansdowne MS 415, fols 8, 18, 20 and 31v; for Thomas Despenser, Farrer, *Honors and Knights' Fees*, II, pp. 58–9; for de Queniburc' in the *cartae baronum* of 1166, *Charters of the Honour of Mowbray*, p. 256, no. 401.

56 For parallel developments, Wales, 'The Knight in Twelfth-Century Lincolnshire', pp. 235–60; for the importance of knightly benefaction to Fountains in the late twelfth century, Wardrop, *Fountains Abbey*, pp. 133, 168–9, 171.

57 An exception was Geoffrey Haget, who had given to Garendon the not inconsiderable benefaction of four carucates in Welby, but simultaneously the Hagets (c.1166–81) gave land in north-east Leicestershire (at Thorpe Dacre, Caldwell and indeed in Welby) to Fountains Abbey as well as founding Helaugh Park and Sinningthwaite Priories: H. Thomas, *Vassals, Heiresses, Crusaders and Thugs: the Gentry of Angevin Yorkshire, 1154–1216* (University of Pennsylvania Press, 1993), p. 150; BL, Lansdowne MS 415, fols 11v, 32v. G. Haget died during 1199: *Early Yorkshire Charters*, ed. W. Farrer and C. T. Clay, 12 vols (Edinburgh and Wakefield, 1914–65), I, pp. 402–3.

58 *Statuta Capitulorum Generalium Ordinis Cisterciensis*, ed. J. M. Canivez, 8 vols (Louvain, 1933–41), I, pp. 117–18.

59 . For the date, I follow J. H. Round, who prints original charters in Historical Manuscripts Commission, *Rutland MSS*, 4 vols (London, 1888–1905), IV, p. 5, no. 16c. BL, Lansdowne MS 415, fol. 10; Nichols, *Leicestershire*, III (ii), pp. 133–5. The date is largely established by Round by the attestation in the first place by

Although this particular acquisition was the most substantial outlay in the late twelfth century, other concealed purchases may have occurred. Particularly ambivalent are references to benefactions made at the time the donor paid relief and married: 'quando releuaui terram meam et uxorem duxi'.[60] There are two possible interpretations here: either the monks assisted in the payment of the relief, through which they acquired land, or the gift simply reflected a rite of passage in the life of the donor which was symbolically marked by a gift or confirmation to the religious. It is not possible to infer anything more concrete.

By and large, the benefactions to the house by knightly families in the late twelfth century appear to be made out of genuine religious commitment, not enforced or concealed sales. No evidence supports the notion of a 'crisis' of this social group to the advantage of the religious house.[61] It appears rather that the knightly families of north and north-east Leicestershire adopted Garendon as the primary religious institution in the region. The house was certainly the most significant in size there – out-ranking Ulverscroft, Charley, and Langley Priory (a nunnery), whilst Belvoir had become a private mausoleum.[62] Since the family of the founders exhibited no interest in Garendon, knightly families perhaps felt a greater involvement through their benefactions, providing almost a multiplicity of patrons. That sentiment may be echoed in the language of corroboration in their charters, in which, before explicit warranty developed, the term *defensores astabimus* was paramount. Even after the introduction of warranty clauses, Robert Putrel – or whoever wrote the charter, but perhaps not without it being informed by his wishes – confirmed the carucate given by his predecessors, with more than conventional piety, referring almost to a tradition of lineage in association with the house. The carucate in Burton-on-the-Wolds, of the honour of Leicester, had,

---

William Basset as sheriff of the county. The alienation was confirmed by the superior lord, styled in the cartulary *W. comes de Albamarl'*, undoubtedly William le Gros (1138–1179). It was confirmed by his successor, who married Albemarle's widow, William de Mandeville, at the Easter Exchequer in 1181: BL, Lansdowne MS 415, fol. 24v; Nichols, *Leicestershire*, III (ii), p. 134. Round also prints charters from Belvoir Castle which are not in the cartulary, including one of de Evermu.

[60] For example, BL, Lansdowne MS 415, fols 6, 9, and 10.

[61] The literature on the question of the fortunes of knightly families is too large to mention in detail, but reference is made to the summary in P. Coss, *Lordship, Knighthood and Locality: a Study in English Society c.1180–c.1280* (Cambridge, 1991), pp. 1–22.

[62] For Belvoir, B. Golding, 'Anglo–Norman Knightly Burials', *The Ideals and Practice of Medieval Knighthood*, Papers from the First and Second Strawberry Hill Conferences, ed. C. Harper-Bill and R. Harvey (Woodbridge, 1986), 35–48, pp. 37, 39, and esp. 42. Charley was dissolved or suppressed – by appropriation to Ulverscroft – in the later middle ages, because its size made it unsupportable.

the charter stated, been given by Henry Putrel *auus meus* and Robert *pater meus*. The corroboration ignored warranty altogether and instead invoked an anathema including the peculiar *defensor astabo,* but more significantly in the same phrase the term *aduocatus*.[63] Putrel was projecting himself as a special protector:

> Si quis predictos monachos inde uexare uoluerit ego / .R. Putrel sicut aduocatus eiusdem elemosine cum eis defensor astabo saluo forinsi seruicio.[64]

Certainly the extent of the protection was limited (to the gift in alms and excluding forinsec service); on the other hand, the phraseology is evocative of a stronger association. The importance of Garendon to lay society was thus established not at its foundation, but by its later adoption by the knightly families of the 'region', in the late twelfth century.

Four principal points emerge from this discussion of the relationship between Garendon and its benefactors. First, the original endowment at the foundation was slender, even marginal, but perhaps not uncharacteristic, and it reflected the political as well as religious motives of the founder. Those political circumstances also help to explain why his honorial baronage were not benefactors of the house. Consequently, the monks had immediately to resort to the acquisition of lands through the land market, in the geographical vicinity of the convent, and facilitated by the troubles of the anarchy. Finally, in the later twelfth century, the house became the focus of common benefactions from the knightly families of north-east Leicestershire, whose inter-relationships were becoming more territorially – and less honorially – based. Concomitantly, the benefactions altered the geography of the estate, since many gifts were both substantial and concentrated in the north-east of the county.

---

[63] For the use of this term in this context, S. Wood, *English Monasteries and their Patrons in the Thirteenth Century* (Oxford, 1955), pp. 17–21, and now, J. Burton, *Monastic and Religious Orders in Britain: 1000–1300* (Cambridge, 1994), pp. 211–12. For another thought on the term, P. R. Hyams, 'Warranty and Good Lordship in Twelfth Century England', *Law and History Review* 5 (1987), 437–503, p. 452 and n. 49. I hope to return to this language of corroboration. For warranty and its language, see now J. Hudson, *Land, Law and Lordship in Anglo-Norman England* (Oxford, 1994), pp. 51–8.

[64] BL, Lansdowne MS 415, fol. 9v; Nichols, *Leicestershire*, III (ii), p. 812. Dr Thompson points out to me that the inclusion of the clause might equally reflect an appeal from the monks for the support of the local knightly families.

Table 1: Counter-gifts in the late twelfth century

Donor	Land	Counter-gift
Robert de Boues	0.5c and 10a	burial of his father
Matthew *filius Willelmi filii Wlrici*	confirm (4b)	fraternity, 2 marks, 2s to his wife
John *filius Radulphi de Constantin*	10b	fraternity/burial
William de Rampeston	selions	burial (*cum corpore suo*)
Hugh Malet	confirm	fraternity
Asketil de Berges	(1) 6a (2) 4c (3) 8a (4) 1c (5) 3c (6) 8a	burial 10s + a horse corrody (for life) 2 marks and 5s 16 marks (services) 16s
Ralph de Queniburc'	confirm + 8a	30s
Thomas Despenser	10b	fraternity
William de Evermu	4c	45 marks (gage)
Richard *filius Turstini*	1c	burial
Luke de Quatremars	confirm + 15a	burial
Robert Arabi	*terra*	his *cognatus* R. Pais entered the house
Nigel de Luuetot	100a	6 marks *ad introitum* (5 to Nigel, 1 to his wife) and a foal for their son
Serlo de Pleseleia	confirm	20s, fraternity
Robert de Jort	confirm	4s, 12s to his wife (the original donor) and 1s each to two sons
Ralph *stabularius*	quitclaim (after litigation)	2 marks, 1 cow, 10 lambs, 1 foal, 1 pig

c = carucate; b = bovate; a = acre; confirm = confirmation (of a gift by either a sub-tenant or a relative)

Texts and Images of Marian Devotion in English Twelfth-Century Monasticism, and Their Influence on the Secular Church

NIGEL MORGAN

Surveys of texts and images of Marian devotion in thirteenth- and fourteenth century England were presented in two earlier papers given at the Harlaxton Symposia in 1989 and 1991.[1] In those papers the bulk of the material was drawn from manuscripts and works of art connected with the secular church, and only occasionally was the monastic contribution to Marian devotions in those centuries mentioned as significant.[2] It was in the preceding centuries that the majority of Marian monastic devotions had been established, and in many cases these were direct precursors of very similar practices taken up by the secular church in the thirteenth and fourteenth centuries. The Benedictines and Cistercians of the eleventh and twelfth centuries were indeed the twin fountains from which most of the hymns and prayers to Mary flowed into the devotional life of the wider society of the church.[3] The influence of the mendicants in the thirteenth century was relatively small in comparison, but

---

[1] N. Morgan, 'Texts and Images of Marian Devotion in Thirteenth-Century England', *England in the Thirteenth Century: Proceedings of the 1989 Harlaxton Symposium*, Harlaxton Medieval Studies I, ed. W. M. Ormrod (Stamford, 1991), 69–103; 'Texts and Images of Marian Devotion in Fourteenth-Century England', *England in the Fourteenth Century: Proceedings of the 1991 Harlaxton Symposium*, Harlaxton Medieval Studies III, ed. W. M. Ormrod (Stamford, 1993), 34–57.

[2] As in the case of the use of the *Ave Maria* and the *Salve Regina*. See Morgan, 'Texts and Images, Thirteenth Century', pp. 73–5.

[3] For general accounts of Benedictine and Cistercian Marian devotions see: P. Bernard, 'La dévotion Mariale dans l'Ordre de Saint Benoît', *Bulletin de la Société Française d'Études Mariales* 3 (1937), 95–143; J. Leclercq, 'Dévotion et théologie mariale dans le monachisme bénédictin', in *Maria*, ed. H. du Manoir, II (Paris, 1952), 549–78; J.-B. Auniord and R. Thomas, 'Notre Dame dans l'histoire de Cîteaux', in *ibid.*, 581–624; J. Leclerq, 'Saint Bernard et la dévotion médiévale envers Marie', *Revue d'ascétique et mystique* 30 (1954), 361–75. An excellent survey of twelfth-century Marian monastic writing is given by H. Graef, *Mary: a History of Doctrine and Devotion*, 2 vols (London, 1963), I, pp. 210–64.

the Augustinian canons may have played an important role in disseminating monastic Marian devotions, particularly in the first half of that century. These influences are above all from monastic texts rather than from the accompanying images. These images in the twelfth century present a more intellectual and theological imagery than the affective humanised image of Mary which emerges in the thirteenth century as a response to the demands of lay piety.[4] Twelfth-century monastic representations of Mary often presented theology through symbolic forms and attributes even though the image was set in a devotional context, but a devotional context where emotional empathy was in the words of the text rather than explicitly conveyed through the form of the image.[5]

The surviving evidence for twelfth-century English monastic Marian liturgical texts is almost exclusively Benedictine.[6] For the Cistercians and Cluniacs the very scanty textual evidence from English manuscripts has to be supplemented by evidence from French sources.[7] For those two orders

---

[4] See Morgan, 'Texts and Images, Thirteenth Century', pp. 93–5; Morgan, 'Texts and Images, Fourteenth Century', pp. 45–7.

[5] This statement inevitably raises the issue of how an image conveys emotion in its particular historical context. Quite possibly these twelfth-century images induced emotional empathy in the eyes of a twelfth-century monastic viewer, even though from a twentieth-century viewpoint they seem detached. As regards the texts of monastic prayers, particularly those of St Anselm, an emotional response, even for a modern reader, is strongly induced by their choice of words and rhetorical phrases.

[6] Two breviaries of St Albans and Winchcombe which contain the Marian offices and hymns (BL, Royal MS 2.A.x; Valenciennes, Bibliothèque Municipale MS 116), several psalters and prayer books containing Marian prayers (BL, Cotton MS Nero C.iv (Winchester); BL, Cotton MS Vespasian D.xxvi (Benedictine modified to Augustinian); BL, Lansdowne MS 383 (Shaftesbury); BL, Royal MS 2.A.xxii (Westminster); London, Society of Antiquaries MS 7 (Durham); Madrid, Biblioteca Nacional MS Vit. 23–8 (Winchester); Paris, Bibliothèque Nationale MS lat. 10433 (Westminster-derived); Verdun, Bibliothèque Municipale 70 (St Albans)) and a hymnal from Durham (Cambridge, Jesus College MS 23). See also the manuscripts containing St Anselm's prayers discussed later in this article.

[7] For the use of the Office of the Virgin by the Cistercians see *The Old French Paraclete Ordinary and the Paraclete Breviary*, ed. C. Waddell, 5 vols, Cistercian Liturgy Series, 3 (Gethsemani Abbey, Kentucky, 1983–5), I, pp. 382–3. For the Cluniac Office of the Virgin, see B. H. Rosenwein, 'Feudal War and Monastic Peace: Cluniac Liturgy and Ritual Aggression', *Viator* 2 (1971), 129–57, p. 139, and E. Bishop, 'On the Origin of the Prymer', in his *Liturgica Historica* (Oxford, 1918, repr. 1962), 211–37, p. 228, with evidence for its restricted use from the time of Abbot Hugh (1049–1109). An important document of English Cistercian Marian devotion is a poem by Roger, a monk of Forde Abbey (Devon): H. Talbot, 'The Verses of Roger of Ford on Our Lady', *Collectanea Ordinis*

liturgical texts were required to be standardised for all their houses, and it is reasonable to assume that the English houses were in close touch with the French mother houses. In the case of the English Cistercians the writings of Aelred of Rievaulx provide some evidence of their Marian devotional attitudes.[8] The other monastic order whose extant liturgical texts from English houses are almost negligible before the thirteenth century are the Augustinian canons, and any conclusions on their importance in the development of Marian devotions before that time remain highly speculative.

Other than liturgical texts and practices an essential expression of twelfth-century monastic interest and attitude to Mary is in the collections of the legendary Miracles of the Virgin which were to become so popular in the secular church in the thirteenth century. The role of the two English Benedictines, Dominic, prior of Evesham and William of Malmesbury, as authors of such collections has been well documented.[9] Another development outside of the liturgy in which the Cistercians played a significant role was through their collections of *exempla*, in which the legends of the Virgin played a part, but the contribution of the English Cistercians to the French Cistercian *exempla* collections still has to be properly defined.[10] The dissemination of *exempla* through their inclusion in thirteenth-century

Cisterciensium Reformatorum 6 (1939), 44–54, and A. G. Rigg, 'Roger of Ford's Poem on the Virgin: a Critical Edition', *Cîteaux* 40 (1989), 200–13.

[8] Most particularly Aelred's sermons on the great Marian festivals; G. Raciti, *Aelredi Rievallensis, Sermones I–XLVI*, Corpus Christianorum, Continuatio Medievalis, IIA (Turnhout, 1989). On his Marian writings see A. Agius, 'St Aelred and Our Blessed Lady', *Downside Review* 64 (1946), 32–8; C. Dumont, 'Aspects de la dévotion du Bx. Aelred à Notre Dame', *Collectanea Ordinis Cisterciensium Reformatorum* 20 (1958), 313–26.

[9] See the work of R. W. Southern, 'The English Origins of the Miracles of the Virgin', *Medieval and Renaissance Studies* 4 (1958), 176–216; J. C. Jennings, 'The Origins of the "Elements Series" of the Miracles of the Virgin', *Medieval and Renaissance Studies* 6 (1968), 84–93; J. M. Canal, 'El libro de laudibus et miraculis sanctae Mariae de Guillermo de Malmesbury, O.S.B. (†c.1143)', *Claretianum* 8 (1968), 71–242; P. Carter, 'The Historical Content of William of Malmesbury's Miracles of the Virgin Mary', *The Writing of History in the Middle Ages: Essays Presented to Richard William Southern*, ed. R. H. C. Davis and J. M. Wallace-Hadrill (Oxford, 1981), 127–66. See also M. P. Gripkey, *The Blessed Virgin Mary as Mediatrix in the Latin and Old French Legend prior to the Fourteenth Century* (Washington, 1938), pp. 45–50.

[10] See the work of B. P. McGuire, 'The Cistercians and the Rise of the Exemplum in Early Thirteenth Century France: a Re-evaluation of Paris BN MS lat. 15912', *Classica et Mediaevalia* 34 (1983), 211–67, especially his conclusion on p. 257: 'The vast amount of material in the Beaupré collection that the compiler claims came from England indicates that England at the close of the twelfth century, especially its Cistercian houses, provided the Continent with a wealth of stories'.

compilations of *exempla* resulted in such monastic writings being transmitted to the laity through their use in sermons.

Mary Clayton's studies of the cult of the Virgin in Anglo-Saxon England have admirably documented the material up to the end of the eleventh century.[11] Her work has shown how new Marian prayers and liturgical forms had been introduced in the tenth and eleventh centuries in the English Benedictine monasteries. Some may also have been in the Norman liturgies introduced in the reforms of the English Benedictine houses after the Conquest, but even if the earlier Anglo-Saxon practices were temporarily abandoned they were to re-emerge in the twelfth century. The liturgical feasts of the Virgin newly introduced in the eleventh century, namely the feasts of the Presentation of Mary in the Temple (21 Nov.) and her Conception (8 Dec.) are a case in point.[12] Evidence from calendars clearly points to the Presentation of Mary being celebrated by the Benedictines at the New Minster at Winchester by c.1030–50.[13] The Canterbury (Christ Church) Benedictional of c.1030 has a blessing for the feast of the Presentation of Mary, and the feast occurs at Christ Church in the twelfth century.[14] By the early thirteenth century the feast had spread to Tewkesbury, Winchester (Cathedral Priory) and Worcester, but it was only adopted by the secular use of Sarum in the closing years of the middle ages.[15] The case of the Conception of the Virgin

---

[11] M. Clayton, 'Feasts of the Virgin in the Liturgy of the Anglo-Saxon Church', *Chaucer Review* 13 (1978/9), 272–83; M. Clayton, 'Feasts of the Virgin in the Liturgy of the Anglo-Saxon Church', *Anglo-Saxon England* 13 (1984), 209–33; M. Clayton, *The Cult of the Virgin Mary in Anglo-Saxon England* (Cambridge, 1990).

[12] On the feast of the Presentation see R. W. Pfaff, *New Liturgical Feasts in Late Medieval England* (Oxford, 1970), pp. 105–9; Clayton, *Cult of the Virgin Mary*, pp. 42–7, 85–7.

[13] *English Kalendars before A.D. 1100*, ed. F. Wormald, Henry Bradshaw Society 72 (London, 1934), pp. 124, 166.

[14] *English Benedictine Kalendars after A.D. 1100*, ed. F. Wormald, Henry Bradshaw Society 77 (London, 1939), p. 78; Pfaff, *New Liturgical Feasts*, p. 105 n. 6; *The Eadwine Psalter*, ed. M. Gibson, T. A. Heslop and R. W. Pfaff (London, 1992), pp. 74–5.

[15] The texts are: Tewkesbury (BL, Royal MS 8.G.vii) of c.1200; Winchester Cathedral (BL, Add. MS 61888) of c.1200; Worcester (Oxford, Magdalen College, MS 100) of c.1210–20. For the reconstruction of the Winchester Cathedral Priory Calendar see N. J. Morgan, 'Notes on the Post-Conquest Calendar, Litany and Martyrology of the Cathedral Priory of Winchester, with a consideration of Winchester diocese calendars of the pre-Sarum period', in *The Vanishing Past: Studies of Medieval Art, Liturgy and Metrology presented to Christopher Hohler*, British Archaeological Reports, International Series 111, ed. A. Borg and A. Martindale (Oxford, 1981), 133–71. For the Sarum feast see Pfaff, *New Liturgical Feasts*, pp. 110–12, for occurrence in the Sarum printed books from 1495 onwards.

was different. It also was introduced by the English Benedictines, and almost certainly as a result of their influence became widespread in the secular church in England by the end of the thirteenth century.[16] In contrast to the feast of the Presentation of the Virgin, that of her Conception became a *cause célèbre* of twelfth-century theological controversy which has been well discussed in the literature.[17] Eadmer of Canterbury, a Christ Church monk, Osbert of Clare, a Westminster monk, and Nicholas, a monk of St Albans were the

[16]   The documentation of this is mostly from the evidence of calendars which from *c.*1250 onwards increasingly include the feast. Hardly any English secular breviaries and missals survive from the thirteenth century to provide evidence. In the *c.*1250 Sarum missals (Manchester, John Rylands Library MS lat. 24, Paris, Bibliothèque de l'Arsenal MS 135) it is in the calendar but not in the sanctoral: J. Wickham Legg, *The Sarum Missal* (Oxford, 1916), p. xxxii. By 1287 the Statutes of Exeter show that it was celebrated there: *Councils and Synods with other Documents of the English Church, II, 1205–1313*, ed. F. M. Powicke and C. R. Cheney, 2 vols (Oxford, 1964), II, p. 1022. Examples of English thirteenth-century secular calendars which contain the feast are: N. J. Morgan, *Early Gothic Manuscripts*, A Survey of Manuscripts Illuminated in the British Isles 4, 2 vols (London, 1982–8), I, *1190–1250*, nos 30, 37, 74; II, *1250–1285*, nos 100, 112, 114, 118, 133, 138, 151, 160, 162, 167, 182. Several others (e.g. *ibid.*, I and II, nos 24, 26, 39, 51, 161) which have the feast suggest derivation from Augustinian calenders.

[17]   E. Bishop, 'On the Origins of the Feast of the Conception of the Blessed Virgin Mary', in *Liturgica Historica*, 238–59; A. W. Burridge, 'L'Immaculée Conception dans la Théologie de l'Angleterre Médiévale', *Revue d'Histoire Ecclésiastique* 32 (1936), 570–97; F. Mildner, 'The Immaculate Conception in England', *Marianum* 1 (1939), 86–99, 200–21; *idem*, 'The Immaculate Conception in the Writings of Nicholas of St Albans', *Marianum* 2 (1940), 173–93; A. M. Cecchin, 'La Concezione della Vergine nella liturgia della Chiesa occidentale anteriore al secolo XIII', *Marianum* 5 (1943), 58–114; S. J. P. van Dijk, 'The Origin of the Latin Feast of the Conception of the Blessed Virgin Mary', *Dublin Review* 228 (1954), 251–67, 428–42; H. F. Davis, 'The Origins of Devotion to Our Lady's Immaculate Conception', *Dublin Review* 228 (1954), 375–92; C. H. Talbot, 'Nicholas of Albans and Saint Bernard', *Revue Bénédictine* 64 (1954), 83–117; C. A. Bouman, 'The Immaculate Conception in the Liturgy', in *The Dogma of the Immaculate Conception*, ed. E. D. O'Connor (Notre Dame, 1958), 113–59; J. Fournée, 'Du "De Conceptu Virginali" de Saint Anselme au "De Conceptione Sancte Mariae" de son disciple Eadmer', *Etudes Anselmiennes* 4 (1984), 711–21. On Eadmer's treatise on the Conception of the Virgin see R. W. Southern, *Saint Anselm and his Biographer* (Cambridge, 1963), pp. 290–6. He points out (p. 295) that only in the early fourteenth century did the treatise, then thought to be by St Anselm, begin to have wide circulation. In the 1328 Council of London it was proposed that the feast of the Conception should be observed by all churches in the province of Canterbury, but from the evidence cited above, n. 16, it was widely celebrated long before that time.

main protagonists.[18] The controversy concerned both the need for a feast day for the Conception of the Virgin and the theological issue of Mary's immaculacy. The feast had been introduced at Christ Church, Canterbury, Exeter, both Winchester houses and Worcester during the eleventh century.[19] The 'campaign' to propagate the feast arose in the 1120s when it was perhaps re-introduced at those places, and shortly after had spread to Bury St Edmunds, Gloucester, Reading, St Albans, Tewkesbury, Westminster, and Winchcombe.[20] It may well have spread to other houses in the same years but we lack the evidence, although some houses evidently continued to oppose its introduction.[21] Their strong support for the feast of the Conception is undoubtedly the most important single contribution of the twelfth-century English Benedictines to the cult of Mary, not only for England but for the church throughout Europe.

A daily mass of the Virgin in addition to a mass for her on Saturdays was introduced by some Benedictine and Cistercian houses during the twelfth century.[22] The Office of the Virgin as an addition to the office of the day,

---

[18] The text of Eadmer's treatise has been published: *Eadmeri monachi Cantuariensis Tractatus de Conceptione sanctae Mariae*, ed. H. Thurston and T. Slater (Freiburg, 1904).

[19] *Kalendars before A.D. 1100*, pp. 125, 167, 223. See also Clayton, *Cult of the Virgin Mary*, pp. 42–7.

[20] For the texts see Bishop, 'Conception', pp. 247–9 and van Dijk, pp. 429–30 (Gloucester, St Albans, Tewkesbury, Winchcombe, Worcester), 433 (Reading). For individual houses: Gloucester (*Kalendars after A.D. 1100*, p. 55); St Albans (*The St Albans Psalter*, ed. O. Pächt, C. R. Dodwell and F. Wormald (London, 1960), p. 44); Tewkesbury (Cashel, Cathedral Lib. MS 1); Westminster (BL, Royal MS 2.A.xxii); Winchcombe (Valenciennes, Bibl. Mun. MS 116).

[21] In the thirteenth century, in addition to the places already mentioned, the evidence of calendars shows that the feast was celebrated at the following houses: Abingdon (CUL MS Kk.1.22); Carrow (Madrid, Biblioteca Nacional MS 6422); Durham (BL, Harley MS 4664; Bodleian, MS Douce 270); Ely (BL, Arundel MS 377, Harley MS 547); Evesham (BL, Add. MS 44874); Norwich (Cambridge, Corpus Christi College, MS 465; Durham, Ushaw College, MS 7); Peterborough (Cambridge, Fitzwilliam Museum, MS 12, London, Society of Antiquaries MS 59) Ramsey (Cambridge, Corpus Christi College, MS 468; BL, Cotton MS Galba E.x).

[22] See P. Draper, 'Seeing that it was Done at all the Noble Churches in England', in *Medieval Architecture and Intellectual Context: Studies in Honour of Peter Kidson*, ed. E. Fernie and P. Crossley (London, 1990), 137–42, pp. 140–1, for several references relating to the English houses. See van Dijk, 'Origin of the Latin Feast', p. 435 for the daily votive mass of the Virgin at Bury St Edmunds for the prosperity of the king, and J. M. Canal, 'El oficio Parvo de la Virgen de 1000 a 1250', *Ephemerides Mariologicae* 15 (1965), 463–75, p. 464 n. 4 for its use at Bury by the time of Abbot Anselm (d. 1148). The text for the latter is in *Eadmeri*

and/or as a regular Saturday observance, became widespread in both the monastic and secular church from the thirteenth century onwards.[23] In 1100 this was not the case, and some English Benedictine texts of the twelfth century provide evidence for its introduction in various liturgical contexts, both public and private, during that century. For this practice of adding the Office of the Virgin to the office every day there is also Premonstratensian and Augustinian evidence, but not specifically from English manuscripts, and it is likely that the Benedictines were not necessarily the main propagators of the practice to the secular church.[24] The Office of the Virgin was recited in three contexts: (i) daily in the communal liturgy as a supplement to the office of the day; (ii) on Saturdays; (iii) in private recitation.[25]

For the use of the Office of the Virgin in the communal liturgy, probably as a Saturday office in addition to the office of the day, the two extant English monastic breviaries of the mid-twelfth century from St Albans and Winchcombe show that these houses had introduced it by the mid-century with a twelve-lesson matins.[26] There is evidence for the Cistercians in France

Tractatus, p. 104. Evidence for a daily mass of the Virgin at Tewkesbury and Rochester in the first half of the twelfth century is cited in S. E. Roper, *Medieval English Benedictine Liturgy: Studies in the Formation, Structure and Content of the Monastic Votive Office c.950–1450* (New York, 1993), pp. 46–7.

[23] The fundamental study is Bishop, 'On the Origin of the Prymer'. See also J. Leclercq, 'Formes successives de l'Office votif de la Vierge', *Ephemerides Liturgicae* 72 (1958), 294–301; J. Leclercq, 'Formes anciennes de l'office marial', *Ephemerides Liturgicae* 74 (1960), 89–102; J. M. Canal, 'Oficio Parvo de la Virgen: Formas viejas y formas nuevas', *Ephemerides Mariologicae* 11 (1961), 497–525; Canal, 'Oficio Parvo de la Virgen de 1000 a 1250', pp. 463–75; P. Lejay, 'Les accroissements de l'office quotidien', *Revue du Clergé Français* 40 (1904), 113–41. A recent full study of the votive Marian office among the English Benedictines is Roper, *Medieval English Benedictine Liturgy*; see pp. 81–4 for the evidence for the daily recitation of the little office in the English Benedictine houses in the thirteenth century.

[24] D. Knowles, 'The Monastic Horarium, 970–1120', *Downside Review* 51 (1933), 706–25, pp. 723–5; Bishop, 'On the Origin of the Prymer', pp. 228–31 for the Premonstratensian and Augustinian evidence.

[25] See Clayton, *The Cult of the Virgin Mary*, pp. 65–7 on these forms.

[26] For St Albans, BL, Royal MS 2.A.x, fols 135–40v; for Winchcombe, Valenciennes, Bibl. Mun. MS 116, fols 257–8. I am grateful to Michael Gullick for his opinion concerning a c.1125–50 dating of the Winchcombe manuscript. For the St Albans Breviary, see R. M. Thomson, *Manuscripts from St Albans Abbey 1066–1235* (Woodbridge, 1982), p. 94, and for that of Winchcombe, V. Leroquais, *Les Bréviaires manuscrits des bibliothèques publiques de France*, 5 vols (Paris, 1934), IV, p. 285. At both Winchcombe and St Albans the 'commemoration' of Mary was a matins office of twelve lessons. For a full discussion of these and the Saturday office see Roper, *Medieval English Benedictine Liturgy*, pp. 96–103.

having introduced daily recitation of the Office during the second half of the twelfth century, and it can but be assumed that the English Cistercian houses followed the lead of the French houses.[27] Premonstratensian canons and Augustinian canons in some of their houses had introduced this practice by 1150.[28] The Saturday office was already celebrated at Worcester before 1100, as evidenced by the Portiforium of St Wulfstan.[29]

The private recitation of an abbreviated version of the public office, the 'little office of the Virgin', was the form which was eventually to achieve popularity in the secular church, becoming the core text of the book of hours. The earliest examples in England of the little office are either in monastic books or in secular books whose textual evidence strongly suggests that they are derived from either Benedictine or Augustinian models. The little office was already in use at two Benedictine houses before the Conquest: Canterbury, St Augustine's and the New Minster at Winchester.[30] Two examples are found in Benedictine (or perhaps more correctly termed Benedictine-derived) books of the twelfth century: two psalters whose liturgical evidence suggests derivation from Westminster and St Albans.[31] Reference to Abbot Anselm's practice at Bury St Edmunds suggests that the little office was recited there in the twelfth century.[32] For the Cistercians

[27]   *Old French Paraclete Ordinary*, pp. 382–3.
[28]   Bishop, 'On the Origin of the Prymer', pp. 229–31.
[29]   See *The Portiforium of Saint Wulfstan*, ed. A. Hughes, 2 vols, Henry Bradshaw Society, 89–90 (London, 1958–60), II, pp. 60–2 (a three lesson matins office). For the monastic tradition of Saturday as a special day devoted to the Virgin see H. Barré, 'Un plaidoyer monastique pour le samedi Marial', *Revue Bénédictine* 87 (1977), 375–99. General discussions are in L. Gougaud, *Devotional and Ascetic Practices in the Middle Ages* (London, 1927), pp. 66–74, and Y. Congar, 'Incidence ecclésiologique d'un thème de dévotion Mariale', *Mélanges de science religieuse* 7 (1950), 277–92. For the case of Worcester see also Clayton, *Cult of the Virgin Mary*, pp. 77–81.
[30]   For these texts see *Facsimiles of Horae de Beata Maria Virgine from English MSS. of the Eleventh Century*, ed. E. S. Dewick, Henry Bradshaw Society 21 (London, 1902) and Clayton, *Cult of the Virgin Mary*, pp. 65–77.
[31]   Paris, Bibliothèque Nationale MS lat. 10433; BL, Add. MS 21927, fols 101v–115v. The full text of the Paris manuscript is given by J. M. Canal, 'Oficio Parvo de la Virgen: Formas viejas y formas nuevas', pp. 510–24. The evidence for the origin of the text of this manuscript from the Benedictines of Westminster is that the calendar is derived from that of Westminster. See C. M. Kauffmann, *Romanesque Manuscripts 1066–1190*, A Survey of Manuscripts Illuminated in the British Isles, 3 (London, 1975), no. 89.
[32]   Canal, 'Oficio Parvo de la Virgen de 1000 a 1250', p. 464 n. 4. The text is in *Eadmeri Tractatus*, p. 104; 'Hic Anselmus duas apud nos solemnitates instituit ... et cotidie unam missam de ea, et post canonicas horas, alias in honorem eius celebrandas decrevit'.

private recitation evidently existed at the time of Abelard.[33] During the early years of the thirteenth century evidence from the *Ancrene Riwle* and several psalters, to whose text it is appended, show that at that time the little office had been taken up by the secular church.[34] It could be said that the lack of surviving texts of the secular church in the twelfth century prevents any firm conclusion that the little office began first in the monastic church, but that it was introduced from monastic texts into the secular church late in that century seems very likely to have been the case.

The same situation of monastic precedents exists for two of the most popular prayers to the Virgin in later medieval lay devotion, the *Salve Regina* and *O beata et intemerata*. *Salve Regina* began as an antiphon in continental monastic circles in the eleventh century.[35] In its late use in secular books of hours it is said at the conclusion of compline, but it is used as an antiphon in a late twelfth century Benedictine Hours of the Virgin in a psalter whose liturgical evidence suggests that its text is derived from Westminster.[36] The prayer *O beata et intemerata* has its first occurrence in England in Benedictine texts, in the *c.*1125 Durham Prayer Book.[37] During the second half of the century it occurs in a Benedictine compilation of prayers.[38] This prayer book was modified for the use of an Augustinian canoness by changes such as in the prayer to St Benedict where Augustine's name is substituted for that of Benedict and 'bishop' for 'confessor'. Another prayer *Intemerata virgo Maria*, not to be confused with *O beata et intemerata*, occurs in the psalter of north French origin, which later belonged to the nuns of Wherwell.[39] Finally *c.*1200

---

33 *Old French Paraclete Ordinal*, p. 383.

34 See Morgan, *Early Gothic Manuscripts*, I, nos 24, 35, 36, 39, all but no. 36 having close connections with the Augustinians, and Morgan, 'Texts and Images, Thirteenth Century', pp. 72–3 where references for the *Ancrene Riwle* are given.

35 See J. M. Canal, *Salve Regina Misericordiae* (Rome, 1963). For the Cistercians see H. Barré, 'Saint Bernard et le "Salve Regina"', *Marianum* 26 (1964), 208–16. For its occurrence in England in the thirteenth and fourteenth centuries see Morgan, 'Texts and Images, Thirteenth Century', pp. 74–5, 79–80 and 'Texts and Images, Fourteenth Century', p. 43.

36 Paris, Bibliothèque Nationale MS lat. 10433. See Canal, *Salve Regina*, pp. 187, 189, 195.

37 London, Society of Antiquaries MS 7. T. H. Bestul, *A Durham Book of Devotions* (Toronto, 1987), pp. 62–3. This is earlier than the manuscript text evidence cited by A. Wilmart, *Auteurs spirituels et textes dévots du moyen age latin* (Paris, 1932), p. 487. In some texts the opening words are just *O intemerata*.

38 BL, Cotton MS Vespasian D.xxvi; see T. H. Bestul, 'The Collection of St Anselm's Prayers in British Library MS Cotton Vespasian D.XXVI', *Medium Aevum* 47 (1978), 1–5, p. 3.

39 Cambridge, St John's College MS C.18; H. Barré, *Prières Anciennes de l'Occident à la Mère de Dieu* (Paris, 1963), pp. 214–15. Wilmart, *Auteurs spirituels*, p. 487 n. 1

O beata et intemerata occurs in the Westminster Psalter.[40] It occurs occasionally in English thirteenth- and fourteenth-century secular devotional books, perhaps as a result of monastic influence, but its more frequent occurrence is only in the fifteenth century as a result of the influence of imported Flemish and French books of hours.[41] The fact remains that the earliest examples of its use in England are in Benedictine books, and that its use in the secular church in the thirteenth and fourteenth centuries may result from the influence of Benedictine texts and practices.

Another Marian devotion which in the thirteenth and fourteenth centuries is associated with the secular church also has its earliest examples in monastic texts of the twelfth century. This is the form of prayer consisting of salutations and joys of the Virgin each beginning with *Ave* or *Gaude*.[42] Facing the well-known full-page picture of the Virgin and Child in the Shaftesbury Psalter is such a devotion in the form of a prayer of twenty-six invocations to the Virgin each beginning with *Ave*.[43] A similar prayer occurs in the Winchester Psalter, the so-called Psalter of Henry of Blois.[44] A hymn, *Ave, mundi spes, Maria*, with repetitive *Ave*s occurs in the Winchcombe Breviary.[45] Prayers with repetitive *Ave*s such as the Psalter of the Virgin, which became popular in the secular church in the thirteenth century, also continue in Benedictine books such as the Reading Abbey Psalter.[46] Also the Joys of the

---

confuses this prayer with *O beata et intemerata*.

[40] BL, Royal MS 2.A.xxii; Morgan, 'Texts and Images, Thirteenth Century', p. 75.

[41] Morgan, 'Texts and Images, Fourteenth Century', p. 43.

[42] The fundamental study is G. G. Meersseman, *Der Hymnos Akathistos im Abendland*, Spicilegium Friburgense, 2 vols (Freiburg, 1958–60). For their occurrence in England in the thirteenth and fourteenth centuries see Morgan, 'Texts and Images, Thirteenth Century', pp. 74–5 and Morgan, 'Texts and Images, Fourteenth Century', pp. 39–41.

[43] BL, Lansdowne MS 383; the text is published by E. Beck, 'A Twelfth-Century Salutation of Our Lady', *Downside Review* 42 (1924), 185–6. The manuscript was apparently not known to Meersseman. Its text is very close, but not identical, to that he prints from two thirteenth-century manuscripts on pp. 162–3.

[44] BL, Cotton MS Nero C.iv; *The Winchester Psalter*, ed. F. Wormald (London, 1973); Kauffmann, *Romanesque Manuscripts 1066–1190*, no. 78. The prayer, on fol. 134v of the Psalter, is the first of a sequence of Marian prayers following *Suscipere digneris*. It has 31 *Ave* invocations as opposed to the 26 of the Shaftesbury Psalter.

[45] Valenciennes, Bibliothèque Municipale MS 116, fol. 260v. Meersseman, *Hymnos Akathistos*, I, pp. 193, 264.

[46] New York, Pierpont Morgan Library MS M.103, fols 138–57; Morgan, *Early Gothic Manuscripts*, II, no. 106. The text of the Psalter of the Virgin in the Reading Psalter was published in a limited edition, *Laudes Beatae Mariae Virginis* (Kelmscott Press, 1896). At that time the book belonged to William Morris. See also Morgan, 'Texts and Images, Thirteenth Century', pp. 74–5.

Virgin, another popular secular devotion in the thirteenth and fourteenth centuries, occurs at Christ Church, Canterbury in the twelfth century.[47] At Canterbury the *Gaude dei genetrix virgo immaculata* devotion occurs in Eadmer's devotional work *De excellentia gloriosissimae virginis matris Dei* written before 1115.[48]

Although these prayers and prayer forms passed from monastic to popular secular use, some of the monastic prayers seem to have remained largely exclusive to them. An example is one of Carolingian origin, which occurred in several pre-Conquest Anglo-Saxon psalters and prayer books, *Singularis meriti sola sine exemplo.*[49] It is often attributed to the eleventh-century Archbishop Maurilius of Rouen, and also sometimes to St Anselm. It occurs in eleven late eleventh- and twelfth-century English Benedictine psalters and prayer books, but did not become a popular prayer in the secular church.[50]

Equally characteristic of monastic prayer collections, but rarely found in secular books, are the three Marian prayers of St Anselm, *Maria tu illa magna Maria, Sancta et inter sanctos post Deum, Virgo mundo venerabilis mater.*[51] These are often set beside other Marian prayers which came to be attributed to St Anselm but were not by him, the so-called Anselmian apocrypha.[52]

47 Southern, *Anselm and his Biographer*, pp. 289–90. On this *Gaude Dei genetrix* see also Wilmart, *Auteurs spirituels*, pp. 330–3.

48 J.-P. Migne, *Patrologiae Cursus Completus. Series Latina*, 221 vols (Paris, 1844–64), CLIX, col. 568b. See Southern, *Anselm and his Biographer*, pp. 289–90.

49 On this prayer see Wilmart, *Auteurs spirituels*, pp. 480–1 and Barré, *Prières Anciennes*, pp. 73–6 *et passim*.

50 Cambridge, St John's College MS C.18, fol. 219; BL, Cotton MS Vesp. D.xxvi, fols 36v–39; BL, Harley MS 863, fol. 115v; BL, Lansdowne MS 383, fol. 166v; BL, Royal MS 8.D.viii, fol. 2v; Soc. Antiq. MS 7, fol. 106; Madrid, Biblioteca Nacional MS Vit. 23–8, fol. 116; Bodleian, MS Auct. D.2.6, fol. 161–162v; Bodleian, MS Laud Misc. MS 79, fol. 110–111; Rouen, Bibliothèque Municipale MS 231, fol. 133; Verdun, Bibliothèque Municipale MS 70, fol. 62v.

51 *Anselmi Opera Omnia*, ed. F. S. Schmitt, 6 vols (Edinburgh, 1946–51), III, pp. 13–25; *The Prayers and Meditations of St Anselm*, trans. B. Ward (Harmondsworth, 1973), pp. 107–26; A. Wilmart, 'Les propres corrections de St Anselme dans sa grande prière à la Vierge Marie', *Recherches de Théologie Ancienne et Médiévale* 2 (1930), 189–204; T. H. Bestul, 'A Note on the Contents of the Anselm Manuscript, Bodleian Library Laud Misc. 508', *Manuscripta* 12 (1977), 167–70; Bestul, 'Collection of Anselm's Prayers'; *idem* 'The Anselmian Devotions in Chicago Newberry Library MS Newberry 8', *Manuscripta* 30 (1986), 205–8; *idem, Durham Book of Devotions*. For the fundamental study on Anselm's Marian writings see J. S. Bruder, *The Mariology of Saint Anselm of Canterbury* (Dayton, 1939).

52 A. Wilmart, 'La tradition des prières de Saint Anselme', *Revue Bénédictine* 36 (1924), 52–71; T. H. Bestul, 'British Library MS Arundel 60 and the Anselmian

Examples of this would be the Winchester Psalter with many added prayers in Madrid.[53] Other twelfth-century English manuscripts of the Anselm prayers were associated with Durham, Buildwas, Reading and other Benedictine houses.[54]

The contemporary imagery and attributes of the Virgin derive partly from the vocabulary of these antiphons, hymns and prayers, but also from the Old Testament prophecies concerning her, and from Marian theological writings which from the late eleventh century had proliferated among the Benedictines and Cistercians. The emphasis on her as a personification of the Church and as Queen was strong in these writings.[55] Even her role as Mother of Mercy, so popular in fourteenth- and fifteenth-century secular devotion, is anticipated in the writings of Eadmer of Canterbury and in English twelfth-century monastic prayers.[56]

Apocrypha', *Scriptorium* 35 (1981), 271–5.

[53]   Kauffmann, *Romanesque Manuscripts*, no. 77.

[54]   Cambridge, Jesus College MS 76 (Durham); Cambridge, Pembroke College MS 154 (Buildwas); Chicago, Newberry Library MS 8; BL, Cotton MS Vespasian D.xxvi (unknown Benedictine house); London, Society of Antiquaries MS 7 (Durham); Bodleian, MS Auct. D.2.6; Bodleian, MS Laud Misc. 79 (Reading); Bodleian, MS Laud Misc. 508; Bodleian, MS Rawl. C.149; Verdun, Bibliothèque Municipale MS 70. Kauffmann, *Romanesque Manuscripts*, nos 31, 75; T. H. Bestul, 'The Verdun Anselm, Ralph of Battle, and the Formation of the Anselmian Apocrypha', *Revue Bénédictine* 87 (1977), 383–9. On the illustrations of these see O. Pächt, 'The Illustrations of St Anselm's Prayers and Meditations', *Journal of the Warburg and Courtauld Institutes* 19 (1956), 68–82 and D. M. Sheppard, 'Conventual Use of St Anselm's Prayers and Meditations', *Rutgers Art Review* 9/10 (1988/89), 1–16.

[55]   H. Barré, 'Marie et l'Eglise du Vénérable Bède à Saint Albert le Grand', *Bulletin de la Société Française d'Études Mariales* 9 (1954), 59–154; H. Coathalem, *Le parallelisme entre la Sainte Vierge et l'Église dans la tradition latine jusqu'à la fin du XII siècle* (Rome, 1954); I. Riudor, 'La realeza de Maria en Eadmero', *Estudios Marianos* 17 (1956), 125–9; H. Barré, 'La Royautée de Marie au XIIe siècle en Occident', *Maria et Ecclesia: Acta Congressus Mariologici-Mariani Lourdes 1958*, 16 vols (Rome 1959), V, 93–119; J. Leclercq, '"Marie Reine" dans les sermons de Saint Bernard', *Collectanea Ordinis Cisterciensium Reformatorum* 26 (1964), 266–76; M. L. Thérel, *Le Triomphe de la Vierge-Église* (Paris, 1984), pp. 117–49, 224–30. See also the important review article of Thérel: P. Skubiszewski, 'Les impondérables de la recherche iconographique. À propos d'un livre récent sur le thème de la glorification de l'Église et de la Vierge dans l'art médiéval', *Cahiers de Civilsation Médiévale* 30 (1987), 145–53. St Anselm in his prayer, *Maria tu illa magna Maria* refers to her as 'Queen of Angels'. She is referred to as Queen of Heaven in the *Ave* prayers in the Shaftesbury and Winchester (Henry of Blois) Psalters, and of course as Queen in the *Salve Regina*.

[56]   H. J. Brosch, 'Die Anrufung Marias als Mutter der Barmherzigkeit bei Eadmer',

The most extensive evidence of the imagery of the Virgin in the English monastic church in the twelfth century is in the form of seals. Two articles by T. A. Heslop have used the seals as evidence of the attributes of the Virgin.[57] From the early years of the century the crowned figure is usual and she frequently holds a foliate stem. In the seal of St Mary's, York, c.1100-20 a star is also present.[58] The star and the foliate stem refer to the prophecies of Balaam and Isaiah concerning the coming of the Messiah: 'A star shall arise out of Jacob and a sceptre shall spring up from Israel' (Numbers, xxiv. 17), and 'and there shall come forth a rod out of the root of Jesse, and a flower shall rise up out of his root' (Isaiah, xi. 1). The crowned figure has precedents in the diadem set on her head in some of the pre-Conquest images, but reflects the increasing tendency to refer to Mary as Queen in hymns and prayers in the twelfth century.[59] She is not only crowned as a seated figure as in the seals of Abingdon and Great Malvern, but also in narrative scenes such as the Pentecost of the Shaftesbury Psalter or the Adoration of the Magi in the St Albans Psalter, Psalm 71 initial, where she also holds a flowering rod.[60] In nearly all cases, as Heslop has argued, the rod she holds is more likely a reference to the flowering rod of Isaiah's prophecy rather than intended as a royal sceptre. The Reading Abbey seal has the flowering rod surmounted by the dove of the Holy Spirit, and the foot of the rod is bulbous, signifying a plant.[61] This latter feature and the dove is also in the illustration of the Virgin and Child in the c.1130-40 Augustine on Psalms from Eynsham Abbey.[62] The

---

De cultu Mariano saeculis VI–XI, Acta Congressus Mariologici Mariani, Croatia (1971) (Rome, 1972), 499–514. She is referred to as Mother of Mercy in the prayer on fol. 135 of the Winchester (Henry of Blois) Psalter: 'O Maria piissima, stella maris clarissima mater misericordie et aula pudicitie'. St Anselm in his prayer *Sancta et inter sanctos* refers to her as 'shrine of mercy'. The twelfth-century texts of the *Salve Regina* begin *Salve Regina misericordie*, the form *Salve Regina mater misericordie* being introduced later.

[57] T. A. Heslop, 'The Romanesque Seal of Worcester Cathedral', in *Medieval Art and Architecture at Worcester Cathedral*, British Archaeological Association Conference Transactions (1975) (Leeds, 1978), 71–9; *idem*, 'The Virgin Mary's Regalia and 12th-century English Seals', in *The Vanishing Past* 53–62.

[58] Heslop, 'Virgin Mary's Regalia', pls 5.1, 5.2.

[59] For the 'diadem' on her head in tenth- and eleventh-century works see: E. Temple, *Anglo-Saxon Manuscripts 900–1066*, A Survey of Manuscripts Illuminated in the British Isles, 2 (London, 1976), nos 77, 84, figs 245, 262.

[60] F. Saxl, *English Sculptures of the Twelfth Century* (London, 1954), fig. Vd; Kauffmann, *Romanesque Manuscripts*, no. 48, fig. 132; Heslop, 'Virgin Mary's Regalia', pl. 5.4; *St Albans Psalter*, p. 230, pl. 63a.

[61] Saxl, *English Sculptures*, fig. VIc; Heslop, 'Virgin Mary's Regalia', pl. 5.5.

[62] Bodleian, MS Bodley 269; F. Wormald, 'A Romanesque Drawing at Oxford', *Antiquaries Journal* 22 (1942), 17–21; Kauffmann, *Romanesque Manuscripts*, no. 52,

dove signifies 'the spirit of the Lord' which shall rest on the rod that shall spring from the root of Jesse according to Isaiah's prophecy of the Messiah (Isaiah xi. 2). In the seals of Abingdon, Great Malvern, Pershore and Worcester she holds a round object, probably a fruit to symbolise the 'fruit of thy womb', a phrase which occurs in both the *Ave Maria* and the *Salve Regina*.[63]

In manuscript illumination and wall painting the crowned figure of the Virgin emerges in the first half of the twelfth century. A female donor kneels before the crowned Virgin in the psalter whose calendar and litany show clear derivation from the Benedictine nunnery of Shaftesbury (Pl. 7).[64] The copy of St Anselm's Prayers and Meditations perhaps made for Premonstratensian canons or Augustinian canonesses, has the crowned Virgin in the initial to the prayer *Virgo mundo venerabilis mater* (Pl. 8).[65] In wall painting at Kempley (*c*.1125–50) and Stowell (late twelfth century), both secular parish churches, the crowned Virgin occurs in the contexts of Christ in Majesty with the Virgin and St Peter, and that of the Last Judgement.[66]

The type of the crowned Virgin in which the crown has finials and is not of diadem form, as in Anglo-Saxon examples, occurs on nearly all the monastic seals. The diadem form, reminiscent of the headgear of a Byzantine empress, had appeared early in the middle ages, above all in Rome. The *c*.700 icon in S. Maria in Trastevere shows her wearing such an object.[67] Probably from the influence of Carolingian or Byzantine images of her wearing this diadem the Anglo–Saxons in the eleventh century portrayed a similar form of headdress. She is so depicted when personifying Ecclesia, the Church, in the Bury St Edmunds Psalter of *c*.1030.[68] This diadem type with added finials continues in some works of the twelfth century such as the figure, again a personification of the Church, in St Augustine's *City of God* from St Augustine's, Canterbury.[69] In this she holds an open book, perhaps signifying

fig. 135.

[63] Heslop, 'Romanesque Seal of Worcester', p. 75.

[64] BL, Lansdowne MS 383, fol. 165v; Kauffmann, *Romanesque Manuscripts*, no. 48; M. A. Farley and F. Wormald, 'Three Related English Romanesque Manuscripts', *Art Bulletin* 22 (1940), 157–60.

[65] Bodleian, MS Auct. D.2.6, fols 156–200, fol. 158v; Kauffmann, *Romanesque Manuscripts*, no. 75, fig. 210. Sheppard, 'Conventual Use', p. 2, fig. 1 considers that the book was originally for the Augustinian canonesses of Harrold.

[66] E. W. Tristram, *English Medieval Wall Painting: the Twelfth Century* (Oxford, 1944, repr. New York, 1988), pp. 135, 147, pls 60, 67–8.

[67] J. Beckwith, *Early Christian and Byzantine Art* (Harmondsworth, 1970), pl. 77.

[68] Temple, *Anglo-Saxon Manuscripts*, no. 77, fig. 262.

[69] Kauffmann, *Romanesque Manuscripts*, no. 19, fig. 50. The diadem with finials also occurs in three Norman depictions of the Assumption of the second half of the eleventh century: a Gospels from Jumièges (BL, Add. MS 17739); a sacramentary

the gospels, and a flowering rod surmounted by a dove. This seems a unique case in England of the Virgin holding such an object when personifying the Church. The likely stimulus for the change from the diadem-type crown to the crown with finials is from Rome, where such an innovation took place c.1120-40, despite the strength there of the old tradition of the diadem.[70] The probable first instance is the now lost 1122-4 mosaic of the enthroned Virgin and Child between Saints Silvester and Anastasius in the St Nicholas chapel of the Lateran Palace, to be followed shortly in c.1140 by the apse mosaic of the Coronation of the Virgin in S. Maria in Trastevere.[71] The figure in the St Nicholas chapel has the symmetrical placing of the Child in front of the Virgin, a feature combined with the crown found in many English monastic seals of the period c.1120-50, such as that of Great Malvern of c.1140.[72] As so often in the history of art, innovations in Rome were quickly taken up elsewhere in Europe.

In spite of these early examples of the crowned Virgin in Rome the subject of the Coronation of the Virgin did not itself begin there, and the earliest example of the theme in European art occurs in a sculpted capital from the Benedictine abbey of Reading of c.1125, significantly in the same decade as the controversy over the feast of the Conception of the Virgin.[73]

from Mont St Michel (New York, Pierpont Morgan Library MS M.641); a homiliary from Jumièges (Rouen, Bibliothèque Municipale MS 1408). For plates see P. Verdier, *Le Couronnement de la Vierge* (Montreal, 1980), pls 66, 67 and Thérel, *Triomphe de la Vierge-Église*, fig. 23. The association of the crown with the Death and Assumption of the Virgin has precedents in the scenes of the Death of the Virgin in the c.980 Benedictional of St Ethelwold and Sacramentary of Robert of Jumièges in which the hand of God holds a crown (with finials) above the dying Virgin. For plates and descriptions see Temple, *Anglo-Saxon Manuscripts*, nos 23, 24, fig. 87 and Thérel, *Triomphe de la Vierge*, fig. 11.

[70]   On this see U. Nilgen, 'Maria Regina – ein politischer Kultbildtypus?', *Römisches Jahrbuch für Kunstgeschichte* 19 (1981), 3-33, with figs 2, 3 of 17th/18th-century engravings and watercolours of the St Nicholas chapel mosaic in the Lateran Palace.

[71]   On the iconography of the S. Maria in Trastevere mosaic see M. Lawrence, 'Maria Regina', *Art Bulletin* 7 (1925), 150-61; G. A. Wellen, 'Sponsa Christi. Het absimosaiek van de Santa Maria in Trastevere te Rome en het hooglied', *Festbundel für F. van der Meer* (Brussels, 1966), 148-59; J. E. Barclay Lloyd, 'Das goldene Gewand der Muttergottes in der Bildersprache mittelalterlicher und frühchristlicher Mosaiken in Rom', *Römische Quartalschrift* 85 (1990), 66-85. I am grateful to my colleague Joan Barclay Lloyd for information on the iconography of the Virgin in Rome.

[72]   Saxl, *English Sculptures*, pl. Vd.

[73]   G. Zarnecki, 'The Coronation of the Virgin from Reading Abbey', *Journal of the Warburg and Courtauld Institutes* 13 (1950), 1-12. The early development of the Coronation of the Virgin is admirably surveyed in Verdier, *Couronnement de la*

With the rise of this theme the Virgin as a crowned figure doubtless became increasingly popular, and even when personified as the Church, Mary is often crowned. This is the case in the initial to Habakkuk in the Lambeth Bible of *c.*1150, either from St Augustine's Canterbury or St Albans.[74] An enigmatic image is the initial to Ecclesiasticus in the Winchester Bible of *c.*1160, a crowned female figure holding a book and an orb.[75] A later hand has inscribed this figure as *Fides*, but this identification seems unlikely, and the Virgin personified as Wisdom (*Sapientia*) seems plausible.[76] Aelred of Rievaulx, in his sermon 21 (*olim* 25) *De Beata Maria* for the feast of the Assumption, likens Mary to the strong and wise woman of Proverbs xxxi. 10, 26, *mulierem quandam fortem, sapientem.*[77] The sermon contrasts Mary as the strong and wise woman with Eve as the weak and foolish woman whose foolishness was taken advantage of by the Devil. The image for Ecclesiasticus in the *c.*1180 Giffard Bible shows Wisdom as a crowned woman holding a sceptre and treading on the lion and the basilisk, symbols of evil, a precursor of the image of the Virgin treading on these creatures found in thirteenth-century England.[78] An analogous image showing the Virgin beside Christ victorious over the Devil, who is under their feet, is in the initial at the beginning of Boethius's *De Musica* from Christ Church Canterbury (Pl. 9).[79]

---

[74] *Vierge.*
Lambeth Palace Library MS 3; Kauffmann, *Romanesque Manuscripts*, no. 70, fig. 193. For arguments for a possible St Albans place of origin see Thomson, *Manuscripts from St Albans*, pp. 31–3.

[75] *Two Winchester Bibles*, ed. W. Oakeshott (Oxford, 1981), p. 57, fig. 63.

[76] For the iconography of Sapientia see M. T. D'Alverny, 'La Sagesse et ses sept filles: Recherches sur les allégories de la Philosophie et des Arts Libéraux du IXe au XIIe siècle', *Mélanges Felix Grat*, I (Paris, 1946), 245–78; 'Sapientia', *Lexikon der Christlichen Ikonographie*, 8 vols (Rome, 1968–76), IV, cols 39–43. An explicit case of the Virgin personified as Wisdom is in the early thirteenth-century Lower Saxon Brandenburg Evangelistary. Surrounded by Prophets, crowned, holding a sceptre with bulb and flower, she bears a scroll inscribed with Ecclesiasticus xxiv. 6; 'Ego in altissimis habitavi et thronus meus in columna nubis'. For a reproduction see G. Schiller, *Ikonographie der christlichen Kunst*, 5 vols in 7 (Gütersloh, 1966–91), IV (i), fig. 172.

[77] Migne, *Patrologiae*, CXCV, col. 353 and Raciti, *Aelredi Rievallensis. Sermones I–XLVI*, p. 64 (Sermon XXI). The old numbering in Migne was XXV.

[78] Bodleian, MS Laud Misc. 752; on the manuscript see Kauffmann, *Romanesque Manuscripts*, no. 103 and *The Giffard Bible: Bodleian Library MS Laud Misc. 752*, ed. J. M. Sheppard (New York, 1986), pp. 130, 159–71, pl. 79 for a discussion of the Ecclesiasticus initial. Sheppard argues for a French origin for the Giffard Bible, and several campaigns of illumination *c.*1150–1210. For the imagery of the Virgin treading on the lion and the serpent (basilisk) in England see Morgan, 'Texts and Images, Thirteenth Century', pp. 89–92.

[79] CUL MS Ii.3.12, fol. 62v; Kauffmann, *Romanesque Manuscripts*, no. 41, fig. 115;

The Tree of Jesse, originating as a pictorial theme in Benedictine and Cistercian circles in France in the 1120s, was taken up almost immediately by the English Benedictines as evidenced by the Shaftesbury and Winchester Psalters and the Lambeth Bible (Pls 10, 11).[80] The possibilities offered by this subject for emblematic symbolism and theological content must have suited the taste for such imagery among the monastic orders. The Virgin in both the Shaftesbury and Winchester Psalters is shown crowned, flanked by prophets with scrolls proclaiming the coming of the Messiah. The figure of the Virgin is absolutely central to the growing plant and is thus the focus of the composition. In the Lambeth Bible the centrality of the Virgin, unusually not crowned, is stressed even more.[81] She is the sole ancestor forming the trunk of the tree between Jesse and Christ. Similarly in the St Augustine's, Canterbury, *City of God*, in the illustration of heaven she personifies the Church triumphant set directly below Christ in the Heavenly City.[82] The Tree of Jesse is another example of a theme which begins in monastic (Benedictine) circles and then spreads to the secular church. In the late twelfth and early thirteenth century it occurs in several secular psalters.[83]

The monastic preference for symbolic meaning in the figure of the Virgin, personifying the Church or as the woman who fulfilled the prophecies of the coming of the Messiah, is also evident in the image of her as Bride of Christ, the *Sponsa-Sponsus* of the Song of Songs so eloquently interpreted in Benedictine, Cistercian and Augustinian commentaries on the text.[84] The only images of the theme which survive from twelfth-century England are Benedictine. In the St Albans copy of Bede's Commentary on the Song of Songs the Bridegroom is clearly intended as Christ in view of the facial type, although the cross nimbus is lacking (Pl. 12).[85] The Virgin as Bride personifies the Church who is wedded to Christ. In the Winchester Bible initial of the Song of Songs the Bridegroom is portrayed as King Solomon, author of the

Thérel, *Triomphe de la Vierge*, p. 181, fig. 80.

[80] A Watson, *The Early Iconography of the Tree of Jesse* (Oxford, 1934), pp. 99–106, pls XV, XVII, XVIII. On these manuscripts see Kauffmann, *Romanesque Manuscripts*, nos 48, 70, 78. For a survey of Tree of Jesse iconography, see 'Wurzel Jesse', *Lexikon der Christlichen Ikonographie*, IV, cols 549–58.

[81] C. R. Dodwell, *The Great Lambeth Bible* (London, 1959), p. 26, pl. 4 for a commentary on the image.

[82] Kauffmann, *Romanesque Manuscripts*, no. 19, fig. 50.

[83] E.g. Morgan, *Early Gothic Manuscripts*, I, nos 23, 30, 72, 74, figs 107, 239.

[84] J. Beumer, 'Die marianische Deutung des Hohen Liedes in der Frühscholastik', *Zeitschrift für katholische Theologie* 76 (1954), 411–39.

[85] Cambridge, King's College MS 19, fol. 21v; Kauffmann, *Romanesque Manuscripts*, p. 38, fig. 40; Thomson, *Manuscripts from St Albans Abbey*, p. 84, fig. 51. For a survey of the iconography see 'Bräutigam und Braut', *Lexikon der Christlichen Ikonographie*, I, cols. 318–24.

Song.[86] Beside him, designated by an inscription, is the 'voice of the Church longing for the coming of Christ'. This too is in the form of the Virgin, crowned and holding the flowering stem so ubiquitous in English twelfth-century Benedictine images of her. In using her as the allegory of the Church which is to come this is an image of her predestination. The predestination of Mary and the Church referred to in the text from Ecclesiasticus xxiv. 14, was frequently used as a reading in the Marian offices and singled out in commentaries as referring to her: 'Ab initio et ante saecula creata sum, et usque ad futurum saeculum non desinam' (created from the beginning and before all ages, and I shall not end even unto eternity).[87] The Puiset Bible from Durham has an initial to the Song of Songs which is lost, but the inscription *Rex et Regina* remains.[88] In the Giffard Bible the *Sponsa* and *Sponsus* are represented as a cross-nimbed Christ standing beside a crowned woman, the pair surrounded by a group of people.[89] The allegorical and symbolic Marian imagery presented in these images, so characteristic of twelfth-century monastic thought, continued on in the thirteenth century in texts, but not much in the form of visual images. The humanising, physically tangible and active images of Mary discussed in my earlier papers came to replace the formal theological type. In a way the emotional embrace of the Bride and Bridegroom in the allegorical image of the St Albans Song of Songs, and the active pose and courtly context of the Bride in the Winchester Bible, show, albeit in the form of allegory, the humanising traits which will be developed in the thirteenth-century images of Mary for the secular church.

It remains to reflect on the way in which the devotional texts and art of monastic communities could have been transmitted to the wider world to influence the secular church. Examples of both texts and images have been taken from several psalters, the Madrid, St Albans, Shaftesbury and Winchester Psalters,[90] whose liturgical contents suggest a close association with the Benedictine Abbeys of St Albans, Shaftesbury and one or both of the Winchester houses.[91] It seems likely that all four books were probably not intended for internal use by the abbeys themselves, but were made for

---

[86]   *Two Winchester Bibles*, p. 43, fig. 34.

[87]   See Clayton, *Cult of the Virgin Mary*, pp. 68–9 for the text in the Winchester eleventh-century office.

[88]   Durham, Cathedral Library MS A.II.1; Kauffmann, *Romanesque Manuscripts*, no. 98. Barré, 'Royauté de Marie', pp. 96, 113, cites the use of the title *Sponsa Regis* by Aelred of Rievaulx.

[89]   Bodleian, MS Laud Miss. 792; *Giffard Bible*, pp. 128–9, pl. 76, but considering the manuscript to be a French product.

[90]   Kauffmann, *Romanesque Manuscripts*, nos 29, 48, 77, 78.

[91]   On their texts and provenance see Kauffmann, *Romanesque Manuscripts*, nos 29, 48, 77, 78; *St Albans Psalter; Winchester Psalter*.

persons, perhaps laymen or laywomen, outside the monastic community. In the case of the St Albans Psalter the recipient was at least in a semi-religious context, the hermitess Christina of Markyate.[92] The elegantly dressed lady who kneels before the image of the Virgin in the Shaftesbury Psalter, presumably the intended owner, is difficult to conceive of as a Benedictine nun.[93] The Madrid Psalter's calendar, although close to that of Hyde Abbey, Winchester, is clearly not a proper calendar either of that house or of the cathedral priory, and a similar but not identical sort of Winchester-derived calendar occurs in the so-called Psalter of Henry of Blois.[94] For the latter I argued many years ago that the book might indeed be for Bishop Henry of Blois, but now tend to think the psalter's visual content, if not its textual content, might be more suitable for a lay person. The one problem about lay ownership for this psalter and the Madrid Psalter is their extensive collections of prayers appended to the psalter text. Such extensive sets of prayers are not characteristic of psalters for lay people but are indicative of a monastic user.[95] If additional prayers are found in lay people's psalters, and the bulk of information admittedly is derived from thirteenth- and fourteenth-century examples, they are few in number and popular in nature, such as the *O intemerata*, *Salve Regina*, the Joys of the Virgin and *memoriae* of the saints derived from lauds in books of hours.[96] The prayer collections in the Madrid and Winchester Psalters seem to be certainly derived from monastic books, and if these two psalters were intended for the laity it must be assumed that little modification of this text element was made. These four psalters provide evidence, perhaps for some of them disputable, that devotional books may have been provided for the laity through some direct link of their patronage with a monastic house whereby the text and pictorial models were either provided from a monastic example, or that the scribes and illuminators worked in collaboration with a monastic scriptorium.[97] Such contacts seem to

---

[92] *St Albans Psalter*, pp. 27–30, 277–9 for Christina of Markyate.

[93] D. H. Turner, *Romanesque Illuminated Manuscripts* (London, 1966), p. 8 describes the woman as 'a lady connected with Shaftesbury Abbey'.

[94] On these calendars see H. Buchthal, *Miniature Painting in the Latin Kingdom of Jerusalem* (Oxford, 1957), p. 123; Morgan, 'Notes on the Post-Conquest Calendar', p. 153.

[95] For the evidence for this from the English psalters of the thirteenth century, in which all the psalters having extensive prayers are Benedictine, see Morgan, *Early Gothic Manuscripts*, I, nos 2, 47; II, nos 111, 140–41 (Benedictine-derived).

[96] Examples of secular psalters with prayers see Morgan, *Early Gothic Manuscripts*, II, no. 118; *idem* 'Texts and Images, Thirteenth Century', pp. 74–6; L. F. Sandler, *Gothic Manuscripts 1285–1385*, A Survey of Manuscripts Illuminated in the British Isles 5 (London, 1986), nos 10, 80 and Morgan, 'Texts and Images, Fourteenth Century', pp. 39–40.

[97] See J. J. G. Alexander, *Medieval Illuminators and their Methods of Work* (London,

have existed not only between lay persons and the Benedictines but also with the Augustinian canons. The famous Copenhagen and Glasgow luxury psalters have Augustinian calendars, but it has been questioned whether they were actually made for internal use in Augustinian houses or alternatively were produced for lay persons, probably patrons of the Augustinian canons, using an Augustinian text model.[98]

For all these psalters firm evidence is lacking for their intended ownership. If they were produced for lay persons, as the character of their text contents suggests, then they provide good examples of how monastic texts and images were transmitted to a wider circle of society in the twelfth century. By the end of the century scribes and illuminators seem to have become more independent of the monastic scriptorium, and the production of books for the laity only rarely involved a monastic house.[99] The evidence from the very large number of extant psalters produced in the thirteenth century makes this quite clear. In the twelfth century the situation seems to have been different, and the circumstances of production of such books provided a link between the Marian devotions of the monastic orders and those of secular society.

1992), pp. 12–22, for the status of scribes and illuminators in the twelfth century.

[98] Copenhagen Royal Library, Thott MS 143.2°; Glasgow, University Library, Hunter MS U.3.2; Kauffmann, *Romanesque Manuscripts*, nos 95, 96; T. S. R. Boase, *The York Psalter* (London, 1962); P. Stirnemann, 'The Copenhagen Psalter', unpublished Ph.D. dissertation (Columbia, 1976), pp. 175–9 suggesting a lay patron linked to the Augustinians.

[99] See Morgan, *Early Gothic Manuscripts*, I, pp. 14–15.

Peterborough, from St Aethelwold to Martin de Bec, c.970–1155

D. F. MACKRETH

The place of Peterborough in history has generally been limited to its refoundation during the Benedictine reform of the later tenth century within Aethelwold's sphere of influence.[1] Moreover, the significance of its name has been ignored. Yet archaeological evidence shows that the use of 'burgh' denoted something tangible, and that the place was once slightly more than just the rather large monastery on the edge of the fens which it remained for the bulk of the four centuries before the Dissolution.

The modern history of Peterborough begins effectively with Aethelwold's introduction of the Benedictine Rule into the monastery. The old story of the destruction of Medeshamstede by the Danes is a twelfth-century fiction: Sir Frank Stenton demonstrated long ago that the archives of Peterborough contained Middle Saxon material, and Hugh Candidus recognised that anything like this surviving from before the supposed destruction needed to be explained away, hence his comment that old privileges were found in a hole in a ruined wall.[2] The Peterborough Chronicle also records the same explanation, incorporating it into a fanciful narrative.[3]

The date of the refoundation is not precisely known. The record of Aethelwold's gifts to Medeshamstede is unlikely to have been as early as 963, and 972 is the date given in the forged Edgar charter.[4] The surviving *vitae* of

---

[1] See for instance Edmund King, *Peterborough Abbey, 1086–1310: a Study in the Land Market* (Cambridge, 1973), p. 6.

[2] F. M. Stenton, 'Medeshamstede and its Colonies', in *Historical Essays in Honour of James Tait*, ed. J. G. Edwards, V. H. Galbraith and E. F. Jacob (Manchester, 1933), 313–26, reprinted in his *Preparatory to Anglo-Saxon England* (Oxford, 1970), 179–92; *The Chronicle of Hugh Candidus, a Monk of Peterborough*, ed. W. T. Mellows and A. Bell (Oxford, 1949), p. 31; *The Peterborough Chronicle of Hugh Candidus*, ed. W. T. Mellows, 2nd edn (Peterborough, 1966), p. 17.

[3] Anglo-Saxon Chronicle, translated in *English Historical Documents, c.500–1042*, ed. D. Whitelock, 2nd edn (London, 1979), 'E', *s.a.* 963.

[4] Peter Sawyer, *Anglo-Saxon Charters: an Annotated List and Bibliography* (London, 1968), nos 1448, 787.

137

the reforming saints are, of course, concerned with these individuals as men of God and, inevitably also, with the wonders performed for whichever house prepared the biography. The energetic Aethelwold received only an ill-balanced record: Wulfstan's *Life*, abbreviated by Aelfric, is mainly concerned with Abingdon and Winchester.[5] However, what can be detected was a complex operation being carried out by a master politician. The latter aspect of Aethelwold's moves is well exemplified in his basically successful attempt to remove the lands given to the reformed houses from the sphere of influence of local lay interests by placing them under the protection of the king.[6] It may be that, at one level, only the Peterborough tradition gives a reasonable account of what was actually carried out.

Hugh Candidus' account of Aethelwold is broader in its scope than the surviving tradition attached to Ely, and neither Crowland nor Thorney has anything of value to relate.[7] Hugh, although concerned with Peterborough, gives notices of Thorney, Ely, Abingdon and the three minsters in Winchester, which he tells us he culled from a *vita*, which was Wulfstan's.[8] The same almost certainly applied to Ely, and the Anonymous of Ramsey is full of the benefactions of Oswald there.[9] Therefore the additional elements in Hugh's story of the foundation should not be lightly disregarded, although writing in the middle of the twelfth century he obviously had no good idea of the workings of the late Saxon state, and even less of the thinking behind the reform movement itself.

He describes Aethelwold's visitation to Medeshamstede: God had appeared and told the bishop to go to Middle Anglia and restore a monastery to St Peter. Aethelwold arrived at Oundle and paused there, thinking that was the place, and began to build, but God appeared a second time and corrected the mistake.[10] Placing this story in the context of the later tenth century, it could be that Aethelwold had a choice of reviving either Wilfrid's monastery or the first monastery in Mercia which still had some record of its past. His

---

5   D. J. V. Fisher, 'The Early Biographers of St Ethelwold', *English Historical Review* 67 (1952), 381–91.

6   D. H. Farmer, 'The Progress of the Monastic Revival', in *Tenth-Century Studies: Essays in Commemoration of the Millennium of the Council of Winchester and Regularis Concordia*, ed. David Parsons (London, 1975), 10–19.

7   *Liber Eliensis*, ed. E. O. Blake, Camden Society 3rd ser. 92 (London, 1962), pp. 72–121; D. Whitelock, 'The Conversion of the Eastern Danelaw', *Saga-Book of the Viking Society* 12 (1937–45), 159–76, p. 174.

8   *Chronicle of Hugh Candidus* (1949), pp. 42–7, (1966), pp. 22–5; Wulfstan of Winchester, *Life of St Aethelwold*, ed. M. Lapidge and W. Winterbottom (Oxford, 1991), pp. cxli–cxlii.

9   Wulfstan, *Life of St Aethelwold*, p. 39 n. 5; Anonymous of Ramsey, in *English Historical Documents*, I, p. 236.

10   *Chronicle of Hugh Candidus* (1949), pp. 27–8, (1966), p. 15.

decision was clear: at the simplest level, he chose the latter and gave the former to it.

Why he chose Medeshamstede is, at the same simple level, unknowable; perhaps local landed interests made Oundle less desirable, or the former had greater customary dues,[11] or a site on the fen edge had the greater economic advantages. However, other factors probably came into play before Aethelwold could even make a decision. The distribution of the reform movement's monasteries has been remarked on in general terms,[12] but the distribution in the southern Danelaw is remarkable: Oswald's Ramsey lies in Huntingdonshire, Thorney belongs to Cambridgeshire, Crowland to Lincolnshire, while Northamptonshire has Medeshamstede. Adding to this, it can be argued that Ely belongs to East Anglia. Surely here is evidence of a policy of providing, in broad terms, one monastery for each shire or region in the southern Danelaw. In this context, it is worth considering that Breedon had been intended by Aethelwold for Leicestershire, although this failed.[13] The late arrival of monasticism in the more strongly Danish areas in the Danelaw and the north suggests that the reformers were aware of the difficulties.

To return to Oundle, the community had passed into oblivion following the death of Wilfrid, but it is mentioned in the annal for 957 in the Anglo-Saxon Chronicle 'D' version: 'in this year archbishop Wulfstan passed away on 16 December and he was buried at Oundle'. The archbishop was Wulfstan I of York: had Oundle reverted to the metropolitan as an estate, or survived in some form to be a standard staging post for archbishops *en route* north or south? Or was it possibly a gift, like that of Southwell to Wulfstan's successor, Oscytel, from Eadwig, which became not only the seat of a minster, but also a staging post for archbishops?[14] Hence it is just possible that Wulfstan had been given Oundle for the same purpose; but the church in which Wulfstan was buried appears not to have been of an ordinary kind.

Rollason, in dealing with the list of resting places of saints in Anglo-Saxon England, has defined two layers in its composition, both eleventh-century in their final form.[15] The two parts are territorially distinct, the

---

[11]   Sawyer, *Anglo-Saxon Charters*, no. 1448.

[12]   Farmer, 'Progress of Monastic Revival'; D. J. V. Fisher, *The Anglo-Saxon Age, c.400–1041* (London, 1973), pp. 288–9; F. M. Stenton, *Anglo-Saxon England*, 3rd edn (Oxford, 1971), pp. 450–2.

[13]   D. Parsons, 'A Note on the Breedon Angel', *Transactions of the Leicestershire Archaeological and Historical Society* 51 (1975–6), 40–3, pp. 40–1; Sawyer, *Anglo-Saxon Charters*, no. 749.

[14]   Sawyer, *Anglo-Saxon Charters*, no. 659.

[15]   D. W. Rollason, 'Lists of Saints' Resting Places in Anglo-Saxon England', *Anglo-Saxon England* 7 (1979), 61–93.

earlier being confined to Northumbria and Mercia in the days of its greatest hegemony, with Wessex and the lands south of the Thames being excluded.[16] Although subject to revision as is any catalogue, the dating of the first part is distinctly tenth century at the latest and probably not later than the mid-ninth.[17] The difference between the layers shows well when it comes to Peterborough: in the earlier stratum, the place is called Medeshamstede and houses St Botulf, who is absent from Hugh Candidus' list of relics;[18] in the second part, the monastery appears as Burh and has saints Florentinus, Cynebergha and Cyneswitha. St Florentinus was acquired during Abbot Aelfsige's attendance on Aethelred II's queen in Gaul in 1013–17.[19] In the earlier layer, Oundle occurs as the burial place of a St Cett who does not figure in any later tradition associated either with Oundle, which became a possession of Peterborough, or with Peterborough itself. As no other entry in the list can be shown to be wrong-headed, there are reasonable grounds for thinking that Oundle had been a notable church property.

Aethelwold's choice, therefore, was not as simple as it looks: Oundle very probably lay in Oswald's hands as archbishop of York. Therefore, these transactions were probably the result of agreement between all parties. The possibility that Oswald had to be compensated for the loss of Oundle provides the perfect background for his singular interest in Ramsey: for all that it was supposed to have been founded by a layman, it was the saint's guiding hand which is obvious.[20] The grand plan suggested above would have required a monastery in Huntingdonshire where no ancient monastery is known, or rather none which could be revived. Therefore, there were no ancient church lands which could be put into the king's hands for redistribution, but a private landowner, with the permission of the king, could grant land away.

The surprising fact about Peterborough is that, while it was well known that there had been no truly corporate life in the town before 1874, no one had asked why 'borough' was part of the name. Little attention has been paid to Hugh Candidus' description of Martin de Bec's deeds which included changing the site of the town, it being assumed that the only town was where the present city centre is.[21] According to this interpretation, the market place lay within a notional burh, one which had all the rights without the obligation of defence, this being inimical to the religious life which was the sole purpose of the community. This was also the basic view taken by King

---

[16] *Ibid.*, p. 66.
[17] *Ibid.*, p. 68.
[18] *Chronicle of Hugh Candidus* (1949), pp. 49–56, (1966), pp. 26–9.
[19] Anglo-Saxon Chronicle, 'E', *s.a.* 1013.
[20] Stenton, *Anglo-Saxon England*, pp. 450–1.
[21] *Chronicle of Hugh Candidus* (1949), p. 122; see below, at n. 83.

who endorsed Bateson's view that Cenulf's wall was probably no more than a boundary pure and simple, owing nothing to late Saxon notions of what a burh should have been.[22] However, before looking at the evidence for there having been a burh as such, we need to establish when it became one formally.

Hugh Candidus attributes the change to Aethelwold's activities.[23] The Peterborough Chronicle interpolator tells us that Abbot Cenulf, 992–1005, was the first to put a wall round the monastery and this was why the name changed.[24] The only hint in Peterborough records that the change of name was early in the life of the reformed house is in the list of those who acted as sureties for the abbey's acquisitions, in which the estate at Peterborough itself is said to be at Burh.[25] However, as the document as it survives is post-Conquest, it may be that the scribe tidied up what was to him an anachronistic name. Fortunately, there are two unimpeachable sources which allow the name to be carried back to Cenulf at least.

Both Wulfstan and Aelfric in their versions of the *Life* of Aethelwold, after dealing with Abingdon and Nunnaminster in Winchester, turn their attention to fenland monasteries. Ely comes first, followed by the acquisition by Aethelwold from the king and the nobles of another place on the bank of the Nene called Medeshamstede, but now customarily called Burh.[26] The epistolatory introduction to Aelfric's *Life* is addressed to Bishop Cenulf and to the brothers at Winchester.[27] Since the bishop had been the abbot (who is credited with the building of the wall), he would surely have corrected the error in the name, had there been one. He died in 1006. Wulfstan's *Life* is earlier and was the text Aelfric used,[28] so that the change in name was already known in Winchester before Cenulf arrived.

The name could not have been given lightly, so that the burden of proof must lie with those seeking to deny the existence of a burh at Peterborough. It can, certainly, be assumed that the purely military needs provided by the Alfredian burhs and those of his son had passed, so that later burhs must have served more civil and administrative functions.[29] The laws of Aethelstan state

---

22   E. King, 'The Town of Peterborough in the Early Middle Ages', *Northamptonshire Past and Present* 6 (4) (1980–81), 187–95, pp. 187–90.

23   *Chronicle of Hugh Candidus* (1949), p. 38, (1966), p. 20.

24   Anglo-Saxon Chronicle, 'E', *s.a.* 963.

25   *Anglo-Saxon Charters*, ed. A. J. Robertson, 2nd edn (Cambridge, 1956), no. 40.

26   Wulfstan, *Life of St Aethelwold*, pp. 40–1, 76.

27   *Chronicon Monasterii de Abingdon*, ed. J. Stevenson, 2 vols, Rolls Series (London, 1858), II, p. 255.

28   Fisher, 'Early Biographers of St Ethelwold'.

29   H. R. Loyn, *The Vikings in Britain* (London, 1977), pp. 119, 121. See further below, n. 54.

that there should be no minting except in a port; it enumerates the greater places with the numbers of moneyers in each, and ends by adding that in each other burh there should be one.[30] Stenton allows this to mean that every burh should, therefore, have had a moneyer, and the converse should be true: if a coin names the place of a moneyer, then that place was a burh. On this count, Peterborough had certainly become a formal burh within the reign of Aethelred II, as a single surviving coin shows.[31] Although Dolley is not prepared to consider that the presence of a mint presupposes a town as such, the use of a mint would have been to service a market.[32] The coin bears MED for Medeshamstede and has what is known as a 'first hand' die dated 979–85.[33] It thus falls almost certainly within Aethelwold's lifetime. There is further evidence for the abbot having a moneyer: the spurious Edgar pancharter says that the king granted a moneyer in Stamford, and a list of further benefactions states that Turkill Hoche gave, as well as lands, a mint in Stamford.[34] If there are genuine elements imprisoned in either or both of these statements, then the coin may not have been minted in Peterborough itself, since, even if the moneyer minted there on behalf of the abbot, the coins should have named the abbot's town and not Stamford. Nevertheless, since the abbot would hardly keep his silver in Stamford in preference to his own house, it is more likely either that there was another moneyer in Peterborough, or that the Stamford moneyer travelled to Peterborough when occasion demanded and minted there.

Being an archaeologist, I looked at the earliest reasonable plans of the town and asked basic questions, the fundamental one being that, if Martin de Bec had indeed changed the site of the town, where had it been before? The knowledge that the original parish church of St John the Baptist had once been east of the precincts seemed to point in that direction.[35] The plan of the town (fig. 5) shows what can be interpreted as a colonised market place having a funnel-like plan issuing from the east precinct wall. Observation and excavation failed to reveal any defences to the north or east of this and all lay

---

[30] Stenton, *Anglo-Saxon England*, pp. 535–6.

[31] R. H. M. Dolley, 'An Introduction to the Coinage of Aethelred II', in *Ethelred the Unready: Papers from the Millenary Conference*, British Archaeological Reports, British Series 59 (Oxford, 1978), 115–33, p. 125.

[32] R. H. M. Dolley, 'A New Anglo-Saxon Mint – Medeshamstede', *British Numismatic Journal* 27 (1954), 263–5.

[33] Dolley, 'Introduction to the Coinage of Aethelred II', p. 120.

[34] *Chronicle of Hugh Candidus* (1949), pp. 35, 70, (1966), pp. 18, 36.

[35] *Peterborough Local Administration: Parochial Government before the Reformation. Churchwardens' Accounts 1467–1573 with Supplementary Documents, 1107–1488*, ed. W. T. Mellows, Northamptonshire Record Society 9 (Kettering, 1939), pp. 218–19.

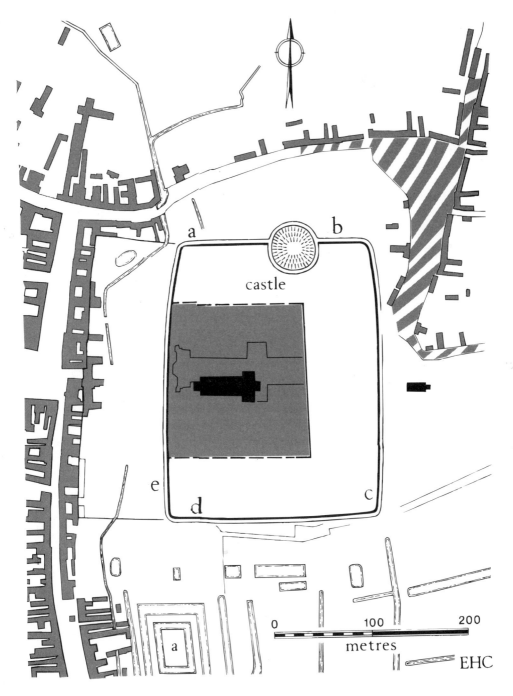

Figure 5: Survey of Peterborough, 1721, with the burh and western extension superimposed.

143

in limbo until an opportunity arose to investigate the date of what was only supposed to be the boundary of Martin de Bec's new western extension. The outcome was unexpected: a medieval pond sealing in the remains of a massive masonry wall set in the front of an earlier rampart, the wall replacing an earlier timber fronting. A major reappraisal of the burh suggested that, if it was encompassed by the present precincts, it was much smaller than had been thought.

Figure 5 shows what is known of the line of the defensive wall and the probable outline – with the estimated shape – of the late Saxon church, as well as the western extension of the precincts attributable to Martin de Bec. The eastern defences have been located at the southern end of the present precinct boundary. There, the rampart sealed in intense occupation immediately predating its creation. Only the back part of the inserted wall was found, the rest having been cut away by de Bec's vineyard wall. The line of the southern defences is constrained by the edge of the flood plain, now largely obscured by modern dumping, but roughly along the edge of the medieval precincts. Work by Ian Meadows outside these found medieval metalled surfaces with cart ruts, almost certainly associated with the wharf by the Bull Dyke, and at the bottom, the outer edge of a ditch. In 1996 he excavated an extension, with the kind permission of the bishop, inside the vegetable garden of the palace and located the front of the rampart and two ditches. The wall had been cut away by a large post-Dissolution pit. The two ditches are of interest: the upper was a recut of the lower and had begun to fill up when the burh wall was demolished, there being a thick layer of its highly characteristic mortar. The lower ditch had a butt end and had also been partly filled before an event which left a strew of burnt stone in it.

In simple terms, the lower ditch is the original and ended next to a feature which could hardly be anything other than a gate; bearing in mind the location nearby of the Bull Dyke, it should have been the Bolhithe Gate forced by Hereward and his companions,[36] and probably eliminated when the ditch was recut, very likely as a response to the troubles of the twelfth-century Anarchy. So far, three sides of the burh have been located. At the same time as the most recent excavations took place, English Heritage undertook a geophysical survey of the bishop's lawn across which the western defences should run, but the results have not been made available.

If the burh has been defined, what lay inside? A test trench in the south-east corner of the precincts revealed fairly intense occupation, with pottery which had an end-date somewhere in the middle of the twelfth century. The layout of the east side of Peterborough before the enclosure (1811–21) shows what looks like a funnel-shaped market place whose end points at the east wall

---

[36] *Chronicle of Hugh Candidus* (1949), pp. 78–9, (1966), pp. 40–1.

of the abbot's vineyard. This market place itself was conditioned by the edge of the flood plain which swings north here, and attention is drawn to the narrow stretch of water on the 1721 survey, the basis for fig. 5, down the east side of the vineyard south of the market place which may have been a relic of the defensive ditch. It would seem possible that the lay service element of the monastery was housed inside the defences, the late Saxon precincts being much smaller than those designed by Martin de Bec.

To a historian, it is possible that the greatest objection to a burh here is its absence from Domesday and the difficulty in reconciling the full needs of the *trinoda necessitas*, fortification, bridge maintenance, and military service.[37] Of the latter, Peterborough certainly had the first, and the only reason why Abbot Leofric could have been at Hastings is because he had led his fyrd there.[38] There is, however, no record of a bridge across the Nene at Peterborough before 1308, yet it seems that the relationship between fortress and bridge was very close.[39] Failing a bridge at Peterborough, the abbot may have had responsibility for a bridge at Wansford; closer to home, however, is the puzzle of the bridge implied by the place-name Botolph's Bridge just west of Peterborough.

Domesday clearly describes an agricultural community, but that it obscures the true nature of the full settlement in the town can be deduced by the accounts of Walter the archdeacon when the king held the abbacy for three years from 1125.[40] After what is basically a straightforward recital of the settlement as it is found in Domesday,[41] he goes on to give: 'Et Alsward tenet .xviii. burgenses, et theloneum de Hordesoca pro .c. et .xv. solidis ... Et milites Abbatis habent .xviii. hospicia in Burgo. Et vi. servientes .vi. hospicia'. The agricultural settlement, listed in Domesday, was the only part which pays anything to the king; the second settlement pays to the abbot and was listed by Walter because, in this instance, the king was taking the profits. Burgesses almost certainly only appear in this document because Walter was familiar with these elsewhere and made a straight equation which no other document supports. This second settlement cannot lie in the agricultural area dignified

[37] N. P. Brooks, 'The Development of Military Obligations in Eighth- and Ninth-century England', in *England before the Conquest: Studies in Primary Sources presented to Dorothy Whitelock*, ed. P. Clemoes and K. Hughes (Cambridge, 1971), 69–84, pp. 69–72.

[38] *Chronicle of Hugh Candidus* (1949), p. 75, (1966), p. 39. See further below on the soke.

[39] *Historiae Anglicanae Scriptores Varii e Codicibus Manuscriptis nunc primi editi*, ed. J. Sparke (London, 1723), p. 163; Brooks, 'Development of Military Obligations', p. 72. See further below, p. 168.

[40] *Chronicon Petroburgense*, ed. Thomas Stapleton (London, 1849), p. 161.

[41] *VCH, Northamptonshire*, I, p. 313.

until modern times with the name of Boongate and, as it predates the new town, should only have been within the burh.

As nothing is really known of the layout of the precincts before the middle of the twelfth century, the layout of the burh is a matter of fine judgement. However, accepting that the burial ground north of the church could hardly have been more extensive than it is now, that is, from the church to the south wall of the dean's garden, there is a strip of ground beyond it running up to the northern defences. The strip would be about as wide as the vineyard, which lay east of the cemetery before that was extended in 1214–22.[42] Repeating the north edge of the cemetery by symmetry on the south side of the centre-line of the Saxon church leaves another strip of about the same width again. It is possible that these strips were occupied by the laity, and the smaller enclave was defined by the north and east edges of the unaltered cemetery and the symmetry implied above, these limits representing the precincts of the late Saxon and post-Conquest monastery. This exercise is far from pointless: the actual defensive wall which belonged to these precincts is very close to one eighth of the whole, and the implications of that are considered when the abbot's soke is discussed.

The first major change to the plan of the burh would have been a castle to cater for Abbot Thorold's knights owing castle-guard at Peterborough. He would have had no difficulty in creating the castle, since all the ground belonged to him and the town had been burnt down the day he arrived. Tout Hill, the motte at the bottom of the dean's garden, represents the central point of the knights' duty and the whole of the northern strip of the burh should then have been barred to the townsfolk. The tradition that Tout Hill is Thorold's castle would carry greater weight if the reference in Hugh Candidus belonged to his stratum of the work. Unfortunately, it is ascribed to the second continuator, Walter of Whittlesey.[43]

Running up the line of the southern defences from the river were a series of 'inlets' best seen on Eyre's survey of 1721 (fig. 5). There are four ditches running up to the precincts, one dividing into two. The two easternmost have been reduced essentially to wide water-filled ditches. King settles on the inlet east of Godfrey de Crowland's double-moated herbarium as the Bull Dyke.[44] There are references in William Morton's book to transport of goods by water involving Bull Gate, which was probably the gate east of the Almoner's Hall.[45] However, in the middle of the fifteenth century the hithe and gate

---

[42]   *Historiae Anglicanae*, p. 109.

[43]   *Chronicle of Hugh Candidus* (1949), pp. 84–5.

[44]   King, 'Town of Peterborough', pp. 192–3.

[45]   *The Book of William Morton, Almoner of Peterborough Monastery, 1448–1467*, ed. W. T. Mellows and P. I. King, Northamptonshire Record Society 16 (Oxford, 1954), pp. 33, 41, 87, 97, 124.

were closely related and the forked layout of the waterway east of the herbarium should have been well suited to loading and off-loading boats.

Traditionally, Edgar gave the jurisdiction of what became the soke of Peterborough to the monastery, but there seems to be no reputable record of such a gift. The spurious charter of Wulfhere implies that Medeshamstede had held full sway over the soke from the earliest times.[46] But the copy of the list of Aethelwold's donations to the newly revived monastery reveals something much more modest: Medeshamstede with its berewics; *Anlafestun* with its berewics; men at Farcet with half of Whittlesey Mere; Oundle with its berewics; Kettering; fens at Well; tithes from the double hundred of Norman Cross; tithes from six tuns or manors in the double hundred on the ness on which Medeshamstede stands; tithes from twenty-four more tuns; finally, an inventory of goods and chattels at Yaxley.[47]

The lands for which sureties were given are clearly additional to the original endowment, and the documents so carefully prepared after the death of Edgar mark a new caution in land acquisition.[48] The dating of the surety lists is fairly uncertain as Ealdulf, the first named abbot of the reformed house, who may only have been the equivalent of prior until Aethelwold's death,[49] carried out most of the transactions, the bishop being present only for a few. Those date to before 984, but the rest date to some time before 992 when Ealdulf was translated to York and Worcester, except for the transaction concerning Peterborough itself which cannot be later than 990 as Earl Aelfwine is involved. The Earl Aelfric referred to in connection with the *Leobrantestun* was possibly Aelfric Cild, earl from 983 to 985. In other words, all these transactions are limited to the period between Aethelwold's gifts – few of his purchases are mentioned – and 992. The point of this digression lies not with purchases, but with two cases of forfeiture; these suggest that the abbot held some form of jurisdiction over the two places concerned of such an order that he received what would have normally passed to the king. It is implied by these two cases that Ealdulf at least had *sac* and *soc* and *infangenetheof* within the double hundred, the form of the soke after the Dissolution.

The Edgar pancharter summarises, in a convenient form, the gifts and early acquisitions of the monastery and gives toll and team at Burh in addition to other powers, and toll and team at Oundle and in the eight hundreds which pertain to it.[50] These inadequate references seem to indicate that the peculiar

46 Sawyer, *Anglo-Saxon Charters*, no. 68.
47 Sawyer, *Anglo-Saxon Charters*, no. 1448; *Anglo-Saxon Charters*, ed. Robertson, no. 39.
48 *Anglo-Saxon Charters*, ed. Robertson, no. 40.
49 Farmer, 'Progress of Monastic Revival', p. 17.

jurisdiction, so greatly enhanced by the thirteenth century that the king's justices had no rights within the abbot's 'realm', was founded in the early days of the reformed monastery. As the abbot resigned to Henry VIII, along with the monastic lands, all his jurisdiction, the term 'soke' has tended to become associated with the jurisdiction given by the king to the new bishop.[51] The hundreds which went to make up the original are deducible from the geldable hidage of the hundreds of Northamptonshire, and the following form a tight unit in the north-east of the county: Nassaburgh (200), Navereslund (200), Huxloe (100), Willybrook (100), Polebrook (100), and Navisford (100).[52]

The importance of this becomes clear when the approximate length of the burh's suggested circuit is examined: the course shown on figure 5, is of the order of 1050-1100 yards (960-1000 metres), depending where the western defences really lie. A test can be applied to see if a length of this approximation is likely: the computations of the Burghal Hidage.[53] Stenton's view was that it was not tenable to argue that the hidages allotted to burhs represented administrative districts.[54] However, the Burghal Hidage belongs essentially to the early tenth century.[55] By the time Medeshamstede had become Burh, the turbulent conditions in which the original burhs had been founded had passed, and the document may represent calculations for determining the length of any new defences by relating it to the number of men owing service in an administrative unit.[56]

The Burghal Hidage includes a table of equivalents of furlongs of wall and the hidage required to serve them: each hide produces one man, and four men are required to defend one pole of wall (five-and-a-half yards); so 160 hides/men are required per furlong (or forty poles).[57] On this basis, the abbot's 800 hides would produce 800 men capable of manning 200 poles or perches, or, neatly, five furlongs of wall. This represents a wall 1,100 yards or about 1,006 metres, at the top end of the measurement of the observed fortifications.

The significance of the five-furlong assessment can be tested further by seeing how well-known administrative districts associated with late burhs also

---

[50] Sawyer, *Anglo-Saxon Charters*, no. 787; Anglo-Saxon Chronicle, 'E', *s.a.* 963.

[51] *Peterborough Local Administration*, p. xlv.

[52] C. Hart, *The Hidation of Northamptonshire*, Leicester University Department of English Local History, Occasional Papers, 2nd ser. 3 (Leicester, 1970), p. 21.

[53] *Anglo-Saxon Charters*, ed. Robertson, pp. 246-9; *Alfred the Great*, trans. S. Keynes and M. Lapidge (Harmondsworth, 1983), pp. 193-4.

[54] Stenton, *Anglo-Saxon England*, p. 265, n. 2.

[55] D. Hill, 'The Burghal Hidage: the Establishment of a Text', *Medieval Archaeology* 13 (1969), 84-92, pp. 91-2.

[56] See also James Campbell, *et al.*, *The Anglo-Saxons* (London, 1982), pp. 152-3.

[57] Hill, 'Burghal Hidage', p. 90.

fit it; a look at the rest of the old county of Northamptonshire may be instructive. Two places are certain to have been burhs in late Saxon times, Northampton and Towcester. Their defensive circuits can be measured with the reasonable certainty that each should be close to the actual lines. The first is about 1,970 yards (1,800 metres), taking the line across the site of the castle.[58] At Towcester, the length is estimated here to have been 1,350 yards (c.1,240 metres) long.[59] Neither figure can be accurate as the actual defences have not been fully established and the published plan of Northampton is to a very small scale. However, using them as a rough guide, Northampton yields 355 perches and Towcester 246 perches and, following the rule of four men/perch, Northampton would need 1,420 hides and Towcester 984, a total of 2,404 hides. If the abbot's 800 are added, the total is too close to the 3,200 hide total of Northamptonshire for coincidence to be ruled out. As Peterborough so closely fits the five-furlong hidage in the computation, Towcester's assessed hides could be 960 to suit six furlongs, and raising Northampton's figure to 1,440 hides would fit nine furlongs, the total for the shire still being 3,200.

Looking at these theoretical allocations in terms of the hundreds of Northamptonshire, Towcester would need either 900 or 950 hides. Taking Hart's eight south-western hundreds, clearly based on Towcester, either a single hundred or a hundred-and-a-half would need to be added.[60] As it happens, the three adjacent blocks, Guilsborough, Nobottle Grove and Wymersley were each of 150 hides, the addition of one of which would fix Towcester at 950 hides. This would leave Northampton with the remaining 1,450 hides in the shire. This does not itself demonstrate that convenient hundreds were allotted to these three burhs, but out of the thirty-three burhs listed in the Burghal Hidage, twenty-five are assessed in such round numbers and hundreds.[61] The probability therefore becomes almost overwhelming that this was the way in which burghal duties were divided up within Northamptonshire.

To add to this in parenthesis, Tait discussed the question of the urban hundred, but his argument is tied up with courts and laws.[62] In a practical sense in the late Saxon period, there could well have been a military

---

[58] J. H. Williams, M. Shaw and V. Denham, *Middle Saxon Palaces at Northampton*, Northampton Development Corporation Archaeological Monograph 4 (Northampton, 1985), fig. 2.

[59] A. E. Brown and J. A. Alexander, 'Excavations at Towcester, 1954: the Grammar School Site', *Northamptonshire Archaeology* 17 (1982), 24–59, fig. 1.

[60] Hart, *Hidation of Northamptonshire*, p. 20, and end map.

[61] Hill, 'Burghal Hidage', pp. 88–90.

[62] J. Tait, *The Medieval English Borough: Studies on its Origins and Constitutional History* (Manchester, 1936), pp. 32–3, 47–52.

component in which the inhabitants apparently supplied the equivalent of a hundred in men. Here may be the context for the apparent one eighth of the circuit forming the west boundary of the monastery itself.

If this kind of arrangement has to be accepted for Northamptonshire, the implications are far-reaching. What Hill sees as a scheme to be applied to West Mercia[63] would be extendable to the southern Danelaw. And if it works there, perhaps the five boroughs should be looked at, as well as East Anglia where Bury St Edmund's is named to distinguish it from *Burgo Sancti Petri*.

All this could cast a different light on a very obscure episode in Peterborough's history. Peterborough's own records suggest a relatively steady growth in prosperity up to the Norman Conquest: there is no suspicion that the place was affected by the only serious set-back which the reform movement suffered. Edgar's death in 975 was followed by attempts to recover some of the land which had been assigned to the new houses. Details are not always clear, but Evesham and Pershore looked upon Earl Aelfhere of Mercia as an enemy and Winchcombe was disbanded.[64] There appears to have been some rivalry between him and Earl Aelfwine of East Anglia, the secular founder of Ramsey, who also appears in Peterborough records.[65] As far as Peterborough is concerned, details of its difficulties are preserved by Ely and Ramsey. Leofsige, of unknown associations, but belonging to Aelfhere's faction, is said to have seized Medeshamstede itself along with Oundle and Kettering, some of the land remaining uncultivated for two years. There was a dispute, with Aethelwold and Aelfwine ranged against Leofsige, and, although the matter was settled in law in London, and confirmed at Northampton and then in front of the eight hundreds who met at Wansford, nothing was resolved until the unrepentant Leofsige was killed by Aelfwine's brother, Aelfwold, who then went to Winchester as a penitent to be raised to his feet by a grateful Aethelwold accompanied by a full celebratory procession.[66] What may really have been at issue was who should control such a valuable military asset, and not a plain protest over the creation of monastic estates.

The well-known pluralist, Leofric, the last abbot before the Conquest and a nephew of Earl Leofric of Mercia, was abbot of Burton-on-Trent, Coventry, Thorney and Crowland as well as Peterborough; Hugh tells us that these favours had been granted by Edward the Confessor. He succeeded Earnwy, who seems to have been persuaded to retire around 1050, although the date is

---

63   Hill, 'Burghal Hidage', p. 92.

64   A. Williams, '*Princeps Merciorum gentis*: the Family, Career and Connections of Aelfhere, Ealdorman of Mercia, 956–93', *Anglo-Saxon England* 10 (1982), 143–72, p. 166.

65   *Ibid.*, pp. 165–6; *Anglo-Saxon Charters*, ed. Robertson, no. 40.

66   *Liber Eliensis*, pp. 84–5; J. Raine, *The Historians of the Church of York and its Archbishops*, 3 vols, Rolls Series (London, 1879–94), I, p. 446.

a little opaque since the Anglo-Saxon Chronicle gives 1052/3.[67] In the context of the time, it can be argued that the act was politically inspired: the abbot would be responsible for his fyrd and his land base was at the frontier of Mercia and East Anglia. The king had no good reason to trust the Godwin family whom he had to welcome back, Earl Harold taking East Anglia into his hands once again. Leofric, being related to the Mercian earl, was unlikely to change his allegiance. It is to his rule that the only reference to any building work before 1107–14 belongs: the dedication of the tower in 1059.[68] Leofric died a bare fortnight after Hastings and the outcome of the battle may have left the monks in a quandary. Hugh says that, for very grief, scarcely anyone could be found to bury him; a more cynical age would argue that none wished to receive any taint from a supporter of the losing side.[69]

The Conquest itself apparently had little effect on the monastery. After a fine example of political equivocation, William confirmed Brand as abbot,[70] but the events of 1069 which ushered in a new system for England also had particular relevance for Peterborough. Aethelric and his brother Aethelwine, both monks of Peterborough, were the last two Anglo-Saxons to hold the see of Durham, in 1042–1056 and 1056–1071 respectively. What is remarkable is that Aethelric retired to Peterborough to be succeeded by his brother almost as though the see was in his gift. The troubles in the north were exacerbated when forces sent by William were destroyed at Durham early in 1069, their leader being burnt to death in Bishop Aethelwine's house. The first brother was tainted by the decision of the second to join Swein and was imprisoned at Westminster, where he died; Aethelwine, captured at the fall of the Isle of Ely in 1071, was imprisoned at Abingdon.[71]

At the critical moment in all these events, Abbot Brand died. As the abbacy had control of 800 soldiers, William could not afford to allow such an important office to remain politically ambivalent and he filled the post with Thorold, abbot of Malmesbury. Thorold's short reign there had not endeared him to the Malmesbury monks and Peterborough, after a rule of twenty-nine years, granted him as near eternal damnation as it Christianly could by reciting his 'misdeeds' in contrast to the eulogies heaped upon his two predecessors.[72] Not only did Thorold arrive at a monastery which had been

---

[67]   *Chronicle of Hugh Candidus* (1949), pp. 65–7, (1966), p. 35.

[68]   Anglo-Saxon Chronicle, 'D', *s.a.* 1059.

[69]   *Chronicle of Hugh Candidus* (1949), p. 75, (1966), p. 39.

[70]   *Chronicle of Hugh Candidus* (1949), pp. 76–7.

[71]   *Chronicle of Hugh Candidus* (1949), pp. 74, 82, (1966), pp. 38, 43; Anglo-Saxon Chronicle, *s.a.* 1071.

[72]   David Knowles, *The Monastic Order in England: a History of its Development from the Times of St Dunstan to the Fourth Lateran Council, 943–1216* (Cambridge, 1940),

despoiled and was deserted, its town – surely the one within the defences – burnt out, but also he was charged with providing for sixty knights out of the estates of the monastery, the heaviest burden of any ordinary monastery save Glastonbury whose burden, in time, was mitigated.[73] Although William's act could be seen as a punishment, Bury St Edmund's, whose abbot was on very good terms with the king, had to support forty knights:[74] no one was to know that Swein's attempt was to be the last effective Danish invasion.[75] In Peterborough's case, the abbot was an acknowledged fighting man and the loyalty of the monastery before his time had been dubious. To some extent the actual quota was a matter of rough agreement between the king and his tenant-in-chief, but not only was the king very powerful in the circumstances, but his Norman tenants-in-chief in any case shared his desire for securing the conquest.[76]

At a stroke burghal defences were redundant. The new system relied upon point of defence and a castle was placed in the north-east corner of the burgh, the motte straddling the wall, which would have been broken down for the ditch around that. Thereafter, it was inertia which allowed the rest of the circuit to survive until at least the end of the Anarchy, during which Peterborough's knights seem to have been able to preserve the house from trouble. However, the uncomfortable relationship between the vill and the monastery must have become more obvious the nearer the new monastic church came to completion. The new west end was to be a twin-towered design of some pretension, and this would have faced the back of an obsolete defensive system.[77] More than that, the great size of the new church would also have emphasised how small the late Saxon precincts were. Martin de Bec simply removed the inconvenience by throwing the boundary of the precincts across the stream and its valley. The whole of the western burh wall and its bank would have been removed and the material used to level the valley to form some kind of forecourt in front of the new church. This was the prelude to the resiting of the town.

The old defences would have provided an excellent quarry for the long lengths of new walling required for the extended precincts, but there is no direct evidence that it was actually Martin de Bec (1132–55) who flattened the

---

p. 105; *Chronicle of Hugh Candidus* (1949), pp. 84–5, (1966), pp. 44–5.

[73] King, *Peterborough Abbey*, pp. 13–16.

[74] Stenton, *Anglo-Saxon England*, p. 635.

[75] *Ibid.*, pp. 601–6, 611; King, *Peterborough Abbey*, p. 18.

[76] H. R. Loyn, *The Governance of Anglo-Saxon England, 500–1087* (London, 1984), p. 181. The most recent synthesis on these negotiations is in Brian Golding, *Conquest and Colonization: the Normans in Britain, 1066–1100* (London, 1994), pp. 135–8.

[77] *VCH, Northamptonshire*, II, pp. 440–1, 444.

whole circuit. The archaeological evidence shows that the burh wall had certainly gone by 1200, which ostensibly allows two candidates other than Martin: William de Waterville (1155–75) and Benedict (1177–93). However, there is a hint in the records that Abbot Martin was responsible: Walter of Whittlesey, in preparing his text of Hugh Candidus' work, and incorporating Swaffham's continuation and the marginal notes in that, added his own, including one to the deeds of de Bec: *castellum destruxit*.[78] This could refer to the motte-and-bailey castle, but Round draws a distinction between a castle as such and a castellum, seeing in the latter a reference to a circuit of defences which might be as much a bailey as a burh.[79] The best evidence, however, that such a drastic change belonged to the rule of Martin de Bec is his act of town planning.

Although it has been doubted that there was a burh or that Hugh Candidus' testimony proves that there was a new town,[80] his meaning is seldom in doubt and he was a witness to Abbot Martin's deeds: Hugh had held offices and was sub-prior.[81] He was almost certainly the Hugo Albus, monk, who stands at the head of the witness list of a document of 1147, in which an infirm knight returned his patrimony to the abbey.[82] The best catalogue Hugh offers for the acts of Abbot Martin reads: 'In the church, in other offices and in many places he was always at work; the gate of the monastery, the market place, the ships' hithe and the vill he changed much for the better, and much he put right'.[83] The layout of the town centre as reconstructed for *c.*1300–10 (fig. 6) shows that the market place and the abbey gate were closely linked, and that Hithegate with the hithe are logical extensions. The change of the gate alone carries all else with it. *Mutauit* has no spiritual meaning:[84] to Hugh, the good that abbots did was directly measurable in terms of the material world.

The rest of the evidence which shows unequivocally that there was a new town is contained in charters. Two contain the term *portam Burgi*. The first concerns land 'quod ego emi coram curia abbatis ad magnam portam burgi'.[85]

[78] *Chronicle of Hugh Candidus* (1949), p. 173.
[79] J. H. Round, *Geoffrey de Mandeville* (London, 1892), pp. 328–33.
[80] King, 'Town of Peterborough', pp. 187–92.
[81] *Chronicle of Hugh Candidus* (1949), p. 95.
[82] King, *Peterborough Abbey*, pp. 27–8; Peterborough Dean and Chapter, MS 1 (The Book of Robert of Swaffham), fol. 115.
[83] *Chronicle of Hugh Candidus* (1949), p. 122: 'In ecclesia et in aliis officinis et in pluribus locis semper operabatur, et portam monasterii et mercatum et portum nauium et uillam multo melius mutauit, et multa emendauit'.
[84] King, 'Town of Peterborough', p. 192.
[85] Peterborough, Dean and Chapter, MS 1, fol. 180; MS 5 (The Book of Charters and Privileges of Henry of Pytchley, junior), fol. 138.

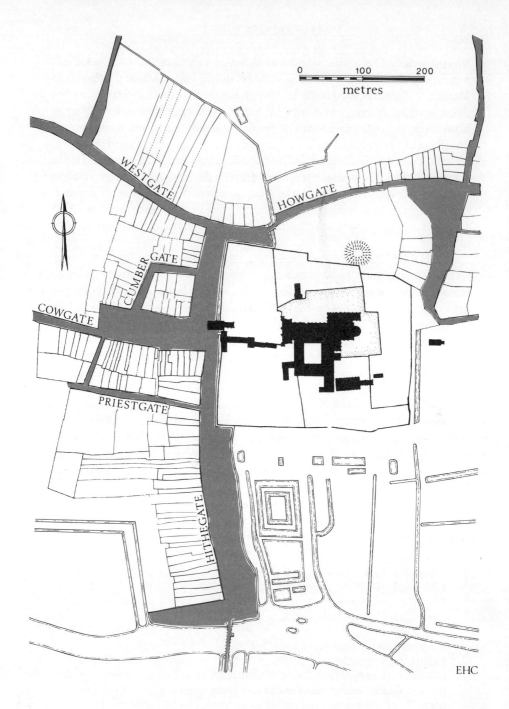

WESTGATE

HOWGATE

CUMBERGATE

COWGATE

PRIESTGATE

HITHEGATE

0   100   200
metres

EHC

Figure 6: The extent of Peterborough, *c.*1310.

The site of the abbot's court is clear: it is the great gate of the burh. The date of the document is the first half of the thirteenth century, as it involves a Norman de Kent and his wife Agnes, identifiable as the widow of William Pudding. The second charter says '... et nominatim hospitali beati Thome martiris ad portam Burgi ...'.[86] The rebuilt chancel of this still stands inside the abbey gate. Reference to 'land and buildings', a formula current only c.1200, indicates that the charter is early thirteenth century at the latest. These references show that the gate was believed to be that of the burh. The subsuming of the old burh into the new precincts did not hide where it had been or the fact that the monastery now occupied all of it and more.

The final piece of evidence lies in two charters belonging to the almoner's lay officer. The first was issued by de Bec's successor, William de Waterville (1155–75), who granted lands and a daily food allowance to William son of Radulph in return for the service due to the almoner, just as his father had received it, including 'unum mansionem in novo vico retro domum Gilberti Secretarii';[87] the residence was in the new town, backing on to the sacrist's. The other charter, issued by Abbot Robert de Lindsey (1214–22), gives to Thomas son of William Almoner de Burg 'tenementa que idem Willelmus pater suus tenuit, scilicet, unum mesuagium in Prestisgate', which he was to hold 'quiete et hereditarie salvis regiis gildis per serganciam in elemosinaria nostra'.[88] Since the tenement was in Priestgate, the *novus vicus* is the present town centre.

The whole of the dual settlement was in the hands of the abbot, the inhabitants owing service and paying their dues to him. That Martin de Bec was intent on ensuring that his own control over the new town was complete is demonstrated by a remarkable memorandum of a transaction dating to 1146,[89] which shows how he coped with the one possible exception: Alsward. For on 22 February, just before the high mass, in front of the great altar in the new church and in the presence of relics of the holy saints, with the abbot, the monks and many witnesses standing by, William and his brother Walter, the sons and heirs of Alsward, redeemed from Geoffrey Spechel the lands of Alsward for forty-two shillings and rendered their inheritence of twenty acres of arable, four of meadow and the houses and tofts of Alsward, to God and St Peter for the work of the church and the ministry of the sacrist, of the charity of St Peter. For this they received a quit rent amounting to twenty-nine shillings.

---

[86]   Dean and Chapter, MS 1, fol. 226; MS 5, fol. 156.

[87]   BL, Cotton MS Cleopatra c.i, fol. 157 (headed fol. 120).

[88]   *Carte Nativorum: a Peterborough Abbey Cartulary of the Fourteenth Century*, ed. C. N. L. Brooke and M. M. Postan, Northamptonshire Record Society 20 (Oxford, 1960), p. 499.

[89]   Dean and Chapter, MS 1, fols 114v–115.

Alsward was the only individual named in Archdeacon Walter's accounts of 1125-8, his holdings including *burgenses*.[90] He may have been the sacrist's lay officer, as the lands were to pass to that obedientiary; but the redeemed land could equally have been used to compensate the sacrist for agricultural income lost from the area needed for the new town site. The unusually elaborate setting for the transaction shows that this was no small occasion. The method of transfer and the details demonstrate that great care was exercised. The presence of thirteen witnesses, including two of the abbot's knights and his chief servants, suggests that the laity were to be made fully cognisant of what was taking place. On the other hand, the absence of a long list of knights suggests that the matter was related essentially to a lower level of society and that nothing pertaining to a knight's fee was involved. The whole transaction smacks of the abbot making sure that there could be no encumbrance on his own rights in his *novus vicus*, and, of course, provides a probable date for that.

By the time Martin died, the monks had been introduced into their new presbytery, the old burh defences had been flattened, the town had been new built, and the whole settlement set on course for a relatively uneventful future. The Peterborough Chronicle, a notable survival of a great Anglo-Saxon tradition, is the last one maintained in the English language and from 1079 is the sole record in that form. A borrowed manuscript was copied in Peterborough in 1121 in the reign of Abbot John de Sees, who began the rebuilding of the monastic church.[91] The last hand used runs from 1132 to 1154, coinciding to a remarkable degree with Martin de Bec's rule; it ends with the notice of his death and the induction of his successor. The burh shared a similar fate: created c.970, it had a wall inserted into its rampart around 992-1005, and was demolished shortly after 1145. What is left of these defences may be in poor physical shape, but they are probably the best dated physical remains of such in the country.

---

[90] *Chronicon Petroburgense*, p. 161; see above, n. 40.
[91] *The Anglo-Saxon Chronicle*, ed. D. Whitelock, D. C. Douglas and S. I. Tucker (London, 1961), p. xvi.

The Relationship Between the Abbey and Town of Peterborough from 1200 to the Reformation

JACK HIGHAM

Many of the great Benedictine houses, of which Peterborough was an important example, were sited in towns, and the relationship between town and cassock inevitably became an important factor in the life of both communities. As David Knowles expressed it, 'In all the cases where a borough lay at the gates of the monastery and was controlled by the monks, it formed one more element, and that an important one, among the many interests and responsibilities, wholly unconnected with religion, that absorbed the minds and employed the various talents of the members of the community'.[1]

Strictly speaking, Peterborough was not a borough in the sense of having received a borough charter, and was wholly under the lordship of the abbot. However, the period from 1200 onwards reveals the development of a kind of borough, through a process by which the town was gradually freed of the dominant lordship of the monastery, a process involving friction which occasionally welled up into confrontation. At the same time, the town existed primarily to serve the monastery, and so again there was a gradual process whereby the town began to pursue its own separate interests.[2]

A third factor is the way in which the monastery, at least in its ideals, was supposed to serve the community. Chapter IV of the Rule of St Benedict, which would have been read in chapter on 18 January, 19 May and 18 September, reminded the monks of our Lord's injunction 'to relieve the poor, to clothe the naked, to visit the sick, ... to give help in trouble, to console the sorrowful'.[3] Chapter LIII, read on 4 April, 4 August and 4 December, dealing with the reception of guests, while acknowledging that 'the respect due to their station is to be shown to all, particularly to those of one family with us

[1] David Knowles, *The Monastic Order in England* (Cambridge, 1940), p. 447.

[2] Susan Reynolds, *An Introduction to the History of English Medieval Towns* (Oxford, 1977), surveys the growth of towns, boroughs and liberties. See also now E. Miller and J. Hatcher, *Medieval England: Towns, Commerce and Crafts, 1086–1348* (London, 1995).

[3] *Regula S. Benedicti*, ed. D. O. H. Blair (Fort Augustus, 1934), p. 28.

in the faith and to pilgrims', yet went on to point out that 'special care is to be shown in the reception of the poor and of pilgrims, for in them especially is Christ received; for the awe felt for the wealthy imposes respect enough of itself'.[4]

The *Regularis Concordia* made these obligations more specific by requiring that 'a place be set apart for the reception of the poor, where daily and without fail the service of the Maundy (*mandati ... obsequium*) may be rendered to three poor men ... and let the same foods of which the brethren partake that day be given to them'. The only member of the community excused from this service is the abbot, but even he is to 'devote himself to this office not only once but as often as leisure or opportunity suggest',[5] an injunction which is unique to the *Regularis Concordia*. Among the thirteenth-century abbots of Peterborough, John of Caux is picked out by the chronicler for special mention in his concern for the local poor, 'whom he loved much and for whom he often provided food and drink, serving them with his own hands'.[6] When the same abbot built the new infirmary, whose ruins survive and whose chapel, adorned with double piscina, is now the drawing room of one of the canons' houses, the chronicler states that on the completion of the infirmary 'he filled the said building with poor people, and abundantly fed them there for three days'.[7] When Cardinal Wolsey spent Holy Week and Easter in the abbey on his journey north following his fall from power in 1530, he personally held a Maundy ceremony at which he washed the feet of fifty-nine men.[8] The way in which this is recorded implies that customarily this work of charity was carried out by the abbot, but by 1530 it seems to have been done only once a year, not daily as the *Regularis Concordia* required.

Therefore another factor which the relationship between abbey and town illustrates is the gradual decline in monastic observance, culminating in a series of scandals involving the world, the flesh and, if not the devil, then the abuse of power and general loss of the high idealism which had been the original motivating force in the founding of the monasteries. The themes which I shall try to draw together, therefore, in the course of this very brief survey of three centuries of the abbey's life, are the process by which the town gradually became free of the abbey, the tensions which that process inevitably created, the way in which the town served the abbey and the abbey

---

[4] *Ibid.*, pp. 138, 140.
[5] *Regularis Concordia*, ed. T. Symons (London, 1953), X, 62, p. 61.
[6] *Historiae Anglicanae Scriptores Varii e Codicibus Manuscriptis nunc primi editi*, ed. J. Sparke (London, 1723), p. 132.
[7] *Ibid.*
[8] G. Cavendish, *The Life of Cardinal Wolsey* (London, 1930), p. 135.

served the town, and the decline in the spirituality of the abbey partly evinced in its connections with the local populace.

The Norman Conquest involved the explicit subordination of the abbey and its property, including the town of Burgh, and the overlordship of the king. It is well known that the abbey of Peterborough had the service of sixty knights imposed on it by the Conqueror, partly as a punishment for the fact that Abbot Brand had paid homage to Edgar Atheling instead of to William I.[9] Edmund King has shown that, in the Northamptonshire Domesday, forty-six percent of the abbey's property was held by knights owing service, but he also points out that only two knights' fees out of the sixty were created within the soke, and those 'in the north and west of the Soke, the area of the poorest agricultural land'.[10] The abbey therefore retained the lordship of the town and of Boroughbury manor.

As King has observed, there were two pressures operating on the abbey's relationship with its tenants. 'The first is the constant pressure on the abbey forcing it to devolve property; the second the necessary adjustment of feudal relationships in the twelfth century as feudal society changed'.[11] King argues that some pre-Conquest freeholders maintained their holdings after the Norman reorganisation, 'amongst whom were a large group of sokemen'.[12] The largest proportion of sokemen in the county recorded in the Domesday survey was in Nassaburgh hundred.[13]

The monastery servants also became land-holders in the twelfth century. Mellows pointed out that the *nativi* or villeins of the town manor originated from the lower grade of monastic servants and added: 'To provide each of them with a customary holding apart from his toft in the Bondgate, the abbot assarted part of the wood of Eastwood and granted holdings each containing about four or five acres of this reclaimed land to these *nativi* of the inner vill'.[14] King, while cavilling at some details of this picture, accepted it as largely true.[15]

With the thirteenth century, changes began to take place. Liberties were particularly important to townsmen because their economic life could be seriously affected by the unrestrained claims of a lord.[16] The key document

---

9   Peterborough, Dean and Chapter, MS 1, fols 11r, 12v; *Historiae Anglicanae*, p. 52.

10   E. King, *Peterborough Abbey 1086–1310: a Study in the Land Market* (Cambridge, 1973), pp. 13ff, 17.

11   King, *Peterborough Abbey*, p. 18.

12   *Ibid.*, p. 55.

13   36% according to H. C. Darby and I. B. Terrett, *The Domesday Geography of Middle England*, 2nd edn (Cambridge, 1971), p. 400.

14   W. T. Mellows, *The Local Government of Peterborough* (Peterborough, 1919), p. 195.

15   King, *Peterborough Abbey*, p. 59.

here is the charter of liberty granted to the town by Abbot Robert of Lindsey between 1215 and 1222, shortly after *Magna Carta*.[17] The essence of the arrangement was the liberation of about 150 tenants from tallage (an annual fee, probably paid at Michaelmas), from merchet (a custom requiring the lord's licence for the marriage of tenants' daughters) and from the duties of carrying hay and reaping grain. Ploughing services are not mentioned, but as Mary Bateson surmised, these 'had probably been released by an earlier grant'.[18] The charter does, however, preserve to the abbot the pleas of portmanmoot, the rent of ovens for baking and 'all our customs due at the river bank and in the market of Burgh'.[19] In return for this liberation from customary services, the total rents payable by the tenants specified rose from £7 0s. 2½d. per annum to £18 9s. 6d. The abbot traded a regular cash income for the reduction of customary services, and the legal status of the tenants thereby improved since they became more free.

The charter makes plain that these arrangements will apply to 'our men of Burgh subsequently listed and their heirs', and it is further provided that 'none may give or sell or alienate any part thereof or take any action whereby the grantors may lose any of the said rents and services and customs'.[20] Miss Bateson was prepared to describe this as 'a borough charter conferring privileged conditions, but of a very humble kind'. She suggested that it is a representative of 'the class of borough charters which offer release from seignorial exploitation, but on the most restricted terms'.[21] It is significant that such a minimal charter does not use the term burgesses, though that does appear for the first time with regard to Peterborough in a survey of 1231.[22]

This important charter, therefore, marks the first step in the liberation of the town. At the same time it indicates that the townspeople were becoming wealthier, if they were able to cope with rents that had been increased to two-and-a-half times their previous level.

The charter lists 147 men and women, which, on the basis of five people to each tenancy, would produce a figure of 735 individuals. To this should be

---

16   For a classic account of the often tense and sometimes violent relations between a monastic borough and its lord, centring on the issue of liberty, see M. D. Lobel, *The Borough of Bury St Edmunds: a Study in the Government and Development of a Monastic Town* (Oxford, 1935); and for urban liberties more generally, see Reynolds, *English Medieval Towns*, pp. 91ff.

17   Peterborough MS 1, fols 227r–229v.

18   M. Bateson, 'The Borough of Peterborough', in *VCH, Northamptonshire*, II, p. 425, n. 20.

19   Peterborough MS 1, fol. 227r.

20   *Ibid.*, fols 227r, 229v.

21   Bateson, in *VCH, Northamptonshire*, II, p. 425.

22   London, Society of Antiquaries, MS 60, fol. 181r.

added about eighty monks, and about as many servants, though some of these may have been listed amongst the inhabitants of the town. On top of this, there would be a further two hundred or so at Boroughbury manor, giving a total population in excess of a thousand.[23]

The list of occupations is rather restricted: three smiths, two carpenters, a glazier, a mason, a cooper, a fisherman, four cooks, two bakers, a butler, an ostler and three tailors, all presumably in the service of the abbey. Unlike Oundle, which was granted a similar charter by the same abbot, no-one was occupied in the making of cloth. When the abbot tried to promote the cloth trade in 1228, an objection was lodged by the lord of Stamford on the grounds that it infringed his town's privileges. The list also suggests a very stable population in Peterborough, as only nine of the surnames imply an origin outside the town.

The mention of the glazier is significant, since we know that it was the same Abbot Robert, grantor of the charter of liberties, who first began to glaze the windows of the abbey, which until his time were 'only stuffed with straw and reed' to keep out the weather.[24] According to Swaffham, he glazed more than thirty windows. The mason and carpenters were presumably working on the completion of the great west front.

In an unpublished article by Donald Mackreth, which he has kindly shown to me, he argues from comparison with other documents that the list in the charter of liberties is actually the abbot's rent-roll 'in the order of tenements on the ground', following the twelfth-century street pattern.[25] An unusual way of obtaining freedom, which Mackreth describes in his article, is demonstrated in the case of Robert Testard, originally from Scotter. The charter of liberties lists him as a former tenant ('toftum quod fuit Roberti Testard'),[26] implying that he missed out on the liberties granted by the charter. But c.1231 his son Peter, who still held land at Scotter, is described as having and holding it freely because of the fact that 'his father was armed to make battle against the men of Kirkton on behalf of the liberty of the house of Burgh'.[27] When the abbey's property was threatened by armed men, the abbot was presumably prepared to grant the privilege of freedom to those of

---

23 For the estimate of 4.5 or 5 persons per average household, see E. Miller and J. Hatcher, *Medieval England: Rural Society and Economic Change, 1086–1348* (London, 1978), p. 29; cf. M. M. Postan, *The Medieval Economy and Society* (London, 1972), p. 32.

24 *Historiae Anglicanae*, p. 107.

25 D. Mackreth, 'Excavations in the Town Centre', unpublished article (kindly communicated by the author), p. 14.

26 Peterborough, Dean and Chapter, MS 1, fol. 229r.

27 *Ibid.*, fol. 155r.

his servants who would engage in a local skirmish in defence of the abbey's interests.

As the obedientiary system developed, it became necessary that they should each be endowed with property. The sacrist, cellarer and chamberlain were established in the twelfth century, in the time of Abbot Martin de Bec (1132-55), as the Peterborough chronicler Hugh Candidus makes clear.[28] The almoner received his main endowment, which included some property in the town, from Abbot Benedict towards the end of that century, but he had already been granted a third of the tithes of Paston church by Benedict's predecessor, William of Waterville,[29] and the cellarer was granted the valuable manors of Alwalton and Fletton shortly afterwards by Abbot Andrew (1194-9).[30] All their revenues were augmented by Abbot Robert of Lindsey in c.1215, when parts of the burgh became assigned to several of the obedientiaries.[31] As Professor Brooke has pointed out, this meant that 'each obedientiary acquired a number of minor tasks unconnected with his original function', and the system was 'not only complicated but incoherent'.[32] Some departments were at times very short of funds, but the system did not easily accept the transfer of monies from one department to another.

Tensions came to a head in 1231, when Bishop Hugh of Wells conducted a visitation which, by doing little more than enjoining the obedientiaries to show reverence for the abbot and provide aid for him when requested, recognised the strength of their position.[33] A more practical answer was to set up the office of a centralised conventual treasurer, at first in 1248 and then more securely under Abbot Richard of London (1274-95), which facilitated transfers of monies between obedientiaries and gradually acquired its own property to strengthen central financial operations.[34] In the following century, however, there was a shift from the direct exploitation of land to a system of farms and fixed rents, which had the effect of restoring to the obedientiaries their fixed incomes and a measure of autonomy. When the income of one

---

[28]   *Ibid.*, fol. 18v.
[29]   For William of Waterville (1155-75), see *ibid.*, fol. 19; and for Benedict (1177-93), see *Historiae Anglicanae*, p. 101.
[30]   *Ibid.*, p. 103.
[31]   *Ibid.*, pp. 111-12; in the case of the cellarer, the increase was necessitated by the enlargement of the monastery from seventy-two monks to eighty.
[32]   C. N. L. Brooke, 'Introduction', in *The Book of William Morton*, ed. W. T. Mellows and P. I. King, Northamptonshire Record Society 16 (Oxford, 1954), p. xx.
[33]   Peterborough, Dean and Chapter, MS 1, fol. 94.
[34]   *Ibid.*, fols 162v, 163v, 165; *Historiae Anglicanae*, pp. 103-4, 126, 147. For monastic treasuries, see R. A. L. Smith, 'The *Regimen Scaccarii* in English Monasteries', in his *Collected Papers* (London, 1947), 54-73.

happened to fall short, it could be made good by another who would eventually have to be repaid, and therefore all these transactions were carefully recorded. The system was cumbersome but it worked.[35]

So far as the tenants were concerned, however, it was a matter of relative indifference which obedientiary they had to pay. One of the most unusual features of Peterborough Abbey is that it has preserved a document containing abstracts of charters made by peasants on the demesne manors of the abbey, the famous *Carte Nativorum*, which was splendidly edited by C. N. L. Brooke and M. M. Postan for the Northamptonshire Record Society in 1960.[36] The book was probably compiled in the mid-fourteenth century by John of Achurch, and although it was known to the seventeenth-century historian Gunton, its significance was not realised until W. T. Mellows showed it to Postan in 1938, with the comment that the title *Carte Nativorum* must be an antiquarian's mistake, since, as all legal historians know, 'villeins could not acquire or transfer property by charter. ... Charters were sealed documents, and only freemen could have a seal' to authenticate transactions.[37] Or that is what Mellows and Postan thought at the time.

As they studied the volume more closely, however, they came to realise that it was in fact a peasants' cartulary, dealing with tiny parcels of land ranging from one rood to one or two acres.[38] The purchasers in many cases were villeins, yet the land they bought was free land, bought from free men. Because they were villeins the land was seized by the abbey and granted back to them to hold at the lord's will, and on being regranted the land they paid an increment of rent. Because these holdings were outside the customary framework, the rent could be increased, and it was therefore in the abbey's interests to make a careful distinction between free land and land held by villeins. Also land held at the abbey's will could not, in principle, be passed on to heirs, so from the abbey's point of view it was essential that the distinction be maintained.

Occasionally a charter includes an act of manumission such as that of William son of Ralph of Thorpe and his heirs by Abbot Andrew (1194–99). For an annual rent of 6s. William, who held fifteen acres in Thorpe and two acres of meadow and the house in which he lived, was set free from all

---

[35] Brooke, 'Introduction', p. xxii; for greater detail on the system, see *Account Rolls of the Obedientaries of Peterborough*, ed. J. Greatrex, Northamptonshire Record Society 33 (Peterborough, 1984), *passim*.

[36] *Carte Nativorum, a Peterborough Abbey Cartulary of the Fourteenth Century*, ed. C. N. L. Brooke and M. M. Postan, Northamptonshire Record Society 20 (Oxford, 1960).

[37] *Ibid.*, p. xxviii.

[38] See King, *Peterborough Abbey*, ch. 6; P. R. Hyams, 'The Origins of a Peasant Land Masters in England', *Economic History Review*, 2nd ser. 33 (1970), 18–31.

customary services: merchet (particularly loathed because it meant peasants were not free even in family matters), the fine for selling a horse, payments for pannage, plough-service, harrowing, reaping and mowing services and all other lay services except a moderate aid (*auxilium ... moderate*) at Michaelmas which was to be seen as distinct from that of the villeins (*non in communi cum rusticis*).[39]

But more usually land was held at the abbey's will in order that the hereditary principle might be obviated and rents increased. However, a change took place towards the end of the thirteenth century. As Professor Brooke has pointed out,[40] we are witnessing the effects of Edward I's statute *Quia Emptores* of 1290. This statute forbade subinfeudation, which was the procedure whereby the recipient or purchaser became tenant of the donor or vendor; instead there had to be a substitution clause whereby the purchaser took the vendor's place and so held immediately of the vendor's lord. The effect of this was that all the conveyances were drafted as if the transactions were in free land.

Paul Hyams has argued that 'by 1300, professional lawyers had arrived on the scene in force' and it may be that 'fear of the lawyers, instigated in the abbot's mind by lawyers themselves' led to the confiscation of the charters and their replacement.[41] The fear was that the old formulae depending only on custom might be shown to be invalid and the landlord's rights would collapse. Better to accept that villeins held quasi-free land on which rent had to be paid than that they held it on legally uncertain terms which might fail to protect the abbey from the forfeiture of all its rights.

Edmund King, examining the evidence, shows that although the market for land free of customary services was fluid at *c.*1300 in Peterborough, attracting considerable numbers of participants, yet 'two generations later the major families had engrossed the lot; eight families, all of them powerful and inter-related, account for all of the land'.[42] These families, Gere, in le Wro, Abbot, Hunne (one of whom was reeve of the manor), Alred, Pappele, atte Grene and Poper of Eye he dubs the 'Peterborough kulaks'. The list of their holdings is item 554 in the *Carte Nativorum*, which King describes as 'the key document in the collection, for it is intended to sum up the material earlier recorded'. It lists the free land held by the villeins of the soke of Boroughbury of which an inquisition was made in 1341-2 by Brother John of Achurch,

---

[39] *Carte Nativorum*, pp. 182-3.

[40] *Ibid.*, p. xvii.

[41] King, *Peterborough Abbey*, p. 104, citing P. R. Hyams, 'Legal Aspects of Villeinage between Glanvill and Bracton' (University of Oxford D. Phil. thesis, 1968); see now his King, *Lords and Peasants in Medieval England* (Oxford, 1980), esp. pp. 217-18.

[42] King, *Peterborough Abbey*, pp. 116-17.

warden of the manors. A key factor was that land was now being passed on from one generation to the next, including younger sons and daughters. Some at least of the peasantry were beginning to be in a position to fulfil the impulse that they should be able to pass on a small degree of independence to their younger sons, and a small dowry, even if it was no more than half an acre, to their daughters.

On a different level again were some of the abbey's officials who used their position to build up considerable personal land-holdings. Perhaps the most outstanding example of social climbing was that of Richard of Crowland, bailiff of the abbey's property in the soke of Peterborough, and son of Benedict of Eye who was born a *nativus* or bondman. Benedict, after manumission, succeeded in making an advantageous marriage with the sister of Abbot Godfrey of Crowland. From this union came young Richard. Abbot Godfrey, against the will of the convent, appointed his nephew bailiff – a literal case of nepotism.[43] In 1305 Richard held a fourth part of the knight's fee of Walton. Later he was granted (or he was able to buy) the Cathwaite tenements of the knight's fee of Barnack and a small portion of the Torpel fee. He was farming two virgates in Boroughbury, some of which he sublet for profit.[44] He also held substantial property in the town and bought a group of ten cottages which he demolished in order to build himself a grand house with hall and solar in Westgate just east of the junction with Boroughbury (Lincoln Road). His social standing was indicated not only by his town house but also by a country house in Walton, which was described in Fr5 Register as 'his mansion'.[45] This was a meteoric rise for the son of a bondman whose initial promotion had at first incurred the disapproval of the abbey.

In the course of the fourteenth century the status of the tenants continued to improve. The account roll survives for the year 1334 when the abbot was Adam de Boothby. It was rendered by Richard Hunne, reeve of Boroughbury manor. From this document it can be seen that some of the virgates had been let at farm rather than being held on the normal customary basis. The case of John Edgar is characteristic. He had paid 10s. 10d. 'for one virgate of land let on farm without its messuage ... for the term of his life, this payment being for all services except boroughwark and sheriff's tourn, and ... 3s. 6d. for one messuage with its curtilage which was wont to pertain to the virgate of land which John Edgar held' and the sum of '£6 10s. 6d. for twenty-nine acres of

[43] *Henry of Pytchley's Book of Fees*, ed. W. T. Mellows, Northamptonshire Record Society 2 (Kettering, 1927), p. 142.
[44] *Ibid.*, p. 125, n. 1; Northamptonshire Record Office, Fitzwilliam Charters 1080; Fitzwilliam Account Roll 2388.
[45] Peterborough, Dean and Chapter MS 7, fol. 107r.; Boughton House, Register of George Fr5, p. 322 (photostat copy in Peterborough Cathedral Library).

meadow in Padholme, sold at 4s. 6d. an acre, by virtue of a concession of Lord Godfrey once Abbot' (the previous abbot, Godfrey of Crowland).[46]

This, and similar documents, reveal that the manorial organisation on the home manor was breaking down. Separate strips had been lumped together to create single holdings which were now being let to tenants for rent. The customary services which the villeins had formerly owed to their lord were being commuted into cash payments, and what remained of the agricultural duties to be performed on the demesne manor were being carried out by farm labourers hired for the purpose by the tenant farmers. As evidence of this last point, the 1334 account records the receipt of '16s. 10d. for the sale of those week-work services which were worth one halfpenny a day-work, 19d. for 19 works which were worth one penny a day-work'.[47]

The next surviving account, that for 1390, shows that this process had continued apace. The demesne was now being farmed by the bailiff, who had taken the place of the reeve, and was acting as farm steward.[48]

The effect of the Black Death may be seen in several ways. In late fourteenth-century accounts the entry 'decassus redditus' begins to appear; it is also apparent that some land had fallen back into the hands of the lord of the manor because the tenants had died without heirs. It now seems that one cause of the Peasants' Revolt of 1381, along with the infamous poll-tax, was the scarcity of labour after the Black Death, resulting in attempts by lords to maintain the services of the villeins at a time when the expectations of peasants and labourers were inexorably rising.[49]

A contemporary account of the effect of the revolt in Peterborough is to be found in the chronicle of Henry Knighton, canon of Leicester.[50] The townsmen joined forces with the customary tenants of the home manor and adjoining manors to attack the abbey. The abbot was Henry de Overton, but there is no record of any retaliation on his part. In the event the revolt was put down with great severity by Henry Despenser, a very martial bishop of Norwich, who by chance was returning from Rutland through Peterborough on the very day that the rebels rose. His company included a few armed servants, eight lances and a few archers. He quickly gathered recruits, probably from among the local gentry and confronted the rebels. Some he killed, some he took prisoner, and some sought refuge within the sanctuary of the abbey church. The warlike bishop followed them in and ran them down

---

[46] Cited by Mellows, *The Local Government of Peterborough*, p. 28.
[47] *Ibid.*, p. 29.
[48] *Ibid.*, pp. 30–1.
[49] The latest survey of the connection between plague and revolt is J. Hatcher, 'England in the Aftermath of the Black Death', *Past & Present* 144 (1994), 3–35, with comments on villeinage at pp. 33–5.
[50] *Knighton's Chronicle, 1337–1396*, ed. G. K. Martin (Oxford, 1995), pp. 224–7.

with lances and swords, some beside the altar. His justification of this breach of sanctuary was reported by the chronicler as 'returning to them the same measure which they had meted out; for they came to destroy the church and churchmen', and therefore 'deserved to perish in the church and by the church by a churchman'. No Benedictine he, but this incident reveals how far some late medieval prelates had strayed from the precepts of Him who taught the love of your enemy and the duty of turning the other cheek.

But it was not a total loss for the peasants. The outcome was that services were not reinstated; rather, even those that survived were now commuted for fixed rents, and the bondsmen improved their status to that of peasant proprietors.[51] Those slaughtered by the bishop of Norwich in Peterborough Abbey were in fact martyrs in the cause of freedom, a cause which their deaths signally furthered.

Turning now to the question of service to the community, especially to the poor, this was of course one element in the Benedictine ideal, and although it was never central, it was always a factor in the relationship of the abbey to the town.[52] Throughout the period covered by this paper, the abbey continued to provide two hospitals. The hospital of St Leonard, at what is now Spital Bridge, was originally founded before 1125 as a leper-house, but by the fifteenth century it had become an ordinary hospital for about eight old bedesmen. The chapel and hospital of St Thomas of Canterbury had been founded by Abbot William of Waterville not long before he was deposed in 1175, and housed eight poor women. The chancel of the chapel still survives and served until recently as the Song School.[53]

It was the almoner who administered these two hospitals, but the annual payments to the occupants (40s. for each man and 33s. 4d. for each woman)[54] are not shown in the accounts of the fifteenth-century almoner William Morton, so presumably this money came from other sources in the convent and from the parishioners of Peterborough. Indeed, despite his title, the almoner was concerned less with the alms of the abbey than with administering his estates, repairing buildings, paying his servants and supporting the monks who were studying at university.

The *Valor Ecclesiasticus* records that the abbey at the end of its life was paying a total of £54 1s. 0d. a year in alms or about three percent of its

51 See above, nn. 47–8.
52 In general see Barbara Harvey, *Living and Dying in England, 1100–1540: the Monastic Experience* (Oxford, 1993), ch. 1.
53 In the autumn of 1994 this building ceased to be the Song School and is now known as the Becket Room.
54 *The Last Days of Peterborough Monastery*, ed. W. T. Mellows, Northamptonshire Record Society 12 (Kettering, 1947), p. 18.

income. This sum includes the payments to the occupants of the hospitals; other specified payments were 4d. a week, amounting to just over £12 a year, issued by the abbot and cellarer, to fourteen poor women; alms of £5 15s. 8d. from an ancient endowment paid out on chief feast days and solemn festivals; 2d. each to 200 poor people at Southorpe on the anniversary of the death of Queen Eleanor; nine quarters of wheat distributed to the poor, five by the almoner and four by the sacrist; and eight quarters of peas distributed by the almoner. The expenses of the Maundy Thursday dole were £2 18s. 4d., and there was an annual distribution of bread on All Souls' day.[55]

Morton's accounts include an item of 3d. for 'a long trough for conserving alms in the refectory', and if Barbara Harvey's evidence from Westminster Abbey may be generalised, this trough must have contained choice items for daily distribution at the east gate.[56] Worn out clothing from the abbey would also be doled out there, and at Peterborough late medieval extensions to the almoner's hall suggest that he may have had a bakehouse to augment the distribution of leftover food to the poor.

Until the early fourteenth century there was no bridge across the river, and the abbey operated a toll where goods and people were landed at the hithe which had been improved by Abbot Martin de Bec in the twelfth century. It is well known that the monks of Thorney, to avoid the Peterborough toll, constructed a road from Norman Cross to Stanground, which they owned, and they operated a ferry onwards from there to their abbey. In 1308 Abbot Godfrey of Crowland built a bridge over the river at the cost of £14 8s. 0d., but the following winter it was destroyed by floating ice. Walter of Whittlesey's Chronicle describes it as *novum pontem*, but there is no evidence of an earlier bridge at this site. For such a low outlay it must have been of wood. The following year he rebuilt the bridge, making it higher and stronger (*altiorem et fortiorem*) at the cost of £18 5s. 0d.; subsequent descriptions of repairs confirm that the second bridge was of wood.[57]

There then followed a series of disputes between the abbey and the town concerning the upkeep of the bridge. A royal inquiry was held on 12 September 1327 whose purpose was to decide 'who was bound to repair and maintain, when necessary, the bridge over the River Nene near the vill of Peterborough, which said river is the boundary between our counties of Northampton and Huntingdon, and who had been accustomed in times past, for what reason and by what right and in what manner, to repair and maintain the bridge'.[58]

---

[55] *Ibid.*, pp. 18f.

[56] *Book of William Morton*, p. 125. Harvey, *Living and Dying*, p. 70, where she suggests that 'as much as 45%' was left 'for the servants and the poor'.

[57] *Historiae Anglicanae*, p. 163.

[58] *Peterborough Local Administration: Parochial Government before the Reformation.*

The witnesses, who were drawn from both sides of the river, swore on oath:

(i) that no person or persons were under any legal obligation to repair the bridge for any reason;

(ii) that no person or persons in times past had been accustomed to repair the bridge at any time, because there was no bridge there before Godfrey, formerly abbot of Peterborough, at his own expense and of his own free will charitably for the first time and newly (*de elemosina sua et ex propria voluntate sua ... caritative primo et de novo*) built a bridge in the fourth year of the reign of Edward II, and for all his time charitably maintained that bridge of his own grace;

(iii) after his death the bridge was broken and ruinous, and remained long out of repair until the visit of the lord king who now is [Edward III] and of the lady queen his mother, out of respect for whom Adam [de Boothby] the abbot of Peterborough who now is repaired the bridge with beams, boards and nails (*lignis, bordis et clavis*) for their passage although he was not bound so to do (*quominus ad hoc non tenebatur*).[59]

On 30 April 1334 Edward III granted to the abbot and convent of Peterborough and the good men of those parts pontage for three years on wares passing over the bridge for the repair of that bridge. A similar document of 10 June 1334, six weeks later, grants the same rights to Peter de Sant Marreys, Master John de Hameldon, parson of the church of Overton Watermill (on the Huntingdonshire side), and to Richard de Lincoln of Peterborough and the good men of those parts for the same purpose.[60] The implication is that the abbot had surrendered the first document, refusing to accept any responsibility for the repair of the bridge, whereupon a group of townsmen undertook the duty. As Mellows points out, 'this is one of the first examples of an independent association of the townsmen outside the abbot's administration of the vill of Peterborough'.[61]

Further legal hearings in 1354 before the steward and marshal of the king's lodging at Peterborough confirmed that the abbot was indeed free of all liability for bridge repairs, and that certain named individuals had been receiving pontage together with individual gifts in cash and in kind for the repair of the bridge. They were ordered to make use of the sums received and proceed with the necessary repairs forthwith.[62] The fact that bridge repairs

---

Churchwardens' Accounts, 1467–1573, with Supplementary Documents, 1107–1488, ed. W. T. Mellows, Northamptonshire Record Society 9 (Kettering, 1939), pp. 236–7.
[59] Ibid.
[60] Ibid., pp. 234–6.
[61] Ibid., p. 180, n. 1.
[62] Ibid., pp. 237–40.

remained the responsibility of the townspeople is shown by occasional entries concerning bridge repairs in the churchwardens' accounts of the parish church of St John in the fifteenth and sixteenth centuries. In 1476 the churchwardens paid 20s. as 'earnest' to a man who had agreed to make a new pier for the bridge, and further entries appear in 1510, 1514 and 1515.[63] Occasionally, the abbey offered a little help; for example, the last abbot, John Chambers, showed his goodwill by giving the parish two trees standing in one of his woods for the repair of the bridge, and the churchwardens' accounts for 1533–4 show a goodwill payment to the abbot's forester of 8d. They further paid 10d. 'to two fellows for felling of the said trees', 2s. 'to William Algar for carrying of the said trees', 12s. 'to John Tailour and Richard Smyth for workmanship of the bridge', 4s. 'for stone and gravel', 2d. 'for sedge', 2d. 'for covering of the same' and 4d. 'for breaking it up'.[64]

Mention of the parish church raises the question of the spiritual provision for the townspeople. The original parish church was east of the abbey, which meant that after Abbot Martin de Bec's town planning exercises the church was in the wrong location. A chapel of ease dedicated to St Botolph was established near Westwood, but during the abbacy of Robert of Sutton (1263–74), William de Thorp, knight, obtained licence from the abbot to remove the chapel to a site in Longthorpe more convenient for the parishioners.[65]

So far as the townspeople of Peterborough were concerned, the old church to the east of the abbey was inconvenient, and often in winter access to it was flooded. The custom became established of using the chapel of St Thomas by the abbey gate as a kind of parish church. On 26 February 1401–2 the abbot and convent wrote to Henry Beaufort, bishop of Lincoln, giving their consent to a request of the parishioners to take down the parish church and build a new one west of the monastery because 'in the winter season when the rains cause floods they could not without the greatest difficulty get to their parish church of St John the Baptist'. The bishop granted his licence for the purpose on 10 May 1402, and the agreement was confirmed by Pope Boniface IX by a document dated 15 November 1402.[66] An agreement dated 1 May 1402 was drawn up between William Genge, abbot, with the convent of Peterborough and John Ankedill, vicar of the parish church of St John the Baptist on the one part, and Thomas Pykewell and twenty-three inhabitants and parishioners of Peterborough in the name of the rest of the said inhabitants on the other part, by which the old church should be taken down 'and that the beams and rafters and all other materials of the said church

[63] Ibid., pp. 21, 93–4.
[64] Ibid., p. 126.
[65] Ibid., pp. 205–6.
[66] Ibid., pp. 225–8.

should be removed to the middle of the Marketstede aforesaid and a new church with chancel in honour of their saint John the Baptist be there completely, decently and honourably constructed within the limits and bounds set and assigned by the said religious with all possible and reasonable speed at their own sole expense'. In order to help forward the work, the abbot and convent gave the nave of the chapel of St Thomas near the abbey gate and provided additional timber from their estates.[67]

In July 1402 the demolition of the old church was begun, and by 1407 the new parish church was complete, the first mass being celebrated by the abbot on 26 June. A further agreement between the abbot and parishioners, dated 9 July 1407, provided for the cemetery on the north side of the abbey to become the burial ground for the parish; this was to remain the sole burial ground for the townsfolk until 1804.[68]

There is a well-known series of visitations of religious houses in the diocese of Lincoln in the fifteenth and early sixteenth centuries published by the Lincoln Record Society, which reveal a general decline in observance and suggest that the Benedictines had strayed far from their ideals.[69] It can, of course, be argued that visitations are called only when there are problems, and that to base an assessment of the quality of monastic life on these visitations is to create a distorted picture. Nevertheless there is enough material to suggest that the original ideals were long forgotten and that for much of the last century of its life, Peterborough Abbey had become a kind of gentlemen's club.

There were several ways in which this affected the abbey's relations with the town. Bishop Gray's injunctions of 1432 required that 'women, especially those concerning whom suspicion may in likelihood arise, in no wise enter the inner offices within the cloister precincts', meaning the dorter, frater and kitchen.[70]

The visitation of 1437 by Bishop Alnwick reveals a weak and elderly abbot, John Deeping (1409–38).[71] Complaints were made to the bishop concerning 'the great and unruly roaming about of the monks and their eating in the town of Peterborough and their suspect conversation with women'. The bishop ordered 'that none of them for any cause whatever shall drink or

---

[67] *Ibid.*, p. 220.
[68] *Ibid.*, pp. 218–19; the first parishioner to be buried was Leticia Godebody.
[69] In general see Janet Burton, *Monastic and Religious Orders in Britain 1000–1300* (Cambridge, 1994); David Knowles, *The Religious Orders in England*, 3 vols (Cambridge, 1948–59), II.
[70] *Visitations of Religious Houses in the Diocese of Lincoln, 1420–1449*, ed. A. H. Thompson, 3 vols, Lincoln Record Society 7, 14, 21 (Horncastle, 1914–29), I, p. 101.
[71] *Ibid.*, III, p. 272–5.

eat under colour of any pretext soever in the town of Peterborough from this time (11 December 1437) until the last day of March next to come, and that they dance not with any women in the same town or bring in any women within the monastery or receive them that are brought in by others to any suspect familiar converse, save only those persons concerning whom the laws have no evil suspicion'. There were complaints that there was 'much late watching and drinking in the evening' during what should have been the greater silence, so that some were 'left indisposed to celebrate on the following days'. The abbot was said to be lax in collecting his rents from the town, and 'the manors and tenements which belong to the abbot's side are going to great and almost irreparable ruin unless heed be taken speedily to their repair'. He was also criticised for his administration of the manor and his commercial judgement; his critics thought there was no profit in making oil out of rape-seed. The tenements belonging to the sacrist were becoming ruinous.

The bishop's injunctions together with the accession of a new abbot, Richard Ashton, were temporarily successful in reforming the monastery, because at the visitation of 1442, almost all the monks reported that 'all things are well'.[72] Indeed their unanimity seems a little suspect, and one senses that Bro. Peter Lynne expressed their underlying feelings when he 'prays that my lord will modify his injunction against going out to the town and drinking therein'. The treasurer still complained that rents for tenements in the town were not being forcefully sought by the new abbot.

Four years later, in 1446, there was another visitation by Bishop Alnwick which revealed very serious problems in the monastery, even though some of the accusations may have been no more than malicious gossip.[73] It seems clear that many tenements were still in as bad a state as ten years before, or rather were becoming even more ruinous. The abbot himself acknowledged that there was an unofficial way from the town into the monastery through the sisters' house (the hospital of St Thomas near the Foregate), and that a newly created garden beside the sisters' house had become a place of rendezvous and drinking for monks and townspeople, who whiled away convivial evenings there together.[74]

There were so many reports of sexual scandals that some credence has to be given to them. The visitation of 1437 had brought one accusation of scandal involving the sacrist and a boy,[75] but the chief complaints had been of a heterosexual nature. In 1446 there were many complaints relating to 'light women and suspect'. The most serious of all these scandals involved the abbot

[72]   *Ibid.*, III, pp. 283–5.
[73]   *Ibid.*, III, pp. 285–302.
[74]   *Ibid.*, III, pp. 285–6.
[75]   *Ibid.*, III, p. 275.

himself (Richard Ashton), who, it was repeatedly alleged, had not one but three mistresses among the married women of the town. As proof of this, it was said that the abbot went out of the monastery at night in secular dress to the house of William Clerk, husband of one of the three women.[76] Also, William Parker's wife was 'decked out' in a fur coat 'beyond her husband's estate';[77] the abbot had given it to her, but it was recognised as the one given by Abbot Deeping, which he 'expressly left to the abbots his successors, to be bestowed upon no-one else'.[78] The prior had advised Ashton to send this woman away, 'and yet he did it not', but instead he proceeded to confer special favours on her husband.[79] Furthermore, William Est's wife had been given a mazer adorned with silver gilt by the abbot, and special favours had been given to her husband by the abbot without the advice of the convent.[80]

It almost seems that the relationship between abbey and town had become a matter of the abbot's own personal relationships, but all these charges he stoutly denied, as did the women. In the end the poor bishop who had to deal with all this set up a board of management to direct the affairs of the monastery and rebuked the abbot, though he did not depose him. The abbot was required to have no further communication with any of the women on pain of excommunication, and the women, with their husbands, were ordered to remove right away from the district.[81]

The truth of the matter was, of course, known only to Ashton and the three women. However, further light on Ashton's character is shed by a letter of his fellow-monk, William Borough, with whom he had studied at Canterbury College, Oxford from 1435 to 1438. On leaving Oxford, the two young monks were given a report from the warden of their college, to be opened by the prior of Peterborough. Borough's letter reveals that they opened the report themselves, and, having found that it accused them of spending much of their time in taverns and with a woman, they naturally destroyed the report. The irony is that nothing would be known of this evidence but for the fact that Borough revealed it in a postscript to a letter to a friend: "Richard begs you to tell no-one the story of the warden's letter addressed to our prior'.[82] William did not stand by his old friend at the 1446

---

[76] *Ibid.*, III, p. 290.
[77] *Ibid.*, III, p. 286.
[78] *Ibid.*, III, p. 293. Cf. pp. 290–1.
[79] *Ibid.*, III, pp. 287, 293, 296.
[80] *Ibid.*, III, pp. 289, 291, 293, 296.
[81] *Ibid.*, III, p. 302. Alice Est, who already lived some distance away in Oundle, was not required to move further, but the abbot was 'to keep from this Alice Est under pain of excommunication' (p. 298).
[82] W. A. Pontin (ed.), *Canterbury College, Oxford*, 4 vols, Oxford Historical Society new ser. 6–8, 30 (Oxford, 1947–85), III, pp. 96–8.

visitation, but agreed with the general view 'that the abbot is blamed of incontinence, for which reason he [William] says that the monastery is greviously defamed by all'.[83]

Finally we come to Robert Kirkton, the penultimate abbot (1496–1528). Having been caught hunting in the king's forest of Cliffe Park, he was summoned to appear in London where he had to pay a fine of £20. His reaction to this was not to give up hunting, which of course has no place in Benedict's rule, but to create his own deer park, of which the Tudor gate survives, plastered with Tudor heraldry as flattery to Lady Margaret Beaufort, whom Kirkton claimed as a friend, and whose intercession had no doubt kept his fine down. In order to create this park, he had, without the consent of the convent, enclosed land adjoining the eastern and northern sides of the abbey and also part of the parochial churchyard, the only place of burial in the town.[84] He had also demolished a number of houses occupied by tenants. This action incensed not only the townspeople but also the monks, who complained to the bishop that their ancient right of way to Oxney for their regular blood-letting had been obstructed by the abbot's park.[85]

Further to this, Kirkton in 1517 sent his servants to drive the townspeople's cattle off Borough Fen which he then proceeded to enclose as pasture for his own livestock ('Et idem dominus abbas opprimit totam communitatem ville de Petirburgh cum catallis suis in eorum communis').[86] The furious townspeople broke open the fences, cut and carried off the grass, and put their cattle back on the fen. In August 1517 they invaded the precincts and were admitted to an interview with the bishop of Lincoln and the abbot in the Lady Chapel. There are two accounts of this meeting;[87] the townspeople claimed that they had acted humbly and reasonably and that the bishop gave them his blessing as he rode away, promising that the 'said inhabitants should be ordered right well and that my lord abbot would be good lord unto his said tenants and inhabitants of the said town'.[88] But the abbot's witnesses asserted that the townspeople used threatening language and gestures: the monk William Boston described 'a great multitude of people of the town amounting as he might in conscience conjecture to the number of xl persons or more, being in a great marvellous fury and anger as it appeared not

[83]   *Visitations of Lincoln*, III, p. 294.
[84]   *Visitations in the Diocese of Lincoln 1517–1531*, ed. A. H. Thompson, 3 vols, Lincoln Record Society 33, 35, 37 (Hereford, 1947), III, p. 79; *Select Cases before the King's Council in the Star Chamber*, II, *A.D. 1509–1544*, ed. I. S. Leadam, Selden Society 25 (London, 1911), p. 128.
[85]   *Visitations 1517–1531*, III, p. 77, 79.
[86]   *Ibid.*, III, p. 78.
[87]   They are recorded in *Star Chamber*, II, pp. 123–42.
[88]   *Ibid.*, II, p. 129.

only by their countenance and gesture but also by their innumerable unreasonable opprobrious words'.[89] The monk offered them a drink to pacify them, but they were not to be put off so lightly. They continued to make threats of personal violence and to rail against the abbot whom they described as having acted 'full Judasly', always eager 'to oppress or undo a poor man'.[90] John Power, gentleman, the leader of the townspeople, was accused of breaking the head of John Holte, one of the abbot's servants.

The townspeople then found a way of paralysing the abbot's power as lord of the manor by controlling the elections of the municipal officers in the manorial courts, the constables, dozeners, ale tasters and searchers of victuals. They put forward their own nominees and rejected the names proposed by the abbot's steward. That this was a real power struggle between abbot and town is to be seen in the fact that the names of those acting for the townspeople include the churchwardens of the parish church and others who would subsequently become churchwardens.

The case passed through the lower court and on appeal the court of the hundred found for the abbot. He then made a complaint to the Star Chamber as the tribunal for the repression of violence. Here the abbot admitted that the townsmen 'had their common of pasture (on Borough Fen) in a reasonable manner too and for a certain number of cattle'.[91] The townspeople on the other hand claimed that 'during the time that no man's mind is to the contrary for the while that they have inhabited in the same town [they] have had and used to have common of pasture in the said waste called Borough Fen for their cattle without any admeasurement'.[92] They complained of the abuse of power by the abbot both in enclosing the fen and enclosing the churchyard 'where their friends were buried'. The determined character of the townspeople's actions probably reflects their awareness that Wolsey had just appointed a commission to inquire into enclosures with a view to enforcing the law against them. Kirkton was already being pilloried as one of the worst offenders.

In the end Bishop Atwater carried out a visitation which revealed that many of the problems of the previous century still persisted. There were more allegations of sexual misdemeanours of various kinds and much drinking, and the tenements were once again in very bad repair, some having been demolished to make way for the deer park.[93] Much else was wrong and Kirkton offered to resign, but the bishop simply admonished him and left him in office. Ten years later Wolsey engineered his resignation and replaced him

---

89   *Ibid.*, II, p. 131.
90   *Ibid.*, II, p. 132.
91   *Ibid.*, II, p. 125.
92   *Ibid.*, II, p. 128.
93   *Visitations 1517–1531*, III, pp. 76–83.

by his own nominee, John Chambers, a wily politician who was able to steer the abbey through the upheaval of the Reformation and the Dissolution, coming out successfully with the town made a city, the abbey transformed to a cathedral and himself as the first bishop.[94] But that is another story.

What emerges from this necessarily brief survey of the relations of abbey and town over three and a half centuries? Monasticism was essentially about withdrawal from the world, but the great Benedictine houses, unlike the Cistercians, were often sited in towns, with the result that the world became an ever-growing influence on the supposedly withdrawn community. This was not always negative, as we have seen. The fact that the town was at the gates meant that there was a constant need to care for the poor and the weak in the true spirit of the Benedictine ideal, and the monks continued this provision throughout the period, though with varying degrees of enthusiasm. There was concern too, for more general needs, such as the provision of a bridge over the river, but this clearly served the abbey's requirements as much as those of the town and was to lead to disputes about maintenance.

On the other hand, the proximity of the town offered occasion for various scandals as the ideals of the monks waned. Also, as the town became freer, it developed a growing resentment against the abbey, particularly over the monks' neglect of the town properties and its abuse of power. Yet, although to some extent the town appears to have served as a temptation for the monastery, one is forced to the conclusion that the community bore within itself the seeds of its own corruption. The history of monasticism is a process whereby the high ideals of its founders are gradually eroded in practice until a reform takes place from within and new zeal is kindled, either within or outside the institution. This cycle is then usually repeated.

In the gospels there is an ambivalence about the term 'world'; it is at once the sphere of 'worldly' influences and yet also the object of God's love. For the monks the town provided both these elements, yet at a deeper level the monks were to learn that withdrawal from the world is never entirely possible, not because the world is at the gates, but rather because the world is never entirely removed from the hearts of those who have sought to make their life within the gates.

---

[94] *Last Days of Peterborough Monastery*, pp. xiv–xvii.

The Almonry Schools of the English Monasteries c.1265–1540

ROGER BOWERS

Not the least striking of the characteristics displayed by the provision of education for the young during the three hundred years prior to the English Reformation is the rich miscellaneity of the institutions through which it was imparted.[1] Among this conspicuous diversity of the means of supply certain of the houses of religious were certainly prominent. However, to attempt an assessment of the contribution made by the late-medieval English monasteries to society at large through their fostering of the education of youth is not a straightforward matter, since it is a study that has enjoyed rather a chequered history.

So long ago as 1655 the historian Thomas Fuller, in the course of a comprehensively hostile and derogatory account of the monks and their monasteries generally, put on record the extent to which, nevertheless, he believed that they had afforded to society at large certain 'Civill benefits and Temporall conveniences'. These included the manner in which:

> They were tolerable Tutours for the education of *youth* (there being a great penurie of other *Grammar-schools* in that Age) and every Convent had one, or moe therein, who [generally *gratis*], taught the children thereabouts. Yea, they, who were loose enough in their own lives, were sufficiently severe in their discipline over others. *Grammar* was here taught, and *Musick*, which in some sort sung her own *Dirige* (as to the generall use thereof) at the dissolution of Abbies.[2]

---

[1] The subject of this article is the education of boys through the agency of monasteries of monks and canons regular. For the education offered to girls through the nunneries, see e.g. N. Orme, *English Schools in the Middle Ages* (London, 1973), pp. 52–4, and sources there quoted, especially E. Power, *Medieval English Nunneries* (Cambridge, 1922). It is a pleasure to record my gratitude to Professor Nicholas Orme and Dr Joan Greatrex for their illuminating and helpful observations upon an earlier draft of this paper, and to the governing bodies of the several institutions concerned for permission to quote from manuscript sources in their ownership and custody.

[2] T. Fuller, *The Church-History of Britain; from the Birth of Jesus Christ, untill the year*

Of the observations so expressed, the first, concerning grammar, passed into the lore of historians who concerned themselves with education, and the last into that of the historians of music. Each in fact did possess a kernel of truth – the former to a point rather more substantial than the latter.

Views derived from Fuller held sway until about the turn of the present century, when A. F. Leach and G. G. Coulton, in seeking to stress the pre-eminence of not the monastic but the secular schools, accomplished a comprehensive belittlement and minimisation of the achievements of the monks and canons regular as purveyors of education.[3] Only quite recently has a more objective assessment of the role of the monasteries in late-medieval education become possible,[4] and the present paper endeavours to build upon these more sympathetic and realistic accounts of the contribution which they were able to make to society at large in this respect.

Much has been clarified over recent years through the recognition of three quite different and distinct regimes of education in which the monastic houses might engage.[5] Of these, one was obligatory but purely internal. Through the permanent or *ad hoc* office of master of the novices, each monastery of necessity trained the most junior of its own members, both prior to and following profession, in the rule of their order and the manner of its local application – no doubt, with varying levels of success. Necessarily, such tuition extended also to the enormous content and myriad complexities of the daily liturgy, the observance of which was the principal reason for their institution's existence.[6]

M.DC.XLVIII (London, 1655), Book VI, p. 297. This history was unusually influential during the nineteenth century, when it was frequently reprinted. For Nicholas Carlisle's amplification of such views in the early nineteenth century, see J. N. Miner, *The Grammar Schools of Medieval England* (Montreal, 1990), pp. 35–9.

[3] See especially A. F. Leach, *The Schools of Medieval England* (London, 1915), and his numerous contributions to the relevant volumes of the *VCH*; the latter are conveniently listed in Leach, *Schools of Medieval England*, p. ix, and Miner, *Grammar Schools*, pp. 333–8. Also G. G. Coulton, 'Monastic Schools in the Middle Ages', *Contemporary Review* 103 (1913), 818–28.

[4] See e.g. Orme, *English Schools*, pp. 5–6, 224–68; *idem*, *Education in the West of England, 1066–1548* (Exeter, 1976), *passim*, esp. pp. 201–15.

[5] Orme, *English Schools*, pp. 233–51. This chapter also deals with instances in which higher education was available internally in a few of the most prominent monastic houses (pp. 233–9). The mendicant orders appear to have been more inclined than the monastics to engage in formal schemes of teaching at grammar school level, though only to boys intended for profession in their respective orders: *ibid.*, pp. 226–33.

[6] Orme, *English Schools*, pp. 239–43. For a plaintively despairing account of the tribulations of an unmusical novice set to learn his plainsong, see (despite the

The two remaining areas of educational enterprise were both of more voluntary and discretionary a nature. These involved arranging for the general education of boys of normal school age to take place on the premises of the monks and under their auspices and patronage, but through the medium of a secular schoolmaster hired for the purpose from beyond the precinct wall. A number of instances are known in which an abbot or prior agreed, through a purely private and *ad hoc* arrangement, to take the sons of influential personages into his household for the inculcation of a gentle upbringing there.[7] However, much the commonest way for the monastic houses to tender a worthwhile education to the young was through their provision of a day and boarding grammar school, and of a qualified secular schoolmaster to teach it,[8] conducted within the almonry premises normally sited on the edge of the precinct.[9] The pupils of this school consisted in part of boys lodged within the almonry or subalmonry,[10] and maintained in food, drink and clothing from the surplus – the alms – of the host monastery itself.[11] However, as will be seen below, in class the numbers of conventional almonry boys were in many

---

inappropriate modern title wished upon it) F. L. Uttley, 'The Chorister's Lament', *Speculum* 21 (1946), 194–7.

[7] N. Orme, *From Childhood to Chivalry* (London, 1984), pp. 60–3; E. J. Gardner, 'The English Nobility and Monastic Education, c.1100–1500', in *The Cloister and the World: Essays in Medieval History in honour of Barbara Harvey*, ed. J. Blair and B. Golding (Oxford, 1996), 80–94.

[8] In no instance is a monk known to have served as master of an almonry school; as expressed in a dictum attributed to St Jerome, 'monachus non docentis sed plangentis habet officium' (Coulton, 'Monastic Schools', p. 819).

[9] See Orme, *English Schools*, pp. 243–7, 249–51. Although this treatment of the almonry schools is brief, Orme is concerned to stress their significance. It may be noted that whenever it is possible to determine the case, the Lady Chapel singing-boys maintained in many monasteries in the period immediately preceding the Dissolution were drawn from among the almonry schoolboys, and did not constitute a second school, a parallel and separate 'song school'. See below, pp. 208–13.

[10] In the larger monasteries, such as Westminster and Peterborough, the part of the almonry premises used and inhabited by the boys and their school was very commonly designated the subalmonry, and placed under the supervision of a monk subordinate to the almoner, the *subelemosinarius*.

[11] For the most vivid surviving description of the organisation and conduct of the residential arrangements of the boys of an almonry school, unfortunately too long to be quoted here, see *The Rites of Durham*, ed. J. T. Fowler, Surtees Society 107 (Durham, 1903), pp. 91–2. At Westminster Abbey a hatch and stairway let into the thickness of the wall, apparently constructed to enable boys to collect their food from the frater and carry it to the site of their new school built in 1461, were discovered in the last century: J. T. Micklethwaite, 'Notes on the Abbey Buildings at Westminster', *Archaeological Journal* 33 (1876), 15–58, pp. 38–9.

cases substantially amplified by the presence of external pupils who were non-resident and came into school each day to attend the lessons in return for the payment of fees.

As is the case with the history of schools generally in the medieval period, absence or loss of sources renders impossible the compilation of any satisfactorily comprehensive account. A survey extending to the relevant secondary sources,[12] much of the printed primary source material, and a substantial proportion of the surviving obedientiary account rolls as yet unpublished, yields a total of some thirty monasteries at which at some time between c.1265 and 1540 an almonry school of both residential boys and a master to teach them in grammar was maintained.[13] However, the sources are undeniably slender. For only four of these schools do the surviving records permit, if not a continuous then at least a reasonably coherent and cogent history to be written. These are the schools of Westminster Abbey, and of the cathedral priories of Canterbury, Durham and Norwich.[14] For a few others – mostly those of the remaining cathedral priories, especially Worcester and Ely – the incidence of surviving references suffices to demonstrate a certain degree of continuity, and occasionally to add descriptive detail. For many schools, however, no more than a couple of chance references, or even only one, are now extant to show that they ever existed at all; and of these references, a high proportion arise only at the very end of the monastic period, in the

---

[12]   To those mentioned in notes 3 and 4 above may be added J. A. H. Moran, *The Growth of English Schooling, 1340–1548* (Princeton, 1985).

[13]   D. Knowles, *The Religious Orders in England*, 3 vols (Cambridge, 1948–59), II, p. 295, considered the almonry school to have been 'common, if not ubiquitous, among the black monks', but this seems to have been an over-generous estimate of their incidence. The tenor of the present article is to suggest that almonry schools were considerably fewer in number, but substantially greater in significance, than has been claimed hitherto. In the case of perhaps a dozen or more further instances beyond these initial thirty, evidence of the maintenance of a group of singing-boys for a Lady Chapel choir is suggestive of the existence of an almonry school for them to have attended for their conventional education, but, in the absence of corroboration, is not conclusive proof. See below, pp. 212–13.

[14]   All four possess published histories, but none is particularly extended. For Westminster see R. D. Bowers, 'Westminster School in the Days of Westminster Abbey', unpublished paper (1993) deposited in the Library of Westminster Abbey; for part of the history of the school of Durham Priory, see *idem*, 'Educational Provision and Policy in a Late Medieval English City: the Grammar Schools and Song Schools of Durham, 1414–1455', unpublished paper (1982) deposited in the Prior's Kitchen, the archive office of Durham Cathedral. I hope presently to take the substance of these papers into a single book dealing with the almonry schools and Lady Chapel choirs of the late-medieval English monasteries in general.

Valor Ecclesiasticus of 1535 or among the papers produced by the Dissolution itself. It seems fair to surmise that in addition to these thirty there was also a now indeterminable number of schools which have left no trace of their existence whatever. Such attenuation of the evidence necessarily inflicts a degree of debilitation upon any attempt to draw conclusions from it, and ensures that analysis cannot be presented as anything other than crude and tentative.

No almonry school is yet known to have been brought into existence prior to c.1265. However, their appearance then was not entirely without antecedents, since one or two prominent houses had already been moved to admit small groups of boys to residential status within the almonry in order to enable them to attend the grammar school in the adjacent town. Apparently in the time of Abbot Samson (1182–1211) it was arranged that during the teaching terms the almonry of Bury St Edmund's Abbey should lodge and feed, free of charge, two boys attending the monastery's grammar school in the town, at the master's nomination. At much the same time, a similar scheme was set up at the almonry of Durham Cathedral Priory in favour of three boys attending the city school.[15] Such arrangements were merely a natural extension to needy schoolboys of the practice of many of the greater monasteries not merely to distribute doles of alms at the almonry gate, but actually to maintain small groups of infirm and elderly poor as residents within the almonry itself.[16] From about the mid-thirteenth century onwards a precedent was also being set by the maintenance of resident schoolboys attending the town school on the part of some of the greater hospital foundations – for instance, Bridgwater (St John), Bristol (St Mark), Exeter (St

---

[15]   *Educational Charters and Documents, 598–1909*, ed. A. F. Leach (Cambridge, 1911), pp. 124, 130. The boys who, with the *conversi*, were to be lodged in a new *hospitale* or almonry built at Bermondsey Priory in 1213 may have been a comparably small number of secular schoolboys for whom food and lodging were being provided: 'Annales Monasterii de Bermundeseia 1042–1432', *Annales Monastici*, 5 vols, ed. H. R. Luard, Rolls Series (London, 1864–9), III, p. 452.

[16]   In the case of Westminster Abbey, A. F. Leach noted that the appearance of the almonry school early in the fourteenth century coincided with a decline in the maintenance of the resident decrepit poor of both sexes, accomplished in fact by 1317 (Westminster Abbey Muniments [hereinafter WAM] 18962*, *Liberacio denariorum*; 18964, *Vadia fratrum*). This allowed him to suggest, very plausibly, that the school was actually replacing the provision for almsmen and women: 'The Origin of Westminster School', *Journal of Education*, new ser. 26 (1915), 79–81, p. 80. Indeed, it is conceivable that the steady increase in independent hospital foundations throughout the thirteenth century was rendering decreasingly necessary the maintenance of the infirm and elderly in monastic almonries, giving scope for the establishment of schools in their place – for which latter, conversely, demand was rising.

John), London (St Katherine), Norwich (St Giles), Ripon (St John) and Winchester (St Cross).[17] Although undoubtedly enterprising when first introduced, therefore, the decision by any monastic chapter to maintain an almonry school of resident boys and a master to teach them represented merely an extension of principles of *caritas* already not unknown among the greater houses.

The earliest certain notices of the existence and maintenance of a formally organised grammar school within a monastic almonry all date from the last third or so of the thirteenth century.[18] Much the most illuminating of these is an extended document arising from the cathedral priory of Norwich. It dates from the priorate of William de Kyrkeby, 1272 to 1288 or 1289, and survives in a copy of about the second quarter of the fourteenth century.[19] It appears to be possible to attribute its original composition to the last few months of Kyrkeby's tenure as prior, in 1288 or 1289.[20]

[17] By the later fourteenth century the secular hospital of St Leonard, York, was maintaining within its premises not only a group of boys but also an internal schoolmaster to teach them in grammar, an arrangement very closely parallel to that of a conventional monastic almonry school: J. A. H. Moran, *Education and Learning in the City of York*, Borthwick Papers 35 (York, 1979), pp. 9–10.

[18] It appears that during that section of the thirteenth century lying between the imposition of minimum ages for admission to the novitiate (itself following the end of the practice of child oblation) and the beginnings of the almonry schools, there were – as a general rule – no young boys associated in any authorised capacity with the English monastic houses.

[19] J. Greatrex, 'The Almonry School of Norwich Cathedral Priory', in *The Church and Childhood*, Studies in Church History 31 (1994), 169–81, pp. 171–3. To the generosity of Dr Greatrex I am greatly indebted both for my acquaintance with this document and for the opportunity to see a text of her article prior to its publication. The document is now Worcester Cathedral Library, Muniment B.680. It is tempting to suggest that this copy was made at Norwich in 1347, at the time of the visitation of Bishop William Bateman (see below, pp. 195–6). Presumably it reached Worcester in error at the time of the return of archives to the newly restored cathedral chapters following the Commonwealth. Further on the school at Norwich, see R. Harries, P. Cattermole and P. Mackintosh, *A History of Norwich School*, ed. Harries (Norwich, 1991), pp. 3–40; the account of the pre-Reformation schools is by Cattermole.

[20] The document ordains that the schoolmaster's salary be paid to him by the almoner: 'Elemosinarius vero stipendium predictis magistro et servienti solvat'. Such a payment appears on none of the eight almoner's accounts that survive for the period up to and including the sixteenth year of Kyrkeby's priorate, 1287–88; it is found for the first time on the next surviving account, that for 1310–11 (Norfolk and Norwich Record Office, Norwich Cathedral Muniments, DCN 1/6/1–9). This indicates that the document's provisions were compiled and put

The document concerns several aspects of the running of a very early almonry school, and indeed its content and terminology alike display a number of features which are consistent with the proposition that this is in fact the founding document ordering the actual inauguration and establishment of the school. Primarily, the opening statement of the decree ordained that 'in dictam elemosinariam ponantur xiij clerici'. That is, at the place in which any ordinance concerning the management of a school already in existence would have been likely to employ the word 'sint' (let there be), this document instead uses 'ponantur'. Rather than select a word implying a steady state, the author chose one conveying an inaugurative instruction – 'let there be placed in the almonry thirteen *clerici*' – which seems to suggest strongly that what was being ordained here was indeed a new venture. There is a conspicuous absence of references to particular instances of past mismanagement now requiring amendment, and indeed the provisions of the document make no allusion to any prior existence of the school. The comprehensiveness of the ground covered by the decree is likewise indicative, including its attention to all the most basic matters to which any founding document would be bound to attend – the number of boys, the hiring and firing of the officers, and the relationship with the parish church. Nevertheless, it has to be acknowledged that there is nothing in the document which would disqualify the counter-proposal that in fact it preserves a set of provisions effecting fine tuning to the management of a school already in existence, or was drawn up to place on a regulated and formal footing practices which had grown up informally in the immediate and recent past; consequently, these possibilities should remain open. However, the balance of probabilities, plus the absence from the almonry accounts prior to 1288 of any mention of the school or of the payment of its master, does perhaps militate considerably in favour of the former proposition.

Many of the provisions made for the Norwich school at this time were to prove eminently durable, and indeed to characterise the whole genre of schools of which it was itself to become, in due course, a very typical example. The ordinance of the Norwich chapter determined that the core personnel of the school consist of a master and thirteen boys, and directed that it be conducted on the premises of the monastery almonry. Numerous references indicate that in all practical respects responsibility for the general oversight of the school resided with a two-man board consisting of the subprior and the almoner. The function of the master of the school was, as bound by his oath, to exhibit diligence in teaching the pupils to the best of his ability *in literatura et in moribus* – that is, in the learning of Latin and in general demeanour and good behaviour. The requirements of the boys

---

into effect at the very end of Kyrkeby's rule as prior.

themselves were that they be of unadvantaged circumstances – *pauper* is the word used – and suitable for, and amenable to, the processes of formal education. It was also stipulated that each boy be *elegantis stature*; it seems likely that this provision was intended to exclude from admission any boy suffering from any of those physical infirmities that would bar him from eventual ordination to the priesthood.[21] Provision was made for the removal of any pupil found to be unsuited to learning or unwilling to learn, any guilty of serious offences and found incorrigible even after warning and punishment, and any who had begun to suffer from incurable illness. Direction was also given for the removal of any unsuitable master, and for his replacement by a successor, all at the discretion of the subprior and almoner.

A servant engaged by the almoner was to assist in the general maintenance of the school and the care of the boys; once these duties were done, his time and service were to be at the discretion of the almoner.[22] He was bound by oath to treat fairly and honestly both with the pupils themselves and particularly with his management of their means of sustenance. His duty was to preserve the alms of the monastery to the use of the boys, and not to distribute elsewhere anything necessary for them and their schoolmaster. Only those items still remaining after their needs were satisfied were to be distributed to the poor on the other side of the almonry gate. The supply of bread alone was not left to merely the chance provision of casual superfluity; of this, an adequate ration was to be supplied directly each day.

The religious duties of the boys were not overlooked. On every Sunday, and on every feast day sufficiently important for lessons similarly to be suspended, the master and boys were duly to be present at divine service – not in the conventual church of the cathedral priory (since the boys were not members of the monastic community) but in the church of the parish in which their almonry residence lay, St Mary in the Marsh.[23] Conveniently, this

---

[21] Such a rule may have been of quite wide recognition and application. For instance, the admission of a boy as a chorister of Lincoln Cathedral in 1424 despite his possessing an extra little finger on one hand was permitted at the time, but presently produced a protest from the chapter that such a departure from propriety should not occur again: Lincoln Archive Office, Dean and Chapter Archives, MS A.2.32, fols 33v, 41r.

[22] 'Predictus vero serviens, officio sibi commisso adimpleto, in aliis Elemosinario obediat': Worcester Cathedral, Muniment B.680.

[23] It has been pointed out that in the Customary of the cathedral priory, apparently compiled from earlier sources between 1257 and 1265, there occur four ostensible references to the presence of boys (*pueri*) in the monastic observance of the *Opus Dei*: Orme, *English Schools*, pp. 245–6 and Greatrex, 'Almonry School of Norwich Cathedral', pp. 170–1, quoting *The Customary of the Cathedral Priory of Norwich*, ed. J. B. L. Tolhurst, Henry Bradshaw Society 82 (London, 1948), pp. 76, 135, 187

was located actually within the close, to the east of the almonry building and not many yards from it.[24] The pupils were not merely to attend but, as young clerks, were to gain from the experience of assisting the parish clergy in the performance of the service. They were to be present from the beginning of the office of matins until the conclusion of high mass – the best part, that is, of the whole morning. The rest of the day was, it appears, holiday in the modern sense of the word.

(bis). However, these references do not constitute evidence for the existence of an almonry school at so early a date. It may be shown that the *pueri* who were present with their masters at the elaborate procession which preceded high mass on Palm Sunday (*ibid.*, p. 76) were not young boys – either secular schoolboys or anachronistic oblates – but the novices. Firstly, it is significant that at the singing of the processional hymn *Gloria, laus et honor* the sections allocated in the secular Uses to performance by the chorister boys, representing the 'children of the Hebrews', are in the monastic Norwich Customary allotted not to the *pueri* mentioned as participating in this procession but to the *iuvenes* – the young monks (*ibid.*, p. 77; cf. W. H. Frere, *The Use of Sarum*, 2 vols (Cambridge, 1898-1901), I, pp. 41-2, 61-2). Had the Norwich *pueri* been genuine boys, it appears certain that they would have been appointed to sing these verses, as the very obvious candidates to represent the *pueri Hebraeorum* in this procession. Rather, these 'boys' can be shown to have been the novices. The mention of the *pueri* arose because of their irregular location on this occasion at the back of the procession ('Pueri vero eant ultimi cum magistris') on its outward journey; the normal rank order in liturgical processions was for the juniors to precede the seniors, not to follow them. On the route back to the cathedral, however, the normal order of procession was resumed. The Customary had to include an instruction to that effect, in order to supersede the previous direction; and it was expressed by the phrase 'noviciis precedentibus' (*Customary of Norwich*, p. 77). The context makes clear that the *pueri* of the first instruction and the *novicii* of the second constituted the same body of personnel. The *pueri* to whom were allocated the purely momentary duties of beginning the simple litany on the eve of the feast of St John Baptist (*ibid.*, p. 135) and of singing the incipit of the opening antiphon of vespers and of matins *de defunctis* at All Saints-tide (*ibid.*, p. 187) were likewise probably the youngest of the novices (see also below, n. 31).

[24] An exact parallel is presented by the case of the boys who, from 1349, were admitted to board and lodging in the chantry house of the Burghersh Chantry at Lincoln Cathedral, while attending lessons at the city grammar school downhill in the city of Lincoln. Notwithstanding the location of their residence within the cathedral close, the boys were required to attend Sunday and feast-day services not in the minster, but in the church of the parish in which the chantry house lay, St Mary Magdalen: R. D. Bowers, 'Music and Liturgy to 1640', in *A History of Lincoln Minster*, ed. D. Owen (Cambridge, 1994), 47-76, pp. 70-1. In most monastic houses, however, the almonry complex did itself contain a chapel; in these cases it was there that the boys attended service on holy days.

By no means, of course, were these boys professionally trained choristers comparable to those of the secular cathedral and major collegiate churches.[25] The boys of the almonry school were expected to contribute to the service simply 'secundum quod deus dederit eis facultatem' – according as God shall have given them the ability. As the liturgy required, the boys at service were divided into two sides, and in one respect they did mimic a standard practice of the greater churches. As a contribution to pre-emption of the onset of sclerosis in the presentation of the liturgy, it was usual in the professional choirs for members of one side, week and week about, to be given responsibility for the reading of the lessons at the eight daily offices, while members of the other side undertook the singing of those complex and elaborate passages of responsorial chant at the office and mass that were committed to a soloist or small group of singers to perform. In St Mary's church likewise the Norwich almonry schoolboys were divided into two sides, though in this case less according to what they could do than to what they could not. One side was to consist of those who had serviceable voices and were able to sing whatever passages of the plainsong service they could manage after tuition, while the other side consisted of those constrained to limit themselves to reading the lessons and chanting the psalms of matins and lauds – all of which were not sung as such, but were little more than merely monotoned to very simple and repetitive musical formulae.[26]

A postscript added to the original document elucidated two further points germane to the good running of the school. Direction was given that a precautionary check on the progress of the boys in learning be made, on at least a weekly basis, by a suitable monk nominated by the subprior. Further, upon each incidence of a vacancy arising from the simple departure of any pupil, or his progress onward to higher studies, the almoner and subprior were to agree on the admission of a new boy, at their discretion, from among those who met the three criteria of physical integrity, suitability for learning and study, and unadvantaged circumstances. That there would be plenty of aspirants to fill each vacant place is suggested by the stipulation that the subprior and almoner were to make their choice uninfluenced by inducements or bribes tendered on behalf of applicants.

Much of the provision thus made rendered Norwich an archetype of monastery almonry schools. Clearly the motive for its foundation can be identified in the common contemporary phrase *intuitu caritatis*: through the

---

25 See below, pp. 209–10.
26 'Predicti vero magister et pueri singulis diebus dominicis et festivis quibus leccioni non vacant ab initio matutinorum usque ad finem misse in ecclesia sancte marie de marisco divinis intersint. Medietas ex una parte cantet, medietas ex alia legentes et psallentes secundum quod deus dederit eis facultatem': Worcester Cathedral, Muniment B.680.

promptings of charity. The arrangements made for the maintenance of the boys in food, the provision of the services of a full-time servant, the direction that they be brought up *in moribus* as well as *in literatura*, and the management of their Sunday and holy-day worship, all make plain that this was a residential school. The requirement that the pupils be *pauper* indicates that the intended constituency was the pool of suitable boys from deserving families which lacked the means to afford education for their sons at the fee-paying schools under episcopal patronage within the city and elsewhere in the diocese. The insistence on physical integrity, and a curriculum that included, as well as grammar, whatever elements from the plainsong service of Sundays and feast-days the master was able to teach, indicates a primary expectation that the boys so educated would ultimately enter the priesthood and be fit to serve cures or be professed to the monastic life, though other uses of a clerkly education were by no means ruled out. If the motive was *caritas*, however, it must be acknowledged that it was a *caritas* characterised less by random altruism than by hard-nosed calculation. In return, the chapter received not merely the warm glow of doing good, but also the capacity to direct thenceforth the best and probably the bulk of their alms to a visible and narrowly circumscribed objective that was wholly under their direction and control.[27] Moreover, the monastery could look forward to the rewards arising from the enrichment of local society thenceforth by its reception of a steady stream of *literati* obligated to the house by gratitude, loyalty and clientage for perhaps the rest of their lives. And whenever any former pupil opted ultimately to take profession as a religious of the house, that no doubt was an outcome affording especial satisfaction.[28]

Intuitus caritatis, so interpreted, probably was no less the motive informing the foundation of other almonry schools in the later thirteenth century. Provision of education for the sons of the laity, apparently by means of an almonry school, was certainly being offered by Guisborough Priory to the society around the southern Tees estuary (Yorkshire, North Riding) by 1266 and at least until 1280.[29] Guisborough was one of the richest of the

---

[27] For a somewhat later consideration of the legitimacy of such diversion of monastic alms to the maintenance of a school, see below, pp. 198-9.

[28] There may well have been a discernible flow of recruitments to the cloister from among former scholars of the almonry, but probably this was rarely large. When at Christ Church, Canterbury, four former almonry boys were received into the novitiate on a single day in 1468, the occasion was sufficiently noteworthy to merit special remark in the private diary of one of the monks: 'The Chronicle of John Stone, Monk of Christ Church, 1415-71', in *Christ Church, Canterbury*, ed. W. G. Searle, Cambridge Antiquarian Society, octavo ser. 34 (Cambridge, 1902), 1-118, p. 106.

[29] C. R. Cheney, 'Letters of William Wickwane, Chancellor of York 1266-1268',

houses of Augustinian canons; at another house of this order, that of Barnwell in the suburbs of Cambridge, an almonry school certainly was thriving by 1296, when there was made the surviving copy of a digest of the responsibilities incumbent upon the almoner in respect of his management of the school.[30] A chance reference on an obedientiary account shows that an almonry school was functioning at Christ Church, Canterbury by 1291-2, and at the neighbouring cathedral priory of Rochester the school of the almonry had already been in existence for some few years by 1299.[31]

English Historical Review 47 (1932), 626-42, pp. 629, 633. Evidently fearing it to be no more than an egregious distraction from the proper work of a house of religious, the archbishop, as visitor, sought subsequently to discourage the monastery from maintaining the school, unless it was accepted by the chancellor of the diocese as plainly advantageous for it to do so: Cartularium Prioratus de Gyseburne, ed. W. Brown, 2 vols, Surtees Society 86, 89 (Durham, 1889-91), II, p. 360. See also Moran, Growth of English Schooling, pp. 97-8, 114, 252.

[30] Text in eighth and last section of BL, Harley MS 3601. Sections 1-7: Liber Memorandorum Ecclesie de Bernewelle, ed. J. W. Clark (Cambridge, 1907), wherein, for the dating of the manuscript, see pp. ix-x; Section 8: idem, The Observances in Use at the Augustinian Priory of St Giles and St Andrew at Barnwell, Cambridgeshire (Cambridge, 1897), pp. 174-5. Given the degree of access to the world beyond the cloister permitted by the rule of their order, it is readily conceivable that it was among the Augustinian canons that there first arose the idea of using the resources of the almonry to maintain a school for secular boys.

[31] Canterbury, Cathedral Library and Archives, A/c Almoner 10, Solid' servientium; Registrum Roberti Winchelsey, Cantuariensis Archiepiscopi A.D. 1294-1313, ed. R. Graham, 2 vols, Canterbury & York Society 51-2 (London, 1952-6), II, p. 841. According to an account of the duties of the several obedientiaries of Abingdon Abbey, compiled apparently towards the end of the thirteenth century, it was to the almoner that the chapter committed the obligation of providing the instruments of chastisement appropriate to the chapter-house and to the school of the boys (scole puerorum): Chronicon Monasterii de Abingdon, ed. J. Stevenson, 2 vols, Rolls Series (London, 1858), II, p. 404. At first sight this appears to be indicative of the existence of an almonry school under the almoner's general supervision. Elsewhere in this document, however, the pueri are recorded as having been in attendance at services in the monks' choir, at least on certain feast-days (ibid., pp. 370, 371, 404; for further references to the pueri see pp. 371, 376, 378, 387, 388). It seems most unlikely that secular boys could have been required to participate in this way in the monks' observance of the liturgy, and consequently it would appear, on balance, more likely that in this document the pueri were in fact not secular schoolboys but the youngest of the novices. (For the similar case of Norwich Cathedral Priory, see above, n. 23.) In the mid-fourteenth century at Bury St Edmund's Abbey, the manuscript list of hand-signals to be used for communication during periods of silence included a signal for 'boy' (pro puero); significantly this followed immediately the signal for 'novice-master' (pro custode noviciorum), suggesting strongly that puer signified 'novice': D. Sherlock

Whatever may have been the original motives informing the inauguration of these earliest almonry schools, it appears that at some point around 1300 there was generated a very specific incentive for their creation rather more widely thenceforth, at least among the houses of Benedictines. Back in 1249 the General Chapter of the Benedictine Order for the province of Canterbury had required all heads of houses to ensure that no monk in priest's orders allow more than four days to elapse without celebrating his private mass, lest by default the souls of benefactors be defrauded of the expected mitigatory benefits.[32] In 1277 this order was re-issued in essentially the same form, but when the whole code was reviewed in the following year the text of this provision was substantially revised. It would appear that anticipation had arisen (or experience had shown) that any high incidence of private celebration among the priested monks might entail compromise in the seemliness and liturgical propriety of the observance. For if each brother was himself celebrating frequently, it might be so difficult to find a colleague sufficiently unoccupied elsewhere to act as his server that a monk might, improperly, celebrate unserved – or use this circumstance as an excuse for not celebrating at all. Consequently, it was decreed in 1278 that no monk in priest's orders should celebrate without the attendance of a fellow monk or some other colleague in religion, or at least of some honest clerk properly vested, to act as server.[33]

At some stage between 1278 and 1338 it evidently became clear that there were many circumstances under which the best solution to the problem of the provision of altar-servers lay in this last option – a ready supply of 'honest clerks properly vested'. No original text of enactment has been found, but when a recension of Benedictine legislation already existing was made and published in 1343, the erstwhile statute which already required no priest to celebrate without the service of a monk or other fellow in religion, or at least of an honest clerk (*aut saltem honesto clerico*), had been amplified with the text following:

> and so that there should be clerks of this kind instantly available for those wishing to celebrate, we decree that in every monastery honest servants (*ministri*) should be appointed to each altar by those in authority, *to whom maintenance should be supplied from the common alms*, or from other sources,

---

and W. Zajac, 'A Fourteenth-Century Monastic Sign-List from Bury St Edmund's Abbey', *Proceedings of the Suffolk Institute of Archaeology and History* 36 (1988), 251–73, p. 261.

[32] *Documents Illustrating the Activities of the General and Provincial Chapters of the English Black Monks, 1215–1540*, ed. W. A. Pantin, 3 vols, Camden Society, 3rd ser. 45, 47, 54 (London, 1931–7), I, p. 45.

[33] *Ibid.*, I, pp. 70–1, 96.

as the superiors shall cause to be ordained.[34]

That is, at some time in the recent past it had been made incumbent on the Benedictine houses in general that from the resource represented by the common alms there should be maintained a permanent team of 'honest clerks', ready in the mornings to act as servers at the side-altars in the monastery church.

It is likely that in fact this legislation had been first enacted at some point between 1301 and 1309. As late as 1301, when Robert Winchelsey, archbishop of Canterbury, adverted to this problem in the injunctions he issued to the prior and chapter of Worcester, he could offer as a solution only the instruction that priested monks celebrating their private masses be served by fellow monks.[35] That the order enshrined in the recension of 1343 had in fact been enacted by 1309 is indicated by the manner in which in that year, already using much the same language as the future text, John Salmon, bishop of Norwich, issued an injunction for his cathedral priory referring to the problem and identifying a very satisfactory solution entirely congruent with the strategy recommended by the General Chapter. His objective was to terminate the prevailing impediment to the celebration of private masses arising from the lack of suitable servers. He decreed that thenceforth there should be appointed by the almoner three of the boys of the existing almonry school, on a weekly rota, to be in attendance in the cathedral church from early morning to the end of conventual high mass, ready to serve those monks wishing to celebrate privately at the side altars while the *Opus Dei* was in progress in the main choir. Only the boys sufficiently mature to perform this service were to be chosen, and after the end of high mass in choir they were to return to school for the rest of the day.[36] Such a solution was of evident utility; clearly the bishop believed it to be practical, and there appears to be no reason to imagine that the scheme so ordered failed to operate.

Indeed, any 'honest clerk' engaged to serve at mass would require training, not only in the liturgical procedure but also in the making of the Latin responses during mass and, especially, in reciting with the priest the ceremony of preparation preceding it. Boys could serve mass just as well as adults, and it may well have been in direct response to the making of the original issue of this legislation, putatively between 1301 and 1309, that it became apparent to a number of the more enterprising of the greater Benedictine monasteries that a very satisfactory way in which to effect

---

[34]   *Ibid.*, II, pp. 32–3: my italics. These provisions were periodically re-enacted thereafter (and see e.g. *ibid.*, II, pp. 83–4) and were re-issued practically *verbatim* in the next (and final) overall codification of General Chapter legislation enacted in 1444 (*ibid.*, II, p. 196).

[35]   Worcester Cathedral Muniments, Reg. A.xii, fol. 118r.

[36]   E. H. Carter, *Studies in Norwich Cathedral History* (Norwich, 1935), pp. 21–2.

compliance with both the letter and the spirit of this legislation was to adopt the device, already anticipated in a handful of houses, of inaugurating an almonry school. Thence could a corps of trained altar-boys, duly maintained on the alms of the house as directed, be readily supplied on demand, the duties and promptings of *caritas* would be agreeably satisfied, and the monastery could look forward to all the other benefits, tangible and otherwise, of running an almonry school.

Notices of the existence of almonry schools do indeed begin to arise in some abundance during the first half of the fourteenth century for the southern part of England. In 1315 the chapter of Ely Cathedral Priory made ordinances for the running of an almonry school already in existence, and the chapter of Christ Church, Canterbury, did likewise in 1320.[37] The earliest notice of an almonry school at Westminster Abbey dates from 1317, and a reference to boys of the almonry at Hyde Abbey by Winchester appears to be datable to *c*.1325.[38] At Whitby the practice of maintaining *pauperes scolares* on the alms of the abbey had had time by 1366 not only to be inaugurated but also, through the negligence of the abbot, to lapse.[39] At Reading Abbey references to almonry schoolboys and their master are to be found on all the earliest surviving almoners' accounts, though these date only from 1375–6 onwards.[40]

Other monastic bodies responded to the General Chapter ordinance by opting to take a somewhat simpler course of action. They undertook the maintenance and lodging of a group of schoolboys within the almonry, but instead of engaging the services of a resident schoolmaster sent the boys to the master of the town grammar school for their education. At some point around the 1330s it was recorded that such an arrangement was being applied at the cathedral priory of Worcester.[41] Elsewhere, in a 'company town' like St

---

[37] S. J. A. Evans, 'Ely Chapter Ordinances and Visitation Records', *Camden Miscellany, XVII*, Camden Society, 3rd ser. 64 (London, 1940), pp. 38–9; BL, Cotton MS Galba E iv, fols 87r, 88v–89v.

[38] WAM 18964, 18965, *Expense elemosinarie*; J. C. Cox, 'The New Minster or the Abbey of Hyde', *VCH, Hampshire*, II, pp. 118–19.

[39] *Chapters of the Black Monks*, III, pp. 281, 291, 301, 304. For lack of boys to serve at the altars, it was alleged, the number of private masses was reduced to barely three or four per day.

[40] BL, Add. Ch. 19641. Leach, *Schools of Medieval England*, p. 218, gave the date of the earliest account in error as 1345/6, and this has been reproduced in subsequent literature.

[41] The town schoolmaster was permitted to nominate three of his pupils for maintenance on the charity of the prior during Lent each year, and was empowered to nominate one pupil for maintenance on the resources of the almonry throughout the teaching terms. He enjoyed these privileges in return for the tuition he provided 'for the kin of the monks and for others maintained of

Alban's, the almoner of the abbey actually maintained the buildings of the town grammar school and appointed the master to it. During the 1330s it was, not surprisingly, to this school that the boys of the almonry were being sent for their schooling,[42] and a corresponding arrangement appears also to have applied at Bury St Edmund's.[43] In relatively small urban communities, where the town and surrounding district might be unable consistently to furnish a clientele sufficient in numbers to maintain two parallel grammar schools, this was a practical and sensible arrangement.

In the northern province of the Benedictine order, matters followed a course somewhat different. There decree was made in 1287 that the use of secular clerks as altar-servers was strictly forbidden. Apparently this rule proved impractical, and it was suppressed six years later,[44] but it was not until 1343, when the thitherto discrete administrations of the two provinces were united under a single body of legislation, that there became effective in the northern province the order that secular clerks maintained on the alms of the monastery be provided to supply the need for trained altar-servers at mass. It is, perhaps, no mere coincidence that very shortly after, from 1348–9 to 1351–2, there arise the earliest notices of the existence of a formal almonry school, incorporating both resident boys and a master to teach them, at the cathedral priory of Durham.[45]

alms' – seemingly a clear reference to boys maintained in the almonry: *Documents Illustrating Early Education in Worcester, 685–1700*, ed. A. F. Leach, Worcestershire Historical Society 21 (London, 1913), pp. xxii, 23. Certain archival entries overlooked by Leach suggest that presently a resident master was engaged for the almonry boys. In 1380/1 a chaplain resident in the almonry was teaching the boys there (Worcester Cathedral Muniments C.176, *Stipendia*; see also *ibid.*, C.183 and C.184, *Exitus grangie*). In 1398 the almoner rewarded one John Ekyngton with cloth for a tunic 'pro informacione puerorum existencium in Elemosinaria' (C.184, *Liberacio denariorum*). In 1535 the *pauperes scholares Elemosinarie* numbered fourteen: *Valor Ecclesiasticus*, ed. J. Caley and J. Hunter, 6 vols, Record Commission (London, 1810–34), III, pp. 226–7.

[42] Ordinance of 1339: *Educational Charters*, ed. Leach, pp. 296–8.

[43] For Bury, see above, p. 181. It was, presumably, for pedagogic services rendered to the almonry boys that by 1444 the master of the town grammar school was lodged *gratis* in the abbey almonry and received from the almoner a stipend of 13s. 4d. per year and livery: A. F. Leach, 'Schools', *VCH, Suffolk*, II, p. 312. The two surviving accounts of the cellarer, of 1514/15 and 1524/5, show that at those dates this obedientiary was spending 26s. 8d. per year on supplying board to the master of the school; for this, however, he received reimbursement in full from the almoner, indicating that an arrangement similar to that of 1444 was still in force: London, Public Record Office [PRO], SC6/3481/70, SC6/Henry VIII/3396, *Forinseca recepta*.

[44] *Chapters of the Black Monks*, I, pp. 258, 263.

Indeed, the provision of servers at the altar remained an important feature within the overall management of the almonry schools, certainly into the fifteenth century – even though only a small number of senior boys, deputed by rotation, was actually needed for this purpose. At Durham Cathedral Priory around the early 1390s complaint was being made that boys who were insufficiently educated to do the job were being deputed to serve the monks' private masses. Apparently these boys were being selected by someone unqualified to choose, and requirement was made that the almoner himself appoint boys to serve at mass henceforth.[46] After 1400 five such boys were regularly deputed to these duties.[47] At Christ Church, Canterbury, it was decreed in 1439 that following breakfast each day the subalmoner depute two of the schoolboys to serve the private masses.[48] Episcopal injunctions delivered to Ramsey Abbey in 1432 required that the almoner supply four boys each day, though subsequent almoner's accounts indicate that three were found to be sufficient.[49] In the same series of visitations, William Gray, bishop of Lincoln, required the prior of the very small monastery of Bradwell (Buckinghamshire) to begin the admission of teachable small boys to be maintained of the alms of the house, expressly to be taught in reading, chant and other 'primitive sciences', and to serve the monks at their celebrations of mass. It was likewise to ensure that the canons celebrating at side-altars be attended by qualified servers that in c.1433 Gray ordered four boys to be

[45] Durham, Cathedral Archives, A/c Hostillar 1348/9, *Expense donorum et oblacionum*; A/c Almoner 1351/2, *Expense*. See also Locellus xxvii, no. 16d (datable to 1354), and R. B. Dobson, *Durham Priory 1400–50* (Cambridge, 1973), pp. 60–1, 169.

[46] For one of the *detecta* of complaint, see Durham, Cathedral Archives, Locellus xxvii, no. 37; for the resulting *compertum*, *ibid.*, Misc. Chrs. 5634 (printed in *Chapters of the Black Monks*, III, p. 83); and for the consequent chapter diffinition, Durham, Cathedral Archives, Locellus xxvii, no. 14.

[47] *Ibid.*, A/cs Terrars 1400/1 et seq., *Expense*; A/cs Sacrist 1414/15 et seq., *Recepte* and *Expense necessarie*.

[48] 'Chronicle of John Stone', p. 23. It was in just the previous year that the Lady Chapel choir of boys' voices had been inaugurated at the cathedral (R. D. Bowers, 'Some Observations upon the Life and Career of Lionel Power', *Proceedings of the Royal Musical Association* 102 (1975–6), 103–27, pp. 117–22), and probably it was the resulting adjustments to the routine of the almonry school that rendered necessary this ruling clarifying the arrangements for the serving of the monks' masses thenceforth.

[49] *Visitations of Religious Houses in the Diocese of Lincoln 1420–1449*, ed. A. H. Thompson, 3 vols, Lincoln Record Society 7, 14, 21 (Horncastle, 1914–29), I, p. 106; BL, Add. Ch. 34703, 34700–1, 34704–7, *Species et iocal'*. Calculation from the data supplied by the *Valor Ecclesiasticus*, IV, p. 275, indicates that in 1535 the boys of the almonry numbered six.

maintained of the alms of Newnham Priory, Bedford.[50]

The sets of regulations produced by the fourteenth-century period of consolidation for the almonry schools, plus the incidence of the payment of stipend to the master recorded on the account rolls, permit some general observations to be made. Certainly the grandest of these schools were for boys who had already mastered the rudiments and had shown aptitude for learning. At Christ Church, Canterbury, no boy was to be admitted unless he was at least ten years old. In addition, each was expected already to have had sufficient education to enable him to contribute immediately to the reading and singing of the services which were held in the almonry chapel by its resident team of six priests and which were attended by the boys on Sundays and feast-days.[51] A similarly advanced level of admission was evidently expected at Ely and St Alban's, where no boy was to occupy an almonry place for more than four and five years respectively.[52] The masters appointed to teach were invariably seculars, commonly but not exclusively priests. Few are more than names; only a small proportion are known to have possessed degrees. Each master enjoyed free provision of food and livery, commonly – but not invariably – free lodging, and a stipend which generally bore some relation to the number of almonry pupils he was expected to teach, but nevertheless often appears very meagre. Commonly it stood at some 13s. 4d. or 20s. 0d. per year, and only rarely did it exceed 26s. 8d.[53] In augmentation of their stipends, of course, those in priest's orders might enjoy the not necessarily particularly lucrative privilege of a modest vicarage or rectory held in plurality.

As observed above, the original motive encouraging the provision of almonry schools may well have been the furtherance of the education of promising boys from unadvantaged backgrounds. In the event, however, it was not long before other considerations began to be felt. No-one could have been unaware that what was being created did in fact constitute potentially a most valuable source of patronage, which the host house could deploy in ways either altruistic or self-interested. This patronage took the form of the capacity to offer free upbringing and education for two particular categories of potential beneficiary – firstly, for the sons of influential personages of the locality

---

[50] *Visitations of Religious Houses*, I, pp. 23, 89.

[51] BL, Cotton MS Galba E iv, fols 87r, 89r, 89v.

[52] Evans, 'Ely Chapter Ordinances', pp. 38–9; *Educational Charters*, ed. Leach, p. 296. At St Alban's five years was allowed 'quia hoc tempus sufficit ad proficiendum in grammatica' (Leach's text adjusted to conform with BL, Lansdowne MS 375, fol. 199r).

[53] See also below, pp. 200–4, for the capacity of the masters to take on, at their discretion, fee-paying day scholars.

whom the chapter wished to influence or reward, and secondly (and in particular), for the sons of the monks' own families and kin. Consequently, within a generation or two, offers to boys of the opportunity to occupy an almonry school place were being made according to principles which supposed that charity best began at home. In contemporary values, the exercise of such a priority was wholly proper, and in its support a respectable and defensible case could readily be produced. Such arrangements were simply consistent with, and flowed naturally from, contemporary Christian teaching that required that every individual make adequate provision in the first instance for the welfare of those to whom he was closest.[54] Plainly, in the light of precepts such as these, modern concepts of 'partiality', or even 'corruption', are utterly inapplicable. The admission of the kin of the monks to the maintained places in the almonry school was simply the natural order of things.

At the cathedral priory of Ely, consequently, when in 1315 the chapter was making an ordinance for the running of an almonry school already functioning, the fundamental premise underlying its legislation was that the school primarily existed to advance those whom the monks wished to benefit. It was for the boys and their master that the best of the alms, in terms of flesh and fish and drink, were to be reserved by the almoner, and no provision was made for the selection of scholars to be effected only from among the unadvantaged. The admission of pupils was to be accomplished not by a selection board choosing from a pool of deserving aspirants; rather, vacancies were to be filled by boys individually presented to the places at the school. This capacity of presentation was available both to members of the house and to certain privileged seculars outside it. These latter were not specifically identified, but presumably consisted of influential neighbours to whom the chapter wished to offer inducement or incentive, or appreciation for services already rendered. A boy presented by a secular patron could be admitted only with the consent of the prior and convent. However, no such inhibition was placed upon those admitted on the nomination of one of the monks, and no attempt was made to identify any particular group or class from among whom the individual monks should make their choice. Not surprisingly, the right of presentation was evaluated as a coveted privilege, and in the interest of the fair distribution of opportunity, no monk was permitted to present again until eight years had elapsed since his last presentation.[55]

One generation further on, the injunctions issued by Bishop William Bateman to his cathedral priory of Norwich following a visitation in 1347

---

[54] For a contemporary jurist's marshalling of the case for the defence of almonry schools, see below, pp. 198–9.
[55] Evans, 'Ely Chapter Ordinances', pp. 38–9.

show the extent to which by then that convent's originally open-handed understanding of *caritas* in the matter of the offer of almonry schooling was being superseded by another of a less disinterested nature. At the time of the visitation the bishop found that a number of the places in the school were being occupied by boys introduced simply by exercise of the authority of certain of the senior obedientiaries of the house. This the bishop believed to be an improper application of their influence. The officers concerned were required to take these boys not from the school, but certainly from the almonry, and to transfer them into their own households for their keep and maintenance thenceforth. The orders which Bateman then proceeded to make for regulation of the procedures of admission did nevertheless represent a recognition of the interests of the monks in securing almonry schooling for their own relatives and kin. No longer was admission to be offered by a selection board to the most promising of the aspirants at the gate. Rather, each successive vacancy arising thenceforth was to be filled simply by a boy nominated to the place by one of the monks. The right of presentation was to circulate by simple rotation, no monk nominating a second time until every one of the others had had his turn. Each was to nominate not entirely at his discretion; his choice was supposed to be made from among the less advantaged members of his own kin. This system was to be inaugurated with the filling of the vacancies created by the removal of the boys introduced by the erring obedientiaries. Nevertheless, the bishop clearly believed himself to be empowered to act in the manner for which he had just seen fit to censure them. He reserved to himself and his successors the right to interrupt the rota of presentation by introducing boys to vacant places at his own will. The addition of the phrase 'in the manner accustomed' appears to indicate that he, and perhaps his predecessors, had already been making use of the almonry school in this way for some time.[56]

In these two cases, that is, the almonry schools had come to be conducted primarily to educate boys who were kin to the monks of the host establishment, or who sprang from families who were clients of the bishop. By 1376 likewise the chapter of Christ Church, Canterbury, was making regulations which incorporated the assumption that at least a significant proportion of the boys of the almonry school had been placed there by presentation of the several monks, and the rest by presentation of secular persons to whom the privilege had been extended.[57] In 1434 or 1435 the

---

[56]   C. R. Cheney, 'Norwich Cathedral Priory in the Fourteenth Century', *Bulletin of the John Rylands Library* 20 (1936), 93–120, p. 112. As founder of Trinity Hall, Cambridge, and midwife to the foundation of Gonville Hall, Bateman stands among the foremost patrons of education in fourteenth-century England.

[57]   Canterbury, Cathedral Library and Archives, MS Domest. Econ. 77. For the reception of a boy presented by Queen Philippa in 1332, see *Literae Cantuarienses*,

diocesan bishop required of the monks of Crowland Abbey that, in accordance with the laudable custom of the monastery, preference in admissions as boys of the almonry should be given to the younger brothers and nephews of the monks, provided they be suitable.[58]

At Durham Cathedral Priory, regulations made for the running of the school likewise presupposed that each of its thirty maintained places was occupied by a boy nominated to it by one of the monks. In 1417, for instance, it appears that circumstances had arisen that suggested to the prior and convent that the time was ripe for a re-consideration and overhaul of the procedures of admission to their almonry school. It was ordered that thenceforth boys be admitted to, and released from, places in the almonry on only a single occasion each year, by means of a formal ceremony conducted each Michaelmas. Hereby each new admittee was presented by the almoner to the prior and three senior monks; the name of each was formally entered on the roll of the almonry, and with his name that of the monk of the house by whom he had been presented.[59] In 1449, indeed, record was made of a formal recommendation that the boys so admitted be chosen, first and foremost, from among the kin of the monks, being themselves suitable to become monks in due course. This rule apparently was intended to discourage too much repetition of recent instances of the admission of boys unrelated to members of the community, in consequence of pressure exerted in their own interest by powerful secular neighbours. Nevertheless, the prior was still empowered to admit boys, when necessary, 'at the instance of lords and magnates whom we may not offend'.[60]

It seems very probable that the admission primarily of the kin of the monks of the host house constituted a convention which rapidly became the norm, and remained prevalent down to the time of the Dissolution.[61] It will

ed. J. B. Sheppard, 3 vols, Rolls Series (London, 1887–9), I, p. 444.

[58] *Visitations of Religious Houses*, I, p. 37. Of the fifty boys maintained of the alms of the abbey of St Mary, York, in 1535, and sent thence to the city grammar school for their education, it appears that thirty were nominated by the monks – six by the abbot, two by the prior, and each of the remainder by one of the twenty-two most senior religious: *Valor Ecclesiasticus*, V, p. 6.

[59] Cambridge, Jesus College, MS 41 (=QB25), fol. 170r.

[60] 'ad instancias et rogatus dominorum et magnatorum quos offendere non possumus': Durham, Cathedral Archives, MS Locellus xxvii, no. 15, m. 3. In February 1448 the prior had found himself yielding to pressure exerted by Sir Robert Ogle, writing that he would 'with good hertt tendre your entennt in resauying [receiving] of that childe to our almose and scoole for whilke yhe haue writen': Dobson, *Durham Priory*, p. 169.

[61] In 1538 a plan to reform the cathedral priory of Coventry included the proposal that the monks should number twenty, of whom each should have his scholar found in the almonry: *Letters and Papers, Foreign and Domestic, of the Reign of*

be recalled that the constitutions granted severally to the New Foundation chapters by which the monks of the cathedral priories were replaced after the dissolutions of 1538–40 all included a specified number of residential scholarship places for boys to enjoy at the associated cathedral grammar schools. Several of the new deans and canons let little time elapse before formalising a rota system among themselves for the nomination and presentation of boys to these foundation scholarships.[62] The alacrity with which they acted does seem to suggest that this practice was then no novelty, but simply a long-standing convention sustained by a venerable tradition long anteceding the Dissolution and now simply re-asserted under the new circumstances.

There was, of course, an ostensible legal impropriety in the practice whereby alms, earmarked according to the rules of the several monastic orders for distribution for the relief of the impotent poor, were applied instead to the maintenance of a school for boys studying grammar. In the early fifteenth century this apparent transgression was considered by the jurist William Lyndwood.[63] Writing in the 1420s he concluded that, in general, ecclesiastical law required that alms indeed be distributed primarily to those unable for any reason to support themselves through the labour of their hands. Nevertheless, he entertained no hostility toward the existence of almonry schools, and he was eager to marshal other considerations and tenets of church law in a way that allowed him to present a legitimation and defence of the use of the monastic surplus to maintain a grammar school for boys, given a single proviso.

The basic principle of such schools was rendered sound by the manner in which the beneficiaries so maintained and educated were usually (*ut communiter*) boys tied to the monks by kinship or other propinquity. For such close kin, the monks were bound by no less than fundamental Christian teaching especially to seek and provide support, more so than for persons

Henry VIII, ed. J. S. Brewer *et al.*, 21 vols in 35 (London, 1862–1910), XIII (2), no. 1198 (p. 504).

[62] *Early Education in Worcester*, pp. 169–71; *The King's School, Ely*, ed. D. M. Owen and D. Thurley, Cambridge Antiquarian Records Society 5 (Cambridge, 1982), pp. 43–4; *The Foundation of Peterborough Cathedral, A.D. 1541*, ed. W. T. Mellows, Northamptonshire Records Society 13 (Kettering, 1941), p. liv; C. S. Knighton, 'Collegiate Foundations 1540 to 1570, with special reference to St Peter in Westminster', Ph.D. dissertation, University of Cambridge (1975), pp. 251–2.

[63] He was compiling a gloss upon a constitution of Stephen Langton (1222), which had required all monastic surplus to be distributed *sine diminutione aliqua* to the poor: W. Lyndwood, *Provinciale (seu Constitutiones Angliae)* (London, 1505), fol. 114, gloss h; also facsimile of edition of 1679 (Farnborough, 1968), p. 209.

unrelated to them.[64] The maintenance by monks of an almonry school for largely (in the first instance) their own kin was therefore entirely defensible. Nevertheless, the fundamental resources concerned were undeniably alms, the need for which by the young and healthy was less than that by the old and infirm, and Lyndwood had to acknowledge this. However, he found that a single proviso, taking cognisance of the promotion of the good estate of the church at large, sufficed to negate this objection. The legitimacy of the maintenance of an almonry school was assured so long as preference in admission to maintained places was given to boys who were attending the school with the purpose of obtaining qualification to enter either religion or the secular priesthood in due course.[65] Nonetheless, it was doubtless in consolidation of the legitimacy of this use of the monastic alms that contemporary references to the boys benefiting from maintained almonry schooling commonly characterised them as 'pauper', irrespective of the real nature of their family background and resources.

Especially for the fourteenth century, the surviving records yield some numbers relating to the pupils attending the several almonry schools. At Norwich Cathedral Priory, as has been seen, the authorised number at the inauguration of the school was thirteen, and this was again given as the recognised quota in 1535.[66] At Ely in 1328-9 there were twenty-three boys (and, uniquely, two masters), but in 1448 provision was made for the teaching of only five.[67] At Westminster the plague years took their toll of the school, and in 1369-70 a master and no more than nine boys were being maintained. Numbers rose steadily thereafter; thirteen boys were recorded for 1373, twenty-eight in 1385, and twenty-two in 1386, 1387 and 1389.[68] Numbers at Reading Abbey extended to ten boys in 1375-6 and 1383-4, eleven in 1389-90, fifteen in 1391-2 and a dozen or so in 1468-9.[69] For the abbey of St Mary de Pratis, Leicester, it was stated in 1440 that the acknowledged

[64] 'Potest tamen pro parte Religiosorum huiusmodi, quantum est ad exhibitionem talium qui, ut communiter, sunt eorum Consanguinei vel alia propinquitate eis ligati, applicari sententia Augu[stini], quam ponit in Libro primo de Doctrina Christiana – ubi dicit quod his qui sunt nobis magis coniuncti, quam his qui quadam forte nobis obveniunt, magis providere debemus': ibid.

[65] 'Et sic ex hoc processu apparet quod his qui Scholatizant in Monasterio ut postea Religionem ingrediantur vel alias Ordinem Ecclesiasticum suscipiant ... prae aliis est talis Eleemosyna facienda': ibid.

[66] See above, p. 183; Valor Ecclesiasticus, III, p. 287.

[67] S. J. A. Evans, 'Ely Almonry Boys and Choristers [sic] in the Later Middle Ages', in Studies Presented to Sir Hilary Jenkinson, ed. J. C. Davies (London, 1957), 155-69, pp. 157-8; Owen and Thurley, King's School, Ely, pp. 25-6.

[68] WAM 31777, 23701, 23712, 23714, 23716.

[69] BL, Add. Ch. 19641, 19643, 19645, 19646, 19656; Custos clericorum et sororum.

complement of boys was twenty-four or twenty-six.[70] At Durham Cathedral Priory in both the fifteenth and sixteenth centuries the number of boys was given as thirty.[71]

Such numbers are valuable for yielding a crude indication of the extent of the charity of the host house. However, they are of but limited use for determining the size of the overall clientele of the schools, since they are no more than partial statistics. What these sources reveal is not the full number of pupils in any school, but merely the number of those for whom the host house was providing free places, in the form of lodging, board, livery and teaching. In addition to these, there is every likelihood that most of these schools included a certain, perhaps a substantial, number of non-foundation boys – day pupils unassociated with the monastery almonry, resident at home or with guardians in the town, who attended the lessons and paid directly to the master the fee appropriate for his teaching. It was, after all, never a characteristic of the provision of schooling in pre-Reformation England that the doors of the schools were closed to any who possessed both the necessary level of intellectual ability and the capacity to pay whatever fees were demanded.[72] Schools that were fully endowed were free and open to all comers; those unendowed were open to all who were able and willing to pay the schoolmaster his fee. Others, endowed or only partially so, might be free of charge to a prescribed number of pupils or to particular classes of pupil, and open to others, at the master's discretion, on the payment of fees. In none of these cases was any formal upper limit placed on total numbers, though, of course, constraints of accommodation inevitably imposed an informal limit.

There appears to be no reason to imagine that the management of the monastery almonry schools incorporated any departure from this fundamental and pervasive premise. In every likelihood the monastic

---

[70] *Visitations of Religious Houses*, II, pp. 208, 209.

[71] Durham, Cathedral Archives, MS 3.3.Pont.9 [1437 or 1438]; *Valor Ecclesiasticus*, V, p. 303 [1535].

[72] Only two classes of school were not characterised by such open entry. One consisted necessarily of those *ad hoc* arrangements for schooling which, when needed, were set up in aristocratic households for the education of the sons of the family, and of the wards and henchmen. The other class consisted of the schools maintained by the secular cathedral and greater collegiate churches for the training and education of the chorister boys who were fully and formally admitted members of the foundation. The closed character of these latter schools arose not as a consequence of any sense of exclusivity. Rather, it was a simple corollary of the fact that the content of the education that was supplied consisted of not only the standard training of the day in grammar, but also a body of specialised and professional knowledge and experience of liturgy. This liturgical training was so extensive that the great bulk of the curriculum offered could have been of no use or value whatever to any boy not a professional chorister.

authorities never imagined that the masters of their almonry schools would teach only the almonry boys. Rather, they merely made an estimate of the number of boys who could be sustained on the alms of their house – or of the number for whose benefit they were prepared to provide and cook a deliberate surplus. For these boys they provided a servant, a dormitory, a schoolroom, and a teacher – and to the latter they paid a stipend appropriate to his teaching of that particular number of pupils. As has been seen, the resulting fee was commonly rather meagre, failing by some way to reach a comfortable income for an educated man who, as the fifteenth century progressed, was increasingly likely to be a secular, married and with dependants to support. There is every likelihood that all concerned expected, as a matter of course, that the master would take on extra fee-paying pupils in addition to the boys of the almonry, at his discretion or up to the limit imposed by the accommodation available.[73]

The existence of such fee-paying scholars would not normally leave much, if any, trace in the surviving archives. Nevertheless, there is a certain amount of evidence offering verification of this proposition. The plainest statement relates to the almonry school at Durham. Here it was observed expressly in 1453 that since a time beyond the memory of man, the master had customarily taught not only the boys of the almonry themselves, but also others wishing to receive instruction there from both within and without the city, undisturbed by impediment or obstruction offered by the master of the city grammar school.[74] A further indication arises from the circumstances under which John Hancock, already for some twenty years master of the episcopal grammar school in the city of Norwich, succeeded in plurality as master of the almonry school of the cathedral priory in 1424, and leased out his interest in the episcopal school to a substitute and *locumtenens*, one John Rikkes. In order, evidently, not to discourage Rikkes with competition too severe, Hancock agreed that as master of the almonry school he would accept for tuition, in addition to the boys residing within the close of the cathedral

---

[73] Not infrequently between 1378/9 and 1436/7 boys supernumerary to the authorised complement of almonry scholars were admitted to full board and lodging in the almonry of Norwich Cathedral, in return for their paying the charges arising: Cattermole in Harries, *History of Norwich School*, pp. 7–8.

[74] Memorandum that the prior and convent do enjoy and have enjoyed the right 'habendi scolam gramaticalem, inibi[que] iuvenes studere scolatizare et instrui volentes tam de monasterio dunelmensi et civitate ibidem quameciam extra admittendi et recipiendi ... sicuti attestari volunt in eventu debite requisiti prefatus dominus prior [William Ebchester] et alii magnates, generosi et presbyteri, et ceteri quamplures Diocesis dunelmensis, qui olim in dicta scola predictorum prioris et capituli in gramatica instructi fuerunt': Durham, Cathedral Archives, MS Locellus ii, no. 4.

(and also any boys from the precinct of the neighbouring daughter house, the priory of St Leonard), further pupils dwelling beyond the precinct wall, whether from the country or from the city, only up to a number not exceeding twelve. He also undertook not to solicit for these extra pupils, but to take on only those who approached him first, either directly or through their friends. The remainder of the potential clientele would thus be available for enrolment at Rikkes's episcopal school. The determination of the number of these supernumerary pupils for the almonry school was, it may be noted, concluded as purely a private transaction between the two men involved; no permission or licence from the prior and convent was deemed to be necessary.[75] This conspicuous absence establishes that under all normal circumstances the enrolment of external pupils was a matter for the sole discretion of the master. It is also clear that it was an act of generosity and self-denial for Hancock to limit himself to the admission of a mere twelve. There is a clear implication that conventionally the number would be much greater; however, the six pounds per year to be received by Hancock from Rikkes under the terms of the lease of the episcopal school evidently sufficed to compensate for the resulting shortfall in Hancock's income from fees.

There is other evidence indicating the extent to which the almonry schools were conventionally open to external scholars. In 1431 the monks of the abbey of St Augustine, located in a suburb of Canterbury just outside the city wall, obtained papal authorisation to establish a grammar school within the precinct, for a clientele identified expressly as not only their own boys brought up on their alms, but also other scholars, lay and unadvantaged, seeking instruction in grammar. The convent had initiated this request to Rome in order to obtain papal authority suppressing in their favour any claim by the schoolmaster of the city of Canterbury to exercise an exclusive monopoly on teaching within the city and its suburbs. The bull therefore expressly extended to all scholars wishing to attend St Augustine's almonry school authorisation to do so without let or hindrance.[76]

In a similar vein, it transpires that at Coventry in 1439 the cathedral priory, for whatever reason, was not currently keeping a grammar school for its almonry boys – an omission which seems to have left the city worthies

---

[75]   Each party possessed a sealed text of the indenture, and in deference to the evident interest of the patron whose school was thus being sub-let, a copy was entered into the episcopal register then current. Transcription and translation: H. W. Saunders, *A History of the Norwich Grammar School* (Norwich, 1932), pp. 93–100.

[76]   *Calendar of Papal Letters: Papal Registers* (London, 1893–), VIII *(1427–47)*, pp. 348–9. The stress laid by the petition on the distance between the abbey and the site of the city school suggests that thitherto the almonry boys had, inconveniently, been sent there for their education.

conscious that the town school could not supply sufficient capacity to meet the demand.[77] The mayor and six of the council were therefore authorised and instructed to approach the prior, 'Wyllyng hym to occupye a skole of Gramer, yffe he like to teche hys Brederon and Childerun off the aumbry'. In the event of his compliance, the worthies of the city court trusted the prior not to demand a monopoly but, without grudging, to acknowledge 'that every mon off this Cite be at hys Fre chosse to sette hys chylde to skole to what techer off Gramer that he likyth, as reson askyth'.[78] The city worthies of the court leet, that is, made their request on the clear assumption that, once established, the almonry school of the cathedral priory would be freely open to any boy of the city and its hinterland desiring education there, seeking simultaneously preservation of the same understanding for the town grammar school.

Hitherto, the monastery almonry schools have generally been considered as closed schools educating only the commonly quite small numbers of boys maintained internally of alms. This position seems to have been merely an assumption; there appears to be no shred of matter actually to support or sustain it. Rather, the evidence pertaining to the issue presented here indicates that in fact the almonry schools were understood to be open schools. Indeed, it seems fair overall to propose that in at least the most successful of these schools the cohort of maintained pupils normally was substantially amplified, and perhaps indeed considerably outnumbered, by the external fee-payers. Some sense of the scale of this admission of external pupils may be yielded by the manner in which at Glastonbury in 1377 the abbey authorities accepted responsibility for paying poll tax on no fewer than forty scholars of the almonry.[79] Properly, poll tax was not payable on persons under fourteen years of age, and normally, it would seem, this rule was applied – as at Lincoln Cathedral, where only four of the twelve chorister boys were charged in 1377.[80] It seems scarcely conceivable that among the pupils maintained of alms

[77] For John Pynchard and William Grene, successively schoolmasters of the town school 1429–1435, see *The Coventry Leet Book*, ed. M. D. Harris, 4 vols, Early English Text Society 134, 135, 138, 146 (London, 1907–13), I, pp. 118, 126, 164, 177 (and cf. p. 101). In 1535 the boys of the priory almonry numbered fourteen: *Valor Ecclesiasticus*, III, p. 51. Further on the almonry school of the cathedral priory, see Miner, *Grammar Schools*, p. 138.
[78] *Coventry Leet Book*, I, p. 190.
[79] PRO E179/4/1, mm. 8–9. Payment was made on thirty-nine, and one (Walter Pride) appeared under *Nomina non solvencium*. The Glastonbury almonry school and Lady Chapel choir are considered in N. Orme, 'Glastonbury Abbey and Education', in *The Archaeology and History of Glastonbury Abbey*, ed. L. Abrams and J. P. Carley (Woodbridge, 1991), 285–99, pp. 291–5.
[80] PRO E179/35/5, m. 1.

at Glastonbury those aged fourteen and above alone amounted to forty. More probably this figure represented the totality of the pupils aged fourteen and over, including a substantial number of fee-paying day-boys as well as the boarders.

Given the prevailing attenuation of the evidence, it is not easy to draw conclusions relating to the discernment of a rationale informing the location and geographical distribution of the almonry schools. To some extent, however, some broad pattern may be identified, since they do appear to have been located less according to chance and whim than to considerations of genuine usefulness and need, and – above all – to the availability of a clientele of fee-paying pupils. The provisional list of some thirty monasteries maintaining these schools includes all but two of the ten cathedral priories, established for the most part in substantial cities;[81] a good number of the urban monasteries located in major cities and towns;[82] a relatively small proportion of the many houses founded in smaller market towns of only local significance;[83] and a certain number of larger monasteries either located close to some very small town in an otherwise irretrievably rural area,[84] or simply founded in or near a village substantially distant from any town.[85] Very roughly, that is, these schools were found in two broad categories of location. The first was composed of major urban centres which, with their immediate hinterlands, could furnish to the school a ready supply of supplementary fee-paying pupils over and above those attending the town school(s). The second consisted of relatively remote areas which otherwise were not readily provided with schools at all, where they were satisfying at least a potential need.

Meanwhile, only a relatively small number of such schools is known to have been established at those monasteries that were located in or on the edge of the towns of only middling size and significance. In a few such locations a school of the monastery almonry was indeed established, and served thereafter as the only school of the town; Evesham, and perhaps also Tewkesbury and

[81] These were Canterbury, Coventry, Durham, Ely, Norwich, Rochester, Winchester and Worcester; the missing two are Bath and Carlisle.
[82] E.g. Bristol (St Augustine), Canterbury (St Augustine), Gloucester (St Peter), Reading, Westminster and Winchester (Hyde Abbey).
[83] E.g. Evesham, Glastonbury and Tewkesbury.
[84] E.g. Forde Abbey near Chard (Somerset), Furness Abbey near Dalton-in-Furness (Lancashire), Crowland Abbey (Lincolnshire), and Ramsey Abbey (Huntingdonshire).
[85] E.g. Barlinch Priory (Somerset), and Thornton Abbey (Lincolnshire). For Barlinch, see N. Orme, 'A School Note-Book from Barlinch Priory', in his *Education and Society in Medieval and Renaissance England* (London, 1989), 113–22.

Glastonbury, may fall into this class.[86] Otherwise, the circumstances that could arise were somewhat diverse, reflecting the manner in which local demand in the smaller towns was unlikely to suffice to sustain an almonry school in addition to a town school already provided under other auspices and pre-dating the period of the foundation of the almonry schools. It was at certain of the monasteries in towns where this circumstance obtained that the option preferred took the form not of the establishment of a self-contained almonry school, but of the maintenance and lodging of boys in the almonry for whom education was provided through attendance at the town grammar school.[87] Indeed, in many monasteries located at lesser urban centres and market towns the pre-existence of a grammar school of the town may well have sufficed to inhibit the establishment of boys of the almonry at all.[88] Close proximity to a major educational metropolis could readily produce the same result,[89] and no almonry school could be expected to flourish where there was scarcely any population at all.[90] In short, that is, the location of the almonry schools was primarily pragmatic. They throve in locations where circumstances were favourable, inasmuch as there existed within the locality at large a demand for schooling which was either not, or not sufficiently, being met.

For even the best documented of the almonry schools, the names of the pupils, whether maintained of alms or fee-paying, are very infrequently

---

[86] For Evesham, see N. Orme, 'Education in an English County: Worcestershire', in his *Education and Society*, 33–48, pp. 39–42, 46–7; see also below, pp. 216–17.

[87] E.g. Bury St Edmund's, Leicester, St Alban's and Sherborne.

[88] Though this is pure speculation, if no school of the almonry is known for any of the important monasteries located in towns such as Christchurch (Hampshire), Cirencester, Colchester, Faversham, Lancaster, Launceston, Lewes, Northampton, Saffron Walden, and Thetford, this lacuna may be the result less of lack of the appropriate monastic records than of the absence of need ever to set up an almonry school which would duplicate a town school (see Orme, *English Schools*, pp. 295–321 *passim*) already existing.

[89] At Eynsham Abbey in c.1365 the abbot and convent opted to authorise the sacrist to appoint and employ two 'honest clerks' (adults) to serve the private masses and execute other chores, to be kept, as required by the Benedictine legislation, on the alms of the house: *Chapters of the Black Monks*, III, p. 44. It may well have been the proximity of the abbey to the city of Oxford, already abundantly supplied with provision for the teaching of grammar, that discouraged this abbey from setting up a school of the almonry in evidently futile competition.

[90] There survive fifteen account rolls of the almoner of the abbey of St Benet at Hulme: Norfolk and Norwich Record Office, Diocesan Archives, boxes EST/2, EST/5, EST/13, EST/14. As might be expected of a monastery set down in a great wilderness of flood and fen, none reveals any trace of the conduct of a school.

recorded.[91] Those most commonly surviving are of the pupils who served as Lady Chapel singing-boys, but these are still rare. Among the major schools, a couple of names survive for Durham Cathedral,[92] the same number for Westminster, and a handful each for Norwich and Christ Church, Canterbury. In consequence, not much can yet be written concerning the uses to which the boys put their education in later life. Of those attending the Canterbury school in the early sixteenth century, however, two did follow the sort of careers that might be considered predictable. Both, in contrasting capacities, remained at the priory. One, Christopher James, at school between 1521 and 1523, became a monk of the house and was professed in 1524.[93] The other, Vincent Fantyng, at school from 1509 to 1512, was taken into the service of the priory in a secular capacity and was serving as an officer of the priory stables by 1517–19.[94] A similar tale is told elsewhere. Of the boys who constituted the Lady Chapel choir of St Osyth's Abbey at Chich (Essex), one, Clement Cuckoo (singing-boy 1526–31), had entered the service of the abbot as a *valectus camere* by 1535;[95] another, Thomas Solmes, a singing-boy in 1521/2, had taken profession as a canon of the abbey at least by 1529. He, however, came to regret it; presently he composed in very respectable Latin a plea to Thomas Cromwell to be absolved from the vows he had taken unwisely (and uncanonically) at the age of thirteen, and achieved release from the monastery in 1536.[96]

Of the nature of the clientele of the almonry schools throughout their history, little or nothing can be said with any assurance. Yet inasmuch as those nominated to places by the religious of the host house probably represented strata of society much the same as those from which their benefactors had themselves sprung, it may well have exhibited some fair degree of homogeneity in terms of family background and general affluence. The Norwich boys whose names are known are said to have been 'drawn

---

[91] For the names of thirty-nine boys attending Glastonbury Abbey almonry school in 1377, see Orme, 'Glastonbury Abbey and Education', pp. 292–3.

[92] Both were future priors of the monastery: Dobson, *Durham Priory*, p. 60.

[93] Canterbury, Cathedral Library and Archives, MS C 11, fols 135v–138r, *passim*; 'Chronicle of John Stone', p. 195.

[94] Canterbury, Cathedral Library and Archives, MS C 11, fols 118v–123r, *passim*; W. A. Pantin, *Canterbury College, Oxford*, 4 vols, Oxford Historical Society, new ser. 6–8, 30 (Oxford, 1947–85), IV, pp. 205, 206. Further on the almonry school of Christ Church, Canterbury, at this time, see G. H. Rooke, 'Dom William Ingram and his Account Book, 1504–1533', *Journal of Ecclesiastical History* 7 (1956), 30–44; Miner, *Grammar Schools*, p. 137.

[95] PRO SC6/Henry VIII/939 no. 10; 943, fol. 15r; 940 (unfoliated).

[96] PRO SC6/Henry VIII/942, fol. 16v; 944, no. 6. Letter: BL, Cotton MS Cleopatra E iv, fol. 25 (calendared briefly in *Letters and Papers*, IX, no. 1157). Release: PRO SC6/Henry VIII/940 (unfoliated).

from the landed and burgess classes of Norfolk and Norwich';[97] the two Westminster boys, brothers, were sons of a Northamptonshire family of gentry.[98] Among boys apparently attending the school of the almonry of Glastonbury Abbey in the 1510s, one is known in later life to have enjoyed the status of a gentleman, another a yeoman, and a third a husbandman.[99] The high social status enjoyed by many of the pupils of the almonry school of Durham Priory was proudly proclaimed in 1453 by the prior; he observed that 'very many magnates, gentlemen, priests and others of the diocese of Durham' – including, not least, himself – were former pupils of the school, and as such were willing to come forward to defend its customs and privileges.[100]

Indeed, eating the same food as the monks, and enjoying the same general ambience of residence in the close, the circumstances of a boarding scholar at an almonry school were not at all disagreeable – indeed, rather enviable. The surviving notices of almonry schools such as those of Canterbury Cathedral, Winchester Cathedral, Hyde Abbey and Westminster Abbey yield glimpses of the manner in which the boys were rewarded for having occupied their spare time in devising diversions with which to entertain and amuse their own senior monks and local ecclesiastical dignitaries.[101] By courtesy of the abbot the chapel boys of Battle Abbey, *c.*1500, were enabled to enjoy the thrill of the cockpit,[102] and of course the annual 'boy bishop' revelry at St Nicholas-tide was ubiquitous. The two or three occasions on which, in fifteenth-century Norwich, the master of the episcopal school achieved a transfer to the almonry school suggest that the latter enjoyed the greater esteem.[103]

And these features are worthy of particular notice. For writing from his lofty perspective as a nineteenth-century gentleman of the Protestant persuasion, educated at Winchester and Oxford, the first historian of English schools, Arthur Leach, habitually apostrophised the almonry schools of the

---

[97] Cattermole in Harries, *History of Norwich School*, p. 7; the evidence on which this statement is based is not given.

[98] See below, note 129.

[99] Orme, 'Glastonbury Abbey and Education', p. 294.

[100] See above, note 74.

[101] Canterbury, Cathedral Library and Archives, MS Misc. A/cs 4, fols 41v, 95r, 142v, 187r. T. Warton, *The History of English Poetry*, 3 vols (London, 1774–81), II, p. 206; III, p. 324. Bowers, 'Westminster School', p. 25.

[102] PRO SC6/Henry VII/1874, fol. 18v.

[103] Cattermole in Harries, *History of Norwich School*, pp. 8–9, 17–20. In 1510 or 1511 the erstwhile master of the city (i.e. Langley) school in Durham likewise transferred his ministrations to the school of the almonry: Leach, 'Schools', *VCH, Durham*, I (1905), p. 373.

Catholic unreformed monasteries as 'charity schools', their pupils as 'mere charity boys', and their teachers as 'rather inferior persons'.[104] He assumed that the clientage of these schools was normally of but menial character and insignificant status, and equally trifling in numbers. Such a characterisation of the almonry schools has become standard orthodoxy – yet it appears to be wholly unsubstantiable. Rather, it seems unlikely that the character of the clientele of the almonry schools was in any respects significantly different from that of the normal run of city and urban grammar schools of the day – except perhaps for sustaining a higher proportion of boys from country families, for whom the boarding element offered by the almonry schools to their internal scholars was evidently a particular attraction. And, when the fee-paying pupils are taken into consideration also, the boys may well have included, as at Westminster and Durham, the sons of gentry and even of the lesser magnatry.

Two developments in the later history of the almonry schools may be discerned. These added to their overall management certain specialised responsibilities that were undertaken by a particular sub-group of boys within the body of maintained pupils. However, these departures gave rise to no fundamental alterations to the nature or working objectives of the schools, and need be only touched upon here.

Towards the end of the fourteenth century there arose among the major secular collegiate churches at large a fad, relatively short-lived, for expanding the duties of the chorister boys who were members of the foundation, and, in the case of churches newly established, for considerably enhancing the numbers of boys.[105] These boys were engaged particularly in the singing of the Lady Mass, the daily celebration of sung mass performed out of choir in the Lady Chapel and rendered votive to the Virgin Mary by its particular choice of texts. The major monastic churches were by no means immune from this movement. Indeed, they were particularly well placed to respond to it, for a supply of unbroken voices was ready to hand from among the younger resident boys of the almonry school. These schoolboys had long been deputed

---

[104] Such observations are ubiquitous in Leach's output. For an especially concentrated example, see *Schools of Medieval England*, pp. 230–4; further, see Miner, *Grammar Schools*, pp. 26–38, 102. Perhaps Leach's low opinion of the boys of religious houses in general was rooted in early acquaintance with the 'quiristers' of Winchester College, for whose lowly and menial position see C. Oman, *Memories of Victorian Oxford* (London, 1941), p. 46. Leach's interpretations also influenced Knowles: see *Religious Orders*, II, pp. 295–6.

[105] R. D. Bowers, 'Choral Establishments within the English Church: their Constitution and Development, 1340–1500', unpublished Ph.D. dissertation, University of East Anglia (1975), pp. 4051–3, 4056–64.

to serve the private masses of monks celebrating at the side altars in the conventual church, and already in some monastic churches certain of the boys were also being engaged to serve the monks celebrating the daily Lady Mass – by 1373 at Westminster, for example, by 1378 at Norwich and by 1383 at Ely.[106] It was not long before a number of chapters were going one step further, taking the decision to engage for the benefit of their church the services of a single professional lay musician, often termed the cantor. In part he was employed to enhance generally the music of the services in the conventual church, but his particular responsibility was to train a group of boys from the almonry grammar school, usually four, six or eight in number, to sing daily the plainsong of the Lady Mass and commonly also that of the evening votive antiphon to the Virgin, sung likewise in the Lady Chapel. This departure was adopted at Westminster in 1384, Worcester by 1396, Winchester in 1402, Ely by 1404, Durham in 1419, and Abingdon and Glastonbury by 1420/1 – to name but a few of the earliest examples.[107] By the time of the Dissolution, the existence of such Lady Chapel choirs at some fifty monastic houses is now known.[108]

This commitment need have distracted the boys concerned but little from their studies. The monastic liturgies extended to only four Lady Masses, changing with the season on a yearly cycle.[109] All was sung to a relatively

[106] WAM 23186, *Soluciones et stipendia*; Norwich, A/cs Almoner 1378/9, et seq. (Norfolk and Norwich Record Office, DCN 1/6/18-24), *Forinseca et dona* – at least, this seems to be the most probable interpretation of the enigmatic references to *pueri* (or *clerici*) *beate marie*; Cambridge University Library, MS EDC A/C Custos Capelle 8, [*Minute*].

[107] Bowers, 'Choral Institutions', pp. 4068-100; idem, 'The Musicians of the Lady Chapel of Winchester Cathedral Priory', *Journal of Ecclesiastical History* 45 (1994), 210-35, pp. 214-19; idem, 'Educational Provision and Policy' [n. 14], pp. 15-23; WAM 18999, 19371, 19871-5, 23188 (Westminster: employment of Walter Whitby as cantor, 1384-8); R. E. G. Kirk, *Accounts of the Obedientiars of Abingdon Abbey*, Camden Society, 3rd ser. 51 (London, 1892), p. 90.

[108] *Pace* Knowles (*Religious Orders*, II, p. 296) and other authors following him, it may be noted that at no stage in their existence should any of the groups of Lady Chapel singing-boys and their cantor be called or thought of as a 'song school'; nor should a cantor be thought of as a schoolmaster. A choir was a unit for musical and liturgical performance, not a school; and a cantor was a musician charged with training a choir and its singers, not a pedagogue teaching school subjects.

[109] As representatives, see *The Ordinal and Customary of the Abbey of St Mary of York*, ed. J. B. L. Tolhurst and the Lady Abbess of Stanbrook, 3 vols, Henry Bradshaw Society 73, 75, 84 (London, 1934-50), I, pp. 56-8; *Missale ad Usum Ecclesie Westmonasteriensis*, ed. J. W. Legg, 3 vols, Henry Bradshaw Society 1, 5, 12 (London, 1891-7), II, cols 1119-29. The four masses were *Rorate celi desuper* (1st Sunday in Advent to eve of Nativity), *Salve sancta parens I* (Nativity to eve of

small repertory of chant, easily learnt; in addition, a conscientious cantor would probably teach the ablest of the boys the musical principles constituting the skill of improvising descant to plainsong, wherewith to add some variety to the daily and somewhat repetitive diet of chant. Little time needed to have been spent in rehearsal, therefore. Singing at mass would take up some forty minutes of the boys' time each morning, and the antiphon some ten minutes in the evening. For the rest of the day they were indistinguishable from their fellows as conventional schoolboys learning grammar. The boys of the Lady Chapel choirs, that is, should not be thought of as constituting a 'song school' separate from the almonry school, but as simply a sub-group of the almonry grammar school boys.

A misapprehension by A. F. Leach has hitherto substantially confused the history of this aspect of the almonry schools.[110] He made a false equation between the almonry grammar schools maintained in the monasteries and the schools established for their choristers (sometimes called 'song schools') by the secular collegiate churches. Indeed, he imagined that the monastic schools were set up from the outset for boys who were already constituting a team of singing-boys for the monastery church. Thereby he missed two points. Firstly, he failed to spot that in fact the earliest almonry schools were established in the first place simply as grammar schools – of which a sub-group of pupils began to constitute a Lady Chapel choir only long after the original foundation had taken place. Secondly, he failed to appreciate that in no sense at all were the singing-boys of the monastery Lady Chapels comparable to the choristers of the secular churches. The latter were fully-fledged, full-time members of the choral body, participating in the totality of the service sung in choir, extending to high mass and some or all of the eight daily offices. The boys of a monastery Lady Chapel choir were not at all participants in the choir service performed by the religious, but were involved only in the relatively modest programme of votive services sung out of choir. Indeed, to no member at all of the regular communities was the term *chorista* or *puer choristarius* ('chorister', 'choirboy') ever applied under any circumstances. In modern writing, therefore, and in conformity with medieval practice and precedent, it appears that the terms 'choristers' and 'choirboys' should never be used of the singing-boys of the monastic Lady

---

Purification), *Salve sancta parens II* (Purification to eve of Resurrection, and Trinity Sunday to eve of Advent Sunday), and *Salve sancta parens III* (Resurrection to eve of Trinity Sunday). The liturgies offered some choice of text and chant for items such as the trope of the Kyrie, and the Alleluia, Sequence and Offertory, especially in the mass *Salve sancta parens II*; in practical terms, it is these variable items that would constitute much of the content of such rehearsal as took place.

[110] See e.g. his *Schools of Medieval England*, pp. 213–30.

Chapel choirs. Their duties, commitments and character were, as contemporaries fully appreciated, in no way comparable to those of the real choristers of the greater secular churches.

However, towards the end of the fifteenth century many of these hitherto modest and small-scale choirs of boys' voices were re-organised on a scale far more adventurous. The incentive was provided by ambition to participate in the execution of one of the greatest glories of the late pre-Reformation English church, namely the extended, florid, virtuosic and technically highly demanding polyphony of the day, written in five parts for boy's treble, alto, two tenor and bass voices.[111] In fulfilment of this objective, teams either of suitably enthused and accomplished religious, or of professional singing-men, or of a mixture of both, were added to the pre-existing voices of the boys. There was nothing lethargic about the monks' adoption of this means of worship once it had been created. It was taken up at Westminster Abbey in 1480 and at Christ Church, Canterbury at about the same time, at the cathedral priories of Winchester in 1482, Worcester in 1486, Durham in 1487, and Ely in 1490, and at Bristol Abbey in about 1492, to give but a few of the earlier examples.[112]

At this point those admitted to the almonry school as singing-boys did indeed become a distinct sub-group within its overall body of pupils, for now their singing commitments required that their educational programme accommodate a sustained and exacting routine of training in repertoire and, in particular, technique.[113] At Winchester the ten singing-boys were especially valued; while their schoolmates continued to eat in the almonry hall on the surplus from the monastic tables, the singers were rewarded by promotion first to the monks' common hall for their meals, and then to the prior's hall.[114] At Westminster in 1507, as the new Lady Chapel built by Henry VII neared completion, a somewhat separate division within the abbey's almonry school was set up for the six singing-boys.[115] Nevertheless, the commitment of

[111] See R. D. Bowers, 'To Chorus from Quartet: the Performing Resource for English Church Polyphony, c.1390–1559', in *English Choral Practice 1400–1650*, ed. J. Morehen (Cambridge, 1996), 1–47, pp. 20–31.

[112] Bowers, 'Choral Institutions', pp. 6042–59; *idem*, 'Musicians of the Lady Chapel of Winchester Cathedral', pp. 223–31; *idem*, 'Westminster School', p. 46.

[113] For a reasonably representative collection of Lady Mass polyphony, composed mostly during the 1530s and 1540s, see BL, Add. MSS 17802–5, nos. 7–32; R. Bray, 'British Museum, Add. MSS 17802–5 (the Gyffard Part-Books): an Index and Commentary', *Royal Musical Association Research Chronicle* 8 (1977), 31–50, pp. 34–6.

[114] Bowers, 'Musicians of the Lady Chapel of Winchester Cathedral', p. 232.

[115] Bowers, 'Westminster School', pp. 46–9. For a description of the arrangements for the singing-boys' tuition in music at Durham on the eve of the Dissolution, see *Rites of Durham*, pp. 62–3.

the boys of these choirs to sing services remained limited to the daily Lady Mass and antiphon, plus a weekly Jesus mass and antiphon on Fridays (a common liturgical innovation of the early sixteenth century). Rehearsal and singing at service need have occupied no more than about a quarter or a third of their working day, and there is no reason why they should not simultaneously have remained an integral part of the almonry school as members of its clientele of scholars learning grammar.[116]

A large number of these monastic Lady Chapel choirs of, or including, boys' voices is now known to have existed, and their emergence gives rise to an intractable problem in the interpretation of evidence. Since the resident pupils of the almonry school were maintained on the surpluses of the host house, their support involved only rare items of expenditure. Consequently their existence is, in general, largely unrecorded on the monastic accounts, the source of potential evidence that has survived in greatest abundance. The maintenance of a Lady Chapel choir, however, did inevitably involve expenditure – on the stipends of the cantor and lay singing-men, for instance, and on the supply and repair of service-books and other necessary equipment. For the existence of a choir, therefore, the evidence may be relatively plentiful. It is, consequently, a result arising simply from the nature of the evidence that a good number of Lady Chapel choirs are known to have existed at monasteries for which there is, as yet, no known trace of the maintenance of an almonry school. It is debatable, therefore, in each of these cases, how far the existence of a Lady Chapel choir also implies the existence of an almonry school.

In a few cases – for instance, at Gloucester Abbey from 1515 until the Dissolution – the cantor was as well qualified to teach an almonry grammar school as he was to be master of the Lady Chapel choir, and his indenture, in effect, required him to do both.[117] Elsewhere, however, there is a dearth of evidence to show how the singing-boys received, beyond the training which a cantor could give them in music, the remainder of their education – not least the tuition in reading and in Latin which they required to support their work in the Lady Chapel. At many of these houses, probably, the singing-boys were, in the usual way, merely a sub-group of the pupils of an almonry school which did exist but has left no conclusive trace of its existence. It would not be safe to assume this in every instance, however, and the possibility remains that at certain of the less prominent monasteries the Lady Chapel singing-boys

---

[116] For any boy whose academic studies were impeded and delayed in consequence of his fulfilment of singing duties, there would be time enough to catch up after his change of voice at the age of fourteen or so.

[117] R. Woodley, *John Tucke: a Case Study in Early Tudor Music Theory* (Oxford, 1993), pp. 21–39, 133–4.

constituted just a group of junior musicians trained by a cantor, to whom no facilities to attend an almonry grammar school could be offered, because none was kept. Consequently, although in many cases evidence for the existence of a group of singing-boys might well be considered *prima facie* reason for believing that a formal almonry school for them to have attended also existed, this conclusion cannot safely be drawn in every case.[118]

A few words should be reserved for the most remarkable of all the almonry schools, namely that of Westminster Abbey.[119] Of the existence of this school the earliest, rather oblique, notice dates from 1317, and further incidental references occur for 1339–40. Thereafter, from the mid-1350s onwards, the grammar master and pupils make regular appearances in the records, in a variety of contexts.[120] The number of pupils maintained on the resources of the monastery was twenty-eight in 1385 and twenty-two between 1386 and 1389.[121]

Until almost the end of the century there is nothing in its history to suggest that this school was in any significant way different from the other almonry schools of the fourteenth century. However, under the abbacy of the industrious William Colchester (1386–1420) there began to be applied to its management a very much enhanced vision of what an almonry school could be. In the first place, at Lady Day 1396 the master's stipend was abruptly doubled – albeit only from 13s. 4d. per year to 26s. 8d.[122] Then the number of maintained pupils underwent steady expansion, until by Christmas 1405 it too had been almost doubled in size. For this particular period, this rise in numbers has to be extrapolated from the abrupt and conspicuous increase in

---

[118] In particular, no almonry school need be presumed to have existed in the case of any monastery which maintained a Lady Chapel choir and was located in the immediate vicinity of a town grammar school to which the singing-boys could be sent. Winchecombe and (apparently) Thetford were examples of this practice.

[119] All published accounts of the school of the pre-Dissolution abbey are brief. Those by Leach, 'The Origin of Westminster School', and L. Tanner, *Westminster School*, 2nd edn (London, 1912), pp. 11–13, are somewhat dismissive; those by J. D. Carleton, *Westminster School* (London, 1965), pp. 1–3, and J. Field, *The King's Nurseries* (London, 1987), pp. 13–16, are rather more perceptive and constructive. There are valuable details in G. Rosser, *Medieval Westminster 1200–1540* (Oxford, 1989), pp. 207–9, and also in B. Harvey, *Living and Dying in England, 1100–1540: the Monastic Experience* (Oxford, 1993), pp. 32, 68, 74–5, 214–15, 249, although in this latter it seems that rather too strong a distinction is perceived between the almonry grammar school and that group among its pupils who served as the Lady Chapel singing-boys. For a detailed account, see Bowers, 'Westminster School'.

[120] Bowers, 'Westminster School', pp. 3–7 (quoting WAM 18964, 18965, 18722, 18981, 18983, 18985, 18990, 18992, 18993 etc.)

[121] See above, note 68.

[122] Bowers, 'Westminster School', p. 18 (quoting WAM 19001, 19002).

the purchases of cloth required to top up the monastic discard wherewith to make the boys' annual liveries, from the regular sum of 36s. 4d. spent each year until around 1400 up to £8 12s. 0d. by Christmas 1405.[123] The overall cohort of boys so maintained in clothing can be calculated to a number very close to forty; and certainly it was recorded that an expenditure on cloth of £10 3s. 10½d. in 1449 was associated with the sustenance of no fewer than forty-four boys that year on the alms of the monastery.[124]

The date of the re-fashioning of the school, which began in 1396, is surely not without significance. The provision of boarding grammar schools for boys can hardly have been other than a lively topic of thought at this time in the immediate wake of the opening of William Wykeham's Winchester College in 1394, and it is hard not to see some spirit of emulation in Abbot Colchester's almost immediate re-ordering and expansion of the Westminster school in the first years of the next century. The abbey could not reproduce Winchester's seventy scholars and two masters, but the exhibition of forty boys and one master was by no means an insignificant gesture to make in deference to the promotion of education in fifteenth-century England.

At Westminster the physical location of the almonry was, unusually, wholly outside the precinct wall. Here there was room for expansion, and in 1421–2 a whole new range was specially built for the conduct of the lately enlarged school. It was a single-storey range of four rooms, each timber-framed but equipped with a hearth and fireplace of stone; the total cost was £22 11s. 8¼d.[125] The number of maintained pupils apparently remained around or in excess of forty, and in 1448–9 extra dormitory accommodation had to be supplied.[126] And in all probability there was added to this complement of maintained scholars some considerable but now indeterminable number of fee-paying pupils.

Presently the political disorders of October 1460 and March 1461 provoked an urgent crisis, for they brought the menacing and ill-disciplined soldiery thrown up by the civil wars to the very walls of the abbey itself. At times of civil tumult, a site in the almonry complex, located beyond the precinct wall and vulnerable to every malevolence minded to descend upon it,

---

[123]   Ibid., pp. 18–21.

[124]   WAM 19059, Minute: 'Et solut' pro panno empto pro magistro scolarum et pueris elemosinarie xliiij hoc anno xli iijs xd ob'. The number was interlined by a contemporary hand which made several similar interpolations on this account, amplifying individual items with greater detail.

[125]   Bowers, 'Westminster School', pp. 26–8 (quoting WAM 19026, Custus domorum). For a diagrammatic plan of the almonry site, see Rosser, Medieval Westminster, p. 70; however, the location of the school is not shown.

[126]   Bowers, 'Westminster School', pp. 32–4 (quoting WAM 19054–7, Firme domorum, Custus domorum).

was clearly no place at which to be conducting a children's boarding school. The erstwhile school building was dismantled, and much of it salvaged for re-use in a far larger new building erected during the summer of 1461 to replace it, well within the monastery precinct on what is now a plot of open space in Dean's Yard.[127] Its cost was £45.7.3; it was only timber-framed, but some idea of its size may be derived from the use of no fewer than 19,000 tiles upon its roof. The accommodation included at least a school-room, lodging for the master, and a chamber for the boys, for which some new beds were made from 400 feet of elm planking. The number of boarders never fluctuated far from forty thereafter, augmented after 1507 by the six singing-boys of the Lady Chapel choir, and this accommodation remained in use as the school until shortly after the Dissolution. Thereupon, at some point between 1540 and 1542, the school removed to new premises,[128] apparently in the stone-built range, vacated in consequence of the extinction of the monastery, that lies parallel with and but a few yards to the east of its erstwhile site.

The school throve without interruption up to the Dissolution, and over the last 130–40 years of its existence it seems clearly to have constituted a very substantial enterprise in the provision of schooling for the sons of the laity through the initiative of the monks of Westminster. The monastery placed upon its secular school a value sufficiently high to justify pouring considerable resources into it, including twice rebuilding in the space of forty years. Quite probably its clientele was national and by no means purely local. Certainly the sole pair of pupils whose names are known, John and Giles Spencer who were at the school in 1531–3, were the sons not of artisans or shop-keepers living in Tothill Street by the abbey gate, but of a gentry family from Badby, near Daventry in Northamptonshire.[129] Indeed, given its location adjacent to

---

[127] Bowers, 'Westminster School', pp. 35–41, quoting WAM 19067, *Custus domorum*. It appears to have been a linear construction occupying the northern end of the eastern edge of what is now the open space forming the centre of Dean's Yard.

[128] Knighton, 'Collegiate Foundations', pp. 44, 262–3. The site for the grammar school shown on Maps I and II in Harvey, *Living and Dying*, pp. xvii, xviii, is that to which the school appears to have removed at this juncture, shortly after the Dissolution of the abbey.

[129] WAM 12257*, *passim*, esp. fols 1v, 17v, 20r. The Spencer boys were fee-paying day scholars who, under the guardianship of their uncle, lodged outside the abbey with a Mrs Parker (*ibid.*, fol. 16r). For the Spencers of Badby see *Warwickshire Grazier and London Skinner 1532–1555: the Account-Book of Peter Temple and Thomas Heritage*, ed. N. W. Alcock, Records of Economic and Social History, new ser. 4 (London, 1981), p. 20, and for the education of this generation of Spencer children see R. D. Bowers, 'Schooling and the Sons of Midlands Gentry in the Early Sixteenth Century', forthcoming in *History of Education*. Doubtless, a high proportion of the first forty scholars of the school of the successor collegiate church, as listed by name early in 1541 (BL, Add. MS 40061, fol. 2v), consisted of

the principal royal palace and to the headquarters of government finance and its associated courts of law, it is not easy to believe that the sort of families whose sons were nominated for the forty free boarding places of its successor school by the dean and canons after 1540 can have been very much different from the sort of families whose sons had been nominated for its forty-odd free boarding places between *c.*1405 and 1540 by the abbot and monks. Westminster, however, is rather an exception. So far as is known, no monastery almonry schools other than those of Glastonbury and Durham even remotely approached it in scale or ambition, and none could vie with it for advantage of locale. After Winchester and Eton it was probably the largest boarding school in the country;[130] equally probably, in many aspects of character and curriculum, and in terms of clientele, it is with those two schools that it may most realistically be compared, no less before the Reformation than after.

The most successful of the almonry schools survived and prospered right up to the Dissolution of their host houses. Some of those in towns where the monastery was not re-founded, such as Evesham, were eventually reorganised under alternative management and were thus preserved.[131] At the re-founded cathedral priories the two erstwhile grammar schools – of the city and of the almonry – were generally merged into one, and it was possible for the last master of the episcopal school to be appointed headmaster of the new cathedral school, and the last master of the almonry school to be appointed usher, as happened at Durham.[132] In some small or declining cities it was only

boys first admitted prior to 1540 as members of the almonry school. However, it has not proved possible to devise a means of identifying precisely which of the names belong in this category.

[130]   In 1535 the abbey of St Mary, York, claimed to be maintaining of alms no fewer than fifty boys; these, however, did not attend an internal school, but were sent for their education to the city grammar school managed under the auspices of the cathedral chapter: *Valor Ecclesiasticus*, V, p. 6.

[131]   In 1462 the abbey was permitted to appropriate the rectory of a deserted parish to provide a grammar master for the novices and for the 'other boys' of the monastery. The latter can only have been the boys of the almonry, and in all probability such a school was conducted within the monastery precinct. However, by the 1530s the abbey was maintaining a separate master to teach the novices, and its grammar school was being conducted in the town; it appears still to have numbered the six boys of the almonry among its clientele. See Orme, 'Education in an English County', pp. 39–42, 46–7; *idem, English Schools*, pp. 240, 248–9, 250–1, 259–60; Leach, 'Schools', *VCH, Worcestershire*, IV, pp. 500–1.

[132]   Leach, 'Schools', *VCH, Durham*, I, p. 375. By 1544 the erstwhile almonry schoolmaster, Robert Hartburn, had succeeded to the headmastership of the cathedral grammar school: J. J. Vickerstaff, 'Profession and Preferment amongst Durham County Schoolmasters, 1400–1550', *History of Education* 19 (1990),

the almonry school which survived to the Dissolution. In Norwich the episcopal grammar school was discontinued in the early sixteenth century, leaving only the almonry school of the cathedral priory to serve the city thereafter.[133] At Ely nothing is heard of the episcopal school after the early years of the fifteenth century;[134] probably it had ceased to function, and it was the last master of the almonry school, Ralph Holland, who became first headmaster of the cathedral school at the re-foundation.[135]

A preliminary listing (appended below) of the English almonry grammar schools yet known to have been in existence at any point between c.1265 and 1540 extends to a little over thirty establishments. The most worthwhile of these represented no small-scale fringe enterprise of only peripheral significance; rather, they appear to have occupied a conspicuous place within the mainstream of the supply of grammar school education in late-medieval England. Nevertheless, their achievement needs to be kept in perspective. While the best of them probably did accomplish really conspicuous records of usefulness and success, it is likely that these were, overall, to be found overwhelmingly among those which were favourably located in the more prominent urban centres. Here alone, with their associated hinterlands, could be found a dependable supply of clientele in the numbers and of the quality necessary to support schools of this type. For monasteries located in rural areas the supply of potential pupils was, by comparison, inevitably far more attenuated and intermittent. The incentive to run an almonry school for the benefit of the kin of the monks might well at some point have been sufficiently strong to cause an inauguration to be undertaken. Thereafter, however, in the presence of any inability (or unwillingness) either to provide more than a few free places on the alms of the house, or to find enough fee-paying scholars in a rural area to attract a good teacher (or any teacher at

---

273–82, pp. 277–8.

[133] This seems to be the only plausible interpretation of the evidence marshalled by Cattermole in Harries, *History of Norwich School*, pp. 9–10, 19–21, 39. Perhaps it was because the almonry school had absorbed the episcopal school that in 1535 the monks claimed Herbert Losinga, first bishop of Norwich (1090–1119), as founder of the almonry school: *Valor Ecclesiasticus*, III, p. 287.

[134] Collations in 1403 and 1405: Cambridge University Library, MS EDR, Reg. Fordham, fols 195v, 201r; Evans, 'Ely Almonry Boys', p. 158.

[135] At the time of the Dissolution Ralph Holland, *magister scole*, was in receipt of an annual corrody of £6 from the almoner: Cambridge University Library, MS EDC 1/C/3, fol. 3r. For his appointment to the new foundation, see Owen and Thurley, *King's School, Ely*, p. 31. The ancient episcopal grammar school of the city of Winchester may likewise have foundered at around the beginning of the sixteenth century (A. F. Leach, 'Schools', *VCH, Hampshire*, II, pp. 256–7), in the face of competition from both the almonry school of the cathedral priory and the grammar school of Winchester College.

all), it might well have proved impossible to generate continuity of supply of the means of sustaining a formal school over a period of time. Such schools may well have achieved only an intermittent and fitful existence; the example set by the school of Thornton Abbey, located in the depths of rural north Lincolnshire, may have been not uncommon among schools established in such areas.[136] Yet others might be subject to management at only the low level of expectation that caused them to be the subject of episcopal injunctions requiring improvement – though the fact that complaint was made at all shows that not everyone was complacent about the poor running of these schools.[137]

Overall, however, many of the greater monasteries were supplying to the society in which they existed a commodity of considerable value. Those located within the cities and towns were offering a means of grammar school education which stood alongside and supplemented that supplied through the auspices of the episcopal authorities, by religious fraternities, or through the bounty of miscellaneous benefactors, secular and clerical. In this respect, it was within the gift of the monastic authorities to play a genuinely constructive role in the society of the later middle ages. It is hoped that the amplitude of the simple trial check-list appended here will demonstrate that their provision of means for the education of the young constituted not the least significant of the contributions made to society at large by the monastic institutions of the later middle ages.

---

[136] *Visitations of Religious Houses*, I, p. 121 (*c.*1422–3); III, pp. 371–80, *passim* (1440).
[137] For examples see St Mary de Pratis, Leicester (*ibid.*, II, p. 208), and Whitby Abbey (see note 39 above).

AFTERWORD

Since the completion of the text of this chapter there has been published an account-book of prior's disbursements from the Priory of St Mary, Thetford (Norfolk), 1482–1540: *The Register of Thetford Priory*, ed. D. Dymond, 2 vols, Norfolk Record Society 59–60 (1995–6). A Lady Chapel choir was maintained here from 1482/3 at the latest until the Dissolution in 1540; it consisted of at least five boys (pp. 74, 414). Probably there was no almonry school at the priory, since some at least of the singing-boys were sent to the town grammar school for their education (p. 653). Among those who can be identified as singing-boys was Edmund Stroger, who occurs in 1535/6 and 1536/7 (pp. 650, 665). In the 1560s a person of this name was closely associated with the choir of St Paul's Cathedral, London, and is known as a composer of keyboard music; he seems very likely to be identifiable with the Thetford singing-boy.

A group of documents arising from the establishment of a Lady Chapel choir of four singing-boys at the cathedral priory of Holy Trinity, Dublin, in 1480–93 is very illuminating for the light which it throws on the procedures necessary to set up such a choir at a monastery where there was no pre-existing almonry school. An edition of these documents will appear in *Music at Christ Church, Dublin, before 1800: Documents and Selected Anthems*, ed. B. Boydell (Dublin, 1998).

A trial listing of monastic almonry schools and Lady Chapel choirs in England c.1265–1540

These listings aspire to offer no more than just an initial attempt to assemble outline data relating to what are in almost all instances very obscure and ill-documented institutions. Little is certain other than that it is very incomplete, and I would be very grateful to receive any notice of errors and omissions which readers may detect.

In few instances are the opening dates given those of actual inauguration, and closing dates are, except where stated, not those of extinction. In the great majority of cases the dates cited are merely those in respect of which some reference to the institution's existence has survived. The various styles adopted for the presentation of dates designate the following:

1317–1540	reasonable grounds for suggesting a continuous existence between the given dates
1397, 1492	isolated references to an institution's existence occur on these dates, between which it may or may not have had a continuous existence
1441–69; 1506–38	the semi-colon separates two periods between which institution appears to have ceased to function
[1402–80]	denotes years during which a Lady Chapel choir existed but consisted of men's voices only, and no educational function for boys was involved
(D)	year of Dissolution
(R)	refounded following Dissolution
1379 (italic)	surviving evidence is suggestive of the existence of this institution at this date, but is not conclusive
1447 (bold)	date apparently of actual inauguration
*	denotes that grammar school teaching was available to Lady Chapel singing-boys through some medium other than an almonry school.
C.P.	Cathedral Priory

Monastery	Almonry boys to town school	Almonry school	Lady Chapel choir
Abingdon		*1390/1*	1420–41
Athelney			[1538]
Bardney		*1379*	
Barlinch		*c.1510*	
Barnwell		1296	1538(D)
Battle			1498/9
Beauchief			1490
Bermondsey	*1213*		
Bradwell		*c.1432*	
Brecon			1537–39(D)
Bridlington*			**1447–52**
Bristol, St Augustine		1491–1512	1491–1512
Buckland			1522–39(D)
Burton-on-Trent			**c.1465**
Bury St Edmunds	*c.1200, 1444, 1514–25*		
Butley			1532–38(D)
Canterbury, St Augustine		**1431,** 1518–39(D)	
Canterbury, C.P.		1291–1540(R)	**1437/8**–1540(R)
Chertsey			1532
Chester		1518–39(R)	1518–39(R)
Cirencester*			1538–9(D)
Coventry, C.P.		1439, 1535	1515–39(D)
Coventry, St Anne	1399, 1535–9(D)		
Crowland		1434–5	
Dover		1535	1530–5
Durham, C.P.	1180, c.1340	1348/9–1539(R)	[1387/8]; **1419**–1539(R)
Ely, C.P.		1315–1539(R)	1404–1539(R)
Evesham	1535	1462	
Forde		1537–9	
Furness		early 16C	
Garendon			1535–6(D)
Glastonbury		1377, 1408, early 16C	1420, c.1510–39(D)
Gloucester, St Peter		1515–39(D)	1515–39(R)
Gloucester, St Oswald	1400		
Guisborough		1266–80	
Hyde by Winchester		c.1325, 1397, 1492	c.1430, before 1492
Ivychurch		1536(D)	
Ixworth		1535	

Monastery	Almonry boys to town school	Almonry school	Lady Chapel choir
Kirkham		*c.1465*	
Lanthony II			1533–9(D)
Leicester, St Mary	1440		1518–37
London, Holy Trinity			1513/14
Missenden			1530
Monk Bretton		*c.1520–30*	
Muchelney			1510–26
Newburgh		*1492, 1538*	
Newnham		*c.1433*	
Northampton, St James	1538(D)		
Norwich, C.P.		**1289**–1538(D)	1441–69; 1506–38(R)
Oseney			1507–*c.*1527
Peterborough		1449–53, 1503–18	1448–63, 1503–39(R)
Ramsey		1355, 1432–48, 1535	[1435–70], 1480–96
Reading		1375–92, 1468/9	1536/7
Rochester, C.P.		1299	
St Albans	1339		[1423], 1525–39 (D)
St Osyth			**1513**–39(D)
Selby		1413–35	1536/7
Sherborne		*1535*	
Spalding		1438	
Taunton			1538–9(D)
Tavistock		*c.1530*	1523–39(D)
Tewkesbury		1535	
Thame			to 1526
Thetford, St Mary			1482–1540(D)
Thornton		1422–40	*1420/1*
Thurgarton			1522–38(D)
Tutbury			1496–1527
Tywardreath		*1522–36(D)*	1522–36(D)
Ulverscroft			1535–9(D)
Walsingham			1483–*c.*1515
Waltham			1540(D)
Westminster		1317–1540(R)	**1384**–1402, [1402–80], 1480–1539(R)
Winchcombe*			**1521**–39(D)
Whitby		before 1366	
Winchester, C.P.		1404–1539(D)	**1402**–1539(R)
Worcester, C.P.	*c.*1335	1380–1539(R)	[1374], 1390–1424, [1424–78], 1478–1539(R)
York, St Mary	1535		

Monastic or Secular? The Artist of the Ramsey Psalter, now at Holkham Hall, Norfolk

LYNDA DENNISON

The question of monastic involvement in the production of illuminated books in fourteenth-century England, on which I here present some preliminary findings, is a complex one.[1] Although further work currently in hand will produce firmer conclusions, some of the details which have so far emerged force one to consider the wider implications of the evidence, which may lead to a revision of current thinking on fourteenth-century workshop practice at a period when the execution of *de luxe* volumes is generally considered to have been almost entirely in the hands of lay craftsmen.

The aim of this paper is to put forward a case in support of the monastic production of illuminated books in the fourteenth century, or at least the close involvement of the religious. It is not unreasonable to take as a pretext the argument that books commissioned by the monastic orders might in some way involve their participation. In his article 'Book Production by the Monastic Orders in England', dealing with the fifteenth century, Ian Doyle is of the view that although it would be unwise to conclude without positive evidence that a manuscript of religious provenance is necessarily of religious workmanship, to ignore this evidence may well be over-compensating. He states that 'it is equally easy to cite separate instances of books written and decorated by individual religious ... as to cite books written and decorated by secular craftsmen for religious houses'.[2] Michael Kauffmann, in the introduction to *Romanesque Manuscripts*, raises the question of where

---

[1]   I should like to express my gratitude to the Francis Coales Charitable Foundation for a generous grant which has enabled me to reproduce the plates with Bodleian Library shelf marks contained in this article. I also wish to thank Mr Sam Mortlock, the librarian at Holkham, for his kindness in facilitating my work on my return visit to the library at Holkham Hall, and Nicholas Rogers for his much valued interest and encouragement.

[2]   A. I. Doyle, 'Book Production by the Monastic Orders in England', in *Medieval Book Production: Assessing the Evidence*, Proceedings of the Second Conference of the Seminar in the History of the Book to 1500, Oxford, July 1988, ed. L. Brownrigg (Los Altos Hills, CA., 1990), 1–19, pp. 2, 3.

illuminated books were produced – cathedral scriptorium, nearby monastery or lay workshop – stating that 'the problem ... should not be allowed to obscure the fact that the majority of manuscripts were still at this period produced in monasteries'.[3]

Similarly, for the thirteenth century, Nigel Morgan states that 'a fair proportion of illuminated and illustrated texts were still produced for Benedictine patrons'; and several 'show marks of ownership or have textual contents suggesting a contact with Augustinian Canons', some with indications that 'their production was in some way supervised by Augustinians possibly for lay people'.[4] Almost half of the manuscripts in his catalogue have been ascribed to ecclesiastical patronage, possibly a conservative estimate since some of those without evidence, as he states, were doubtless intended for ecclesiastical destinations. To add to these findings there is the unequivocal evidence of the 1277 statute of the English Benedictines, reiterated in 1343 and 1444, which prescribed that monks must occupy themselves according to their abilities in various tasks, such as studying, reading and writing, correcting, illuminating and binding books.[5]

Whereas Doyle is aware that such evidence in favour of monastic production might be found in chronicles, obituaries, financial accounts, visitation reports, wills and inventories, he asserts that 'the majority of evidence is in or on the surviving books'; he highlights colophons, inscriptions and palaeographical characteristics.[6] I shall extend this list of physical features to embrace individual artistic hands, borders, *mise-en-page* (lay-out of the page), and iconography; indeed, all codicological and decorative aspects of illuminated books. It is on this basis that I have arrived at my conclusions. To this end, I am focusing on a psalter, now MS 26 in the library of Holkham Hall, Norfolk (Pls 13, 15, 17, 21, 23),[7] commissioned for the

---

[3]   C. M. Kauffmann, *Romanesque Manuscripts, 1066–1190*, A Survey of Manuscripts Illuminated in the British Isles, 3 (London, 1975), pp. 12–16, especially p. 15.

[4]   N. J. Morgan, *Early Gothic Manuscripts*, A Survey of Manuscripts Illuminated in the British Isles, 4, 2 vols (London, 1982–8), I (*1190–1250*), pp. 12–13.

[5]   See *Documents Illustrating the Activities of the General and Provincial Chapters of the English Black Monks, 1215–1540*, ed. W. A. Pantin, 3 vols, Camden Society, 3rd ser. 45, 47, 54 (London, 1931–7), I, pp. 38, 74; II, pp. 51, 205, 228; see also D. Knowles, *The Religious Orders in England*, 3 vols (Cambridge, 1948–59), II, p. 233; and Doyle, 'Book Production by the Monastic Orders', p. 3.

[6]   Doyle, 'Book Production by the Monastic Orders', p. 2.

[7]   The manuscript has received little art-historical attention to date. It is briefly referred to in W. O. Hassall, *The Holkham Library*, Roxburghe Club (Oxford, 1970), pp. 6, 34, pls 2–7. See also L. F. Sandler, *Gothic Manuscripts, 1285–1385*, A Survey of Manuscripts Illuminated in the British Isles, 5, 2 vols (London, 1986), no. 143; L. E. Dennison, 'The Stylistic Sources, Dating and Development of the Bohun Workshop, *ca.* 1340–1400', unpublished Ph.D. dissertation (University of

Benedictine house at Ramsey, a location attested by the calendar which, amongst other features specific to Ramsey, contains the abbey's dedication on 22 September.[8] But the question of this illuminator's monastic or secular origins cannot be answered by reference to the Holkham Psalter alone, and this illuminator's other works and artistic context will be discussed.

The Ramsey Psalter, which has a ten-part division of the text,[9] is generally considered to date to the last quarter of the fourteenth century, a time when the production of illuminated psalters was on the decline. The style has a certain naïveté; the monumentality of this illuminator's figures and the iconography of the historiated initials differ fundamentally from the small-scale style and narrative idiom of the approximately contemporary Bohun manuscripts.[10] Indeed, in terms of page layout, border structures, ornamental motifs and iconography it holds more in common with psalters of the first quarter of the fourteenth century; in other words, it has a greater affinity with pre-Black-Death manuscript production. In these respects, it is surprisingly similar to the so-called Psalter of Richard of Canterbury (now Glazier MS 53 in the Pierpont Morgan Library, New York), a work of the central Queen Mary Psalter group of c.1320.[11] No single page is an exact copy of the other, but the Holkham artist seems to be drawing heavily on the Queen Mary Artist's repertoire of border structures and ornamental motifs, as the *Beatus* page in each manuscript demonstrates (Pls 13, 14). Although in Plate 21 the Holkham illuminator has extended the borders to enclose the text completely, apparent in the work of both artists is the same combination of organic and rectilinear structures (Pl. 22), the straighter borders demonstrated well by the *Beatus* folio in Glazier 53 (Pl. 14).[12] Furthermore, they share

London, 1988), pp. 217–23, 233, 234, 235, 236, pls 620–6, 632, 644. This manuscript will be referred to as either the Holkham or Ramsey Psalter.

[8] The calendar will be the focus of discussion below, pp. 244–5.

[9] The page of Psalm 26 is now missing; the initials to Psalms 52 and 80 are defaced and the initial to Psalm 109 is partly mutilated.

[10] For illustrations of the Bohun manuscripts, see principally M. R. James and E. G. Millar, *The Bohun Manuscripts: a Group of Five Manuscripts Executed in England about 1370 for Members of the Bohun Family*, Roxburghe Club (Oxford, 1936); Sandler, *Gothic*, nos 133–41; see Dennison, 'Bohun Workshop', *passim* for suggested dates of these manuscripts.

[11] For discussion of this manuscript and further bibliography, see L. Dennison, 'An Illuminator of the Queen Mary Psalter Group: the Ancient 6 Master', *Antiquaries Journal* 66 (2) (1986), 287–314, pls XL–LX, in particular pp. 295–6 and n. 51. See also Sandler, *Gothic*, no. 57.

[12] In the calendar of the Holkham Psalter, where the border ornament occupies only one full margin, with prolongations in the upper and lower margins, further parallels are apparent. The various calendar pages can be compared with the marginal decoration for Psalms 26, 38, 80, 97 and 101. Conversely, further

distinctive motifs, such as daisy and dragon forms; and examination of the iconography highlights further close parallels, the subjects of the historiated initials being almost identical, except for the *Beatus*.[13] The monastic destination of the Psalter of Richard of Canterbury is attested by textual evidence and by the figure of the Benedictine monk who kneels outside the initial to Psalm 119.[14]

With regard to the Holkham Psalter, a further unusual feature is the size of the initial to Psalm 109. It occupies eleven lines (Pl. 15), second only to the *Beatus*, of fourteen lines; the others are of nine lines or less.[15] By this date, no such distinction was usually made for the first psalm sung at Sunday vespers, and for parallels it is necessary to look back to a period when it was more usual. The twelfth-century Shaftesbury Psalter (BL, Lansdowne MS 383), probably produced in a monastic scriptorium, singles out Psalm 109, giving it greater prominence than those at the other psalm divisions, with the exception of the *Beatus*, a process which is repeated in other twelfth- and thirteenth-century examples.[16]

parallels can be made between the fuller borders in Glazier 53, such as those for Psalms 68 and 109, as well as the decoration for the opening of the Office of the Dead on fol. 150, all of which share certain basic structural elements with all the principal pages of decoration in the Holkham Psalter.

[13] The other exception is the iconography for Psalm 68, which in the Holkham Psalter has David kneeling in prayer in water, whereas the manuscripts of the Queen Mary group have Jonah and the whale. The Holkham Psalter shares other points in common with manuscripts of the first half of the century: the delicately pounced design of coiling sycamore branches, used by the Holkham illuminator for the grounds of the initials, is identical to that employed by the English Bohun Artist (see Dennison, 'Bohun Workshop', *passim*) and, in turn, derives from an earlier fourteenth-century tradition (see *ibid.*, p. 218, n. 42 for a list of examples).

[14] For an illustration, see J. Plummer, *The Glazier Collection of Illuminated Manuscripts* (New York, 1965), pl. 34.

[15] Psalms 38, 52 and 68 are of 9 lines, Psalm 97 has 8 lines, and Psalms 51 and 101 each have 5.

[16] For the Shaftesbury Psalter of *c.*1130–40 see Kauffmann, *Romanesque*, no. 48. This manuscript has three historiated initials at Psalms 1, 51 and 109 (that for Psalm 101 has been excised); Hereford Cathedral Library, MS O.6.xii, a glossed psalter of *c.*1140, probably produced at the cathedral (*ibid.*, no. 62), also has four historiated initials, those at the normal tripartite divisions (1, 51 and 101), and one at Psalm 109; Bodleian, MS Auct. D.2.4 (*ibid.*, no. 81), a mid twelfth-century glossed psalter of New Minster, Winchester, has the same four initials; and there are other instances where prominence is given to Psalm 109. For the thirteenth century, Cambridge, St John's College, MS K.30 (see Morgan, *Early Gothic*, I, no. 15) has ornamented initials, except for Psalm 1 (*Confitebor*), and Psalm 109, which has a king within the initial; BL, MS Arundel 157 (*ibid.*, no. 24), apart from Psalm 1, has an initial for Psalm 109 which is larger than the others; and New York,

What conclusions might be drawn from this conservatism in design and general concept? One hypothesis might be that the Holkham illuminator had access to earlier models provided by the patron or the workshop. The evidence so far suggests that these models had a monastic source.

In order to work towards identifying a monastic or secular origin for this artist it is appropriate to establish the extent of his *oeuvre*. The single illuminated folio in a copy of Higden's *Polychronicon* (Bodleian, MS Bodley 316) is unquestionably by this illuminator.[17] The border structures and individual forms are identical, as a comparison between the *Dixit dominus* folio from the Holkham Psalter and the *Polychronicon* illustrates (Pls 15, 16). In the lower border on the *Cantate* page there are paired columbines, a comparatively rare motif which also occurs in the *Polychronicon* border; this is, moreover, a characteristic form of the central Queen Mary group, of which the Psalter of Richard of Canterbury is a key member.[18] The *Polychronicon* initial is now partially defaced but enough remains to indicate that the figure style is of the same monumental type as in the Ramsey Psalter, with its heavy draperies and well-defined hands and feet. Although the *Polychronicon* has an inscription on fol. 2 stating that it was given by the duke of Gloucester to the College of the Holy Trinity which he and his wife, Eleanor de Bohun, founded for secular priests at Pleshey Castle, Essex, in 1394, Neil Ker has demonstrated that this volume is part of another (now BL, Harley MS 3634), which bears a Norwich Cathedral Priory pressmark, indicating that it was not initially produced for Thomas of Gloucester.[19] Ker's findings place it directly

---

Pierpont Morgan Library, MS Glazier 25 (*ibid.*, no. 50), has nine ornamental initials at the liturgical divisions, except for Psalms 101 and 109 which are figural.

[17] On this manuscript, dated 1394–7, see J. Taylor, *The Universal Chronicle of Ranulf Higden* (Oxford, 1966), pp. 107, 125, 149, 156; O. Pächt and J. J. G. Alexander, *Illuminated Manuscripts in the Bodleian Library Oxford*, 3 vols (Oxford, 1966–73), III, no. 674, pl. lxx; N. R. Ker, 'Medieval Manuscripts from Norwich Cathedral Priory', *Transactions of the Cambridge Bibliographical Society* 1 (I) (1949), 1–28, pp. 18–19; Sandler, *Gothic*, discussed under no. 143; Dennison, 'Bohun Workshop', pp. 218–20; F. Avril and P. D. Stirnemann, *Manuscrits enluminés d'origine insulaire VIIe–XXe siècle*, Bibliothèque Nationale, Département des Manuscrits, centre de recherche sur les manuscrits enluminés (Paris, 1987), referred to under no. 207.

[18] It occurs in a psalter, Longleat House, Wiltshire (collection of the marquess of Bath), MS 11; in the Psalter of Richard of Canterbury; and in London, Dr Williams's Library, MS Ancient 6. For illustrations of some of the above see Dennison, 'Ancient 6 Master', p. 292 (Longleat Psalter); pl. XLIa (left-hand border on fol. 105v of Ancient 6, where the binder has all but excised the motif); and pl. LIIb (fol. 102v of the Psalter of Richard of Canterbury).

[19] Ker, 'Medieval Manuscripts from Norwich Cathedral Priory', pp. 18–19. It should be noted that the *Polychronicon* initial illustrating the Trinity would thus

in a monastic *milieu*. A further *Polychronicon* in a closely related style, though probably not by the Holkham artist, is now in Paris; it, too, bears a Norwich Cathedral pressmark.[20]

Two further *Polychronica*, as yet undiscussed in an art-historical context, can be assigned to the illuminator of the Ramsey Psalter. One, CUL, MS Ii.2.24, was produced for St Augustine's, Canterbury.[21] A cursory examination is sufficient to establish its familial relationship to the two *Polychronica* associated with Norwich Cathedral Priory (Pls 16, 19). The borders contain the easily recognisable repertoire of forms of paired, elongated daisy buds, large sycamores, serrated cabbage leaves and dragons biting into rectilinear stems, but above all the paired columbines, ultimately derived, as I have suggested, from the 'central' Queen Mary workshop. To be noted is the kneeling monk, although in different positions, in the two examples illustrated.[22] In the Cambridge example the *retardataire* nature of these border forms is, as to be expected, reinforced by the figure style which bears the characteristic 'hip-shot' sway, first current some eighty years earlier (and prolonged until *c.*1340–45) (Pl. 19). On stylistic grounds this manuscript is datable to the mid- to late-1390s.[23] Above all, it exhibits the highly distinctive palette of bright crimson and azure, both touched with white, and an orange-red, all integrated with a matt burnished gold which is found in this artist's late works – the Ramsey Psalter and the Bodleian *Polychronicon*.

The other *Polychronicon*, BL, Royal MS 14.C. ix (Pl. 20), was produced for Ramsey Abbey,[24] the same destination as the Holkham Psalter. As can be

---

have equal relevance to both the Pleshey foundation and Norwich Cathedral Priory, also dedicated to the Trinity. The lower border bears the arms of the priory – *Argent a cross sable* – adjacent to a praying monk.

[20] Paris, Bibliothèque Nationale, MS lat. 4922, for which see Avril and Stirnemann, *Manuscrits enluminés*, no. 207, with bibliography.

[21] Mentioned in A. B. Emden, *Donors of Books to S. Augustine's Abbey*, Oxford Bibliographical Society, Occasional Publication 4 (Oxford, 1968), p. 5. See also M. R. James, *The Ancient Libraries of Canterbury and Dover* (Cambridge, 1903), p. 297; Taylor, *Higden*, pp. 45, n. 3, 91, 106, 152.

[22] Taylor, *Higden*, p. 91, suggests that the kneeling monk (identified as Arnold) was the scribe.

[23] Taylor, *Higden*, p. 91, dates the text to the fifteenth century, but the illumination suggests a date towards the end of the fourteenth.

[24] On this manuscript see G. F. Warner and J. P. Gilson, *British Museum: Catalogue of Western Manuscripts in the Old Royal and King's Collections*, 4 vols (London, 1921), II, p. 136. This manuscript was owned by John Warboys, abbot of Ramsey and Bachelor of Divinity of Oxford, in 1519. The *Polychronicon* was clearly a book favoured in monastic circles; indeed, Higden, the compiler, was a Benedictine monk of Chester. Continuations were made by other scholar-monks. See also Taylor, *Higden*, pp. 67, 99, 106, 155, and frontispiece, illustrating the map

seen from a comparison of the opening pages from the Ramsey, Norwich Cathedral and St Augustine's, Canterbury *Polychronica*, they share identical border forms and structures (Pls 16, 19, 20); they also agree in having the same distinctive palette.[25]

The decoration of the four *Polychronica* and the Holkham Psalter further relates to that in a *Flores historiarum* by Matthew of Westminster, which belonged to Henry Despenser, bishop of Norwich from 1370 to 1406,[26] thus reinforcing an East Anglian emphasis for this group of manuscripts. The Holkham illuminator is possibly identifiable in a fragment of a psalter-hours, now MS B.3.2 in Trinity College Library, Dublin,[27] working in the section comprising the Canticles, as well as executing the initial and border at Psalm 109 depicting the Trinity. Although representing a later manifestation of the Holkham illuminator's style, suggested by certain leaf forms, the facial types and border structures indicate that it is the work of this artist.[28]

---

on fols 1v–2 of BL, Royal MS 14.C.ix. For the popularity of the *Polychronicon* in this environment, see *ibid.*, pp. 149–51.

[25] Another apparently monastic-produced book, although not by the artist of the Holkham Psalter, but utilising *retardataire* border elements, in this instance derived from *de luxe* manuscript production, focused in Norwich in the first quarter of the fourteenth century, such as the Gorleston Psalter and the Stowe Breviary, is the so-called Norwich Domesday Book. This is discussed in P. Lasko and N. J. Morgan, *Medieval Art in East Anglia 1300–1520* (Norwich, 1973), no. 47, with bibliography. The Domesday Book contains a survey of all the parishes in the diocese of Norwich, the possessions of the prior and monks of the cathedral priory, and the religious houses within the diocese. See also *The Eastern Counties Collectanea*, ed. J. L'Estrange, I (Norwich, 1872–3), pp. 159–62; and 'Domesday Book', *Friends of Norwich Cathedral, 17th Annual Report* (1947), 8–16.

[26] BL, Cotton MS Claudius E.viii, for which see Lasko and Morgan, *Medieval Art in East Anglia*, no. 41. The borders utilise motifs from the Lytlington Missal workshop and at the same time employ the dragon forms typical of the *Polychronicon*, but would seem not to be by the artist of the Ramsey Psalter at Holkham.

[27] For references to this fragment, see T. K. Abbott, *Catalogue of the Manuscripts in the Library of Trinity College, Dublin* (Dublin 1900), no. 92 (p. 12); M. L. Colker, *Trinity College Library Dublin: Descriptive Catalogue of the Mediaeval and Renaissance Latin Manuscripts*, 2 vols (Aldershot, 1991), I, no. 92 (pp. 165–8). See also Dennison, 'Bohun Workshop', pp. 216, 217, 220, 221, 222, 223. There is no evidence of provenance for this fragment.

[28] The partial border accompanying the *Deus deus meus* initial on fol. 23v, with the climbing figure at the top of the shaft in the Dublin manuscript (Dennison, 'Bohun Workshop', fig. 616), can be compared in its structure with a number of pages in the Holkham Psalter, such as those in the calendar (*ibid.*, fig. 617) and minor borders (*ibid.*, fig. 632), as well as the right-hand marginal bar on the *Dixit insipiens* folio and the left-hand marginal bar on the *Cantate* folio (*ibid.*, figs 623,

Examination of other manuscripts not traditionally assigned to this illuminator may shed further light on his monastic or secular origins. The Holkham Psalter was shown in 1946 to Otto Pächt who noted that its artist was rather like the Master of the Egerton Genesis, but he concluded that it was not the Genesis hand.[29] In 1943 Pächt had added the so-called Derby Psalter (Bodleian, MS Rawlinson G.185) to the *oeuvre* of the Genesis illuminator, whose existence had been established by M. R. James in 1921, when he published a facsimile edition of the Egerton Genesis (BL, Egerton MS 1894). An addition had been made to this artist's work by E. G. Millar in 1938, with the discovery of the manuscript now called the James Memorial Psalter (BL, Add. MS 44949), and in the same year as Pächt's publication Francis Wormald added the Crucifixion and Christ in Majesty miniatures in the Fitzwarin Psalter (Paris, Bibliothèque Nationale, MS lat. 765).[30]

Despite Pächt's reservations the Egerton Genesis Master and the Holkham illuminator do appear to be one and the same; but two factors need to be borne in mind when making stylistic parallels in support of this theory. Firstly, there is the artist's development, which would indicate a move away from the Italianisms apparent in the Genesis-related material towards a reassertion of English stylistic tendencies in the Holkham Psalter-related works. For instance, in what are apparently his latest works there are no markedly foreshortened figures, aerial or backview, and an interest in three-dimensional structures, as in the Fitzwarin Psalter, is absent not only from the Holkham Psalter but from the Derby and James Memorial Psalters as well. Secondly, the iconographic model available to the artist may have given rise to stylistic anomalies. In securing these attributions to the Holkham artist's *oeuvre* there is only scope to touch on a limited number of comparisons. There is a close correspondence between the head of David in the Holkham *Beatus*, with his clearly defined upper eyelids, and the heads in

---

625).

[29] Pächt's unpublished observations are preserved in the library at Holkham Hall, Norfolk.

[30] O. Pächt, 'A Giottesque Episode in English Mediaeval Art', *Journal of the Warburg and Courtauld Institutes* 6 (1943), 51–70, pp. 69–70 (see also pp. 57–69 for his discussion of the Egerton Genesis cycle); M. R. James, *Illustrations of the Book of Genesis*, Roxburghe Club (Oxford, 1921); E. G. Millar, 'The Egerton Genesis and the M. R. James Memorial MS', *Archaeologia* 87 (1938), 1–5, pls. i–iv; F. Wormald, 'The Fitzwarin Psalter and its Allies', *Journal of the Warburg and Courtauld Institutes* 6 (1943), 71–9, p. 73, pls 22d, 23b. For further discussion of this group of manuscripts, particularly the James Memorial Psalter, see L. Dennison, 'The Suggested Origin and Initial Destination of London, British Library, Additional MS 44949, the M. R. James Memorial Psalter', *The Legacy of M. R. James: the Proceedings of the 1995 Cambridge Symposium*, ed. L. Dennison (Stamford, forthcoming), *passim*.

the top left-hand section of the composite miniature on fol. 8 of the Egerton Genesis (Pls 13, 33). In comparing the *Dixi custodiam* initials in the Holkham and Derby Psalters it can be seen that the figure of the Holkham David has been radically transformed (Pls 23, 24). In the Derby Psalter the artist is clearly adhering to the bulkier, more conventional types. Both figures, however, have similar hands and gestures; in each the drapery falls in heavy folds and clings around the lower leg at the base, and the head of God suggests that it is the same hand. Added to these specific parallels, the general monumentality of the Derby Psalter figures relates to those of the Holkham illuminator, as does the technique and palette; and these being illuminated lectern psalters, a comparative rarity after *c*.1350, the general format and conception of the two books are similar. Furthermore, the *Gnadenstuhl* Trinity of Psalm 109 in the Derby Psalter has both a stylistic and iconographic parallel in the Bodleian *Polychronicon* (Pls 34, 16). The specific dragon type used by the Egerton Genesis Master in the James Memorial Psalter recurs in the *Polychronica*, thus reinforcing the attribution. It is also found in Bodleian, MS Fr.e.22,[31] which is probably by the hand of the Holkham illuminator; the borders in MS Fr.e.22 in turn relate to those in the Derby Psalter. The two- and four-line pen initials which occur in the James Psalter are identical to the single-pen initial found on fol. 55v in the Holkham Psalter.

The origins of the border structures and some of the ornament in Holkham MS 26 have been demonstrated above to derive apparently at first-hand from a Queen Mary model. For this reason it does not precisely relate to the Derby Psalter, the borders of which seem to arise from those of the Fitzwarin Artist, as in a psalter, now Bodleian, MS Liturg. 198;[32] yet it is curious that aspects of the border decoration of the latter ultimately originate in that of the Queen Mary group, although the reliance on those forms is seemingly less direct.[33]

31 Pächt and Alexander, *Bodleian Library*, III, no. 703, pl. lxxi, who note its similarity to Bodley 316. See also Dennison, 'Bohun Workshop', p. 219. The manuscript has no figural illumination, but illuminated initials and borders occur on fols 14, 28v, 40v, 53, 63 and 75.

32 Comparison can be made between fol. 20 in the Derby Psalter and fol. 20v in Liturg. 198. On Bodleian MS Liturg. 198, see Wormald, 'Fitzwarin Psalter', pp. 71, 73, 74, 78–9, pl. 26a, b; Pächt and Alexander, *Bodleian Library*, III, p. 59 (no. 651), pl. lxv, with further bibliography; L. Dennison, '"The Fitzwarin Psalter and its Allies": a Reappraisal', in *England in the Fourteenth Century; Proceedings of the 1985 Harlaxton Symposium*, ed. W. M. Ormrod (Woodbridge, 1986), 42–66, figs 1–28, pp. 43, 44, 45, 46, 49, 65, 66, figs. 4, 33; Sandler, *Gothic*, no. 121.

33 Although less refined than the Queen Mary group of manuscripts, Liturg. 198 uses the specific vocabulary of daisy, marigold and strawberry flowers, as well as interlace and serrated cabbage leaf forms, as in the products of the central Queen

What evidence does this extended group of works provide for a location of production and the monastic or secular origin of the illuminator I will now rename the Genesis/Holkham Master?

The Egerton Genesis has no internal indicators for ownership or provenance,[34] but the James Memorial Psalter and the Derby Psalter are more informative. Geoffrey Hand has positively demonstrated that the Derby Psalter has a calendar of Christ Church Cathedral, Dublin, and a colophon secures Prior Stephen of Derby's ownership.[35] Although there is a maximum of nine *lectiones*, the calendar is clearly for monastic use. Of special significance in the present context is not the Irish location but the Augustinian destination of the manuscript. This is fully attested in the form of an absolution on fol. 143 which is specifically intended for the canons of the priory.[36] A quite different destination is indicated by the James Memorial Psalter, the calendar and litany of which point to Durham.[37] The full significance of the extension to the Genesis/Holkham Master's *oeuvre* becomes apparent when it is noted that this artist is found working in three manuscripts which have strong monastic associations, albeit Augustinian in one instance, Benedictine in two. The question of whether this artist was monastic or secular might be indirectly served by considering the two miniatures, assigned to this hand, in the Fitzwarin Psalter, one a Crucifixion (fol. 22), the other a Christ in Majesty (fol. 21v).

In my 1985 Harlaxton paper I put forward a case in support of the Egerton Genesis Master as not being contemporaneous with the hand I named

---

Mary group, such as the Longleat Psalter by the Ancient 6 Master, and the Psalter of Richard of Canterbury by the Queen Mary Artist, where, moreover, some of the structures, although modified, resemble those of Liturg. 198.

[34] Nor do Dublin, Trinity College, MS B.3.2 or Bodleian, MS Fr.e.22.

[35] G. F. Hand, 'The Psalter of Christ Church, Dublin (Bodleian MS Rawlinson G.185)', *Repertorium Novum* 1 (1955-6), 311–22. It is perhaps worth noting that in comparison with another Christ Church book, a martyrology of the second half of the fourteenth century, Hand concludes that there is a stronger English element overall in the saints invoked (*ibid.*, pp. 312–14 for list of saints). The colophon of ownership, 'Frater Stephanus de Derby prior ecclesie Sancte Trinitatis Dublin' cathedralis istud psalterium ordinavit et fieri fecit. Sit benedictus. Amen', occurs on fol. 142.

[36] For sins against their rule, that of St Augustine according to the customs of Arrouaise making special mention of the abuse of private property (Hand, 'Psalter of Christ Church, Dublin', p. 314). As Hand has demonstrated (*ibid.*, pp. 314–22), the psalter contains, in addition, a considerable number of entries concerning affairs of the priory from 1368 to 1416.

[37] As demonstrated by Millar, 'Egerton Genesis', p. 3. This calendar is further discussed below, but is given more detailed treatment in Dennison, 'M. R. James Memorial Psalter', *passim*.

the Fitzwarin Artist, who illuminated the entire Fitzwarin Psalter, except for the bifolium of the two miniatures painted by the Egerton Genesis Master.[38] On account of various factors, I concluded that collaboration was unlikely, especially since no other extant manuscript shows these two artists working together.[39] Indeed, examination of extant works by these illuminators indicated that they functioned largely independently of other artists, a factor which in itself may point in the direction of a monastic *milieu*.[40] In addition to the attributions made by Francis Wormald to the Fitzwarin Artist, which are the Fitzwarin Psalter itself (with the exception of the two miniatures by the Egerton Genesis Master), the historiated initials in Liturg. 198, and a *bas-de-page* in the Carew–Poyntz Hours,[41] I added a further *bas-de-page* in the same hours, a single folio in the Bohun Psalter in Vienna (National Library, Cod. 1826*), and some of the initials in a psalter, BL, Harley MS 2888.[42] At the same time I tentatively assigned to this illuminator all the decoration in a missal, Bodleian, MS Don. b.5, an attribution I now unreservedly confirm.[43] Comparison of a decorated initial from this missal and a partial border by the Fitzwarin Artist from the slightly later Vienna Bohun Psalter (Pls 27, 28) reveals the use of identical pigments, techniques and foliage forms; and if the opening page of the missal is compared with a typical folio from the Derby Psalter (Pls 25, 26) the borders can be seen to be almost identical in structure and shape as well as features of ornament. Much of the common ground between them, however, appears to be in a mutual influence from the Queen Mary Psalter group. It can be concluded that a Queen Mary repertoire of forms permeates the works of the Fitzwarin Artist and that it was communicated by exemplars which in turn found their way into the Genesis/Holkham Master's vocabulary. Thus, no actual working contact was

---

[38] See Dennison, 'Reappraisal', pp. 46–8. This was in opposition to the view expressed by Wormald ('Fitzwarin Psalter and its Allies', pp. 71–9).

[39] Firstly, the Egerton Genesis Master's miniatures occur in the same bifolium, separated from the other fourteen illuminated by the Fitzwarin Artist; secondly, unlike the other miniatures, the two occur in a diptych arrangement; and thirdly, the Egerton Genesis Master's Crucifixion repeats the same subject painted on fol. 14 by the Fitzwarin Artist, thus suggesting that the bifolium was inserted at a later date. For further discussion, see Dennison 'Reappraisal', p. 47.

[40] It seems to have been customary in the fourteenth century to work in collaboration with one or more illuminators. For a discussion of two such partnerships, see Dennison, 'Ancient 6 Master', *passim* and *eadem*, 'Bohun Workshop', in particular chs 4, 7.

[41] Wormald, 'Fitzwarin Psalter', pp. 71–9.

[42] Dennison, 'Reappraisal', pp. 44, 45.

[43] *Ibid.*, p. 62, n. 105. For further bibliography on Bodleian, Don. b.5 see Pächt and Alexander, *Bodleian Library*, III, no. 668, pl. lxv.

necessary. The question of how such patterns may have been transmitted will be the subject of later discussion.

In the Bodleian Missal, as in the Fitzwarin and James Memorial Psalters, there is emphasis on decorative, rather than historiated, initials, except for the opening of the text which in all three cases has figural illumination. This may be an indicator, along with other conservative features, that it was prepared in a monastic scriptorium using more archaic models, and not a cost-cutting exercise; there is a high standard of execution throughout. Similarly, there are fine pen initials accompanying the musical notation, reminiscent of those in Harley 2888 by the Fitzwarin Artist. They further recall those in the Derby Psalter by the Genesis/Holkham Master. This concentration on decorative pen initials may be a further indication of monastic workmanship, as might the gathering of the folios in quires of twelve leaves, rather than the customary eight, which is a feature of some of these manuscripts.[44]

The missal was produced for Buckland church, about twelve miles south-west of Oxford.[45] The calendar has Frideswide on 19 October, Milburga on 31 August and Hugh on 6 October; Augustine is given prominence in the litany, which excludes Benedict. Another manuscript not intended for monastic use but evincing monastic influence is the Helmingham Breviary, commissioned for a church near Norwich in the early fifteenth century.[46] Janet Backhouse has suggested that Benedictine influence is probably reflected in the status given to the translation of St Benedict on 11 July. The original

---

[44] Bodleian, Don. b.5 is gathered in twelves, as are the BL *Polychronicon* (see n. 24), except for the first and last quires, and the Cambridge *Polychronicon*, except for the last quire (now incomplete) which was of ten leaves, whereas the Fitzwarin Psalter is in eights. The James Memorial Psalter, apart from the prefatory cycle and calendar and some material at the end, is gathered in twelves from fols 38 to 289v. The Holkham Psalter is gathered in eights and tens, which it shares with the Derby Psalter; while Liturg. 198 is mostly gathered in eights,.except for two-to-three quires at the beginning which are of twelves. Gatherings in twelves are sufficiently uncommon at this date to be possibly significant in the present context. See also n. 65.

[45] See *Friends of the Bodleian, Eighth Annual Report* (Oxford, 1932–3), pp. 15–16, pl. IV. See also no. 293 in Sotheby's *Sale of the Meade Falkner Library* (December, 1932), pp. 12–14. The property and advowson of the church at Buckland, Berks., were acquired in 1353/4 by the Bonhommes of Edington Priory who followed the rule of St Augustine; see *The Edington Cartulary*, ed. J. H. Stevenson, Wiltshire Record Society, 42 (Devizes, 1987), pp. xxiii, 136–7. I am indebted to Benjamin Thompson for this reference. Although the Buckland Missal appears to date to the 1340s, it could have been passed to the Bonhommes from an Augustinian source.

[46] J. Backhouse, 'The Helmingham Breviary: the Reinstatement of a Norwich Masterpiece', *National Art Collections Fund Review* (1993), 23–5.

patron was probably one Robert, who appears to be mentioned twice in the inventories of the Benedictine priory of St Leonard. Since the small monastic community at St Leonard's was responsible for services in the neighbouring church of St Michael-on-the-Mount, this link provides a context for the transmission of monastic influence to a book apparently designed for a secular setting. Moreover, Backhouse makes the crucial point that a monastic contact would provide special models not available elsewhere, and cites famous examples such as the Lytlington and Sherborne Missals.[47] It is just this sort of monastic influence in a non-monastic manuscript that one detects in the Buckland Missal.

This huge volume shows no division of labour; it was entirely illuminated by the Fitzwarin Psalter Artist. Indeed, none of the manuscripts in which this artist participated testify to actual collaboration. This sense of isolation is further borne out by his fleeting appearance in the Carew-Poyntz Hours and the Vienna Psalter, where no actual collaboration is codicologically or stylistically tenable.[48]

The Fitzwarin Artist again appears alone in Harley 2888, possibly his earliest extant work, where he completed around 1340 a manuscript started approximately ten years before. A destination in the diocese of Lincoln seems likely for this book in which the feast of St Hugh's translation occurs on 6 October, Oxford then being in the Lincoln diocese. The calendar has the feast of Augustine on 28 August, although it does not have the rarer octave on 4 September, and this saint occupies a high rank in the litany. A patron in the southern part of the Lincoln diocese is suggested by Erkenwald on 30 April and Mildred on 13 July, but curiously it lacks Frideswide. Perhaps further suggestive of monastic influence are Albinus on 1 March, which it shares with the Augustinian Isabella Psalter (Munich, Staatsbibliothek, Cod. gall. 16) and the Augustinian Derby Psalter;[49] Leufred on 21 June, which it again shares

[47] However, Backhouse concludes (p. 25) that the breviary was 'most probably produced in a professional commercial workshop, very likely in Norwich'.

[48] See n. 40 above. The liturgy cannot be taken into account in these two manuscripts since the calendars belong to later campaigns. For discussion and bibliography see Dennison, 'Reappraisal', pp. 43–6.

[49] It also occurs in the Dominican Psalter-Hours of Elizabeth de Bohun, countess of Northampton, in all probability written out at the priory in Shrewsbury, although not apparently illuminated there, for which see Dennison, 'Reappraisal', pp. 52–5 and passim. For further discussion of this manuscript, see Christopher de Hamel in Sotheby's Sale Catalogue, The Astor Collection of Illuminated Manuscripts (London, 21 June, 1988), lot 52 (pp. 16–17) (the present whereabouts of this manuscript are unknown); Sandler, Gothic, no. 111; and Dennison, 'Bohun Workshop', principally chs 1–2 passim, and appendices VII.i, VIII. For the Isabella Psalter see D. D. Egbert, The Tickhill Psalter and Related Manuscripts (New York, 1940), especially pp. 82–9, 149–74.

with the Derby Psalter; and Pantaleon on 28 July, which also occurs in the Augustinian Isabella Psalter and the Benedictine Ramsey Psalter at Holkham. These saints which have been highlighted all occur in the Augustinian calendar of Guisborough Priory.[50] A monastic, specifically Augustinian, *milieu* is further reinforced by the illuminator of the earlier material in Harley 2888;[51] and the psalter contains musical notation, suggesting perhaps that it was not prepared for a layperson.

In Bodleian, MS Liturg. 198 the Fitzwarin Artist again worked totally independently. It is a manuscript which lacks a calendar but has a litany with the double invocation of Augustine, perhaps suggesting that it was prepared under Augustinian influence, but for a laywoman with Augustinian connections, as indicated by the presence of a kneeling female in secular dress in the donor initial on fol. 93v.[52] Unlike Harley 2888, but like the James Psalter by the Genesis/Holkham Master, the limited liturgical evidence, most notably Ebba of Coldingham in the litany, points to the north-east of England.

The Fitzwarin Psalter itself indicates a central destination, again on account of the feast of the translation of Hugh on 6 October. The psalter was made for the Fitzwarin family around 1345 when they were living in Wantage, some fifteen miles south-west of Oxford.[53]

Some interesting facts emerge from studying the case histories of the Fitzwarin Artist and the Genesis/Holkham Master, between whom there are some as yet unexplained connections. Whereas the apparently late works by the Genesis/Holkham Master suggest a focus of activity in East Anglia, those of the Fitzwarin Artist, with whom there appears to be some link, point to a centre in the southern Midlands, possibly to Oxford.[54] Although no working

---

[50] For which see F. Wormald, 'A Liturgical Calendar from Guisborough Priory, with some Obits', *Yorkshire Archaeological Journal* 31 (1934), 5–35.

[51] The artist who initiated the decoration in this book appears to be that of the Du Bois Hours (New York, Pierpont Morgan Library, MS M.700). See Sandler, *Gothic*, no. 88, who refers (p. 97) to some possible 'Augustinian influence, as Augustine's deposition and translation (on 28 February) are both included'.

[52] A possible monastic origin for a manuscript provided for a laywoman is also suggested by the Du Bois Hours, for discussion of which see Sandler, *Gothic*, no. 88.

[53] See Dennison, 'Reappraisal', for a stylistic dating, which is further supported by the heraldic evidence discussed in N. Rogers, 'The Original Owner of the Fitzwarin Psalter', *Antiquaries Journal* 69 (2) (1989), 257–60. Although clearly produced for lay ownership the calendar of the Fitzwarin Psalter preserves grading of 3 and 9 *lectiones* for some of its feasts, reminiscent of the Augustinian grading of the Derby Psalter and, incidentally, Queen Mary's Psalter. The calendar in the James Memorial Psalter is also graded. See n. 121, below.

[54] In 'Reappraisal' I made a case for the Fitzwarin Artist's activity being confined to

contact was seemingly made between these two illuminators an Oxford destination for the Fitzwarin Artist might afford a clue as to the origin of the Genesis/Holkham Master. The Fitzwarin Psalter, which contains work by both artists, seems to hold the key to the enigmatic connection between them.

It is reasonable to assume that the owner of the Fitzwarin Psalter procured the additional bifolium from the same establishment in the Oxford region. The later work shows influence from the earlier since the Egerton Genesis Master seems to have made every effort to conform to the Fitzwarin Artist as to the general style and layout of the miniatures. However, even without the instance of the bifolium in the Fitzwarin Psalter, the two illuminators have in common a number of characteristics, not least of which is their independent working method, which in total might point to their having evolved from the same, possibly monastic, *milieu* – in this instance perhaps an Augustinian house in Oxford, either St Frideswide's (now Christ Church Cathedral) or Oseney Abbey.[55] Firstly, it is of interest to note that they participated in works of a northern destination,[56] despite their southern orientation; secondly, they provided illumination for manuscripts with monastic, largely Augustinian, associations; and thirdly both artists show certain formal and stylistic relationships, as comparison between the *Beatus* page in the Fitzwarin Psalter by the Fitzwarin Artist and that in the James Memorial Psalter by the Holkham Master indicates (Pls 31, 32).

Moreover, the two psalters share a conservative approach to the decoration of the main psalm divisions, in that they are entirely ornamental, with the exception of Psalm 1. I know of no other *de luxe* psalter of the fourteenth century that follows this practice. The so-called Astor Psalter-Hours, of *c*.1345, made for Elizabeth de Bohun, which was probably written out at the Dominican priory of Shrewsbury, has conventional foliage for the divisions of the hours, although not for the psalms.[57] In the case of both the Fitzwarin and James Memorial Psalters the argument of economy is hardly appropriate for they both have 'expensive' prefatory cycles, which in themselves are *retardataire* for their date. This, like other features already highlighted, reflects certain archaising tendencies, pointing to earlier, possibly

---

the period before the 1348/9 outbreak of the Black Death, suggesting that he died as a result of the plague, whereas the activity of the Genesis/Holkham Master post-dates this outbreak of the pestilence.

[55] On Oseney Abbey and St Frideswide's, see D. Knowles and R. W. Hadcock, *Medieval Religious Houses: England and Wales*, 2nd edn (London, 1971), pp. 169–70. St Frideswide's relics were at the Oxford priory dedicated to her.

[56] Bodleian, MS Liturg. 198 (by the Fitzwarin Artist), and BL, Add. MS 44949 (by the Genesis/Holkham Master).

[57] For bibliography on this manuscript see n. 49 above.

monastic, models.[58] Indeed, the use of ornamental decoration for the large initials seems to be a survival from the period when the narrative illumination appeared in prefatory cycles, rather than as historiated initials in the main text. For viable precedents it is again necessary to look back to the twelfth century when ornamental initials were customary.[59] In the thirteenth century, when historiated initials had become more standardised for the main psalm divisions, the use of ornamental initials, which may have been based on a monastic model, is still preserved in some luxury examples, such as the Glazier Psalter (New York, Pierpont Morgan Library, MS Glazier 25), possibly textually derived, as Nigel Morgan suggests, from the psalter made for the Benedictine monks of Westminster, now BL, Royal MS 2 A.xxii.[60]

[58] Lucy Sandler (*Gothic*, no. 120) has remarked how archaising the figure poses are, citing as an early parallel the twelfth-century Winchester Psalter, for which see Kauffmann, *Romanesque*, no. 78. See also Wormald, 'Fitzwarin Psalter', p. 72, pl. 246, who suggests that the two manuscripts exhibit a parallel tendency to caricature; but might the parallels between the two books be more tangible and could the Fitzwarin Artist have had access to the Winchester Psalter, or a related exemplar, produced at the Benedictine houses of either Hyde Abbey or St Swithun's, Winchester, Kauffmann (*Romanesque*, p. 105) favouring St Swithun's as the place of manufacture?

[59] E.g. Kauffmann, *Romanesque*, no. 62, which has four decorated initials; no. 77, which has two miniatures and eleven decorated initials; no. 78, the Winchester Psalter, which, apart from a prefatory cycle of thirty-eight miniatures, has a historiated *Beatus* and two decorated initials; no. 81, which has three decorated initials at Psalms 1, 51 and 109, Psalm 101 having a bust of Christ (Bodleian, MS Rawl. G.185, the Derby Psalter, as a point of interest, has numerous initials containing busts of Christ); and no. 94, which as well as a cycle of sixteen miniatures preceding the text has a mixture of three historiated and eight decorated initials.

[60] See Morgan, *Early Gothic*, I, no. 50, where he notes (p. 97) that 'the absence of historiated initials for most of the liturgical division psalms is unusual for the period and may support the conclusion from the full-page miniatures that some late 12th-century model like the Westminster Psalter was used'. Of further interest, two out of the nine large initials which are not ornamental include that for Psalm 109, thus giving it greater prominence. Other examples include Cambridge, Trinity College, MS B.10.9 (Morgan, *Early Gothic*, I, no. 7), where eight out of the nine remaining initials are predominantly ornamental; BL, Royal MS 2.A.xxii (*ibid.*, no. 2), where six out of the ten initials are ornamental; Bodleian, MS Auct. D.2.1 (*ibid.*, no. 8) has ornamental initials for Psalms 1, 101 and 109 and a historiated initial for Psalm 51; Leiden, Bibliotheek van de Rijksuniversiteit, MS lat. 76A (*ibid.*, no. 14) has initials which are entirely ornamental; Cambridge, St John's College, MS K.30 (*ibid.*, no. 15) has mostly ornamental initials; Edinburgh, National Library of Scotland, MS 10000 (*ibid.*, no. 29) has eight large initials, six of which are ornamental. Of these, nos 2, 14 and 50 have prefatory cycles.

Both the Fitzwarin and James Memorial Psalters therefore have been shown to be extremely conservative in approach to many aspects of design and content, therefore agreeing with the *retardataire* nature of Holkham MS 26.

Other possible monastic elements in the Fitzwarin Artist's *oeuvre* are found in Harley 2888, Liturg. 198 and the Fitzwarin Psalter. These have blue and red pen initials and simple line-fillers of abstract patterns and animal forms (Pls 29, 31) probably executed by the scribe, the fish being particularly distinctive, contrasting with the illuminated type which are more common at this date.[61] For comparative examples it is again necessary to look to the early thirteenth century and focus on manuscripts such as Munich, Staatsbibliothek Clm. 835 and BL, Arundel MS 157, both psalters of likely Oxford provenance, produced *c*.1200–10, where the line-fillers consist of simple linear patterns such as animals, birds and fish – the exact repertoire of the Fitzwarin Artist (Pl. 30).[62] Although there are no *lectiones* indicated in the calendar of Arundel 157, or monastic divisions for the psalms, Augustine heads the confessors in the litany, suggesting, as Nigel Morgan points out, some monastic involvement, if not in the illumination itself, then in the preparation of the text.[63] It is also interesting that Arundel 157 preserves the larger initial

---

[61]   This might support the case that the book was either prepared by a monastic scribe who completed all the minor decoration, especially if it were to be farmed out to a lay workshop, or executed by an itinerant illuminator, secular or monastic. A monastic scribe would perhaps be more likely to decorate the minor initials in pen and coloured inks and not consciously allow for an illuminator, unless there were a monastic illuminator to hand.

[62]   See Morgan, *Early Gothic*, I, no. 23 for the Munich Psalter, and no. 24 for Arundel 157, to cite but two examples.

[63]   Morgan, *Early Gothic*, I, no. 24, where Augustinian involvement is suggested by Augustine heading the confessors in the litany, citing two other Augustinian manuscripts with minor decoration by the same artists, BL, Harley MS 2905 and a missal at the Victoria and Albert Museum, MS L. 404–1916. Further examples include Morgan, *Early Gothic*, I, no. 14, where the calendar is based on an Augustinian model ('many luxury psalters of the late 12th and early 13th centuries on the evidence of their Calendars and Litanies have Augustinian connections'); no. 23, the Munich Psalter, which has an Augustinian litany, although a Benedictine calendar ('most other books by the workshop have Augustinian textual features which suggest this order was in some way involved in directing the workshop or providing text models'); no. 29, Edinburgh National Library, MS 10000 ('as Augustine heads the Confessors and some prayers are in the female gender an intended destination for the Augustinian nunnery of Iona seems certain'); no. 35, Berlin, Kupferstichkabinett MS 78.A.8, whose 'text model suggests an Augustinian house ... Augustinian canons were in some way involved'; no. 39, BL, Lansdowne MS 431 ('the Calendar and Litany suggest that the Psalter was intended for an Augustinian house in East Anglia'); and no. 51, Cambridge, Trinity College, MS B.11.4, with an Augustinian calendar of the

for Psalm 109, as in the Holkham Psalter. Could these factors be further evidence of monastic models?

It is possible to conclude thus far that, although the Genesis/Holkham Master may have begun his career in Oxford, his apparently later works suggest, where evidence is available, that he gravitated to a centre, or centres, in East Anglia. It is worth noting that the Fitzwarin Artist seems to have made a similar move, just before the Black Death, apparently from Oxford to Cambridge.[64] The evidence accumulated seems to be indicating that both the Fitzwarin Artist and Genesis/Holkham Master were itinerant for at least part of their careers. In the case of the Genesis/Holkham Master, there is also an observable shift in patronage. Whereas the Derby Psalter is Augustinian, the Ramsey Psalter and the four *Polychronica* are Benedictine.[65] To judge from this

---

London diocese ('the Calendar is Augustinian – 4 September, Octave Augustine – of the London diocese').

[64] This is discussed in Dennison, 'Reappraisal', p. 62 and *passim*.

[65] There is a precedent for this in the form of the 'Abbot Simon Master' (see Kauffmann, *Romanesque*, nos 90, 91, 96) who, as well as working for the Benedictine monastery of St Albans, appears to have participated in a psalter produced for a house of Augustinian canons in Yorkshire (see also Morgan, *Early Gothic*, I, p. 14).

Possible communication of models, or indeed illuminators, between monastic establishments of different orders, namely Augustinian and Benedictine, is tentatively hinted at in the relationship between the style of the Fitzwarin Artist and the illuminator of two historiated initials at the beginning of the author's commentaries to Books I and II of the Decretals of Gregory IX, BL, Royal MS 10 E.vii (Warner and Gilson, *Royal and King's Collections*, I, p. 335), which originally belonged to St Albans Abbey. The opening page has a border with several figures including St Alban holding the arms of the abbey, and a kneeling Benedictine. This border relates closely to those of the Fitzwarin Artist, as demonstrated by the *Beatus* folio in Bodleian, MS Liturg. 198 (cleaning of the St Albans volume has revealed the bright pigments and thus an even closer relationship to the Fitzwarin Artist); and the small pen initials in each book are of the same type. Furthermore, the St Albans manuscript agrees with Don.b.5, the James Memorial Psalter and certain other related manuscripts listed in n. 44 above in being gathered in twelves. A good case, further details of which I plan to publish at a later date, can be put forward in support of the St Albans manuscript having been written out at that house, and this might in turn support the preparation in a monastic *milieu* for the aforementioned works. It further hints at possible connections, in this case between an Augustinian house in Oxford and the Benedictine house at St Albans. Alternatively, Gloucester College (see also n. 70 below) may have acted as an intermediary (there were certainly connections between the two establishments in the fifteenth century, for which see D. R. Howlett, 'Fifteenth-century Manuscripts of St Albans Abbey and Gloucester College, Oxford', in *Manuscripts at Oxford: R. W. Hunt Memorial Exhibition*, ed.

alone, the artist, monastic or secular, was not tied to a single centre, nor apparently to a single order. The indications so far seem to suggest a semi-itinerant illuminator who travelled from one centre to another, but equally had a stable base at one or possibly two centres or monastic houses. This would account for the presence of the same illuminator in manuscripts of disparate destinations – an enigma which constantly presents itself to the historian of manuscripts.

Owing to the strong monastic affiliations of these books it is worth pursuing the possibility that the nucleus of this activity is monastic. Michael Kauffmann refers to instances of artists, such as the Alexis Master, moving from one monastery to another seeking work, and Nigel Morgan has put forward other cases.[66] However, owing to the varied patronage of the books discussed in this paper, it would appear to have been a monastic centre where lay persons and the secular clergy could also order books. I touched on this question in the conclusion to my last Harlaxton paper, suggesting that ecclesiastical establishments seem to have acted as catalysts in setting up commissions, preparing the texts and possibly even illuminating them, providing itinerant illuminators from their own communities, or possibly operating a network by which itinerant lay illuminators could function over a wide area.[67] Strongly suggestive of such arrangements is the variety of scribes encountered, indicating varying locations, and not a single or stable workshop base. Invariably, where the illuminator is constant, the scribe is not, indicating

---

A. C. de la Mare and B. C. Barker-Benfield (Oxford, 1980), 84–7). See Dennison, 'Bohun Workshop', p. 72 for a stylistic discussion, where I link the St Albans manuscript to the artist of Baltimore, Walters Art Gallery, MS W.105, and Dublin, Trinity College, MS F.5.21. Both these manuscripts have the comparatively rare feast of St Damasus on 11 December, which occurs in the Augustinian calendar of Guisborough Priory, the James Memorial and Derby Psalters (see also n. 92 below), and in several Benedictine calendars (*English Benedictine Kalendars after A.D. 1100*, ed. F. Wormald, 2 vols, Henry Bradshaw Society 77, 81 (London, 1939–46), *passim*).

[66] Kauffmann, *Romanesque*, pp. 15–16. The 'Alexis Master' of St Albans appears to have worked at Bury to illustrate the life of St Edmund (no. 34). See also Kauffmann's discussion of another St Albans artist (no. 83) who collaborated on the Winchester Bible. For the thirteenth century, see Morgan, *Early Gothic*, I, no. 47, London, Society of Antiquaries MS 59, where he states that 'probably the artist of the Peterborough Psalters travelled widely while formulating his style, and on the basis of the artistic connections suggested he could have been predominantly involved with Benedictine patrons'.

[67] L. Dennison, 'Some Unlocated Leaves from an English Fourteenth-Century Book of Hours now in Paris', in *England in the Fourteenth Century: Proceedings of the 1991 Harlaxton Symposium*, ed. N. Rogers (Stamford, 1993), 15–33, pls 13–45, pp. 31–3.

that it is the illuminator who travels and the scribe is provided by a given monastery.

Further support for this hypothesis is provided by one of the patrons, John Wells. It was this monk, later to become prior of Ramsey Abbey, who commissioned his *ex libris* to be painted alongside a St Christopher at the opening of his miscellaneous collection of texts, now Bodleian, MS Bodley 851 (Pl. 36).[68] This St Christopher and the figure wearing a short tunic who is standing in the lower right-hand section of the composite miniature on fol. 5v in the Egerton Genesis are strikingly similar in respect of the facial type, large figure proportions and the monochrome water-colour technique of their execution (Pls 35, 36). The rather broad, angular draperies worn by the adjacent figure in the Genesis miniature relate to those of the St Christopher, the substantial figure of which in turn compares with the Goliath in Psalm 1 of the Derby Psalter.[69] They are clearly by one and the same hand.

It may have been John Wells who was instrumental in directing the Genesis/Holkham Master to Ramsey. They could have made contact when Wells was a scholar at Gloucester College, Oxford.[70] It will be recalled that the two leaves from the Fitzwarin Psalter, having miniatures by the Holkham Master, were presumably added in the Oxford region, probably at Oxford itself. Wells received his doctorate in theology in 1376. It could take up to seventeen years for a monk to earn this degree, that is an M.A. of eight years duration, followed by a doctorate of nine years.[71] This indicates that Wells was in Oxford from as early as *c.*1359, the decade in which the Genesis/ Holkham Master appears to have begun his artistic career. This tinted

---

[68] On fol. 6v; Pächt and Alexander, *Bodleian Library*, III, no. 650, pl. lxvi; Dennison, 'Bohun Workshop', p. 220. The *ex libris* reads: 'Iste liber constat fratri Johanni de Wellis monacho Rameseyensi'. For details concerning John Wells see A. B. Emden, *A Biographical Register of the University of Oxford to A.D. 1500*, 3 vols (Oxford, 1957–9; repr. 1989), III, p. 2008. Bodley 851 comprises Walter Map, *De nugis curialium*, miscellaneous poems, and William Langland, *Vision of Piers Plowman*.

[69] For an illustration of the Goliath in the Derby Psalter, see Dennison, 'Bohun Workshop', fig. 638.

[70] Emden (*Oxford*, III, p. 2008) refers to John Wells in connection with Gloucester College. This institution had been founded in 1283 when John Gifford granted a house to the Benedictines of the province of Canterbury so that thirteen monks might study there, the number being increased later. It was first affiliated to Gloucester, but became the common house of studies under the abbots-president of the province in 1291; it was then staffed by other abbeys besides Gloucester and monks from Whitby were admitted. Such an establishment could have engendered contact of the type suggested. For further details concerning the college, see Knowles, *Religious Orders*, II, pp. 14–28.

[71] See Knowles, *Religious Orders*, II, p. 22.

drawing in Bodley 851 not only provides a viable link between the two personalities, but it secures Oxford as a likely centre for their contact. Owing to the highly personal nature of the *ex libris* it is worth postulating that here lies an explanation for the artist's shift in allegiance from Augustinian to Benedictine patronage. Indeed, it was possibly Wells who made provision for this artist to illuminate books for monastic patrons in the East Anglia region, specifically at Ramsey Abbey. It is this tinted drawing with an assured Ramsey provenance, although it could have been executed during the illuminator's sojourn in Oxford, which supports my contention that the Egerton Genesis Master and the Holkham Master are identical, and it serves as well to strengthen the monastic *milieu* of this group of manuscripts.

What is emerging is that this illuminator, who was probably secular, held a special working allegiance to monastic establishments.[72] On this basis, the Genesis/Holkham Master seems to have been operating in Oxford until the late 1360s, where he benefited from predominantly Augustinian patronage, the Augustinian Derby Psalter doubtless having been executed before his move to East Anglia. There is tentative documentary evidence in favour of a date in the mid 1360s for the Derby Psalter on the basis of some added notes on fol. ii verso, dated 4 November 1368, and on fol. 142v, dated 1375.[73]

It is now appropriate to speculate which products of this Master's *oeuvre* were executed before his presumed departure for East Anglia. Having eliminated on the one hand those works which seem to speak for Oxford, namely the two miniatures added to the Fitzwarin Psalter, and the Derby Psalter, because of its Augustinian connections, and on the other hand those which point to East Anglia, which are the Ramsey Psalter now at Holkham and the *Polychronica* with Norwich and Ramsey associations,[74] this leaves the Egerton Genesis itself and the M. R. James Memorial Psalter. The *ex libris* of St Christopher, despite its Ramsey destination, and because of its association with Wells who spent a considerable period at Oxford, could have been executed at either location. As noted, this drawing relates in style to both the Egerton Genesis and the Derby Psalter.

Owing to the lack of internal evidence for dating both the Egerton Genesis and the James Memorial Psalter some estimate of respective dates can only be made on stylistic grounds. Both the style and technique of the Genesis seem to suggest a date of production between the additions made to the

---

[72]   For the suggestion of a similar practice, see Morgan, *Early Gothic*, I, no. 33, which will be the subject of later discussion, below.

[73]   See Hand, 'Psalter of Christ Church, Dublin', p. 311. Although these notes do not provide a guaranteed *terminus ante quem* for the book, a date in the early- to mid-1360s is consistent with this illuminator's artistic development.

[74]   The relevance of the *Polychronicon* belonging to St Augustine's Abbey, Canterbury, will become apparent in later discussion.

Fitzwarin Psalter and the Derby Psalter, dating to c.1355–65. The James Memorial Psalter similarly has much in common with the style of the apparently earlier manuscripts in the chronology, although there are certain linear devices which suggest that he was moving away from them. On balance, an earlier position seems more likely because of its close formal and stylistic relationship with the pre-Black-Death Fitzwarin Psalter; it is therefore datable on stylistic grounds to c.1355–60. This can be demonstrated simply by comparing the *Beatus* page in each manuscript (Pls 31, 32). The James Memorial Psalter's intimate stylistic relationship with the Derby Psalter is apparent not only from the principal illumination but also from the minor decoration; they both share particularly distinctive line-fillers, clearly painted by the artist himself. Additionally, despite the varying final destinations of the two books, the Derby Psalter for Christ Church, Dublin, and the Memorial Psalter for somewhere in north-east England, the calendars have in common certain elements, not least Frideswide on 19 October,[75] which may be pointing to an identical exemplar to which the appropriate regional modifications were made. Where they are especially compatible is in a strong Augustinian emphasis, sharing a number of feasts with the Isabella Psalter and the calendar of Guisborough Priory, both Augustinian and discussed earlier.[76] They share Emerenciana (23 January);[77] Projectus (25 January);[78] Oswald (28 February);[79] Chad (2 March);[80] Patrick (17 March);[81] Guthlac (11 April);[82] Leo

---

[75] In the James Memorial Psalter Frideswide appears immediately below Ebba in the litany.

[76] See nn. 49, 50 above.

[77] This also occurs in the Ramsey Psalter at Holkham and Bodleian, MS Barlow 22, based on a Ramsey model; the Augustinian calendar of Guisborough Priory (for which see Wormald, 'A Liturgical Calendar from Guisborough Priory', pp. 5–35); Bodleian, MS Rawl. G.170; London, Dr Williams's Library, Ancient MS 6; and Paris, B.N. MS lat. 1332 (the latter two Franciscan).

[78] This also occurs in the Holkham and Barlow Psalters and the Guisborough calendar, as well as BL, Add. MS 49622 (the Gorleston Psalter); Bodleian, MS Lat. liturg. e.6 (the Chertsey Breviary); and Cambridge, Corpus Christi College, MS 53 (the Peterborough Psalter and Bestiary).

[79] A feast they also share with Barlow 22, Corpus 53, as well as the Augustinian Isabella Psalter (see Egbert, *Tickhill Psalter*, pp. 82, 84–5; the calendar is fully transcribed on pp. 153–5).

[80] Which as well as occurring in the Isabella Psalter, the Guisborough calendar, Rawl. G.170 and Barlow 22, is also found in certain Queen Mary group manuscripts, such as the Psalter itself (BL, Royal MS 2B.vii), Ancient 6, the Chertsey Breviary, and CUL, MS Dd.4.17.

[81] As in the Isabella and Guisborough calendars.

[82] Guthlac is also in the Holkham, Barlow and Isabella Psalters.

(also 11 April);[83] Peter Martyr (29 April);[84] Translation of Nicholas (9 May);[85] Potenciana (19 May);[86] Eligius (25 June);[87] Mildred (13 July);[88] Radegund (13 August);[89] and Thomas of Hereford (2 October).[90] Perhaps especially indicative of having been written out at Oxford is the appearance of Frideswide (19 October) in both the James and Derby Psalters.[91] Finally, they also share Damasus (11 December).[92] Variations of this type, held in common by books in which the same, or related, illuminators are present, become meaningful.

Since both St Frideswide's in Oxford and the nearby priory of Oseney were Augustinian, the involvement of the Fitzwarin Artist and the Genesis/Holkham Master with either, or both, of these establishments is therefore possible. It is in the context of the Munich Psalter group, probably located in Oxford, that Nigel Morgan has suggested the Augustinians were in some way involved in directing, or providing text models for, the workshop.[93] Clearly, illuminators would have attached themselves to the source of work, thus explaining the diversity of liturgical evidence often apparent in the various manuscripts executed by a given illuminator, which again raises the question of itinerant practices.

The Ramsey Psalter shows a number of characteristics which place it late in the career of both Wells, who died in 1388,[94] and the Genesis/Holkham Master. It was probably produced in the late 1380s, or even the early 1390s,

---

[83] Leo also occurs in Barlow 22 and the Guisborough calendar.

[84] Agreeing again with the Isabella Psalter, the Dominican Astor Psalter-Hours, the Gorleston Psalter and various Queen Mary group manuscripts.

[85] This feast is not usually included in English calendars of the fourteenth century, although it also occurs in the Benedictine Chertsey Breviary.

[86] This is also found in the Isabella, Barlow and Gorleston Psalters, as well as in the Dominican Astor Psalter-Hours and various manuscripts of the Queen Mary group.

[87] In the case of the Derby Psalter it is accompanied by Vindicianus.

[88] Which they share with BL, Yates Thompson MS 13.

[89] This also occurs in the Guisborough calendar and the Chertsey Breviary.

[90] This feast is also found in BL, Egerton MS 2781 and Bodleian, MS Lat. liturg. e.41 (the Zouche Hours).

[91] Although it has to be acknowledged that this saint also occurs, for example, in the Isabella Psalter, Longleat House MS 11, Queen Mary's Psalter, CUL, MS Dd.4.17, and BL, Add. MS 42130 (the Luttrell Psalter). I discuss the special significance of Frideswide for the James and Derby Psalters in 'M. R. James Memorial Psalter'.

[92] Significantly agreeing with the Ramsey Psalter at Holkham; it further occurs in the Guisborough calendar, the Isabella Psalter, as well as in the Vatican Hours, Rome, Biblioteca Apostolica Vaticana, Pal. lat. 537.

[93] Morgan, *Early Gothic*, I, no. 23, discussed more fully under n. 63 above where other examples of Augustinian influence are noted.

[94] Emden, *Oxford*, III, p. 2008.

after Wells's death. Both the Ramsey Psalter and the closely related *Polychronica* introduce several new constituents, such as an intensive palette,[95] coupled with a more painterly rendering of form, relying less on outline, a naïve monumentality and an enriched border style, containing some new motifs, which seem to be a synthesis of the Bohun and Queen Mary styles. It is at this point in the artist's career that he begins to come under the umbrella of the Bohun style, localisable to East Anglia, and the Lytlington Missal style, probably localisable to London, thus witnessing to new 'contacts' such as a change in location might engender.[96] But he largely remains an aloof artistic figure.

Having proposed Oxford as the likely centre of the Genesis/Holkham Master's activity in the period *c.*1355–75, which monastic centre in East Anglia might have been the focus of his later activity?[97] In order to work towards an answer to this question it might be profitable to consider whether

---

[95]   For the execution of the Derby Psalter, the Genesis/Holkham Master had access to some particularly unusual pigments: a luminous green, deep viridian, scarlet, silver and mosaic gold. For discussion of the artist's later palette see above, pp. 228–9.

[96]   The Genesis/Holkham Master's possible presence in Dublin, Trinity College, MS B.3.2, discussed earlier (p. 229), provides a link with the artist of the Bohun Psalter-Hours (Edinburgh, National Library of Scotland, MS Adv. 18.6.5), who also participated in the work, a manuscript which can be linked on stylistic grounds to the Woodstock/Norwich Cathedral *Polychronicon* by the Genesis/Holkham Master. Contacts formulated via Bohun patronage could well explain the Genesis/Holkham Master's acquaintance with the Edinburgh Psalter-Hours Artist. Possibly Thomas of Woodstock forged links with monastic establishments when his 'in house' illuminators, discussed at pp. 244–6, below, died. The Edinburgh Psalter-Hours Artist is later found working in the Carmelite Missal (BL, Add. MSS 29704, 29705, 44892, where he is the most conservative of the illuminators involved), and at an earlier stage had collaborated (in Keble College MS 47) with one of the artists who produced the Benedictine Lytlington Missal (Westminster Abbey Library, MS 37). Both the Carmelite and Lytlington Missal associations further expand this monastic *milieu* (see also nn. 140, 142 below). For discussion of the complex inter-relationships between these manuscripts see ch. 9, 'Relatives of the Bohun Manuscripts', in Dennison, 'Bohun Workshop', with the proviso that the Holkham Psalter Artist (see pp. 232–5) can no longer be straightforwardly assigned a single centre of activity and that his 'semi-permanent' base at this date is perhaps more likely to have been Ramsey or Norwich rather than London. For the Lytlington Missal, see in particular A. J. Robinson and M. R. James, *The Manuscripts of Westminster Abbey* (Cambridge, 1909), pp. 7–8; and for further bibliography, see Sandler, *Gothic*, no. 150.

[97]   For a map of Benedictine houses in the area, see Knowles and Hadcock, *Medieval Religious Houses*, map I.

any of the monastic centres in the region had a tradition of producing illuminated books in the fourteenth century, at the same time bearing in mind the evidence provided by the Genesis/Holkham illuminator's *oeuvre*. It will be recalled that the Holkham Psalter itself, a *Polychronicon*, and the St Christopher *ex libris* of John Wells are associated with Ramsey Abbey, and two *Polychronica* have links with Norwich Cathedral Priory.

In the first quarter of the fourteenth century a series of liturgical books was produced principally for monastic patrons, centring around the Peterborough Psalter, now MSS 9961-2 in the Royal Library, Brussels, commissioned for Peterborough Abbey.[98] One related psalter, now divided between New York, Pierpont Morgan Library MS M.302 and Sankt Paul im Lavanttal, Carinthia, Austria, Cod. XXV/2 19, was produced for Ramsey; it contains some iconography especially significant to the abbey.[99] Naturally, the monks themselves would have been in the best position to advise on iconography and to prepare specific texts. In weighing up the possible location for the Peterborough Psalter workshop Lucy Sandler put forward convincing evidence in support of Ramsey but decided on a centre in London; but she now refutes this, leaving the question still open.[100] Ramsey is certainly worth considering, at least as a place where texts were prepared, even if illuminated by lay artists, based there for the duration of the work.

There are equally tempting, though circumstantial, strands of evidence which point to Norwich Cathedral Priory as the seat of a monastic-influenced workshop in approximately the same period (*c*.1310–30), with a group of books, again strongly monastic in ownership, which centre upon the skilled illuminator of the greater part of the Ormesby Psalter, an artist who, like the Egerton Genesis Master, was the focus of Pächt's 1943 study.[101] The

---

[98] See L. F. Sandler, *The Peterborough Psalter in Brussels and Other Fenland Manuscripts* (London, 1974); Sandler, *Gothic*, nos 40, 41, 42, 91.

[99] Such as a series of miniatures relating to the history of Ramsey Abbey, scenes from the life of St Benedict, the dedication of the abbey and its foundation. For a detailed description and full reproduction of this manuscript, see Sandler, *Peterborough Psalter*, pp. 39–47, 116–19 containing discussion of the calendar, 147-9, 162-9; see also Sandler, *Gothic*, no. 41.

[100] For her discussion of the evidence for Ramsey, see Sandler, *Peterborough Psalter*, pp. 133–4, 143 n. 2 (ch. V), on the basis that place of execution might be identical with its provenance; and for her conclusion as to London as the centre of production, see *ibid.*, p. 135, which tends to over-simplify this complex issue. For her revised conclusion as to the location of artistic activity for this group of manuscripts, see Sandler, *Gothic*, I, pp. 24–5, 29. It should be noted that Ramsey had a magnificent library, for details of which see *VCH, Huntingdonshire*, I, p. 382.

[101] For Pächt's discussion of the Ormesby Psalter Artist in question, see 'Giottesque Episode', pp. 54–6. See also S. C. Cockerell and M. R. James, *Two East Anglian*

Ormesby Psalter is a complex book because it was worked on over a number of years in what appear to have been three or four campaigns, the artist in question being responsible for the portion datable to c.1310–20, which comprised the illumination for all but two of the main psalm divisions.[102] This psalter has a calendar and second litany of Norwich Cathedral Priory, and it is well known that it was presented to the bishop by Robert of Ormesby, the Benedictine monk who is seen kneeling in the form of a patch-like addition to an earlier, then discarded, *Beatus* page.[103]

The Ormesby illuminator of c.1320 has been identified in three other works, all with monastic provenances in the Norwich region, two Benedictine, the third Cluniac.[104] The two Benedictine commissions, a Gregory, *Moralia in Job*, now Cambridge, Emmanuel College, MS 112, and an Apocalypse, Dublin, Trinity College Library, MS K.4.31, contain material very specific to monastic usage, strongly suggesting monastic intervention.[105] James noted that the *Moralia* came to Emmanuel College together with other volumes of Norwich provenance, and conjectured 'that the book was written at or for a Benedictine monastery', thus supporting the conclusion that Norwich Cathedral Priory was the place where the *Moralia* was prepared.[106]

Psalters at the Bodleian Library, Oxford. The Ormesby Psalter. The Bromholm Psalter, Roxburghe Club (Oxford, 1926); Lasko and Morgan, *Medieval Art in East Anglia,* no. 21 (pp. 18–19), where further bibliography is cited; and Sandler, *Gothic,* nos 43, 47, the latter by a follower.

[102] I discuss the campaigns of this complex book in an entry in a forthcoming encyclopaedia, to be published by Garland, where I estimate that there were three or four separate campaigns spanning some fifty to sixty years (c.1280–1330/40).

[103] I first drew attention to the later dating of this material in Dennison, 'Reappraisal', p. 50 n. 36, comprising the Douai Psalter (Douai, Bibliothèque Municipale, MS 171); the miniature added to the Gorleston Psalter (BL, Add. MS 49622); the added donors and *Beatus* page in the Ormesby Psalter (Bodleian, MS Douce 366); Cambridge, Trinity College, MS R.7.3, a Bede, *Historia Ecclesiastica* (hitherto unassigned); and the St Omer Psalter (BL, Yates Thompson MS 14), with the suggestion that this stylistic phase is datable not earlier than c.1330, and that a progression through that decade and beyond was likely. For further discussion, see Dennison, 'Bohun Workshop', pp. 54–5.

[104] See Cockerell and James, *Two East Anglian Psalters*; M. R. James, *The Dublin Apocalypse,* Roxburghe Club (Cambridge, 1932).

[105] The *Moralia* has the iconography of a devil pulling a monk's habit, Gregory and a Benedictine and supplicating Benedictines in the margins. See Sandler, *Gothic,* no. 45, for the *Moralia in Job,* and James, *Dublin Apocalypse,* where he notes (p. 22) that the text of the *Moralia,* which is rather Italian in character, recalls that of the law books and is 'a hand not unlike that of the meditations at the end of the Apocalypse'.

[106] See M. R. James, *The Western Manuscripts in the Library of Emmanuel College: a Descriptive Catalogue* (Cambridge, 1904), no. 112, specifically p. 98, with reference

Furthermore, this artist (the main Ormesby illuminator) was clearly inclined towards unusual pictorial subjects, as might be engendered by a monastic environment, and, as Sandler suggests, 'the design of a cycle of illustration for a rarely illustrated text was a task he might have approached with enthusiasm'.[107] This observation strikes a familiar chord with the Genesis/Holkham Master whose 'Genesis' is exceedingly unusual.[108]

A further notable feature of the Ormesby illuminator is his independent nature of working, with no obvious collaboration throughout his career. It has been noted that the isolated and exclusive nature of the Genesis/Holkham Master might point to an association with monastic, rather than lay, workshop production. James, in his introduction to the facsimile edition of the Egerton Genesis, saw that this illuminator's distinctive stylistic and technical traits put the 'artist in a place by himself'.[109] It is surely more than mere coincidence that the Fitzwarin Artist, the Ormesby illuminator and the Genesis/Holkham Master, singled out for special discussion for the apparent affinities between them, all pursued this independent method of working.

Furthermore, both the Ormesby and Genesis/Holkham artists are unique amongst fourteenth-century illuminators in having a style so profoundly influenced by a specific type of Italian art, that of Bolognese decretals.[110] In the

to nos 91 and 142, the latter (p. 111) coming from Norwich Cathedral Priory.

[107] Sandler, *Gothic*, II, p. 52, under her discussion of no. 45.

[108] See James, *Illustrations of the Book of Genesis*, pp. 2–4, who refers to the book as 'the most puzzling' illustrated manuscript he had ever seen, the pictures of which were 'the work of so original a hand'; and in the same context Pächt ('Giottesque Episode', p. 57) asserts that 'the style of these miniatures is so uncommon, the whole aspect of the book so extraordinary that when it was first published it was not recognized as an English work of art ... It is still an outsider in the family circle of English art'; and Wormald, 'Fitzwarin Psalter', p. 74, is of the view that the Egerton Genesis Master's style and miniatures 'seem exotic and strange to those having no certain knowledge of the origin of his style'.

[109] James, *Illustrations of the Book of Genesis*, p. 4. See also Pächt's comments in 'Giottesque Episode', pp. 69, 70.

[110] Other fourteenth-century English illuminators were influenced by this style of painting, but not as significantly as the two in question. It is well known that Bologna was the centre for the production and distribution of books on canon and civil law. They were conveyed in large numbers throughout Europe by export and the passage of scholars returning home after a period of study at the University of Bologna. For the transfer of books by students, see E. Cassee, *The Missal of Cardinal Bertrand de Deux: a Study in 14th-Century Bolognese Miniature Painting* (Florence, 1980), pp. 9–10. J. J. G. Alexander, in 'An English Illuminator's Work in some Fourteenth-Century Italian Law Books at Durham', in *Medieval Art and Architecture at Durham Cathedral*, British Archaeological Association Conference Transactions for the year 1977 (London, 1980), 149–53, pls XXVID–XXV, pp. 151–2, refers to a mandate of Bishop Hamo which clarifies

case of the Ormesby illuminator this manifests itself in corporeal figure forms, solidly modelled, and certain border motifs. The same sort of 'borrowing' had preoccupied the Genesis/Holkham Master at an early stage in his career, but in addition the artist then employed figures which are variously positioned in extreme foreshortening, and especially ambitious aerial and back views.[111] Even a cursory examination of monastic library catalogues indicates the prolific ownership of decretals, not least at Ramsey Abbey.[112] If the Ormesby and Holkham artists were monks they could well have studied decretal manuscripts at first hand. Conversely, if they were not monks but lay illuminators working within a monastic *milieu*, whether 'in house' or on a circuit, decretals would have been readily accessible for their consultation.[113]

Given the Genesis/Holkham Master's likely monastic *milieu*, it is worth considering the possibility that the artist derived iconography for the Genesis

---

the purpose of these law books and why they existed, and still survive, in such numbers in cathedral libraries. See also Pächt, 'Giottesque Episode', pp. 55–7; and M. Salmi, *Italian Miniatures* (London, 1957), p. 21. Italian influence in English miniature painting in the period *c.*1340 to 1400 is discussed in chapter 10 of Dennison, 'Bohun Workshop', where I suggest (p. 249) that the Bolognese miniature was probably the strongest underlying continuous channel of Italian influence on English manuscript painting in the fourteenth century.

[111] These features occur in works estimated to date to before *c.*1370, whereas the Holkham Psalter dates to the late 1380s or 1390s. They are demonstrated by the historiated initial on fol. 68v in the Derby Psalter, which can be compared with the style of Nicolò da Bologna, whose output was prodigious throughout the fourteenth century. For discussion and reproduction of the work of Nicolò da Bologna in its various phases, see P. D'Ancona, 'Nicolò da Bologna, miniaturista del secolo XIV', *Arte Lombarda* 14 (1969), 1–22; for additions to his *oeuvre*, see E. Aeschliman, 'Aggiunte a Nicolò da Bologna', *Arte Lombarda* 14 (1969), 23–35. See Dennison, 'Bohun Workshop', p. 246, for specific discussion of the Egerton Genesis Master and Bolognese influence, and *ibid.*, p. 241 n. 19 for further bibliography on Niccolò da Bologna.

[112] For Ramsey Abbey library, see *Chronicon Abbatiae Rameseiensis*, ed. W. Dunn Macray, Rolls Series (London, 1886), pp. 356–67. For Christ Church, Canterbury and Dover, see James, *Ancient Libraries of Canterbury and Dover, passim.* For the abbey of Bury St Edmunds, see M. R. James, *On the Abbey of S. Edmund at Bury* (Cambridge, 1895), pp. 7–8, 30, 65, 71, 103. For St Augustine's, Canterbury, see the following note.

[113] Emden, *Donors of Books to S. Augustine's Abbey* lists numerous benefactions of the monks which mention what seem to be the customary decretals, some of which at least had no doubt been illuminated before leaving Italy. It was Richard, monk of St Augustine's, Canterbury, who owned the *de luxe* psalter illuminated by the Queen Mary Artist, one of the finest illuminators in England at that date (*c.*1320). It is therefore not unreasonable to speculate that Richard, and other like-minded monks, possessed finely illuminated volumes.

at first-hand from a representative of the Cotton Bible tradition in a monastic library in England, whether at Ramsey, Norwich or Canterbury.[114]

Returning to the question of a centre of artistic activity for the later career of the Genesis/Holkham Master, owing to the artist's association with both Ramsey Abbey and Norwich Cathedral Priory either centre is viable, given that both of these houses could have been centres of production in the first quarter of the fourteenth century. Alternatively, no single centre may have been the focus of this illuminator's production, but commissions, for a lay as well as monastic clientele, could have been facilitated by a monastic circuit between establishments in East Anglia.[115]

Apart from the material so far outlined, there is further tangible evidence in favour of the existence of what might be described as a monastic circuit. The indisputable affiliation between the *mise-en-page* in the Ramsey Psalter and that in the Psalter of Richard of Canterbury alone suggests the operation of an inter-monastic library loan system, in this case between the Benedictine houses of Ramsey and St Augustine's, Canterbury.[116]

---

[114] Pächt ('Giottesque Episode', pp. 64–5) thought that it was not impossible that the Egerton Genesis Master knew and used this class of manuscript as a model and that 'it was actually the very same venerable codex which twice at an interval of four centuries gave inspiration to English artists', noting that James, in the context of illustrations of the Old Testament, had surmised that St Augustine's, Canterbury, was the place where 'an ancient picture Bible might have found a home' (S. C. Cockerell and M. R. James, *A Book of Old Testament Illustrations of the Middle of the Thirteenth Century*, Roxburghe Club (Cambridge, 1927), p. 22). It will be recalled that the Carolingian Utrecht Psalter came at an early date to Canterbury and was repeatedly copied there over three centuries.

[115] And in the case of this artist's earlier activity, Augustinian establishments in Oxford as a focus of activity, providing books for patrons widely spread. As noted, both the Fitzwarin Artist and the Genesis/Holkham Master supplied illumination for books with an apparently northern destination when seemingly based in Oxford. Nigel Morgan (*Early Gothic*, I, no. 29) provides an interesting precedent for a book ordered at a distance, coincidentally produced in Oxford, a psalter of *c.*1210 for a Scottish nun of the Augustinian house at Iona.

[116] J. Burton, *Monastic and Religious Orders in Britain, 1000–1300* (Cambridge, 1994), echoes this possibility. She refers (pp. 192–3) to the copying of manuscripts in the monastic scriptorium, either as duplicates or from books borrowed from other religious establishments. It should be noted that her observations are based on sources prior to 1300, although it should not be assumed that there was a radical change thereafter. See also M. W. Sheehan, 'The Religious Orders 1220–1370', in *The History of the University of Oxford*, I, *The Early Oxford Schools*, ed. J. I. Catto (Oxford, 1984), 193–221, especially pp. 208–9, with reference to the circulation of books in and among mendicant houses by an inter-library loan system.

It is surely more than a coincidence that the Queen Mary Psalter style occurs in another manuscript of assured Canterbury provenance, an early fourteenth-century hymnal for Christ Church, Canterbury, added to a thirteenth-century psalter made for St Augustine's (Bodleian, MS Ashmole 1525) (Pls 38, 39).[117] There is a close correspondence between the ornamental initials and partial borders in the hymnal and those in the Psalter of Richard of Canterbury (Pls 14, 22, 37). The minor decoration, comprising one-line pen initials and line-fillers, especially the repertoire of the latter, agrees precisely. The figural illuminator – who occurs only once in the initials that survive – although very familiar with 'Queen Mary' forms, is not a hand I recognise (Pl. 39). There is, however, a strong indication that the same scribe participated in both; and apart from these two examples this scribe is apparently not identifiable in any other Queen Mary group manuscript. Since the thirteenth-century psalter was already in use at Canterbury, in all probability the added hymnal was also made there, at either St Augustine's or Christ Church,[118] and the itinerant or 'in house' illuminator was called on to decorate the textual additions. The fact that the scribe in the hymnal and that in the Psalter of Richard of Canterbury appear to be one and the same gives support to the theory that the text of Richard's Psalter was possibly prepared at St Augustine's, or Christ Church, Canterbury, and that the 'Queen Mary'-related illuminator, probably secular, was called upon to execute the decoration. Owing to the central Queen Mary Psalter group's likely London

---

[117] See Morgan, *Early Gothic*, I, no. 33, for a discussion of the thirteenth-century material. He is of the opinion that whereas the calendar of the thirteenth-century psalter was produced for St Augustine's, the litany is of the cathedral priory of Christ Church, and considers that the style of the hymnal portion has 'some resemblance to the earliest work of the Ormesby Psalter' (Bodleian, MS Douce 366), but this seems unlikely. Michael Michael ('Some Early Fourteenth-Century English Drawings at Christ's College, Cambridge', *Burlington Magazine* 124 (1982), 230–2, pp. 231–2, is of the view that the hymnal's initials are 'almost identical to those found on the "Three Living and Three Dead" page of the De Lisle Psalter (f. 127)'. Although there are close similarities with the artist of the minor decoration in the De Lisle Psalter, probably a closer relationship exists with the Psalter of Richard of Canterbury; and this, as will be revealed, has the support of the text and one-line verse initials. The strongly Queen-Mary-related style of the single surviving head in an initial (see my plate 39) does not occur in the De Lisle Psalter. If, however, the two marginal illuminators are one and the same then an undiluted version of the Queen Mary Psalter style is apparent in the De Lisle Psalter. The distinctive daisy and marigold buds occur in the Ashmole manuscript, and not in the De Lisle Psalter, which strengthens the case in favour of a Queen Mary-related hand.

[118] Both Christ Church and St Augustine's had a tradition of producing books in the Romanesque period (Kauffmann, *Romanesque*, pp. 12 ff.).

base, it is possible that the Benedictine house at Westminster, which incidentally initiated the production of the Lytlington Missal later in the century,[119] may have been a catalyst in instigating the St Augustine's commission, as well as a breviary produced by this 'workshop' for a Benedictine abbot of Chertsey.[120]

Indeed, the complex network of 'central' and 'subsidiary' Queen Mary workshops might be more readily explained by a monastic attachment.[121] On the one hand, the central Queen Mary group patronage (as well as workshop practice) indicates a professional, lay arrangement, while on the other hand there are strong hints of connections with monastic establishments.[122] The hymnal supports the theory that there was a close liaison between monastic and supposedly secular workshops, a situation which would not exclude their working for a variety of lay and ecclesiastical patrons.[123] This, in turn, helps to explain the phenomenon of Queen Mary border forms and iconography continuing to be influential long after the period of their currency. This

---

[119] For the Lytlington Missal, see n. 96, above.

[120] For discussion of the breviary, see Dennison, 'Ancient 6 Master', pp. 288–9 and *passim*, where further bibliography is cited. See also Sandler, *Gothic*, no. 62 a, b.

[121] The very specific monastic destination of the Psalter of Richard of Canterbury is attested not only by the iconography of the kneeling monk mentioned earlier, but also by the division of the psalter according to the monastic divisions, the Benedictine calendar (having up to twelve *lectiones*) and the two comparatively rare historiated initials, one showing David in prayer for Psalm 143, marking the beginning of the section of the psalms sung at Friday vespers in Benedictine use, and another showing the sacrament of Extreme Unction given to a dying monk. See Sandler, *Gothic*, no. 57. The grading of 3 and 9 *lectiones* in Queen Mary's Psalter may thus ultimately reflect a non-secular model (see also n. 53 above). Like the Psalter of Richard of Canterbury, a close stylistic counterpart, it may have been conceived and written in a monastic environment. It is too early to state with confidence whether the illumination was done in this context, but a central Queen Mary group involvement is strongly hinted at by the evidence presented thus far. For research to date on the Queen Mary group, see the bibliography in L. Dennison, 'The Apocalypse, British Library, Royal MS. 19 B.XV: a Reassessment of its Artistic Context in Early Fourteenth-Century Manuscript Illumination', *British Library Journal* 20 (1994), 35–54, pls 1–7.

[122] An equally tantalising dichotomy exists between a probable stable base in London, possibly at Westminster – with the provision of books for monastic establishments in other parts of south-east England, as evidenced by the central Queen Mary group – and the possibly itinerant version of the style, provided by the 'Subsidiary' Queen Mary Artist, whose focus of activity appears to have been East Anglia, but with some London contacts.

[123] Indeed, it is Nigel Morgan's view (*Early Gothic*, I, no. 33) that the thirteenth-century texts may have been written out in the monastic scriptorium but illuminated by a secular artist.

would appear to be the case not only in monastic circles but also apparently in mendicant ones too. The group of manuscripts around the Queen-Mary-derived Vatican Hours (Rome, Biblioteca Apostolica Vaticana, Pal. lat. 537) have certain indicators in their calendars of mendicant influence.[124] The divergence of geographical destination for the Vatican Hours and related manuscripts within an Oxford–Cambridge–London orbit is readily explained by a mendicant circuit of the type I have here postulated for monastic houses.[125]

The Canterbury Hymnal gives further support to the notion of a monastic circuit in that the set of collects in the attached thirteenth-century psalter is known to occur in only two other fourteenth-century manuscripts – the Benedictine Ormesby Psalter and the Augustinian Tickhill Psalter.[126] The latter, according to a fifteenth-century inscription, was written and gilded by John Tickhill, prior of the Augustinian monastery of Worksop, near Nottingham.[127] Could this be suggesting an interchange of textual exemplars, and by implication iconographic and ornamental models, between these two monastic orders which have been the primary focus of this paper?

A further facet of the production of luxury books in the fourteenth century is the patronage of religious establishments by noble families and the various interrelationships thus engendered. What better evidence is there, although mendicant, of such connections than the Austin Friars and Bohun patronage?[128] Well known documentary evidence shows that at least one of

---

[124] This is touched on in Dennison, 'Some Unlocated Leaves', pp. 31–3, but I intend to deal with this question more fully in a later publication. For the Vatican Hours, with bibliography, see *ibid.*

[125] Dennison, 'Some Unlocated Leaves', pp. 28–33.

[126] Morgan, *Early Gothic*, I, no. 33. See also Egbert, *Tickhill Psalter*, p. 12.

[127] Egbert, *Tickhill Psalter*, p. 5. The implication is that, as well as writing the book, Tickhill had a hand in the illumination. Since more than one figural illuminator is present, Egbert's interpretation (p. 7) that professional artists were hired for the purpose and that the 'gilding' merely refers to the smaller text initials seems likely, and accords with my tentative conclusions from the works discussed in this paper.

[128] For a discussion, see L. Dennison, 'Oxford, Exeter College, MS. 47: the Importance of Stylistic and Codicological Analysis in its Dating and Localization', in *Medieval Book Production*, ed. Brownrigg, 41–59, Figs 1–39, pp. 55–6. See also *eadem*, 'Bohun Workshop', pp. 255–6, 270–4 (the Bohun family and the Austin Friars). Two other pertinent instances of mendicant involvement are Ancient 6, illuminated by one of the artists of the central Queen Mary group for Queen Philippa around 1327/8 (see Dennison, 'Ancient 6 Master'), which has a Franciscan calendar; and Elizabeth de Bohun's Psalter-Hours of Dominican use (see n. 49 for bibliography). This manuscript, although apparently written out at the Dominican priory at Shrewsbury, was probably illuminated in Cambridge.

the central illuminators of the Bohun workshop was an Austin Friar who worked at the Bohuns' castle at Pleshey in Essex.[129] It is worth noting that the Austin Friars had a house at Huntingdon, some eight miles from Ramsey.[130] John de Tye, the Austin Friar and illuminator named in the will of Humphrey the sixth earl,[131] could have been a member of the Huntingdon, or possibly the Cambridge, convent.[132]

The Bohun manuscripts are very useful for the indisputable evidence they provide of the religious orders being involved in illuminating on a 'commercial' (in the narrow sense of the word) basis. Although the two key illuminators can be identified as being involved over some thirty years in their production, there is not the same consistency on the part of the scribes.[133] Although illuminated at Pleshey, the texts themselves could have been prepared by the scribes at the nearby houses of Austin Friars at Huntingdon or Cambridge. Huntingdon is more likely since there is some suggestion that this is the convent to which the Bohuns' family confessor, William of Monkland, had an attachment.[134] The Austin Friars' involvement with the production of the books in part offers an explanation for the selection of detailed iconographic cycles from the Old Testament for their illustration.[135] These cycles deviate little from the Vulgate text, but the selection of what are often fairly obscure points in the narrative, which have no apparent visual precedent, can be more readily understood given the clerical backgrounds of William of Monkland and John de Tye who must have acted equally as iconographic advisers.

The Vienna Bohun Psalter, to which the Fitzwarin Artist added a single leaf, was curtailed at the outbreak of the Black Death (Pl. 28).[136] The severe

---

Such a transfer could have been facilitated by a mendicant circuit, an area I intend to discuss further in a later publication.

[129] For discussion of this evidence see Dennison, 'Bohun Workshop', pp. 255-6, with bibliography.

[130] Knowles and Hadcock, *Medieval Religious Houses*, pp. 240, 241.

[131] See J. Nichols, *A Collection of all the Wills, now known to be extant, of the Kings and Queens of England* (London, 1780), p. 50.

[132] See the discussion in the context of n. 134 below.

[133] With the notable exception of the five closely-related books, discussed in ch. 7 of Dennison, 'Bohun Workshop', pp. 157-75, in particular pp. 173-4.

[134] For Monkland, see Dennison, 'Bohun Workshop', pp. 270-2, and for his possible attachment to the Austin Friars' convent at Huntingdon (to which I suggest John de Tye may also have been attached, Dennison, 'Bohun Workshop', p. 272), see A. Gwynn, *The English Austin Friars in the Time of Wyclif* (Oxford, 1940), pp. 107-13, who consulted Torelli's *Secoli Agostiniani*.

[135] For a list of Old Testament subjects in the various Bohun manuscripts, see Dennison, 'Bohun Workshop', pp. 315, 316-21, 327-8, 330-4.

[136] For discussion, see Dennison, 'Reappraisal', pp. 45 ff. Having raised the question

loss of illuminators in the Pestilence might be accounted for by some at least being monks or friars – or lay artists working within a monastic or mendicant *milieu*. Knowles, in his discussion of the effects of the Black Death on the religious orders, observes that individual groups might totally escape or be annihilated.[137] At St Albans they lost their abbot, prior, subprior and forty-six monks, and the Norwich Dominican house was emptied to the last friar.[138] It is of some significance in the monastic context of this paper that when the production of illuminated manuscripts did revive in the mid-1350s, under Bohun patronage, a religious order, albeit a mendicant one, was amongst the prime movers in this development.[139]

Further evidence for the existence of a monastic circuit between Ramsey Abbey, Norwich Cathedral Priory and St Augustine's, Canterbury, is provided by the four *Polychronica*, all of which derive from almost identical exemplars despite their varying destinations. Significant, however, is that there is apparently a different scribe in each of the *Polychronica* of approximately the same date. This would reinforce the suggestion that it was the illuminator and not the scribe who undertook the travelling. The Genesis/Holkham Master's apparent mobility accounts for the use of an up-to-date palette, since here the artist is using pigments associated with the probably London-based Lytlington Missal group of *c*.1380 to 1400, which a monastic circuit could well explain; but in many ways this illuminator was insular at this date, becoming increasingly conservative, having moved away

---

of mendicant involvement there is tentative evidence in support of workshop or patronage links between the Augustinians and Austin Friars. The Friars may have been instrumental in putting the Fitzwarin Psalter Artist, who apparently had been active in an Augustinian *milieu* in Oxford in the mid 1340s, in contact with Humphrey de Bohun, the 6th earl of Hereford, just before the 1348/9 outbreak of the Black Death, when he wanted his psalter, now in the Austrian National Library, completed in a presumed Cambridge location. However, at this stage in research it can only be conjectured that the earl's illuminators in the 1340s were connected with the Austin Friars.

[137] Knowles, *Religious Orders*, II, pp. 8–13.

[138] *Ibid.*, pp. 10, 11.

[139] It is also worth noting in the context of the transfer of Bolognese decretals to English libraries (see n. 110 above), that the Austin Friars acquired large convents at both Oxford and Cambridge. In 1318 the general chapter decreed that at Oxford and Cambridge, as at Paris, there should be two masters of theology, with the result that during the next sixty years friars from Germany and Italy, where the order was strongest, frequented the English universities (see Knowles, *Religious Orders*, II, p. 148). See also Gwynn, *English Austin Friars*, pp. 96–105, on the activity of the Italian friars at Oxford and Cambridge in the 1350s. Bolognese decretals were doubtless conveyed to England by visiting Italian monks and friars, or by English monks or friars returning after a stay in Italy or Avignon.

from the complexities of foreshortened forms and three-dimensional architectural devices. Indeed, English illumination of c.1365/70 to c.1395/1400, the Lytlington Missal group being no exception, is characterised by a growing conservatism in these respects.[140]

Further links between Benedictine centres, namely Ramsey, Norwich and Canterbury, and another monastery – Durham – on the projected circuit, are hinted at by a copy of Nicholas of Lyra's *Postillae in Pentateuchum* (Durham, Dean and Chapter Library, MS A.1.3) of 1386 (Pl. 18).[141] Although not by the Genesis/Holkham Master, the characteristic border forms on fol. 1, including columbines, are closely derived from his repertoire and are not those associated with 'commercial' production (if, in fact, it was) in London at this date.[142] But seemingly by the Genesis/Holkham Master, and adding support to the existence of a monastic circuit, is a line-drawing of a zodiac man, rendered in this artist's typically monumental style. It occurs in the margin of fol. 25v in Bodleian, MS Douce 129, a copy of Johannes de Sacro Bosco, *Compotus*, given to Thomas Dune, monk of Durham, by Johannes Manbe, subprior, in the late fifteenth century.[143] This drawing appears in a quire of four folios, comprising a different, finer quality vellum, and is possibly of a slightly earlier date (the 1390s) than the rest of the manuscript, the text of which is of the early fifteenth century. But its significance lies in the fact that a seemingly East Anglian illuminator has produced an isolated drawing in a monastic volume destined for a monk of Durham, although admittedly the original destination is not secured.[144]

---

[140] It is of interest that the Lytlington Missal and related manuscripts also utilise the Queen Mary border forms of daisy buds, sycamores and lion masks, thus perpetuating indigenous English trends in border decoration, which contrast with the *avant-garde* ornamental vocabulary imported in the early fifteenth century by the foreign artists who worked in the Carmelite Missal. It is the conservative (English) artist of the Carmelite Missal (see n. 96 above) who seemingly had contact with the Genesis/Holkham Master.

[141] Listed in E. Millar, *English Illuminated Manuscripts of the XIVth and XVth Centuries* (Paris, 1928), p. 86, no. 259. It has been noted (see Doyle, 'Book Production by the Monastic Orders', p. 18, n. 45) that the initial showing St Cuthbert with St Oswald's head and the illuminated border are of a style which occurs in Lambeth Palace Library, MS 23, belonging to Durham, offering further clear evidence that this is the sort of text favoured, like the *Polychronicon*, in monastic circles (see also Doyle 'Book Production', p. 8).

[142] I am referring here to the Lytlington Missal and related manuscripts, for which see n. 96 above.

[143] For an illustration, see Pächt and Alexander, *Bodleian Library*, III, no. 707, pl. lxxi.

[144] See footnote 151 below for a possible explanation.

A monastic circuit of the type strongly indicated by these strands of evidence provides an explanation for the appearance of illuminators in manuscripts for patrons spread over a wide area. For instance, it has seemed puzzling that an artist associated with the Tickhill Psalter group in the 1310s, which provided books for patrons in the region of Nottingham, should be identified in the c.1320 campaign of the Ormesby Psalter, associated with Norwich Cathedral Priory.[145] No centre for the Tickhill Psalter group's artistic activity has as yet been identified, although Egbert's suggestion that these artists worked for patrons in the houses of Augustinian Canons in the diocese of York seems viable in the light of conclusions reached thus far.[146] It moreover testifies to what clearly seem to be the itinerant working methods of these monastic circuit illuminators. However, since the Ormesby illuminator in question is seemingly swapping allegiance, as did the Genesis/Holkham Master, from Augustinian to Benedictine patronage, it would seem to reaffirm that the artists were secular and not monastic, unless there were a reciprocal arrangement between the two orders, that is an 'artist on loan'; but the need to be mobile would surely rule out this possibility. Maybe these apparently secular illuminators were in the permanent employ of the Benedictines (or, where appropriate, Augustinians). A precedent for this is to be found in the twelfth century, with Master Hugo, who was employed for a considerable period at Bury Abbey.[147] A thirteenth-century precedent might be the so-called Sarum Master, presumably lay, but whose patronage, where known, was provided by monastic institutions in Wiltshire and ecclesiastics elsewhere.[148]

What is undeniable is that the Genesis/Holkham Master, and other artists highlighted in this paper, were working in a monastic, or sometimes mendicant, environment, in which books were probably commissioned, planned, prepared and written, within a system served by a thriving network of communications. Such an arrangement did not necessarily exclude secular commissions. This is amply borne out by the Tickhill Psalter group, the products of which, as suggested, were in all probability produced in a monastic environment, although mostly for a lay clientèle, and the

---

[145] Namely the Tickhill Artist who worked on fols 154 and 191v in the Ormesby Psalter; see Cockerell and James, *Two East Anglian Psalters*, pls XXI (discussed pp. 24–5), pls XXVIIIc (discussed p. 31). See also Egbert, *Tickhill Psalter*, pp. 112–16 (for conjecture on the possible circumstances) and appendix VII (pp. 209–18).

[146] Egbert, *Tickhill Psalter*, pp. 3–4, 121–2. Sandler, *Gothic*, I, p. 26 leaves this question open.

[147] For discussion of Master Hugo, see Kauffmann, *Romanesque*, pp. 14, 15, 89.

[148] For the Sarum Master, see N. Morgan, *Early Gothic*, II, p. 21, nos 98–103.

illumination in all likelihood by secular artists.[149] It has been noted that Nigel
Morgan observed for the thirteenth century the possible intervention of the
Augustinians in the production of manuscripts for non-monastic patrons.[150]
The same seems to apply for the fourteenth century, but with the
Benedictines taking equal prominence.[151] The execution of illuminated books
within this specific context appears to have been a two-way process, between
religious establishments and lay patrons on the one hand, and between
religious establishments and lay workshops on the other, a factor which has
perhaps not been sufficiently emphasised in the past.[152] For instance, the
central Queen Mary group was probably secular, but with a well organised set
of contacts on the monastic circuit, serving a wide clientèle – scholarly,
monastic, clerical, lay and official – throughout southern England.[153]

At the same time, a number of commissions were clearly for monastic
consumption and one cannot totally exclude the possibility that in certain
instances monks were involved as illuminators. Perhaps there has been too
much emphasis in the past on the notion that only the lay professionals could
produce books of fine workmanship, conservative though some of the
monastic models may have been. There was no doubt some contact between
monastic and secular illuminators. The issue is certainly not as clear-cut as

---

[149] For a detailed discussion of the owners of the various manuscripts of this group,
see Egbert, *Tickhill Psalter*, *passim*; Sandler, *Gothic*, nos 26, 27, 30, 31, 34. For
additions to the group since Egbert's study, see *ibid.*, nos 28, 29, 32, 33, 35.
Whether or not Tickhill was responsible for the illumination is not at issue; the
mere involvement of the Augustinians is sufficient evidence to suggest a working
collaboration between the laity and the religious.

[150] Morgan, *Early Gothic*, I, p. 13. See also my n. 63 above.

[151] A monastic network could well have been facilitated by establishments such as
Gloucester College, Oxford, and by the similar houses established at Oxford by
Durham and Christ Church, Canterbury, monastic houses which have figured in
this discussion. For information on these institutions, see Knowles, *Religious
Orders*, II, pp. 14–15 ff. Doyle ('Book Production by the Monastic Orders', p. 9)
notes that copying appears to have been particularly encouraged at Durham and
Durham College, Oxford. Books could have been produced and circulated by this
method. I discuss this area further in 'M. R. James Memorial Psalter' (see n. 30,
above).

[152] Doyle ('Book Production by the Monastic Orders', pp. 3–12, 14) appears to have
formed comparable conclusions and cites instances for the fifteenth century of
monastic-prepared manuscripts, illuminated by peripatetic craftsmen, lay or
religious.

[153] For discussion, see Dennison, 'Ancient 6 Master', and *eadem*, '"Liber Horn",
"Liber Custumarum" and Other Manuscripts of the Queen Mary Psalter
Workshops', in *Medieval Art, Architecture and Archaeology in London*,
Transactions of the 1984 Conference of the British Archaeological Association,
ed. L. Grant (London, 1990), 118–34, pls XXVIA–XXXIXB.

imagined. Contrary to current opinion, it is my contention that the fourteenth century was not so exclusively the period of the so-called professional artists in lay workshops, set apart from monastic establishments.[154] As Ian Doyle noted, it is possible that consciousness of the rise in lay book production 'has tended towards an underestimation of the amount of continued literary activity in monastic communities'.[155] From the examples Doyle has studied he refers to instances of both monastic and lay co-operation and itinerant craftsmen, lay or religious, working in monastic houses.[156] Illuminators in the main may well have been secular, but links with monastic establishments were clearly sustained throughout the late medieval period.[157] Ecclesiastical establishments were doubtless the nuclei for such interchange.

A monastic circuit not only explains the migration of artists, three instances of which have been cited in this paper, but also why manuscripts illuminated by the one artist should indicate from their liturgical evidence such widely diverse destinations, and yet preserve certain unusual feasts common to them all. It also explains the way in which motifs can be perpetuated from one generation to another, even after such a catastrophe as

---

[154] As implied in M. A. Michael's survey of documentary references from published sources, 'English Illuminators c.1190–1450: a Survey of Documentary Sources', *English Manuscript Studies 1100–1700* 4, ed. P. Beale and J. Griffiths (London, 1993), 62–113, with interpretation of the evidence at pp. 62–77. Useful though these references are, as Michael himself admits (*ibid.*, p. 63), they should be interpreted with caution. It is thus rather surprising that he concludes categorically (*ibid.*, p. 72) 'that monastic scriptoria were no longer centres of illumination in the later middle ages'. Although the script and layout of the Rochester Chronicle and *Commendatio Edwardi I* (discussed *ibid.*, n. 34, p. 112) suggest execution by the same scribes who prepared *Liber Custumarum* and *Liber Albus* and therefore is in all likelihood secular (see Dennison, '"Liber Horn", "Liber Custumarum"', *passim*), the illumination, even the under-drawing, as Michael suggests, bears little relation to the 'central' Queen Mary figure and border forms (for a discussion of which see Dennison, 'Ancient 6 Master', *passim*) and thus has no direct bearing on the Psalter of Richard of Canterbury, its closest relationship being with the *Liber Custumarum* decorators. What the Rochester Chronicle does seem to support, however, is the existence of a monastic circuit involving Queen-Mary-related exemplars.

[155] Doyle, 'Book Production by the Monastic Orders', p. 1.

[156] For instance, he refers to a cartulary written by a peripatetic craftsman, lay or religious (Doyle, 'Book Production by the Monastic Orders', p. 12).

[157] Morgan, *Early Gothic*, I, no. 33, supports my tentative conclusion that although secular illuminators were probably involved, a text might be prepared within the establishment, especially if it were for monastic consumption. See also Kauffmann, *Romanesque*, pp. 14, 15, for an identical view for the twelfth century, where he gives examples such as Master Hugo, the artist of the Bury Bible.

the Black Death.[158] Of further interest, all the Benedictine establishments central to the discussion lie within the eastern half of England, the houses in East Anglia, such as Ramsey and Norwich, possibly providing intermediary links between Durham in the north and Westminster, Chertsey and Canterbury in the south. Oxford may well have been an important catalyst in forging artistic links between the Augustinian and Benedictine orders. A further factor which supports a monastic, rather than secular, focus for the manuscripts covered in this paper is that there is not a high degree of codicological compatibility; different vellum, ruling patterns and gathering structures are found and there is no consistency of scribe, thus suggesting that the locations for the work vary, telling against a commercially-run enterprise.

I reiterate Doyle's comments quoted in the introduction to this paper; I share the view that continuing analysis of minor aspects of decoration, although painstaking and time-consuming, will lead to further evidence for the influence or even the close involvement of monastic communities in the production of illuminated books in the fourteenth century. And further research will inevitably yield yet more links between books, and thus serve to reinforce the concept of a monastic circuit postulated here. Although this paper has touched on matters both tenuous and tentative, these arguments have seemed worth putting forward since they may have a parallel in the findings of others at periods where, as here, a number of coincidences cannot be ignored or easily explained, but which cumulatively amount to tangible evidence. Clearly, a monastic and mendicant thread is woven throughout much luxury, as well as more commonplace, production of illuminated books in the fourteenth century.[159]

---

[158] The strand of central Queen Mary workshop influence in the border forms of both the Fitzwarin Artist and the Genesis/Holkham Master and, indeed, the Lytlington Missal group seems, therefore, to testify to the monastic origin of some of their models. A similar influence is also detectable in the group of apparently London, or possibly Oxford or Cambridge, manuscripts of the 1330s, including BL, Egerton MS 2781 and the Vatican Hours, which have mendicant elements in their calendars. If a similar circuit were in operation for the mendicants, it would explain the difficulty in assigning this group to one particular centre, for which see Dennison, 'Some Unlocated Leaves', pp. 28–31.

[159] I am planning other publications which will attempt to elucidate further the various issues raised in this paper.

Monuments to Monks and Monastic Servants

NICHOLAS ROGERS

At Parkminster Charterhouse 'the faithful monk, when his call comes, is buried - not in a coffin, but clothed in his habit as he lived, and lying on a bare board. A nameless wooden cross surmounts his grave; he is as unknown in death as he was in life'.[1] What is still current Carthusian practice would have been the norm for most members of most religious orders during the middle ages. Burial in the monastic cemetery, in an undifferentiated grave, was the ultimate expression of communal identity. Monastic customaries often prescribe a daily commemoration of the departed, as well as the keeping of specific anniversaries.[2] At Syon the nuns gathered round an open grave after Tierce while the abbess recited the *De Profundis*.[3] More usual was the custom described in the *Rites of Durham*:

> Also the mounckes was accustomed euery daie aftere thei dyned to goe thorowgh the cloister, in at ye vshers dour and so thorowghe the entrie in under the priors lodginge and streight in to ye centorie garth wher all ye mouncks was buried, and ther did stand all bair heade a Certain longe Space praieng amongs the Toumbs & throwghes for there brethren soules being buryed there, and when they hadd done there prayers then they did Return to ye cloyster.[4]

The names of individual monks, including those of affiliated houses, as well as confraters and benefactors, could be entered in the *Liber Vitae*, to be placed on the altar at Mass. A note at the beginning of the New Minster *Liber Vitae* (BL, Stowe MS 944) reads: 'In this due order follow the names of the brethren and monks as well as friends and benefactors, that they may be inscribed into the pages of the heavenly book by the recollection from time to time of this

---

[1]   *St Hugh's Charterhouse* (Parkminster, Sussex, 1963), p. 10.

[2]   On these commemorations see *The Monastic Breviary of Hyde Abbey, Winchester*, ed. J. B. L. Tolhurst, 6 vols, Henry Bradshaw Society 69–71, 76, 78, 80 (London, 1932–42), VI, pp. 72–81. On the Office of the Dead in monastic liturgy see *ibid.*, pp. 107–13.

[3]   *The Bridgettine Breviary of Syon Abbey*, ed. A. Jefferies Collins (Worcester, 1969), pp. xvi, 27.

[4]   *Rites of Durham*, ed. J. T. Fowler, Surtees Society 107 (Durham, 1903), p. 87. There were similar customs at Evesham and St Alban's (*ibid.*, p. 269).

script'.[5] The theology of this passage informs the famous drawing of the Last Judgement in the manuscript.[6] Less well-known is the fact that this manuscript remained in continuous use until the 1530s, and contains an unparalleled list of the monks of Hyde Abbey.[7] Similar lists survive from other monasteries, such as Durham, Canterbury and Thorney.[8] Somewhat different in character is the *Liber Vitae* compiled in 1380 by Thomas Walsingham for St Albans, and added to until the sixteenth century.[9] Not surprisingly, in view of the historiographical tradition of the abbey, the entries take the form of brief biographical citations, detailing the services of those commemorated. However, this book performed the same function as the New Minster *Liber Vitae*. Amundesham tells us that it was 'daily placed upon the high altar of the monastery during the solemnities of the Mass, that for the expiation of their sins the Victim of the holy altar may continually be offered to the Lord, and that they may be commended by the celebrants with pure minds piously remembering them'.[10] The inclusion of portraits of the principal benefactors (Pls 40, 41) reinforces the shift towards individual commemoration, which is mirrored by the development of funerary monuments.

Three categories of religious might be honoured by intramural burial: those noted for their sanctity, monastic superiors, and distinguished obedientiaries. The first class lies largely outside the scope of this paper, belonging to the history of the development of shrines. However, mention

5   BL, Stowe MS 944, fol. 13.

6   J. Gerchow, 'Prayers for King Cnut: the Liturgical Commemoration of a Conqueror', in *England in the Eleventh Century: Proceedings of the 1990 Harlaxton Symposium*, Harlaxton Medieval Studies II, ed. C. Hicks (Stamford, 1992), 219–38, p. 231, pl. 10.

7   Printed in full in *Liber Vitae: Register and Martyrology of New Minster and Hyde Abbey, Winchester*, ed. W. de Gray Birch, Hampshire Record Society 5 (London, 1892).

8   The Durham list is printed in *Liber Vitae Ecclesiae Dunelmensis; nec non obituaria duo ejusdem ecclesiae*, ed. J. Stevenson, Surtees Society 13 (Durham, 1841). It is discussed in Lynda Rollason's article in this volume. Names from the Christ Church Obituary in Lambeth Palace MS 20, fols 157–249, Cambridge, Corpus Christi College MS 298, and Thomas Cawston's Obituary (Canterbury Cathedral MS D.12) are printed in *Christ Church, Canterbury*, ed. W. G. Searle, Cambridge Antiquarian Society octavo ser. 34 (Cambridge, 1902), 153–96. The Thorney confraternity list is in BL, Add. MS 40000.

9   A. Gransden, *Historical Writing in England*, 2 vols (London, 1978–82), II, pp. 123, 126, 401, n. 73, pl. IV; L. F. Sandler, *Gothic Manuscripts 1285–1385*, A Survey of Manuscripts Illuminated in the British Isles, 5, 2 vols (London, 1986), no. 158.

10   *Annales Monasterii S. Albani, a Johanne Amundesham ...*, ed. H. T. Riley, 2 vols, Rolls Series (London, 1870–1), I, p. 432.

must be made of some of those cases where holiness was honoured, but there does not seem to have been any public cult. In the 1428 description of the monuments in St Albans mention is made, for example, of Dom John Gyldeford, *custos* of the nuns of Sopwell, 'whose goodness of life earned for him burial' in the south transept.[11] At Bury St Edmunds the bones of the monk Egelwin, who had zealously looked after the body of St Edmund during the Danish invasion of the early eleventh century, together with those of Abbot Leofstan and the devout woman Oswen, were kept in a wooden chest at the foot of St Edmund's shrine, apparently resting on two columns.[12] The account of the 1465 fire records that this chest became miraculously immobile, its occupants refusing to forsake the saint to whom they had been devoted in life.[13] The brass of a monastic anchorite which survives in large part as a palimpsest at St John Sepulchre, Norwich, was probably occasioned by a life of particular sanctity.[14]

The tombs of abbots and priors are also outside the scope of this paper, but a few preliminary remarks about their character may provide a context for those of the brethren over whom they ruled. Although some places, such as St Augustine's, Canterbury, provide early examples of the intramural burial of monastic superiors,[15] it was not until the eleventh century that this practice became common. At first the preferred place of burial was the chapter-house, as at St Albans,[16] or along a walk of the cloister, as at Westminster Abbey,[17] but by the thirteenth century there was a shift to the abbey church, a favoured position being before the high altar or the choir altar. This was facilitated by the development of incised slabs and monumental brasses. The choice of a floor-slab rather than a raised monument could in itself be an expression of monastic humility. In my survey of English episcopal monuments between 1270 and 1350 I noted that none of the abbatial brasses of that period seems to have been associated with a table-tomb.[18] Later on

---

[11]   *Amundesham*, I, p. 437.

[12]   M. R. James, *On the Abbey of S. Edmund at Bury* (Cambridge, 1895), p. 137.

[13]   *Ibid.*, p. 207.

[14]   M. Norris, *Monumental Brasses: the Memorials*, 2 vols (London, 1977), p. 272, fig. 305; J. Page-Phillips, *Palimpsests: the Backs of Monumental Brasses*, 2 vols (London, 1980), p. 79 (18N1-2), pl. 142.

[15]   On the early intramural burials at St Augustine's, Canterbury, see W. St J. Hope, 'Recent Discoveries in the Abbey Church of St. Austin at Canterbury', *Archaeologia* 66 (1915), 377–400.

[16]   *Amundesham*, I, pp. 434–5; M. Biddle and B. Kjølbye-Biddle, 'Excavation', in *Lasting Letters*, ed. R. McKitterick and L. Lopes Cardozo (Cambridge, 1992), 17–32.

[17]   F. Anderson, 'Three Westminster Abbots: a Problem of Identity', *Church Monuments* 4 (1989), 3–15.

[18]   N. Rogers, 'English Episcopal Monuments, 1270–1350', in *The Earliest English*

Figure 7: Brass of John Artur: north choir aisle, Milton Abbey, Dorset.

there are some instances of high tombs with sculptured effigies, but these are very much the exception to the rule. Two occasional practices which testify to a sense of historical continuity in monastic communities are the erection of retrospective monuments and the sequential numbering of tombs, as at Lesnes and Bisham.[19]

Any evaluation of the monuments of obedientiaries and other monks, and of lay monastic servants, is considerably hampered by the wholesale destruction of those monuments at the Suppression. Most dissolved monasteries were so thoroughly robbed that the very grave-slabs, as well as brass inlays, were stripped from the site.[20] Even where the monastery was a cathedral priory or was transformed into one of the Henrician cathedrals, monastic monuments were peculiarly vulnerable, as representatives of the old order. Typical is the fate of the grave stones in the 'Centorie garth' at Durham, which the Calvinist Dean Whittingham

> did cause to be pulled downe and dyd breake and deface all such stones as had any pictures of brass or other imagerie worke or challices wrought vpon theme. And the Residewe he caried them all awaie, and did occupie theme to his owne vse & did make a washinge howse of many of them for women Landerers to washe in, so that it cannot be decernyd at this present that euer any hath bene buried in the said Centorie garth yt is maid so plaine and streight for he could not abyde anye auncyent monuments, nor nothing that apperteyned to any godlie Religiousnes or monasticall liffe.[21]

Apart from the small group of monastic brasses at St Albans, to be considered later, the only surviving brass still *in situ* to a member of a monastery other than the superior is a simple inscription at Milton Abbey, Dorset, commemorating John Artur, monk (Fig. 7).[22] A few brasses survived to be

---

Brasses: Patronage, Style and Workshops 1270–1350, ed. J. Coales (London, 1987), 8–68, p. 20.

[19]   On the indent of Elias, 9th abbot of Lesnes, *c.*1300, see A. W. Clapham, *Lesnes Abbey* (London, 1915), p. 63, fig. 9c; on the brass of Adam Wergrave, 5th prior of Bisham, see Page-Phillips, *Palimpsests*, p. 42 (85L1), pl. 23.

[20]   J. Bertram, *Lost Brasses* (Newton Abbot, 1976), pp. 16–17.

[21]   *Rites of Durham*, p. 60.

[22]   W. de C. Prideaux, 'The Ancient Memorial Brasses of Dorset', *Proceedings of the Dorset Natural History and Antiquarian Field Club* 28 (1907), 226–44, pp. 230–1,

discovered amid the ruins, such as the head of a nun found on the site of Kilburn Priory, and now in St Mary's, Kilburn,[23] or the figure of a nun of Barking, found – and lost – in the eighteenth century.[24] Here and there indents of monastic brasses can be found: a full-length figure in the north aisle of the nave at Winchester Cathedral;[25] a badly worn demi-figure of a nun at Romsey;[26] the beautiful crosses in the ambulatory at Ely;[27] and various indents in the ambulatory at Westminster, many now reduced to little more than patterns of rivets.[28] But despoiled slabs such as these have been, and still are, vulnerable to the tidy minds of official vandals. Incised slabs, such as that of John Vinsay from Meaux Abbey,[29] have survived at several rural monastic sites, especially in north and central England, where there was not the imperative to remove all 'useful' materials. But these, when in exposed ruins, are prone to the action both of weather and of unofficial vandals. The fifty-six incised slabs found when Bardney Abbey was excavated between 1909 and 1914 soon succumbed to frost and the stone-throwing antics of local youths; what survived to 1931 was preserved by the complete backfilling of the site.[30]

A very few monuments to monks and nuns survived because they were located in parish churches. At Heydon in Norfolk is an inscription commemorating Thomas, son of John Dynne, a monk at St Benet's Hulme, who died in 1492,[31] while at Hilburgh in the same county are early sixteenth-century brasses to Anne Sefull and Olive Walsham, both simply styled *sancte monialis*.[32] It is just possible that these were transferred at the Dissolution from some nearby convent, much in the way that the Curson monument was moved from the Austin Friars at Oxford to Waterperry[33] or

pl. opp. p. 230.

23 H. K. Cameron, 'The Brasses of Middlesex. Part 21: Islington', *Transactions of the London & Middlesex Archaeological Society* 32 (1981), 140–50, p. 150, fig. 5.

24 'Portfolio of Small Plates', *Transactions of the Monumental Brass Society* 13 (5) (1984), pl. 3 (p. 468).

25 A. G. Sadler, *The Indents of Lost Monumental Brasses in Dorset & Hampshire* (Ferring-on-Sea, Sussex, 1975), p. 31.

26 *Ibid.*, p. 21.

27 C. J. P. C[ave], 'Ely Cathedral: List of Brasses, &c.', *Transactions of the Monumental Brass Society* 3 (2) (1898), 88–106, pp. 89, 99–100.

28 J. S. N. Wright, *The Brasses of Westminster Abbey* (London, 1969), p. 43.

29 'Portfolio of Small Plates', *Transactions of the Monumental Brass Society* 13 (6) (1985), pl. 2 (p. 559).

30 F. A. Greenhill, *Monumental Incised Slabs in the County of Lincoln* (Newport Pagnell, 1986), pp. xx–xxi, 6–15.

31 M. Stephenson, *A List of Monumental Brasses in the British Isles* (London, 1926), p. 339.

32 *Ibid.*, p. 339.

33 J. Todd, 'The Palimpsest Brass in Waterperry Church', *Transactions of the*

the brass (and coffin) of Geoffrey Barbur translated from Abingdon Abbey to the parish church of St Helen.[34]

Most monastic brasses were destined for the melting pot, but there was also widespread re-use of the metal for new brasses engraved on the reverse. Of the some 350 sixteenth-century palimpsest brasses discovered so far a good proportion are anonymous fragments of figures, forming a frustrating jigsaw puzzle with half the pieces missing.[35] For example, at Okeover, Staffs., the shields form part of a cowled figure of mid-fifteenth-century date. That this may have come from Westminster Abbey is suggested by the presence also of a portion of the arms of Edward the Confessor.[36] Inscriptions were more likely to be kept intact, simply being reversed for other inscriptions, and several can be assigned to monastic sources. The only ones which have so far been localised all commemorate superiors: a prior of Bisham,[37] an abbot of Bury,[38] and a *rara avis*, a Carthusian prior of Sheen who became bishop of Llandaff.[39] Nevertheless, it is possible to make some deductions about the four other monastic inscriptions so far discovered. Earliest in date, c.1440, is a metrical inscription in two columns at Norbury, Derbyshire, beginning '[En Tho]mas quondam prior hic tellure quiescit', which can almost certainly be linked with a section of a cowled figure, re-used in the same monument to Sir Anthony Fitzherbert (d. 1538).[40] Another palimpsest portion of the Fitzherbert brass has been identified as having come from Croxden Abbey, but this was not necessarily the source of Prior Thomas's brass. The most that can be said is that since the Fitzherbert brass was engraved in a midlands workshop, that of Prior Thomas almost certainly came from that region.

At Aldenham, Herts., the figure of Joan Warner, which has been dated c.1538, is cut from an inscription referring to a priest-monk called Bewford, who died on 30 August 1485, and his mother Agnes Bewford, buried at his feet.[41] The formula used, beginning *Memorandum*, suggests a link with a written record such as a chronicle or *liber vitae*, such as we will see later existing at St Albans. The association of parents in the spiritual benefits of

---

Monumental Brass Society 8 (6) (1949), 246–50.

[34]   Bertram, *Lost Brasses*, p. 16.

[35]   For a complete catalogue see Page-Phillips, *Palimpsests*.

[36]   Page-Phillips, *Palimpsests*, p. 41 (82L2-5), pl. 21.

[37]   Adam Wergrave, d. c.1420, palimpsest at Haddenham, Bucks. (Page-Phillips, *Palimpsests*, p. 42 (85L1), pl. 23).

[38]   Thomas Totyngton, d. 1312, brass engraved c.1490, palimpsest at Hedgerley, Bucks. (Page-Phillips, *Palimpsests*, p. 44 (103L2), pl. 29).

[39]   John Ingylby, d. 1499, palimpsest at Edlesborough, Bucks. (Page-Phillips, *Palimpsests*, p. 49 (137L5), pl. 47).

[40]   Page-Phillips, *Palimpsests*, p. 88 (21M10), pl. 158.

[41]   *Ibid.*, p. 41 (79L1), pl. 17.

their children's monastery, which was expressed liturgically in a collect of the Office of the Dead,[42] is also reflected in one of the incised slabs at Bardney, commemorating both Thomas Cle, subprior (d. 1527), and his father Richard Bovell, who was a confrater of Bardney.[43]

It was not until 1568 that the inscription marking the grave of Dom John Awncell, who died on 9 April 1511, was re-used for a brass to a yeoman of the guard at East Wickham, Kent.[44] Although there must have been a glut of metal in London workshops during the Reformation, the late date suggests that this most probably came from somewhere such as a cathedral priory where the process of despoliation was a gradual one. The name Awncell is a Kentish one,[45] but Joan Greatrex, to whom I am most indebted, has not found a John Awncell at either Christ Church, Canterbury, or Rochester. Equally tantalising is the inscription found on the reverse of a 1546 brass at Sonning, Berks., in 1987. Although undated, the epigraphy suggests a date c.1510. The inscription refers to a third prior, suggesting a provenance in one of the major abbeys, but unfortunately it is defective at a vital point, so we cannot say whether his name was Thomas Hawke, or Thomas Hooke, or Thomas Hewke.[46]

Further information about monuments to obedientiaries and other monks can be gleaned from monastic chronicles. Of these undoubtedly the most valuable is that kept by John Stone, monk of Christ Church, Canterbury, which records the deaths of the members of that community between 1415 and 1471.[47] This reveals a clear differentiation of areas for burial. Since archbishops and high nobility clustered round the shrine of St Thomas and on either side of the sanctuary, the usual place for the priors was the nave. Of John Elham (d. 1449) it is specifically recorded that he is *sepultus*

---

[42] 'Deus qui nos patrem et matrem honorare precepisti', *Monastic Breviary of Hyde Abbey, Winchester*, V, fol. G68v.

[43] Greenhill, *Lincoln*, pp. 12–13 (no. 43).

[44] Page-Phillips, *Palimpsests*, p. 60 (212L3–4), pl. 84.

[45] For Awncells living in Faversham, Fordwich and Mersham see *Index of Wills and Administrations now preserved in the Probate Registry at Canterbury, 1396–1558 and 1640–1650*, ed. H. R. Plomer, Kent Archaeological Society, Kent Records 6 (London, 1920), p. 17. For Auncells in Rochester see *Index of Wills proved in the Rochester Consistory Court between 1440 and 1561*, ed. L. L. Duncan, Kent Archaeological Society, Kent Records 9 (Canterbury, 1924), p. 8. John Auncell was baker and bailiff of Fordwich for St Augustine's, Canterbury (C. Cotton, 'St. Austin's Abbey, Canterbury. Treasurer's Accounts 1468–9, and others', *Archaeologia Cantiana* 51 (1939), 66–107, pp. 89, 104).

[46] 'Palimpsests: 4th issue of addenda', *Monumental Brass Society Bulletin* 50 (Feb. 1989), p. 26, pl. 206.

[47] 'The Chronicle of John Stone, Monk of Christ Church, 1415–1471', in *Christ Church, Canterbury*, ed. Searle, 1–152.

... *cum aliis prioribus*.[48] But some archbishops – Islip, Wittlesey, and Arundel – chose to be interred in the nave, and there was also competition between archbishops and priors in the north-west transept, the site of St Thomas's martyrdom, which was first selected by a prior in 1391.[49] There may be a subtle allusion to the need to stake out space for burial in the scriptural quotation used by John Stone to describe the interment of Thomas Goldstone I (d. 1468) in his new Lady Chapel 'in monumento suo novo quod exciderat de petra, ubi nondum quisquam positus fuerat'.[50]

In view of the apparent difficulty in finding suitable places even for the monuments of monastic superiors, where were distinguished obedientiaries and other monks interred at Canterbury? In two instances Stone records burial before crypt altars,[51] but for the most part any intramural interments took place in the infirmary chapel. At Canterbury this was an aisled building with a chancel, about 100 feet long, and separated from the infirmary proper by a wall pierced by a door.[52] It contained at least two altars, that of Sts Leonard and Benedict, before which were placed the almoner Henry Sutton, William Chart, and James Grove, who had held various offices in the monastery, and that of Sts Agnes and Agatha, the resting-place of the sacrist John Molond and the subprior John Wodenysbergh.[53] Another monk accorded the honour of burial in the infirmary chapel was John Kynton (d. 1416), a late vocation who had previously been secretary to Henry IV and chancellor to Queen Joan.[54] The chapel fell into ruin at the Dissolution, but the badly broken indent of a monastic brass can still be seen on the site, confirming that at least one of those buried there was commemorated by a monument.[55]

On one occasion Stone records the place of burial of a layman associated with the monastery. In 1445 the famous composer Lionel Power, who is styled *armiger istius ecclesie*, was laid to rest next to the cemetery gate.[56] This

---

48   *Ibid.*, pp. 45–6.
49   Prior John Finch, who was commemorated by a brass (C. E. Woodruff and W. Danks, *Memorials of the Cathedral & Priory of Christ in Canterbury* (London, 1912), p. 165).
50   'Chronicle of John Stone', pp. 104–5. Cf. John xix.41.
51   William Stone, granger (d. 12 Nov. 1415), 'before the altar of Sts Catherine and Mary Magdalene', and Henry Cranebroke (d. 20 Sept. 1430), 'before the altar of St Nicholas' ('Chronicle of John Stone', pp. 7, 15).
52   R. Willis, *The Architectural History of the Conventual Buildings of the Monastery of Christ Church in Canterbury* (London, 1869), p. 52, pl. 3.
53   'Chronicle of John Stone', pp. 14, 15, 16, 68.
54   *Ibid.*, pp. 7–8.
55   A. G. Sadler, *The Indents of Lost Monumental Brasses in Southern England, Appendix III* (Ferring-on-Sea, Sussex, 1986), p. 23.
56   'Chronicle of John Stone', p. 37.

can be compared with the privilege granted to John Rackett and Lionel Elmeden, gentlemen in the retinue of the prior of Durham, of burial within the monastic cemetery, so as to be 'neare vnto that holy man Sainct Cuthbert'.[57] At Bardney, although 20 of the 39 identifiable grave slabs, mostly in the nave, were those of lay folk, none is actually identified as having an official role in the life of the abbey. This reflects parochial use of the nave, similar to that documented by Janet Burton at Kirkham Priory.[58] In most of the greater monasteries parochial services had been transferred by the late middle ages either to a chapel adjoining the nave, as at St Albans and Ely,[59] or to a *capella ante portas*,[60] thereby limiting secular intrusions into monastic life. These parishioners might still request burial in the nave.[61] Moreover, not surprisingly, it is in the mitred abbeys and cathedral priories that one finds most evidence of a secular curial structure involved in the management of the abbey and its estates.

It is only at St Albans that we can get a reasonably complete view of the pattern of burial in a major English Benedictine monastery (Pl. 42). The principal source of information is the account of the altars and tombs compiled in 1428, and appended to John de Amundesham's *Annales*.[62] This is supplemented by the biographical information in the *Liber Vitae*, to which the 1428 account refers at several points. Furthermore, despite despoliation, neglect and restoration, no fewer than nineteen brasses or portions of brasses and thirty-eight brassless indents can be found there.[63] Of the nineteen brasses, three are of abbots, five of obedientiaries and other monks, and two of the remainder can be identified as laymen who held an official role in the abbey. Several of the indents can be identified by comparison with the descriptions in the 1428 account or rough sketches made by John Philpot in 1643.

Virtually all the monuments considered so far date from the late fifteenth or early sixteenth century, but St Albans provides much earlier instances of

---

57   *Rites of Durham*, pp. 59–60.

58   See the penultimate essay in this collection, below.

59   On the history of the parish of Holy Cross or Holy Trinity at Ely see *VCH, Cambridgeshire*, IV, pp. 82–3.

60   E.g. St Nicholas at Abingdon, St James and St Mary at Bury St Edmunds, St Laurence at Reading, and St Nicholas at Rochester.

61   E.g. Thomas Edon (d. 1495 or 1496) and his wife Agnes (d. 1506), who willed to be buried in the abbey church of St Edmund at Bury (Suffolk Record Office, IC 500/2/4, fols 44, 178v). A portion of the Edon brass survives as a palimpsest at Hedgerley, Bucks. (Page-Phillips, *Palimpsests*, p. 44 (103L3), pl. 29).

62   Printed from BL, Harley MS 3775 in *Amundesham*, I, pp. 431–50. For an English translation with commentary see *An Account of the Altars, Monuments, & Tombs, existing A.D. 1428 in Saint Alban's Abbey*, ed. R. Lloyd (St Albans, 1873).

63   W. Page, 'The Brasses and Indents in St Alban's Abbey', *Home Counties Magazine* 1 (1899), 19–25, 140–61, 241–7, 329–32.

the honouring of obedientiaries. Adam the cellarer, who died c.1180, was rewarded for his diligence by burial *inter abbates* in the chapter-house.[64] A visual counterpart is the placing of his image *inter abbates* in the *Liber Vitae* (Pl. 40). It is recorded that devout folk used to take chips from his tomb, which when reduced to powder and drunk in draught cured various ailments.[65] This first tomb was a raised coffin-slab, but because it was inconvenient to passers-by it was replaced by Abbot Thomas de la Mare (1349–96), who substituted a marble stone with keys engraved thereon, and placed the original tomb on one side of the chapter-house.

The earliest surviving monument to an obedientiary at St Albans would appear to be an indent in the south transept, datable on stylistic grounds to the 1320s or early 1330s. It shows a bust-length effigy superimposed on a floriated cross resting on a small beast like a Scottie dog, under a crocketed canopy, with a marginal inscription fillet.[66] Assuming that the slab is still in its original position, then it can be identified as that of Prior Robert Norton, described by Amundesham as a marble slab with the demi-effigy of a monk under a tabernacle.[67] It is known that Robert Norton died during the abbacy of Richard de Wallingford (1326–35), which accords neatly with the stylistic evidence. Another fourteenth-century bust-length indent, cut down and partly obscured by cement, can be found in the north transept (Fig. 8). One cusp of a canopy can be discerned, so this also fits Amundesham's description of the Norton monument. However, the stone is Tournai marble, indicating that this, like the grand brasses ordered by Thomas de la Mare for himself and his predecessor Michael Mentmore in the 1350s, was made in Flanders. A date in the immediate aftermath of the Black Death, when the London workshops were reduced to incompetence, is plausible.[68] The north transept, adjoining the sacristy, was the usual burying-place of the sacrists. Of those mentioned in the 1428 account, the most likely candidate is Dom Hugh Langley, sacrist under Abbot Wallingford (1326–35), who is described as being buried 'under a marble stone, decorated, but without an epitaph'.[69] The demi-figure format is unparalleled, to the best of my knowledge, in Flemish brasses, and must be a special request. There seems to be something of a monastic tradition of half-effigies. At St Albans there is also a badly worn demi-figure brass of an

[64] *Amundesham*, I, p. 435; *Account of the Altars*, pp. 8 (no. 23), 36; BL, Cotton MS Nero D.vii, fol. 16v.

[65] *Amundesham*, II, p. 304.

[66] Page, 'Brasses', p. 245 (no. 58), pl. opp. p. 246.

[67] 'Media figura monachi infra tabernaculum superposita' (*Amundesham*, I, p. 436; *Account of the Altars*, pp. 9 (no. 29), 38).

[68] J. Bertram, 'An Unnoticed Flemish Indent in St. Albans Abbey', *Transactions of the Monumental Brass Society* 13 (6) (1985), 536–7.

[69] *Amundesham*, I, p. 440; *Account of the Altars*, p. 12 (no. 53), 46.

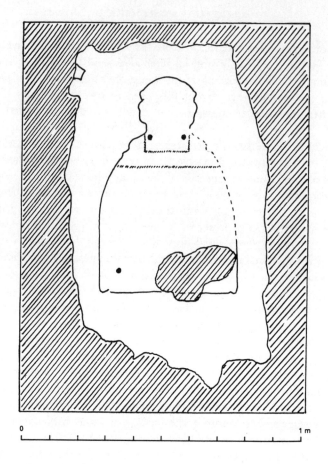

Figure 8: Indent, probably of the brass of Hugh Langley:
north transept, St Albans Abbey

anonymous monk of c.1450–75,[70] and elsewhere we have the Romsey indent, already mentioned, and the brass of Friar William Jernemuth, which survives almost intact as a palimpsest at Halvergate, Norfolk.[71] I do not think that this format, used on occasion for episcopal brasses, was chosen primarily for reasons of economy.[72] It is possible that, as in certain thirteenth-century low-relief effigies, the half-length figure is to be read as a resurrected body emerging from the grave.[73]

[70]   Page, 'Brasses', p. 144 (no. 20).
[71]   R. Greenwood and M. Norris, *The Brasses of Norfolk Churches* (Holt, Norfolk, 1976), p. 38, pl. 38; Page-Phillips, *Palimpsests*, p. 80 (22N1), pl. 144.
[72]   H. Haines, *A Manual of Monumental Brasses* (Oxford, 1861), p. cxxxiv.
[73]   E.g. the coffin slab at Penshurst, Kent (J. Newman, *West Kent and the Weald*, 2nd edn (Harmondsworth, 1976), p. 454, pl. 19). There may also be links with a type

Also in the north transept is the indent of a full-length figure under a canopy, with foot inscription, marginal inscription and a scroll presumably directed to the image (of the Virgin and Child, or possibly a Pietà) set immediately under the arch of the canopy. The position, immediately before the altar of St Zita, corresponds to that recorded for the monument of the lay brother William Stubbarde, a noted stone carver, who worked on the cloister, the prior's seat and various other works.[74] He was working during the abbacy of Thomas de la Mare, which accords with the date in the late 1380s indicated by the form of the canopy. Amundesham records a two-line verse inscription, which could well be that at the foot. The only doubt is introduced by the size of the brass, some seven feet long. Would a lay brother, however talented artistically, have been honoured by such a grand monument?

Several of the brasses which are, or were, at St Albans are individual in their iconography, making specific reference to the devotions of those they commemorate. As at Ely, there is a range of cross brasses, perhaps the most unusual being one in the presbytery, in which a monk kneels before what resembles a processional cross, with figures of the Virgin and St John mounted on the arms.[75] The diction of the verse inscription,

Salva Redemptor plasma tuum nobile
Signatum sancto vultus Tui lumine
Nec lacerari sinas fraude demonum
Propter quos mortis exsolvisti precium

is reminiscent of epitaphs which have been reliably attributed to John Whethamstede, abbot for two turns between 1420 and 1465.[76]

More conventional in form are the two mid-fifteenth-century full-length standing figures of monks. Little can usefully be said about one, apparently originally in the north aisle of the presbytery, beyond noting that there is no sure ground for the traditional attribution to Reginald Bernewelt.[77] However, there are several points of interest about the other, marking the grave of Robert Beauver in the presbytery. If only the indent of this brass had survived, there would have been no way of telling that he was shown holding the Sacred Heart, sprinkled with drops of blood.[78] Comparison can be made with the incised slab of Abbot Richard Horncastel at Bardney, who is shown

of low-relief effigy in which the figure is partly covered by an inscription plate or shield (K. Bauch, *Das mittelalterliche Grabbild* (Berlin, 1976), p. 88, Abb. 59, 130, 131).

[74] *Amundesham*, I, p. 440; *Account of the Altars*, pp. 12 (no. 54), 46; Page, 'Brasses', pp. 246–7 (no. 65), pl. opp. p. 247.
[75] Page, 'Brasses', p. 147 (no. 22), pl. opp. p. 147.
[76] Haines, *Manual*, p. xciv.
[77] Page, 'Brasses', pp. 241–2 (no. 42), pl. opp. p. 243.
[78] *Ibid.*, pp. 147–8 (no. 23), 331, pl. opp. p. 148.

holding a shield bearing the Sacred Heart.[79] Beauver's union with Christ is
further expressed by the use of the versicle 'Cor mundum in me crea Deus' on
the scroll. The inscription points to a two-fold motivation for special
commemoration. It reads:

> Here lies brother Robert Beauver, formerly monk of this monastery, who,
> for forty-six years and more continuously ministered in divers offices, greater
> and less, of the convent of the monastery aforewritten, that is to say, in the
> offices of third prior, kitchener, refectorer, and infirmarer, and in the offices
> of sub-refectorer and spicerar of this convent. For whose soul may you
> deign, O most dear brethren, to pour out prayers to the Most High Judge
> and the Most Pious Lord Jesus Christ, that he may grant to him pardon for
> his sins. Amen.

It is not known when Beauver died, but in 1454 he is stated to be aged seventy
years and more. At a time when the life expectancy at Westminster Abbey has
been calculated as 29 to 30 years at age 20, such longevity was worthy of
note.[80] It is not, however, the number of years since his profession which is
recorded, but the period for which he served as an obedientiary. The careful
enumeration of the variety of posts he filled serves as implicit praise of his
versatility. Where epitaphs provide more than a versified prayer for the soul
of the deceased, they might single out some meritorious action or unusual
skill. Thus Bartholomew Wendover, who had previously been rector of
Schaxtone, is praised for having paved the cloister in which he was buried.[81]
William Trent, described by Amundesham as 'a profound grammarian and
chief instructor of the monks', and appropriately buried in the north walk of
the cloister, is hailed as *alter Donatus*.[82] In other cases there is a conventional
recitation of appropriate virtues. Of Dom Richard Bevere, buried within the
enclosure at the eastern end of the nave, we read:

> He whom a stone covers, was a diligent Sub-prior;
> He when alive was a devout monk.[83]

The location and form of monastic monuments were dependent on abbatial
or capitular decisions. Thus we read that Dom John Gyldeford was buried in
the south transept 'by the leave of' Abbot Whethamstede.[84] Occasionally a
more active abbatial initiative is indicated. Dom Nicholas Radcliffe, 'amongst

---

[79] Greenhill, *Lincoln*, p. 5, frontispiece, pl. 10.
[80] B. Harvey, *Living and Dying in England 1100–1540: the Monastic Experience* (Oxford, 1993), p. 128.
[81] *Amundesham*, I, p. 435; *Account of the Altars*, p. 8 (no. 24).
[82] *Amundesham*, I, p. 436; *Account of the Altars*, p. 9 (no. 25).
[83] Supprior hic fuerat, quem saxa premunt, operosus;
Hic dum vivus, erat claustralis religosus.
Amundesham, I, pp. 440–1; *Account of the Altars*, p. 13 (no. 56).
[84] *Amundesham*, I, p. 437; *Account of the Altars*, p. 10 (no. 33).

theologians a most brave opponent in his days of John Wyclyf, the heretic', was 'provided with a marble stone and an epitaph at the cost of' Abbot William Heyworth.[85] Abbot de la Mare's provision of monuments points to a conscious programme of commemoration, of which the commissioning of the *Liber Vitae* in 1380 is another reflection.[86] It comes as something of a surprise to read that in the early fifteenth century Dom John Savage, sub-cellarer and forester, and Dom William Alnewyke, sub-prior and archdeacon, in turn 'chose for themselves' burial in the south transept 'near the book of the bled', *juxta librum minutorum*, where they were commemorated by a 'marble stone beautifully adorned with effigies and verses'.[87] This suggests that by this date obedientiaries at St Albans enjoyed a prescriptive right of intramural burial in the place of their choice, but such autonomy may be more apparent than real. It is more likely that there was an appreciation of the particular devotions of monks, as when William Heron, prior of Wallingford, described as 'one most fervid in devotion to the Virgin', was interred before the image of the Virgin 'which is called "Beautiful"'.[88] Similarly, the unusual position of the tomb of the almoner Dom William Wyntyrshulle, halfway down the nave, is explained by his attachment to the nearby Chapel of the Blessed Virgin at the Pillar, which he furnished.[89]

The individuality of William Wyntyrshulle's place of burial is noticeable because the nave, west of the nave altar enclosure, was used for lay folk connected with the abbey. The concessionary nature of this provision is indicated in the account of Alan Midelton (d. 1420) in the *Liber Vitae* (Pl. 41), where it is stated that this collector of the rents of various obedientiaries 'earned' burial in the nave because of the prudent way in which he executed his duties without molesting or injuring anyone.[90] Little can usefully be said about the appearance of the monuments in the nave, since the indents there have been swept away. Two civilian figures of the 1460s now mounted on a board in the Whethamstede Chantry may have come from the nave, but defy identification.[91] John Crosby, a former shield bearer to Henry IV who had become a corrodian of the abbey, was commemorated by a punning

[85] *Amundesham*, I, p. 436; *Account of the Altars*, pp. 9 (no. 38), 38. He died between 1396 and 1401 (A. B. Emden, *A Biographical Register of the University of Oxford to A.D. 1500*, 3 vols (Oxford, 1957-9), III, p. 1539).
[86] *Gesta Abbatum Monasterii Sancti Albani, a Thoma Walsingham ... compilata*, ed. H. T. Riley, 3 vols, Rolls Series (London, 1867-9), III, pp. 389-90.
[87] *Amundesham*, I, p. 439; *Account of the Altars*, pp. 11 (no. 46), 44.
[88] *Amundesham*, I, p. 436; *Account of the Altars*, pp. 9 (no. 27).
[89] *Amundesham*, I, pp. 442-3; *Account of the Altars*, p. 14 (no. 82).
[90] BL, Cotton MS Nero D.vii, fol. 145v.
[91] Page, 'Brasses', pp. 21-2 (nos. 1, 4), pl. opp. p. 21.

cross-brass.[92] Those commemorated were mostly either domestic servants, such as John Quyntyn, servant to the refectorer, or William Henewyke, clerk of the infirmary, or legal officials, such as Master Ralph Gardiner, notary public, who witnessed the election of Abbot de la Moote in 1396.[93]

A further degree of honour was paid by allowing burial in the presbytery or near the shrine of St Alban. The inscriptions of the brasses found here are reticent about the precise links of the deceased with the abbey; the position says it all. That of Bartholomew Halley and his wife Florence simply asks in English for a *Pater* and *Ave* for their souls. There is no allusion to his role in defending the abbey's rights to St Nicholas, Pembroke, at the 1453 parliament.[94] Similarly Robert Fayrfax, whose monument was restored in 1921 on the basis of a Philpot sketch, is styled Doctor of Music, but there is no indication that the composer of the *Missa Sancti Albani* had been *informator chori* at the abbey.[95] On his brass in the north aisle by the door leading to the shrine of St Alban, Thomas Fayreman, who died in 1411, is identified as bailiff of St Albans. But it is necessary to turn to the *Liber Vitae* to learn what is implicit in this position at the heart of the abbey, that he and his wife Alice were *confratres* and substantial benefactors.[96]

The fragmentary nature of the evidence makes one hesitate to draw conclusions about monastic monuments in medieval England. It is clear that practice varied not only according to the charisma of the order, but from house to house within an order according to local circumstances. Similarly, the pattern of lay burial in monastic churches varied widely, but seems to have mirrored the degree of lay involvement, parochial or curial, in the life of a house. A well-placed monument, inducing the prayers of the community, was a most potent reward for special benefactors, whether of goods or services. As the word *memoriale* on the 1521 brass of sub-prior Thomas Rutlond at St Albans reminds us,[97] the usefulness of monuments as a historical record as well as an incitement to devotion on behalf of the souls of the dead was appreciated in houses with a tradition of historical writing. Above all, it seems to have been in those houses with the strongest sense of identity as a community that the individual was most often commemorated.

---

[92] *Amundesham*, I, p. 443; *Account of the Altars*, pp. 15 (no. 85), 49.

[93] *Amundesham*, I, pp. 441, 442; *Account of the Altars*, pp. 13, 14 (nos 64, 77, 78), 46.

[94] Page, 'Brasses', pp. 152, 154 (no. 31), pl. opp. p. 152; J. C. Wedgwood and Anne D. Holt, *History of Parliament: Biographies of the Members of the Commons House, 1439–1509* (London, 1936), pp. 409–10.

[95] Page, 'Brasses', pp. 159–61 (no. 38).

[96] *Amundesham*, I, p. 439; *Account of the Altars*, pp. 12 (no. 49), 45; Page, 'Brasses', p. 241 (no. 41), pl. opp. p. 242.

[97] Page, 'Brasses', p. 244 (no. 55), pl. opp. p. 245.

The Liber Vitae *of Durham and Lay Association with Durham Cathedral Priory in the Later Middle Ages*

LYNDA ROLLASON

It is a commonplace of the study of religious houses in the middle ages that lay interest was considerable and that the lay patron was very influential. Indeed, it is inconceivable that a great foundation like Durham Cathedral Priory should have functioned apart from the secular world with which it had constantly to deal, or that the monastery should not make use of valuable contacts with that world to its own advantage in conducting its affairs. Although information about founders of religious houses is not rare, it is quite unusual to be able to look in detail across the spectrum of the 'friends' of a great house like Durham. In the survival of the *Liber Vitae* of Durham we have a manuscript which has claims to be a list of the 'friends' and benefactors of the house from its first foundation at Lindisfarne through to its dissolution at the Reformation. Thus not only is it theoretically possible to consider the 'friends' of the house in any one period but also to discuss changes and developments in this group over time. In this paper I wish briefly to consider the development of the manuscript, to place it in some sort of context by discussing its possible functions, and to outline how my own study of it has modified my ideas about its contents and how the manuscript can be used to illuminate lay association with the priory. My work on this manuscript is in its very early stages, so I shall concentrate my attention on the last part of the book and consider what light it sheds on lay involvement in the later middle ages.[1]

The *Liber Vitae* (*LV*) now forms fols 15-84 [12-81][2] of London, British Library, Cotton MS Domitian A.vii, being bound together with

---

[1] My work on the *Liber Vitae* has been made possible, first, through a grant by the Society of Antiquaries in 1993 for computer equipment and, secondly, through the generosity of local Durham specialists, most notably Mr Alan Piper, who has placed his work on the Durham monks at my disposal and made helpful suggestions at all stages.

[2] The *Liber Vitae* has been twice foliated, once in ink and once in pencil. The ink foliation was used in the printed edition by Stevenson (below, n. 3), but the pencil foliation is that now current. In this paper I shall use the pencil foliation but

twelfth-century extracts from the gospels (fols 4–14v).[3] The *LV* is quite small in scale, roughly 205 mm high and 140 mm wide, although it was evidently somewhat larger before being trimmed in a rebinding. The *LV* is itself composite. Fols 15–45v [12–42] represent the original compilation: a list of some 3,150 names classified according to the bearers' rank in the world and in the church, for example 'kings and dukes', 'queens and abbesses', 'anchorites', 'abbots with the rank of priest'. It is written in insular majuscule, on good quality vellum, three columns to the page. The beauty of the pages is enhanced by the employment of red headings and the use of gold and silver alternately for the names. This section seems to be a fair copy of the list written in the mid-ninth century at the monastery of either Lindisfarne or Monkwearmouth-Jarrow.[4]

Fols 46–84 [42–80] represent additions made to the manuscript between the tenth and sixteenth centuries. This part of the text is also predominantly lists of names. The earliest of these reflect the original form of the book. There is no continuation of the gold and silver writing nor are the entries categorised by the use of headings, but the entries are made in columns and the script is regular. Later additions are increasingly disordered, written in columns or blocks, the pattern changing even on a single page. At the same time, entries were made, apparently randomly, in the earlier parts of the manuscript, as if to use spare parchment. The *LV* must have been with the Community of St Cuthbert at Chester-le-Street in the early tenth century when Athelstan's name was appended to the list of kings (fol. 15 [12]), presumably at the time of his visit to the shrine of the saint in 934. The manuscript must have travelled to Durham with the community in 995, for important land grants in favour of St Cuthbert at Durham were added to it.[5]

---

include the ink foliation in square brackets.

[3] E. M. Thompson and G. F. Warner, *Catalogue of Ancient Manuscripts in the British Museum*, 2 vols (London, 1881–4), II, pp. 81–3. The *Liber Vitae* has been published in its entirety twice by the Surtees Society, first in a printed edition by J. Stevenson, *Liber Vitae Ecclesiae Dunelmensis...*, Surtees Society, 13 (Durham, 1841), and secondly in a facsimile edition by A. H. Thompson, *Liber Vitae Ecclesiae Dunelmensis*, Surtees Society, 136 (Durham, 1923). The early part of the manuscript is discussed and edited by Jan Gerchow, *Die Gedenküberlieferung der Angelsachsen, mit einem Katalog der Libri Vitae und Necrologien*, Arbeiten zur Frühmittelalterforschung 20 (Berlin and New York, 1988), pp. 109–54, 304–20.

[4] A. G. Watson, *Catalogue of Dated and Datable Manuscripts, c.700–1600, in the Department of Manuscripts, the British Library* (London, 1979), p. 101, where the date is given as mid-ninth century; Jan Gerchow, *Die Gedenküberlieferung*, pp. 109–54; and *The Making of England 600–900*, ed. L. Webster and J. Backhouse (London, 1991), p. 132, where the vellum is described as purple-tinted.

[5] H. H. E. Craster, 'Some Anglo-Saxon Records of the See of Durham', *Archaeologia Aeliana*, 4th ser. 1 (1925), 189–98, at pp. 189–93.

But it was only after the refoundation of the monastery of Durham in 1083 that the *LV* came to be regularly used. The names of the monks of the new foundation were entered,[6] and this list subsequently continued; from that time until the Reformation monastic professions were regularly noted. A major feature of the post-Conquest section of the manuscript is that the names of increasing numbers of lay people of both sexes were added to it, until in the end these predominated. The resulting folios are not a fair copy, like the early part of the book, but a constantly updated text with material added in many hands over the course of 450 years.

Before the lists of names entered in the *LV* can be used in a discussion of the history of Durham Cathedral Priory or of the impact of lay association on that house, the questions of why the lists were drawn up, what they were recording and how they were to be used need to be addressed. The *LV* does not contain any internal indication as to its function. There are two generally current views as to what the lists represent. The first is that the lists record benefactors of Durham Cathedral Priory.

This assumption rests principally on a description of the *LV* in another Durham book, written at the end of the sixteenth century, describing the furnishings and ceremonies of the late medieval priory. This book, known as the *Rites of Durham*, includes the following passage about the *LV*:

> There did lye on the high altar an excellent fine booke verye richly couered with gold and silver conteininge the names of all the benefactors towards St Cuthbert's church ... the very letters for the most part beinge all gilded as is apparent in the said booke. Till this day the layinge that booke on the high altar did show how highly they esteemed their founders and benefactors and the dayly and quotidian remembrance they had of them in the time of masse and diuine service did argue not only their gratitude, but also a most diuine and charitable affection to the soules of theire benefactors as well dead as livinge which booke is yett extant declaringe the sd use in the inscription thereof.[7]

This description of the *LV* as a high-status book, recording the names of founders and benefactors of the church of Durham and used in a daily commemoration during divine service, must, however, be an over-simplification, if only because lists of professed monks form a prominent proportion of the later sections. The second assumption is that the lists are the names of those who entered into confraternity with the monastery.[8] Before

---

6   A. J. Piper, 'The Early Lists and Obits of the Durham Monks', in *Symeon of Durham: Historian of Durham and the North*, ed. David Rollason (Stamford, 1998), 161–201.

7   *Rites of Durham*, ed. J. T. Fowler, Surtees Society, 107 (Durham, 1903, reprinted 1964), p. 16.

8   David Knowles, *The Monastic Order in England*, 2nd edn (Cambridge, 1963), p.

either of these assumptions can be accepted it is necessary to compare the *LV* with other books and documents of generally similar character which survive, in order to make clear that medieval religious houses encouraged a variety of associations with a wide circle of secular and ecclesiastical persons and that these were variously recorded and were differently treated.

The first and perhaps most obvious type of association was indeed that of benefactor. Gifts of land, money or buildings, furniture or fittings were frequent. To remember one's benefactors was an important obligation on a religious house, seriously entered into, and manuscripts specifically recording benefactions do survive. The *Liber Benefactorum* of St Albans (BL, Cotton MS Nero D.vii), which was written in 1380 at the direction of Thomas Walsingham, lists benefactors to the abbey according to their position in the world, including kings, queens and popes, and each entry details the individual gifts to the house of each benefactor. Further the *Liber Benefactorum* instructs that the names of benefactors are to be remembered three times a day and includes the collects to be used in their commemoration.[9]

Different abbeys had varying customs as to the methods by which they commemorated their benefactors. William of Malmesbury describes the elaborate nature of the services at Glastonbury: 'On the anniversaries of kings, bishops, abbots and ealdormen who helped to build the church, the brethren were obliged to celebrate mass for their souls at each altar, and, in particular, in the presence of the whole convent, to do so respectfully using the ornaments that they had given to the church'.[10] The fragmentary thirteenth-century list in BL, Add. MS 17450, fol. 5v, which records benefactors of Glastonbury, is arranged to facilitate such commemoration.[11]

The *LV* is not primarily a book of this type. The entries do not include any details of gifts large or small. There can be no doubt of course that many and well-known benefactors of Durham are in fact included in the *LV*. The addition of Athelstan's name to the list, in the tenth century, no doubt showed that the community appreciated the king's gifts and wished to record

---

476.

9   L. F. Sandler, *Gothic Manuscripts 1285–1385*, A Survey of Manuscripts Illuminated in the British Isles, 5, 2 vols (London, 1986), no. 158 (II, pp. 180–1); Watson, *Dated Manuscripts*, no. 546 (p. 105); and Sir William Dugdale, *Monasticon Anglicanum*, ed. J. Caley, H. Ellis and B. Bandinell, 6 vols in 8 (London, 1817–30), II, 209ff. I owe my information on this manuscript to Dr Rebecca Reader.

10   William of Malmesbury, *De antiquitate Glastonie ecclesie*, quoted by M. Blows, 'A Glastonbury Obit List', in *The Archaeology and History of Glastonbury Abbey: Essays in Honour of C. A. Ralegh Radford*, ed. Lesley Abrams and J. P. Carley (Woodbridge, 1991), 257–69, p. 257.

11   Blows, 'A Glastonbury Obit List', p. 258.

his generosity in a fitting way, although the list of his gifts was recorded elsewhere.[12] The later prominent inclusion of members of the Neville family can be ascribed to a sustained friendship as a result of which that family made handsome gifts to the priory, including the Neville screen, a note concerning which is recorded in the *Rites*.[13] It is not clear, however, that the manuscript lists exhaustively all such benefactors of Durham. Notable supporters of Durham such as Kings James I and II of Scots, for example, who were defenders of Durham's interest in Coldingham, are not included.[14] These omissions might be due to the loss of leaves from the manuscript. The profession lists of the monks of Durham are certainly incomplete for the fourteenth century, and the quire structure of the manuscript is very irregular. On the other hand, contemporaries of the kings of Scots are included, so not all the relevant folios can be missing.[15] A further reference in the *Rites* suggests that Durham once possessed a second book closer to the St Albans *Liber Benefactorum*:

> There is also another famous booke: as yett extant conteininge the reliques Jewels ornaments and uestments that were giuen to the church by all those founders for the further adorninge of gods seruice whose names were of record in the said booke that dyd lye upon the high altar, [i.e. the *LV*] as also they are recorded in this booke of the afore said reliques and Jewells to the euerlastinge praise and memorye of the giuers and benefactors therof.

But unfortunately this second volume does not survive.[16] In considering the omissions of benefactors from the *LV*, it is possible that, if two books really

---

12   Simon Keynes, 'King Athelstan's Books', in *Learning and Literature in Anglo-Saxon England: Studies Presented to Peter Clemoes on the Occasion of his Sixty-Fifth Birthday*, ed. Michael Lapidge and Helmut Gneuss (Cambridge, 1985), 143–201, pp. 172–7.

13   *Rites of Durham*, p. 6.

14   For an account of the Coldingham question see R. B. Dobson, *Durham Priory, 1400–1450* (Cambridge, 1973), pp. 316–27, esp. pp. 322, 324.

15   For the quire structure of the manuscript see Gerchow, *Die Gedenküberlieferung*, p. 114. Contemporaries of the kings of Scots included in the *LV* are discussed below, pp. 288–9.

16   *Rites of Durham*, pp. 17, 208n. As this volume is lost it cannot be certain what form it actually took. Further, it is not known who the author of *The Rites* was, but it seems clear that he had not been a monk and that he was writing some decades after 1540; thus his recollections about and understanding of the status and nature of the book may not be entirely accurate. In the note on this passage (p. 208), Canon Fowler equates this second book with 'the great book of the high altar' alluded to in other contemporary sources. But this appears to have been a gospel book to which were added documents and a chronicle; see H. H. E. Craster, 'The Red Book of Durham', *English Historical Review* 40 (1925), 504–32, especially pp. 519ff.

were kept at Durham, the transference of names from one book to the other was less than complete, which would reinforce the impression that the *LV* is not primarily a benefactors' book.

The names in the *LV* are not organised as are those in the fragmentary Glastonbury list or the extensive lists which survive from Christ Church, Canterbury, as obit lists to facilitate the celebration of anniversaries.[17] The *LV* lists are therefore distinct in type from those created during the eleventh and twelfth centuries at Durham in the Cantor's Book, which includes a copy of Usuard's martyrology, the *Rule of St Benedict*, Lanfranc's *Constitutions* and a kalendar.[18] It was the cantor's responsibility to enter obits and this was done initially in the kalendar (fols 6–11) and subsequently in the martyrology (fols 12–39v), a section of which was read each day in Chapter. The number of names recorded in the *LV* far exceeds the numbers recorded in the Cantor's Book and suggests that there were two sorts of commemoration practised, one centred around the anniversaries recorded in the Cantor's Book, another around the *LV*. The lack of overlap between the two is brought into sharp focus by the unusual inclusion in the *LV* of the record of a grant to Malcolm king of Scots, his queen Margaret, and their children, of full participation in the good works of the priory, and commemoration after their death with thirty offices of the dead and celebration of their anniversary in the same way as that of King Athelstan (fol. 52v [48v]). The date of the anniversary is recorded in the martyrology under 13 November (fol. 36v).

Surviving benefactors' lists and obit lists record the names of relatively small groups of people closely associated with monastic houses which considered individual commemoration of their 'friendship', daily or on the anniversary of their death, suitable and appropriate. The *LV* with its thousands of names, whilst it includes many of the names of such persons as were favoured by the community of Durham, represents a rather different sort of association. Its form is closely paralleled in the *Liber Vitae* of New Minster and Hyde Abbey,[19] and more distantly in the Thorney Abbey

---

[17] Blows, 'Glastonbury Obit List'; R. Fleming, 'Christchurch's Sisters and Brothers: an Edition and Discussion of the Canterbury Obit Lists', in *The Culture of Christendom: Essays in Medieval History in Commemoration of Denis L. T. Bethell*, ed. M. A. Meyer (London, 1993), 115–53.

[18] Durham, Dean and Chapter Library, MS B.IV.24. The manuscript is discussed by A. J. Piper, 'The Durham Cantor's Book (Durham, Dean and Chapter Library, MS B.IV.24)', in *Anglo-Norman Durham 1093–1193*, ed. David Rollason *et al.* (Woodbridge, 1993), 79–92, and the obits in Piper 'Early Lists and Obits of the Durham Monks'. The obits are printed as an appendix to Stevenson's edition of the *Liber Vitae*, pp. 135–52.

[19] BL, Stowe MS 944. *Liber Vitae: Register and Martyrology of New Minster and Hyde Abbey, Winchester*, ed. W. de Gray Birch, Hampshire Record Society, 5 (London,

confraternity lists, incorporated into the preliminary leaves of a tenth-century gospel book.[20] The character of these books is instructive. The Thorney Abbey lists, amounting to some 2,300 separate entries, were added in groups in various hands between c.1100 and c.1175. Some of the entries apparently preserve an earlier list or lists but most of the names are those of contemporaries. The *Liber Vitae* of New Minster and Hyde Abbey was begun in 1031-2 as a display book, celebrating the connections between the abbey and the Anglo-Saxon kingdom and incorporating older material. It was continued through the middle ages, like the Durham book, with names being added on spare and incorporated leaves.

What all have in common is the apparently unordered nature of the lists they comprise. It is assumed that they represent those people who sought confraternity with the monastery. Admission into confraternity entitled those so admitted to full participation in the benefits and prayers of the affiliated house. Durham made confraternity agreements with other religious houses, notably in the eleventh and twelfth centuries, which agreements were entered in the *LV*,[21] but others were made later, for example with the Bridgettine community of Syon in 1455 and again in 1516.[22] Agreements were also made with individual religious and with seculars, both men and women. Lanfranc's *Constitutions*, which presumably formed the basis of Durham custom on this matter, outline a ceremony conducted in the chapter-house, enabling the confrater to take his seat among the brethren.[23] The agreement was recognised by individual letters to the recipient of the privilege, which when returned to the monastery on the holder's death triggered the ceremonies for a deceased

---

1892); Gerchow, *Die Gedenküberlieferung*, pp. 155-85; *The Liber Vitae of the New Minster and Hyde Abbey Winchester*, ed. S. Keynes, Early Manuscripts in Facsimile 26 (Copenhagen, 1996).

[20]   BL, Add. MS 40,000. Gerchow, *Die Gedenküberlieferung*, pp. 186-97; Cecily Clarke, 'BL Additional MS 40,000, ff. 1v-12r', *Anglo-Norman Studies* 7 (1984), 50-64.

[21]   For example, on fol. 52 [48] there are agreements between Durham and Westminster, Fécamp, St Stephen's Caen, St Peter's Gloucester, the cathedral priory of Winchester, Christ Church Canterbury, Glastonbury, Selby, Lastingham and Hackness.

[22]   Brief details are included in *The Obituary Roll of William Ebchester and John Burnby: Priors of Durham*, ed. James Raine, Surtees Society, 31 (Durham, 1856), p. 111.

[23]   *The Monastic Constitutions of Lanfranc*, ed. and trans. David Knowles (London, 1951), pp. 114-15. For a discussion of the admission of persons into confraternity see E. Bishop, 'Some Ancient Benedictine Confraternity Books', in his *Liturgica Historica: Papers in the Liturgy and Religious Life of the Western Church* (Oxford, 1918), 349-61, and most recently, *Liber Vitae of New Minster*, ed. Keynes, pp. 49-65.

brother which were the *raison d'être* of the association. If the *LV* is a record of those granted confraternity with Durham then the names of the lay persons in it would be entered as they were accepted, just as the names of professed monks were entered. Unfortunately, comparison of the *LV* with the surviving letters shows a marked discrepancy between the two. For example, of the thirty-one letters surviving from between 1500 and 1510 I have so far found only two names that are certainly also entered in the *LV*. The most prominent omissions are those of Lady Margaret Beaufort, admitted into confraternity in 1502, and Henry VII, admitted probably in 1508.[24]

Lanfranc's *Constitutions* implies that admission was open to all, but the surviving letters from Durham suggest that confraternity was considered a special honour granted in respect of 'past kindnesses' to the monastery at Durham or one of its cells – in effect, the recognition of a special relationship. It seems unlikely that all the people recorded in the *LV* could have claimed any such relationship. The apparent lack of correlation between the surviving letters and the *LV* suggests that *confratres*, like other benefactors, were separately remembered. However, it is clear that in the later middle ages letters of confraternity were often issued by monastic houses, hospitals and guilds in great numbers, to a standard pre-written form which could be purchased for money like an indulgence and the name of the recipient inserted in the spaces left on the letter.[25] Although the *LV* does not contain indications of payment, it has been suggested that the *Liber Vitae* of New Minster and Hyde Abbey does.[26] If the entries in the *LV* are records of people purchasing fraternity, it seems unlikely that they were all admitted with the full ceremony in the chapter-house. Perhaps it would be reasonable to suggest some sort of sliding scale of recognition and relationship amongst those associated with Durham in the later middle ages.

Neither the Durham *LV* nor the Thorney lists make clear the purpose of their compilation, but the *Liber Vitae* of Hyde Abbey includes an extended passage explaining its purpose, which is worth quoting in full:

> Here follow in their appropriate order the names of the brethren and monks [of the monastery of New Minster], and also of the friends and benefactors, whether living or dead, so that, by the making of a record on earth in this written form, they may be inscribed on the pages of the heavenly book, by whose alms-giving, through the bounty of Christ, this community is sustained from day to day. And may the names be entered here of all who commend themselves to its prayers and fraternity, in order that there may be

---

[24]   *Obituary Rolls*, pp. 114–15.

[25]   W. G. Clark-Maxwell, 'Some Letters of Confraternity', *Archaeologia*, 2nd ser. 25 (1926), 19–60, and 'Some Further Letters of Confraternity', *Archaeologia*, 2nd ser. 29 (1929), 179–216.

[26]   *Liber Vitae of the New Minster*, ed. Keynes, p. 104.

a commemoration of them every day, in the holy solemnities of the Mass, or in the harmonies of psalmody. And may the names themselves be presented by the sub-deacon every day before the holy altar at the Morrow or principal Mass, and may they be read out by him in the sight of the Most High, as time permits. And, after the offering of the oblation to God, placed on the holy altar at the right hand of the principal priest who is celebrating Mass, during the mysteries of the sacred Mass, may they be most humbly commended to Almighty God. So that, just as commemoration of them is made on earth, so too in that life, by the bounty of Him who alone knows how all are, or are to be, there, may the glory be augmented of those who are of greater merit in heaven, and may the cause be smoothed in the hidden judgements, of those who are of lesser merit. Rejoice and be glad, because your names are written in heaven.[27]

Monks and lay brethren, founders and benefactors are clearly included in the Winchester book, just as at Durham; and, in the case of the benefactors, their contribution to the welfare of the community is recognised. But what is notable is the phrase 'And may the names be entered here of all who commend themselves to its [i.e. the monastery's] prayers and fraternity' with the specific hope that through daily commemoration of all, by association rather than individually 'may the glory be augmented of those who are of greater merit in heaven, and may the cause be smoothed in the hidden judgements, of those who are of lesser merit'. It would appear that many of those named are seeking benefits from the abbey rather than being its benefactors in any real sense. The Hyde Abbey *Liber Vitae* and, I would suggest, the Durham *LV* are in reality collective chantries; they do contain the names of those who were benefactors and confraternity members, but they are predominantly composed of the names of those seeking prayers.[28] The lists in these books are therefore explained. Daily, and largely anonymous or collective, remembrance of persons living or dead required no ordering or structure in the manuscript, the names so included, whenever this happened or in whatever part of the book, becoming a part of the constant round of prayer provided by the monastery. Inclusion is neither exclusive nor indicative of any particularly close relationship with the religious house, excepting a general desire to be included in the round of prayers for the good of one's soul. If these conclusions about the structure and scope of the *LV* are correct, an examination of entries in the Durham *LV* should show benefactors, confraternity members and others, probably the majority, who in purchasing association expected to benefit from the prayers of the monks.

---

27 *Liber Vitae of the New Minster*, ed. Keynes, pp. 82–3.
28 The distinction may prove to be a false one as benefactors offer support so as to benefit from the prayers of the monks, and at all periods there is evidence of the purchase of prayers.

Entries which can be shown to have been those of prominent benefactors and confraternity members are not difficult to identify. On folio 77v [73v] (Pl. 43) we have, by the standards of the later parts of the book at any rate, quite a well laid-out page. It was not written all at one time, nor all in the same hand. Even this folio has suffered subsequent insertions and additions; thus the names of John Rakett and Margaret his wife are interlined, those of Richard Lilborn and others are added on the right, whilst lower down those of William Ryddylle and his wife are also inserted. Further, it seems to be the case that the setting-out and plan of the page were not fixed when it was begun. Thus, the first entry fills three lines, and is in a larger script:

> Lady Joan de Neville, countess of Westmorland, Lord Richard Neville, earl
> of Salisbury, and Lady Alice, countess of Salisbury, his wife.

This is followed by several entries, one to a line, in several hands:

> Lady Elizabeth, countess of Westmorland
> Lord Robert Babthorpe, knight
> Lord Alexander Seton, lord of Gordon
> William Seton, brother of the Lord Alexander
> Robert Seton, nephew of the aforesaid Lord Alexander
> Roger Thornton and Elizabeth, his wife
> William Hoton and Joan his wife
> John Kempe, cardinal priest of St Balbina and archbishop of York
> Thomas Hoveden, knight, and Elizabeth his wife
> Katherine Chewpayne, anchoress of Standforth

The entries lower on the page generally adopt a block format.

The names recorded at the head of the page represent benefactors of the priory by any standard. The first entry is for Joan Neville, countess of Westmorland, who was Joan Beaufort, daughter of John of Gaunt and Catherine Swynford. She married before November 1396 Ralph, lord Neville of Raby, who was created earl of Westmorland in September 1397. He died in October 1425.[29] She had a close relationship with the priory and was granted confraternity on St Cuthbert's day, 1430.[30] She showed great interest in the priory's benefices, and she spent the last two years of her life on the bishop of Durham's manor at Howden. The bishop of Durham at that time was her son, Robert, elevated in 1438. She died on 13 November 1440.[31]

Richard, earl of Salisbury, was the eldest of Joan Beaufort's sons by her marriage to Ralph Neville. He married, in or before 1420/1, Alice, who was daughter of Thomas Montague, earl of Salisbury, and who was *suo jure* countess of Salisbury. Richard assumed the title earl of Salisbury after his

---

[29] G.E.C., *The Complete Peerage*, ed. V. Gibbs *et al.*, 12 vols in 13 (London, 1910–59), XII.2, p. 547.

[30] *Obituary Rolls*, p. 109.

[31] Dobson, *Durham Priory*, p. 187.

father-in-law's death in 1429.[32] He enjoyed close relations with the then prior of Durham, John Wessington, receiving letters of confraternity in April 1431, letters which do not include his wife.[33] This folio, then, is likely to have been begun after 1429, the date of the assumption by Richard of the title of earl. Perhaps the most likely date would be 1430 or 1431, the dates of Joan's and Richard's confraternity agreements.

The entry for Lady Elizabeth, countess of Westmorland, could be for one of two women. One possibility is that it was for Elizabeth Holland, the wife of John Neville, first son and heir of Ralph Neville, first earl of Westmorland, and his first wife Margaret Stafford. Elizabeth and John were married at Brancepeth, near Durham, in 1394, but he died in 1420 and she was dead by 1422/3.[34] It is more likely that the entry was for Elizabeth, the wife of Ralph Neville, second earl of Westmorland, grandson of Ralph, the first earl. A daughter of Sir Henry Percy ('Hotspur'), she and Ralph were married in 1426 and she died on 26 October 1437.[35] The second identification is more likely, first, because of the placement of Elizabeth's name after an entry which must have been made after 1429, by which point Elizabeth Holland was dead; secondly, because her name is linked in the list with that of Sir Robert Babthorpe, who, as lay steward of the priory's collegiate church at Hemingbrough, received confraternity letters in 1434, and whose family owed feudal allegiance to the house of Percy.[36]

The entry for William Hoton was for William Hoton of Hardewick, who was lay steward of Durham from 1437 to 1446, and not only served the monastery in this capacity but loaned the prior considerable sums of money on easy terms.[37] This entry must be dated between 1437 and 1446, the year of Hoton's death.

John Kempe, whose name and title are entered in a markedly different hand, was the son of a Kentish gentleman, a fellow of Merton College, Oxford, and ultimately a doctor of laws who practised in the higher ecclesiastical courts. He combined an ecclesiastical and political career and had some connections with Durham. In 1416, he was archdeacon of Durham, rising to become, in 1426, archbishop of York. In 1439 Pope Eugenius IV appointed him cardinal priest of Santa Balbina. In 1452, he became archbishop of Canterbury and he died in 1454. During his time as archbishop of York the

[32] Complete Peerage, XI, p. 395.
[33] Dobson, Durham Priory, pp. 187–8; Obituary Rolls, p. 109.
[34] Complete Peerage, XII.2, p. 548. It is unlikely that she would have been styled countess of Westmorland.
[35] Complete Peerage, XII.2, p. 550.
[36] The History and Antiquities of the Parish of Hemingbrough, ed. J. Raine, Yorkshire Archaeological Society (York, 1888), pp. 174–5; Obituary Rolls, p. 109.
[37] Dobson, Durham Priory, pp. 128–9.

then prior, Wessington, enjoyed unusually cordial relations with him.[38] This entry must have been added after 1439 but before 1452, the date of Kempe's elevation to Canterbury.

These people were not just the givers of gifts to the priory; their support and good will were essential and they were intimately connected to the priory by political and social ties of the greatest complexity. The juxtaposition in the *LV* of the names of Joan Beaufort and Richard, earl of Salisbury, with Elizabeth, countess of Westmorland, for example, disguises an explosive situation, in which the priory was deeply and embarrassingly involved, although it tried through Prior Wessington to be a friend to both sides, and was finally the means of mediation. Elizabeth was married to Ralph Neville, grandson of Ralph Neville and his first wife Margaret Stafford. Joan Beaufort was Ralph Neville's second wife and, on his death in 1425, she managed to ensure that the bulk of her husband's estates outside County Durham passed to her own children at the expense of those by his first marriage. The situation threatened open war and created, to quote Professor Dobson, 'a definite two-party grouping in the North during Wessington's priorate'. Wessington tried to keep on good terms with both sides and, after Joan's death in 1440, was instrumental in bringing about a negotiated settlement between the two branches of the family.[39]

While the priory might have had to tread warily in a morass of local feuds and politics, it was also concerned more generally in national politics and most especially with the complex relations with Scotland. The priory had been concerned in the long negotiations which finally saw the ransom and release of King James I of Scots in 1424, after a captivity of eighteen years. The final treaty was formally ratified in the chapter-house at Durham, after discussions between the two sides lasting over a fortnight. The entertainment of the notables concerned cost the prior over £100.[40] It is perhaps surprising that this occasion has left no record in the *LV*; neither the name of the king of Scots, nor that of his queen, a relative of Countess Joan, is inscribed in it. But connections between Durham and Scotland at this time account for the inclusion of the names of Alexander Seton, Lord Gordon, his brother William and nephew Robert, together with that of Master Johannes Methfene, secretary to the king of Scotland. These names must have been recorded subsequent to the treaty of 1424 because Methfene was secretary to James II rather than James I, but there was continuous activity across the border after 1424 as envoys were exchanged and truces concluded and extended. Master John was an envoy as early as 1437, and was at Durham to arrange a truce in

---

[38]   *Dictionary of National Biography*, ed. Sir Leslie Stephen and Sir Sidney Lee, reissued edn, 22 vols (1908–9), X, pp. 1272–6.

[39]   Dobson, *Durham Priory*, pp. 185–7.

[40]   Dobson, *Durham Priory*, p. 108.

May 1444 and again in 1449, when he was involved in discussions which took place in the cathedral, concerning the status of Berwick and Roxburgh during the truce.[41]

The entry for Alexander Seton could be either for the first or second lord of Gordon. The first Alexander Seton was the second son of Sir William Seton and married in 1407/8 Lady Elizabeth Gordon. His active career was closely involved with that of James I, king of Scots. He was one of the negotiators for the king's release and spent a year in England as a hostage for him, being released in 1425. He was often employed on embassies to England. He died in 1440/1.[42] The second Alexander Seton succeeded his father in 1441, and was created earl of Huntley in 1444 or 1445.[43] I have as yet been unable to trace either William Seton or Robert Seton, listed in the *LV* as respectively a brother and a nephew of Alexander, which would resolve the matter. But a William Seton became a monk of Durham around 1430, which may be significant.[44] The other persons on the list may also appear there as a result of the Scottish connection. The Setons and Methfene must have known Countess Joan as the aunt of James I's queen, another Joan Beaufort. They must have had many dealings with Richard, earl of Salisbury, as warden of the western marches towards Scotland, and with Archbishop Kempe, both as a member of the council of regency for the infant Henry VI and more especially in 1436 when he was joined by the bishop of Durham and the earl of Northumberland in relieving Roxburgh which was being beseiged by James I. Even Babthorpe, who died in 1436, could have been known to the first Alexander Seton, as a prominent member of the Normandy campaign under Henry V, comptroller of the king's household and executor of the king's will.

It thus becomes clear that these names display a multitude of associations which demonstrate the priory's involvement at various levels with major patrons, on a personal level, a regional level, and a national level. Such people, powerful in both the secular and ecclesiastical worlds, would have been necessary contacts and allies for the priory.

No doubt the desire to promote a trusted servant to an advantageous position caused Countess Elizabeth to push for the appointment of William Hoton, who was a servant of the Nevilles, to the lay stewardship of Durham,

---

[41] *Calendar of Documents Relating to Scotland A.D. 1108–1509*, ed. J. Bain, 4 vols (Edinburgh, 1881–4), IV, p. 226 where he is joined with Alexander Seton on a commission to conclude a truce with England (pp. 237, 246).

[42] *The Scots Peerage*, ed. Sir James Balfour Paul, 9 vols (Edinburgh, 1904–14), IV, pp. 518–20.

[43] *Scots Peerage*, IV, pp. 521–6.

[44] A. B. Emden, *A Biographical Register of the University of Oxford to A.D.1500*, 3 vols (Oxford, 1957–9), III, pp. 1671–2. Seton was admitted to Durham College as a scholar in 1431–2.

but the reason given for her support may have been real. She wrote to the prior recommending Hoton for the post and saying: 'and for so much as he [Hoton] is my said worshipfull lord's steward, he shall cause more good acord and peis betwen his tenandis and youres at all tymes'. The countess's brothers-in-law, Sir John and Sir Thomas Neville, also wrote to the prior recommending Hoton.[45] In the event Hoton proved to be worthy of his trust, for at his death Prior Ebchester wrote that this 'deede is to me and my brethren ... savying the displesaunce of Gode, the most hevynesse and losse of oon that ever befell to us or to the monastery of Durham'.[46]

A second group can be shown to be those of the families of the monks of Durham. The *LV* includes the names of professed monks throughout the period. At first, they appear as a series of discrete blocks of four to six names, each entered as a group (for example fol. 79 [75]). Then the system of recording changes and the monks are listed in larger but still discrete groupings (fol. 79v [75v]). Finally, their names are entered amongst those of lay persons and often with remembrances of their mothers and fathers. An obvious example of the practice is on fol. 80 [76] where there is an entry which reads:

> Master Thomas Carre and Master William Carre with their parents, brothers and sisters

Thomas and William Carre were both monks of Durham in the early sixteenth century, Thomas dying in 1520 and William in 1512 or 1513.[47] The association of monks with their families in the *LV* was far more frequent than appears at first sight. Because of the informal methods of recording, some groupings which look unrelated on the page (i.e. groups of names in the same hand but bearing different surnames) are in fact family or kin groups of the monks. It was quite common, although not universal, for men who became monks to change their surnames on entering religion. There seems to have been no compulsion to do so, nor is there any clear pattern. Alan Piper suspects that some men at least adopted the maternal surname, although some may have adopted the name of their birthplace, as many surnames are also local place-names.[48] The clearest evidence for the practice of name-changing at Durham comes from those monks who lived through the Dissolution to receive firstly a pension and then appointment as the first canons of the new

45 Dobson, *Durham Priory*, p. 129.
46 Dobson, *Durham Priory*, pp. 125–6.
47 For my information on the monks of Durham I am grateful to Alan Piper for permission to use his research, which will be published shortly under the aegis of the Surtees Society.
48 Dobson, *Durham Priory*, pp. 56–7.

cathedral foundation, under their paternal names. Thus on fol. 83 [79], bottom left, the entry reads:

William Robinson and Alice his wife
Henry Heghyngton Isabella his wife
Dom C. Heghyngton Dom Thom.
Robert Heghyngton and Johanna his wife
Henry Robynson and his wife.

This entry is all in the same hand with two sets of brackets associating the persons named, Robinsons and Heighingtons. Dom C. Heghyngton is Cuthbert Heighington who entered the priory at Durham about 1509 and lived across the Dissolution, dying on 29 January 1549. He was assigned a pension under the name of Robinson. In 1533 his brother Robert Robinson was in the almoner's infirmary. Robert is not included in the *LV* entry unless he is to be identified with the Robert Heighington married to Johanna.

In one instance a modification to the entry in the manuscript reinforces the presupposition of name-changing. The entry at the top right of fol. 83 [79] reads:

Joh. Robynson of Newcastle and Maiona his wife.
Dom Edward Hebburn their son
Dom Henr. Hebburn

Edward Hebburn was a monk of Durham, entering the priory around 1521 and disappearing from the record in 1532/3. He is clearly identified by the entry as the son of John and Maiona Robinson, and indeed his surname seems originally to have been entered as Robinson, but this was altered by being overwritten with the name Hebburn.[49]

On folio 79v [75v], Robert and Richard Heryngton are both entered amongst professions of the monks. Robert entered the monastery around 1486 and is last recorded in 1529. Richard survived across the Dissolution and was awarded a pension under the name of Jonson. In the lower part of the same folio is a group of entries

John Jonson
Annes Jonson
William Jonson
Thomas Jonson
Richard Heryngton
Robert Heryngton

It would appear therefore that Richard and Robert Heryngton have been entered a second time in the *LV*, this time in conjunction with members of their family.

---

49   I am grateful to Alan Piper for pointing this out to me.

Even where there are several different surnames in a group, it may nevertheless be possible to perceive family connections between them. On folio 82v [78], for example, is an entry with a box around it headed 'Richard Wheldon monk'. The names which follow are:

John Felton
John Peyrson
Elizabeth Peyrson his wife
Robert Thomson
Robert Peyrson
Margaret Browelle
Robert Browelle
Margaret Browelle his wife
Agnes Felton

The grouping here suggests some form of association, but does not show of what sort. We know from the feretrar's accounts, however, that Richard Wheldon, a monk of Durham between *c.*1510 and 1539, was the son of Isabella Peyrson, who gave a tenement in Claypath to the feretrar's office in 1536–7. Although she is not named in the *LV*, it seems reasonable to regard the Peyrsons of the entry in question as members of Richard Wheldon's family, while the use of the box suggests that he was also related to the Thomsons, Feltons, and Browelles.

There are other examples in the *LV* where such family relationships can be postulated. It is not always clear exactly what sort of association these relatives of the monks had with the priory. It is possible that some were truly benefactors. Thus it may be that John Robinson of Newcastle, father of Edward Hebburn, monk of Durham, was the man granted confraternity in letters issued on 7 June 1475.[50] This John Robinson had given the prior and convent a tenement in Pilgrim Street, Newcastle, and in return he and his wife received confraternity, and a pension of six marks yearly. The letters, however, record the name of Robinson's wife as Johanna and the *LV* as Maiona, so this may not be the same family. In the case of the Wheldon/Peyrson family the one known benefactor of the priory, Isabella Peyrson, is not recorded in the *LV*, either as part of Wheldon's extended family or independently. One can only suggest that as family of professed monks they might have some claim to the generosity and prayers of the monks. There is some suggestion that this extended to practical charity, for Robert Robinson, brother of Cuthbert Heighington, was received into the almoner's infirmary. Confirmatory evidence of these associations and the nature of the relationships with the priory may be quite difficult to find; for, if, as Barrie Dobson has suggested, the monks of later medieval Durham derived not from the gentry class but from the upper reaches of the peasantry, there will have been

---

[50]   *Obituary Rolls*, p. 113.

few wills and no family pedigrees.[51] Stray references in the priory archive may suggest further associations of this sort. At present it seems reasonable to suggest that far from men leaving their families on entering religion, the latter became associated with the priory which made itself responsible for their spiritual and bodily well-being.[52]

Numerous names in the *LV* can be shown to have been of tenants of priory property in Durham City. One example should suffice. A line on folio 78 [74], which is written in a single hand, reads:

Willelmus Chamer   Johanna his wife   Robertus Patson.

From the tenement documents we learn that in 1500 the widow of William Chalmer, afterwards widow of Robert Pateson, holds one burgage in Alvertongate, which was once held by the same William Chalmer.[53] Here we have three local people, tenants of the priory, and in this case we can see something more of their relationship. It seems unlikely that the arrangement in the *LV* is fortuitous: a woman named after her then husband, with the name of her future husband next. Here must be represented not a family, which would have precluded marriage amongst them, but the close relationships of friends, neighbours and/or business associates. It is not really clear why their names have been entered. In November 1476 Robert and Johanna Patson were granted confraternity.[54] The entry in the *LV* on folio 78 cannot record this event, if when it was made Johanna was the wife of William Chalmer. On the other hand neither Johanna nor Robert is entered a second time in the *LV*. This single entry highlights the difficulties of considering all the names in the *LV* to be *confratres* of the priory.

Since it is clear that many of the names recorded in the *LV* were tenants of the priory, it is difficult to see them all as benefactors, but rather easier to envisage their purchasing prayers from the monastery. However, in this aspect the *LV* appears a very intimate book with considerable significance for the immediate locality. For example, many of the people associated with a tenement held by Johanna Chalmer appear in *LV*. The tenement was granted in 1443 by one William Artays to Robert Sotheron, chaplain. In the same year Sotheron granted it to William Chambre, then described as mason. In her will, Johanna Chambre, then Pateson, granted the property to John Nesse, chaplain, and Roger Moreland. All these people are recorded in *LV*. After this, however, the trail runs cold; the next holder, Thomas Dobynson, and his

---

51   Dobson, *Durham Priory*, p. 58.
52   Dobson, *Durham Priory*, pp. 58–9 and note for further instances.
53   Margaret M. Camsell, 'The Development of a Northern Town in the Later Middle Ages: the City of Durham, *c.*1250–1540' (unpublished Ph.D. dissertation, University of York, 1985), II/i, p. 21.
54   *Obituary Rolls*, p. 113.

associates, are not recorded in the book. Cecily Clarke's work on the confraternity records of Thorney demonstrated that the people commemorated lived in geographical proximity to the abbey, turning to it presumably as their closest religious centre.[55] There does appear to be a similar pattern in *LV*, as shown by the entries on folio 77 [73], where there is a group of three entries in the same hand at the top left hand of the page:

> John Bowman
> Margaret Bowman
> William Bowman

This is followed, in a different hand, by the name:

> Thomas Ryhale

and then in a third hand by the name:

> John Binchester, chaplain

These names are not obviously a group. They are not all in the same hand, nor related by boxes or brackets in the text. All these people, however, were local to Durham and associated with the priory's land-owning in the city. Evidence of this is provided by the tenement histories of the city researched by Margaret Bonney. In 1411 Margaret Bowman granted a burgage plot in Alvertongate jointly to Alan Hayden and John Binchester, chaplains, and to Thomas Ryhale. In 1419 these men leased it to the prior for forty years.[56] Although Alan Hayden's name does not occur in *LV*, the names of all the other persons involved in these transactions do. This confirms that, as in the case of Thorney, the *LV* contains names of people who were from the immediate area of the priory and involved in its affairs.

It remains to be discovered precisely how far the geographical range of the *LV* extends through the north-east. The involvement of the priory in the wider politics of the region together with its group of dependencies, including Coldingham in Scotland, might suggest a wider geographical range, which the inclusion of the Nevilles and Percys would support, but there is also a local Durham city concentration. Perhaps it will prove that the benefactors and confraternity members come from a wider area than those seeking prayers, especially in the later middle ages. It will be interesting to know how far urban centres such as Newcastle are represented in the *LV*, as the city provided alternative possibilities for both benefaction and the purchase of prayers.

In conclusion, it appears that the *LV* does not include, especially for the later middle ages, a comprehensive list of either the priory's benefactors or its

---

55   Cecily Clarke, 'The *Liber Vitae* of Thorney Abbey and its Catchment Area', *Nomina* 9 (1985), 53–72.
56   Camsell, 'Durham City', pp. 16–17.

confraternity members. Indeed it is possible that the manuscript was not maintained after 1083 with the aim of recording these persons. Rather it comprises hundreds of names of people who were remembered in the prayers of the community. Only with further research can we hope to identify sufficient of them to comment adequately on their relationship with the priory.

Chaucer's Two Nuns [1]

MARSHA L. DUTTON

The great anomaly in Geoffrey Chaucer's frieze of human society, *The Canterbury Tales*, is the presence of two nuns, who should not be there at all, but at home in their monastery.[2] Chaucer's portrayal of the Prioress and her chaplain, the Second Nun, with their overlapping prologues and similar tales, violates the otherwise clearly established pattern of each pilgrim's representing a different occupation, a different place in medieval society. Among those on the journey these two are the only duplicates: there is one knight, one cook, one monk, one miller, one clothmaker – and two nuns.

Little attention has been given to Chaucer's purpose in creating this duplication, perhaps because no one knows what to think or say about nuns, how to evaluate the quality of their thought or how to judge what they say or do.[3] While many have discussed the Prioress and her Tale, agreeing that her portrait is highly ambiguous and that her devotion to the Virgin is beautifully expressed and charmingly sincere, most have abandoned examination of her Prologue right there.[4] And the tacit agreement until relatively recently to ignore her companion and chaplain, the Second Nun, indicates that she is as faceless and uninteresting – boring, even – to modern readers as to her fellow pilgrims. Even the careful symmetry of their prologues and tales has evoked no interest.

---

[1] I am grateful to Mona Lagordo, Marilyn Miller, Robert E. Mory, and Paul Schaffner for their assistance to me during my days of work in the *Middle English Dictionary*. I also owe special thanks to Emily K. Stuckey, Kate Douglass, Carole Hutchison, Kristin Cole, and my colleague Steven Jobe for assisting me with the research and writing of this paper.

[2] See E. Power, *Medieval People*, 10th edn (New York, 1963), p. 94.

[3] See, however, J. B. Holloway, 'Convents, Courts, and Colleges: the Prioress and the Second Nun', in *Equally in God's Image: Women in the Middle Ages*, ed. J. B. Holloway, C. S. Wright, and J. Bechtold (New York, 1990), 198-215. N. A. Eliason has argued that Chaucer intended the Second Nun's tale as a second tale for the Prioress, never meaning to include a second nun among the pilgrims ('Chaucer's Second Nun?', *Modern Language Quarterly* 3 (1942), 9-16).

[4] But see S. Ferris, 'The Mariology of *The Prioress's Tale*', *American Benedictine Review* 31 (1981), 232-54.

But Geoffrey Chaucer created the Second Nun in her silence and invisibility as surely as he created the Prioress in her verbal and visual excess, and the distinction his narrator makes between them in the General Prologue becomes dramatically significant when they themselves begin to speak, in their separate but similar prologues and tales, linked even through their shared use of rhyme royal.[5] Then the Prioress shows herself intellectually and verbally incompetent, linguistically and doctrinally muddled, what C. Wood has called 'a nun who is no nun'.[6] The Second Nun, however, is a nun, and a good one, who perfectly realises her vocation and carries out her office as chaplain to her superior, not merely as secretary and lady's maid but as a spiritual and moral guide. She is doctrinally sound, intellectually solid, rational, and articulate. Where the Prioress pretends to be a romantic heroine, ornamenting her sober cenobitic garment with jewelry betokening romantic love, the Second Nun veils herself in the silence and facelessness of her habit and vocation, invisible, nameless, and uninteresting even to the garrulous and ever-curious narrator.[7] Where the Prioress is childish, the Second Nun is an adult. She knows who she is and what she is about.

Chaucer's depiction of the difference between this mature woman and her childish superior reveals his awareness of the ways in which Mme Eglentyne fails to fulfil her monastic vocation. Further, it suggests his care and rhetorical skill in using not only the General Prologue but the Prioress's Prologue and Tale to delineate her character and to create a dramatic interaction between the two women.

While the Second Nun offers to her superior doctrinal and moral guidance, her Prologue and Tale also resolve some of the ambiguity of Chaucer's portrait of the Prioress as a woman characterised by childishness and confusion. But the Second Nun does not exist merely for the sake of the Prioress, even while she serves as her intellectual and spiritual guide. As surely as she exists dramatically for the instruction of the Prioress and her fellow pilgrims, she speaks for the intellectual and spiritual instruction of Chaucer's audience, articulating the spiritual reality that the journey to Canterbury is part of the journey to the heavenly Jerusalem. This humble and learned woman is one of those pilgrims who offers up the *sententia* of *The Canterbury Tales*; she with St Cecilia reminds those who ride with her and those who

---

5 See C. D. Benson, 'The Aesthetic of Chaucer's Religious Tales in Rhyme Royal', in *Religion in the Poetry and Drama of the Late Middle Ages*, ed. P. Boitani and A. Torti (Cambridge, 1990), 101–17.

6 C. Wood, 'Chaucer's Portrait of the Prioress', in *Signs and Symbols in Chaucer's Poetry*, ed. J. P. Hermann and J. J. Burke, Jr., Alabama Symposium on English and American Literature (University, AL, 1981), 81–101, esp. p. 100.

7 All references to *The Canterbury Tales* come from *The Riverside Chaucer*, gen. ed. L. D. Benson, 3rd edn (Boston, 1987).

attend to her words that this life of exile and pilgrimage, of error and effort, is only a transitory stage to be succeeded at last by 'bettre lif in oother place' (VIII.323), 'oother lyf ther men may wone' (VIII.332).

The Prioress appears in every way to be what people expect in a nun. She is scrupulously polite and clean, tender-hearted, dressed in a habit with a properly pinched wimple, and recognised even by her fellow pilgrims for her singing of the 'service dyvyne' (I.122). She swears the most ladylike of oaths and speaks a French apparently learned in the convent. Her Prologue begins with material familiar to her from her daily office, and she narrates a Marian tale about a virgin martyr. She is, at first glance at least, unexceptionable.

At the same time, however, the Prioress systematically violates assumptions about who nuns ought to be, even by her presence outside the monastery. Every element of her portrait shows her neglect of monastic regulation and discipline. However religious her jewelry, she should not be wearing it; however touching her tenderheartedness, she should be more concerned for hungry and suffering humans than for lap dogs. And she should not be on pilgrimage at all.

Most significantly, when the Prioress speaks she reveals her essential confusion about the content and meaning of Christian doctrine, of moral and Incarnational theology. She also shows herself unable to sustain a logical train of thought, to anticipate her end from her beginning or remember her beginning once she has accidentally attained an end. She wanders, repeats herself, confuses subject and object, before and after, up and down. She appears to be indeed, as she freely confesses, 'as a child of twelf monthe oold, or lesse' (VII.484). But of course she is not a child. As Chaucer himself notes in the General Prologue, 'hardily, she was nat undergrowe' (I.156). And she is the Prioress of a monastic community with all its responsibilities.

The conflict between the wilful and satisfied childishness and infancy of the Prioress and her actual age, status, and effort 'to ben estatlich of manere, / And to ben holden digne of reverence' (I.140–1) lies at the heart of her portrait. For in her failure to emerge from infancy she ignores all that St Paul and St Augustine require of spiritual adults. 'When I was a child I thought as a child, I spoke as a child, I reasoned as a child, but when I became an adult I put away childish things', wrote Paul (1 Corinthians xiii. 11). And Augustine echoes: 'We are tender-hearted and bear with [infant faults] because we know that the child will grow out of them... . The same faults are intolerable in older persons'.[8]

---

[8]   *Confessiones*, 1.7.28; ed. L. Verheijen, Corpus Christianorum, Series Latina 27 (Turnhout, Belgium, 1981); R. S. Pine-Coffin, *Saint Augustine: Confessions* (London, 1961), p. 28. See on this topic M. L. Dutton, '"When I Was a Child": Spiritual Infancy and God's Maternity in Augustine's *Confessiones*', in *Collectanea*

The Prioress's linguistic incompetence first reveals her lack of knowledge and the long journey between her and Christian maturity.[9] Vain about her unenviable linguistic skills, the Prioress unnecessarily and badly speaks French and translates from Latin when she lacks competence in both, thereby revealing herself as also grammatically insecure in English.

Early in the description of the Prioress in the General Prologue Chaucer-pilgrim remarks on her French, praising it and then qualifying that praise by identifying its dialect:

And Frenssh she spak ful faire and fetisly,
After the scole of Stratford atte Bowe,
For Frenssh of Parys was to hire unknowe. (I.124-6)

While travelling on this English pilgrimage in the company of English pilgrims, the Prioress has, apparently, found the occasion to speak a great deal of French, enough for at least one of her fellows to discern its quality.

Her Latin is, not surprisingly, even worse than her French.[10] Although she does not attempt to speak it, except perhaps to entune her office, she begins her Prologue with a paraphrase of the first two verses of Psalm 8, prefacing them with their Latin beginning, *Domine dominus noster*. These verses would have been profoundly familiar to her, not only from the monastic psalmody but from the opening lines of matins in the Little Office of the Virgin, said daily in private.[11] But she presents a halting, repetitious, and error-ridden translation that ends with the voices of infants, fails to give God the credit for their praise of him, and omits the words of God's enmity to the avenger, words with particular relevance to the tale she is to tell. The Latin that the Prioress attempts to translate reads as follows:

1. Domine Dominus noster, quam admirabile est nomen tuum in universa terra! Quoniam elevata est magnificentia tua, super caelos.

Augustiniana, ed. J. C. Schnaubelt and F. Van Fleteren (New York, 1989), 113-40.

[9] In *De doctrina christiana* Augustine defines knowledge, to be gained from the study of Scripture, as the third step on the road to Christian perfection, urging the learning of languages in order to understand 'literal signs', the words, of Scripture: 'against the unknown literal sign the sovereign remedy is a knowledge of languages' (*De doctrina christiana* 2.7-15.9-22; trans. D. W. Robertson, *On Christian Doctrine* (Indianapolis, 1958), 38-50, p. 43).

[10] Power comments that 'She would read ... in her psalter or in such saints' lives as the convent possessed, written in French or English; for her Latin was weak, though she could construe *Amor vincit omnia*'; *Medieval People*, p. 80.

[11] B. Boyd, *Chaucer and the Liturgy* (Philadelphia, 1967), pp. 68-75; see also *The Prymer or Lay Folks' Prayer Book*, ed. H. Littlehales, Early English Text Society orig. ser. 105 (London, 1895), pp. 2-3.

2. Ex ore infantium et lactentium perfecisti laudem propter inimicos tuos, ut destruas inimicum et ultorem.

But she exclaims:

> O Lord, oure Lord, thy name how merveillous
> Is in this large world ysprad ...
> For noght oonly thy laude precious
> Parfourned is by men of dignitee,
> But by the mouth of children thy bountee
> Parfourned is, for on the brest soukynge
> Somtyme shewen they thyn heriynge. (VII.453–9)

The errors of this translation begin to appear at the end of the second line, with the insertion of the past participle *ysprad*, changing the free-standing copula *is* into part of a passive construction. So the Lord's name, whose praise in the psalm controls a complete and self-contained sentence, becomes the subject of a passive verb, syntactically the recipient of its action, no longer independently glorious but now made so by those who proclaim it. The addition of *ysprad* also makes the adjective *merveillous* ambiguous as it is not in the Latin, especially in its position at the line break. In the first two lines *merveillous* functions as an adjective modifying *thy name*, like *admirabile* in the psalm. But in conjunction with the passive verb it may be read as an adverb modifying *is ... ysprad*, praising no longer the name of the Lord but the action of those who spread it.

The Prioress also omits the second half of the first verse of the psalm, in which the psalmist extols the Lord's glory as raised above the heavens, inserting in its place 'men of dignitee' to supplement the psalmist's *lactentium* 'unweaned infants', in her version 'children ... on the brest soukynge'. In Latin *infantium et lactentium*, 'infants and sucklings', denotes those unable of their own accord to voice God's praise because of their age; the amplification clarifies the phrase, making the age of the infants more precise. But the Prioress transforms the unweaned into those physically inhibited from singing; 'children ... on the brest soukynge' must praise God with muted voices.[12]

Finally the Prioress stops short before completing the second verse of the psalm, which declares that God raises up his praise from the mouths of infants 'because of his enemies, that he may destroy the enemy and the avenger'. The Prioress's combined errors of translation and her failure to complete the verse suggest that she does not understand the meaning of the verses she daily

---

[12] Dante's rendering of this line may have influenced Chaucer's translation. In *Paradiso* 33, which contains Bernard of Clairvaux's hymn to the Virgin Mary, the source for the Second Nun's hymn and through hers the Prioress's, Bernard confesses himself as inarticulate 'che d'un fante/ che bagni ancor la lingua alla mamella' (ll. 107–8).

recites, which identify the avenger with God's enemy, and that she has not connected these verses with the common biblical reservation of vengeance to God.[13]

The Prioress thus reveals herself not merely a poor translator, incompetent in both Latin and English, but also one unaware of the psalm's meaning. Her paraphrase subordinates the Lord to those who praise him, rather than with the psalmist acknowledging that their very ability to praise is his doing, and omits the warning of his hatred of vengeance.[14]

In the Tale that follows the Prioress again shows her inability to read and understand biblical texts, compounding her linguistic inadequacies in Latin and English with a theological misunderstanding of the hierarchy of grace. In the fourteenth stanza of the Tale, almost its centre, she briefly apostrophises the martyred 'litel clergeon', her protagonist, in words translating Revelation, xiv. 3-4 into logical and syntactic impossibility:

O martir, sowded to virginitee,
Now maystow syngen, folwynge evere in oon
The white Lamb celestial ...
Of which the grete evaungelist, Seint John,
In Pathmos wroot, which seith that they that goon
Biforn this Lamb, and synge a song al newe,
That nevere, flesshly, wommen they ne knewe. (VII.579-85)

The biblical text portrays the blessed as singing before the throne of God, the four beasts symbolising the evangelists, and the elders of the church, then identifies them as virgins who follow the Lamb, that is, Christ, wherever he goes. But this version omits the throne, the beasts, and the elders, leaving only the 'white Lamb celestial'. While it says that the child will sing while following the Lamb, it links him with those martyrs who, the Prioress says, sing a new song while going before the Lamb. Her mistranslation, and misunderstanding, allow the 144,000 to precede the Lamb (an image that suggests the leaders glancing over their shoulders to see where the Lamb is about to go), while the murdered child apparently goes both before and after. It again reveals the Prioress's poor Latin, her weak logic, and her inability to understand either the Latin source or her own English sentence.

In both the Prologue and the Tale Chaucer takes care to insist that the faulty translation is the Prioress's rather than his, each time at the point where it goes wrong. So in the second line of the Prologue, after the *ysprad* that destroys the substance and syntax of the psalm, and again in the second line of this passage after 'the white Lamb celestial', the narrator breaks in with the words 'quod she', reminding the audience whose translations these are. Twice

[13]   Cf. Romans, xii. 19; Matthew, vii. 1.
[14]   An opposing point of view appears in Ferris, 'Mariology of *The Prioress's Tale*' (see note 4, above).

then in the Prioress's brief venture into public speaking, both times as she struggles to render familiar biblical passages in English, Chaucer calls attention to the fact that it is she who speaks, she who provides the words and the syntax, alerting listeners and readers to her words while absolving himself of responsibility for them.

The Prioress's inept Latin translation also exposes her grammatical and syntactic problems in her own language, problems that continue even when she has no Latin to contend with. In the last stanza of her Tale she commits one final grammatical error when she appeals to Hugh of Lincoln to 'Preye eek for us, we synful folk unstable' (VII.687), acknowledging herself as one with all sinners; the repetition of the plural pronoun emphasises that identification.

But the stumbling repetition is also a last proof of her linguistic inadequacies. The Prioress is not sure, it seems, whether a pronoun used as object of a preposition is in the objective or nominative case. That she stumbles is remarkable enough, but that she stumbles from the correct *us* to the incorrect *we* underlines the level of her English usage, offering up a linguistic or syntactic parallel to her assumed gentility of manner and attire. So she shows her English, like her French, to be provincial in origin and form.

The intellectual and theological weakness revealed by the Prioress's linguistic inadequacies in all three languages also affects the development of her Prologue and Tale, where she exalts the Virgin Mary over the Lord, celebrating her miraculous power at the expense of her mercy as intercessor with her Son. In the Prologue she quickly loses the thread of both her psalm and of her praise to God, beginning accurately enough with 'O God, our God', but distractedly trailing off in praise of Mary and managing to persuade her readers and herself that she intended such a hymn all the time. In commenting on this passage F. N. Robinson mentions the convention he believes she follows: 'It was a regular literary convention to prefix to a miracle or saint's legend an invocation to Christ or the Blessed Virgin'.[15] Florence H. Ridley concurs: 'A prologue such as this is conventional in saints' lives and miracles of the Virgin'.[16]

But the Prioress's Prologue is not in fact a hymn to the Virgin, or at least not intended as such. Although she starts in praise of the Lord, by the second stanza she has wandered from the theme, perhaps distracted by a word reminding her of the Virgin whom she does not yet address:

Wherfore in laude, as I best kan or may,

---

[15] *The Works of Geoffrey Chaucer*, ed. F. N. Robinson, 2nd edn (Boston, 1957), p. 735.

[16] *Riverside Chaucer*, p. 913.

Of thee and of the white lylye flour
Which that the bar, and is a mayde alway,
To telle a storie I wol do my labour. (VII.460–3)

The modal verb in the first line of this stanza seems to recall to the Prioress the noun *may* 'maiden', commonly used in Middle English reference to or invocation of the Virgin Mary.[17] As she is already familiar with this psalm's place in the daily Office of the Virgin, she probably thinks of it as properly directed to the Virgin as much as to God; it is no wonder that her mind turns here from God to the one who was both maid and mother.

In the three stanzas that follow the Prioress not only praises the Virgin but again exalts her over the Lord. As she inadvertently moves from praise of God's name into a fragmentary hymn to the Virgin, she mentions Jesus, the Virgin's son and God's, only as an afterthought, within a phrase naming the Virgin as 'herself ... honour and the roote / Of bountee, next hir Sone, and soules boote' (VII.465–6).

By the third stanza the Prioress has entirely forgotten the Lord, now addressing her praise directly to the Virgin, whom she praises not as one selected by God as an agent of his love for and mercy toward humankind, but as the grasper rather than the recipient of the flame of the Holy Spirit. While hymning the Virgin's purity and humility, the characteristics for which medieval theologians and poets conventionally celebrate her, the Prioress presents that humility as the virtue by means of which she was able to ravish the Holy Spirit from the Godhead, so bringing about the conception in herself of Christ, God's Wisdom:

O bussh unbrent, brennynge in Moyses sighte,
That ravyshedest doun fro the Deitee,
Thurgh thyn humblesse, the Goost that in th'alighte,
Of whos vertu, whan he thyn herte lighte,
Conceyved was the Fadres sapience,
Help me to telle it in thy reverence! (VII.468–73)

In giving Mary here the upper hand over God himself, the Prioress inverts the economy of salvation, making Mary the initiator, crediting to her rather than to God the power to choose and to ravish.

In the last two lines of the Prologue, however, the Prioress recollects herself, ending triumphantly with two plural pronouns of address: 'and therfore I yow preye, / Gydeth my song that I shal of yow seye' (VII.486–7). This retreat to the plural *yow* from the nine singular pronouns of address to Mary in the previous stanza shows the Prioress to have noticed her error,

[17] *The Middle English Dictionary*, ed. Hans Kurath *et al.* (Ann Arbor, MI, 1967–), *s.v. mai* n. See, e.g., *The Man of Law's Tale*: 'Now, lady bright, to whom alle woful cryen, / Thow glorie of wommanhede, thow faire may / ... / Rewe on my child' (II.850–3).

remembering whom she had begun by addressing; now she gracefully retreats, hymning the Lord with the Virgin.

In her Tale the Prioress persists in her theological and syntactic confusion. Once again she slides inadvertently from celebration of God's might to the Virgin's; further, inverting a popular medieval Marian legend, she portrays the Virgin as an agent not of mercy but of vengeance. Thus the Tale, like the Prologue, reveals the theological confusion of its teller.

In this legend a seven-year-old Christian boy has his throat cut by Jews angry at his insistent singing of the *Alma redemptoris* as he walks between his home and school. Thrown by his murderers 'in a wardrobe ... / Where as thise Jewes purgen hire entraille' (VII.572-3), the boy is miraculously preserved from immediate death by the Virgin so that he may continue to sing her praise. His song leads Christians to him; having learned of his fate they torture and kill the Jews 'by the lawe' (VII.633-4).[18] Although the boy still sings, no effort is made to heal him or save his life; all Christian haste is applied to exacting vengeance. The miracle has only violent consequences.

Although the Jews are punished as murderers, the Christians do not seem to recognise the child's continuing to sing as a miracle until it delays his burial. Only then does the Christian abbot inquire into the reason that the boy still sings even though 'thy throte is kut to my semynge' (VII.648), allowing the boy at last to explain the miraculous event as the gift of the Virgin:

> This welle of mercy, Cristes moder sweete, ...
> To me she cam, and bad me for to synge
> This anthem verraily in my deyynge,
> As ye han herd, and whan that I hadde songe,
> Me thoughte she leyde a greyn upon my tonge.
> Wherfore I synge, and synge moot certeyn
> In honour of that blisful Mayden free
> Till fro my tonge of taken is the greyn. (VII.656-66)

The grain removed, the boy is at last allowed to die; the abbot and convent fall to the ground 'Wepynge, and herying Cristes mooder deere' (VII.677-8).

As a miracle of the Virgin this tale ought properly to show the Virgin as above all merciful. The many medieval Marian legends consistently show her interceding for those who love her, but especially for the guilty among them.[19] Indeed in the Tale the child-protagonist refers to her as 'this welle of

---

[18] See for discussion of the legal status of this vengeance R. Rex, 'Wild Horses, Justice, and Charity in the Prioress's Tale', *Papers in Language and Literature* 22 (1986), 339-51.

[19] See examples in *The Middle English Miracles of the Virgin*, ed. B. Boyd (San Marino, CA, 1964).

mercy', and the Prioress concludes with a prayer that insists that mercy –
God's and the Virgin's – is its end and meaning:

> Preye eek for us, we synful folk unstable,
> That of his mercy God so merciable
> On us his grete mercy multiplie
> For reverence of his mooder Marie. Amen. (VII.686–90)

The Prioress thus understands the need of sinful humans for God's mercy and
knows that the Virgin intercedes with the merciful God for that human need,
but her understanding reaches only as far as her own need and that of her
friends, not to the unknown stranger or enemy.

Most of the analogues to this tale studied by Carleton Brown show the
child to be healed and restored to the community; many include conversion
of the Jews nearby as well.[20] Butin this tale the Virgin shows no mercy, in her
own person or in intercession with her Son. She does not save her young
devotee, either before his murder or after, but only makes possible his
continuing praise of her, and his friends' vengeance on his slayers. Chaucer's
emphasis here, accented by the Prioress's closing words, appears to be not
only the general absence of charity shown by the Prioress and the Christians
of whom she speaks, but the absence of all mercy, on the suffering child or on
those who suffer because of his murder.[21]

As the primary effect of the miracle is not mercy but vengeance, it links
the Virgin and the Christians of the Tale with the enemies of God, against
whom Psalm 8 says he raises up praise. Whether one takes the words of the
psalm to mean that vengeance is reserved to the Lord or that the Lord
considers the avenger one with his enemies, the vengeance of this tale violates
them. Although the question of the Prioress's anti-semitism has been much
discussed, Chaucer is clearly less concerned that the murderers are Jews, the
usual medieval scapegoats, than that they are both the villains and the victims.
There could be no vengeance had there been no wrong done, but the wrong is
in the murder committed, not in the murderers' being Jews. Chaucer's
concern is not anti-semitism, but vengeance, emphasised by the Prioress's
repeated use of a psalm that condemns what her tale proclaims.

---

[20] See C. Brown in *Sources and Analogues of the Canterbury Tales*, ed. W. F. Bryan
and G. Dempster (1941; rpt. New York, 1958), pp. 462–3. See also M. H. Statler,
'The Analogues of Chaucer's Prioress's Tale', *Publications of the Modern Language
Association* 65 (1950), 896–910.

[21] Brody's discussion of vengeance in Chaucer's *Man of Law's Tale* and its parallel in
the *Prioress's Tale* is instructive here, especially in his reference to 'the primitive
delight in vengeance felt by' the two pilgrims; S. N. Brody, 'Chaucer's Rhyme
Royal Tales and the Secularization of the Saint', *The Chaucer Review* 20 (1985),
113–31, p. 120.

It is a commonplace that the protagonist of this tale represents the Prioress herself. But the similarities between them underline their differences, for the clergeon is only seven, while the Prioress is an adult. Both she and the 'litle clergeon' speak words whose meaning they cannot understand, she mistranslating familiar biblical passages and he praising the Virgin in words learned by rote: 'Noght wiste he what this Latyn was to seye' (VII.523). He sings a song that does no good and much harm, he understands the words but not the meaning of Christian doctrine, he feels rather than thinks: he is entirely a child. And as he is a child, he is not to be judged for his childish faults 'because we know that the child will grow out of them.'

But the Prioress, who has had ample opportunity to leave behind her childish faults, has not done so. She tells a Marian tale not of mercy, forgiveness, healing of the sinner, conversion of murderers, or even rescue of an adoring child, but instead one of merciless vengeance carried out by Christian monks resident in Christian society. She aligns herself consciously with 'children on the brest soukynge' rather than with 'men of dignitee'. And as she is like them, as she chooses to be like them, she remains always a spiritual child, spiritually if not physically 'undergrowe'.

In contrast to the lengthy and detailed introduction of the Prioress in the General Prologue, the other nun receives only the barest mention: 'Another Nonne with hire hadde she, / That was hir chapeleyne, and preestes thre' (I.161–2). This nun affects the reader as she does the narrator: she seems a nameless, faceless woman present only as a shadowy companion of her more decorated and decorative superior. Even syntactically the Second Nun is twice subordinated to the Prioress, entering the scene only as the object of the verb of which the Prioress (*she*) is the subject and described only in relationship to her. The Second Nun has neither a whole sentence nor indeed a whole syntactic unit to herself.[22]

But the few words devoted in the General Prologue to the Second Nun define her for the audience as precisely as do the Prioress's forty-four lines, for in her failure to do anything that might attract the attention of those who meet her, the Second Nun does just what nuns ought to do. She reveals no charming traits, no gentle *faux pas*, no delightful hints of femininity. Of her name, her table manners, and her social origins nothing is known. She is a perfect nun, hidden within her habit and her service to the Prioress.

In her Prologue and Tale this nun's words confirm the audience's initial inferences about her character, revealing her understanding of Incarnational

[22] F. N. Robinson explains the brevity of the Second Nun's introduction by speculating that 'Chaucer very likely started to describe the Second Nun and stopped with the word *chapeleyne*; then somebody else completed the line... ' (*Chaucer's Works*, p. 654).

theology and Mariology, her competent Latinity, and her clarity of English style. That she is more competent in Latin than the Prioress appears in her own claim in the Prologue to have translated her Tale, the Life of St. Cecilia, from Latin.[23] She is also more theologically aware and articulate than the Prioress: her hymn to the Virgin presents an accurate explication of Mary's role in the economy of salvation, and her tale of martyrdom appropriately presents the saint as an imitator of Christ and an exemplar of Christian charity and evangelism. She correctly understands Mary as subordinate in her human life and history to Christ, addressing her as 'doghter of thy Sone' (VIII.36) and 'doghter deere of Anne' (VIII.70), and shows a proper ordering of grace in naming Mary's son 'Creatour of every creature' (VIII.49). Finally the miracle in her Tale allows teaching, preaching, and founding of a church rather than vengeance.

The Prologue to this Tale combines four stanzas on sloth with seven stanzas of a hymn to the Virgin, followed by a stanza acknowledging that the Second Nun is the translator, not the author, of the tale that follows. While humble and self-effacing in her apology for what she has not done, her explanation also signals her learning, her linguistic ability, and her concern with the meaning within the words she speaks:

Foryeve me that I do no diligence
This ilke storie subtilly to endite,
For bothe have I the wordes and sentence
Of hym that at the seintes reverence
The storie wroot, and folwen hire legende. (VIII. 79–83)

The Second Nun's insistence here on reporting not only the words but the sentence of her Tale reminds the audience that stories, and especially stories of saints, have *sententia*, meaning, and alerts listeners to the presence of that meaning in the Tale that follows. She then shows the way meaning resides in and informs words by explicating the multiple meanings of the name *Cecilia*, so demonstrating her ability to translate from Latin into English while reminding her audience of the necessity to look beyond the words into their significance if they are to find the *sentence* of her Tale.

The core of this Prologue is, like the Prioress's, a hymn to the Virgin, but intentionally rather than accidentally. The Second Nun titles that portion *Invocacio ad Mariam* and begins with direct address to the Virgin: 'And thow that flour of virgines art alle' (VIII.29). This hymn, unlike the Prioress's, insists on Mary's mercy; the Second Nun reminds the audience that Mary is

---

23   The Second Nun's translation is also, as S. Reames has shown in her identification of the source, a close and accurate translation of the Life of St Cecilia from what she calls 'the Franciscan abridgment', 'A Recent Discovery Concerning the Sources of Chaucer's "Second Nun's Tale"', *Modern Philology* 87 (1990), 337–61.

most likely to extend that mercy to the innocent and the sufferer.[24] Addressing Mary in the words of the Prioress's clergeon as 'Thow welle of mercy, synful soules cure' (VIII.37), she identifies herself in personal need of that mercy, herself an exile, a sinner, a child of the Fall:

> Now help, thow meeke and blisful faire mayde,
> Me, flemed wrecche, in this desert of galle; ...
> And though that I, unworthy sone of Eve,
> Be synful, yet accepte my bileve. (VIII.57–8, 62–3)

Like the Prioress, the Second Nun tells a legend of a virgin saint martyred for her articulation of Christian truth but continuing to speak although her throat is cut. For Cecilia both virginity and martyrdom are a matter of choice rather than circumstance. On her wedding night she persuades her bridegroom to live in chastity with her, and she is martyred for teaching and converting pagans, through high-spirited, intelligent, and often witty argument. She converts men of her own station, not only her husband Valerian and his brother Tiburce but Maximus, 'that was an officer / Of the prefectes' (VIII.368–9).

In her encounter with Almachius the prefect she goes even further, arguing with him and mocking his attempt to match her intellectually. When Almachius demands that Cecilia sacrifice to pagan gods and abandon Christianity she derides him:

> At which the hooly blisful faire mayde
> Gan for to laughe, and to the juge sayde:
> 'O juge, confus in thy nycetee,
> Woltow that I reneye innocence
> To make me a wikked wight?' quod shee. (VIII.461–5)

When Almachius petulantly complains 'I reeche nat what wrong that thou me profre, / For I kan suffre it as a philosophre' (VIII.489–90), Cecilia retorts:

> O nyce creature!
> Thou seydest no word syn thou spak to me
> That I ne knew therwith thy nycetee
> And that thou were in every maner wise
> A lewed officer and a veyn justise. (VIII.493–7)

In these passages Cecilia becomes an imitator of Christ, like him in the days before and after his arrest pursuing her own course of martyrdom, arguing, mocking pomposity, and refuting pseudo-philosophy. Cecilia's eventual martyrdom comes at her own insistence and as a consequence of her perseverance in good working and 'charity ful brighte' (VIII.118). As she has

---

[24] For similar Chaucerian passages depicting the Virgin as one with special concern for the needy and suffering see *The Man of Law's Tale* (II.841–54) and 'An ABC', *Riverside Chaucer*, pp. 637–40).

earlier told Tiburce that the promise of 'oother lyf ther men may wone' (l. 332) means they need not fear loss of present life, she scoffs at Almachius's threat of death, saying 'Thou, that ne mayst but oonly lyf bireve, / Thou hast noon oother power ne no leve' (VIII.482–3).

At last, inevitably, it is her insistent words that bring her end, and the beginning of that 'oother lyf':

Thise wordes and swiche othere seyde she,
And he [Almachius] weex wroth, and bad men sholde hir lede
Hom til hir hous, and ...
'Brenne hire right in a bath of flambes rede.' (VIII.512–15)

Cecilia's death is in many ways like that of the Prioress's protagonist. She too suffers in a subterranean cell, though hers is a steam bath. She too for some time survives having her throat cut by her tormentors, for after failing to die in the steam bath, she receives 'Thre strokes in the nekke' (VIII.526); when these three also fail to kill her, the law forbids a fourth. Thus Cecilia remains for three days 'half deed, with hir nekke ycorven there' (VIII.533).

Meanwhile, the Second Nun recounts, Cecilia teaches, preaches, and provides not only spiritually but physically for her spiritual children, those whom she has led to the faith:

Thre dayes lyved she in this torment,
And nevere cessed hem the feith to teche
That she hadde fostred; hem she gan to preche,
And hem she yaf hir moebles and hir thyng,
And to the Pope Urban betook hem tho. (VIII.537–41)

The Second Nun's description of Cecilia's plight echoes the Prioress's description of her child martyr:

Ther he with throte ykorven lay upright,
He *Alma redemptoris* gan to synge
So loude that al the place gan to rynge. (*Prioress's Tale*, VII.611–13)

The parallel here is intentional: both Cecilia and the clergeon lie with neck 'ykorven', and as they lie near death both continue the proclamation they made when fully alive. As the Second Nun emphasises that this martyr purchases her delay in dying with her torment, she reminds the audience that the clergeon also suffered as he continued to sing during the days that his friends sought for him, found him, executed his murderers, and carried out his funeral.

The two miracles differ, however, in their purpose and effect. Whereas the child's death is delayed not at his wish but through the intervention of the Virgin, to praise her and bring death to his slayers, Cecilia's miraculous delay in dying is, like her virginity and martyrdom, the result of her own mature choice, and Cecilia's lingering on this side of death brings conversion and enduring service to Christ. Cecilia informs Pope Urban that she herself requested the miracle that preserves her through three days of suffering, not to bring vengeance on her tormentors but to carry out her responsibilities to her fellow Christians, to continue in charity toward them:

> I axed this of hevene kyng,
> To han respit thre dayes and namo
> To recomende to yow, er that I go,
> Thise soules, lo, and that I myghte do werche
> Heere of myn hous perpetuelly a cherche. (VIII.542–6)

As the results of Cecilia's miraculous deeds are the point of this story, the Second Nun concludes her Tale with them:

> Hir hous the chirche of Seint Cecilie highte;
> Seint Urban halwed it, as he wel myghte;
> In which, into this day, in noble wyse,
> Men doon to Crist and to his seint servyse. (VIII.550–3)

As Cecilia is martyred for her efforts on behalf of the Gospel rather than merely suffering because of childish fecklessness, she is miraculously saved, for a while, to care for her converts and create a church where God's worship may continue to ring out. The Second Nun thus makes clear to her audience the proper role of the saint in furthering the faith and responding to persecution not with hate and vengeance but with forgiveness. By her inversion of the Prioress's tale, which climaxes and ends in violence, the Second Nun celebrates not only the cause and meaning of martyrdom – adherence to the Gospel in word and spirit through the practice of love for God and for neighbour – but the meaning of, reason for, and result of miracles.

The Prologue and Tale of the Prioress represent an inverted world view in which the Creator is subordinated to his creatures, dependent on them for his praise, chosen rather than choosing. The Virgin Mary accomplishes the Incarnation through her virtue, and Christ's meaning and importance seem to rest primarily in his relationship to her; martyrs in beatitude precede Christ the Lamb rather than singing before God's throne while a child martyr goes both before and after; and the humble Mary, 'welle of mercy', allows mass murder with the miracle through which her follower suffers so that her praise may be heard a little longer. This world is turned upside down by logical and syntactic inconsequence, shaped and confused by Eve's Fall, through which humans lost the ability to know the good and to choose it. Her Christians conform to the society of the 'greet citee' 'in Asye' (VII.488) in which they live rather than being transformed from it by the renewal of their minds in Christ's love.[25] They do murder in return for murder and take an eye for an eye, a hundred Jewish lives for the life of one Christian child, explaining their vengeance as justified 'by the lawe'. They, like the Prioress, seem unaware of the effects of Christ's Incarnation.

The Second Nun's Prologue and Tale, however, turn the world again right side up. The Virgin is not only Anne's daughter but daughter of her son, chosen by God to bear his son. And that only-begotten son of God is with his father Creator of all creatures. Those who suffer for their proclamation of the Gospel act in charity and witness to God's love. For the Second Nun writes of a world in which Christians transcend their pagan society, renewed indeed in Christ's love and witnessing for that love to their neighbours, like the Second Nun herself.

The Second Nun thus restores the correct order to the relationship of God and humankind, presenting a world in which Christians proclaim God's love, live in chastity, and exercise charity and mercy while rejecting wrath and vengeance, a world characterised by divine grace rather than divine ire. She presents an alternative world of Christian effort, though not one in which Christians live safely and without torment: Cecilia risks all in her decision to live as a chaste bride of Christ and to lead others to imitate her, and finally she suffers all. But as she has chosen to follow Christ at whatever cost to herself, she follows him in her dying as in her living, knowing that this life is not the only life, that there is other life beyond, and that whoever bereaves the Christian of this life only opens the door to the eternal one that follows. So the Second Nun turns the Prioress's Prologue and Tale on their head, turning the Prioress's theology upside down and getting it right.

Does the Prioress hear her? Probably not. Everything Chaucer has said about her suggests that her attention is always in the wrong place. But all her chaplain can do is to keep trying. And if any of the other pilgrims hear her, or if Chaucer's audience hears her, she has done her job.

For that is the Second Nun's other responsibility in this work, to guide all her fellow pilgrims on the road to Canterbury and, says the Parson, 'Of thilke parfit glorious pilgrymage / That highte Jerusalem celestial' (X.50-1). So the Second Nun speaks to her larger audience as to her immediate one, reminding all in Cecilia's words that:

> ... ther is bettre lif in oother place,
> That nevere shal be lost, ne drede thee noght,
> Which Goddes Sone us tolde thurgh his grace. (VII.323-5)

---

[25]   Romans, xii. 2.

Rabbits and Eels at High Table:
Monks of Ely at the University of Cambridge, c.1337–1539

JOAN GREATREX

The presence of Benedictines at Oxford and Cambridge from the late thirteenth century to the Dissolution of the monasteries is well documented. Detailed studies of particular groups of monks are, however, far from complete, although Dr Pantin made an impressive contribution in his four volumes on Canterbury College, Oxford.[1] Research is currently being focused on various medieval communities in England, both urban and rural, including social groups and classes, baronial, knightly and peasant, and also ecclesiastical associations and orders; and the results to date have significantly enlarged our horizons of knowledge and understanding in these areas. The monastic presence in medieval society was manifest in outward and visible form in the impressive building complexes surrounding both the abbey churches that dotted the rural English landscape and the cathedral churches, some of which were in the care of monks, that were predominant features of the urban scene. Although their inhabitants were not confined to the enclosure it was the centre of their daily life of prayer and worship, study and manual work; it would be true to say that in a limited sense their communities were a society in microcosm. The procurement of food supplies and other essential commodities, the supervision of monastic properties from which their income was largely derived and a number of other business concerns necessitated their involvement with secular affairs and people in the world outside; but their sorties were usually of limited duration. In exceptional cases a select few were

---

[1] W. A. Pantin, *Canterbury College, Oxford*, 4 vols, Oxford Historical Society, new ser. 6-8, 30 (Oxford, 1947-1985). See also J. Greatrex, 'Monk Students from Norwich Cathedral Priory at Oxford and Cambridge, c.1300-1530', *English Historical Review* 106 (1991), 555-83; eadem, *Biographical Register of the English Cathedral Priories of The Province of Canterbury, c.1066-1540* (Oxford, 1997). An earlier draft of this paper was read at a meeting of the Medieval Society at the University of Cambridge in 1993. Many of the amendments incorporated here were prompted by the judicious comments of Barbara Harvey of Somerville College, Oxford.

allowed longer periods of absence, advanced studies in a university setting being one of these.

It is my intention to examine in some detail the lives and careers of one of these select groups, namely the privileged monks of Ely Cathedral Priory who were chosen to go to Cambridge. While their counterparts at Norwich began to take up places at Gloucester Hall in Oxford in the last decade of the thirteenth century, there is no evidence of Ely participation in this new venture for another forty years. It would be surprising if a few Ely monks had not been involved at an earlier stage but there was probably no regular policy until the late 1330s.[2] At this time, probably because of the initiative of Prior John de Crauden (1321–41), whose interests and achievements extended beyond an ambitious building programme within the Ely cloister, arrangements were made for the accommodation of the brethren studying at Cambridge. The exact date of the founding of Crauden's Hostel is uncertain, although James Bentham, an eighteenth-century antiquary and canon of Ely, suggested 1340.[3] It was located on the site of what in 1350 became Trinity Hall, when Bishop Bateman of Norwich purchased the hostel and other adjacent tenements from Crauden's successor, Prior Alan de Walsingham, in order to make his own foundation. The Ely monks were then probably lodged in Spalding's Inn, also known as Borden's Hostel, in St Michael's parish (nos 9 and 10 Trinity Street).[4] About 1414/17 the provincial chapter allocated the sum of £12 to the prior of Ely 'pro novo manso Cantabrigg'; but by the late 1420s a common house of study for Benedictines had come into being on the forceful urging of two priores studentium worn down by their responsibilities for a community that remained physically scattered, and on the initiative of several Benedictine prelates among whom the abbot of Crowland was the dominant figure.[5] This was the hostel which went by the

---

2 Oxford seems to have been an almost unmentionable word, to judge from the silence of the Ely records, with the possible exception of John de Swaffham who incepted in 1289/90 at an unnamed institution and received gifts from the Ely chamberlain; Cambridge University Library [CUL] EDC 5/3/5. The only reference to Oxford occurs on the pittancer's account in 1320/1 when he reported sending a 7s. contribution towards a papal levy for the stud[ia] apud Oxon, CUL EDC 5/8/5.

3 James Bentham, *The History and Antiquities of the Conventual and Cathedral Church of Ely*, 2nd edn (Cambridge, 1812), p. 220.

4 H. P. Stokes, *The Medieval Hostels of the University of Cambridge*, Cambridge Antiquarian Society, octavo ser. 49 (Cambridge, 1924), pp. 9, 72, 87–8. The 'Monks' Building' is that part of Trinity Hall closest to Clare College; A. W. W. Dale, *Warren's Book* (Cambridge, 1911), p. 67.

5 *Documents Illustrating the Activities of the General and Provincial Chapters of the English Black Monks, 1215–1540*, ed. W. A. Pantin, 3 vols, Camden Society 3rd ser. 45, 47, 54 (London, 1931–7), III, p. 180, II, p. 149; R. W. McDowell, 'Buckingham

name of 'Monkis Place', and by 1483 was known as Buckingham College, and subsequently became absorbed in Magdalene College.[6]

It is probably no coincidence that the impetus for Prior Crauden's initiative on behalf of his monk students came in the wake of Pope Benedict XII's bull, *Pastor bonus* (1335), and the decree *Summi magistri* (1336) which was addressed specifically to the black monks. This papal legislation included some new prescriptions with regard to the setting up of a common house of studies within the university to which one monk in twenty was henceforth to be sent.[7] Even before this date the prior and chapter of Christ Church, Canterbury had leased a hall in Oxford in order to provide accommodation for several of their monks whom they had sent to study there.[8] Crauden, too, must have been moved by practical considerations and by the need to maintain monastic life and discipline, which would have been impossible had the monks been placed in any of the existing secular hostels. He was, no doubt, reluctant to send his brethren unnecessarily far away to that other place, although the Norwich monk-students' association with Oxford, despite the distance involved, does not seem to have caused any problems.

It is a truism to observe that answers given depend on questions asked, but medievalists, on occasion, need to be reminded that the questions which may be asked are directly dependent on the quantity and the type of surviving records. At Ely, for example, we, alas, know little of the work that was carried on in the monastic scriptorium, and only a pitiful number of manuscripts remain from what must have been a well-stocked library. On the other hand, from the last two centuries preceding the Dissolution about 380 obedientiary account rolls survive, albeit many in a fragmentary and fragile state. These are the main source of information for monk-scholars for the simple reason that the cost of their accommodation and maintenance was shared among the obedientiary offices. However, any questions we put to these accounts must directly relate to expenditures incurred on the student's

---

College', *Proceedings of the Cambridge Antiquarian Society* 44 (1950), 1–12, p. 1; *VCH, Cambridgeshire*, II, p. 312. The sum of £12 0s. 22½d. [sic] given to the prior of Ely exactly matched, and probably therefore cancelled out, the Ely contributions to the chapter over a three-year period.

[6] Buckingham College at Cambridge corresponds to the much earlier Gloucester Hall/College at Oxford; for a survey of its history by Peter Cunich see P. Cunich, D. Hoyle, E. Duffy and R. Hyam, *A History of Magdalene College Cambridge, 1428–1988* (Cambridge, 1994), pp. 1–30.

[7] The bull *Pastor bonus* laid down regulations for the setting up of this common house of studies, and all religious houses were expected to make regular contributions; see *Chapters of the Black Monks*, II, pp. 77–8, 231.

[8] *Literae Cantuarienses*, ed. J. B. Sheppard, 3 vols, Rolls Series (London, 1887–9), I, nos 380, 397, 401.

behalf by his brethren at home in the cloister; and it is worth repeating the comment that, unfortunately, the annual financial statements were prepared with a view to passing the scrutiny of the monastic auditorial board and not with any concern for the future questions of historians.

A few basic facts and figures are the necessary prelude to an encounter with the students themselves in order to secure the background of their activities and endeavours, and to provide some basis for evaluation and judgement. First, then, the size of the cathedral priory. On the eve of the Black Death numbers stood just above 50; after a sharp drop to about 28 they rose to 40 within a decade, and for the next seventy years the average number was close to 45, with fluctuations ranging between 39 and 47. There follows a gap in statistical records for almost fifty years, but at the close of the fifteenth century there were 42 monks, and as late as 1534 there were 34 or 35. If we arbitrarily assume the monastic life span of the average monk after profession to be twenty years – and I have abundant evidence that this is a low estimate – we arrive at a total of about 450 professed monks of Ely during the two centuries between the 1330s and the Dissolution. If these calculations may be accepted as reasonably accurate, we may conclude that I have tracked down and entered to date about four-fifths of this number – some 370 – in my *Biographical Register*.[9] The fact that most of these monks were known by their toponymic provides us with the clue to their local origin and, although few of their relatives can be identified, it is safe to assume that their family backgrounds were undistinguished.

For my purposes in this present investigation there are two categories of Ely monk-students: those known to us by name and those whose names are not recorded; we shall need to scrutinise both. Of the named group at Cambridge there are 37, that is one monk in every ten among those entered in my register. This places Ely only just below Worcester which averaged one in nine; Norwich and Canterbury had a slightly higher record of about one in seven and one in eight respectively.[10] It has frequently been observed that few

9   For the *Register*, see note 1. These statistics are mainly compiled from the unprinted account rolls of the Ely chamberlain, CUL EDC 5/3/1-34 and CUL Add. MS 2957, fols 25-36; see J. Greatrex, 'Some Statistics of Religious Motivation', in *Religious Motivation*, Studies in Church History, 15 (1978), 179-86, pp. 182-3. For the first two centuries of its existence the population of the cathedral monastery had been considerably higher – there had been about 70 monks at the time of the creation of the bishopric and the reconstitution of the abbey as a cathedral priory in 1109 – but records of this period are sparse, with the result that only 170 names have so far come to light and the biographical details are few.

10   See my *Biographical Register* (note 1, above). This figure revises the position assigned to Ely in my article on the Norwich monk-students (note 1 above); at

monks remained at the university long enough to take a degree because the reasoning that lay behind the decision to send them in the first place, and to assume the financial burden which this necessitated, was not learning for learning's sake but for the practical purposes of instruction and preaching. At Norwich just over a third of the named monks obtained degrees; at Ely the number is over half: nineteen obtained degrees out of thirty-seven, which is astonishingly high. However, it should be pointed out that, if the number of unnamed Ely monks who spent short periods of study at Cambridge could be assessed or some of them identified, the ratio would no doubt be more in line with Norwich where over twice as many monk-students are known by name.[11]

As to the size of the group of anonymous students whose numbers as well as names have escaped us, it is possible to make some meaningful estimates as follows.[12] Of the accumulation of obedientiary accounts, which would have increased by thirteen each year (one for each of the major obedientiary offices, 2,600 in two centuries), there remains at least one account for about 165 of these 200 years. Many of them, regrettably, either make no reference to monk scholars or are too damaged to be legible; and some of them survive only in Bentham's eighteenth-century transcripts.[13] Nevertheless, by combining two factors – (1) the total number of years during which both named and unnamed monk-scholars occur and (2) the total number of years during which the twenty graduates must have been at the university in order to comply with academic requirements (allowing six to seven years for a first degree and ten for a doctorate) – we may conclude that there were probably fewer than 30 years in the two centuries when no Ely monk was at Cambridge.[14]

Contributions toward the expenses of the monk-students were shared among the Ely obedientiaries, as was also the case at Norwich. They consisted of regular payments that went to make up an annual pension, which in 1363 the provincial chapter set at £15 plus travelling expenses for each monk; but none of the Ely accounts provide sufficient detail for corroboration of this

that time I was not aware of the comparatively late arrival of Ely on the university scene.

[11] Greatrex, 'Monk Students from Norwich', esp. pp. 579–83 where 82 Norwich names are listed, 29 of them with degrees.

[12] It is not possible, however, to deduce numbers of monk-students from entries on the account rolls where the abbreviation is *scol*'.

[13] These transcripts are in CUL Add. MSS 2950, 2956, 2957.

[14] However, there are many pitfalls. What for example, are we to make of these two statements on two accounts of the year 1483/4: the precentor made a contribution of 22½d. to two scholars, but the granator reported no payment to scholars because there were none, CUL EDC 5/4/7, 5/9/9.

amount.[15] There were also some payments for particular needs such as clothing, as well as occasional gifts. Some of the pension contributions were allocated according to a predetermined rate which may have varied from year to year and must have been calculated on the basis of the income of the individual obedientiary office. For example, the cellarer paid John de Bekkles *pro generali* for an eight-month period in 1341 and 1342 at the rate of 3½*d.* per week (9*s.* ½*d.*) and in addition another 8*s.* ½*d.* based on a levy of ½*d.* in the £.[16] Obedientiaries sometimes specified the particular purpose for which their contribution was intended; John Feltwell received 37*s.* 10*d.* from the treasurer for bread and ale in 1423/4, when he was described as the 'third scholar' at Cambridge. The other two scholars between them were paid £8 4*s.* 2*d.*[17] Inceptions proved to be costly occasions, when the monk–graduate was expected to provide a feast for the regents and other university dignitaries; at such times the obedientiaries came to the rescue with offerings in cash and kind. Roger de Norwich I and Edmund de Totyngton were two such recipients of the generosity of their brethren, who rallied round to support them on their day of academic triumph. In 1383/4 Roger de Norwich I received 13*s.* 4*d.* from the chamberlain and 20*s.* from the cellarer, who also gave a further sum of 10*s.* as a gift (*exhennium*); and for the feast itself 260 rabbits were sent up from the priory warrens at Lakenheath. Only one detail of Edmund de Totyngton's inception in 1396/7 has been preserved, namely that the precentor contributed two eels costing 16*d.* for the feast.[18]

Other interesting facts concerning those Ely monk students who are identified by name can be extracted from the sources provided that we confine ourselves, as already noted, to posing questions capable of being answered. Among these I suggest the following: at what age and at what stage of their monastic life were Ely monks sent to Cambridge, what evidence is there as to length of stay for both graduates and non-graduates, and to what offices were they assigned on their return?

There is a clearly discernible policy with regard to the most appropriate time to send the chosen monks to university; it can be determined fairly accurately on the basis of an examination of the known dates of admission to the priory and of the dates of ordination to minor and major orders. The general pattern during the two centuries seems to have shown little change: the monks who were considered suitable for further studies were sent up to

15 *Chapters of the Black Monks*, II, p. 78.
16 CUL EDC 5/2/7, 8, CUL Add. MS 2957, fol. 3.
17 CUL EDC 5/13/12, CUL Add. MS 2957, fol. 73.
18 CUL EDC 7/15/acct, CUL Add. MS 2957, fol. 46. The provincial chapter had decreed in 1343 that a grant of £20 should be made for inception expenses from the common fund for theologians and 20 marks for canon lawyers, *Chapters of the Black Monks*, II, p. 23.

Cambridge either a year or two before or shortly after their ordination to the priesthood, at which time, we may presume, they were between 22 and 25 years of age. By then they had spent an average of four or five years in the monastery, for, although few admission or profession dates have survived at Ely, these were generally coincident with or followed almost immediately by ordination as acolyte or subdeacon.[19] In this initial period these novices or juniors would have been required to learn to take their part in the divine office and to become familiar with monastic routine as well as with the Benedictine Rule and customs. They would also have been required to study under a senior monk or lector in order to prepare themselves for later responsibility in the form of teaching and preaching, and in some cases further study. Surviving Ely sources have preserved only a meagre scrap of evidence about the claustral studies of the young monks in the form of recorded payments to Roger de Norwich I, a Cambridge graduate to whom reference has already been made. When dates of ordination and commencement of study are both unknown some doubt remains, but even in many of these cases the outline of the general pattern suggests itself. John de Sutton II, Henry de Madyngle and Walter de Walsoken are among the typical examples of the prevailing policy. Sutton was sent up a year or two after his ordination to the priesthood, while Madyngle had very likely been allowed to begin his university studies some time in the three years during which he remained a deacon; Walsoken was probably at Cambridge shortly before being ordained priest.[20] In the later fifteenth and early sixteenth century monk-deacons, and occasionally subdeacons, are found more frequently at the university; Robert Colville, later prior, provides an example among Ely monks, but he had been in the monastery for at least three or four years.[21] The length of the study

---

[19] Profession was usually one year after admission and clothing in the monastic habit. Intervals between the four ordinations varied between a few weeks and several years.

[20] Sutton was ordained priest in September 1421 and by 1423/4 was a student at Cambridge, CUL EDR G/1/3 (Reg. John Fordham), fol. cix^v; CUL EDC 5/13/12; Madyngle's priesting occurred in April 1408 and he was at Cambridge the following year, CUL EDR G/1/3 (Reg. Fordham), fol. 247; CUL EDC 5/2/29; Walsoken's ordination took place in September 1338, CUL EDR G/1/1 (Reg. Simon de Montacute), fol. 102; and he was receiving a student's pension this same year, CUL EDC 5/3/4.

[21] Colville was tonsured, but perhaps not yet clothed as a monk in 1463, ordained acolyte three years later and deacon in 1469, the year he left for Cambridge, CUL EDR G/1/5 (Reg. William Gray), fols 210v, 211, 214; CUL EDC 5/13/-. John Pynchbeke of Winchester Cathedral Priory was at Oxford a few months before being ordained deacon in 1477, *Compotus Rolls of the Obedientiaries of St Swithun's Priory, Winchester*, ed. G. W. Kitchin, Hampshire Record Society 7 (London, 1892), p. 456; his ordination as deacon is in Hampshire Record Office, A1/14

period allowed varied greatly and seems to have followed no fixed pattern. Moreover, Ely monk-students tended to be more subject to interruptions – during which they were recalled to assume responsibilities in the cloister – than monk-students of other cathedral priories. Simon de Banham, for example, is known to have been at Cambridge over a twelve-year period, probably intermittently, before his inception in 1366; John Feltwell's studies spanned some fourteen years in the 1420s and 1430s; and John de Yaxham was trekking back and forth between Ely and Cambridge for about seventeen years beginning in the mid-1390s.[22] The occupations of this group of long-term students during their periods at home in the cloister will be considered in conjunction with their later careers in office. Another group represented by John Fyncham and John de Hatfeld were given only a year or two before being recalled for good.[23] There were also some monks who were allowed longer periods of study but do not appear to have proceeded to a degree.

In this last group there are at least six whose known lengths of stay at Cambridge would have been sufficient for them to have graduated as bachelors. John de Bekkles and Walter de Walsoken are two of these, who are entered on the surviving account rolls as students between 1337 and 1343; they are the two earliest students known by name and were presumably among the first to take up residence in Crauden's Hostel. In their case we have details of the actual length of some of their periods of residence; for example, Bekkles spent at least eight or nine months of the year in Cambridge for at least three of these years, while Walsoken, who was studying canon law, spent six months in Cambridge in 1339/40 and nine months in 1343, further evidence of part-time studies. These two were joined by a third monk, John de Sautre, in 1339/40, who pursued his course of study during the next seven or eight years. Edmund de Thomeston received grants as a student between 1389/90 and 1396/7 but may well have arrived at Cambridge at an earlier date as he had been ordained priest in 1380. John Ward's university career in the

(Reg. William Waynflete), II, fol. 178v. Anthony Wotton of Christ Church Canterbury, was at Oxford and a subdeacon at the time of his death in 1508, Pantin, *Canterbury College, Oxford*, I, pp. 87–8.

22 Banham was at Cambridge in 1354/5, *Sacrist Rolls of Ely*, ed. F. R. Chapman, 2 vols (Cambridge, 1907), II, p. 167; his inception is entered on CUL EDC 5/4/14a and 5/3/15. Feltwell was third scholar in 1423/4, CUL EDC 5/13/12 and obtained his B.Th. in 1436/7, CUL Add. MS 2957, fol. 31. The earliest and latest dates of Yaxham's study period at Cambridge are in CUL EDC 5/13/10 and *The Register of Henry Chichele, Archbishop of Canterbury 1414–1443*, ed. E. F. Jacob, 4 vols, Canterbury and York Society, 43, 45–7 (Oxford, 1937–47), IV, pp. 126–7.

23 CUL EDC 5/2/29 (1409/10 for Fyncham) and 5/9/6 (1371/2 for Hatfeld) are the only references.

early sixteenth century spanned at least ten years (1518/19 to 1528/9), the treasurer's payments to him suggesting that he too was resident in Cambridge for only part of the year.[24]

A few individual case studies, followed by some pertinent comments on the small group of university-trained priors and on the attractions of canon law, should prepare the background for an answer to the final question regarding post-university office-holding and occupations. Henry de Madyngle, already mentioned, will provide the first example. He made his profession before Prior William Powcher in November 1404, was ordained acolyte the following month, and in April 1408 Bishop Fordham ordained him to the priesthood. The earliest record of his having been sent to Cambridge occurs during the next year, but since his university studies continued until his inception in theology in 1416/17 it is possible that he actually first went up c.1406/7 while still a deacon. If so, he may have had only three preliminary years in the community before his departure for Cambridge.[25] Madyngle was a younger contemporary of Edmund de Walsingham, a future prior, who had been priested in 1402 and had perhaps begun his studies a few years before Madyngle; they both incepted in the same year, a heavy financial burden for the Ely chapter. Walsingham stayed on at Cambridge for another year but then returned to Ely on account of his election as prior (1418–1425). It is not surprising to learn that later on during his priorate, very likely at about the time when the provincial chapter was establishing a common house of study for monks in Cambridge, he was consulted by the presidents who requested him to nominate a *prior studentium* for the Benedictines, now at last to be under one roof.[26]

Robert Colville, another future prior (1500–10), entered the priory around 1463–5 while still in his teens and was selected for study at Cambridge some five or six years later, either just before or shortly after his ordination to the diaconate. However, his stay appears to have been brief since, by 1473, the year of his receiving priest's orders, it must have been decided that his talents lay elsewhere, for he was back in the cloister and had resumed the organ

---

[24] For Bekkles and Walsoken see CUL EDC 5/3/4, 5/2/6, 7 and 8, 5/3/6a, and for Sautre see also 5/3/10. Thomeston's study period is recorded on CUL EDC 5/13/8, 10, and Ward's on CUL EDC 5/3/34, 5/13/18–20, CUL Add. MS 2957, fols 75, 79, 80.

[25] Madyngle's profession and ordination dates are in CUL EDR G/1/3 (Reg. Fordham), fols 198v, 244, 247; his known Cambridge dates extend from 1409/10 to 1416/17, CUL EDC 5/2/29, 5/3/29.

[26] Walsingham was ordained priest by Bishop Fordham, CUL EDR G/1/3, fol. 242. He was elected prior before 25 July 1418, CUL EDC 7/8/3 (court roll), and was consulted about the *prior studentium* in 1423 x 1426, *Chapters of the Black Monks*, III, p. 102.

studies which he had begun the year after his admission.[27]

William Wells II, a third prior-to-be (1430–60), and, like Edmund Walsingham, elected while still at Cambridge, arrived at Ely priory at an unknown date before 7 June 1419, the day of his ordination as acolyte. He must have been at the time 19 or 20, as by September of that year he was in deacon's orders. Four years later (1423/4) he and John Sutton II were at Cambridge receiving maintenance of £8 4s. 2d. from the treasurer, and in 1428/9 the two were provided with £6 17s. 6d. These amounts, barely half of the £15 sum laid down by the provincial chapter, require comment. While it remains unknown in the case of these two monk-students, and of the others, what total contributions would have been forthcoming, it appears from the surviving evidence that the sums paid by other obedientiaries were small and taken together would not have matched the treasurer's payment. Thus, it is reasonable to suggest that these monks were in attendance at Cambridge for only part of the year. Since William Wells II obtained a first degree in canon law about 1430 he had probably begun his studies by or before 1423/4 (the first year in which he was recorded as a student), especially if these studies were only part-time. He was given permission to continue towards a higher degree, but his academic career came to an abrupt end with his election as prior within the year, when he was probably only in his early thirties. The university authorities saw fit to fine him £40 'quia non continuavit lecturam suam in iure canonico post admiscionem suam ad gradum baculariatus'.[28]

Finally, the later stages of Roger de Norwich I's university career deserve notice. Although his academic pursuits seem to have been interrupted while he served a term in the office of almoner, he was allowed to resume his studies and to proceed to a higher degree in 1384/5. Contributions to his inception expenses, including the feast at which the guests were served roast or perhaps stewed Lakenheath rabbit, came not only from the gifts previously mentioned but also through procurations paid over a three-year period by the same obedientiaries. The prior and chapter gave Norwich leave to continue his studies; there were further contributions from the chamberlain and granator *pro regencia sua*, and in 1389/90 from the treasurer who provided him with a maintenance grant of 36s. 7d. and described him as *legens in theologia*. During these years he was also giving instruction to the juniors.[29]

---

27 See note 21 above. Colville's organ studies are recorded on CUL EDC 5/9/8, 5/13– (1473/4).

28 Wells was ordained acolyte and deacon by Bishop Fordham, CUL EDR G/1/3, fols 272, 272v; his presence at Cambridge is recorded on CUL EDC 5/13/12 and Public Record Office SC6/1257/4; his fine occurs in CUL Cambridge Univ. Reg. 1.2.1.

29 He served as almoner in 1377/8, CUL EDC 5/1/10; his inception is entered in CUL Add. MS 2957, fol. 35, CUL EDC 7/15/acct; his regency is in CUL EDC

Among the Ely monk-graduates there are eight doctors of theology, or *sacre pagine professores* as they were often called. Although there appear to have been no doctors of canon law, half of the monks who attained first degrees did so in canon law, and one, John Cottenham, achieved both degrees: B.Cn.L and B.Th., the former in 1505/6 and the latter some eight years later, in 1513/14, when he was granted the grace to proceed towards inception in theology. He seems to have had more than his fair share of university education over about twenty years, possibly more, although there were interruptions while he held office in the priory. In 1516 his brethren brought his studies to an end by choosing him as their prior.[30]

The two unusual instances of Ely monks being elected priors while still students are not sufficient – even with the addition of two others, the previously mentioned Robert Colville and John Cottenham – to allow us to conclude that the community of St Etheldreda displayed a marked preference for university-educated priors. While the Canterbury and Durham cathedral chapters tended to choose university graduates in the fifteenth and sixteenth centuries, at Ely, of the eleven priors during its last 140 years only four were graduates; the proportion of graduates among the priors of Norwich in this period is slightly higher than Ely and that of Worcester, surprisingly, lower.[31]

There is probably some explanation for the surprising emphasis on, or popularity of, canon law studies which attracted a third of the graduates at Ely; at Norwich the number was less than a quarter and at Worcester there were none. Pantin pointed out that canon law was less exacting than theology and suited practical men of affairs such as, for example, Prior Thomas Chillenden of Christ Church, Canterbury.[32] Moreover, William Courtenay claims to have found that by the end of the fourteenth century there had been a shift at Cambridge away from theology towards law; but it seems somewhat unlikely that this popular preference would have had much impact on Benedictine study patterns.[33] From the surviving evidence at Ely there is no clear indication that the monk-lawyer's training was put to practical use on his return to the cloister, but it is conceivable that the programme of studies

---

5/13/8 and his post as instructor in CUL EDC 5/3/21, 23.

[30] For Cottenham's degrees see the entry in A. B. Emden, *A Biographical Register of the University of Cambridge to 1500* (Cambridge, 1963), which did not locate many of the obscure manuscript references to Ely monks.

[31] These were Edmund Walsingham (*c.*1418–24), William Wells (1430–61), John Cottenham (1516–22) and Robert Wells or Steward (1522–40). In addition there was one more, Robert Colville, already named, who studied for a year or two at Cambridge, but was no longer young when elected.

[32] Pantin, *Canterbury College Oxford*, IV, p. 63.

[33] W. J. Courtenay, *Schools and Scholars in Fourteenth-Century England* (Princeton, 1987), p. 52.

for a degree in canon law at Cambridge was more suitable for those who were only able to be present on a part-time basis. Of course, it may be that this remarkably high percentage of canon law graduates known at Ely results from the chance survival of medieval documents; but the marked contrast with the other cathedral priories renders it likely that in this respect Ely was different.

There has never been any doubt that, although the monastic horarium, centred on the daily mass and office, took precedence, Benedictines held study and learning in high regard and stressed the practical fruits of teaching and preaching. Sufficient evidence of both these activities exists at Worcester and elsewhere to allow us to presume that the same was true for Ely, although only two instances of monastic preaching survive, both within the university setting. In May 1415 Archbishop Chichele licensed four Ely monk-students to preach in any church appropriated to Ely Cathedral. I assume that this refers to churches in or near Cambridge, St Andrew's for example, of which the sacrist was patron.[34] These preaching assignments would have served a two-fold practical purpose to the benefit both of the young monks themselves who needed experience and of those responsible for providing preachers. In addition, Cambridge church-goers who listened attentively to these young homilists in training might also have benefited from the freshness of their exegesis. The other example is that of Richard Swaffham, monk-student in the 1470s and 1480s until his inception as D.Th. in 1486/7; he was appointed to give the Palm Sunday sermon on 4 April 1479 in Ely Cathedral, and in the year in which he obtained his doctorate he was called upon to preach in the cathedral both on Good Friday and on Easter Day (13 and 15 April 1487).[35] At Worcester, the precentor was charged with the travelling costs of monks returning from Oxford to preach on major feasts, but at Ely any similar expense would have been minimal; for this reason, we may assume, there were few payments to record, and therefore fewer records to provide evidence for the historian.

Evidence gathered from cathedral priories has revealed the outline of a discernible pattern of office-holding among the university-trained monks upon their return to the cloister. It has appeared that they were seldom, if ever, given the chief administrative positions like those of treasurer/bursar, cellarer or sacrist. At Worcester, Norwich and Canterbury, for example, the returning monks seem to have been less frequently burdened with the offices which controlled finance and administration, or those which had the responsibility of procuring provisions for the house or of supervising building construction and renovation; they tended to be appointed to serve as

---

34 These were Henry de Madyngle, Edmund de Walsingham, John de Yaxham and John de Stunteney, *Reg. Henry Chichele*, IV, p. 126.

35 For his inception see the entry in Emden, *Biographical Register, Cambridge*; his preaching assignments are in CUL EDC 5/10/36, 40.

precentors (librarians), subpriors and penitentiaries, and in the case of Durham and Norwich as priors of the outlying cells. Although here again one must be aware of the traps set by chance survival, the Ely pattern proves to be an exception. Examples will serve to illustrate both the trends and the problems.

A glance at the monastic 'career' of Thomas de Dounham I after attaining his B.Cn.L. *c.*1380/2, shows that, in addition to being licensed by the bishop as a penitentiary in the city and diocese of Ely and as confessor to the nuns at Chatteris, he served for some years in the demanding role of almoner and for at least six months in that of cellarer. Henry de Madyngle was appointed to the important post of land steward (*senescallus terrarum*) shortly after his return to Ely with his D.Th., in 1419/20, while Edmund de Totyngton, also D.Th., served for several years as sacrist (and *custos operum* at Ely) following his inception in 1396/7.[36] Almost immediately upon his return, John Feltwell (B.Th., 1436/7) was given the office of land steward for a term of two years, followed by three years as sacrist and finally an appointment as subprior, while John Soham (B.Cn.L. by 1444) served successively as treasurer, granator, sacrist, infirmarer, land steward and subprior.[37] Thomas Wells II had a series of assignments both before and after his B.Cn.L. The date of his commencement at Cambridge is unknown, but, since his studies were intermittent, he probably made his first appearance as a student soon after his ordination to the priesthood in 1458. Between that date and his *introitum* in canon law in 1473/4, he was in charge of the Ely estates as land steward for two periods of two years each (1462/4, 1467/9) and for one year served as *custos* of the Lady Chapel (1466/7). The year of his degree he was precentor, two years later feretrar, followed by another four- or five-year stint as land steward.[38] These examples lend further weight to the prevalence of part-time

---

[36] Dounham was B.Cn.L. before 19 September 1383, CUL EDR G/1/2 (Reg. Thomas Arundel), fol. 48, penitentiary, *ibid.*, fol. 46, confessor, CUL EDR G/1/3 (Reg. Fordham), fol. 189v; his office holding is in CUL EDC 5/1/11, and CUL EDR G/1/3 (Reg. Fordham), fols 189v, 192. Madyngle's office of land steward is recorded in CUL EDC 5/2/30. For Totyngton as sacrist see *Calendar of Papal Registers: Papal Letters* (London, 1893–), *1396–1404*, p. 506, CUL EDC 5/10/24–6, CUL Add. MS 2956, fols 165, 166.

[37] Feltwell's offices are in CUL 7/15/acct, 7/16/34 (land steward); CUL Add. MS 2956, fol. 168, Add. MS 2950, fol. 76, CUL EDC 5/10/34 (sacrist); CUL EDR G/1/5 (Reg. Gray), fol. 46v (sacrist and subprior). The first reference to each of Soham's offices in chronological order is as follows: CUL EDC 5/12/5 (treasurer); EDC 5/4/37 (granator); CUL EDR G/1/5 (Reg. Gray), fol. 46v (sacrist); CUL EDC 5/13– (infirmarer; 1465/6), CUL EDC 5/13– (land steward, 1473/4), CUL EDR G/1/5 (Reg. Gray), fol. 80v.

[38] Wells was ordained priest by Bishop Gray, CUL EDR G/1/5, fol. 205; land steward and *custos* of the Lady Chapel, CUL EDC 5/4/40–42; CUL Add. MS

study and also to the advantage of naming a deputy or *socius* for all the obedientiaries, a custom which, in the form in which it is recorded on the heading of almost every account roll, seems peculiar to the Ely obedientiary system.

It is true that Ely monk-students on their recall from university are often found as penitentiaries, precentors and subpriors like their counterparts at other cathedral priories; and like them they were frequently named as proctors to carry out various legal and financial negotiations, to represent the prior and chapter at Convocation and to attend the triennial provincial chapters in Northampton. This last duty was frequently assigned to the Norwich and Worcester monk-students at Oxford, who are noted by Pantin in the useful list found in his *Chapters of the English Black Monks*, where, however, there are no references to Ely. To his list we may now add five Ely monks, all university students at the time or previously: John Yaxham was sent to Northampton in 1429; Thomas Wells II went with one of the eleven or twelve John Elys, probably VIII, in 1474; and Thomas Wells II and Richard Swaffham were there in 1477.[39]

This abundance of biographical detail of the Ely monks' later careers has been presented in order to highlight what is surely a striking contrast to the pattern already observed in other cathedral priories. At Ely, it has become clear that monks returned to play a full part in the day-to-day running of the priory and shared the weight of administrative responsibility with their brethren who had remained in the cloister. This fact suggests that Ely was a more integrated community than, say, Norwich, where there are signs of a division between sixteenth-century university and non-university monks.[40] The difference may be related to the geographical proximity of Cambridge to Ely in contrast to the long distance between Norwich and Oxford. Ely monks' absences from the community and community life were, it seems, never long enough to cause problems, and some monk-students had to interrupt their studies at Cambridge in order to assume office, while, no doubt, trying to keep up their reading at home until they were released from their duties and allowed to return.

There are several conclusions that may be drawn from these investigations. First, the reiteration of an earlier general remark that there is no substitute for what are sometimes described as 'in depth' studies. Secondly, that these have revealed that Ely should now be added to David Knowles's list of the religious houses most assiduous in their academic service in the

---

2957, fol. 62; precentor, CUL EDC 5/13/– (1473/4); feretrar, CUL EDC 5/11/7; land steward again, CUL EDC 5/13/16, 5/10/36, 7/15/acct.

[39] PRO SC6/1257/4, Yaxham; CUL EDC 5/13– (1473/4), Wells and Ely; CUL EDC 5/13/16, Wells and Swaffham.

[40] Greatrex, 'Norwich Monk Students', p. 578.

university setting, since we have found that, with relatively few exceptions, almost every year during the two centuries before the Dissolution saw two or three, and occasionally even four, monk-students at Cambridge. Moreover, Ely monks were not hampered, as Knowles assumed, by a university education which made them overqualified and unfit to assume office in the cloister; and his fear that the unity of the common life would be broken by periods of study leave at university seems, for Ely at least, to have been unfounded.[41] There is another aspect to be taken into account, which should not escape our notice through lack of factual evidence, namely, the unknown consequences of the monk-students' contacts with contemporary Cambridge students, and the lasting friendships that must have developed between some of them to the enrichment of the lives of both. Finally, there is the striking fact that Ely had a remarkably high proportion of university graduates of whom one third obtained degrees in canon law.

In conclusion, at Ely and elsewhere, as it has frequently been remarked, there are no visible signs that the two centuries of adherence to the educational directives of Benedict XII, implemented by the English Benedictine chapter, produced any brilliant monastic teachers or preachers or led to the breaking of new ground in original scholarship. Without tangible results there are no means of measuring intellectual activity and so evaluating the effect of this long-standing university connection. However, the enduring fidelity to this tradition may be regarded in itself as a kind of sign, notably when it receives endorsement from other sources that indicate rejuvenation and new growth. At Ely the latter can be perceived in the mid-1530s by the presence of four monk-students at Cambridge, at least three of whom were being supported simultaneously by a community numbering only about 35;[42] and at the same time by the presence of new life in this community with the recent profession of ten young novices and juniors.[43] Forced to submit to their sudden and unexpected demise by Henry VIII and Cromwell, the Benedictines were prevented from adapting to the new world of which those monks in the university setting of lively debate and exchange would probably have been among the first to become aware. The monastic influence on society at large had been on the wane through the later fourteenth and the fifteenth centuries and intimations of resurgence among the Benedictines in the sixteenth century were short-lived. What they might have done had they been allowed to survive would have surely reflected the aims of the successive

---

[41] David Knowles, *The Religious Orders in England*, 3 vols (Cambridge, 1948–59), II, pp. 18–19, 355, 359.

[42] These were Robert Hamond, Robert Skelsyn, Thomas Wilberton and William Wisbech, CUL EDC 5/10/33, CUL Add. MS 2957, fol. 81.

[43] The last ten names listed on the visitation return in September [1534] were not yet priests, CUL EDR G/1/7 (Reg. Thomas Goodrich), fol. 90v.

generations of monks, who had perseveringly striven to pass on the goals and fruits of a learning which had been sustained and guided by, while remaining subordinate to, the monastic life of prayer.

Appendix

Ely Monks at Cambridge

Note: the few entries marked * are noted in Emden, *Biographical Register ... Cambridge to 1500*, but some of these need to be supplemented by my *Biographical Register* (see footnote 1). References have been omitted here because some have been provided in the text and accompanying footnotes, and the remainder are available in my *Biographical Register*. Earliest recorded dates are given and some have been calculated on the basis of a degree obtained.

Simon de Banham, between 1354/5 and 1366 when he incepted D.Th.

John de Bekkles, between 1337/8 and 1343.

Robert Colville, in 1469/70.

*John Cottenham, between *c*.1491 and 1513/14; in 1505/6 he was granted B.Cn.L. and by 1513/14 had obtained a B.A., and was given grace to proceed towards inception in theology.

Thomas de Dounham I, between 1371/2 and 19 Sept. 1383 when he was described as B.Cn.L.

*John Ely VIII (?alias Ingram), described as B.Th., *tempore* Prior Henry Peterborough, 1462 x 1478.

John Feltwell, between 1423/4 and 1436/7 when he was named as B.Th.

*John Fyncham, in 1409/10.

Robert Hamond, between 1528/9 and 1535/6.

John de Hatfeld, in 1371/2.

Thomas de Lincoln, in 1347/8.

*Henry de Madyngle, between 1409/10 (or probably earlier) and 1416/17 when he incepted D.Th. or D.Cn.L.

[Peter] de Norwich II, incepted D.Th. by 1364/5; the Christian name is absent.

*Roger de Norwich I, incepted D.Th. in 1384/5, went on to do his regency and was still at Cambridge in 1389/90.
    Note: there is sufficient evidence to make it clear that these two monks are distinct.

Richard Overton, in 1510/11.

John de Sautre, between 1339/40 and 1347/8.

John Skelsyn (or Skyle), between 1532/3 and c.1534/5.

*John Soham I, before 1455 when he was described as *bacularius*; in a later reference this is amplified by *in decretis*.

John Stretham I, in 1420/1.

John Stunteney, in 1415.

John Sutton II, between 1423/4 and 1436/7; he incepted D.Th. in 1435/6.

[John de Swaffham, incepted D.Th. in 1289/90, probably at Oxford.]

*Richard Swaffham, between c.1476/7 and 1486/7 when he incepted D.Th.

*John Swanton, in 1420.

Edmund de Thomeston, between 1389/90 and 1396/7.

Edmund de Totyngton, between 1389/90 and 1396/7 when he incepted D.Th.; he was probably a student by c.1386/7.

*Edmund Walsingham, probably between c.1406/7 and 1416/17 when there are references to his *introitum* and his *inceptionem*.

Walter de Walsoken, between 1337/8 and 1343; his studies were in canon law.

John Ward, between 1518/19 and 1528/9.

Geoffrey de Wellington, between c.1400 and 1407/8 when he was admitted B.Cn.L.

Robert Wells, between 1510/11 and c.1522; in 1520 he was described as M.A.

*Thomas Wells II, between c.1466/7 and 1473/4 when he was admitted B.Cn.L.

*William Wells II, between 1423/4 and 1430 when he was described as B.Cn.L.

Thomas Wilberton (alias Outlaw), between 1535/6 and 1539.

William Wisbech, between 1535/6 and 1539.

Laurence Wittlesey, between 1523/4 and 1527/8.

John de Yaxham, between 1396/7 and 1415; he was admitted B.Cn.L. at an unknown date.

Priory and Parish: Kirkham and its Parishioners 1496–7

JANET BURTON

Kirkham Priory was one of the first generation of Augustinian houses to be founded in the north of England, being established *c*.1122 by Walter Espec, lord of Helmsley. Espec is perhaps more famous for a later foundation, the Cistercian abbey some miles away at Rievaulx, but his earlier house became and remained the family monastery of his heirs, the Ros family. A number of its members were buried in the priory church, and the family arms can be seen on the fine late thirteenth-century gatehouse there. Two 'foundation charters' for Kirkham – issued in fact a decade or two after the event – reveal that in common with many other Augustinian houses Kirkham numbered among its endowment several churches: the parish church of Kirkham itself, recorded in Domesday Book, which formed the nucleus of the new religious house, those of Helmsley, Kirbygrindalythe and Garton, and three churches on Espec's Northumberland estates.[1] To these were later added a moiety of the York churches of St Peter, Walmgate, and St Mary, Castlegate, and the churches of Crambe, Westow and Burythorpe.[2] An actum of Archbishop William FitzHerbert, which can be dated quite precisely to between April and June 1154, confirmed to the church of Holy Trinity, Kirkham, and the canons serving God there, *inter alia*, their Yorkshire churches: the parish church (*ecclesiam parrochiariam*) of Kirkham, and Helmsley, Garton, Kirbygrindalythe, and St Peter, Walmgate, with their possessions.[3] Papal

---

[1] The foundation charters of Kirkham are printed in *Cartularium Abbathiae de Rievalle*, ed. J. C. Atkinson, Surtees Society 83 (London, 1889), pp. 159–61, 243–5; on the problems of chronology connected with the early records of Kirkham, see D. Baker, 'Patronage in the Early Twelfth-Century Church: Walter Espec, Kirkham and Rievaulx', in *Traditio-Krisis-Renovatio aus theologischer Sicht: Festschrift Winfried Zeller*, ed. B. Jaspert and R. Mohr (Marburg, 1976), 92–100. For a discussion of the history of Kirkham see Janet Burton, *Kirkham Priory from Foundation to Dissolution*, University of York Borthwick Paper no. 86 (York, 1995).

[2] Oxford, Bodleian Library MS Fairfax 7 (15th-century cartulary of Kirkham, much abbreviated) fols 9r and 33r; see also the confirmation of Archbishop William FitzHerbert, below, note 3.

[3] *English Episcopal Acta, V: York 1070–1154*, ed. J. Burton (Oxford, 1988), no. 91,

confirmations were received from Celestine III (1198) and Innocent III (1199), which in addition gave licence for the appropriation of any or all of the churches named, and for them to be served either by canons of the priory, or suitable chaplains.[4] In the 1290s vicarages were established in the churches of Westow (*alias* St Mary *de Mora*, of the Moor), Garton, Kirbygrindalythe, Helmsley and Crambe,[5] and in May 1311 Archbishop Greenfield confirmed that Kirkham had indeed appropriated that group of churches in the vicinity of the priory.[6]

It is with two of these churches, the parish church of Kirkham which was part of the priory, and that of Westow, three-quarters of a mile to the south-east of the monastery, that this essay is concerned.[7] It is based on an examination of a cause paper, which contains documents generated by a case heard in 1496–7 by the officials of the consistory court of York.[8] The case concerned the claims and counterclaims of the churchwardens of Westow and the parishioners of the small hamlet known as Kirkham Roo or Raw, which lay outside the gates of Kirkham Priory.[9] It is clear from the charges brought by the inhabitants of Kirkham Roo that the churchwardens had been claiming that they were parishioners of Westow and therefore liable to contribute to the upkeep of the fabric of the church. They maintained, on the contrary,

pp. 72–4.

[4] The bulls are printed from the abbreviated versions in Bodleian, MS Fairfax 7, in *Papsturkunden in England*, ed. W. Holtzmann, 3 vols (Berlin, 1930–52), III, no. 294, pp. 416–17. Fuller texts appear in the cause paper which forms the basis of this paper: see below, note 8.

[5] Bodleian, MS Fairfax 7, fol. 15r–v.

[6] *The Register of William Greenfield, Lord Archbishop of York 1306–1315*, ed. W. Brown and A. Hamilton Thompson, 5 vols, Surtees Society 145, 149, 151–3 (London, 1931–40), III, pp. 196–7.

[7] The vicarage at Westow had been established by 23 May 1294, when Archbishop John le Romeyn instituted Stephen de Amunderby, priest, to the vicarage of St Mary on the Moor on the presentation of the prior and convent of Kirkham: *The Register of John Le Romeyn, Lord Archbishop of York 1286–1296*, ed. W. Brown, 2 vols, Surtees Society 123, 128 (London, 1913–17), I, p. 234.

[8] York, Borthwick Institute of Historical Research, Cause Paper CP F 307. My attention was first drawn to this cause paper a number of years ago by Professor David Smith, Director of the Borthwick Institute, and I would like to acknowledge his generous assistance in the preparation of the present paper.

[9] The English Place-Name Society volume for the East Riding does not record the name Kirkham Roo/Raw (*The Place-Names of the East Riding of Yorkshire and York*, English Place-Name Society 14 (Cambridge, 1937), pp. 143–4). The element *Raw* or *Roo* is recorded, however, meaning a hamlet. The name Kirkham Roo could refer to the village of Kirkham, which lies to the east of the priory, or it could signify a small settlement to the north, quite literally outside the gatehouse of the priory.

that they were parishioners of Kirkham, and used the nave of the conventual church as their parish church. The cause paper is extensive: it comprises copies of those archiepiscopal and papal confirmations to which reference has already been made, and which were produced in evidence; the allegations; a list of witnesses to be heard; and the depositions of over forty people whose evidence was given in the nave of Kirkham Priory on several dates between December 1496 and March 1497.[10] There is a mass of evidence, only portions of which can be touched on in this short paper. But it is clear that what we have gives a detailed picture of the parochial use of the priory, and relations between priory and parish, monastery and local society, in the last decade of the fifteenth century. I am going to concentrate on a few main themes: lay worship and the administering of the sacraments in the priory church; baptism, marriage and burial; the obligations of the Kirkham parishioners with respect to parts of the priory church; and finally the part played by the Augustinian canons of Kirkham in the cure of souls.

The starting point for this discussion, however, must be the one document which is earlier than the rest. On 11 March 1467/8, Thomas, prior of Kirkham, appeared before a notary public in his conventual church in order to exhibit an indenture sealed with the seal of John Dalton, chaplain, which contained a series of agreements between Dalton and the canons.[11] The prior remarked that he had had cause to exhibit the document on several occasions to maintain the rights of his monastery; and he now requested that it be copied into a public instrument by the notary who was present. The agreement stated that the prior and convent had, at the instance of Robert, eldest son and heir of Lord Ralph, baron of Greystoke,[12] appointed John Dalton, chaplain, as their assistant (*coadiutor*), to serve them in respect of the cure of souls of the inhabitants living outside the gates of the monastery *super lez pentez Raw*, administering the sacraments to them, and giving them burial.[13] Dalton was to hold this office for the term of his life unless he should

---

[10] There are three sets of depositions, only one of which is numbered. For convenience, I have designated the lists A, B and C, and give details below, as an appendix to this paper.

[11] The prior was Thomas Urton, or Irton (1462–70).

[12] Robert de Greystoke predeceased his father, dying in 1483. Ralph de Greystoke, Lord Greystoke and Lord FitzWilliam, died on 1 June 1487. His will, dated 27 May of the same year and proved on 30 July, requested that his body be buried in the chancel of Kirkham in the presence of the altar: Borthwick Institute, Reg. 23 (Reg. Rotherham), fol. 334r; see also *The Complete Peerage*, ed. V. Gibbs *et al.*, 13 vols (London, 1910–59), VI, pp. 197–9.

[13] I take *pentez* to be related to the word *pentis*, and variants, meaning 'shed, or lean-to added on to a building; a projection, sloping roof etc. ... to provide protection against the weather'; see *pentis* n., *Middle English Dictionary* (Ann Arbor, 1967–). *The English Dialect Dictionary*, ed. J. Wright, 6 vols (London,

resign or be promoted to another post. There followed detailed financial arrangements from which it appears that John Dalton's reward for his service was a small proportion of the offerings of the inhabitants and a clothing allowance. The added testimony of John Dalton – that there had been no coercion through force or fear or fraud – suggests that there was a history behind this agreement, and he ended by swearing that those who lived *super lez pentez Raw* outside the gates were as much parishioners of Kirkham as those who dwelt inside the monastery. The agreement was confirmed, as Prior Thomas requested, by John Akers, clerk of the diocese of Durham and notary public. The document, evidently produced in evidence in 1496–7, gives a foretaste of the dispute which was to erupt thirty years later.

The point at issue in the cause paper was not so much that the nave of the priory church was used by the laity. This seems not to have been in question, nor would it have been unusual; many abbey and priory churches were used by the laity, and it is quite clear from the documentary evidence that Kirkham had been a parish church before the establishment of the priory and that a parochial status had been retained. The question was rather: to which parish did the inhabitants of Kirkham Roo belong? In order to determine this, witnesses were asked to respond to a number of articles put forward by the proctor of the residents of Kirkham Roo against Thomas Nawton, James Nawton, Robert Sissotson, and John Wodcok, churchwardens of Westow. These were:

1. That there had been a parish church in the vill of Kirkham, within the conventual church, from time immemorial – twenty, thirty, forty, fifty, sixty years and more – and that it had been duly and legitimately constructed and dedicated.
2. That it had a baptismal font and a cemetery enclosure, and other attributes of a parish church.
3. That the inhabitants of Kirkham Roo and their predecessors were, from time immemorial, parishioners of Kirkham not Westow.
4. That they had a peaceful right to a resident parish priest to administer the sacraments.
5. That the charges (*onera*) from the inhabitants of Kirkham Roo and the rest of the parishioners of Kirkham were due to Kirkham not Westow; these were their obligations in respect of the repair of the nave of the parish church and its windows, lights, chalices and other ornaments, the provision of holy bread, the stipend of the parish clerk, and the maintenance of the cemetery enclosure.

1898–1905), IV, p. 471, also notes the sense of 'shed', or 'hut'.

6. That if, in the past, the inhabitants of Kirkham Roo had made any offerings to the vicar of Westow, the vicar had then shared them with the prior and convent as proprietors of Westow, and any such payments had moreover been made out of charity not obligation.

7. That the vicar of Westow was bound to account for all the offerings and other ecclesiastical oblations to the prior and convent as proprietors of the church.

8. That the inhabitants of Kirkham Roo and the other parishioners of Kirkham were not obliged to contribute to the repair of the nave of Westow nor to the provision of ornaments there.

9. That these matters were well known round and about.

There are depositions of forty-three individuals, all men, ranging in age, so they claimed, from 'about thirty-five' to seventy-three. Their testimony is, apart from odd words and phrases, recorded in Latin. Some of the depositions are incomplete, some survive in both draft and fair copy.[14] The witnesses were drawn, as would be expected, from a small geographical area. Eleven came from Crambe, eight from Westow, six from Whitwell, three from Malton, and individuals from Langton, Terrington, Helmsley, Firby in the parish of Westow, Menethorpe, Sand Hutton, Hutton on Derwent (High or Low Hutton), Howsham, Foston, Burythorpe and Barton. There is, at first sight, a surprising lack of witnesses from the community most closely involved, Kirkham itself, but this may be explained by the accident of survival. Among the papers there is a list of thirty-eight people who were evidently intended to be summoned as witnesses, but the testimony of only nineteen of them survives among the forty-three depositions, and several of those who were meant to be heard were inhabitants of Kirkham.[15] The witnesses divided in their opinions but the balance of those whose testimony has survived tipped in favour of Kirkham Roo, with twenty-five people agreeing with the propositions, compared with seventeen for the churchwardens of Westow and one apparently neutral.

Clearly the use of this kind of oral testimony presents problems. It relies on human memory rather than written evidence – although some documents were produced – and the witnesses were asked about the situation as it had been over many years. Some gave conflicting, although not necessarily irreconcilable, answers. However, there are a number of reasons why the evidence may be treated as reliable in its broad outline if not its detail. What we have here is the corporate memory of the community. It is clear that

---

14 See below, appendix.
15 In fact depositions from only two Kirkham witnesses, Henry Grane and William Towres, survive. This was clearly not a complete list of witnesses to be heard.

evidence was given in public, and there would have been ample opportunity for challenges to be made as to the identity, evidence, or partiality of those deposing.[16] The survival of the papers generated by this case enables us to observe relations between priory and parish and the interaction of monastery and local community in the later middle ages. Instead of merely stating that the nave of Kirkham had a parochial use, we can see something of the nature of that use. The case offers a vivid recreation of the lay community around the priory in that snapshot of history.

In response to the first question, about the parish church within the priory, some witnesses gave a yes/no/do-not-know answer. But others chose to be more expansive, and in so doing shed some light on the internal arrangements of the priory, the building itself. One or two stated that the parish church was built in honour of the Holy Trinity, the same dedication as the priory, and that it adjoined (*est adiuncta*) the conventual church.[17] William Towres of the parish of Kirkham revealed that within the nave there was an altar dedicated to the Blessed Virgin Mary, and it was there that he himself had married: 'ipse iuratus fuit nuptus ad dictam ecclesiam que est in naui ecclesie conuentualis ibidem ad altarem beate Marie virginis'. Henry Grane, aged 40, who said that he had lived at Kirkham within two miles of the priory since he was three years old, described how the parish church was divided from the conventual one by doors beneath the rood screen, 'divisa ab ecclesia conventuali per ostia sub lez rode'. William Adyson of Crambe used the same phrase, and added that for that reason it was deemed to be 'a palmesonday feld': 'navis ecclesie conventualis de Kyrkham, separata per ostia ab ecclesia conuentuali sub lez rode, est ecclesia parochialis de Kyrkham et sic fuit reputata a palmesonday feld ad presens de vera scientia sua'. The meaning of 'Palm Sunday field' is not absolutely clear, but Palm Sunday was one of the main feast days of the church's year when processions involving both clergy and people took place, and the allusion may be to the ritual during which they visited parts of the church and churchyard.[18] Other witnesses mentioned that the two doors below the rood had locks and keys, and could therefore be opened and closed at the will of the convent: 'ecclesia ... est disiuncta ab

---

[16] Some witnesses deposed that, on certain points, they agreed with previous witnesses, indicating that they had been present during their testimony. Moreover in one of the sets of depositions, list B, there is record that the witness was required to state whether he was an employee or tenant of the priory.

[17] E.g. the deposition of Roger Bell of Langton. In the extracts quoted from the depositions all contractions have been silently expanded.

[18] G. R. Owst, *Preaching in Medieval England* (Cambridge, 1926), pp. 199–200; D. M. Owen, *Church and Society in Medieval Lincolnshire*, History of Lincolnshire 5 (Lincoln, 1971, repr. 1981), p. 107. See also M. Rubin, *Corpus Christi: the Eucharist in Late Medieval Culture* (Cambridge, 1991), pp. 244–5.

ecclesia conuentuali quia sunt ostia que claudi & apperiri possunt cum voluerint'.[19] The nave evidently had a bell-tower, and this and the bells and bell-ropes were maintained by the offerings of the inhabitants.[20]

Monastic rectors of appropriated churches could do one of three things. They could serve the church by one of their own number; they could have a vicarage instituted, and appoint a vicar; or they could put in a stipendiary chaplain. Westow was appropriated and served by a vicar presented by the prior and convent. The agreement of 1468 makes it clear that at that point the canons had – for Kirkham – opted for the third choice: John Dalton was appointed as parochial chaplain to serve the cure of souls of those dwelling inside the monastery – the servants and corrodians – as well as in the hamlet. But was this always the case? There are some interesting comments. Roger Bell of Langton deposed that there was a parochial chaplain appointed by the prior, and that, except in the time of John Dalton, the custom had been for the chaplain to be a *religiosus*, a canon of the house. This would seem to have been confirmed by other witnesses, although one witness stated that John Dalton was preceded as chaplain by John Furster, vicar of Westow.[21] John Dalton then became vicar of Westow, and the depositions enable us to suggest the sequence of chaplains after him as Robert Semar, and the present chaplain, Stephen Rowley.[22] It would appear, then, that until the 1450s or 1460s a canon was responsible for the cure of souls. Then, according to a seventy-three year old from Firby, first John Furster then John Dalton was appointed chaplain by agreement with the prior for this reason: that the prior was unwilling for a canon to leave the cloister, 'eo quod prior noluit quod canonici sui exirent claustrum pro cura ministranda'.[23] Another witness went further and deposed

---

[19] See, for instance, the evidence of William Towres; also that of John Morley, which refers to the doors *sub clauibus et seris*.

[20] Testimony of Roger Bell and John Todde. William Adison of Crambe, however, maintained that the prior and convent repaired the bell tower and bells, and William Towres stated that it was the sacrist.

[21] Testimony of John Elwyn of Firby.

[22] William Towres stated that he had known Lord Robert Semar, parochial chaplain of Kirkham, for many years; Roger Bell mentioned Semar as chaplain in the time of Prior Urton (d.1470). Henry Grane and John Stevenson knew Robert Semar and then Stephen Rowley, parochial chaplains at the invitation of the prior; and William Adison confirmed that Rowley was chaplain at the present time (1497). Richard Syth, aged 70, said that for 40 years and more he had been confessed by Richard Colynson, canon of Kirkham, with licence from a certain Richard Bonsay, then parochial chaplain. It is not certain where he fits into the sequence, but it is probable that the chaplains were: Richard Bonsay (?c.1455), John Furster, John Dalton (before 1467), Robert Semar (between 1468 and 1470) and Stephen Rowley (1496–7).

[23] Deposition of John Elwyn.

that this was because of the plague, 'quia pestis tunc fuit'. Yet another was even more explicit: there was a plague and the prior was unwilling that canons should minister to outsiders 'lest they infect the whole convent', 'eo quod pestis erat et noluit quod canonici sui ministrarent ne inficerent totum conventum'.[24]

A further detail about the spiritual provision made by the priory for its parishioners, not mentioned in the agreement of 1468 but emerging from the depositions, is that there was a chapel at the gates of the priory. This was described by John Eleson and others as *extra portas prioratus*, and by William Towres as *super lez Kirkham Roo*. William Marshall, aged fifty-one, stated that the inhabitants of Kirkham Roo heard mass there every feast day at least, and that a canon of the priory celebrated there at the will of the prior. However, his testimony may be compared with that of John Eleson of Whitwell, aged sixty, who maintained that the parochial chaplain celebrated there daily and distributed holy bread and water weekly. It was claimed that the villagers maintained the chapel, except for the choir which was the responsibility of the prior. We are given no clue as to how long the chapel had been there, but John Eleson suggested a reason for its construction: lest the parishioners, gathered in the parish church, that is the nave, should by their tumult impede the canons in the performance of their services: 'dicit quod hoc fit ibidem ne parochiani in ecclesia parochiali viz naui ecclesie conuentualis congregati per tumultum impedirent canonicos in seruicio suo'.

The chapel is mentioned in other contexts, sometimes in connection with the activities of the parish clerk. This was another test of parochial status, and thus a point of dispute, since it was one of the contentions of the Westow party that their parish clerks visited Kirkham Roo to carry out their functions. Some witnesses stated that the inhabitants of Kirkham had their own parish clerk to whom they paid a stipend; one was able to name William Cowper as parish clerk of Kirkham for over thirty years.[25] John Eleson of Whitwell and others further stated that the inhabitants gave holy bread weekly at the chapel outside the gates of the priory, and this seems to be a

---

[24] Deposition of Robert Ecclesfeld, aged 48, and Robert Marshall of Crambe, 66.

[25] Roger Bell, Robert Ecclesfeld, Thomas Newton, vicar of Crambe, and John Eleson all testified that the inhabitants of Kirkham Roo had their own parish clerk; cf. the testimony of John Spynk of Malton, and of John Spynk of Westow, who claimed that when he was about 12 he had been taught by Richard Clerc, the parish clerk of Westow, and had accompanied him to Kirkham on the eve of St Nicholas and saw him receive the customary dues of a parish clerk. John Watson said that his own father had been parish clerk of Westow, and that when he was aged about 6, he had gone to Kirkham with his father on the feast of St Nicholas to collect the parish dues, and had carried the holy bread for Kirkham *super dorso suo*.

reference to the distribution of the Holy Loaf – a lay version of the Eucharist – which generally took place after the Sunday mass.[26] Another parish custom alluded to briefly is the *somergame*, the summer festival or entertainment.[27] William Smorgyng of Westow, who supported the contention that the inhabitants of Kirkham Roo – or some of them – attended the parish church of Westow and paid their offerings there, attested that the parishioners of Westow 'kept the summergame', *seruabant lez somergame*, in the chapel of Kirkham and *super lez Kirkham Roo*. Thomas Botrell of Menethorpe agreed, but maintained that this was for the support of the church of Westow.[28]

What the evidence seems to suggest is a gradual separation of priory and parish. Until the mid-fifteenth century the lay community within and outside the priory precinct was apparently served by one of the canons, though we cannot assume that this had been the case consistently through the centuries. After that the separation is manifest in two ways: the appointment of a parochial chaplain who was not a canon, and the construction of a chapel to remove lay worship from the priory itself. This chapel evidently became the focus for parochial worship and the taking of the sacraments, as well as parochial customs and festivities. But this is not to say that the priory ceased to involve itself with the spiritual care of its parishioners, since it appears, from another source, that Stephen Rowley, parochial chaplain at the time of the dispute, was indeed a canon of Kirkham.[29]

---

[26]   On this practice, see R. N. Swanson, *Church and Society in Late Medieval England* (Oxford, 1989), p. 280.

[27]   This is one instance where the depositions use a vernacular in preference to a Latin word.

[28]   There are three witnesses who mention the summergame, and in each the emphasis is different. In the draft of William Smoryng's deposition the sentence *parochiani de Kyrkham Roo seruabant les somergame in capella...* has been altered to read (as it does in the fair copy) *parochiani de Westow*, stressing, perhaps, that the chapel was also used by the parishioners of Westow. The force of the testimony of Thomas Botrell was that the inhabitants of Kirkham Roo and Westow celebrated the summergame together (location not specified), for the benefit of the church of Westow, while Thomas Kildwick or Kylwyk deposed that the inhabitants of Kirkham Roo celebrated the festivity with the other parishioners of Westow; he knew this because he himself had been chosen as king one year, and Elizabeth Calton of Kirkham as his queen – giving us just a hint of what the nature of the *somergame* might have been. See Janet Burton, 'New Light on the "Summergame"', *Notes and Queries* 240 (1995), 428–9. For further references, one of them to the 'sommerr lordes and ladyes', see *Records of Early English Drama: York*, ed. A. F. Johnson and M. Rogerson, 2 vols (Toronto and Manchester, 1979), I, pp. 219, 358.

[29]   Stephen Rowley, canon of Kirkham, was ordained priest on 28 February 1460/1: Borthwick Institute Reg. 20 (Reg. Booth), fol. 447r.

In the list of articles, it was stated that the nave of Kirkham had the attributes of a parish church, especially a font and a cemetery. The witnesses divided in their opinions as to where the villagers baptised their children. Witnesses could be found to swear that they had seen Kirkham babies baptised at Westow, while others deposed that they had seen children baptised at Kirkham within the nave of the priory. The acid test of Kirkham's parochial status was, however, that it possessed a baptismal font. There was no doubt that there was a font there – that would have been quite apparent to all those gathered in the nave over the winter of 1496 and early spring of 1497: the question was, how long had it been there? Here the vagaries of human memory led to several different answers being given. John Adyson of Crambe, aged sixty, recalled that a certain John Delaryn, who lived at Kirkham Roo, had removed the old font and caused a new one to be built about twenty years before (i.e. about 1475). John Elwyn did not mention Delaryn but suggested that the present font had been there about 46 years, that is, from about 1450. William Towres stated that he had known John Delaryn well, and that after he had provided a new font, he himself had on many occasions seen parts of the old one lying in the church. William Adison of Crambe agreed that there was a font, and added that his wife, now aged sixty years and more, remembered seeing the old font *cum lez topynet* where the new font now stood.[30] Some added physical descriptions: Robert Marshall of Crambe, aged sixty-six, recalled the old font, built some fifty years ago according to his memory (*c*.1445). And, he said 'it had a cover like a little bell-tower': 'et habuit unum cooperortorium ad instar unius campanilis parui'. But perhaps the clearest detail was provided by Roger Bell of Langton, at thirty-eight one of the youngest witnesses, who quite incidentally and casually let slip that he had been to a school held in the nave of the church. In his youth, he said, he went to school with the late Sir John Kyllom within the space of five feet of the font.[31] Here the deposition gives one of its very rare lapses into the vernacular: 'and then it was an old font like a litle stepill with a lynne cloth on it like a surples. And þat he in his child game cast stonys at the toppe of it many tymes'. He had seen a new font erected in the time of Prior Urton (1462–70) when Sir Robert Semar was parochial chaplain. This suggests that the witnesses who placed the provision of the new font by John Delaryn around twenty years before were the more accurate in their recollections.

Marriages also took place within the nave of the priory church. Mention has already been made of one witness who stated that he had been married at

---

[30]   *Topynet* could be a variant of *tapnet, topnet*, meaning a basket of rushes, here used in the sense of a bed of rushes; see *OED tapnet, topnet*; or a form of *tapet*, 'a piece of figured cloth used as a hanging, table cover, carpet or the like': *OED tapet*.

[31]   John Killom, canon of Kirkham, was ordained subdeacon on 25 February 1463/4: Borthwick Institute, Reg. 20 (Reg. Booth), fol. 458v.

the altar of the Blessed Virgin Mary. Others also recalled their wedding. John Todde of Malton, aged forty-two and a widower, had married his wife in the parish church of Kirkham around twenty-two years earlier. John Stevenson of Whitwell, about sixty years of age, recalled giving his daughter in marriage to Robert Bonfair at the door of the church thirty years before. A number of witnesses deposed that residents of Kirkham Roo had married at Westow, but this does not contradict the fact that the priory church was used for weddings: it raises the more general question of which parish the parties chose for their nuptials.[32]

As with marriages, no witnesses denied that the burial of the dead took place at Kirkham: again the issue was whether this was the final resting place of the inhabitants of Kirkham Roo.[33] William Towres, at the age of forty-six, claimed to have seen over eighty villagers of Kirkham Roo buried in the cemetery and the church – a suspiciously large number for a small community. But it must have been hard to contradict those who maintained that they had buried their own within the nave or the cemetery enclosure. John Todde of Malton stated that his wife was buried within the church as her parish church – he had also married her and had four children baptised there – and Richard Kellet, rector of Burythorpe, swore that his brother's daughters had been both baptised and buried at Kirkham. And several witnesses stated that William Wyndres, in the name of the parishioners living in Kirkham Roo, repaired a fourth part of the cemetery enclosure. Thomas Syth, when asked what repairs Wyndres had carried out, replied that he had enclosed *cum lez pale*, that is, with ditches or fences, as much space as belonged to the parishioners, which was the greater part of the cemetery. The voluble Roger Bell recalled that Collysonn, who lived at Kirkham Roo, repaired that part of the cemetery not adjoined by houses, with ditches or fences, at his expense and that of the villagers. As parishioners of Kirkham, the inhabitants of Kirkham Roo shared the responsibility for the maintenance of a portion of the cemetery enclosure.

The dispute was evidently not new, for it was already an issue in 1468 and perhaps earlier. It was not resolved then, and raised its head in the 1490s. We can conjecture a fairly obvious reason for this re-emergence: that the church of Westow was then in need of repair. According to witnesses its tower had

---

[32] See, for instance, the depositions of William Watson, William Smoryng and Robert Botrell.

[33] A number of witnesses, John Botrell and John Bauys among them, said that they had seen residents of Kirkham Roo buried at Westow. Thomas Botrell claimed that there was a pot, *olla*, which was the mortuary of the residents of Kirkham Roo, still at Westow, and John Middylton and John Watson both identified an *olla* at Westow as the mortuary of a man named Mowbray of Kirkham Roo, who had been buried at Westow.

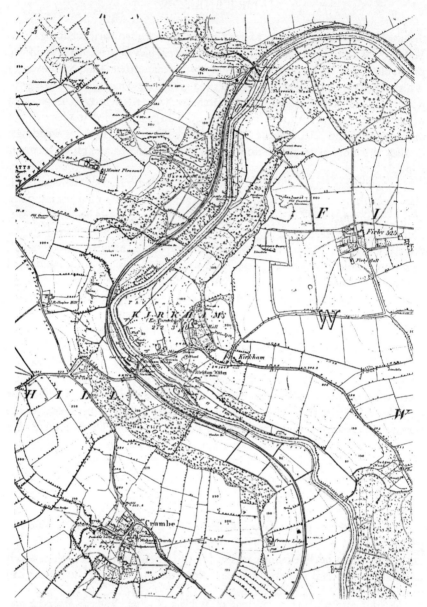

Figure 9: Map of Kirkham, from the Ordnance Survey 6", sheet 141 (1856).

been finished some forty-eight years before, that is in the late 1440s, but there
may now have been a further financial reason for the churchwardens to renew
their claims for contributions.[34] One deposition however, suggests another

<hr>

[34]   See, for instance, the deposition of Robert Watson of St Michael's parish, Malton:

clue why the issue had become more contentious in the last years of the fifteenth century, and this may lie with the man with whom this discussion opened, John Dalton. It will be recalled that the agreement under which he became parochial chaplain of Kirkham demanded his resignation in the event of his promotion to another post. The evidence of one of the witnesses suggests that when John Furster – who had also administered the cure of souls at Kirkham Roo by agreement with the prior – ceased to be vicar of Westow, John Dalton wished to have the benefice, but the prior was unwilling for him to have the post until he had released the inhabitants of Kirkham Roo.[35] But John Dalton was instituted as vicar of Westow on 6 December 1467, and so the agreement exhibited the following March was a response to his unwillingness to relinquish his chaplaincy at Kirkham.[36] Could the fact that at least two of the vicars of Westow had also been parochial chaplains of Kirkham have caused confusion in the minds of the churchwardens of Westow, and others, as to the parochial status of those who dwelt outside the monastery gates?[37]

Although the surviving documentation contained in CP F 307 is considerable, one thing the cause paper lacks is the sentence. Moreover, the date of the cause coincides with a gap in the extant act books of the consistory court, so we have no record of the final decision. However, there is reason to believe that the inhabitants of Kirkham won their case. In 1822 Kirkham was described as extra-parochial; there had been no church there since the dissolution of the priory, and the seven inhabitants of its three houses attended Westow church.[38] On the six-inch Ordnance Survey map of 1856 the area to the north of the gateway is still marked as extra-parochial (Fig. 9). This suggests that the villagers of Kirkham Roo proved their point to the satisfaction of the court, and that the area was recognised as part of Kirkham, and not Westow, parish.

The Augustinian canons, as a clerical as well as a monastic order, had a special relationship with the parish churches of medieval England. They were not the only religious group to be endowed with churches, far from it. The

campanilis ecclesie parochialis de Westow quod fuit edificatum & finitum circa xlviii annos.

[35] Evidence of Robert Botrell.

[36] Borthwick Institute, Reg. 22 (Reg. Neville and Booth), fol. 28r. John Dalton had resigned as vicar by 6 November 1470 (ibid., fol. 125r); see Fasti Parochiales, V: Deanery of Buckrose, ed. N. A. H. Lawrance, Yorkshire Archaeological Society Record Series 143 (1983), pp. 60–2.

[37] There is no evidence to connect Dalton's successors John Nawton (instituted 6 November 1470) and Richard Nabiller/Stabiller (instituted 19 October 1477) with Kirkham: Borthwick Institute, Reg. 22, fols 125r, 265r; Fasti: Buckrose, p. 61.

[38] T. Langdale, A Topographical Dictionary of Yorkshire (Northallerton, 1822), p. 178.

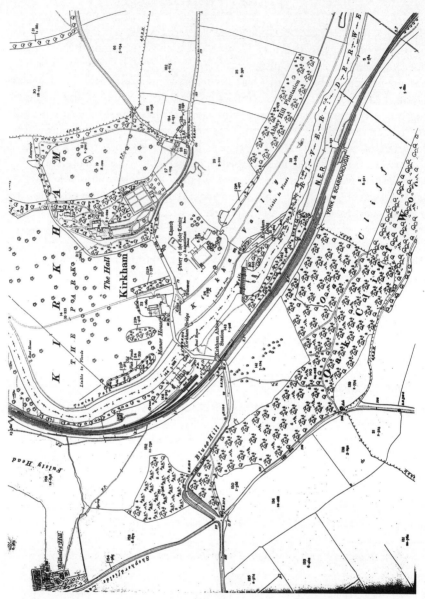

Figure 10: Map of Kirkham, from the Ordnance Survey 25", sheet 141/8 (1910).

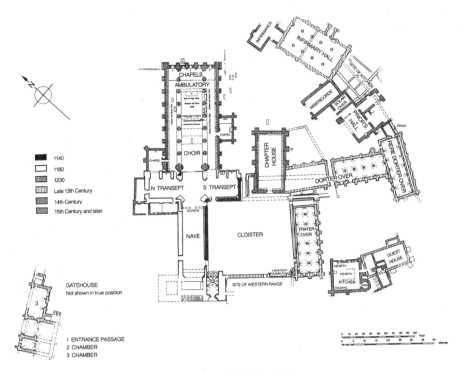

Figure 11: Plan of Kirkham Priory,
from *Kirkham Priory*, English Heritage, 1992 edition, pp. 6–7.

black monks benefited from the movement to transfer the advowson of parish churches from lay to ecclesiastical hands, and the Cistercians, despite an official ban on the acceptance of churches, also came to hold them, although in smaller numbers.[39] Much of what we know of the relationship of a religious house to its parish churches concerns financial matters, for whether a monastery held the patronage and presented an incumbent to the bishop, or appropriated and served the church through one of its members, or instituted a vicarage, the church was on one level a financial asset. The Kirkham cause paper allows us to see another aspect of monastic involvement with parish churches. For the purposes of this paper the outcome of the court case of 1496–7 is less important than the light shed by the depositions on the parochial use of the nave of Kirkham Priory. An analysis of the evidence allows us to deduce the chronology of the chaplains who served the cure of souls of the laity who lived within the priory and in the hamlet which had

---

39   On some aspects of monastic involvement in the parish churches of the north, see J. Burton, 'Monasteries and Parish Churches in Eleventh- and Twelfth-Century Yorkshire', *Northern History* 23 (1987), 39–50.

grown up to serve the needs of the community; to examine developing relations between priory and parish, and the changing status of the spiritual care offered by the canons; and, through the chance reference by one witness, to catch a glimpse of the Augustinians providing education for the young of the village. It is well-known that parts of conventual churches were used by laity – but rarely do we get this chance to reconstruct quite so vividly a picture of parish life, both spiritual and social, within the context of the religious orders.[40]

[40] In this respect it is worth drawing attention here to two sixteenth-century cause papers which concern Kirkham Priory. Details of York, Borthwick Institute CP G 601–602, were printed by J. S. Purvis many years ago (*Select XVI Century Causes in Tithe from the York Diocesan Registry*, ed. J. S. Purvis, Yorkshire Archaeological Society Record Series 114 (Wakefield, 1949), pp. 78–96). Although dated 1556 the case, with its numerous depositions, sheds much light on the history of Kirkham Priory in the years before the Dissolution, and on its relationship with the surrounding parishes. See Burton, *Kirkham Priory*, pp. 26–7.

APPENDIX

York, Borthwick Institute of Historical Research, cause paper, CP F 307
Depositions

There appear to be three sets of depositions, one (for convenience here designated A) apparently a fair copy, and two (B and C) which appear to be drafts. In one of the draft lists (B), the depositions are numbered. List A contains eighteen depositions, of which seven also appear in draft on list B, and eleven on list C, and these are not in chronological order of the appearance of witnesses. List B contains twenty-six depositions (in chronological order), numbered, of which nineteen are unique. List C contains drafts of the first eleven depositions in A, and six others. As in B these are in date order of appearance. The depositions usually give the place of residence and age, as well as the name of the witness, but B adds at the end a notice of whether the witness is a tenant or servant of the prior. The following list attempts to reconstruct the order of the depositions, and notes on which list/s the witness appears. There exists among the documents of the cause paper a list of witnesses to be summoned. There is one set of twenty names, then a heading: *testes compulsi ut sequitur*, followed by another eighteen names. The depositions of nineteen of these thirty-eight have survived, and are indicated in the list below by an asterisk.

10 December 1496
Robert Watson, pa. St Michael, Malton, 57, sworn on behalf of the churchwardens of Westow (AC)
John Botrell, pa. Westow, 70 (AC)
John Bauys, 54 (AC)
Robert Turnay/Tornay, pa. Crambe, about 60 (AC)

28 January 1496/7
William Watson, pa. Westow, 50 (AC)
John Spynk, Malton, over 40 (AC)

31 January 1496/7
Roger Bell, Langton, 38 (ABi)*
William Marshall, Terrington, 51, tenant of a parcel of land *super lez Wald* belonging to the prior (ABii)*
John Adyson, pa. Crambe, 60, tenant of the prior (ABiii)*

345

1 February 1496/7
Edward Harkey and William Pole, pa. Helmsley (ABiv)
William Towres, pa. Kirkham, 46, baker at Kirkham Priory (ABv)*
John Todde, Malton, 42 (ABvi)*
Henry Grane, pa. Kirkham, 40, servant and stipendiary of the prior (incomplete in A; Bvii)*
William Adyson/Adison, Crambe, 60, tenant of the prior (Bviii)*
John Stevenson, Whitwell, about 60, tenant of the prior (Bix)*
John Morley, Whitwell, over 50, tenant of the prior (Bx)*
Richard Webster, Crambe, 50, tenant of the prior (Bxi)*
Thomas Syth, Whitwell, about 35, tenant and servant of the prior (Bxii)*

1 March 1496/7
John Elwyn, Firby, pa. Westow, 73, servant of the prior (Bxiii)

2 March 1496/7
Robert Ecclesfeld, Whitwell, 48, servant of the prior (Bxiv)*
Robert Thomson, Whitwell, 60, servant of the prior (Bxv)*
Lord Thomas Newton, vicar of Crambe, 48 (Bxvi)
Robert Marshall, Crambe, 66, servant and tenant of the prior (Bxvii)*
John Wederherd, Crambe, 54, tenant of the prior (Bxviii)*

6 March 1496/7
William Smoryng, Westow, 71 (AC)
Robert Botrell, Westow, 50 (AC)
John Spynk(e), Westow, 40 (AC)
Thomas Botrel(l), Menethorpe, 47 (AC)
Thomas Kildwick/Kylwyk, Menethorpe, about 50 (A (incomplete) C)
John Myddylton, Westow, 72 (C)
John Watson, Sand Hutton, 40 (C)

9 March 1496/7
John Eleson, Whitwell, 60, tenant of the prior (Bxix)
Richard Syth, Barton, 70, servant of the prior (Bxx)*
John Tayliour, Crambe, 60, tenant of the prior (Bxxi)*
Thomas Wyly, pa. Crambe, 53 (Bxxii)*
Robert Dawtrie, Foston, 60 (Bxxiii)
Richard Sheppard, Crambe, 50, tenant of the prior (Bxxiv)*
Edward Jacsoun, Crambe, 40, tenant and servant of the prior (Bxxv)
Lord Richard Kellet, rector of Burythorpe (Bxxvi)

10 March 1496/7
John Barthrop, Hutton on Derwent, 50 (C)
John Milum, Howsom, over 48 (C)
Thomas Bradshaw, Westow, over 40 (C)
Robert Brinham, pa. Westow, 36 (C)

Witnesses summoned
Those who were summoned but for whom there are no depositions are:
Master John Dalton of York; Thomas Smythson of pa. Bossall; Robert Aton,
John Nelson and John Lawson of Crambe; William Wyndryse of Kirkham;
and from the compulsory witnesses, John Sissotson, Thomas Sissotson,
Richard Stevenson, John Firth and William Sawtre of Crambe, and Robert
Mathew, Robert Sclater, John Marton, John Welburn, Richard Sandwich,
John Benson, Milo Leper and John Cristelow of Kirkham.

English and Welsh Monastic Bishops:
the Final Century, 1433–1533

BARRIE DOBSON

'The end is where we start from'.[1] Needless to say, not many of the innumerable admirers of medieval Christian monasticism have ever thought it at all profitable to follow T. S. Eliot's celebrated advice. Indeed for a historian to open this particular symposium with a discussion of the last monastic bishops of medieval England and Wales may seem to some an act of deliberate perversity. With hardly an exception the nineteen monks and regular canons who sat on the episcopal bench during the hundred years between 1433 and Henry VIII's break with Rome in 1533 are completely forgotten today: and on the face of it their careers may now seem among the least significant and perhaps the least prepossessing features of the last century of the medieval English church.[2] Even Dr Derek Baker, one of the most sympathetic advocates of late medieval monasticism, was tempted to apply to the senior English religious of the fifteenth century a very different quotation from T. S. Eliot: 'shape without form, shade without colour, paralysed force, gesture without motion'.[3] Perhaps so; but then it must always be worth asking whether an apparent lack of form, colour, force and motion is in fact an historical illusion, the consequence less of human weakness than of a paucity of surviving records. Even more than the other members of the Lancastrian, Yorkist and early Tudor episcopal bench, the handful of monk-bishops can only be known 'in faint outlines':[4] but it may still be possible to discover

---

[1]   T. S. Eliot, *Four Quartets* (London, 1944), p. 42.

[2]   The bishops discussed in this paper comprise all the monks and regular canons who held English or Welsh sees after the death of Robert of Lancaster, bishop of St Asaph, on 26 March 1433 and before the election, unconfirmed by the pope, of John Salcote or Capon to the diocese of Bangor between November 1533 and January 1534. See John le Neve, *Fasti Ecclesiae Anglicanae, 1300–1541*, revised edn, 12 vols (London, 1962–7), XI, *The Welsh Dioceses*, pp. 5, 38.

[3]   D. Baker, 'Old Wine in New Bottles: Attitudes to Reform in Pre-Reformation England', in *Renaissance and Renewal in Christian History*, Studies in Church History 14 (1977), 193–211, p. 193.

[4]   A. H. Thompson, *The English Clergy and their Organisation in the Later Middle*

whether their diverse careers have – or have not – a general message to impart. For here, at the very least, is a unique opportunity to examine the lives of a small and exceptional group of late medieval regulars who escaped the confines of their local contexts to play a very public role in national and ecclesiastical affairs. Hardly ever criticised in their own time for doing so, were they in practice ever able to make a significant and distinctive contribution to the pre-Reformation church? What, if anything, do they tell us about the realities of English medieval monasticism in its final century?

The study of the monk-bishop in medieval England and Wales is, almost by definition, always the study of a small minority. Even if one were to include for consideration, which this paper does not, those English monks (by no means completely identified) who served in a humble capacity as suffragan bishops *in partibus* or as resident and non-resident bishops in Ireland and elsewhere, the numbers of medieval English religious who held bishoprics will always be too small to defy sophisticated prosopographical analysis. Since at least 1066 this had always been so. As the late Dom David Knowles pointed out when correcting a common misapprehension over fifty years ago, the proportion of English bishops of monastic provenance declined rather than increased after the Norman Conquest: there had been at least six monastic bishops in 1062–3 but there were only three by 1100.[5] A century later, after the number of English dioceses had stabilised at seventeen (with the foundation of Carlisle in 1133) and the four Welsh dioceses of Bangor, Llandaff, St Asaph's and St David's had been brought under the metropolitan authority of the archbishop of Canterbury, the number of monastic bishops in the country had dropped to one or even zero. From 1216 to 1340, as Knowles again made clear, the number of regulars among the twenty-one bishops of England and Wales continued to fluctuate at a very low level and between comparatively narrow limits (six to none). By the mid-fourteenth century members of the mendicant orders (not to be considered in this paper) were admittedly being consecrated as bishops in considerable numbers, although nearly always to Welsh sees. Of the twenty-nine regular bishops appointed to English and Welsh dioceses between 1216 and 1340, only seven were friars: but of the forty-four regulars made bishops between 1340 and 1485, as many as thirty-one were mendicants. Much more remarkably, however, during the forty-eight years between 1485 and 1533, friars comprised only a third of the fifteen regulars who sat on the episcopal bench.[6]

Ages (Oxford, 1947), p. 41.

[5]   David Knowles, *The Monastic Order in England, 940–1216*, 2nd edn (Cambridge, 1963), pp. 697–701, 709–10.

[6]   *Ibid.*, pp. 709–10; Knowles, *The Religious Orders in England*, 3 vols (Cambridge, 1948–59), I, pp. 321–2; II, 369–71; III, pp. 492–3. Of the several general surveys of the English episcopate at particular periods during the later middle ages, see

It seems clear enough that although the mendicant bishop was a not inconspicuous figure in late fourteenth- and early fifteenth-century England, the proportion of monks and regular canons as opposed to friars on the episcopal bench actually increased in the last century of English monasticism. For reasons which this paper must try to explore, bishops of monastic as opposed to mendicant origins tended to be valued somewhat more rather than less by the English crown and church as the middle ages drew to a close.

It is, however, possible – and necessary – to be more precise. Dom David Knowles's belief that throughout the later medieval centuries the average number (approximately three or four) of regulars on the episcopal bench remained 'curiously constant' conceals some intriguingly varied demographic trends in the case of the monk-bishops themselves.[7] Between 1400 and 1435, five monks became bishops in England or Wales. During the thirty-five years from 1435 to 1470 that figure fell to four; but between 1470 and 1505 it rose to no fewer than twelve. During the twenty-eight years after 1505, however, no monk or regular canon was elevated to an episcopal see within the English or Welsh church with the solitary exception of Thomas Skevington, the Cistercian abbot of Beaulieu who was provided to Bangor in 1509. Skevington was the last monk to be promoted to a diocese within the kingdom until John Salcote or Capon succeeded him at Bangor twenty-four years later as the first English religious to be appointed bishop under royal rather than papal authority.[8] It would certainly be dangerous to draw too many conclusions from so small a sample of statistics; and it can go without saying that the selection of the nineteen monk bishops discussed in this paper tended to depend less on royal attitudes to monasticism in general than on personal encounters and accidental circumstances now often impossible to recapture. It may well be coincidental, for example, that three monks were provided to episcopal sees (Richard Redman to St Asaph; Thomas Mylling to Hereford; and Richard Bell to Carlisle) during the reign of Edward IV.

However, it can certainly not be a coincidence that no fewer than ten monks (Henry Deane to Bangor, Salisbury and Canterbury; William Senhouse to Carlisle and Durham; Michael Diacony to St Asaph; John Ingleby to Llandaff; Miles Salley to Llandaff; Thomas Pygot to Bangor;

---

especially J. R. L. Highfield, 'The English Hierarchy in the Reign of Edward III', *TRHS*, 5th ser. 6 (1956), 115–38, and R. G. Davies, 'The Episcopate', in *Profession, Vocation and Culture in Later Medieval England*, ed. C. H. Clough (Liverpool, 1982), 51–89.

[7] Knowles, *Religious Orders*, II, p. 369. The several omissions in Knowles's various lists of 'Regulars as Bishops' can be most readily rectified by recourse to the volumes of Le Neve, *Fasti, 1300–1541*.

[8] A. B. Emden, *A Biographical Register of the University of Oxford to A.D. 1500*, 3 vols (Oxford, 1957–9), III, pp. 1707–8; Le Neve, *Fasti, 1300–1541*, XI, p. 5.

Dafydd ab Iuean to St Asaph; Dafydd ab Owain to St Asaph; John Penny to Bangor and Carlisle; and Thomas Skevington to Bangor) were elevated to bishoprics in the reign of Henry VII. Here, among the many other factors in play, may be indirect confirmation of the first Tudor monarch's well known commitment to the reformation of the religious life in his kingdom. What more appropriate a way for Henry VII to 'reawaken devout laymen's fervour for monastic life' than the appointment of a handful of monk-bishops (and even a monastic archbishop of Canterbury) who might act as publicists for that life?[9] Henry VII's experiment in increasing the representation of monks and regular canons on the English episcopal bench was, however, too tentative to be anything but abortive; and it was certainly not at all an experiment continued by his son until, as will be seen, the very different conditions of the 1530s. Nevertheless the ideal of the monk-bishop, admittedly very different from its Tudor reality, could hardly be entirely ignored by the many would-be reformers of the English church during the generation immediately before Erasmus's sardonic indifference to the monastic life began to exercise its dispiriting effect. For that generation the *reformatio* of English monasticism was still often seen as a desirable and perhaps essential pre-condition for the regeneration of the Christian religion as a whole.[10]

Not, one supposes, that Henry VII and his contemporaries would have expected the regeneration of the monastic life within his kingdom to begin in the comparatively remote dioceses of Hereford, Carlisle and (above all) those in Wales. In the selection of the great majority of the sees to be held by the monk-bishops of Yorkist and Tudor England more material and less worthy considerations continued to be paramount. The twenty-six dioceses ruled at some time or other between 1433 and 1533 by the last nineteen monk-bishops of medieval England were markedly concentrated at either Hereford (three), Carlisle (three), Coventry and Lichfield (two) and, above all, in Wales (twelve). With a very few exceptions, of whom Richard Redman and Henry Deane – who died as bishop of Ely and archbishop of Canterbury respectively in 1505 and 1503 – are perhaps the most obvious, members of the religious orders were always likely to be promoted to the least wealthy and well-endowed sees in the country. Ever since the twelfth century the lucrative preferment needed to reward the crown's senior secular clerks, the leading

9   A. Goodman, 'Henry VII and Christian Renewal', in *Religion and Humanism*, Studies in Church History 17 (1981), 115–25; cf. R. L. Storey, *The Reign of Henry VII* (London, 1968), p. 63.

10   M. Bowker, *The Henrician Reformation: the Diocese of Lincoln under John Longland, 1521–1547* (Cambridge, 1981), pp. 17–28; M. K. Jones and M. G. Underwood, *The King's Mother: Lady Margaret Beaufort, Countess of Richmond and Derby* (Cambridge, 1992), pp. 138, 143, 147, 180–2, 194–8.

administrators of the English state, had inevitably relegated monastic bishops to the financially less desirable and sometimes positively barbarous dioceses. Thus the fifteenth-century monk-bishops of Carlisle, Rochester, Hereford and Coventry and Lichfield, although certainly less ludicrously impoverished than their Welsh counterparts, presided over four of the five least wealthy English dioceses as they were valued in 1535.[11] As for the four notoriously impecunious Welsh sees, only St David's – the diocese least frequently held by a regular – seems to have enjoyed an annual income of much more than £150 in the later middle ages. Within an *ecclesia Anglicana* where a single cathedral prebend (Masham at York Minster) might be valued at over £160 per annum, it was therefore hardly likely – to state the obvious – that a diocese in Wales would arouse much interest among the most senior secular clergy of the period.[12]

For that very reason the four medieval Welsh dioceses were bound to offer more prospects of promotion to aspirant monk-bishops than any sees in England itself. Indeed it would hardly be an exaggeration to state that the study of the late medieval English monastic bishop is primarily an aspect of the history of the established church in Wales. As is well known, during the fourteenth and fifteenth centuries the latter – like native Welshmen themselves – had gradually been reduced to quasi-colonial status; and the English crown increasingly debarred Welshmen from becoming bishops in their own country. For many decades after the Glendower rebellion had revived English fears of insurrection west of the marches, 'not a single Welsh-speaking Welshman was made bishop of a Welsh see'.[13] It followed, until the early years of the sixteenth century at least, that all the monk-bishops of the kingdom were Englishmen – with the intriguing exception of a native of Normandy, Michael Diacony, who had been prior of St Helier's, Jersey as well as Henry VII's confessor, when he was provided to St Asaph in 1495.[14] Whether or not in gratitude for the support of his fellow countrymen in 1485, Henry VII was soon prepared to go further still and become the first king for over a century to relax the practice of always appointing non-Welsh

---

[11]   D. Knowles and R. N. Hadcock, *Medieval Religious Houses: England and Wales*, 2nd edn (London, 1971), p. 447.

[12]   *A History of York Minster*, ed. G. E. Aylmer and R. Cant (Oxford, 1977), pp. 52–62; cf. Thompson, *English Clergy*, pp. 38–9.

[13]   G. Williams, *The Welsh Church from Conquest to Reformation*, 2nd edn (Cardiff, 1976), p. 301.

[14]   *Ibid.*, p. 302. Diacony (also known – somewhat confusingly – as Deacon or Diacre) was granted English denization a few months before his provision to St Asaph: see *Calendar of Patent Rolls* (London, 1891–), *1494–1509*, p. 25. He died in late 1499, *Calendar of Papal Letters: Papal Registers* (London, 1893–) [*CPL*], *1495–1503*, p. 380.

bishops to Welsh sees. Thomas Pygot, abbot of Chertsey when provided to Bangor in 1500, was a native of Denbighshire. More remarkably still, between 1500 and 1513 the diocese of St Asaph was allowed to pass into the hands of two powerful Welsh Cistercian abbots, Dafydd ab Iuean ab Iorwerth and Master Dafydd ab Owain. Surviving Welsh poetry of the early sixteenth century makes it clear that these two bishops were indeed highly popular and perhaps dangerously charismatic figures in North Wales.[15] It may not be too difficult to understand why Henry VIII immediately abandoned his father's experiment, with the inevitable if not insignificant consequence that there was no Welsh representation on his episcopal bench when the latter faced its hours of greatest trial and decision in the early 1530s.[16]

The crown's continued discrimination against native Welsh clergy accordingly explains why senior English monks and regular canons often had a greater opportunity to become bishops in late-medieval Wales than they had in England. Small wonder, however, that when Henry VI recommended Reginald Boulers, abbot of Gloucester, to the see of Llandaff in November 1440, Boulers refused the appointment almost immediately and preferred to wait for as long as ten years for the much more attractive proposition of the bishopric of Hereford.[17] But whether in the Welsh or the poorer English sees nearly all monk bishops would be confronted by acute financial problems. Making all allowances for the near impossibility of making an accurate estimate of the real income and expenditure of any of these bishops, it seems abundantly clear that their most serious problem was usually the inadequacy of their revenues. To take only one but critical example, so few and so impoverished were the churches in the patronage of many of these monk-bishops that they found it difficult to make suitable provision for their own ecclesiastical officials. Thus Bishop Richard Bell of Carlisle was forced to institute his registrar, Robert Fisher, to both the rectory of Cliburn and the vicarage of Torpenhow because the revenues of only one of these churches would have failed to maintain him.[18] At Carlisle, as in Wales, the bishops'

15   CPL, 1495–1503, pp. 380–2; Williams, Welsh Church, pp. 302, 306, 382–7, 404–11, 429; Emden, Oxford, I, p. 549.

16   Le Neve, Fasti 1300–1541, XI, pp. 5, 23, 39, 55–6; Williams, Welsh Church, pp. 302–6.

17   Correspondence of Thomas Bekynton, ed. G. Williams, 2 vols, Rolls Series (London, 1872), I, pp. 22, 27–9, 31; Emden, Oxford, I, p. 229.

18   R. B. Dobson, 'Richard Bell, Prior of Durham (1464–78) and Bishop of Carlisle (1478–95)', Transactions of the Cumberland and Westmorland Antiquarian and Archaeological Society, new ser. 65 (1965), 182–221, p. 217, reprinted in R. B. Dobson, Church and Society in the Medieval North of England (London, 1996), 135–62, p. 159. Cf. H. R. T. Summerson, Medieval Carlisle, 2 vols, Cumberland and Westmorland Antiquarian and Archaeological Society, extra series 25

resources were usually more restricted than those of their powerful local magnates.

In such circumstances one might well ask why any members of the monastic orders were actually prepared to accept the impoverished bishoprics that tended to be offered to them. Some no doubt hoped for rapid translation into other and richer dioceses. If so, most were to be disappointed; of the nineteen last monastic bishops of medieval England and Wales, only five (Reginald Boulers, Richard Redman, Henry Deane, William Senhouse and John Penny) migrated to wealthier sees. Moreover, by the fifteenth century the prospects of any monk enjoying the fruits of an outstandingly rich diocese had become even more restricted because of the final collapse of the long-contentious electoral powers of the eight English monastic cathedral chapters. During the thirteenth and fourteenth centuries these chapters had at least occasionally been allowed to have their way and choose one of their own number as their titular abbot. Between 1300 and 1400, for example, there had been five monk-bishops at Rochester, four at Ely and one at Norwich.[19] However, the very last member of an English cathedral priory to become spiritual superior in his own see was Prior Alexander de Totyngton, elected to the bishopric of Norwich in September 1405; and even Totyngton found himself imprisoned at Windsor Castle before a papal provision in the following January put his claims to his episcopacy beyond doubt.[20] Significantly enough, only one of the last nineteen monastic bishops of medieval England was a member of a cathedral chapter; and in 1478 Richard Bell, this solitary exception to prove the rule, became bishop not of his own community at Durham but of the Augustinian canons of Carlisle Cathedral.[21] No doubt the complete disintegration of the ability of monastic, and indeed secular, cathedral chapters to impose any of their own candidates on the *cathedrae* of fifteenth-century England testifies to the increasingly irresistible authority of the crown in the matter of senior ecclesiastical appointments. However, such a development also had the obvious secondary effect of ensuring that the last generations of monastic bishops in England probably owed comparatively little to the prestige and influence of their mother houses as such; rather they had to attract the attention of the crown (and sometimes the papacy) through their own personal reputations and/or political services to the crown.

(Kendal, 1993), II, pp. 590–607.

[19] W. A. Pantin, *The English Church in the Fourteenth Century* (Cambridge, 1955), p. 19.

[20] H. Wharton, *Anglia Sacra*, 2 vols (London, 1691), I, pp. 415–16; Le Neve, *Fasti, 1300–1541*, IV, *Monastic Cathedrals*, p. 24.

[21] Dobson, 'Richard Bell', pp. 209–11.

But how – to return to the major problem at issue – were the last nineteen monk-bishops of late medieval England induced to accept appointment to the most impoverished dioceses of the kingdom? The answer undoubtedly and increasingly lay in the proliferation of the practice of *commendam* by papal licence. In one or other of its various manifestations, the custom of *commendam* (first mentioned by St Ambrose) had long been a controversial feature of church life: in 1274, for example, the General Council of Lyons had ordained that no clerk might hold more than one parish *in commendam*, and then only for no more than six months.[22] By the fifteenth century however, the practice was increasingly restricted to benefices which a bishop or other dignitary was permitted to hold, usually permanently, together with his see. Although the intricacies of *commendam* as practised in late medieval England still await their historian, there seems to be no doubt that it was during the decades after 1450 that English bishops began to be positively importunate – and usually successful – in their requests for *commendams* from the papacy. As early as 1410 the Cistercian Robert of Lancaster had been permitted to hold his abbey of Valle Crucis *in commendam* with his new bishopric of St Asaph; but by the close of the fifteenth century nearly every monk or regular canon who attained episcopal status was following his example.[23] In 1472 Richard Redman had papal licence to retain his abbey of Shap (together with one other benefice) *in commendam* with the see of St Asaph, a precedent to be followed by Thomas Pygot who continued to be abbot of Chertsey after becoming bishop of Bangor in 1500. Similar examples of papal permission to continue as abbot of one's community after elevation to a bishopric are provided by Henry Deane in 1500 (prior of Llanthony by Gloucester), John Penny in 1505 (abbot of Leicester) and Thomas Skevington in 1509 (abbot of Beaulieu). More surprisingly still, William Senhouse was allowed to hold St Mary's Abbey, York, *in commendam* for seven years after his promotion to the see of Carlisle in 1495.[24] Even more startling, for it certainly startled contemporaries, was the audacious attempt of Richard Bell, prior of Durham, to 'hath the prialite in a commendam' when he was provided to the see of Carlisle in February 1478: only the intervention of Edward IV finally reassured the Durham monks that their late prior's 'auctorite over you is now utterly expired and extincte'.[25] The practice of *commendam*, in other words, was much more common in

---

22   J. R. H. Moorman, *Church Life in England in the Thirteenth Century* (Cambridge, 1945), pp. 32–3.

23   *CPL, 1417–31*, pp. 117, 177, 364.

24   *Ibid., 1471–75*, p. 316; *1495–1503*, pp. 219–20, 385; *Cal. Pat. Rolls, 1494–1509*, pp. 56, 77, 625, 299; Emden, *Oxford*, III, pp. 1458, 1529, 1669, 1707–8.

25   Durham, Dean and Chapter Muniments, Reg. IV, fol. 182; Reg. Parv. III, fols 182, 186v; Dobson, 'Richard Bell', pp. 210–11.

pre-Reformation England than has usually been supposed. But whatever its irregularity and its adverse effects on those religious houses which suddenly found themselves without an effective superior, by 1500 the additional emoluments made possible by *commendam* had become more or less essential to the sustenance of the large majority of monastic bishops.[26]

The papacy's increasing readiness to allow monk-bishops to hold their previous abbacies *in commendam* with their new sees naturally made it even more likely than it already was that those sees would seem especially attractive to heads of wealthy religious houses. It is indeed very apparent that unless one was the superior of a rich Benedictine or Cistercian monastery the prospects of becoming a monastic bishop at all were minimal to a degree. Of the nineteen monastic bishops between 1433 and 1533, all were black monks except for three Cistercians, two Augustinian canons, one Premonstratensian and one Carthusian. By the time of their promotion to the bishoprics of St Asaph and Bangor between 1500 and 1509, all three Cistercian monks, two of them Welsh, had long been prominent figures in monastic life as abbots of particularly distinguished religious houses within their order. Similarly the elevation of the two Augustinian canons in question to the episcopal bench (Henry Deane to Bangor in 1494 and John Penny to Bangor in 1505) is largely explicable in terms of their long experience of public affairs as the heads of their respective monasteries of Llanthony by Gloucester and St Mary de Pre, Leicester.[27] Much more unusual was the unique career of Richard Redman, the only medieval English Premonstratensian canon ever to become a bishop. As the abbot of Shap who in 1459 had secured a commission for life as the abbot of Prémontré's representative in England, he went on to become bishop of St Asaph (1471), Exeter (1495) and finally Ely (1501–5).[28] Although 'no other English white canon had a career approaching Redman's in importance', the reasons for the meteoric rise of this remarkably zealous and efficient administrator are not altogether impossible to conjecture.[29] The same can hardly be said of the single most startling promotion of a member of a religious order, a Carthusian no less, to a bishopric in the late medieval kingdom. The provision to the diocese of Llandaff in June 1496 of John

---

[26] Little evidence survives to assess whether the common papal requirement that grants of *commendam* should not lead to 'a decrease in divine worship and the usual number of monks and ministers in the monastery' was in fact observed (*CPL, 1495–1503*, p. 385).

[27] Emden, *Oxford*, I, p. 554; III, p. 1458.

[28] H. M. Colvin, *The White Canons in England* (Oxford, 1951), pp. 224–7, 254–6, 363–4.

[29] *Collectanea Anglo-Premonstratensia*, ed. F. A. Gasquet, 3 vols, Camden Society, 3rd ser. 6, 10, 12 (London, 1904–6), *passim*; Knowles, *Religious Orders*, III, pp. 39–51.

Ingleby, presumably a descendant of the John de Ingleby of Ripley in the North Riding of Yorkshire who had founded Mount Grace in 1398 and therefore a one time brother of Mount Grace himself, is no doubt an incidental tribute to the incomparable prestige enjoyed by his order at the end of the fifteenth century, but is otherwise by no means easy to understand.[30]

By contrast, the dominance of members of the Benedictine order among the ranks of the monk-bishops of the fifteenth and early sixteenth centuries is not only very striking but comparatively easy to explain. Apart from their prospects of retaining their abbacies *in commendam*, the superiors of the major houses of black monks were ideally placed not only to acquire sophisticated management skills within the largest business corporations of the country but also to act as hosts to many of the most influential lay and ecclesiastical personalities of the age. It is accordingly not particularly surprising, to take the most obvious example, that three monk-bishops of this period (Thomas Spofford, William Wellys and William Senhouse) had previously been abbots of St Mary's, York, the richest monastery in the north of England.[31] Much better documented is the way in which Richard Bell, as prior of Durham between 1464 and 1478 (when he was provided to the diocese of Carlisle), was in regular personal contact and regular correspondence too with 'diverse lords of right high estate'.[32] At a more general and perhaps imponderable level, and despite a prevailing belief to the contrary, it could well be argued that the largest Benedictine communities in the country became more rather than less assured of their position in English church and state during the course of the fifteenth century. For good or ill, many black monks tended to play a more influential role as preachers, penitentiaries and spiritual mentors outside their precincts than they had probably ever done before.[33] To take only one but surprising example, the number of identified Benedictines serving as suffragan bishops in English dioceses (a role usually and naturally associated with the friars and, to a lesser extent, the Augustinian canons) appears to have increased considerably during the early sixteenth century. Of the twenty-five or so suffragan bishops in England hitherto identified between 1400 and 1500, only two were Black Monks and at least eighteen were friars. Between 1500 and 1533, however, the

---

30 Le Neve, *Fasti, 1300–1541*, XI, p. 23; A. J. Pollard, *North-Eastern England during the Wars of the Roses* (Oxford, 1990), pp. 180–2.

31 Emden, *Oxford*, III, pp. 1669, 1744, 2012; cf. R. B. Dobson, 'Cathedral Chapters and Cathedral Cities: York, Durham and Carlisle in the Fifteenth Century', *Northern History* 19 (1983), 15–44, p. 43.

32 Durham, Dean and Chapter Muniments, Reg. Parv. III, fol. 168v; Dobson, 'Richard Bell', p. 206.

33 R. B. Dobson, 'English Monastic Cathedrals in the Fifteenth Century', *TRHS*, 6th ser. 1 (1991), 151–72.

number of mendicant suffragan bishops fell to seven while the Benedictines who served as suffragan bishops rose to at least six.[34] For this handful of suffragans, as for the monk-bishops who are the subject of this enquiry, perhaps the words of Sir Richard Southern increasingly applied: 'No one looked to them for new ideas or new forms of spiritual life: they looked to them for stability, pageantry, involvement in the aristocratic life of the upper classes, and a visible display of continuous religious and family history'.[35]

To those not inconsiderable qualifications for episcopal office at any time, the senior black monks of late fifteenth-century England could add one more. With the obvious exception of the friars, no religious order of the period was more successful than the Benedictines in providing its most academically talented members with the opportunity to receive a university education. Whereas there had been no fewer than three Benedictine *studia* (eventually known as Durham, Canterbury and Gloucester Colleges) at Oxford since the late thirteenth century, it was only after the 1440s that the English Cistercian monks and Augustinian canons gradually began to colonise less impressive Oxford *mansiones studentium* of their own.[36] As study in the university schools, and indeed the acquisition of a higher degree in theology or canon law therein, had long been more or less essential qualifications for entry into the episcopacy, the Benedictines were always likely to produce many more bishops than their rival monastic orders. In the event, and with the possible exceptions of William Heyworth (bishop of Lichfield, 1420–47) and Dafydd ab Iuean ab Iorwerth (bishop of St Asaph, 1500–3) as well as the almost certain exception of John Ingleby (bishop of Llandaff from 1496 to 1499), all nineteen monk-bishops holding English sees between 1433 and 1533 were university graduates. Although one or two of these bishops had Cambridge connections, like John Penny who received a present of 6s. 8d. from the university there in 1506–7, they were probably all alumni of Oxford University too.[37] The acute shortage of suitable halls and colleges for

[34] *Handbook of British Chronology*, ed. E. B. Fryde, D. E. Greenway, S. Porter and I. Roy, 3rd edn (London, 1986), pp. 284–7; but for the prospects of eventually amplifying these lists see D. M. Smith, 'Suffragan Bishops in the Medieval Diocese of Lincoln', *Lincolnshire History and Archaeology* 17 (1982), 17–27.

[35] R. W. Southern, *Western Society and the Church in the Middle Ages* (Harmondsworth, 1970), p. 237.

[36] R. B. Dobson, 'The Religious Orders, 1370–1540', in *The History of the University of Oxford*, II, *Late Medieval Oxford*, ed. J. I. Catto and T. A. R. Evans (Oxford, 1992), 539–79; cf. W. A. Pantin, 'General and Provincial Chapters of the English Black Monks', *TRHS*, 4th ser. 10 (1927), 195–263.

[37] *Grace Book B*, ed. M. Bateson, 2 vols, Cambridge Antiquarian Society, Luard Memorial Series 2–3 (Cambridge, 1903–5), I, p. 218. No clear evidence seems to exist for Venn's belief that Archbishop Henry Deane was a Cambridge graduate (Emden, *Oxford*, I, p. 554).

university monks resident in Cambridge, only gradually ameliorated in the decades before the Reformation, made it inevitable that the university of Oxford was always the major training ground of the monk-bishops of late-medieval England.[38] Moreover most of these future bishops probably spent several, and sometimes many, years as students at Oxford. Much the best documented case is yet again that of the Durham monk, Richard Bell, who was sent to Oxford by Prior John Wessington in 1432 when he was approximately twenty-two years old. Bell was a resident fellow of Durham College for the next eight years, serving as one of the college's two bursars from 1435 to 1440: later in his career he returned to Oxford, this time as warden of his college from 1450 to 1453.[39] How many of the other monk-bishops of the later middle ages studied at Oxford for as long as eleven years is impossible to know; but there can be little doubt that for most of them it was as young university students that they first began to establish a reputation within their orders as scholars, as men of affairs and (not least desirable for a future bishop) as eloquent preachers and orators.

Not in fact that many or indeed any of the last nineteen monk-bishops of medieval England can be proved to have achieved a great deal in the cause of academic learning. Somewhat surprisingly, none seem to have been canon lawyers; and the great majority were graduates of the Oxford faculty of theology. It seems extremely unlikely, for instance, that the Thomas Pygot who was described as a scholar of civil law when granted a university grace in February 1459 can be identified as the future prior of Chertsey Abbey and bishop of Bangor.[40] However, at least five future monk-bishops (William Wellys, Reginald Boulers, Robert Tully, Thomas Myllyng and Michael Diacony) undertook the lengthy and strenuous academic labour necessary to secure a doctorate in theology; while Richard Bell of Durham College supplicated for the baccalaureate in theology towards the end of 1450.[41] By the standards of the fifteenth-century episcopal bench as a whole, this is hardly an outstanding record of attainment in the acquisition of higher degrees; but then there can be little doubt that many of these university monks also possessed exceptional administrative skills which led to their peremptory recall from Oxford to their mother houses earlier than they may have wished. Such a practice had been a frequent cause of criticism from the presidents of the chapters of the English black monks since at least the time of Cardinal Adam

---

38   Dobson, 'Religious Orders'.
39   Durham, Dean and Chapter Muniments: Durham College Accounts, 1435–40; Reg. Parv. II, fol. 88; cf. Dobson, 'Richard Bell', pp. 186–94.
40   Register of the University of Oxford, I, 1449–63, 1505–71, ed. C. W. Boase, Oxford Historical Society, 1 (Oxford, 1885), p. 33; Emden, Oxford, III, p. 1529.
41   Emden, Oxford, I, p. 228; II, p. 1283; III, pp. 1912, 2012, 2170; Dobson, 'Richard Bell', p. 192.

Easton. However, it is easy to appreciate why a future bishop like Richard Redman, who was incorporated as M.A. in 1455 but became the effective superior of all the Premonstratensians in England only four years later, could hardly be allowed to linger among the academic delights of the Oxford schools.[42]

No doubt the cares of monastic, and later episcopal, office also help to explain why so few monk-bishops in the century after 1433 seem to have been creatively learned or indeed to have written anything at all except for often eloquent Latin correspondence. The evidence here is admittedly seriously deficient, not least because wills survive for only some of the bishops in question. However, it seems clear enough that the last English monk-bishop to qualify as a demonstrably original writer and thinker was Philip Repyngdon, also the last medieval English monk to be made a cardinal.[43] Ironically enough, Repyngdon's scholarly reputation rested primarily on his early controversial sermons in support of Wyclif's eucharistic doctrines.[44] Like his fellow monk-bishops of the fifteenth century, Repyngdon apparently found little time to study, let alone to write, after he joined the episcopal bench. Nor is there much evidence that the last nineteen monastic bishops of England and Wales left significant collections of books to posterity. Here again the best recorded example is that of Richard Bell of Durham, whose personal collection of manuscripts included a thirteenth-century Bible and works by Anselm, Geoffrey de Vinsauf, Peter of Blois and Robert Grosseteste; but all these volumes were passed on to the common monastic library or to younger Durham monks before Bell became bishop of Carlisle in 1478.[45] There seem to be more substantial grounds for supposing that the monk-bishops of late medieval England were sometimes important patrons of learning and scholarship. In 1480 Bishop Thomas Myllyng of Hereford was thanked by the university of Oxford for his support to deserving graduates; and in the early 1450s the preface of a new English copy of Cencio Romano's version of the pseudo-Platonic *Axiochus* was addressed to Reginald Boulers when the latter was bishop of the same diocese.[46] Otherwise, and by an irony

---

[42] Colvin, *White Canons*, pp. 363–4.

[43] Whether Repyngdon ever accepted (or was allowed to accept) the cardinalate to which he was appointed by Gregory XII in September 1408 remains, however, an uncertain matter; he was not accorded the title of cardinal in English official documents (Emden, *Oxford*, III, p. 1566).

[44] See, e.g., M. Aston, *Faith and Fire: Popular and Unpopular Religion, 1350–1600* (London, 1993), pp. 38, 41–2, 63, 70–1.

[45] Durham, Cathedral Library, MSS B.III.26, fol. 2v; B.IV.41, fol. 290v; B.IV.42, fol. ii; Dobson, 'Richard Bell', pp. 193–4.

[46] *Epistolae academicae Oxon.*, ed. H. Anstey, 2 vols, Oxford Historical Society 35–6 (Oxford, 1898–9), II, pp. 459–60; R. Weiss, *Humanism in England during the*

which contemporary Welshmen would have been quick to appreciate, much the most influential founts of literary patronage among the monk-bishops of the later middle ages seem to have been the two Bishops Dafydd who held the see of St Asaph between 1500 and 1513. The learning as well as piety and devotion of Dafydd ab Iuean were celebrated at extravagant length by his two poets, Guto'r Glyn and Gutun Owain; while of Dafydd ab Owain it could be said that Welsh poets 'flocked to him as to no other patron'.[47] No English monastic bishops of the later middle ages received – or seem to have deserved to receive – so fulsome a tribute.

It is in any case hardly likely that the Lancastrian, Yorkist and early Tudor monarchs deliberately advanced members of the monastic orders to the more marginal dioceses of their kingdom in order to promote literature and learning there. Nor is it much more probable, except perhaps for a few years during the reign of Henry VII, that many monks were elevated to the episcopal bench just because they were monks. More specific and sometimes conflicting motives were clearly at stake. In the first place, the crown sometimes abandoned its customary initiative in the matter of episcopal appointments and yielded to the machinations and pressures exerted by an ambitious abbot eagerly intent on attaining episcopal status, especially if he could retain his abbacy *in commendam*. Here the classic case is undoubtedly that of Prior Richard Bell of Durham whose agents at the curia are known to have been scheming quite openly to acquire a bishopric on his behalf several years before he was finally provided to Carlisle in 1478.[48] Bell has been alleged, somewhat implausibly, to have aspired to the papacy itself; so it is as well to be reminded of a fifteenth-century monk-bishop who obviously deeply regretted that episcopal greatness had been thrust upon him. Thomas Spofford, abbot of St Mary's, York, for sixteen years before he became bishop of Hereford in 1421, began petitioning Martin V for permission to resign his see and return to the monastic life as early as 1429. Only twenty years and many heart-rending petitions later was he allowed to return to his mother house as a witness to the fact that not all monk-bishops found their lot a congenial one.[49]

Spofford had owed his own bishopric to his much valued eloquence at the council of Constance and to the sponsorship of his *protector singularissimus*, Cardinal Beaufort; but then most future monk-bishops of the period naturally attracted the personal attention of their king while performing political and

    Fifteenth Century, 3rd edn (Oxford, 1967), p. 176, n. 4; Emden, *Oxford*, I, p. 229.

[47]   Williams, *Welsh Church*, pp. 404–6.

[48]   Durham, Dean and Chapter Muniments, Reg. Parv. III, fols 156–7; *The Priory of Coldingham*, ed. J. Raine, Surtees Society 12 (London, 1841), pp. 232–5; Dobson, 'Richard Bell', pp. 208–9.

[49]   *Bekynton Correspondence*, I, p. 1; Emden, *Oxford*, III, p. 1744.

administrative services on his behalf. Here the most dramatic if exceptional career is undoubtedly that of Prior Henry Deane of Llanthony by Gloucester who became one of Edward IV's chaplains in 1477 and survived the collapse of the Yorkist monarchy to be chancellor and deputy-governor of Ireland in 1494–6; four years later he was no less than keeper of the great seal of England, an office he still held when provided to the archbishopric of Canterbury in May 1501.[50] A generation earlier Reginald Boulers and Robert Tully had both owed their promotion to the episcopal bench to their staunch, and unpopular, support of the Lancastrian monarchy.[51] By contrast there can be no doubt that Thomas Myllyng, prior and then abbot of Westminster, secured the bishopric of Hereford in 1474 because of his adherence to the Yorkist cause. Already well known to Edward IV, not least as a preacher, it was during the king's short involuntary exile in 1470–71 that he sheltered Queen Elizabeth Wydeville from the Lancastrians in his own lodgings at Westminster; and it was there too that the future and ill-fated Edward V, the future bishop's godson, was soon to be born.[52]

Even if no other monk-bishop of the period was called upon to assist the royal family at quite so dangerous a moment of crisis, personal service to the ruling monarch was always the most certain route to the episcopal bench. If so, did the kings of late medieval England have any precise views about how these bishops might enhance royal authority in the more marginal sees within the realm? Once again the question is easier to pose than to answer. It seems clear enough that the Yorkist and early Tudor monarchs were disinclined to promote monks and regular canons of high aristocratic birth, not that there were many of these available in the religious houses of late medieval England.[53] On occasion, however, and particularly in the case of the strategically important diocese of Carlisle, there might be obvious advantages to the king in appointing monk-bishops who were of local origins and

---

[50] S. B. Chrimes, *Henry VII* (London, 1972), pp. 107, 242, 254, 263–4; cf. A. Way, 'The Will of Henry Dene, Archbishop of Canterbury', *Archaeological Journal* 18 (1861), 260–1; Emden, *Oxford*, I, p. 554.

[51] R. J. Knecht, 'The Episcopate and the Wars of the Roses', *University of Birmingham Historical Journal* 6 (1958), 108–31, p. 113; Emden, *Oxford*, I, p. 229; III, pp. 1912–13.

[52] C. L. Scofield, *The Life and Reign of Edward the Fourth*, 2 vols (London, 1923), I, pp. 541, 546; II, pp. 5, 273–4; Emden, *Oxford*, II, pp. 1282–3.

[53] Several, but probably not a majority, of the monastic bishops discussed in this paper were of gentry origins. The two individuals most distinguished by birth were perhaps Richard Redman (who was probably the grandson of Sir Richard Redman of Harewood, speaker of the House of Commons in 1415; Colvin, *White Canons*, p. 363) and Reginald Boulers (who claimed to be connected to the family of Butler, of which James, earl of Wiltshire, executed in 1461, was then the head; Emden, *Oxford*, I, pp. 228–9).

experience. Richard Bell, although a prior of Durham, had much knowledge of northern politics and Anglo-Scottish relations before he became bishop of Carlisle in 1478; and his successor, William Senhouse, was probably a member of a cadet branch of the Senhouse family of Seascale in Cumbria.[54] Otherwise most new monastic bishops must have known very little indeed about their new dioceses – especially if they were in Wales – before they were enthroned there. Thereafter, as with all late medieval bishops, their effectiveness as both political and spiritual leaders of their sees must naturally have much depended on the vexed issue of their residence. As only nine episcopal registers (three of them published) survive for these twenty-six different pontificates, any attempt to generalise on this subject is bound to be impressionistic to a degree. That some monk-bishops, like Thomas Myllyng at Hereford from 1474 to 1492, were frequently absent from their dioceses, seems fully confirmed by their registers; and it seems inconceivable too that Richard Redman's strenuous responsibilities for the welfare of his Premonstratensian order can have allowed him to visit his see of St Asaph at all frequently between 1471 and 1495.[55] For less worthy reasons, Bishop Skevington of Bangor was allegedly a notorious non-resident, described by one of his enemies as the 'richest monk in England'.[56] No doubt episcopal absenteeism was always liable to be most rampant in the Welsh sees; but even there, and certainly in the diocese of Carlisle, many monk-bishops clearly dedicated themselves to the administrative and pastoral work of their office for very long and at times more or less uninterrupted periods.[57]

It might in any case be unwise to expect too much in the way of dynamic spiritual leadership from monastic bishops who were often elderly when they came to office. What is notable is their intense commitment to the building and renovation of their cathedrals and, even more, their episcopal palaces. It is unfortunately one of the greater architectural tragedies of the later middle ages that so few of these palaces, especially in London, survive in an authentic state or indeed survive at all. Nevertheless the visitor to Rose Castle in Cumbria can still examine the *novum opus* built by Bishop Richard Bell in the late 1480s: his building works there comprised not only a new chapel with an elaborate roof but also a tower still known by his name.[58] Most impressive of all was the contribution of fifteenth-century monastic bishops to the

---

[54]   Summerson, *Medieval Carlisle*, II, pp. 592, 597, 601.

[55]   D. M. Smith, *Guide to Bishops' Registers of England and Wales* (London, 1981), *passim*; Colvin, *White Canons*, pp. 363–4.

[56]   Even Cardinal Wolsey was allegedly scandalised by Skevington's non-residence (Williams, *Welsh Church*, p. 306).

[57]   Summerson, *Medieval Carlisle*, II, pp. 591–5; Dobson, 'Richard Bell', pp. 211–21.

[58]   J. Wilson, *Rose Castle* (Carlisle, 1912), pp. 125–6, 212–19; Dobson, 'Richard Bell', p. 214.

restoration of the four Welsh cathedrals, all in a state of severe disrepair since at least the Glendower rebellion. St Asaph, in particular, had allegedly remained in a state of ruinous neglect until Bishop Redman restored its transepts and choir (adding elaborate canopied stalls) between 1471 and 1495. At about the same period, Bishop Robert Tully inserted twenty-eight choir stalls into the newly roofed choir of St David's. Even greater effort and expense were devoted to Bangor Cathedral. Between 1496 and 1500 Bishop Henry Deane completely repaired the transepts and choir there, to be followed a few years later by Thomas Skevington who thoroughly rebuilt the nave and erected a new west tower, still commemorated by a Latin inscription of 1532 over the doorway below.[59] Not alone among the Welsh diocesan bishops of the late fifteenth and early sixteenth centuries in their concern for the fabric of their cathedrals, the monk-bishops of the period made much the most important contributions to that cause. Even today those cathedrals still remain their greatest memorials.

With a few exceptions (like Richard Bell's magnificent brass in the choir of Carlisle Cathedral or Richard Redman's flamboyant chantry chapel at Ely), the more personal memorials of the monk-bishops of late medieval England are now harder to find. Not that those bishops failed to take considerable pains about the future location of their mortal remains. Here indeed they were faced with a difficult choice. Would it be preferable to seek burial (like Bell, Redman, William Wellys and Henry Deane) within the cathedrals where they had recently been enthroned in state? Or was it more appropriate to be interred (like Thomas Spofford, Thomas Mylling, William Senhouse and John Penny) in the abbey churches of their original monastic *alma mater*?[60] Where, when faced with the eventual prospect of the Day of Judgement, should their greater loyalties lie? No easy question to answer perhaps; and it was probably best solved by the very last of the monk-bishops of medieval England and Wales, Bishop Thomas Skevington, who bequeathed his heart to Bangor Cathedral but left the rest of his body to his old Cistercian abbey of Beaulieu.[61] In its somewhat macabre fashion Bishop Skevington's decision may

---

[59] D. R. Thomas, *The History of the Diocese of St Asaph*, 3 vols, 2nd edn (Oswestry, 1908–13), I, p. 70; Williams, *Welsh Church*, pp. 430–3; cf. *Blue Guide to the Cathedrals and Abbeys of England and Wales* (London, 1984), pp. 272–306.

[60] Emden, *Oxford*, I, pp. 161, 554; II, pp. 1283–4; III, pp. 1458, 1669, 1744, 2012. As Robert Tully so rarely visited his cathedral church of St David's while alive, he chose to be buried in the parish church of Tenby when dead (*ibid.*, III, p. 1913). Not surprisingly, the most spectacular funeral ceremonies ever held to commemorate any of these nineteen bishops were those which followed the death of Archbishop Henry Deane in 1503: see *A History of Canterbury Cathedral*, ed. P. Collinson, N. Ramsey and M. Sparks (Oxford, 1995), pp. 145, 487–8, 493.

[61] Emden, *Oxford*, III, p. 1708.

serve to provide a fitting final comment on the divided loyalties inherent in the life of any monastic bishop. But for other reasons too Skevington's death – 16 or 17 August 1533 – must mark the end of this paper. Less than a dozen years after his demise no fewer than twenty-four ex-religious (most of them Black Monks) would be found among the bishops and suffragan bishops of the post-medieval Henrician church.[62] For those monks and regular canons of the 1530s, their end was so literally their beginning that they present a different and even more complicated story. But then perhaps they also present the strangest of possible paradoxes too. In the history of England and Wales monk-bishops were to be most numerous and most influential when monasticism itself was no more.

---

[62] See Le Neve, *Fasti, 1300–1541* and *1541–1857, passim*. Of the many ironies of these years perhaps the least expected is the way in which Robert Holgate, a Gilbertine canon from Watton in Yorkshire who became an absentee bishop of Llandaff in 1537, should eventually find himself (in 1545) the first post-Reformation archbishop of York: see A. G. Dickens, *Robert Holgate, Archbishop of York and President of the King's Council in the North*, St Anthony's Hall Publications 8 (York, 1955), pp. 4–18.

APPENDIX

Monks and Canons Holding English and Welsh Sees, 1433–1533

1.	*William Heyworth* O.S.B.	Abbot of St Albans 1401–20	Lichfield 1420–47
2.	*Thomas Spofford* O.S.B. (Sch.Th.)	Abbot of St Mary's, York 1405–21	Hereford 1421–48
3.	*William Wellys* O.S.B. (D.Th.)	Abbot of St Mary's, York 1423–36	Rochester 1436–44
4.	*Nicholas Ashby* O.S.B.	Prior of Westminster Abbey 1435–41	Llandaff 1441–58
5.	*Reginald Boulers* O.S.B. (D.Th.)	Abbot of Gloucester Abbey 1437–50	Hereford 1450–3 Lichfield 1453–9
6.	*Robert Tully* O.S.B. (D.Th.)	Monk of Gloucester Abbey c.1440–60; Prior Studentium, Oxford 1451–3	St David's 1460–82
7.	*Richard Redman* O.Prem.	Abbot of Shap c.1458–1505	St Asaph 1471–95 Exeter 1495–1501 Ely 1501–5
8.	*Thomas Myllyng* O.S.B. (D.Th.)	Abbot of Westminster Abbey 1469–74	Hereford 1474–92
9.	*Richard Bell* O.S.B. (B.Th.)	Prior of Finchale Priory 1456–64, Prior of Durham Cathedral 1464–78	Carlisle 1478–95
10.	*Henry Deane* O.Can.S.A. (Sch.)	Prior of Llanthony 1467–1501, King's Chaplain 1477, Irish Chancellor 1494–6	Bangor 1494–9 Salisbury 1500–1 Canterbury 1501–3
11.	*William Senhouse* O.S.B.	Abbot of St Mary's, York 1485–1502	Carlisle 1495–1502 Durham 1502–5
12.	*Michael Diacony* O.S.B. (D.Th.)	Prior of St Helier's Jersey 1495, King's Confessor 1495	St Asaph 1495–9

13. *John Ingleby* O.Carth.	Monk of Mount Grace Priory	Llandaff 1496–9
14. *Miles Salley* O.S.B.	Abbot of Eynsham 1499	Llandaff 1499–1517
15. *Thomas Pygot* O.S.B.	Abbot of Chertsey 1479–1504	Bangor 1500–4
16. *Dafydd ab Iuean* O.Cist.	Abbot of Valle Crucis *c.*1490–1503	St Asaph 1500–3
17. *Dafydd ab Owain* O.Cist.	Abbot of Conway 1503–8	St Asaph 1503–13
18. *John Penny* O.Can.S.A.	Abbot of Leicester 1496–1508	Bangor 1505–8 Carlisle 1508–20
19. *Thomas Skevington* O.Cist.	Abbot of Waverley *c.*1478–1508 Abbot of Beaulieu, 1508–33	Bangor 1509–33

Dr. DANIEL WILLIAMS

It is with bitter regret that we have to announce the sudden death of our colleague, Dr. Daniel Williams, English Medieval Historian at the University of Leicester. Daniel Williams was a member of our Steering Committee from the beginning, and a paper from him, on 'Simon de Montfort and his adherents', appeared in our first volume of 1984. He went on to edit the volumes of 1986, 1987 and 1988, covering the Twelfth and Fifteenth Centuries as well as the Early Tudor period, and to contribute a further four papers to later Symposia. His work on 'The Croyland Chronicle, 616–1500' appeared in our 1986 volume; that on 'The Peverils and the Essebies' in 1988; and on 'Matthew Paris and the thirteenth-century prospect of Asia' in 1991. Last July he gave a further paper, redolent with the dry humour and perceptive comment we had come to expect, on 'Trouble in the Cathedral Close: Archbishop Boniface's 1258 visitation of the priory of Christ Church, Canterbury'. It was, as always, a polished performance, and we look forward to seeing it in print.

The Harlaxton Symposium had become, therefore, one of Daniel Williams' major contexts, and its interests, covering a wide inter-disciplinary range, were very much his own. He also published extensively elsewhere in the field of English, especially Midland, medieval studies. He edited the *Transactions of the Leicestershire Archaeological and Historical Society* from 1978 to 1989. He will be long associated with the interpretation of the Battle of Bosworth, where he was ever ready to draw swords with alternative reconstructions. His was the Bosworth Museum, and his book on the battlefield, first written in 1978, was revised in '75, '84 and '96. Perhaps his generous hours as editor, his skirmishes at Bosworth, and above all his devotion to his thirty years of loyal students, have deprived us of his *Magnum Opus*. Richard III eludes us yet, for his final and definitive biography was to have crowned the retirement Daniel Williams never lived to enjoy. That retirement would have been marked by his so-young lease of personal happiness. We will sorely miss a highly valued colleague and friend. Generations of students are mourning a teacher as kind as he was inspiring. But our greatest sympathy goes to his family, so swiftly and cruelly bereaved.

Pamela Tudor-Craig

1 (Henderson) Inscription carved in relief, Tarbat, Ross & Cromarty (Trustees of the National Museums of Scotland)

2 (Henderson) SS Paul and Anthony breaking bread in the desert; on the shaft, spiral ornament of a type found on a slab at Applecross, Ross & Cromarty: cross slab, St Vigeans, Angus (copyright: T. E. Gray)

3 (Henderson) The raven delivers a loaf of bread to SS Paul and Anthony: cross slab, Nigg, Ross & Cromarty (copyright: Cameron MacLean)

4 (Henderson) Pictish symbols and ceremonial hunting-scene: slab, Hilton of Cadboll, Ross & Cromarty (photo: T. E. Gray, copyright: Trustees of the National Museums of Scotland)

5 (Henderson) David saves the lamb, and a lion hunt: corner-slab shrine, the St Andrews Sarcophagus, Fife (crown copyright: Royal Commission on the Ancient and Historical Monuments of Scotland)

6 (Henderson) Hybrid creature flanked by predators: architectural sculpture, Meigle, Perth & Kinross (copyright: T. E. Gray)

7 (Morgan) Woman before the Virgin and Child: Shaftesbury Psalter,
BL, Lansdowne MS 383, fol. 165v (photo: Conway Library, Courtauld Institute,
University of London)

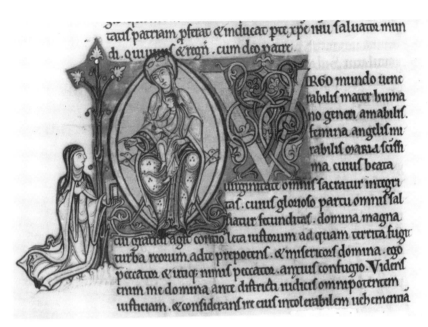

*tatis patriam pstac & inducac pxe xpe mu saluaroi mun
di. qui mm & regm . cum deo patre.*

*ERGO mundo uene
rabilis mater huma
no geneu amabilis.
femina angelis mi
rabilis oraria sctissi
ma cuius beata
uirginitate omnis sacracur integri
tas. cuius glouoso partu omnis sal
uacur fecundiras. domina magna
cui gratias agit coelo tera iustorum ad quam tertia fugit
turba reorum. adte prepotens. & misericors domina. ego
peccator & unq̃ nimis peccator. anxius confugio. Videns
enim me domina ante districti iudicis ommpotentem
iustiaam. & considerans ire eius intolerabilem uchementia*

8 (Morgan) Woman before the Virgin and Child: Meditations of St Anselm, Bodleian MS Auct. D.2.6 fol. 158v (photo: Conway Library, Courtauld Institute, University of London)

9 (Morgan) Virgin and Child: Boethius, *De Musica*, CUL, MS Ii.3.12, fol. 62v (photo: Conway Library, Courtauld Institute, University of London)

12 (Morgan) Sponsa-Sponsus: Bede on the Song of Songs: Cambridge King's College, MS 19, fol. 21v (photo: Conway Library, Courtauld Institute, University of London)

10 (Morgan) Tree of Jesse: Shaftesbury Psalter, BL, Lansdowne MS 383, fol. 15
(photo: Conway Library, Courtauld Institute, University of London)

11 (Morgan) Tree of Jesse: Psalter, BL, Cotton MS Nero C.iv, fol. 9 (photo: Conway Library, Courtauld Institute, University of London)

13 (Dennison) Holkham Hall, Norfolk, MS 26, fol. 7
(photo: Conway Library, Courtauld Institute, University of London,
and by kind permission of the earl of Leicester)

Eatus uir qui nõ
abiit in consilio im
piorum: ꞇ in uia pct
catorum nõ stetit. et
in cathedra pestilentie
non sedit
Sed in lege dñi uo
luntas eius: ꞇ in lege
eius meditabitur die ac nocte
Et erit tanquam lignum qð plantatum est
secus dccursus aquarum: qð fructum suum
dabit in tempore suo.
Et folium eius nõ defluet: ꞇ oñia quecunq;
faciet semper prosperabuntur.
Non sic impii non sic: set tanqm puluis
quẽ proicit uentus a facie terre.
Ideo non resurgunt impii in iudicio: neq; pec
catores in consilio iustorum.
Qm nouit dominus uiam iustorum: ꞇ iter im
piorum peribit.

14 (Dennison) New York, Pierpont Morgan Library, MS Glazier 53, fol. 6
(photo: Conway Library, Courtauld Institute, University of London,
and The Pierpont Morgan Library, New York)

16 (Dennison) Bodleian, MS Bodley 316, fol. 8
(photo: copyright The Bodleian Library, Oxford)

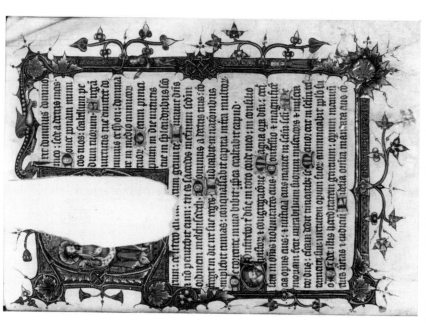

15 (Dennison) Holkham Hall, Norfolk, MS 26, fol. 56
(photo: Conway Library, Courtauld Institute, University of London,
and by kind permission of the earl of Leicester)

18 (Dennison) Durham Cathedral Library, MS A.1.3, fol. 1
(photo: by kind permission of The Dean and Chapter of Durham)

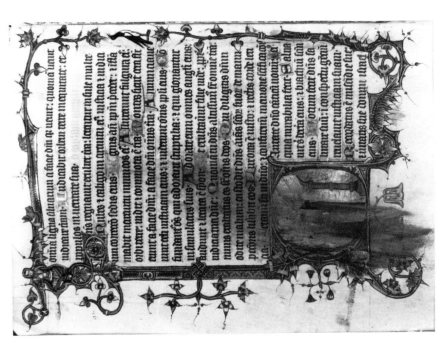

17 (Dennison) Holkham Hall, Norfolk, MS 26, fol. 48v
(photo: Conway Library, Courtauld Institute, University of London
and by kind permission of the earl of Leicester)

19 (Dennison) CUL, MS Ii.2.24, fol. 13
(photo: by permission of the Syndics of Cambridge University Library)

20 (Dennison) BL, Royal MS 14 C.ix, fol. 9
(photo: copyright the British Library Board)

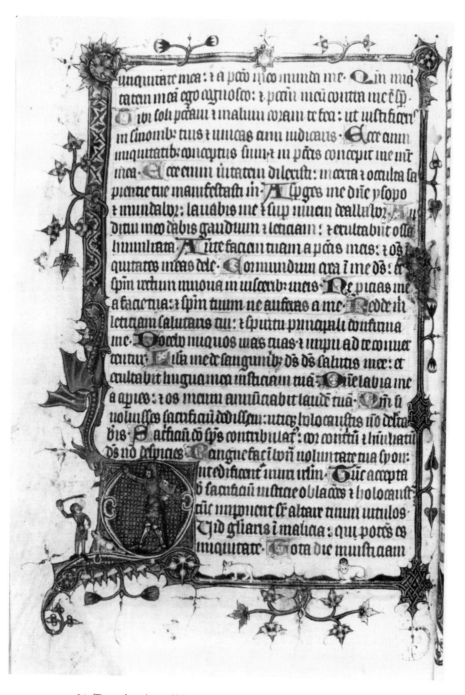

21 (Dennison) Holkham Hall, Norfolk, MS 26, fol. 27v
(photo: Conway Library, Courtauld Institute, University of London,
and by kind permission of the earl of Leicester)

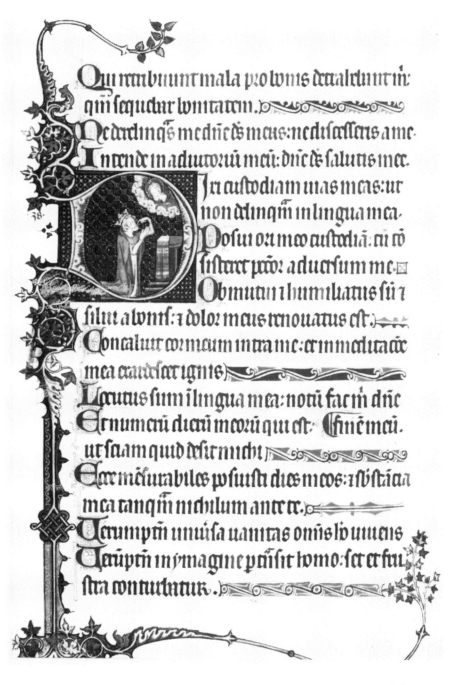

Qui retribuunt mala pro bonis detrahebunt mi
qm sequebar bonitatem.

Ne derelinquas me domine deus meus: ne discesseris a me.
Intende in adiutorium meum: domine deus salutis mee.

Ita custodiam uias meas: ut
non delinquam in lingua mea.
Posui ori meo custodiam. cum co
sisterer peccator aduersum me.

Obmutui humiliatus sum 7
silui a bonis: 7 dolor meus renouatus est.

Concaluit cor meum intra me: et in meditacione
mea exardescet ignis.

Locutus sum i lingua mea: notum fac mihi dne
Et numerum dierum meorum qui est. finem meum.
ut sciam quid desit michi.

Ecce mensurabiles posuisti dies meos: 7 substancia
mea tanquam nichilum ante te.

Verumptm uniuersa uanitas omnis homo uiuens
Verumptm in ymagine praeterit homo: sed et fru
stra conturbatur.

22 (Dennison) New York, Pierpont Morgan Library, MS Glazier 53, fol. 36v,
detail (photo: Conway Library, Courtauld Institute, University of London, and
the Pierpont Morgan Library)

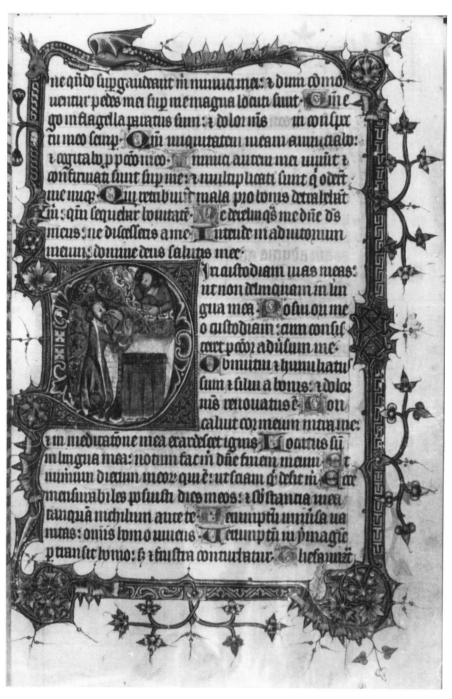

ne quo supgaudeant in nuntia mea: z dum comino
uentur pedes mei sup me magna locuti sunt. Qui e
go in flagella pacatus sum: z dolor mis in conspe
tu meo semp. Qui iniquitatem meam annunciabo:
z cogitabo p peccato meo. Inimici autem mei uiuunt z
confirmati sunt sup me: z multiplicati sunt q oderūt
me inique. Qui retribuit mala pro bonis detrahebant
mi: qui sequelar bonitate. Ne derelinqs me dūe ds
meus: ne discesseris a me. Intende in adiutorium
meum: domine deus salutis mee.

In custodiam uias meas:
ut non delinquam in lin
gua mea. Posui ori me
o custodiam: cum consif
teret peccator aduersum me.
Obmutui z humiliatus
sum z silui a bonis: z dolor
mis renouatus e. Con
caluit cor meum intra me:
z in meditatione mea exardescet ignis. Locutus su
in lingua mea: notum fac mi dūe finem meum. Et
numerum dierum meorum que e: ut sciam qd desit mi. Ecce
mensurabiles posuisti dies meos: z substantia mea
tanquam nichilum ante te. Veruntamen uniuersa ua
nitas: omnis homo uiuens. Veruntamen in imagine
ptransit homo: sed z frustra conturbatur. Thesaurizat

23 (Dennison) Holkham Hall, Norfolk, MS 26, fol. 22
(photo: Conway Library, Courtauld Institute, University of London,
and by kind permission of the earl of Leicester)

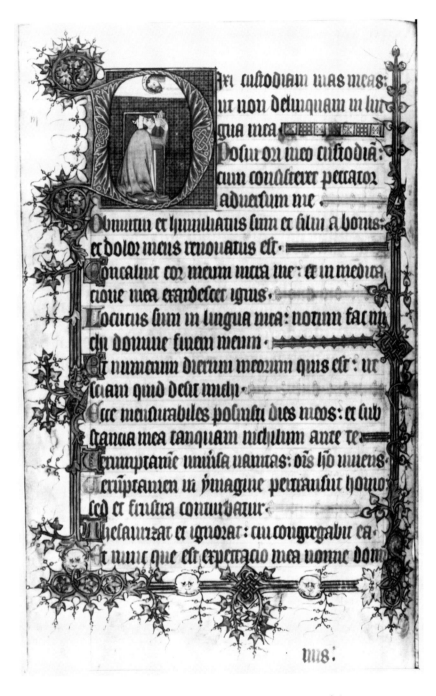

24 (Dennison) Bodleian, MS Rawlinson G.185, fol. 32v
(photo: copyright The Bodleian Library, Oxford)

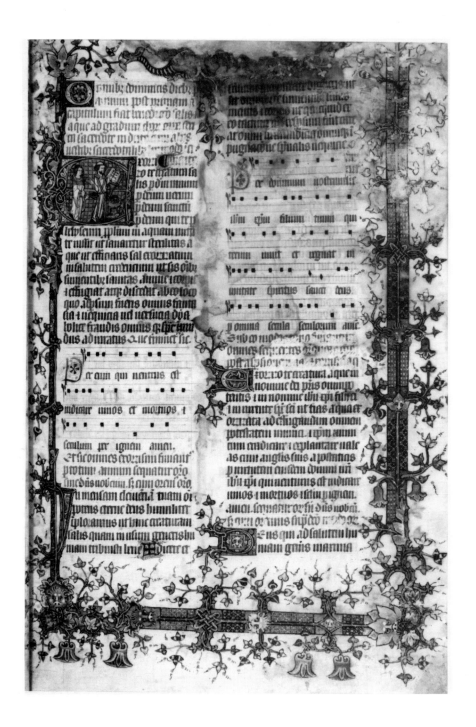

25 (Dennison) Bodleian, MS Don. b.5, fol. 7
(photo: copyright The Bodleian Library, Oxford)

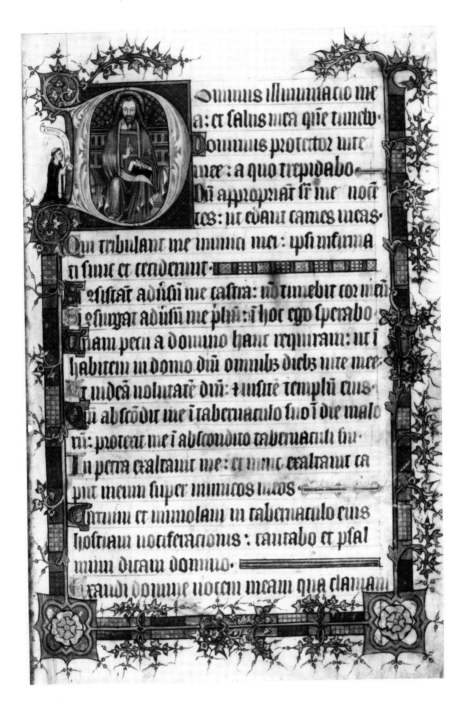

26 (Dennison) Bodleian, MS Rawlinson G.185, fol. 20
(photo: copyright The Bodleian Library, Oxford)

27 (Dennison) Bodleian, MS Don. b.5, fol. 172v, detail
(photo: copyright The Bodleian Library)

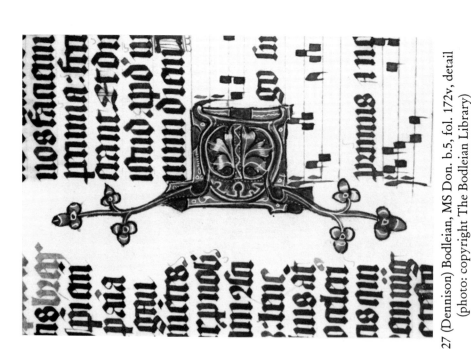

28 (Dennison) Vienna, Österreichische Nationalbibliothek,
Cod. 1826*, fol. 50, detail (author's photo:
reproduced by kind permission of the Austrian National Library)

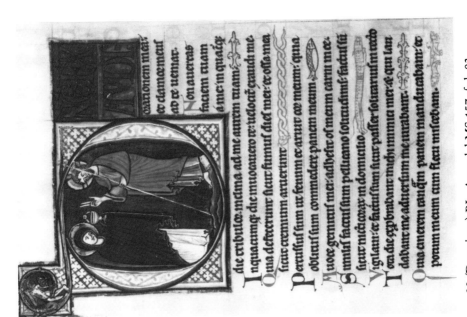

30 (Dennison) BL, Arundel MS 157, fol. 83
(photo; copyright the British Library Board)

29 (Dennison) Bodleian, MS Liturg. 198, fol. 46
(photo: The Bodleian Library, Oxford)

31 (Dennison) Paris, Bibliothèque Nationale, MS lat. 765, fol. 23
(photo: copyright, the Bibliothèque Nationale, Paris)

Eatus uir qui non
abiit in consilio impi
orum ⁊ in uia peccator’
non stetit : ⁊ i cathedra
n. iudicio. pestilencie
n. falsitatis non sedit.
Beneit soit le bier
que ne foreie el consail
de sen grees ⁊ ne estuet
en la uoie des pecchie

ours : ⁊ ne siet el iuggement de fausine
Set in lege domini uoluntas eius ⁊ in lege
eius meditabitur die ac nocte.
Mais sa uolentee fust en la lei nre sire : et
pensera en sa lei par iour ⁊ par nuit
Et erit tanquam lignum quod plantatu est se
cus decursus aquarum. quod fructum suu
dabit in tempore suo.
Et il serra si com arbre q plauntee ioust les
cours des eawes q soun fruit dorra en so trps
Et folium eius non defluet : ⁊ omnia quecu
q faciet prosperabuntur.

32 (Dennison) BL, Add. MS 44949, fol. 39
(photo: copyright, the British Library Board)

34 (Dennison) Bodleian, MS Rawlinson G.185, fol. 97, detail
(photo: copyright The Bodleian Library, Oxford)

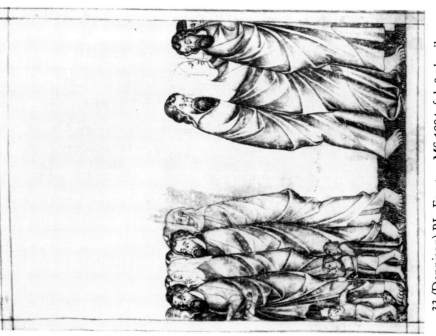

33 (Dennison) BL, Egerton MS 1894, fol. 8, detail
(photo: copyright the British Library Board)

36 (Dennison) Bodleian, MS Bodley 851, fol. 6v, detail (photo: copyright The Bodleian Library, Oxford)

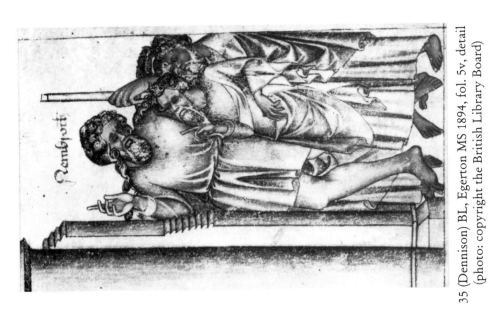

35 (Dennison) BL, Egerton MS 1894, fol. 5v, detail (photo: copyright the British Library Board)

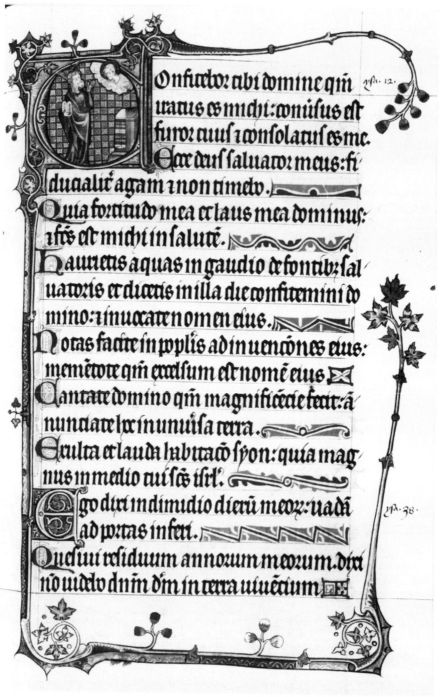

37 (Dennison) New York, Pierpont Morgan Library, MS Glazier 53, fol. 132
(photo: Conway Library, Courtauld Institute, University of London,
and Pierpont Morgan Library)

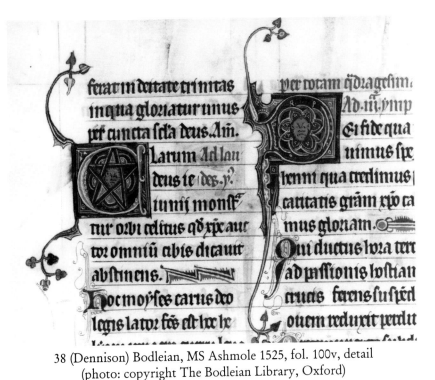

38 (Dennison) Bodleian, MS Ashmole 1525, fol. 100v, detail
(photo: copyright The Bodleian Library, Oxford)

39 (Dennison) Bodleian, MS Ashmole 1525, fol. 164v, detail
(photo: copyright The Bodleian Library, Oxford)

40 (Rogers) Adam the Cellarer, *Liber Vitae*: BL, Cotton MS Nero D.vii, fol. 16v
(by permission of the British Library)

41 (Rogers) Alan Midelton, *Liber Vitae*; BL, Cotton MS Nero D.vii, fol. 145v
(by permission of the British Library)

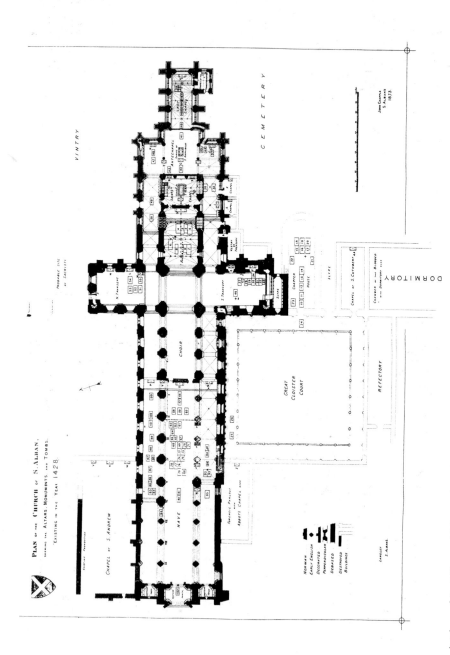

42 (Rogers) Plan of St Albans Abbey, showing burials: *An Account of the Altars, Monuments and Tombs...* ed. R. Lloyd (St Albans, 1873)

43 (Rollason) Durham *Liber Vitae*; BL, Cotton MS Domitian A.vii, fol. 77v
(by permission of the British Library)

The Late Daniel Williams